Across God's Frontiers

Across God's Frontiers

Catholic Sisters in the American West, 1850–1920

ANNE M. BUTLER

UNIVERSITY OF NORTH CAROLINA PRESS • CHAPEL HILL

This volume was published with the assistance of the Greensboro Women's Fund of the University of North Carolina Press.

© 2012 THE UNIVERSITY OF NORTH CAROLINA PRESS

Designed by
Jacquline Johnson
Set in Adobe Caslon by
Tseng Information Systems, Inc.
Manufactured in the
United States of America

Founding Contributors: Linda Arnold Carlisle, Sally Schindel Cone, Anne Faircloth, Bonnie McElveen Hunter, Linda Bullard Jennings, Janice J. Kerley (in honor of Margaret Supplee Smith), Nancy Rouzer May, and Betty Hughes Nichols.

The paper in this book meets the guidelines for permanence and durability of the Committee on Production Guidelines for Book Longevity of the Council on Library Resources.

The University of North Carolina Press has been a member of the Green Press Initiative since 2003.

Library of Congress Cataloging-in-Publication Data
Butler, Anne M., 1938–
Across God's frontiers : Catholic sisters in the American West, 1850–1920 / Anne M. Butler.
    p. cm.
Includes bibliographical references (p.   ) and index.
ISBN 978-0-8078-3565-4 (cloth : alk. paper)
1. Nuns—United States—West—History.
2. Monasticism and religious orders for women—United States—West—History. 3. Monastic and religious life of women—United States—West—History. 4. Catholic Church—United States—West—History. 5. West (U.S.)—History. 6. West (U.S.)—Church history. I. Title.
BX4220.U6B88 2012
271′.90078—dc23
                                                    2012005083

16 15 14 13 12   5 4 3 2 1

With love and admiration

for my children,

Daniel Ryan Porterfield

and

Katherine Anne Porterfield

Contents

Illustrations

Abbreviations for Religious Congregations of Women

ASC	Adorers of the Blood of Christ
BVM	Sisters of Charity of the Blessed Virgin Mary
CCVI	Sisters of Charity of the Incarnate Word
CDP	Sisters of Divine Providence, San Antonio, Texas
CSA	Sisters of St. Agnes
CSC	Sisters of the Holy Cross
CSFN	Sisters of the Holy Family of Nazareth
CSJ/SSJ	Sisters of St. Joseph of Carondelet; Sisters of St. Joseph
DC	Daughters of Charity of St. Vincent de Paul
DCJ	Carmelite Sisters of the Divine Heart of Jesus
FSM	Franciscan Sisters of Mary (formerly Sisters of St. Mary)
FSPA	Sisters of St. Francis of Perpetual Adoration
HJ	Hermanas Josefinas
LSP	Little Sisters of the Poor
MCDP	Missionary Catechists of Divine Providence, San Antonio, Texas
MSC	Missionary Sisters of the Sacred Heart of Jesus (Cabrini Sisters)
OP	Dominican Sisters, Sinsinawa, Wisconsin; San Rafael, California; Edmonds, Washington; Galveston, Texas
OSB	Benedictine Sisters of Pontifical Jurisdiction; Benedictine Nuns; Congregation of Benedictine Sisters of Perpetual Adoration; Olivetan Benedictine Sisters
OSF	Sisters of St. Francis of Assisi, Milwaukee, Wisconsin;

	Sisters of St. Francis of the Holy Family; Sisters of St. Francis of Philadelphia; Sisters of St. Francis, Congregation of Our Lady of Lourdes, Rochester; Sisters of St. Francis of Clinton, Iowa; Franciscan Sisters of Chicago; Franciscan Sisters of the Immaculate Conception; Franciscan Sisters of Oldenburg, Indiana; School Sisters of St. Francis; Missionary Franciscan Sisters of the Immaculate Conception
OSM	Servants of Mary (Servite Sisters)
OSP	Oblate Sisters of Providence
OSU	Ursuline Nuns of the Roman Union; Ursuline Nuns of the Congregation of Paris
PBVM	Sisters of the Presentation of the Blessed Virgin Mary
RGS-CGS	Sisters of the Good Shepherd
RSCJ	Society of the Sacred Heart
RSM	Sisters of Mercy
SBS	Sisters of the Blessed Sacrament for Indians and Colored People
SC	Sisters of Charity of Cincinnati
SCL	Sisters of Charity of Leavenworth, Kansas
SCN	Sisters of Charity of Nazareth
SHF	Sisters of the Holy Family of San Francisco
SHSp	Sisters of the Holy Spirit and Mary Immaculate
SL	Sisters of Loretto at the Foot of the Cross
SMP	Sisters of Mary of the Presentation
SNDdeN	Sisters of Notre Dame de Namur
SNJM	Sisters of the Holy Names of Jesus and Mary
SP	Sisters of Providence
SSA	Sisters of St. Anne
SSF	Sisters of the Holy Family of New Orleans
SSM	Sisters of the Sorrowful Mother
SSMO	Sisters of St. Mary of Oregon
SSND	School Sisters of Notre Dame
VHM	Visitation Nuns

Preface

In this work, I again turn to the American West, the magnificent region that most draws my historical interest. On this occasion, across exquisite and fractious western landscapes, Roman Catholic nuns and sisters, studies in black and white—gossamer veil sliding across a shoulder, starched coif framing the face, silver crucifix resting on a short cape, ebony rosary beads folding into floor-sweeping serge skirts—caught my attention. Among the diverse women of the West, perhaps these nuns of distinct appearance and demeanor harbored gender secrets that would further illuminate a western history once dominated by masculine voices.

Catholic nuns have not garnered

much note, even in the limited accounts of female westerners. "Real" women partnered with men for a truly fulfilled life. Even if a woman delayed marriage for factory employment, artisan pursuits, or professional endeavor, most ultimately accepted domesticity, linked arms with a husband, followed his lead, and bore and raised his children. These wives and mothers kept family central to the western narrative of every culture.

In the popular imagination, nuns lived by the antithesis of this familial American West. With their rejection of the secular community and its social moorings, nuns appeared to be simple, slightly boring women of little impact. Although their relief services won praise during crises, nuns and sisters served as targets for various kinds of mean-spirited jokes, usually relating to disciplinary cruelty or sexual frustration. Caricatures depicted nuns as dissatisfied, morose women so embittered by a broken romance or inconsolable after a suitor's death that they retreated to a convent to mourn the lost male lover and grieve forever their stunted womanhood.

In this overall gender insult that placed intimacy with a man as the only route to contentment, nothing in these shallow platitudes acknowledged there could be satisfying female choices that *intentionally* excluded men. Nuns and sisters, according to some, were too few in number, obsessed with religion, naïve about life, and shocked by earthiness to figure in the accounts of women who shaped so much of the American story. Nuns and sisters, however, were neither silent nor secluded, disinterested nor ingenuous, warped nor winsome. Rather, they were movers and shakers in the religious and secular spheres. Their histories offer an excellent opportunity to understand more about the complex realities of the women's West. The records held in convents across the United States affirm that assertion.

Sisterhoods intended that convent records and annual chronicles follow a set scheme, generally written into the institute's constitution. For example, the Sisters of the Holy Cross in their 1855 rule book outlined procedures for maintaining mission histories, responsibilities of the recording secretary, and standards for entries into house journals. The directions stipulated appearance and content, charging that events be described as they occurred and that introductory pages explain the origins of the mission. Events inside the convent constituted the applicable topics, with mention of remarkable public or secular happenings allowed in the briefest terms. The scribe employed simple and neutral language, so the account could be read aloud without embarrassment for speaker or audience. Should a "scandal" occur, only the superior could authorize naming the involved parties. This carefully directed annalist, along with domestic assignments, professional work, and prayer obligations, produced two identical handwritten copies of the house chronicle—one sent to the motherhouse and the second stored at the local mission.[1] The job of house annalist measurably increased duties for that sister, but this clear template for subject matter and focus facilitated the assignment.

Each year, the mission superior added to the record by sending various supplemental reports to the motherhouse. These might include house expenses, health information, details of religious exercises, descriptions of school or hospital happenings, or the initiation and conclusion of secular business arrangements. The motherhouse archivist, in turn, organized and kept all mission chronicles, papers, financial statements, and legal documents, as well as the equivalent materials generated at the motherhouse.

As a congregation stabilized and assignments regularized, the duties of the secretary to the mother general expanded to include the compilation of a general community annals. In this task, the secretary summarized the annual reports and chronicles submitted from each of the mission stations, blending them into the motherhouse record, usually with an overlay of piety. In some congregations, this effort occurred years after the daughter houses submitted their annals, and once the master document was in place, some archivists discarded the originals from the missions; while much is woven into these extensive and diverse records, the dangers of purposefully manipulated narrative lurked among the pages. In addition, the point of view frequently shifted, as administrations changed and new secretaries were directed to correct, augment, expand, or delete earlier entries. A hardback ledger replaced a flimsy copybook and unmarked newspaper clippings insinuated themselves onto chronicle pages, which are notable for conflicting data, mismatched numbering, and inconsistent dating. Clearly, unraveling these documents and establishing their authenticity can be challenging; chronicles and annals, compelling as they can be, are best scrutinized, winnowed, and examined in concert with other sources. In contrast, congregations faithfully preserved legal papers, hospital statistics, financial ledgers, school enrollments, personnel files, minutes of chapter meetings, letters from clergy, and the correspondence of mother generals. Thus, across religious congregations, the plethora of records, even those compromised, represent massive primary collections about women.

Sister Emerentiana, the first archivist of the Sisters of the Holy Cross, wrote about the frustrations of trying to organize reams of shuffled papers. Her congregation arrived in the United States in 1843 but procrastinated about its formal accounting, even though directives had been written in 1855. It was not until 1893, fifty years after the Sisters of the Holy Cross had come to America and the year that Emerentiana assumed her duties, that the congregation, goaded by its early intentions, authorized a systematic overhaul of the records. The newly charged archivist confronted the reality that, despite long-standing regulations, overextended mission sisters had ignored paperwork. Mission houses failed to submit written reports in a regular fashion, leaving Emerentiana with an untidy assortment of incomplete and muddled documents. She said of her chore: "This was attended with much difficulty. . . . I had to depend on the personal recollections of the . . . sisters. . . . The memories of no two . . . agreed . . . , especially on dates, hence I was often compelled to choose the statement that seemed most likely to be true, and no doubt the reader may find . . . the same sister mentioned as being in two places at the same time!"[2]

During my research, I found that most convent archivists, like the hardworking Sister Emerentiana, fulfilled an assignment that nearly overwhelmed them. Typically, I met elderly, even grievously unwell, sisters who agreed to oversee the archives after retiring from a long convent career. Rarely did a congregation archivist have experience with documents, training in records conservation, or university degrees relating to archival procedures. A California archivist told me she was newly appointed, knew nothing about paper preservation, and had found files of over 100 years randomly stacked on the floor of a single room. Not surprisingly, the physical plants, resources, staff, and protocols of archdiocesan archives far surpassed those with a single amateur caretaker, who with grit and devotion performed her duty as well as possible.

By the 1990s, Catholic archivists came to realize the necessity of sharing professional strategies and building strength through unity. An initiative to address those ideals came with the formation of the St. Louis Area Religious Archivists (SLARA) organization, spearheaded by the indefatigable Marylu Stueber of the Franciscan Sisters of Mary. Through lectures, workshops, and regular communication, this association has significantly advanced the management and protection of congregational records, making St. Louis Catholic repositories the standard for the operation of the small private religious archives. Sister Emerentiana would be relieved and gratified.

The spirit among the members of SLARA matched that of the sister archivists I met across the West. All displayed the same three traits: a deep love for their sisterhood, an abiding respect for the documents, and a passionate desire to spread the history of the congregation. I became the beneficiary of those sentiments, for the sister archivists in every location, regardless of various constraints—monetary, educational, or geographic— eagerly facilitated my work.

From an original 125 letters of inquiry to various congregations with western missions, I received responses from more than ninety. Of these, only two dissuaded me from coming to the archives, one declaring nothing could be published without prior approval from the mother general, the other bemoaning the disorder in her files. Over twenty years, the former, removed from my research itinerary, was the only to mention a publication restriction. Rather, in the main, the sister archivists mirrored one elderly nun, who, throwing open her locked cupboards, announced: "Here is the record. It is all yours."

My correspondents invited me to work in the archives, reside as long as I needed at the convent, bring my husband, take meals in the dining room, and visit among the sisters. Many nuns, based only on my initial inquiry, sent documents or a rare book with the request, "Please return this to me, when you have finished, as it is our only copy." It was an awesome start.

Subsequently, I made many research trips to convent archives. Some records were maintained in state-of-the-art facilities; others were in Hollinger boxes along shelves in the community recreation room. Some archivists excelled at professional organization; others did not understand internal order for collections but could lay a hand on any document. Most congregations kept critical original documents in a vault, although one had cordoned off a basement, close to the boiler and two sump pumps, and piled all the ledgers on the floor or bookcases under the water pipes; all was illuminated by overhead bare electric bulbs, the sockets connected by yards of extension cords. The tenacious archivist argued for and received better quarters. In one congregation, a chagrined archivist opened the handiwork of her predecessor—a donated, musty 1950s wallpaper sample book, in which the sister randomly glued every letter, newspaper article, report, teaching note, or grocery list she could find. It was an archival disaster that a later leadership team corrected. Once I flew to a distant city for a scheduled visit, only to be turned away because a nun had broken her leg; her hospital bed had been wheeled to the archives so the caregiver, doubling as archivist and nurse, could manage. Medical privacy topped research, which had been forgotten in the melee.

Despite such human glitches, my work progressed because archivists unlocked offices at odd hours, tracked down western materials, and taught me to read between the lines of seemingly innocuous documents. They hosted my husband and me for meals, introduced us to their companions, shared witty and frank conversations, welcomed us for days in their guest apartments; fees for board and services, if they existed at all, remained embarrassingly small. Many entrusted cherished records to a researcher from the secular community for the first time in the history of the congregation, and they did so with honesty and openness. I am forever in the debt of these religious women who contributed so fully to this project. Some sisters who assisted me continue as the congregation archivist or have retired, but several have died, as indicated with (+) before the name. I thank the following:

(+)Helen Streck ASC, Wichita; (+)Inez Blatz OSB, St. Joseph, Minnesota; Frances Briseno OSB, Boerne, Texas; Mary Walker OSB, Bismarck, North Dakota; Margaret J. Clarke OSB and Richard Boo OSB, Duluth, Minnesota; (+)M. Louis George OSB, Tulsa, Oklahoma; Maria Espiritu McCall SBS and (+)Margaret O'Rourke SBS, Bensalem, Pennsylvania; Genevieve Keusenkothen DC, St. Louis; Margaret Ann Gainey DC and M. William Vinet DC, Los Angeles; Deanna Carr BVM and (+)M. Clara Bormann BVM, Dubuque, Iowa; (+)Josephine Kennelly CCVI, San Antonio; (+)Seraphine Sheehan SCL, Leavenworth, Kansas; Charlotte Kitowski CDP and (+)M. Paul Valdez CDP, San Antonio; Lois Hoh OP and Marie Walter Flood OP, Sinsinawa, Wisconsin; Jo Ann Niehaus OP, Galveston, Texas; (+)Gerald LaVoy OP, San Rafael, California; Helen Jacobson OSF and (+)Marita Egan OSF, Aston, Pennsylvania; (+)Grace McDonald FSPA, La Crosse, Wisconsin; (+)Alcantara Schneider OSF, Rochester, Minnesota; Michaela O'Connor SHF, Fremont, California; Rosemarie Kasper SNJM, Portland, Oregon; Miriam Mitchell SHSp, Anne Finnerty SHSp, and Mary Pius X Gorman SHSp, San Antonio; Patricia Rose Shanahan CSJ, Los Angeles; Charline Sullivan CSJ, St. Louis; Mary Kraft CSJ, Minneapolis; Marylu Stueber FSM, St. Louis; Joy Weideman OSM and (+)Adolorata Watson OSM, Omaha; Mary Katherine Doyle RSM, Auburn, California; Marilyn Gouailhardou RSM, Burlingame, California; (+)Edna Marie LeRoux RSM, Farmington Hills, Michigan; M. Jeremy Buckman RSM and (+)M. Joseph Scanlon RSM, St. Louis; Susan Dunwald RSM, Cedar Rapids, Iowa; Gabriel Ann Tamayo MCDP, San Antonio; Constance Fenwick OSP and (+)M. Reparata OSP, Baltimore; Marlyss Dionne SMP, Valley City, North Dakota; Maureen Walker PBVM and (+)Mary Jo Hasey PBVM, Fargo, North Dakota; Barbara Miner SCSC, Milwaukee; Sarita Genin SSND, Milwaukee; Mary Ann Kuttner SSND, Mankato, Minnesota; Carol Marie Wildt SSND and Judith Best SSND, St. Louis; Kathleen Padden OSU and (+)Rose Marie Kaupp OSU, Toledo, Ohio; (+)Christine Wolken OSU, Paola, Kansas; and Charlene Herinckx SSMO, Beaverton, Oregon.

In addition, I thank these archivists: Jeffrey M. Burns, San Francisco Archdiocese Archives; Kevin Cawley and Sharon K. Sumpter, University of Notre Dame Archives; J. Norman Dizon, Seattle Archdiocese Archives; Roberta Doelling, Sisters of Mercy Archives, St. Louis; Mary A. Grant Doty, Portland Archdiocese Archives; Loretta Z. Greene and Peter F. Schmid, Sisters of Providence Archives, Seattle; (+)Peter E. Hogan SSJ, Josephite Fathers Archives, Baltimore; Ronald M. James, Preservation Officer, State of Nevada; David Kingma, Gonzaga University Archives; Monte G. Kniffen, Sisters of Mercy Archives, Omaha, Nebraska; Edward J. Loch SM, San Antonio Archdiocese Archives; Margaret Lichter, Dominican Sisters of Edmonds, Washington, Archives; Stephanie Morris, Sisters of the Blessed Sacrament Archives, Bensalem, Pennsylvania; Kathleen O'Connor, Sisters of Notre Dame de Namur Archives, Belmont, California; (+)Kinga Perzynska, Catholic Archives of Texas, Austin; Mark G. Thiel, Marquette University Archives, Milwaukee.

Research funds from several agencies provided crucial aid, including Michael Karchmer of the Gallaudet Research Institute with a summer research award; the Cushwa Center at the University of Notre Dame, a Hibernian grant; Utah State University, a faculty research grant; the Irish American Cultural Institute; the National Endowment for the Humanities, a summer stipend; and the Utah Humanities Council, the Albert J. Colton Fellowship.

In other areas, I owe many. For mighty office assistance, I thank Lynne Payne at Gallaudet University and Barbara Stewart at Utah State University (USU). There are not enough words of gratitude for Carolyn Doyle, who ran the *Western Historical Quarterly* office at USU with high-quality professionalism and efficiency, even as she meticulously and cheerfully prepared my manuscripts for publication. For this one, Carolyn returned to my life, fixing every problem, relieving worries, assuring me I could meet my deadline, and guaranteeing that I did so. Thank you.

At USU, scholarly days were better because of Carol A. O'Connor, Clyde A. Milner, and Ona Siporin, each generously reading chapters of this manuscript. These three helped me to sharpen my ideas, asking better questions of my material and myself. In the face of a blizzard of pressing demands and heavy burdens, they promoted this work and me with spectacular enthusiasm and gigantic friendship.

Students from USU enhanced my teaching and did the same for this manuscript. Heather Block Lawton and Michael J. Lansing motivated me to stay on task. They read early chapters and traveled to Florida, making critiques more forceful and fun by their presence. From Alaska, John W. Heaton, and from South Dakota, Matthew Pehl, both with a devotion to rigorous scholarship, inspired me with their high standards, professionally and personally. The life of every mentor should be graced with superior students and treasured friends the likes of these four.

I thank other outstanding associates, who in various ways aided in making this a more thoughtful book. Michael E. Engh SJ, Gerald McKevitt SJ, Louis L. Renner SJ, and the late Thomas W. Spalding CFX pointed the way to critical scholarship in Catholic history. Carol K. Coburn and Roberto R. Treviño read the entire draft with care, offering the rich insights and core assessments so necessary for a scholarly project. Their assistance meant more than these few words convey. I also thank Glenda Riley, Suellen Hoy, Margaret McGuinness, Donna F. Ryan, Terrence J. McGovern, and Susan Devore—all of whom insisted that western sisters deserved their place in the canon and urged me to see them there.

At the University of North Carolina Press, I had the good fortunate to work with senior editor Charles Grench, who supported this manuscript from our first conversation over dinner in Denver. At the press, I also thank Jay Mazzocchi and Sara J. Cohen, whose encouraging manner and meticulous attention eased every phase of production. I, of course, remain solely responsible for the content of or any error in my work.

I extend affection and thanks to my high school teacher and debate coach, Kyllene Bodum SSND; my late cousin, Jordan Buckley CFX; and my late professor, Virgina Geiger SSND. Each loved academics and, as educators, prodded me toward the world of letters. In addition, the friendship and hospitality of Bill and Marlene Eckert, Doris and Warren Moos, Nelson and Joan Cooney, and Jane M. Martin lifted my spirit over many years.

The late Charlotte and Delbert Theall, my legal guardians for fourteen years, homesteaded as newlyweds on the Canadian prairie. As older people with a New England farm, they boarded children from derailed circumstances. For the Thealls, I was family; they made the good childhood a life taken for granted and set me on a steady path to the future. Sprawled by their fireplace, I found their worn, leather-bound album of Alberta scenes mesmerizing. With images of tar-paper shacks, Norwegian immigrants, barley harvests, Native families, and the streets of old Calgary, the neatly captioned black-and-white photographs imprinted the West in my heart and mind. Not only did these extraordinary people open home and hearth, they whetted the intellectual curiosity that drove my professional life. I also thank their grandson Peter G. Manson, my brother Edward E. Oligney, my sister Barbara O. Britz, and my cousins Ruth Maroney Young and Carolyn Christmas Centuori—always a spectacular, albeit unconventional, family.

On Amelia Island came new champions. Rose Gladney, with her intellectual passion and sense of justice, deepened my vision. Every Tuesday, Maurine Lenahan arrived with warmth and charm, never complaining about my unsightly den. In the face of distraction, Carolee Zdanis added merry wit, a thousand kindnesses, and daily ballast. From David Burghardt, I learned more about the fragile beauty of historical photographs. Gary Gaskill, who also loved antique images, and the late Chuck Zdanis used patience and skill on my temperamental computer; I appreciate Gary, miss Chuck, and thank them both.

My deepest affections go to immediate family. Stepdaughters Amy Barsanti and Jennifer Butler always applauded my endeavors. Nine grandchildren—all girls—spurred me to add another piece to western gender history. Jay Butler buoyed me with his faith, energy, and merriment. Jay has been an exceptional spouse, advocate, and companion, especially for one who fell accidentally, but cheerfully, into the unusual world of historical scholarship. Finally: my children, Daniel Ryan Porterfield and Katherine Anne Porterfield. Dan and Kate sustained all my history journeys and life adventures; I lovingly dedicate this work to them.

Across God's Frontiers

*The sea is so rough that it is
with difficulty that we can
remain in bed. To add to our
terror, the ship takes fire.*

—Oregon Chronicles,
20 October 1859, Archives
of the Sisters of the Holy
Names of Jesus and Mary,
Portland, Oregon

Introduction

In 1836 a small band of Sisters of St.
Joseph of Carondelet, under the leadership of Mother Febronie Fontbonne, left
Lyons, France, to begin a mission in St.
Louis, Missouri. In 1852 Sister Francis
and six Daughters of Charity of St.
Vincent de Paul departed from Emmitsburg, Maryland, for San Francisco,
California, where within weeks the five
surviving nuns opened a school. In 1856
Mother Joseph of the Providence sisters of Montreal, Canada, and two other
French-speaking sisters launched the
first hospital in the Washington Territory. In 1857 Sister Willibalda brought a
handful of Bavarian Benedictines safely
to St. Cloud, Minnesota, where they
established a monastery in what they
could only describe as "wilderness."

Hardship in travel, illness of body, peril to spirit, poverty on poverty—these colored each of the ventures above. Yet together, these fragile groups, harbingers of thousands to come, planted a place for themselves, their congregations, and their church in the American West. These few nuns were not the first to labor in North America, nor even the first west of the Mississippi River. Mercy sisters and Presentation sisters from Ireland, Ursulines and Religious of the Sacred Heart from France had all sent earlier missionaries. Operating on convent directives and faith incentives, the women journeyed to settings they had never imagined, established "convents," went about their service work, and waited to greet and succor the next wave of professed religious making the fearful transition from "Old World" to "New."

The sorties of Catholic sisters into many western corners etched out unique spaces for convent life in the West. Individually and collectively, their stories cobbled together a spiritual scaffolding on which the western pioneer experiences of religious congregations of women rest. Energized by western life, the women discarded many of the weighty constraints inherent in their vowed rituals, reshaped their identity, and moved on, renewed. Yet, for all they introduced to America, all their activity, all their womanhood, these nuns hardly originated monastic life and convent routines. That complex story preceded cloister building in the American West.

European history included the phenomenon of women desiring a religious life set apart, beginning with fourth-century ascetics in the deserts of North Africa. Buoyed by the examples of holy men, religiously motivated women cast aside the family structures in the known cities for the self-exploration and self-denial of rocky caves. Rather than regarded as a punishment, spiritual reclusiveness lured ancient women with its freedom from domestic and sexual obligations and the opportunity to test intellectual, religious, and physical stamina.[1]

The women's lives failed to bring pious anonymity. Rather, they sparked interest and speculation among the less devout, even as they promoted the ideal of committed religious profession. By the fifth and sixth centuries, the cross-pollination of religious traditions between Western and Eastern civilizations had blossomed into an altered European spiritual lifestyle—monasticism—for both women and men.

With that movement, however, came significant restrictive gender attitudes. Male religious leaders and desert ascetics passionately preached avoidance of females as necessary for piety and purity, a notion that gained purchase in Europe. When the single hermits abandoned austere isolation for the brotherhood of shared community, they elbowed women religious physically, as well as intellectually, from the centers of spiritual power.

Organized religious life emerged, but with a masculine resonance. It called on authoritative male voices to decide the boundaries and routines of communal life. To achieve personal sanctity, religious men, the founders argued, should wander among the populace, beg for sustenance, preach Christian reform, and, even in poverty, derive intellectual benefit from contact with the evolving economic and political structures of society. The ascent of a few European abbesses aside, prominent diviners of religious rules, such as Benedict of Nursia (ca. 480–ca. 547), Dominic of Osma (1170–1221), and Francis of Assisi (ca. 1181–1226), diluted female spiritual autonomy by forming a gendered set of regulations for vowed women.

For women, the emphasis by founding fathers on mandatory walled enclosure, severe prayer schedules, banned public connections, and the imposition of the "grand silence" retarded social knowledge, legitimated religious segregation by gender, truncated female leadership in the church, and denied access to the stimulations of the larger community. By the Middle Ages, women living under these masculine monastic rules endured further hindrances from family feuds, political alliances, and land holdings in a society driven by church and state competition.

Not the least of that convoluted story involved the physical campus where professed women lived and prayed. The European monastery evolved over many years into an imposing assortment of purposefully placed buildings. Here stood the gatehouse and reception parlor, there the private quarters of the abbess, an imposing chapel with a cemetery conveniently close by, nuns' dormitories, a chapter house for administrative business, a main kitchen, and an infirmary discreetly located to isolate the infected. Livestock, gardens, and orchards dotted about the perimeter, while the cloister itself—an open-air center quad surrounded by a covered walkway—assumed an institutional character that influenced the construction of convents, churches, and universities for hundreds of years. Walled monasteries, with their nearly self-sufficient residents, conveyed their fierce message of barricaded space; the world was not welcome to enter freely, the residents not at their leave to depart. These locked spiritual enclaves pulsated with coercion, where women pressured by family and clergy wedded themselves to lifelong service in their church, as defined by the male hierarchy of their faith.

But America invigorated professed religious life for Catholic women and challenged these European models. Powerful social, economic, and political factors outside the ancient structures of European Catholicism spun a novel humanity for nuns and sisters in America. With these changes came a blow to the very institution most closely associated with cloistered life for women: the sealed-off monastery. Nowhere would the resulting transformations be more evident or more clearly delineated than in the American West.

When post–Civil War America turned to the economic and political horizons of the West, the nation generally overlooked the Catholic nuns already a part of that scene. Somehow, quiet cloister gardens and praying women appeared at odds with the boisterous and bloody stories—successes and failures, contests and combatants—associated with a vast region of North America. Nobody seemed to remember the arrival of the Sisters of St. Joseph in St. Louis or the Daughters of Charity in Los Angeles. Yet, those sisters and others who made their way into the American West in the early days of its Anglo-European incursions, and the women who inhabited those primitive "convents," added to western community building, for good and ill. Nuns often acted with parochial ignorance and cultural blindness, even as they made specific contributions to regional and national events. At the same time, their western experiences touched sisters deeply, producing life-changing epiphanies for individuals and congregations.

For decades, convent histories lagged, as nuns, usually in an "obedience," wrote about sister colleagues in publications that used a common template. In sentimental language, each vouched for the holiness of the founding mother, enthused about the paternal bishop who served as the spiritual director, and recited in meticulous detail the decisions of various superiors of the order. Disagreements and defections, arrogance and ambition— these the congregational apologists obscured. A careful reading between the lines might imply, but only faintly, that the local bishop's "fatherly concern for his daughters" really meant the sisters thought the prelate an overbearing bully who controlled their every move and every penny. Further, the historical landscapes on which congregational events occurred seldom mattered in these accounts, and scholarly analysis eluded the text. Amid the narrative, alleged "holy" conversations between nuns added literary invention, designed to inspire with the cheerful "saintliness" of the subjects. All in all, the finished product appealed only to a limited audience.

In fairness, those who wrote early congregational histories knew that no Catholic manuscript reached a printer without the ornate stamps of the *Nihil Obstat* and *Imprimatur*. All church publications passed under the careful scrutiny of congregational administrators, a committee of outside judges, and the bishop to earn these flyleaf embossments. Realistically, no nun historian, well acquainted with this gauntlet of censorship, expected her work to be published if it cast an unfavorable light on or questioned the behavior of bishops, priests, or congregational leaders.

There are exceptions within the genre, works aimed at the larger canon of history. The following three heightened my appreciation for the efforts of nun historians to produce measured, well-researched studies.

In 1948 Mary Evangeline Thomas published a detailed monograph titled *Footprints on the Frontier: A History of the Sisters of Saint Joseph, Concordia, Kansas*, in which she argued her congregation should be viewed within the framework of Frederick Jackson Turner's 1893 frontier thesis. Thomas, a meticulous academician, faulted Turner for his failure to value the religious aspects of the western movement of white society, although, oddly, she made no comment on his parallel neglect of women of any persuasion. Despite a focus on one sisterhood, Thomas made the point that women religious belonged in the history of the American West.

In *As God Shall Ordain: A History of the Franciscan Sisters of Chicago, 1894–1987* (1989), Anne Marie Knawa traced the bumpy road to stability for one congregation. Searching out far-flung repositories and tracking slim leads, Knawa, with an exhaustive array of correspondence, illuminated the forgotten but important intermingling of sisterhoods. Thus, Knawa showed congregations as owners of primary documents laden with gender history.

Finally, Mary Richard Boo's *House of Stone: The Duluth Benedictines* (1991) enlarged the academic maturity emanating from the history of American religious women. Enriched by extensive research and crafted into a graceful narrative, *House of Stone* shaded the personalities and actions of its main characters, many of whom in very human ways challenged the "piety" model of earlier publications. This author confronted the politics and controversies endemic to congregation building without censure or sentiment, creating a realistic assessment of convent leaders and followers.

These books pointed to the evolving paradigms in writings about women religious. Over five decades, women religious attending to their own history wrestled with the hagiography of an earlier time and pushed themselves, their scholarship, and their congregations toward mainstream academia. Still, newer works generally ignored the wider field of women's history and did not apply the implications of feminist scholarship to nuns and sisters.

One notable exception, *Building Sisterhood: A Feminist History of the Sisters, Servants of the Immaculate Heart of Mary* (1997), broke the mold for writing by religious women. A collaborative publication by members and associates of the congregation, this volume intentionally and specifically embraced all aspects of the Immaculate Heart of Mary experience from a feminist perspective. It explored learned gender roles inside the congregation, the assumption and rejection of identity, the honing of an intellectual and spiritual philosophy, the phases of reaching an inner sense of personal freedom, and the consequences of interactions with a male-dominated clergy. As such, it stands alone in the contribution made to the history of women religious, laying out the cycles of life for a congregation and its members.

With the convergence of women's history and a feminist perspective, religious congregations appeared poised to enter a new era of scholarship. The volume above suggested other congregations would hurry toward a fresh assessment of themselves, one based on emerging ideas about the history of women.[2] In addition, the subject sounded like a natural for secular scholars, especially those grounded in feminist thinking. Some few have answered that call. I have found the ideas of the following individuals useful.

Shortly before the appearance of the Immaculate Heart of Mary essays, Jo Ann Kay McNamara, in her magisterial study *Sisters in Arms: Catholic Nuns through Two Millennia* (1996), set a scholarly standard for writing about women religious. In a sweeping opus that embraced Christianity across the ages, McNamara opened a Pandora's box of religion, releasing dark clouds of gender history. From era to era, she examined the place and role of professed women in the Catholic tradition. McNamara argued that gender differences constituted the essential ingredient in an ideology that promoted male authority. She allowed no quarter to the masculine church, insistent on forcing women to chastity and cloister even as it feared that a community of sequestered females might discover and develop autonomy. McNamara traced the earliest female spirituality in the African deserts to womanly prospects in modern society, always probing the church denial of the intellectual and spiritual capacity of women. Although, across the centuries, a disheartening theme of oppression darkened her conclusions, McNamara assembled a stunning mosaic of womanhood and an anthem to the religious courage and tenacity of professed women.

I am also influenced by the scholarship of Margaret Susan Thompson, who examined the way that sisters enabled the early American Catholic Church to embrace its diverse constituency. Thompson cast a feminist religious mantle over nuns of the past but shook it out as a blanket for reflection, rather than as an artificial cloak over sisters' lives. Thompson, author of "Discovering Foremothers: Sisters, Society, and the American Catholic

Experience," and whose supporting analysis unified the feminist essays of the Sisters, Servants of the Immaculate Heart of Mary, stressed the integrity of a charism in dealing with a congregation's history.

According to Thompson, charism, a term gaining broad usage since Vatican II, is "the spiritual impetus that impelled it [the congregation] into existence and thereby enables it to make a unique contribution both to Catholicism and to the wider religious culture."[3] In calling for a faithful presentation of charism, Thompson emphasized that authors compromise the "collective legitimacy as a religious congregation" when by omissions and inventions they distort the record, thus undermining the very justification for a sisterhood.[4] Margaret Susan Thompson, brushing aside the works of piety, unfurled a new banner for those writing the history of nuns.

In the philosophical realm, I am drawn to the work of Terrence W. Tilley. In his monograph, *Inventing Catholic Tradition* (2000), Tilley examined theories applicable to the historical experiences of nuns and sisters. His discussion that questions whether traditions are made or given touched directly on the lives of nuns and sisters who traveled into and worked in the American West. On the surface, it might appear that nuns lived by an immutable code and behaved in an equally unchanging manner. Yet everything that happened to nuns in the American West contradicted those assumptions, even as the sisters themselves believed they held to old traditions and passed them intact to new members. Although I would not attempt to incorporate the full complexity of Tilley's philosophical argument into my historical narrative, his ideas shadowed me as I considered this work.

Important as these scholars have been to me, as a western historian I see these issues about women religious somewhat differently and in a multifaceted regional setting. For me, there are elements that set Tucson, Arizona, apart from Baltimore, Maryland, or Helena, Montana, apart from Richmond, Virginia. For that matter, Tucson is not Helena, the singularities and oddities of each reinforcing the attraction for using the word "West" in the plural, encompassing as it does one distinct region after another.

In these western places, as well as other locations, I see differing collections of economic and political circumstances shaping the lives of people constantly in transition. Further, the West, with its reliance on white masculine imagery and action, offers a compelling environment in which to sort out racial divides and gender patterns. In the West, the varied associations swirling between and among groups of people is unmatched in America—for horror and humanity.

I am aware that discussions about what constitutes "the West" have sharpened over the past twenty years, especially since the emergence of the "New" western history. When I began graduate studies at the University of Maryland, professors ran a pointer along a map of the United States, traced the length of the Mississippi River, swept over the pink and yellow states to the Pacific Ocean, and told the class: "This is the West." Courses labeled as the history of the "Cis-Mississippi" or of the "Trans-Mississippi" confirmed that easterners with the Atlantic Ocean at their backs saw the West according to white political and cultural institutions.

The appearance of many critical publications and the occasion of many heated discussions paused the use of such geography and history. Western historians began to question the worn tropes of "pioneer," "Wild West," or "frontier," with exciting results. Listening to new voices, many from indigenous women and men, a West as a place defined and understood by its own peoples rearranged our historical vision. Arbitrary boundaries by Rand McNally did not make sense when the peoples of color, standing in and on their own land, questioned those wedded to definitions written with the pens of nationalism and imperialism.

Accordingly, my West as a subject for scholarly research has changed many times over, even to a point of weariness. Yet, I recognize the necessity to set fences for a historical work, giving order to where and when the author travels. The reader will find here many Wests; these Wests include the continental United States bounded by the Pacific Ocean and the Mississippi River but also touch down, be it briefly, in Ohio, Pennsylvania, Wisconsin, Indiana, and Alaska.[5] Readers may assert that I have simply become uncertain about the West the longer I have wandered through its compelling and majestic geographies, listening to its mingle of voices.

That charge may be true, but as I pursued the records of the many religious congregations serving in these diverse regions, it became apparent that regardless of discussions today, my subjects believed themselves to be "in the West." They held this conviction at the time they generated their documents and later in life when they recalled earlier years in those locations. The peoples with whom the nuns associated also nurtured a personal understanding of place and knew themselves the owners of these spaces. These forests and plains, mesas and valleys were homelands, once not overrun by invading armies, snatched away by land-grabbers, divided up among religions, or controlled by an absent white government. Natives and newcomers agreed that the landscapes on which they accepted and rejected one another pulsated with a western ambience and a western history that did not belong to the East. It seemed fair to honor that perception.

I intended the time frame of this work to fall between 1865 and 1920, a decision that soon revealed fault lines. How could the Sisters of the Holy Names or the Sisters of Providence simply "appear" in Oregon and Washington? The reader needed a context for understanding that French Canadian sisters made arduous treks by wagon, steamer, and donkey from Canada, through New York, along the Atlantic coast, across the Isthmus of Panama, and north on the Pacific coast to set those convents into motion. The nuns produced a narrative in reaching those places, one that influenced their lives as they took up missions far from their Canadian motherhouses; so I have supplied some accounts before 1865 to anchor sisters in the West. In 1908 the United States closed as "mission territory" and began sending nuns out of the country, rather than receiving them regularly as missionaries. In 1917 a rewritten Canon Law—something like a religious cousin to the U.S. tax code—showed the futility of definitive statements about enclosure, further freeing sisters' choices. Plenty of poverty, isolation, and hardship continued inside convents, but by 1920 many American sisterhoods planned sophisticated futures of national and international public-service activism.

Although "nun" and "sister" appear in the glossary, in the interests of clarity, I state here the differences in the two words and explain how they are used in this book. The terms are often confused, and commonly many persons say "nun" when "sister" would be more precise. Nuns pronounced solemn permanent vows, resided for life in one house under the rule of enclosure, and were obligated each day to recite or chant the Divine Office, a closely regulated liturgical prayer reflecting the canonical hours, from which come such terms as "matins" and "vespers." Sisters pronounced simple vows and abjured enclosure and daily chant, developing an active ministry with less-rigorous prayer routines and frequently transferring from one convent to another. Nuns joined religious orders; sisters joined congregations or institutes. Prayerful contemplation versus prayerful service roughly distinguishes the two categories.

Several terms are interchanged to reduce word repetition. Frequently, "nun" and "sister" appear in tandem to account for the possible status of all the women discussed. Also, the words "order," "congregation," and "institute" are used for variety. "Community" is another reference to a sisterhood, but in most cases it is reserved to mean secular people near a convent.

Inside the American Catholic community, one hears, as with all cultural subsets of society, language peculiar to the group. Catholics converse about their church, faith practices, and religious congregations of men and women in a shorthand. For example, a member of the Sisters of Charity of the Blessed Virgin Mary would be known as a "BVM," the initials after each sister's name; more than one Catholic refers to the School Sisters of Notre Dame as "the SSNDs." Catholics know this jargon, but the terms can be mystifying for the uninitiated. To help with the maze of Catholic administrative and institutional vocabulary, a glossary follows the text.

The names of nuns can be confusing, especially as many of them represented masculine or Latin forms intended to evoke thoughts of revered popes, sacramental devotions, saintly martyrs, or church feasts and liturgies. At the same moment, unrelated sisterhoods might include a "Sister Pancratia" or a "Mother Cornelius." Also, most congregations prefaced each name with a version of "Mary" but abbreviated it, as in "Sister M. Dorothea." Within a congregation, just as in intimate family groups, authority figures gave out one name at a time. When a sister died, her name returned to the novitiate pool for future members. Generally, I have identified a sister's congregation and included a family surname, if available. In subsequent references, I may have reduced the personal or congregational name for literary economy. Thus, Mother Mary Amadeus of the Sacred Heart Dunne, compressed to Mother Amadeus, Amadeus, or Dunne. A list of congregations named and their abbreviations precedes the preface.

This book argues that Roman Catholic nuns and sisters represented a significant part of the American narrative of women, religion, and the West. Roman Catholic sisterhoods sustained far-flung, small convents of single women who, outside the normative structures of marriage and family, carved a social, economic, and political place for themselves, their congregations, and their church in the American West. In their convents, women, bonded by spiritual commonalties and across a wide range of ages and nationalities, accommodated a shifting religious environment.

The Roman Catholic Church operated on a long-developed system of patriarchy. In its religious tenets and human administration, the church privileged men over women in every instance. Nuns and sisters participated in advancing this patriarchy and also resisted its power. Given these realities, this book specifically does not suggest that all bishops and priests conspired to be villains, suppressing religious women. Nonetheless, by intent and accident, the general interaction between male clergy and religious women advanced gender discrimination.

Riding on the great waves of European immigration, Catholic nuns cut their first American paths as outsiders and newcomers come to find employment and a life. They built on those initial convent ventures to attract young American women to religious life. Through skilled administration, financial acumen, and congregational purpose, they found ways to support themselves and to build institutions that offered multifaceted services to indigenous groups and displaced migrants—families, bachelors, widows, other single women, children—often before territorial, state, or local government offices could do so. Typically dressed in church-fashioned habits of a style that set them apart from other women, sisters in the West encountered rapidly changing convent routines, as they accommodated the demands of the populations around them, expanded their social agencies, and answered to the administrative and spiritual expectations of a motherhouse hundreds of miles away in the East or Europe.

Further, most sisters missioned to the West wrestled with congregational, clerical, and secular tensions exacerbated by poor communication networks, great distances, conflicting goals, power disputes, national rivalries, and various kinds of discrimination. Despite these handicaps, in the American West, Catholic nuns served as conduits in the shaping of institutions and in the exchange of culture between indigenous and invading peoples. The configurations of convent lives shifted, as the sisters responded in positive and negative ways to matters of race, class, and gender within their convents and among western peoples. Ultimately, Catholic nuns and sisters influenced community building in the West, and the West energized change in the practice of religious life for Catholic women in America. Overall, this narrative suggests the ways in which the West played a major role in the transformation of the European cloister into the American convent. Accordingly, it is the aim of this regional account of Roman Catholic nuns and sisters to enlarge the history of American religion, American women, and the American West.

RESURRECTION SISTER
(Author's collection)

*I was a young lady of the
world before I came to the
convent. I had tasted of its
sweets and bitters. . . . The novitiate was a haven of peace,
a renewal of youth.*

—Sister Colubkille McEnery,
Memoirs of Pioneer Sisters,
Archives of the Sisters of
Divine Providence,
San Antonio

Nuns for the West

Sister Colubkille McEnery once
thought only to remain in the comfortable surroundings of her native Ireland,
close to kith and kin. Ultimately, this
spirited woman chose differently, left
her familiar world, and traveled more
than 4,000 miles from the Emerald
Isle. She ventured into the alien landscapes of the American West and the
unknowns of a convent world. She bid
farewell to her Irish home and journeyed to the remote town of Castroville, Texas, approximately twenty-five
miles south of San Antonio, where she
redefined herself as a religious sister in
the Congregation of Divine Providence.
Rejecting her life as a "young lady of
the world," she chose to be "nun within
a cloister," eschewing husband and

family, embracing duty and obedience, and following daily routines guided by church regulations, spiritual rituals, self-denial, and community work. She accepted devotion to the Divine Providence ideals shaped more than 125 years earlier in the eighteenth century, ideals centered on educating poor children in rural areas, which now she found aplenty in the countryside of Texas.[1]

Although they shared religious affiliation under the mantle of the Roman Catholic Church, nuns and sisters represented a broad assortment of women. Their religious congregations, social profiles, national loyalties, spiritual goals, and personal expectations gave them diversity. Their youth, zest, and intellectual curiosity drew them together in commonalty. As unmarried women living in western Catholic convents and mission stations, they added to the race, class, and gender complexity that marked all areas of the West. Ultimately, the multiple factors that shaped these nuns produced a unique band of pioneering women who, while balancing carefully circumscribed public and private roles, wove a significant and complicated gendered thread through the fabric of the American West.

Crossing Borders for Convents

In earlier decades of the nineteenth century, prior to Sister Colubkille's life-changing move, women from other nations launched similar religious quests directed toward the United States. In the 1870s, Mother Mary Odilia Berger, the older of twin girls from a Bavarian family of three such sets, and her five religious companions arrived in St. Louis, Missouri, after tumultuous years in France and Germany.[2] In 1872 Mother Odilia, despairing of the secular European climate, had written to Gustave Wegman, her American contact, that "the present state of affairs with regard to religious and convents especially, is so discouraging that we feel inclined to cross the ocean."[3] Convinced that Europe promised only unmitigated repression for Catholics, especially nuns, Berger hoped in America to reenergize her congregation, which was devoted to the spiritual dictates of Francis of Assisi and committed to nursing service in the homes of the sick.[4] In mid-August of 1874, Sister Mary Anselma Felber and four Swiss Benedictine companions said their farewells to the nuns around them and inched along the craggy, steep descent from their mountain-high abbey. Selected for missions in the American West, the nuns rested one night in Lucerne, Switzerland, took a train to Paris, France, and boarded a ship that bore them across the Atlantic Ocean. Three weeks later, the Swiss nuns, who ranged in age from twenty-three to thirty-five, arrived in Maryville, Mis-

souri. There, in a rural spot where no promised convent waited, the destitute sisters, whose languages included fluent Swiss, limited German, and
less Latin, undertook the study of English, hoping to open a school.[5]

At the beginning of 1893, the Servants of Mary in London, England,
agreed to a second attempt at mission work in the United States and released
five sisters, led by Sister Mary Gertrude Guinaw and Sister Mary Xavier.
The sisters first returned to Wisconsin, scene of the earlier failed effort,
but relocated to Indiana and ultimately moved further west to Omaha,
Nebraska.[6] Searching for employment, they started a kindergarten, where
they relied on European pedagogy for their classroom methods.

In 1902 twenty-eight-year-old Sister Marie Agnes, born Victorine
Bagot in Plénée, France, and four companions of the Sisters of Mary of
the Presentation began a school in Wild Rice, North Dakota. It was the
first of several missions in the United States for these Presentation sisters,
who, on leaving chaotic circumstances in France, journeyed to Manitoba,
Canada, before crossing the border to the United States and locating south
of Fargo.[7] Assessing their future, a priest supporter advised: "There are no
French sisters in the diocese of Fargo. . . . You will be able to expand into
many other parishes. . . . For the moment, you need no English diplomas."[8]
Local residents reinforced those words for Sister Marie Agnes, when in
Wild Rice she was told, "We want French sisters to teach our children our
holy religion and our old French tongue."[9]

West of North Dakota, in Colorado, Mother Frances Xavier Cabrini,
as she had done in other locations, closely examined the immigrant Italian community. Directed by the Vatican to focus on expatriates in several
countries, Cabrini, founder of the Missionaries of the Sacred Heart, specialized in operating social-service centers for Italians in many arenas. In
Denver, Mother Cabrini, touched by the hardships of the miners and their
families, wrote to her sisters in Rome that "the very great number of Italians . . . here renders our mission . . . more necessary."[10]

In the United States, the number of foreign immigrants rose to nearly
100,000 by 1840 and then roared past 20 million by 1920. In their choices,
Sister Colubkille McEnery, Mother Odilia Berger, Sister Mary Anselma
Felber, Sister Mary Gertrude Guiwan, Sister Marie Agnes Bagot, and
Mother Frances Xavier Cabrini—women of Irish, German, Swiss, English, French, and Italian heritage—and other women religious participated in this massive story of people on the move. These nuns and sisters
came from many countries, and like their secular fellow travelers, they explored strange locales, pursued promising employment, and then settled
into various pockets of the United States. Accordingly, the lives of Catho-

In 1893 the English Servants of Mary sent just two immigrant nuns to the West
but ultimately established a motherhouse in Nebraska, welcoming others from abroad,
building their reputation as educators, and accepting local young women to
the novitiate. (Courtesy Servants of Mary, Omaha, Neb.)

lic sisters reflected the tumultuous but interesting path of the American
immigrant experience.

The West, whether encroached on by religious women or secular families, sheltered a piebald assortment of people, welcoming them in varying degrees and pitting one group against another in the brutal battle for
economic advantage and control of land.[11] By 1890, among foreign-born
westerners, almost 170,000 were German, the tally for Irish tilted toward
115,000, and Mexicans accounted for more than 75,000. Italians, fewer
than 30,000 in 1890, by 1910 had climbed to almost 125,000, whereas over
200,000 residents of Mexico crossed into U.S. territory.[12]

In addition, migrants other than the foreign-born circulated through
the West looking for new prospects or escaping the land-grabbing outsiders. Anglo-Americans set forth from a family plot in the East to try
for farms, or gold, or cattle. Thousands of Native Americans, confronting cataclysmic political and economic disruptions, abandoned their home

places or hunkered down on small reservations, courtesy of government coercion. This restless cross-cultural movement of people raised the dust of the West and changed its social face, altered local demographics, and left institutional voids for all communities.[13]

Other newcomers joined the European immigrants sweeping into many regions of the West. Restless neighbors to the north and south also participated in the human stampede. In the post–Civil War West, Mexicans and Canadians augmented the incoming western populations—no less enticed by the employment opportunities, no less driven to leave uncomfortable political tensions, no less impelled to find increased advantage for their families than Europeans.[14]

In 1883 Mother St. Pierre Cinquin supported the initiative to "assist [the Spanish sisters and postulants] . . . in spiritual and material matters" and looked to Mexico as an ongoing source of recruits for her congregation.[15] By 1889, always happy to increase the size of her Texas sisterhood, she reported with satisfaction that "Mexican postulants . . . came in large numbers."[16]

Women who entered convents inside Mexico also emigrated north to the American West. The Daughters of the Purity of Mary organized as a congregation in Aguascalientes, Mexico, in 1903, but some sisters later emigrated permanently to Kingsville, Texas.[17] In 1914, traveling under the protection of U.S. soldiers, an entire congregation—Sisters, Servants of Mary of Vera Cruz, Mexico—immigrated to Galveston, Texas, later establishing their foundation in Louisiana.[18]

To the north, Canadian women interested in religious life also carried that desire across borders into the United States. From 1852 through 1910, the Sisters of St. Joseph in St. Paul, Minnesota, accepted approximately 796 candidates for the novitiate, of whom 418 were native to America, 371 were foreign-born, and 7 could not name their homelands (although they almost certainly were non-American). Of those from outside the United States, 153 listed Canada as their place of birth, so that approximately 41 percent of the foreign-born applicants for the Sisters of St. Joseph stepped over a neighboring international boundary for a convent life that emulated the language of home and the traditions of hearth.[19] In addition, from 1852 through 1910, of the 418 American-born candidates, 267, or almost 65 percent, hailed from Minnesota, indicating the growing attraction of joining an order close to kin. Primarily, though, these figures underscored the initial prevalence of foreign immigrants, in this case approaching 50 percent, entering American convents.

The original band of St. Joseph sisters who left France for the United

States settled in St. Louis. Surprisingly, the Minnesota branch house, with its nearly 800 candidates, did not grow on those origins through French-born applicants. North of St. Paul, however, declining agricultural prosperity and increasing civil friction between the English and French pointed Franco-Canadians toward the United States. Although the greatest number of French Canadian immigrants settled in New England, many turned toward the western Canadian provinces. Eventually dropping south into Minnesota and Wisconsin, these French-speaking families searched for better farming chances and less political hostility.

In convent choices, potential candidates apparently did not think better prospects and less cultural animosity would be found in a German congregation. These convent-bound French women, born in Canada or the United States, rejected a flourishing German-based Benedictine sisterhood in Minnesota, favoring the Sisters of St. Joseph, whose lives more closely matched their own French roots.[20] National divisions aside, those bypassed Benedictines recorded their own growth, welcoming ninety-five candidates in just over twenty-five years. Only one Benedictine claimed Canada as home, while almost 40 percent of the foreign-born applicants came from German-speaking regions of the United States or Europe.[21] Women with German ancestry showed themselves as purposefully drawn to their cultural identity as those from a French background.

National origins influenced the convent choices of young women. Increasingly, congregational demographics shifted as members native to America overtook the foreign-born. Nonetheless, the cultural themes of Europe, Canada, and Mexico cast a long shadow over individual sisterhoods for many years.

Immigration and Convent Numbers

One estimate placed the number of Catholic sisters in the United States at about 5,000 in 1860, rising to 32,000 in 1890 and approaching 50,000 by 1900, although these figures seem unreliable, as Catholics possessed no standardized system for self-enumeration.[22] In the mid-nineteenth century, the *Sadlier's Catholic Directory*, an early attempt to compile statistics by dioceses, suffered from haphazard data collection, partial documentation, and inconsistent reporting styles. For example, the 1865 volume provided only the number of convents in the diocese of St. Louis: "Religious Houses of Females, 21." An exception, the Sisters of Mercy in that city, listed nineteen members, counting professed and lay religious and those in formation. Other congregations—the Sisters of St. Joseph, the Sisters of

Charity, the Society of the Sacred Heart, the Sisters of the Good Shepherd, the Carmelite Nuns, and the School Sisters of Notre Dame—had separately and in concert built a St. Louis presence for over thirty years, but no numerical data quantified their presence.[23]

By the mid-1890s, a competing almanac published as *Hoffman's Catholic Directory* somewhat clarified national data about religious women. It relied, however, on one source for information, inadequate questionnaires, and voluntary responses to a lone editor working without a staff. Its numbers remained problematic, given the directory's lack of a consistent collection methodology and standards for measuring populations.

This directory, even with these weaknesses, presented a more accurate count of professed women.[24] In 1900 it listed residents in women's congregations west of the Mississippi River as 10,807 professed sisters and novices and 491 postulants, totaling more than 11,000 women in western Catholic religious life.[25] The figure suggested that by 1900, over 20 percent of the nation's estimated 50,000 nuns and sisters, with novices and candidates, lived in the American West.

Surely, such a tally understated the actual number of nuns in the West. Even so, with the exception of the Southwest and borderlands, the West never struck a particularly Catholic note in its history. One's imagination did not see images of Catholic nuns leading the oxen of wagon trains, rowing across rivers, or strolling through mining camps. Cloisters and rosaries did not mesh with the raucousness or the isolation of western spaces. Convent bell towers rarely breeched the stark horizons; veiled women intent on a spiritual life surely shied away from the brutal days that came to shape all regions of the West.

Those assumptions have been in error. Nuns and sisters, as regional workers living in same-gendered community, engaged the private and public aspects of western life. They acquainted themselves with the Anglo-European West and its peoples in several different ways and over many decades. More than 10,000 strong, the sisters stepped into the "women's West," where they stood on a female front. Yet more than any other group of women, nuns and sisters were ostracized and vanished from the collective memory and printed records of western life.

In 1850 one French Dominican nun arrived in California; by 1900 more than 130 vowed women worked in thirteen institutions of the congregation. In 1851 seven French-based Notre Dame de Namur sisters began a California school, their professed nuns reaching almost 250 and their students nearly 6,000 by the 1920s. In 1859 twelve Sisters of the Holy Names arrived in the Oregon Territory from Canada; fifty years later, 126 women had taken vows, twenty-seven candidates were in formation, and twenty-two sisters had died. In 1863 in Philadelphia, Mother Agnes, a Catholic convert, took charge of two missions and nine professed Franciscans; forty-three years later, at the end of her administration, the congregation numbered 900 and operated sixty missions, with some in Oregon, Washington, Kansas, Wyoming, and Oklahoma. In 1864 seven Sisters of Mercy arrived in Nebraska from New Hampshire, building the congregation number to ninety-eight by 1914. In 1875 three Mercy sisters settled in Cedar Rapids, Iowa, and by 1895 drew on the work of thirty-four professed sisters and seventeen women in the novitiate. In 1881 three Swiss Benedictines established themselves in South Dakota and by 1900 counted 125 professed sisters. In 1883 six Sisters of St. Joseph organized an independent community in Kansas, and by 1914, 232 professed nuns and forty-six women in formation continued the work. In Texas, the Sisters of Divine Providence grew from ninety-five women in 1886 to 250 by 1903.[26]

Member by member and with steady increments, nuns built a presence in the American West. Although some of the congregations above may never have exceeded more than 500 to 800 women during their peak years, some groups sustained substantial populations. The Sisters of St. Joseph of Carondelet expanded so rapidly after they opened their 1836 motherhouse in St. Louis that they planted four other American foundations, including one at St. Paul, Minnesota, and another in Los Angeles, California. The three western houses alone totaled over 1,000 sisters in 1900 and then soared to more than 2,500.[27] The Sinsinawa Dominicans began their congregation with thirteen sisters in 1847 and each decade more than doubled their number, from 1900 to 1910 admitting almost 350 women.[28]

Similarly, after 1858, when four School Sisters of Notre Dame arrived in St. Louis, the SSND congregation spread rapidly, mushrooming in several U.S. locations.[29] The first sisters in America left German-speaking European convents, coming to the United States as professed nuns. Other SSND foreign-born sisters arrived in the United States as children, relocating with their immigrant parents, growing to adulthood on American soil, and then choosing the Notre Dame convent.[30] Between 1865 and 1900, 809 American entrants versus 132 foreign-born spoke to the coming cultural face of the sisterhood. In totality, these numbers meant that approximately 1,000 women (born before 1900) entered the St. Louis SSND congregation, giving it numerical strength, greater U.S. flavor, and more nuns for the West across the second half of the nineteenth century and deep into the twentieth.[31]

As applicant numbers rose in the nineteenth-century West, congregations formalized admissions with an annual entrance day. The welcoming event might include a studio portrait in candidate's attire, such as of this postulant for the School Sisters of Notre Dame in Missouri. (Author's collection)

Even with these numbers, Mother Caroline Friess, the SSND provincial, worried about competition from other exiled nuns, noting: "Most of the sisters of religious orders who have been driven from Europe . . . have come to America, with their sincere piety and solid performance . . . have been . . . patronized and . . . found good acceptance as teachers and trainers of children."[32] Mother Caroline sought American placements but, aware that her immigrant nuns retained strong feelings for home, comforted those longing for their native land, writing *Kulturkampf* "destroyed" the original European convent, and "that same shock has ruined many of our houses in Poland." "In America," she noted, "[we have] the consolation of extending our field of labor."[33] Her words foretold the way ahead for her congregation, as well as others.

Youth Makes Its Mark

To implement the extension of that labor through America, congregational superiors dispatched a youthful squad of immigrant and native-born sisters to hundreds of western locations. Of ninety women admitted to the Daughters of Charity in their West Central Province from 1850 to 1920, all were between age seventeen and thirty-four, with the average just over twenty-three and a half years.[34] The Sinsinawa Dominicans also sought young women: well over half of their 229 candidates between 1904 and 1910 were within the ages of fifteen and twenty-six.[35]

In Minnesota between 1880 and 1910, the Franciscan Sisters admitted 275 women, their ages falling between fifteen and forty-six. Of the 275 candidates, 257 ranged in age from fifteen to twenty-nine; only eighteen women over the age of thirty entered the Rochester Franciscans for a thirty-year period, and of them, two were in their forties.[36]

Beside documenting congregational growth, the samples revealed the individual life choices of young women. Nineteenth-century mores, legalities, and religious sentiment valued marriage as a private and public good.[37] These attitudes crossed economic lines and included the daughters of the wealthy, as well as working-class immigrants employed in factories and domestic service.[38] While those women came from different social strata, marriage and motherhood gave them a common gender standard. For all women, motherhood took on new meaning as a cherished vocation to which society assumed all should aspire.[39] Financial security, social standing, cultural traditions, female identity, sexual opportunity, maternal emotions, and flowering notions about companionate marriage all pulled young women toward matrimony.

Still, women with educational interests or family work obligations stalled on a marriage commitment. Various priorities helped them avoid a hasty decision, and some estimates placed the average age for nineteenth-century brides to be almost twenty-two.[40] Elongating a societal expectation of a reasonable marriageable age to between twenty and twenty-six, thousands of women rejected the advertised benefits of matrimony. They declined the romantic attentions or monetary attractions of men and removed themselves from the marriage pool, closing a convent door on secular values.

The cousin of one Sister of Charity recalled that around 1860, her extremely social relative affected a "very dressy" appearance, favoring "long trains, very high heeled shoes and slippers," and refused two marriage proposals. Before she entered the convent, the future nun was regarded as "faddish" and "very fastidious with no domestic taste, did not sew, [and] had not even hemmed a handkerchief."[41] This popular woman, who in death was eulogized as "one of the great educators of the West," rather than defining her life along conventional avenues aimed at social and economic self-improvement, chose an unmarried state in a cloister.[42] Nothing about her stylish, self-centered manner hinted she would replace fashionable society with convent austerity.

In 1914 a similar personality described a young Irish woman inquiring about the Dominican sisters in Texas. Little about her indicated she would be a natural for monastic life. She appeared for her Dublin interview in a striking lavender suit and a black velvet hat decorated with sprightly red roses, causing the bishop to dismiss her as a serious prospect. Thirty-eight years later, after a distinguished record as an educator, the now Mother Adeline Tierney became mother general of the Galveston Dominicans.[43] These unlikely nuns-to-be, outwardly no different from thousands of other single, marriage-age Catholic women, dispelled the image of drab women jilted by suitors and disappointed in romantic relationships as the standard for convent material.

Rather, a convent presented young women with a singular, often exciting opportunity that might well involve international travel. Of the first thirty-seven professed nuns of the Sisters of the Holy Ghost in San Antonio, thirty-three were born in Ireland. Among this group of Irish immigrants, thirty gave their ages as between fifteen and twenty-eight years at the time of admission to the convent. These unmarried women from County Cork, Tipperary, and Kilkenny found a way to leave the confines of family and the low prospects of home, travel as single females, emigrate safely to the United States, and take advantage of the professional work offered by the Sisters of the Holy Ghost in Deep South Texas. Among these immigrants, one, Sister Mary Evangelist, a twenty-eight-year-old from County Galway, rose to be the second mother superior of the congregation, symbolizing the roadway to power and status for youthful nuns of the West.[44]

Besides the many Sister Evangelists, a few women, with no vocation interest, used the travel protection of a congregation as a means for reaching the United States. At least one sisterhood dismissed a novice who admitted she came to America to be married. After the groom's mother prevented the wedding, reportedly the young woman, "out of spite . . . entered the convent."[45] The episode suggested the wisdom of caution before investing convent funds in European women who too easily volunteered to travel as postulants.

Such risks aside, young women focused on convent vocations had the wherewithal to influence the development of western religious life. In 1852 Mother Benedicta Riepp, twenty-seven years of age, led two other Benedictine women from their Bavarian monastery to the wilderness of Pennsylvania. There, Mother Benedicta, who insisted on the financial and monastic rights of women religious, confronted the punitive leadership of the ruling male Benedictines, forty-three-year-old abbot Boniface Wimmer. Wimmer enjoyed the advantages of age, authority, gender, and American experience, all of which he leveraged against the tubercular Benedicta.

To counter Wimmer's autocracy and contain his sweeping control over the sisters, Mother Benedicta sent her nuns to Minnesota and then went to Rome to appeal for relief from the abbot. Finally the nun, her strength depleted by mortal illness and spiritual harassment, managed to reach her sisters in Minnesota. There, ten years after she introduced Benedictine women to America, Mother Benedicta—exhausted by deadly disease, poor nutrition, and emotional assault—died at thirty-seven, having launched, in spite of adversity, a sisterhood destined, out of its Minnesota foundation, to become one of the most powerful in the West.[46]

Like the doggedly strong Mother Benedicta, other young sisters rose quickly in western environments. In 1869, for example, when the Texas bishop C. M. Dubuis sent the Sisters of the Incarnate Word from Galveston to San Antonio to open a hospital, he placed the twenty-three-year old Sister M. Madeline Chollet in charge.[47] In 1872 Dubuis, trying to reduce the administrative size of his immense diocese, elevated Madeline's companion, Mother St. Pierre Jeanne Cinquin, age twenty-seven, to superior of the San Antonio group. Dubuis's efforts, which could be defended as entirely practical, nonetheless split the congregation of the Incarnate

Word, leading to decades of strained feelings between sisters in Galveston and San Antonio. Mother St. Pierre, however, seized on her appointment and emerged as an aggressive expansionist who traveled widely, built connections in Mexico, ruled her congregation with an intensely personal manner, and solidified the place of the San Antonio Incarnate Word sisters in the Southwest among Anglos and Mexicans. When Mother St. Pierre died in 1891, having fallen out with clergy overseers, she had opened schools, hospitals, and orphanages across Texas and Mexico; she was forty-six years old.

Mother St. Pierre was not the only Texas nun to have administrative responsibilities descend on her at a young age. In 1886, when the Texas bishop J. C. Néraz forced the ouster of the superior general of the Sisters of Divine Providence, he chose twenty-eight-year-old Sister Florence Walter for the position, a nun who since the age of twenty-three had served as superior of a San Antonio convent.[48] Youth, with its energy and "can-do" spirit, proved to be an asset, leading to early promotion for nuns taking their personal vision into the West.

Humor in All Things

The large collections of young women migrating into the West, traveling in odd circumstances, and living together in dire conditions bolstered themselves with a lively, unrestrained sense of humor. Their letters and journals belie the somber countenances that nuns turned to a photographer's lens or the impressions of those watching sisters on trains and in stores. True, nuns received explicit instructions that around secular people, they "shall keep their eyes modestly cast down . . . [and] abstain from childish levity, immoderate laughter."[49] Public constraints aside, in private, nuns devised many ways to keep merriment in their lives.

Novitiates, despite their emphasis on sisterly perfection, encouraged candidates and novices looking for laughter. Regulations seldom muzzled a good time in the convent. Fifty or more young women living and working simply could not resist those zany moments that enlarged congregational lore and left sisters chuckling for decades.

Music was a natural outlet for humor, and any occasion could be an excuse for the postulants and novices to hastily assemble a chorale. In 1894 the professed nuns gathered in the novitiate of the Sisters of Charity of the Blessed Virgin Mary in Dubuque for "a program of playful nonsense . . . delightfully carried out." One novice performed a pantomime "relating to the triumph of a turkey gobbler over a haughty young goat." Two others entertained with a "laughable" skit, "Bettie and the Bear." A rendition of "Good Night" closed a musical evening in which "the old sisters laughed until they cried."[50]

Holidays gave another chance for festivities, and the novices devised clever ways to celebrate, laugh, and stay within convent behaviors. Religious holidays elicited the usual observances, but each congregation relished its own traditions, often expressions of customs from the home country. On Christmas Eve at the Franciscan Sisters of Perpetual Adoration, the candidates and novices were "ordered" to retire early; then the professed sisters finished the specialty food preparations and decorated the refectory. At each place setting, the mother superior left a basket baked from dough and filled with popcorn, cakes, an apple, an orange, and a holy card. The following year, the celebration began a week earlier, when "Santa Claus called and asked to be admitted." Costumed angels also appeared, each delivering a solo, until the "Christkindchen sang 'Stille Nacht,'" an event leaving the nostalgic German sisters remarking that "such . . . never visited us before."[51]

Holidays, customs, and nostalgia went hand in hand. At the St. Peter's novitiate of the Montana Ursulines, the novices received Christmas stockings filled with treats and a plum pudding from the Toledo motherhouse.[52] The Sisters of St. Mary in St. Louis numbered only fifty-nine in 1889, but they managed a holiday celebration in "the usual jovial manner," with a Christmas tree for their hospital patients and gifts of nuts and candy. By 1900 the convent had grown to 140, and the festivities had enlarged correspondingly; each sister held a lighted candle, adding to the glow of the tree, and joined in the hymns and carols.[53]

Even a mother superior stressed by cantankerous clergy, staffing shortages, and financial woes could appreciate humor from the sisters. A contemporary of Mother Caroline Friess, superior of the SSND, recalled, "When all were full of life and glee, particularly the candidates, she was highly pleased." One sister remembered: "When . . . I played the role of Mother Caroline, giving her orders and treating her as *my subject*, she enjoyed the joke, especially when I succeeded in imitating her manners." In the afternoon, when the bishop stopped for a visit, the young sister continued her mimic of Mother Caroline, "ordering" the real superior to "entertain his lordship in my name." Reportedly, Mother Caroline cried out, "Bravo, bravo," saying to the bishop, "We must let these young folks have their fun."[54]

Charades and musical numbers often formed the basis for novitiate recreation, but amusing spontaneity did not always guarantee approval. A reluctant novice, aware of her limited singing ability, resisted calls to audition for the sisters' choir. At last coaxed to the front of the room, the savvy young sister belted out in her poorest voice for the nuns. She chose a bawdy sea chanty that began, "Oh, the captain with the whiskers; Took one quick glance at me"—thus ending her musical career but creating a favorite convent story that passed among the sisters for years.[55]

Still, mirth dominated in novitiates, even in serious moments. An elderly sister recalled that as a novice, her biggest stumbling block was the assignment to read aloud to the community. She dreaded her turn, as her tongue invariably twisted the words. Among her legendary flubs, she garbled the thoughtful evening meditation "Examine yourselves and see" into "Examine your sleeves and see," sending ripples of laughter through the chapel. Always flustered, the young nun incited more chuckles when, during a supper reading for senior nuns, a passage about a monk who for his meal had "taken the wing of a pheasant" became "he took the wing of a peasant."[56] The laughter that accompanied such gaffes and the enjoyable memories they generated showed that young women kept their humor intact after entering the convent. Indeed, one novice in Kansas wrote to her father: "If you want to learn to laugh, come to our novitiate and see how we do it."[57]

Departure from the novitiate and assignments to miserable western missions, rather than dampening laughter, generated more occasions for humor and manufactured group fun. If anything, exuberance and levity increased as sisters entered into challenging physical environments. At bare missions, sisters relied on making holidays festive, foibles funny, and disasters amusing as ways to deflect hardship.

On the birthday of George Washington, two nuns "highly delighted" their Native students with a surprise sleigh ride to one of the Indian home camps, a simple outing that released everyone from the frigid schoolhouse.[58] In mid-December, two Franciscans at a Native school merrily announced that "Santa Claus was in the bakery" and refused to allow peeks at their preparations. On 6 January, the date of "Little Christmas," the annalist reported that amid the parties, "Santa Claus has made his appearance several times today."[59] In Oregon, the French Canadian Sisters of the Holy Names piled donated gifts under the two decorated trees in their school. After the boarding students presented a tableaux of the Nativity, with one student as the infant Jesus, the presents were passed to the children. Recitations, songs, and music rounded out the entertainment. The following holiday season, the superior granted the nuns, whose duties scattered them about the school, several days of recreation during the vacation, causing one to note, "We are so seldom united . . . that this privilege is heartily appreciated."[60] These celebrations held more cultural meaning for the nuns than for their Native students, but the pleasure of distractions and gifts charged life with shared laughter.

Travel, with its inevitable contacts with the secular community, usually gave sisters more excuses for laughing. In 1888, after a lengthy trip by train, stagecoach, and horse-drawn wagon, the weary sisters who arrived at the isolated Red Lake Indian mission reported: "We had a grand recreation till ten o'clock in the evening." Their reunion gave them plenty to joke about, including "a good laugh about the *old man*, he is a good *old fellow*."[61] Which male—priest, conductor, stage driver, or Native wagon hauler—prompted this mirth and why remained a mystery, but the stressed travelers extracted some bit of humor from their outrageous journey.

Nuns assigned to western outposts always injected mirth into the simple and mundane. A nun recalled that as a young sister, she and her companion made an "endless trip" by passenger coach and freight cars, stopping at every hamlet to unload watermelons. Hours later, the two climbed into a horse and buggy for the last segment of the miserable trip. Jolting along, they incessantly pestered the driver with the age-old query of the young: "Are we there yet?" With the convent finally in view, one sister hid herself in the bottom of the wagon. As the driver drew up to the kitchen door, a nun anticipating the much-needed help dashed out to greet them. Horrified by the petit sister standing before her, the older missionary exclaimed: "'You little thing! What can you do?'" With that, the second newcomer, Sister Otilda, "popped up in the buggy!" The startled Sister Hildegund shouted, "Oh, *there* is the cook!"[62] Horseplay around a superior hardly aligned with conduct for junior nuns, especially in front of a male driver, but the giddy sisters got mileage from the prank for years, laughing at themselves and the overwrought Sister Hildegund.

Tricks of hiding or jumping out to surprise another sister appeared to be popular forms of fun. Even Mother Katharine Drexel, a figure of considerable dignity and decorum, allowed herself to be part of a joke on sisters. Arriving at the St. Michael's mission in Arizona, Mother Katharine and two other nuns blocked the sight lines into their wagon, allowing one sister to hide from the mission staff. The St. Michael's faculty hailed the nun they expected to join them, but the visitor recalled, "Sister moved away and a greeting I received that I do not know how I got out of the wagon. As for myself, I was laughing and . . . could not keep the salt water bags closed."[63]

Students' antics especially challenged sisters to suppress laughter and hold to teacher solemnity. Yet funny moments overtook nuns, and they barely kept a serious face when students indulged themselves in jokes. At St. Catherine's school in New Mexico, when one of the older Native boys slipped out of the building and deliberately frightened a group of sleeping Indians, the ensuing ruckus terrified an Irish caretaker. In the morning, the superior listened to the long complaint of the outraged Irishman and dutifully took the offending student aside for a scolding. The youth, still pleased with his results the evening before, tried to appear contrite, but instead he "hung his head and almost went into convulsions," while the nun, charged to be the stern disciplinarian, confessed: "Really I laughed till my sides ached."[64]

In times of danger and fear, nuns typically called on their well-developed sense of humor to dispense with the tension. Even disastrous events, such as the December 1907 fire that destroyed the girls' dormitory and threatened the rest of the campus at St. Catherine's in Santa Fe, prompted nuns to look for the humor in misfortune. As the flames raged, nearby residents raced to contain the blaze, and men, women, and youngsters formed a bucket brigade. Other helpers dashed from attic to cellar, tossing all possessions "pell mell" from the windows. In the days following, the sisters groaned over the private items found by the citizenry, as "hidden things were brought to light. . . . 'Confidentials' galore! Unmentionables! . . . A fault book was an interesting reading for a large boy." "Fires are not especially good for the nerves," observed a nun, but then conceded, "if only I had time to tell the amusing incidents."[65]

Finding amusement and including themselves in the joke stayed with sisters young and old. When a railroad strike stranded Blessed Sacrament sisters traveling to Santa Fe, they took refuge in an empty Pullman car for the day and entertained themselves with memories, especially of one friend famous for her pranks. Indeed, remarked one nun, "Sister Veronica, God bless us, would play tricks on the Holy Father himself." Sister Veronica's jokes even earned names among the nuns—such as the "famous" "Wilcox" and "Tea decanter" episodes. One nun regaled the others with an account of Sister Veronica directing her to catch a small pig and another mishap when manure smeared the helpful novice's white veil after she grabbed a cow's tail. The stories of home led one to "hold her sides with laughter," but the sister assured the motherhouse that no public harm was done, for "we can retell these little jokes, as we have the whole car to ourselves."[66]

This quickness to laugh at themselves and each other gathered steam over the years for the Sisters of the Blessed Sacrament. For example, on a trip to a mountain town in New Mexico, the wagon driver asked his three passengers to vacate the carriage as he crossed a wide watery ditch. The nuns agreed, and two managed to clutch a low hanging branch and heave themselves over the muddy chasm. One hung back, prompting the irritated driver to shout, "Jump!" Instead, as "Sister didn't want him to see her 'spindles,'" she walked out of sight for her turn and then hurled herself into space, missing the bank and landing in the mud. The heavy habit stayed dry, but the petticoat absorbed muck to the waist, a soggy mess she kept secret until evening. When the nun raised her skirt to show the disaster, her companions hooted in disbelief, saying they had wondered at her odd gait. Nuns rarely indulged vanities or foibles, and these two saw only humor because one hid her legs from a man and "laughed heartily" at the whole story.[67]

Sisters corresponding with a motherhouse employed humor to describe many of their mission experiences, figuring that a laugh covered bizarre situations. In New Mexico, these same Sisters of the Blessed Sacrament tried to capture by letter their extensive preparations for an afternoon visit from Archbishop Chapelle and the famed Cardinal James Gibbons of Baltimore, Maryland. The sisters fully appreciated the orchestrated nature of such an event and the required protocols for high-ranking company. In case they had overlooked these, the local prelate sent no-nonsense instructions that the clergy would arrive "promptly at one o'clock and would sit down *immediately* to dinner."

Such an occasion represented a festive day for sisters who did not have many social diversions or opportunities to entertain cardinals of the church. To display their celebratory feelings, the sisters draped the dining room with the national and papal colors and set up two easels (borrowed from a local furniture store), placing on one a painting of the Last Supper and on the other a copy of the Declaration of Independence. Nor did they limit the decorations to the dining area. White-and-rose bunting and many evergreens festooned the outside steps, where the carriages would stop.

After laying out a rich description of this scene, Sister Evangelist continued, "Now I must tell you the joke." At about noon, an hour ahead of the archbishop's schedule, a handsome team trotted toward the convent. Sister Evangelist made no secret that with this early arrival, she "was 'blessing' the archbishop," as the nuns hastily removed their aprons, rolled down their sleeves, straightened their habits, and prepared to greet the cardinal and his entourage. "There we stood, eleven of us to meet his eminence and the archbishops . . . but I could hardly restrain from laughing," for rather than the expected dignitaries, six uninvited priests emerged from the carriage and announced they wished a tour of the famous St. Catherine's Indian School.

Once the expected guests arrived, the nuns served an elegant meal, though not one entirely pleasing to the cardinal. He requested "a very sweet wine or whiskey" rather than the claret and burgundy on the table. Then he "asked for beef or mutton, two kinds of meat we did not have." Events tumbled along, as the prelate, spearing a piece of meat from a platter held by a nun, inquired about a local band's musical selection, "Sister, is that the Rocky Mountain Nightingale?" The nervous young nun hurriedly answered, "No bishop, it is venison."[68] Finally a request for a bed, so that the cardinal, who suffered from indigestion, might rest after his meal, flustered the self-possessed Sister Evangelist. Later she admitted that in a day of disasters, she found the nightingale exchange completely hilarious.

Nor did nuns only laugh about the clergy or the exasperating demands they could make. Fully engaged in life, sisters understood humanity. They knew of the biology of men and women and could be a bit randy over a seemingly taboo subject.

For example, sisters required to administer feminine hygiene care in the women's ward of their hospital developed a regular routine, complete with laughter. Daily, the nuns administered a vaginal douche to every patient. This procedure called for a gallon of warm water, a rubber bed pad, a bucket, and a wooden frame on which to suspend the pail to catch the runoff matter. These young sisters, dressed in heavy woolen habits, with waist-length capes, wide sleeves, starched cuffs, and large brown-striped aprons, laboriously made their rounds, assembling and dismantling the cumbersome equipment, giving the treatment at each bed, and laughing at themselves as "the hook and ladder company."[69] Although they probably did not share this humor with their female patients, among the sisters, earthy joking kept the work bearable.

These nuns were not so unusual, for beyond public ears, sisters chuckled about a range of "risqué" subjects. In Texas, one sister, known for outlandish additions to her garb and infamous for her lusty manner, relished her role as the shocking member of her small convent. As she steamed about the house, tackling heavy labors, the nun lightened her load and distracted her colleagues with unorthodox tunes, whose refrains ran to such as "Oh, for a man, a man to saddle the horse."[70]

Humor such as this permeated the narrative of a congregation, creating shared memories of laughter, even in times of privation. The sunny personality of Sister Pancratia Studer of the Adorers of the Most Precious Blood of Christ influenced generations of other members during her eighty years in the convent. Only fourteen when she entered religion, Sister Pancratia viewed the world through a jovial lens, so that hearty amusement colored her life. Whether as a fifteen-year-old postulant wandering lost in a town, a cook keeping chickens under a bushel basket, or a novice dragged across stones by a cow, Pancratia described everything as, "Here is another funny thing that happened." She set off a fire alarm by ringing the steeple chimes instead of the convent supper bell, batched beer that "shot clear to the ceiling," baked fresh lemon pies that she hid in her suitcase, and laced the bishop's pumpkin pie with so much whiskey, it could "walk to the table by itself."[71] While not every nun was graced with as much humor as Sister Pancratia, jokes, laughter, and a wry sense of self-deprecation permeated the lives of religious women who went to the West.

That sense of the merry carried sisters alone and together into uncertain situations. It kept them from coddling each other and prevented them from taking themselves too seriously. Humor served to build a congregational memory grounded in affection, humility, and humanity. In the West, those qualities could be useful for survival, and the nuns and sisters came well prepared for this aspect of western life.

The Lure of Learning

Zeal for education and academic achievement characterized the women who came to the West as nuns and sisters. In the formative days of congregations, many immigrant girls arrived on American shores with what passed for elementary school training, and fewer of them boasted completion of secondary studies. Even those who carried the imprint of European educational training contended with the barriers of language once they landed in English-speaking America, a drawback that hindered their early progress.[72]

In America, swiftly evolving pedagogical values rose before young nuns. After the Civil War, the support for broader literacy, insistence by former slaves for long-denied education, clamor among immigrants for American survival skills, and an 1884 edict by the U.S. bishops for a nationwide system of parochial schools elevated attention to formal instruction.[73] Both in secular society and Catholic circles, religious congregations saw that the eagerness of postulants and novices for learning meshed with growing trends in American intellectual life.

Initially, domestic work dominated, and candidates attended to their books only after completing all physical daily labor. In addition, sister leaders felt a duty to prepare candidates and novices first and foremost in religious life, and some feared the introduction of too much secular learning.[74] Yet as nuns answered the call to the West, their employment contracts showed that parishes wanted higher standards, requiring sisters to instruct in at least one European language, English, reading, writing, arithmetic, Bible history, and religion.[75]

This placed a substantial burden on small congregations, and they responded by meticulous organization. The dual education of young sisters was not left to chance, with congregational rules detailing the spiritual and academic programs for new members. One rule, intended to identify potential strengths in sisters, instructed the mistress of postulants to recognize and develop the "habits and talents" of each candidate.[76] Anxious to guide minds toward congregational excellence, superiors devised careful procedures for academic and personal development, such as advising young sisters to "use the books and follow the method of teaching that has been pointed out to them."[77] The intention "to help the sisters in teaching" included a directive for each to "carefully prepare the lessons and recitations to be taught."[78]

These novitiate exhortations fell on fertile ground with postulants and novices eager to excel in their assignments. In 1876 the Sisters of St. Joseph in St. Paul celebrated the twentieth anniversary of their girls' boarding school, St. Joseph's Academy, where they had consistently furthered the most current academic training for students. The Sisters of St. Joseph exposed students to a more inclusive curriculum than might be true of many finishing schools, with subjects not necessarily associated with female education: religious instruction; orthography; reading; writing; grammar; geography; mathematics; the globe; prose and poetical composition; sacred and secular history; astronomy; rhetoric; botany; intellectual and natural philosophy; chemistry; bookkeeping; French; German; Latin; music on the piano, melodeon, and guitar; vocal music; drawing and painting in oil, watercolors, and pastels; plain and ornamental needlework; tapestry; embroidery; hair and lace work; and the making of artificial fruits and flowers.[79]

The course of study conveyed the range of intellectual interests that should attract female scholars, and it succeeded. As a beginning high school student, Sister Wilfrida Hogan boarded at St. Joseph's Academy and followed this program for a single academic calendar. She then returned home, but, longing for the disciplined studious environment at St. Joseph's, she returned two years later and entered the novitiate side of the academy. As an elderly nun, Wilfrida recalled, "The novitiate really was the 'House of Study,'" with morning and afternoon ninety-minute oral recitation periods. The subjects included Christian doctrine, reading, rhetoric, grammar, mathematics, astronomy, philosophy, physics, elocution, music, writing, and drawing.[80]

The intensity of this routine exceeded Sister Wilfrida's experiences as a boarding student, and from the point of view of the sister administrators, that was for good reason. Congregations saw preparation of teaching nuns as a serious responsibility. Mother Caroline Friess SSND, who carried Catholic education through the West, exhorted nuns: "Let your general endeavor be . . . your continued improvement as teachers." Lest there be any misunderstanding, she told them, "As our congregation is exclusively devoted to the education of youth, every sister . . . will deem it a sacred duty to perform her task in thoroughly systematic order."[81] Mother Emily Power of the Dominicans, a fierce advocate for academic learning among religious, wrote to her sisters: "The day is not far distant when every inefficient and indifferent teacher will be shut out from school work. Let none of these be found among us."[82]

As educators, teaching sisters wanted to graduate academy students whose learning reflected well on the congregation, and they determined to prepare students to be women of stature in society. When students returned as candidates for the congregation, these same teachers exacted an even higher performance, so that as professed sisters they could face any teaching exigency on the missions. As the country broadened its call for a literate citizenry, devotion to learning and appreciation for its place in upward mobility grew within women's congregations.

Sister Mary Buckner, the young woman remembered by her cousin as a flighty social butterfly "who had not even hemmed a handkerchief," toured the Montana mining camps on horseback and lived to be "a naturalist . . . an expert in botany . . . [who] knew and could give the scientific classification of every flower, tree, and shrub that grows in the mid-West; [a teacher who] made general astronomy a most fascinating and interesting subject"; and one who "excelled as a writer and critic of English, and possessed an extensive knowledge of history."[83] In the convent, Sister Mary, who had displayed little interest in learning as a girl, found an atmosphere that allowed her to engage her full intellect. Once she entered the convent, Sister Mary unleashed her academic curiosity, using every opportunity to advance in learning.

In like fashion, Mother Angelique Ayres of the Congregation of Divine Providence in Texas came to the convent from a limited educational background and a family scarred by economic upheaval, sudden death, complicated relationships, and constant relocation. Out of this unsettled background, as a postulant, Mother Angelique studied piano, theology, and German. Within three years, her superiors assigned her to classes in physics, history, political science, Latin, German, and methods of education. By the age of thirty, she listed a lengthy number of summer-school classes and correspondence courses, in-residence evaluations, and Texas state examinations when applying for approval of a bachelor's degree and admission to a master of arts program. She served as a music instructor, editor of a congregational magazine, high school faculty member, founding dean of Lady of the Lake College in San Antonio, and general superior of her religious community. Angelique Ayres devoted her entire religious life to improving her own academic credentials and furthering the formal knowledge of her sisters and the students in the Divine Providence schools.[84] Although her personal history deserved applause, it rather generally mirrored the thirst for learning and the academic ambition that drove women religious who turned to the American West for their professional careers. Whether postulant, novice, or professed, religious women committed themselves to personal enlightenment and professional advancement through formal studies.

The fact that these European and American women of youth, humor, and learning added to western populations and influenced local institutions apparently missed the casual observer. Other westerners easily overlooked the unusual characteristics of the nuns moving through and settling in their communities. Sisters—dressed in uniform clothing that hid individuality and disguised personality—came and went from their western assignments without drawing interest from neighbors. Near a nondescript convent in Sequin, Texas, or Butte, Montana, residents had little reason to notice the distinct personalities and intellectual interests of nuns.

True, the sisters interacted with local Catholics and operated schools and hospitals essential to local communities, but their presence as women did not attract attention as one of overall regional importance. Perhaps immigrant families were too poor to notice that the canvas ceiling of the schoolhouse provided a haven for bats, or that the defection of the pastor and friction between German and Irish parishioners left a school in chaos.[85] Perhaps in hospitals, patients completing their own journeys from Italy, Germany, Canada, Sweden, and Denmark were too preoccupied with their pneumonia, rheumatism, crushed leg, or fractured hand to think about the nuns who cared for them.[86] Yet thousands of nuns, many of them young, with merry hearts and intellectual curiosity, infiltrated all regions of the West, promoting organized religion, building civic institutions, framing new identities, and maintaining attitudes of race, class, and gender that undergirded Anglo-European America.

Race, Class, and Gender

As Catholic nuns and sisters developed American convent life and turned to the West for employment, their worldview generally matched that of the society around them. Although the essence of their theology centered on deep concepts of social justice, sisters did not always question the cultural trends of the nineteenth century. Their views of major societal forces, in the main, did not set them apart from other Catholic men and women.

In matters of race, Catholic sisters acted in concert with the ideologies of European and Christian superiority as they began their western lives. In 1727 the Ursuline nuns who arrived in New Orleans came to a colony that only three years earlier issued the *Code Noir*, a governing law for black slaves. It laid out stringent rules for blacks that not only bound them to coerced labor but to the Catholic Church.[87] As the Ursuline nuns built their economic stability in Louisiana, like other white property holders, they did so as slave owners. Unlike many southern whites, the nuns vigorously endorsed the religious precepts of the *Code Noir*, supporting the Catholic conversion, blessed marriages, and protection of family life of black slaves.[88]

Other congregations, apparently with ease, incorporated American racial views about black slavery into their early years, as well. Prior to the Civil War, the Sisters of Charity of Nazareth, Kentucky, with priests in the area, purchased slaves and used their labor to improve a congregation farm and school campus.[89] In 1845 the French-speaking Sister Marie Therese Maxisa Duchemin, a woman of color, withdrew from Baltimore's Oblate Sisters of Providence and moved to Monroe, Michigan, to form a new sisterhood. Thirteen years later, church politics, national rivalries, cultural divisions, and race prejudice drove Duchemin to a Canadian convent, and her foundress role was excised from her congregation's written and oral records.[90]

These responses to bondage and African Americans generally reflected the racial views tolerated and defended by the Catholic Church. In the nineteenth century, authorities at the Vatican remained cool to the rising cry of American abolitionists that slavery be outlawed immediately. In 1839 Pope Gregory XVI condemned the international slave trade but fell short of a sweeping indictment of slavery.[91] In America, the bishops, with black slavery hanging like a dank fog, likewise kept silent, until a civil war threatening the nation prompted one to state that, "in return for a lifetime of work, we must give these unfortunate people . . . the bread and clothes necessary to their material life . . . and . . . their just share of truth."[92]

Nuns and sisters entered into an America deeply mired in racism that few assessed in its fullness. Racism and its octopus arms enveloped their church. Dedicated to the educational and "moral" elevation of people of color, nuns, snared by these tentacles of racial injustice and their paternalism, intentionally and unintentionally perpetuated slavery in many environments.

When those environments shifted to the home regions of Native American people, the octopus arms did not untangle, but instead tightened and enveloped large and small missions. Christian missionaries saw paganism, idolatry, and superstition in the sacred traditions of Native people in every crevice of the West. With forced conversions and cultural repression defined as "beneficial" for Indians, race hatred aimed at blacks in the East and South flowed into the West for other persons of color. There, with a history of European racism directed at indigenous peoples dating to the 1600s, military, government, and religious policies conspired to place Natives at a disadvantage in every endeavor. It required generations for both groups to loosen the fetters of the resulting damages.

In areas relating to class, a European monastic heritage influenced the thinking of nuns. For generations, monastery life functioned through a class division that evolved over several hundreds of years. During that time, church authorities repeatedly attempted to devise a scheme for total enclosure. Several arrangements, including extern monks and servant women, came and went, but each proved unsatisfactory for some reason. Eventually, monastic life succumbed to a sort of religious rigor mortis that dictated the behaviors of the choir sisters and the lower sisters who served them.[93] As a result, the inner machinery of a monastery operated through a clear system of class segregation. Choir sisters, who entered a given religious house for life, held the highest rank within the priory. This system that privileged choir sisters but divorced them from the secular world produced an awkward arrangement that prohibited access to the normal functions of life.

Work routines were handed over to lower-class women, and some congregations divided their lay sisters between domestic sisters who labored inside the cloister and extern sisters who transacted all business with the outside world. Because the extern sisters mingled between the secular and cloistered societies, strict and sometimes contradictory rules governed their admission to the congregation and their conduct on public errands. Regulations concerning the lay sisters spun a confusing web, but increasingly they became more sequestered. In any case, the daily religious obligations of the worker sisters lessened compared to the choir sisters, so that the many tasks of running a monastery could be accomplished.

By the nineteenth century, the religious protocols for the extern sisters in some European institutes had taken on more uniformity. The women spent a year in novitiate, professed simple vows to the abbess, recited a reduced daily prayer obligation, dressed somewhat differently from the choir sisters, and observed fewer days of fast. Individual monasteries permitted or prohibited the extern sisters in the actual cloistered sections of the priory.[94] The work of the lay sisters in the outside world for the choir sisters remained essential for the smooth operation of the monastery and the continuation of a church policy based on gender inequality for religious women.

When European nuns embarked for America, they transported the customs of their particular congregations concerning the division of the choir and lay sisters. Among the twelve Sisters of the Holy Names who left Montreal for Oregon in 1859 were two of the lay rank, both from French families.[95] Those first two lay sisters, ages twenty-two and twenty-four when they arrived in Oregon, lived through the same desperate circumstances as the ten choir nuns. Oregon stripped away constructed differences, the twelve missionaries relied on each other in all aspects of mission life, and the two garnered enormous respect for their long domestic service in the Northwest, as did several cooks and gardeners who followed.[96]

Despite this appreciation for the extreme work duties undertaken by the lay sisters in pioneer regions, and even with all the democratic impulses surging through American society, many congregations retained their distinctions between choir and lay sisters. Different work responsibilities brought different cultural exposure for the two rankings. In 1882, more than thirty years after the congregation first arrived in the United States, Mother Caroline Friess implied the educational differences between the two groups when she fretted about a mission that did not have regular access to a German-speaking priest "because several lay sisters can confess in English only in a pinch."[97]

Just as they perpetuated ideas about class, Catholic nuns and sisters projected the prevailing nineteenth-century affections for gender. Grounded inside a religious organization that actively denied the equality of women, nuns reinforced that attitude in their personal conduct and professional actions. Yet even as nuns appeared to accept gender prescripts, the many societies around them impinged on the presumptions of their church.[98] Regardless of the lived and intellectual separations between professed religious and secular women, ideas that percolated out of the latter group wafted into the world of the cloister. An inevitable conflict between past values and present forces loomed.[99]

Further, as Catholic nuns and sisters turned to the many Wests of North America, gender definitions for women shifted and realigned in ways that defied prediction. The groundswell of insistence by women that their lives meant more than a presumed existence in the world of domesticity touched females of every social class and religious persuasion. For some, the dramatic dictates brought assertive acquisition of new skills, educational achievement, and professional lives. For others, the promotion of a new female identity was threatening and encouraged retrenchment and a hardening of old ideas.

Nuns entering into the West faced perplexing choices, caught as they were between the two standards. How could they abandon the centuries of male-led religious practice, and did they wish to do so? How could they defend their own contradictory public behaviors to these same male religious leaders, their own women superiors, and themselves? To what end would their youth and attraction to learning lead them? In what ways would western life clash with religious life, and how would nuns resolve these issues that increasingly hinged on power and personal agency?

Armed with conservative perspectives in matters of race, class, and gender, Catholic nuns entered into a human cauldron and rare geography destined to alter the patterns of religious life. Like most cataclysmic changes, these came about through accident rather than premeditation. Mother Caroline inadvertently commented on how unexpected outcomes would occur, saying: "Because the sisters had arrived from three different places they did not know each other. I feared this might cause some strange feelings and a holding back in their relationship. . . . I found I was mistaken. . . . Friendliness prevailed. . . . Neither cultural background nor speech nor heritage was a barrier."[100] As events crossed their path, sisters learned that American convents sheltered the forces of diversity that would redirect their thinking and experience as nuns and as women.

In the matters of race, class, and gender, the force of personal faith played a role in the actions of nuns and sisters. Invisible and inexplicable, the beliefs of religious women meant more than the external trappings of veils and cloaks, more than the accident of family baptism. The faith of the nuns, intangible as it might be, accounted for who they were, how they assessed themselves, and what they did while they remained professed

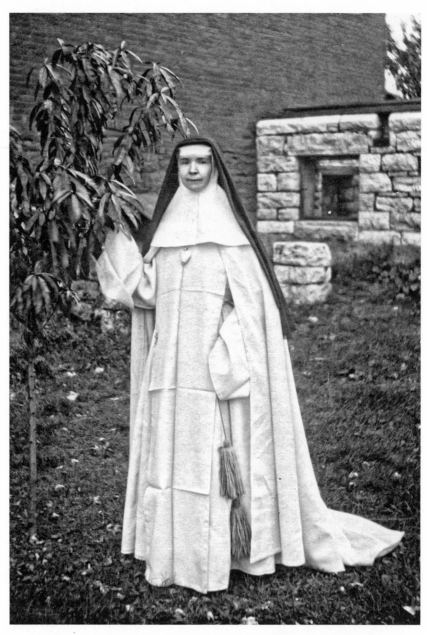

Despite an elegant appearance that evoked Old World monastic images,
the Sisters of the Good Shepherd—living in several western cities, including
St. Louis and St. Paul—cooperated with the justice system by sheltering criminal
women and "wayward" girls, thus countering violence and abuse with stability,
education, and vocational training. (Author's collection)

women of a religious congregation. Their day-to-day decisions and expectations attached directly to their understanding of the Catholic faith and the viability of their congregational charism. Through the charism, sisters defined the uniqueness of their congregations, centered their spiritual identity, and channeled their faith, both individually and collectively.

This devotion to a specific theology and a congregational impulse produced concrete results that had little to do with overt piety. Language filled with religious images, sacred rituals as the calendar of life, and behaviors rigidly aligned to an expected standard in fact revealed nothing about inner belief and personal spirituality. Core tenets of Catholicism and their meaning within the context of professed religious life apparently explained some motivation driving individual nuns and sisters as they faced west. Faith defies explicit measurement, but its presence in these particular lives illuminated the gossamer iron of religious belief and the way it contributed to the choices of these women.

Catholic nuns and sisters headed into the American West with as many complexities as other groups of pioneers. Frequently members of immigrant communities, they plowed their way through dislocation, homesickness, poverty, and the barriers of language. Still, as insiders both by religion and nationality, they circulated among other newcomers in the West, connected with them, and took part in their immigrant lives. Membership among the immigrant communities of America provided but the first step into other relationships that influenced nuns in the West.

Regardless of any secular associations they formed or heartaches they shared, as single women, nuns stood far outside the typical western pioneer model. European- and American-born, they mixed up the demographics of the West with their same-gender convents and decisions to make their way in life by permanently foregoing marriage and motherhood. As unmarried young women, they walked with a buoyant spirit, looking for laughter and chances to enliven their intellects. With all this singularness as nineteenth-century women, they generally clung to the conservative race, class, and gender attitudes of country and church. Nonetheless, personal spirituality and faith informed their thinking and their actions, leaving open the possibility that new experiences would dislodge old attitudes and fresh insights would eradicate set assumptions.

As nuns and sisters made their way into the West from many different directions, all its regions and all its cultures awaited them. Nuns came to change western people, but inside rural cabin or urban home, other thoughts prevailed. On bare mesas and in lush valleys, beside swollen rivers and atop sweeping mountains, outside saloons and across prairies, the West watched to see what these untried sisters would make of convent life under new skies and with newer people. In response, through unusual travel and demanding work, Catholic nuns began their discovery of the West, its unmatched diversity in people and place, and the meaning of an American sisterhood.

*[W]e entered the Rocky Range
. . . a frightful and desolate region; nothing . . . but snow-clad
mountains of rock. . . . The cars
pass over frightful chasms, the
rails are laid on logs resting on
pillars, whose only support are
the craggy rocks beneath.*

—Journal of the Sisters of
St. Joseph en Route to
Arizona, 1870, Archives of
the Sisters of St. Joseph of
Carondelet, St. Louis

Travels

On a sweltering morning in May 1870,
seven parched and trail-weary Catholic nuns watched as their guides loaded
a primitive towboat that would carry
the group over the turbulent Colorado
River just west of Fort Yuma, Arizona.
With but two men on the opposite side
to haul the raft ropes through the dangerous waters, the lead driver explained
that only one crossing could be made.
He ordered the nuns to climb into the
wagon, crammed with baggage and
provisions. Thus it came that the seven
women were in the overloaded carriage when the driver urged the skittish
horses forward at the very moment the
small craft lurched away from the river-
bank. One sister, in the moments of the
unfolding disaster, managed to leap

onto solid ground, but the others remained trapped. In the ensuing chaotic jumble, one horse lost its footing and fell onto the raft as the wagon crashed to its side, teetering out over the rushing currents. The heavy weight of the downed animal prevented the carriage, with its cargo of sisters, trunks, and baskets, from rolling into the formidable Colorado River. The fearsome scene and the near drowning were but the latest calamities in the unlikely travels of these seven sisters.[1]

Only three weeks earlier, Sister Monica Corrigan and six companions, amid tender farewells, left their Sisters of St. Joseph of Carondelet convent in St. Louis, Missouri, to open a school in Tucson, Arizona. The trip of the sisters from their Carondelet home to a western mission took them over new terrain and through hazardous environments, bringing perils and experiences that few, including the nuns themselves, would have associated with convent life.[2] These Sisters of St. Joseph, as well as nuns from other congregations, journeyed into the American West as migrants, soaking in the self-knowledge and personal enlightenment that energizes travel. The sisters entered the western world, where, despite uncertainties and trepidations, they adapted to an unpredictable and unforgiving American West.

Catholic nuns melded with the traditional "pioneer West," associated with multiple nineteenth-century cataclysms for the region, its newcomers, and its indigenous peoples. White settlers—native or foreign-born and backed by the power of the United States—contributed to and capitalized on regional destabilization in pursuit of personal success and prosperity. Nuns shared in that larger dynamic, but they also stood apart from many of the corporate and political forces that rearranged western life.[3]

Although sisters established permanent convents in many western areas, as a group they were regional vagabonds, assigned and reassigned to missions in many locations. Sisters spent their work lives moving in, around, and out of the West. Among nuns, as individuals and as members of organized religious orders, migration and settlement represented expectations defined and experienced differently than the secular impulses driven by conquest and gain. In three ways—physical, cultural, and intellectual—nuns negotiated the West on terms particular to their life choices.

Sights and Sounds

Moving into and about many western spaces immersed the sisters in multifaceted situations that countermanded their lifestyle, which had evolved in European monastic regimens grounded in class distinctions and constricted feminine decorum.[4] Raucous days and noisy nights, typical for immigrants traveling into western regions, contrasted with European abbey atmospheres.[5] Steamboats and wagons, stagecoaches and carts jostled along with more of the same. The warring stenches of garlic-tainted sweat, pungent cigars, human vomit, rotten eggs, and spoiled chicken affronted everyone, but for nuns, these public assaults of humanity clashed with the sedate design of convent living and introduced the women to a collection of dilemmas. Social interactions, language complexities, daily hardships, human intimacy, and personal danger all contributed to the demands placed on nuns and sisters by life in the West.

Although the sisters willingly accepted the charge that took them from cloister to roadway, the public journey—where cautious phrases and prudent behaviors seldom reigned—rubbed against the monastic seclusion of many years and called for personal and congregational adjustments. One sister, less than two weeks removed from an Ohio cloister secured by locked grills, wrote about her new Montana convent, a small house with five open rooms: "How beautifully useful are *grates*, for when people once get in, they never know when to go." Another noted of shopping in the business district: "How strange it seemed to go into the different stores."[6] In California, the Sisters of the Holy Family hosted eight Ursuline nuns, among them one who had not stepped outside of her convent in thirty-three years and, previous to her current travels, had never seen a railroad.[7] As Sister Monica, en route to Arizona, perceived, women religious felt keenly these new days, musing that a cold repast in a passenger coach differed from a hot supper in the refectory, or that a night seated upright in a crowded railroad car bore no resemblance to the privacy of one's cell at the motherhouse.[8]

Language also affected sisters dealing with the newness of travel. Like other migrants, the nuns climbed into railcars, where cacophony filled the air. Many foreign-born immigrant families, new to America, possessed but a smidgen of English and might not hear their familiar mother tongue from any other traveler. Nuns, fluent in their native German, Italian, French, or Flemish, experienced this same isolation, which was exacerbated by their reluctance to approach secular strangers. A Dominican sister, who labored in California for over forty years, early in her American days had written, "I came here . . . knowing neither English nor Spanish and not being able to speak to anyone, because I met no French people during . . . eight years."[9]

For traveling nuns, however, more than close-by humanity and language deficiencies clashed with their former daily lives. In the typical cloister, sisters lived by disciplines that discouraged individual choice or personal spontaneity while requiring adherence to two documents: the rule and the constitution.[10]

Spatial separation was not intended to promote indifference to congregational regulations—quite the opposite. Every exhortation focused on intensifying loyalty to the community left behind. Further, the obedience vow meant that traveling sisters pledged adherence to the final directives of a mother general or a local bishop. At the same time, when missioned sisters entered, even temporarily, into the geographic jurisdiction of another prelate, the women were bound to honor his ecclesiastical authority.

In and of themselves, these inherently conflicting hierarchies could lead to confusing situations for emigrating sisters scrambling to keep all superiors satisfied. Western travel, with its great distances, regional isolation, and faulty communication systems, presented further obligations—whether spiritual or temporal—for nuns and sisters who set forth determined to abide by their many instructions and avoid inciting displeasure in any of their religious superiors. In spite of these constraints, after a few early problems, sisters adapted well to public travel, even as they wrestled with nun-styled privacy, convent behaviors, and clerical protocols that matched up poorly with the West.

Some sisters lived through hard lessons before they became confident about responding to western circumstances.[11] Unpredictable problems en route to a destination could and did arise almost routinely. Obedience to a mother superior and maintenance of rules for public behavior remained powerful edicts, and sisters did not ignore them casually. Yet the immediacy of the unexpected threw rules and customs into question, more and more influencing nuns to uphold the spirit of the regulations but search for a practical route out of the difficulty.

For example, in 1894 a group of Sisters of the Blessed Sacrament on their first mission discovered the importance of autonomy when train engineers, responding to a labor protest, rerouted passenger cars to a side rail. After six hours, railroad officials, falsely asserting the strike represented merely a local dispute, announced a replacement train would arrive in the morning. Marooned in Kansas City as it filled with agitated strikers, the women debated whether to walk through dark streets searching for a friendly convent or remain at the depot overnight. Among themselves, and thinking of their superior in Pennsylvania, they posed the question: "What would Mother wish us to do?"

Their decision to sit in the waiting room with street veils lowered while one sister guarded the baggage—a scene certain to draw public attention—

would not have pleased their Mother Katharine. From the perspective of those stranded in Kansas City, however, this choice avoided an aimless hunt for a nameless convent, afforded a lighted depot over unfamiliar sidewalks, devised a way to fashion a semiprivate space in a public world, and protected the currency of the train tickets. The group's travel savvy for the moment at hand was affirmed when a substitute train took them out of Kansas City only thirty minutes later.[12]

Such episodes heightened self-reliance among nuns and sisters, teaching them and those who followed that they should riddle out for themselves the obstacles of the West. After a few blunders, religious women on their own in the West learned to select the sensible solution and defend their actions at a later date. These sisters assessed their options, considered the rules that guided them, pondered the will of the mother superior, and then acted on the choice best suited to those conflicting priorities, certain they could justify the circumstances that elicited their personal agency.

Still, an easy beginning deceived more than one group of sisters headed for the West. For the first 250 miles of the 1870 Arizona journey, Sister Monica and her companions traversed a familiar route that belied the difficult road ahead. After leaving the St. Louis motherhouse, the sisters looked forward to reunions with other nuns from Carondelet and stopped twice with St. Joseph compatriots in nearby convents. Their journey thus began as something of a social outing, filled with exciting plans and soothing receptions among members of their own congregation. Ahead in Kansas City, Missouri, lay St. Teresa's Academy, a school opened in 1866 by other nuns from the St. Louis motherhouse.[13] The new missionaries anticipated, correctly, spending another worry-free night among women they had known for many years.

They were not disappointed, but a convivial evening with the academy staff inevitably gave way to the hour of departure. With adieu came the realization that everything of their secular and religious past was about to fade away. Even the announcement that Mother St. John Facemaz and Sister Lucina of St. Teresa's would travel as far as Omaha did not relieve a sad awareness that long-term, if not permanent, separation from spiritual family in St. Louis would now inflate the sorrow of biological relationships previously severed.[14]

Their gloomy spirits lifted in Omaha, though, when the sisters discovered they had missed their connection to San Francisco. Although such a development would provoke most travelers, the postponement meant more hours with Mother St. John. Thus, the stranded Sisters of St. Joseph picked their way through town to Mount Saint Mary's Academy and Convent of the Sisters of Mercy and sought overnight refuge with that congregation.

These Omaha nuns lived in bitter circumstances, but, under the leadership of Sister Mary Ignatius, they received their surprise guests with warmth and hospitality.[15] Fewer than ten Mercy sisters, their academy perched on a lonely hill, had operated the drafty school and convent since 1865 despite the constant poverty. The arrival of the stranded Sisters of St. Joseph offered the gifts of diversion and sociability. The Sisters of Mercy knew well the quirks of travel; it had taken them several hectic weeks to reach Omaha during the closing days of the Civil War, when chaotic crowds of former soldiers and displaced citizens milled through the cities and along the riverfronts. Under the cover of darkness, the Mercy nuns crept into Omaha far more informed about western travel than when they set forth from their motherhouse in New Hampshire.[16]

The hospitality of the Sisters of Mercy in Omaha mirrored a fortuitous aspect of travel for nuns on many trails. Delayed in unfamiliar towns and strapped by limited pocketbooks, mission teams often found sanctuary with the sisters of another congregation. Typically, those throwing wide a western convent door in friendship had, within recent memory, waded through the same uncertainty, exhaustion, uneasiness, and confusion troubling their guests.

Their own epic journeys completed, these mission groups settled into lonely lives—four or five women, far from home, housed along the edges of a town, hard put to keep a small school or hospital solvent and the trajectory of their religious lives focused. The opportunity to entertain other sisters provided spontaneous conviviality, broke the monotony of work, and softened the abrasive domestic exchanges that inevitably arose under the harsh living conditions. Guests at least temporarily swept aside the dual foes of poverty and homesickness that crept into small convents. As a mother superior in the Northwest remarked about such tensions, the spring and summer months brought "a greater sense of contentment, more open heartedness, and pleasant relations."[17]

For sisters on the road, the convent of another religious order promised meals, simple though they would be, eaten in the style of the refectory; common prayer shared at matins or vespers; and the luxury of privacy for daily hygiene and care of the habit. These occasions encouraged the local superior and the traveling one to suspend the rule of evening silence, allowing companionship—conversation, ritual, song, gossip, laughter. The guests might bring news of Philadelphia, St. Louis, or New York; the resident sisters might have travel advice or hints about dealing with frontier bishops. The benefits of such soothing balm and critical information could not be measured for either the stressed hosts or the weary visitors.[18]

Among its benefits, this cross-community support spun webs of friendships and spiritual solidarity from one religious congregation to another. In Oregon, Sisters of the Holy Names missioned from Canada commented: "Four of our dear Sisters of Providence have arrived. . . . The time is so pleasantly spent that . . . we forget we are in a land of exile."[19] In Canada, the mother superior of the Sisters of Providence wrote about the Holy Names sisters: "Give them as much help as possible."[20] In Arkansas, Benedictine sisters spending frequent weekends with the School Sisters of Notre Dame prompted the annalist to write that "these . . . two very dear sisters . . . feel very much at home with us."[21] Sisters of Charity of Leavenworth stayed with the Sisters of Mercy in Nebraska, and Ursulines of Toledo found shelter in the hospital of the Leavenworth charity sisters in Montana.[22] Contacts bridged the congregational divides and improved spirits, as one sister noted in her diary, *"Deo Gratias—*Two Franciscans came . . . to pay us a visit. They took dinner and left by the 2:40 train."[23] In the West, nuns from many congregations depended on the social contact with sisters from other missions.

In some situations, intercongregation visits extended over several weeks or even months, but such was not so in 1870 for the Sisters of St. Joseph moving to Arizona to open the first western school for the motherhouse.[24] The Nebraska morning ended the relaxation for these two groups of worn women. The Sisters of St. Joseph would not see these Sisters of Mercy again. Now the missionaries, their train crawling out of the Omaha station and their mother general standing on the platform, were on their own, and hour by hour, new vistas underscored the distance from urban St. Louis.

As the train entered Wyoming, it began a deceptively gentle ascent into the first front of the Rocky Mountains. When the train pulled into the wind-beaten depot of Sherman, Wyoming, the highest point on the rail, the passengers looked out on a desolate assortment of buildings—a newspaper office, two small hotels, one saloon, and a milliner's shop. If the nuns questioned why a seamstress chose this remote and dreary hamlet to open a fashion business, they did not comment on the store's more likely function as a brothel for Union Pacific road crews.[25] In any event, the stop was brief and the train moved on.

With Sherman behind them, the nuns plunged into a West they had not seen before. Like other first-time travelers into the Rocky Mountains, they could hardly grasp the enormity of the towering and jagged rock that rose

The reunion of these probable siblings, an Oregon Sister of St. Mary (left) and a Minnesota School Sister of Notre Dame (right), suggested the transient histories of immigrant families, explaining how biological sisters, separated in age, came to select religious congregations based hundreds of miles from each other. (Author's collection)

on each side. Dazzled though they were by nature's grandeur, the women fixed more on the rough tracks. Inching along the rickety uprights, the cars seemed certain to hurtle off into the space below. Little surprise that few passengers appreciated the nineteenth-century engineering craftsmanship that produced the railroad scaffolding—one that measured precisely, amid this jumble of boulders, each foot between the uprights and the cross ties.

Regardless, little in the makeshift appearance of the timbers or screeching of the rails inspired admiration among those captive in the carriages. One sister, unable to tolerate the scene, shook her napping companion who, startled to see the gaping maw, slept no more. She, with all the silent passengers, succumbed to the tense atmosphere as the cars passed over the groaning and weaving supports. Not until they saw the train on firmer ground did the travelers—men and women alike—relax, bursting into chatter and laughter with heartfelt exclamations of relief.[26]

Finally arriving in San Francisco, the sisters agreed to take several days to recover from the arduous journey. The constant swaying of the railcars sickened all seven with a persistent dizziness. Personal toilet had been as elusive as sleep on the train, and the nuns wished to bathe and clean their religious garments. Fatigued and ill, they once more sought help in a convent of the Sisters of Mercy.

The women in the Mercy convent had been in San Francisco since 1855 and were led by two legendary missionaries from Ireland, Mother Baptist Russell and Mother Gabriel Brown.[27] By 1870, after early years of poverty and illness, this California community was well situated, allowing it to extend hospitality to passing sister missionaries. As in Omaha, sisters of the Mercy congregation outdid themselves with kindness; Mother Gabriel arranged an outing to the countryside, packed a food basket for the road, and sent the St. Joseph sisters by carriage to the docks, where they boarded a ship for a rough ocean voyage.[28]

When their vessel anchored in San Diego, the sisters, again victims of vertigo, retired to a boardinghouse to recover before the final segment of their journey. Once restored, they hired a driver with a small enclosed wagon for the overland trip to Tucson. Although by now it would seem that dangerous roadways and towering waves had deadened the sisters to fear and illness, the California mountains and deserts presented new obstacles.

Within hours, a relentless sun wilted the women with a furnacelike heat, but when light slid away, the temperature plummeted to a bone-crunching cold. As darkness fell and coyote yipping filled the night, the nuns clutched summer shawls about their shoulders and scavenged along the rocks and brush, vainly seeking a level patch for sleep. Now regretting the notions of humility and poverty that impelled them to decline extra provisions from the Mercy pantry, the sisters parceled out food and tea with care, fearful they would finish the meager rations before they reached a ranch or trading post.

On the second travel day, the driver, battling the steep pitch of the trail, saw that his team lacked footing and unloaded the wagon by ordering the nuns to walk. One by one the sisters, poorly attired for such a strenuous endeavor, climbed down from their seats and turned toward the mountain slope. They scratched and clawed over stones and brambles, grasping for firm ground as they pulled themselves to a height of more than 4,000 feet. As the nuns crawled on hands and knees, behind them the guttural shouts from the driver, creaking protests of the wooden wagon, bawling cries of terrified beasts—hoof and harness gouging tree and rock—echoed in the mountain air, a racket of suffering and savagery.

Overcome from the fearsome climb and brutish scene, the severely dehydrated women fell about on the mountain crest, gasping for breath in the thin air, barely able to contemplate the descent to the desert floor. The drop appeared to be so perfectly perpendicular that the sisters could see no path before them. Locking hands in teams, the sisters flung themselves into the air, falling and bumping down the mountain at pell-mell speed, sliding past carcasses of horses and cattle, earlier victims of the punishing trail.[29] As the nuns crashed and rolled to the bottom, a putrid stench from the mineral-laden desert floor rose to fill their nostrils. Immersed in death on a western trail, the sisters staggered past the shallow graves of earlier migrants, many who, like their draft animals, had perished on the wicked pathway. Spent from the effort, one nun collapsed, pulling off her bloody stockings to remove dozens of thorns, souvenirs from a mountainside thicket of cactus. The dispirited nuns regrouped, waited for the wagon driver, and then limped on, one sister labeling the deadly place the "Abomination of Desolation."[30]

Like these Sisters of St. Joseph, other nuns found that western journeys produced horrors greater than they anticipated. It took some years and trial by error for congregations to realize a trip that began in comfort might shift precariously, producing treacherous conditions surprising in their suddenness and severity. Danger commonly disrupted trips, forcing inexperienced sisters to confront the West as it existed, not as it was rumored to be. In the moment of peril, retreat promised no less risk than continuing forward and, in either event, such decisions rarely rested with the nuns.

Mercurial weather changes threatened all westerners, but for sisters, limited in their knowledge of nature, the risk intensified when led by one impervious to the deadliness of the fickle climate. For example, on Halloween night 1864, three Sisters of Loretto, persuaded to open a school in Mora, a small town nestled high in the Sangre de Cristo Mountains of New Mexico, found themselves in a crisis not of their making. The women traveled "under the protection" of the Mora parish priest, Jean Baptiste Salpointe, French-born and destined to become the second archbishop of Santa Fe.

Fairly recent to the Southwest, Salpointe brushed off warnings of an approaching winter storm and insisted the nearly thirty-mile trek from Sapello to Mora could be completed by marching over mountain roads through the night. Conditions mocked his bravado when, an hour beyond the town of Sapello, fair skies turned to rain, quickly followed by thick, pelting snow, so usual to western mountains. High winds and early darkness added to the hazards, as the horses sliding on ice and straining through drifts could no longer advance.

Almost immediately, the poorly conceived plan of an all-night mountain caravan collapsed. In the swirling blizzard, all semblance of the roadway disappeared. Further, the rapidly mounting snow made it impossible to know where the side of the path ended and open space to the ravines below began. Safety required that the party immediately stop in its tracks, literally not risking another step forward.

The stranded group, improbably happened upon by another fabled Catholic missionary of the Southwest, Joseph P. Machebeuf, hunkered down for the night with a small fire and the nuns' biscuits and apples as supper. Shortly, a thundering avalanche of wet snow, strong enough to strip bark from tree trunks top to bottom, crashed near the site. Later, Salpointe casually noted that, as he drifted off to sleep, he heard the potentially deadly pile strike closest to the nuns' wagon, a fact that did not appear to interrupt his rest. The sisters passed these bitter hours wrapped in blankets inside their carriage, apparently so displeased with the turn of events that they refused to join the priests at the campfire for the skimpy meal of bread and fruit.[31]

At dawn, Salpointe and Machebeuf directed everyone to use branches snapped by the avalanche to clear a path for the horses. The futility of this burdensome effort brought a decision to abandon the Mora run and return to the Sapello parish. This proved to be an equally impossible task, as branches applied to the opposite direction cleared the hip-deep snow no more successfully. After several hours, the exhausted group was rescued by a number of men—Anglo farmers or Mexican shepherds—living in the mountains and eventually straggled back into Sapello.[32] Some days later, the Sisters of Loretto reached their new assignment at Mora, where perhaps they agreed that their arrival was due more to good fortune than good guidance.

In common with these Sisters of Loretto, as well as the Sisters of St. Joseph, other nuns also faced the danger and uncertainty of nineteenth-century western travel. In Texas, a sister remembered, "the horses shied and ran against a big stone. Sister . . . was thrown out and the top of the buggy fell on her head."[33] Another sister of the same congregation reminisced, "The trip was not a very pleasant one for the rain came down in torrents and the creeks and ditches we had to cross through the pitch dark forest were very dangerous."[34] In Oregon, a Sister of the Holy Names wrote: "Great was our anxiety and fear . . . when we passed over rugged mountains and on the brink of steep precipices with the accelerated speed to which the horses were forced by a merciless driver."[35] En route to Yankton in the Dakota Territory, a stagecoach carrying Presentation sisters flipped, requiring the nuns to crawl through a window of the vehicle.[36] On the Mississippi River, Mother Caroline of the School Sisters of Notre Dame and Sister Mary Ellen of the Daughters of Charity were among the survivors of a gigantic steamboat explosion that killed almost 350 passengers. Caroline recalled: "There was a tremendous crash and the bolted cabin door burst open . . . I stood aghast for a moment, till the fire, crackling beneath my feet, warned me to make my escape."[37] In Montana, Ursulines wrote of crossing William's Ford on the Tongue River: "The river . . . had a very swift current [and] the water . . . was very high. . . . We felt danger but resolved to show no signs of fear."[38]

In general, "resolved to show no signs of fear" described the reaction of nuns to hazards caused by the western environment. In 1904, when Sister Mary Clare of the Sisters of Charity of Leavenworth left Grand Junction, Colorado, for a begging trip, she anticipated that a coach at the rail depot would convey her into the town of Carbondale. Instead, because of the overdue train and extreme cold, the stage had departed, a fact the conductor overlooked as he let the woman off and the cars rolled into the night. In the snow, "without a human being in sight and [only] a dim lamp . . . in the distance on the railroad track," the nun decided that she and her companion, a young girl from the sisters' orphanage, best move along before the frigid temperatures won the night.

In "gloom, darkness, [and] dismay," with the rushing Roaring Fork

River living up to its name, the two set off, "expecting death at every turn." Unwittingly, they turned away from Carbondale and toward open livestock range. They barely escaped death when they mistook the dark water for a roadway, and twice, silent cattle crowded against them, panicking the child, who again stumbled toward the tumultuous river. The nun—privately admitting, "if I had been wandering through the woods of Australia, I could not feel more lost" but trying to reassure the youngster—joked that gentle-natured cows "would not touch good little girls."

Her jest failed to deflect the child's fear, as the youngster then exclaimed with greater panic, "What if we should meet a man?" The nun recalled answering, "A man? A man is just the being I am wishing to meet. There is not one in Colorado tonight who would not have pity on us. He would show us the way to Carbondale and relieve us of our heavy satchels."[39] Whatever ill ease crept over Sister Mary Clare on the dark and cold Colorado countryside, she determined she had a twofold responsibility: remain calm for her young orphan and find the way to Carbondale. This pragmatic undergirding helped Sister Mary Clare and other nuns in the West to solve dilemmas within the best available context of convent standards. In doing so, they revealed a composure and sturdiness that allowed some westerners to form new opinions of religious women.

Then, too, some nuns relished precarious western travel, which they defined as "adventure." In March 1877 a St. Joseph sister in an army convoy from Fort Fetterman enthused about crossing the Powder River: "A freshet has washed away the bridge. . . . We were taken over in a new and novel ferry of no less than a tub, with a seat in the center, a piece being cut out of the front, two ropes fastened to the sides. . . . Thus, we crossed, one at a time; and I can assure you we enjoyed the ride."[40] This lighthearted approach to the West and its dangers further layered the public image of Catholic nuns, diluting stereotypes of the humorless sequestered ascetic.

It proved to be the usual in western travel for nuns: physical adversities overtook them in an environment where personal sensibilities might be affronted. In the interests of survival, their notions of dignity, or their desire for excitement, they camouflaged their inner feelings, suppressed fear, and stepped along. In repeated cases, sisters managed to make their way and sometimes acted with lifesaving alacrity, perhaps startling themselves, for nothing in their convent commitments prepared them for the vicissitudes of western society. As single women traveling in small groups, they overcame public inexperience, personal timidity, and the absence of convent superiors to resolve problems and support each other. Convent formation stressed acceptance without complaint and a contained public demeanor, and so they depended on both—often while confronting the daunting extremes of travel to the American West.

Peoples and Places

Exposed to the sights and sounds of the West, sisters communicating with eastern and European motherhouses wrote a special insiders' narrative of western history. Thus, traveling nuns served as cultural journalists documenting the natural landscapes and the diverse humanity of the region. In the nineteenth and early twentieth centuries, many sisters were women of education and expressed themselves eloquently through the written word. The West complemented these talents, giving sisters rich materials for their correspondence. Since the letters and diaries circulated almost exclusively within a congregation, the collective perceptive insights and appreciative commentaries of sisters rarely reached the larger society.

For example, in 1877 a Sister of St. Joseph exclaimed about Wyoming: "I wish that more of our delicate Sisters could take this trip. . . . The scenery here is picturesque and beautiful. Our tents are on the brink of a stream, which is lined with cottonwood trees. Lively May flowers are here in abundance. I enclose the rattles of a rattlesnake one of the men killed yesterday."[41] Nearly two decades later, a sister en route from Pennsylvania to New Mexico wrote about a dawn in Colorado: "I watched the sun rising over the eastern plains . . . the grassy land . . . invested with new beauty, caused by the mellow light . . . the soft clouds across the sky, fringed with pink . . . stealing its way through the purple, and forming streaks of purple, pink, and blue all along for a great distance." She incorrectly lamented that she lacked the poetic skills of a Robert Burns, for "words would gush from my heart to describe the scene."[42]

Her rapture replicated that of Mother Amadeus Dunne, an Ursuline from Ohio who established the first Catholic convent in Miles City, Montana, where the exacting West changed the worldview of the middle-aged nun. In March 1884, after three months marked by cold, rain, and floods, Mother Amadeus led three of her group to the Cheyenne settlements, located in the southeastern corner of the territory. On this trip, Mother Amadeus journeyed onto rugged turf far removed from the urban setting of a Toledo or a Miles City.

Traveling over slick paths and fording dangerous waters under the protection of a Fort Keogh military escort, the Ursulines felt the force of their new environment. Gazing out from the military ambulance transport,

Mother Amadeus looked far across the panoramic stretches of scenery, barely able to discern the distant soldiers sent ahead to prepare the evening camp. Something about the shifting visuals, as the convoy closed the gap between the two groups, stirred her ascetic sense. The surreal tableau reinforced an earlier comment from Amadeus to the Toledo convent: "Everything out here is far different than we imagined it."[43]

For Mother Amadeus, the trip appeared to unleash a deep love for the western environment and a willingness to engage the West at its edgiest. She never ceased to exalt in excursions that took her through remote reaches in all hours of the day and seasons of the year. In Helena, Montana, during an 1884 stop at the hospital of the Sisters of Charity of Leavenworth, Amadeus enthused: "Here we are in the heart of the great Rocky Mountains. On every side we see them towering around us with their snow-capped tops."[44] Her legendary travels were far from over; more than twenty-five years later, Mother Amadeus, sixty-four years old and hobbled by an assortment of ailments, joined her Ursuline missionaries on Kings Island, Alaska, where, on Christmas night, she "beheld the Aurora. . . . The dancing lights had gathered into one broad semi-circle of gold encircling our tiny cabin. We stood in the center of all this celestial splendor."[45]

Sisters in other locations also documented their first impressions of new places in the West. A Sister of Charity of Leavenworth traveling from Colorado to Wyoming wrote to her Kansas motherhouse: "Could you but see the Great Laramie Plains. . . . How grand and great they are!"[46] In 1864 Holy Names sisters leaving Portland for the Dalles watched with the scientist's eye, writing:

> We did not notice our transition from the Willamette to the Columbia . . . until the grandeur of the mountain scenery overwhelmed us. . . . The day passes in . . . an ever changing panorama, towering cliffs, immense boulders of fantastic shape, waterfalls, snow-capped summits in the distance, all is marvelous, for here, the Columbia, breaking through the Cascade Range, has cut . . . a canyon 4,000 feet deep, through the overlaying lava. . . . The vegetation along the river is almost tropical in luxuriance . . . [though] to our intense regret, the immediate vicinity of our new home is as dry, rocky, and barren as a desert.[47]

More than ten years later, a new crew of Holy Names sisters journeying east of Portland to Baker City continued the academic tone, noting: "We pass through a desert of sand; the luxuriance of green foliage for which western Oregon is remarkable has disappeared; an occasional tree attracts attention and much to our disappointment we have become acquainted

Like these Kentucky Sisters of Loretto, visiting Seven Falls in Colorado Springs, Colorado, nuns unfamiliar with the flora and fauna of their new mission life engaged and studied the scenic West as a way to broaden their regional knowledge. (Author's collection)

with the Oregon sage (*Origanum vulgare*) which in color and profusion tires the eye."[48] The next morning, one sister added, "There is a prodigality of Nature's gifts in the Valley of the Grand Ronde, presenting a striking contrast to the scanty flora of the Umatilla and Pendleton. The Blue Mountains form an exception here, towering pines and firs intermingle with a variety of shrubs and flowers in making it an enchanting scene."[49]

The West did not elicit lush and scientific verbiage from every nun. Sister Monica, on her 1870 journey to Arizona, commented of the terrain: "On the right lies a great salt lake, supposed to have been part of the ocean, [but] being hemmed in by the mountains, could not recede. . . . On the left rise ugly mountains of volcanic rock and red sand."[50] The following day on the desert brought further misery, for Sister Monica recorded: "Traveling . . . is rendered dangerous on account of the sand storms. . . . When the sun is at meridian height the sand is hot enough to blister. . . . We could get water only in one place . . . not only hot, but so full of minerals that we suffered more after taking it than before."[51]

Everywhere in the West, sisters through literary device captured western nature in its usual and unusual forms. From Texas, Mother St. Pierre informed her congregation that after a flood, the sisters in Galveston were "completely blockaded by the waters of the Gulf." In Oregon, the Sisters of St. Mary remembered of their first views of Beaverton: "Within a thousand feet of the buildings, there was a second growth of pines and firs with dense shrubs of hazel bushes and vines, making a natural forest for protection." Mother Joseph, who rode horseback from Missoula, Montana, to Vancouver, Washington, wrote about a mishap in an isolated Rocky Mountain campsite: "The fire . . . meant to keep the wolves at bay began to threaten. . . . A burning forest seemed to surround us. . . . Great branches fell . . . [and] the howl of the wolves . . . redoubled. . . . We battled burning cinders and blinding smoke. . . . The trees had been too damp for a widespread forest fire." A Presentation sister close to the Canadian border reported to her motherhouse in France: "The temperature varies from extreme heat to extreme cold, but is healthful because the air is dry. . . . Summer with its frightful electric storms, its hot destructive winds; . . . without transition, snowstorms with temperatures of twenty to forty degrees below zero." In California, a Dominican new to San Francisco told her motherhouse that "the wind blew such a quantity of sand through the cracks of the floor, as to make our work almost useless. . . . Open one of the windows and you will have enough [fresh air] to blow you across the bay." In Minnesota, a Benedictine explained to her European patron that over a two-year period, the poverty of her rural convent worsened because "innumerable flying hordes of thieves, [that is] grasshoppers destroyed everything." An Irish postulant in Dakota Territory wrote to her mother: "This is real prairie land—something you could never envision. Trees are miles apart and very sparse. Hills and valleys do not exist here, and one is often awakened at night by howling of the prairie dogs and coyotes."[52]

Like all Anglo-European immigrants to the West, nuns also learned nature could be as treacherous as it was beautiful, lessons that influenced their future approach to western work. For example, in 1888, during a decade of some of the worst winters recorded on the Dakota plains, a twenty-five-year-old Swiss-born nun lost her bearings as she left the laundry shed and headed across the yard for noon dinner, misjudging that a white-out snowstorm obliterated direction and distance. As the midday hour passed and Sister Wilhelmina had not arrived from the laundry, the other nuns, with no hired hands or neighbors for assistance, organized their own search.

Fearing the whipping wind and the blowing snow, the sisters tied themselves to a long rope, secured it firmly to the porch rail, and crawled on their hands and knees, calling the missing woman. Through a bitter afternoon, the voices of the hunters floated over the yard, as the stinging snow piled up over the body of the hunted. Late in the day, the searchers bumped against the mounded drift that was the moribund Sister Wilhelmina. Blinded by the snow, she had huddled against a fence for protection. Exhausted and shocked, the distressed nuns retrieved the ice-weighted body, dragging and pushing their near-dead companion to the convent. Within moments, Sister Wilhelmina died, and her overwhelmed friends rallied to bathe and dress her for burial. The cruel event traumatized the small household of isolated Swiss Benedictines, but they stayed on the plains. The women grieved, and in response, they sharpened their precautions against deadly winter in open country and over the next twenty years cut an educational path in the demanding environments of eastern and central South Dakota.[53]

Some weather disasters were of such magnitude that they intensified the public involvement of nuns, bringing the sisters into intimate partnerships with citizens. For example, the September 1900 killer storm that struck Galveston, Texas, showed that into the twentieth century, nature remained dominant in western life. With weather predictions largely a product of local speculation, unprepared Texans watched a threat of rain and a rumor of storm transform into a catastrophe of rising waters and hurricane winds, lumbering with deadly slowness over the Gulf of Mexico and Galveston Bay.

During the worst hours, the Dominican sisters and their boarding students at Sacred Heart Academy saw their barricades of furniture collapse, as water and wind ripped apart the roof, walls, and windows of the convent property.[54] At a beachfront Ursuline school, the nuns, after their seawall failed, turned the convent remains into a haven for more than 1,000 victims. The sisters literally plucked survivors from the dark waters pounding past the upper floors of the damaged building.[55]

This hurricane, snuffing out 6,000 to 8,000 lives, created lifelong nightmarish memories for nuns, students, and citizens at these Dominican and Ursuline sites, but it also traumatized the Sisters of the Incarnate Word at St. Mary's Infirmary and their separate orphanage. As at the Dominican academy, the walls of seemingly invincible buildings disintegrated before the very eyes of the nuns. Dawn revealed the hospital yard littered with debris and bodies. At the orphanage, however, the savage hurricane pulverized the site, leaving neither structure nor inhabitant. Of the ninety children and ten sisters lost, rescuers pulled only a few broken bodies of nuns from the mud. Using a clothesline, which in the storm looped into a deadly noose, each had lashed one or two toddlers to herself, apparently hoping adult ballast would save the smallest orphans.[56] Like other nuns who survived a regional maelstrom, the Galveston sisters carried for decades the pain of helplessness and the scarring memories of unleashed western nature.

Less than six years later, nuns more than 2,000 miles from Texas learned the same lessons about the western environment, linking convents to the public through a natural phenomenon. On 18 April 1906 at 5:15 A.M., as many sisters filed into their chapels for morning devotions, a massive earthquake rocked San Francisco. The magnitude of the quake—toppling buildings, cracking streets, setting fires—took shape quickly, and just as quickly Catholic sisters reacted to the civic turmoil. In nearby San Jose, the Sisters of Notre Dame de Namur used the teacher's friend for orderly lines in classroom and chapel—a wooden clicker—to guide 125 terrified students silently down three flights of swaying stairs, out of the crumbling dormitory, and onto the campus lawn.[57]

In San Francisco itself, the Sisters of the Holy Family, formed in 1872 to introduce social-work programs into the neighborhoods of the poor, responded instantly, for the city's needs meshed with their sense of mission. Unlike the hysterical thousands desperately trying to escape the devastation, the sisters searched for the hardest-hit parts of San Francisco.[58] They began at Mechanics' Pavilion, bringing sheets, pillows, and blankets from their convent; sorting out the dead from the dying; assisting the wounded;

and encouraging the disoriented. When roaring flames forced rescuers and injured to fall back from the pavilion, some of the sisters rode by wagon to the emergency hospital at Alamo Plaza, while others walked to the Holy Family convent to open another aid post. In the days that followed, these sisters—whose property losses included three day-home buildings and part of the main convent, for financial reversals of nearly $40,000—took their nursing to North Beach, the Howard Street Pier, and the Potrero.[59] As tent cities for the homeless sprouted in open spaces, the Holy Family sisters circulated among survivors, gathering children—parted from their parents by death or confusion. They organized kindergarten activities and sewing classes, distributing the aprons, shirts, and shawls made by youthful seamstresses to nearby victims.[60]

Neither the hurricane at Galveston nor the earthquake at San Francisco could be cataloged as "frontier" events, but they were decidedly western natural disasters, fueled by local climatology and geology. Inside these two urban centers, sophisticated communities with the latest conveniences, the West displayed its inexorable power. Within moments, natural forces destroyed regional communication and transportation modes, tossing western cities into a retrograde era of isolation and separating them from the better-connected municipalities of the United States. With their links to the larger society shattered, western urbanites found themselves more than usually removed from the nation's main arteries and reminded of the strength of the environment in which they lived.

Thus, the West in diverse spaces and regions—deserts and rivers, mountains and valleys—could surprise its residents in several different ways. For Catholic nuns, whether in urban or rural settings, submersion into western nature elicited insight and memoir. The sisters excelled as keen observers of the western world, documenting its beauty, uniqueness, and danger. They responded to this natural world in unprecedented ways for cloistered women, accruing new experiences, developing skills as westerners, engaging their secular neighbors, and applying their life lessons to future endeavors in the West.

In addition, nuns absorbed more than the natural world of the West, studying the lives of other westerners. The West attracted nuns for the express purpose of supporting burgeoning communities. It was not odd that religious women devoted careful thought and attention to other Anglo-Europeans whose paths they crossed.[61] As one of the Holy Names sisters in the original mission trip from Canada to Oregon remarked about the importance of embracing secular society, "How true it is that we must have a knowledge of persons and things."[62]

Perhaps nobody pursued that knowledge more thoroughly than Mother Caroline Friess, who, during an 1848 exploratory tour that ultimately saw the German School Sisters of Notre Dame situated in Missouri, Minnesota, and Texas, cast a critical eye over the people and places she visited. Of her overall impressions of the United States, Caroline lamented: "At the supper table we noticed once more the American sameness in the menu; in every hotel the meals are prepared the same way, even in the country, with the exception that the city cooking is more delicate and pastry is added." Mother Caroline saw this dullness in food preparation as one more indicator of a general national tendency toward uniformity, adding: "The cities, streets, wells, and pumps are all of the same kind. In the whole country one finds only a single style of kitchen utensils, house and garden implements. A sameness is also to be found in the country itself; everywhere may be seen hills, woods, uncultivated land and neglected rivers."[63]

It was, however, the youth of America that interested the visiting educator, recalling of her steamboat ride across Lake Erie: "On board were entire families whose children made much noise and showed themselves very disobedient. The mothers, however, had not the least worry, because here, the fathers take the place of nursery maids."[64] Mother Caroline thought there could be some adjustment in the behavior of Americans she met on her travels, writing that "the dear children are like young horses. . . . Their fiery and passionate, also, restless and fidgety temperaments prevent all undisturbed or uninterrupted instructions."[65]

Still everywhere she ventured, Caroline looked to the future in America, where education would be the principle employment for her sisters. She decried the destitution of immigrants, writing to the European motherhouse: "Our work here is made . . . difficult because girls 10 to 18 come from the woods without knowing . . . any letters of the alphabet." Repeatedly, Mother Caroline labeled financial constraint as the foe of education: "Their poverty permits them to attend class only three to six months"; "It was a most difficult problem to train and to teach those children [because of their] poverty, listlessness, and dislike for learning"; "Many children must go about in bare feet and threadbare clothing"; "the Germans in America are generally poor."[66] Thus, before the middle of the nineteenth century, Mother Caroline identified a theme that dominated among Catholic sisters who followed her: Anglo-European people in western communities lived and worked at the economic margins.

Nuns from many congregations echoed that refrain. Franciscan Sisters of Philadelphia, who opened a private school in Oregon, saw irregular employment and inadequate wages crushing families living in shacks scattered about the district. To counter this, the sisters, after the paid semesters concluded, opened their private academy, offering free summer classes for children too poor to attend school during the academic year. As one sister observed, "so extreme is their poverty that for some clothing must be provided before they can even leave home."[67]

The poverty, endemic to the boom-and-bust cycles of the West, was not confined to Oregon or the missions of the Philadelphia Franciscans. At St. Scholastica's Benedictine monastery in Atchinson, Kansas, a prioress noted that 1874–75 had included failed crops, swarms of locusts and worms, and an extreme winter, with the result that "every day, young strong Germans come begging, because they have had no work for months and are starving."[68] In Texas, a sister looking back to her first 1899 assignment mused: "I was too green to notice its poverty." A colleague recalled that another Texas mission was "a solitary spot with many privations." A third sister, sent to open a school in Oklahoma, remembered that in 1902, "nearly all were Protestant and very poor."[69] In Windthorst, Kansas, Dominican sisters and Adorers of the Blood of Christ, both of whom served at the Immaculate Heart of Mary parish, found that over two decades, a tax of twenty-five to sixty cents per student for the school operation placed a burden on families with more than one child.[70] In Yakima, Washington, a superior suggested withdrawing from a mission because "there is no money in circulation."[71] A Dominican sister in Anaconda, Montana, wrote that the closing of the copper smelter for several months "caused great hardship for the people who were poor and had large and young families."[72] In Virginia City, Nevada, the superior anticipated reduced donations for the orphans, "considering the poverty at large."[73] In Aberdeen, Washington, Dominicans summed up the widely recognized reality for sisters missioned to the West: "The Catholics were few and far between and most of them very poor."[74]

These circumstances meant that sisters, rather than standing distant from the complicated and constantly fluctuating economy of the nineteenth- and early twentieth-century West, interacted closely and deliberately with workers—often the poorest people of a community. For example, when those Dominican sisters came to Aberdeen in 1890, they arrived in a rough-edged town newly shaped by the industrial exploitation of its resource-rich coastal region enhanced by nearby lush timber stands. Along with the fishing boats and transport vessels anchored off the shore, lumberyards and mills peppered the town, and ten miles east in the Chehalis River valley lived the skilled and unskilled loggers who cut, split, and hauled the trees destined for Grays Harbor, the shipping point at

Aberdeen. Although an atmosphere of promising industry prevailed, the workers themselves accumulated limited cash, indebted as they were to a company store in the mountain camp and local vice businesses in the harbor town.

In this place, with its scant financial support from the town or the parish, the nuns set about to establish a presence, renting three unstable shacks raised on stilts over the smelly tidal flats of Grays Harbor. The sisters converted one building into a simple schoolhouse, a second they opened as a rudimentary hospital, and the third they made their bleak residence. In late September 1890, the sisters welcomed thirty pupils across all grades, calling the primitive shack "St. Rose School." The same day, they admitted the first person—their prototype patient, a victim of an industrial accident—to the hospital cabin now known as "St. Joseph's." To heat the ramshackle buildings, which shifted precariously from either wind or water, the nuns waded into the high tides for the rotting drift lumber that clogged the shoreline. Other times, they scoured the nearby forest for fallen timbers they could heft into a wheelbarrow, which they maneuvered back to their "convent." In these ways, the Dominicans placed their public mark on Aberdeen.

Their inadequate facilities, however, could not meet the needs of the community. Most urgent was the call for a professional hospital for workers injured on the docks, in the mills, or at the logging camps. Anxious to introduce better care and to leave the unsanitary rentals they called "school, hospital, and home," the Dominicans undertook a fund-raising campaign supported, in part, through numerous begging tours. They pinned their hopes for cash on Montesano, the mountain labor camp that fed timbers to the waiting transport ships. To reach the forested spot, the nuns depended on the logging train, boarding the rough conveyance at the Grays Harbor terminal.

The engine left the depot and ran along a roadbed that hugged a mountain on the right and dropped off into a ravine on the left. On the ascent, the single engines, with no heavy freight, reached surprising speeds, frequently jumping the tracks and tipping precariously on the skinny road. The engine had no benches, so the sisters sat on the floor or, when so ordered, stood on a small exterior step, where they clung to the grab bar, dreading a spill—which in either direction threatened lethal results. Even on the smoothest runs, limbs of the overhanging trees whipped along and through the engine windows, forcing the nuns to dodge and duck the stinging pine needles and cudgel-like branches.

At the end of the line, the sisters stepped into the din of one of the least accessible and little known of western industries. Here, the two women moved among loggers—some just adolescents—who gathered in all-male hamlets rigidly monitored by company managers, cooks, and foremen. For the lumberjacks, exhausting hours, death-defying jobs, and raw living typified their regimens. The sisters could not miss the utter beastliness of these lives: bloody injuries resulting in lost hands and legs occurred routinely when open gears and moving belts snagged the loose clothing of workers; overcrowded, shoddy cabin dormitories infested with fleas and other vermin produced unhealthy and stench-ridden quarters; and the absence of basic institutions opened a societal vacuum within the pines, making the youngest and the weakest vulnerable to the physical and emotional cruelties of the seasoned and the bully. In this unvarnished masculine setting of grueling work and human depravity, the two sisters, unlike romanticized nuns of fiction, carried out their begging surrounded by coarse verbal harassment laced with crude expletives and sexual innuendo. They then boarded the log-laden train for the harrowing descent to Grays Harbor.[75]

Within two years, the sisters opened St. Joseph's Hospital, which flourished along with the general economic upturn brought to Aberdeen by the robust health of the lumber industry. The new brick building, with its operating rooms and in-house pharmacy, rose above Aberdeen as its most imposing edifice, a marked improvement over the original dilapidated cabin hospital.[76] Despite the upgrading of this mission and the local public praise for its excellence, the sisters, in various communications, never forgot the poverty and hostility of the early years at Aberdeen and Montesano: "Much could be written of the trials and hardships endured"; "Poverty, crosses, and trials were the portion of the sisters"; "The pioneer church in Aberdeen . . . was very poor and small."[77]

As a result of placements similar to Aberdeen, many sisters lived close to the turbulent work dynamics of changing regional economies. These associations, often more hedonistic than mannerly, connected nuns to the people of the West. The sisters absorbed reality and used it to energize and justify their social-service response to human needs in the West.

For example, Blessed Sacrament sisters from Pennsylvania headed for New Mexico lived through the Pullman Strike of 1894 at the center of its happenings.[78] The May protest originated in Chicago, but it had snowballed, especially throughout the West, by the time of the nuns' trip in late June. Near Kansas City, Kansas, the nuns took a delay in stride, unaware that local workers identified with an uprising against the business practices of George W. Pullman, the imperious railroad entrepreneur. By the time they reached Dodge City, the sisters began to see a larger problem, when, in a swift move, the engineer and the fireman joined the strike by uncoupling the cars, abandoning the passengers, and riding off with the engine.[79]

Finally pulling into La Junta, Colorado, the nuns learned that strikers had cut all the telegraph wires. The women began to grasp the magnitude and complexity of the protest, which emerged as a landmark moment in American labor history. In La Junta, a raucous crowd—strikers, sympathizers, U.S. marshals, railroad officials, private police, and curious onlookers—swelled to nearly 5,000, most milling about the depot day and night. As general disorder and physical confrontations escalated, a conductor advised the sisters to lock themselves inside the Pullman accommodations. Since the strike centered on an industrywide refusal to move Pullman cars, which were overturned and burned in some locations, the nuns might have hesitated at this suggestion. Having, however, just passed the day sandwiched in among shouting, angry men who jumped on and off their coach, the sisters accepted the solitude, reporting calmly: "We . . . are now as retired as if we were in our convent."[80]

As the number of confused passengers, law officers, and striking workers grew, demands for food and drink inflated accordingly. The sisters, no less hungry than others, decided to leave the locked Pullman car for the public dining room. With their seventy-five-cent complementary railroad food passes, the sisters stood for an hour pressed into a crowd of more than 100 waiting impatiently outside the depot's Fred Harvey Hotel restaurant.

When finally seated at the linen-covered tables, the guests may have chosen from the famous Harvey menu of roast beef, quail, raw oysters, cheeses, and fresh fruits. Perhaps after such a fine meal, the pie with ice cream and a cup of the distinctive Harvey House coffee relaxed the harried travelers, who, looking on "nuns" as universal confidants, began to unburden a litany of personal difficulties.[81] One worried about an aging parent, another feared for a dying husband.[82] The Sisters of the Blessed Sacrament, despite the unorthodox social arrangements, did not fall short of their dinner companions' expectations—comforting, advising, and promising prayers.

Within a day, the sisters, immersed in a public drama of extraordinary national proportions, had set aside, among other practices, their convent refectory rules. Not only had they appeared in a restaurant, but they dined with secular people, welcomed public conversations, listened to family intimacies, and offered the empathy expected of nuns. As for the sisters in this nontraditional setting, one conveyed to the motherhouse the unusual news that the nuns had enjoyed an evening supper with four U.S. marshals, "all refined and perfect gentlemen."[83]

Yet the sisters did not allow the charming dinner companions from law enforcement to cloud their broader societal concerns; instead, they increasingly worried about the railroad employees who were under attack from authorities and strikers. Their conductor reported that at Raton, New Mexico, miners and railroaders, an alliance that suggested the expanding nature of the labor protest, stopped a maverick train and half lynched the engineer and fireman, releasing them with dire warnings for other strikebreakers. Their uneasy informant concluded his account to the nuns with a disquieting assurance that "the passengers do not stand any danger, as the mob will not harm them."[84]

According to a new bulletin, after the Raton episode, strikers stopped the next train at Trinidad, Colorado, overtook the cars, and disarmed the deputy escort. With reports of the violence escalating only 100 miles to the southwest, the nuns studied the chaotic La Junta depot scene, concluding that the 200 U.S. marshals "seem to be afraid to take any action, or else are in sympathy with the strikers."[85] By the time that their train, crammed with soldiers—guns and fixed bayonets in each window and the engineer's cab—departed, Sister Mercedes admitted: "We did not feel homesick leaving La Junta, but we did feel scared."[86] At Trinidad, the last stop before Raton, the sight of a hastily constructed tent city housing an additional 350 soldiers likewise failed to instill confidence, especially when two sisters were threatened at rifle point for walking near the disabled telegraph office.

Still, the sisters, intent on fulfilling their travel obedience to the motherhouse, continued onward with aplomb, ignoring rumors that once the cars entered the Raton tunnel, protesters would set off massive dynamite charges.[87] Such did not occur, and so this small group of Sisters of the Blessed Sacrament rode the first train to pass Raton, New Mexico, in the Pullman Strike of 1894, reaching Santa Fe in the early hours of 8 July.[88] Two days later, the emerging labor leader, Eugene V. Debs, and others of the American Railway Union were arrested; by the middle of July, the union and the boycott of the Pullman Palace Car Company had collapsed, but four young Catholic nuns, now focused on starting a school in New Mexico, had been involved directly, at least briefly, with someone from every quarter of this seminal American labor event.

Eight years later, Italian immigrant nuns in Colorado replicated these attitudes about working people, as they searched out laborers in unlikely places. To reach their countrymen working the mines, the sisters picked their way along slick, smelly passageways or clutched steel ropes as they were lowered in buckets hundreds of feet down narrow, pitch-black shafts. Once at the bottom, the nuns flattened themselves against the rock as the crews passed with loaded wheelbarrows to dump dirt and ore into the buckets the women had just ridden. Here, in the literally poisonous world of miners, the sisters crept through the small spaces and spoke Italian, using religious encouragement "to bring a good word to those poor men . . . where breathing is laborious and the only light from a few tallow candles."[89]

Events such as these kept ordinary people of the West close to Catholic sisters, as industrial growth, economic need, political developments, ethnic frictions, and labor discrimination enveloped nuns in different areas and eras. Circumstances of the moment positioned the sisters at the center of western humanity and raised before religious women the voices of contest and protest. The nuns rethought their regional impressions, scrutinized the societies around them, and developed into one-of-a-kind cultural journalists.

Local Communities and Expectations

The diverse populations of the West directly affected the choices nuns made about the communities in which they lived and worked. In addition, western experiences melded into the thinking of professed women, shaping their development and future goals. In combination, these elements touched patterns of convent life in the West and beyond.

Mother Caroline Friess cast a wide net in her determination that German immigrants would find a rallying place as Germans in the presence of the School Sisters of Notre Dame in the West. She was energized by mission trips to small communities, during which German settlers crowded about her and called out, "Give us teachers for our children!"[90] She believed in the power of an "imposing" school building to build confidence among American newcomers. With her strong Germanic roots, Caroline argued that the majority of her countrymen in America were poor and that many years would pass before they could acquire wealth. A solid school, in the literal sense, could be a beacon of hope for "the poorer or middle classes."[91] She saw these compounds of school, convent, church, and rectory as cultural "ornaments" that could uplift immigrant families. Mother Caroline's administrative policies defined convents and schools as tangible symbols of national identity around which immigrants could organize. As a result, sisters, in highly visible ways, were to function as instruments of stabilization for nascent Anglo-European communities. Mother Caroline intended that this stabilization would improve the immigrant experience in America, but it would do so with forceful German guidance.

Mother Frances Cabrini would have agreed with Mother Caroline, applying the German sister's vision to Italian immigrants. During a missionary trip to Seattle, Mother Cabrini decried the fact that in one Italian community, some residents had not attended church for fifty years. Cabrini, who stayed with the Sisters of the Holy Names while she sought mission privileges from the bishop, reported that Catholic immigrants around Seattle insisted they did not want to go where "they don't speak to us like our churches in Italy."[92] That, she told her sisters, meant the American Catholic parishes conveyed a Protestant ambiance because "they use the English language." Cabrini's solution sent teams to the scattered homes of the immigrants, two sisters personally walking the workers and their families back to the Italian church to participate in rituals. She declared that "I expect this mission will bear much fruit," as the sisters had restored the use of "their mother tongue," and the parish resurrected the feasts of familiar Italian saints and reintroduced religious processions akin to home.[93] Thus, Cabrini credited the direct action of Italian sisters in a well-established immigrant community for a cultural and religious regeneration.

By the close of the nineteenth century, waning spiritual identity for ethnic groups in the American West was evident in more places than Seattle. In El Paso, Texas, a spate of nationalities stretched the resources of the Catholic Church called on to service Mexican, European, and American congregants. The Daughters of Charity, whose primary work emanated from the Hotel Dieu Hospital, responded by enlarging their El Paso mission, carrying soup and food by buggy to the poor. Given the Daughters' cross-cultural charitable activities outside the hospital, even the rumor of the superior's reassignment prompted pleadings for reconsideration to the motherhouse in St. Louis. One correspondent argued: "Being so far from religious centers, our religious forces are very weak and so little to impress our public with the exception of your admirable order under the able generalship of Sister Regina."[94]

The secular community often had not anticipated that the presence of a convent would have such a supportive impact. In a parallel manner, sisters who came to the West as "greenhorns" perceived over time that, despite their initial reluctance, their unpredicted western lives changed them. A young Sister of Charity, after many horrific frights while moving between Colorado and Wyoming, wrote to her Kansas motherhouse: "I felt like saying in an extremely loud voice to be heard at all points of the compass, 'Oh all you sisters, safely sheltered in your convents, *stay there*, if you can!'"[95]

She hardly took her own advice, for the following year saw her with a companion on an extensive begging tour through California and Nevada. Over a period of nearly twelve months, the two nuns made their way from San Francisco to Oakland, San Jose, Gilroy, Los Angeles, and back. Despite the difficulty of travel, the sister who had once called for nuns to stay in their convents now enthused about the "meadow-lark, linnet, quail, and robin," "the wheat-fields . . . glorious to behold," "exquisite flowers," and "some pine-trees . . . indescribably pretty."[96] This sister turned the unknown into practical knowledge and a spirit of human and western appreciation.

Of the overarching impressions from her begging mission, the sister remarked: "When I am Mother Superior, which will be the day after never, I will send every Sister on her turn to beg . . . to let them learn by experience, and to let them see how the two classes of people are divided in this world. . . . The rich man will close his hand on his dollar, while the poor man will give *half* of his."[97] This sister, who once thought of "shelter" in convents, now, having traversed a great portion of the Far West, spoke of "adventures" and the character of humanity. The following year, the Sisters of Charity of Leavenworth selected this itinerant missionary, perhaps to her astonishment, to be superior of a small convent in a remote pocket of Kansas City.[98]

Catholic nuns, like this one, often dismissed the life moments that changed their thinking and altered their personal accomplishments. They were not, however, dim-witted. Out-of-the-ordinary circumstances ultimately caused sisters to reassess the boundaries of their abilities, their prospects in religious life, and the reaches of womanhood. Out of such experiences nuns began to sense the transformations within themselves. Despite setbacks, arbitrary clerical decisions, and the West itself, sisters in both rural and urban environments found that religious life allowed them to carve out a gendered and often exciting space in the American West. In the process, the sisters came to see themselves as part of the West and central to its Catholicism.

In southeastern Montana, for example, less than two months after three Toledo Ursulines moved to a stark outpost, the priest announced he was withdrawing from the Cheyenne mission work, heading for Miles City, and continuing home to Ohio.[99] The young man cited his health, imperiled by the bitter environment and worsened by the absence of medical care, for his decision to abandon the women without any supporting arrangements from church or government. The three formerly cloistered nuns—totally unacquainted with a reservation where Indian families starved, government provisions and relief allotments failed to materialize, and white ranchers aggressively intruded onto Native land—could hardly believe his words. The sisters noted, not unkindly, that the priest, the first of two to desert them, "cried bitterly" but accepted the few foodstuffs and sweets sent to the women from the Toledo motherhouse. Baffled as to how they would interact with local federal employees or live among the Cheyennes, whose language the women had only begun to study, the sisters assured the motherhouse: "We are all determined not to give up. . . . We are willing to bear anything for the work."[100] In Miles City, Mother Amadeus, reflecting on the events at the Cheyenne mission, wrote to the same superiors: "You would not believe what a strange place this is and what a change it has made in us."[101] Her attitude invaded other western newcomers. A Presentation sister from Ireland mused that "more than an ordinary vocation is necessary for Dakota life."[102] It was a reminder that the American West required something fresh of religious women, who, in turn, found themselves adjusting their personal aspirations for life in a convent.

Certainly, the West did not become "home" to every nun, and some returned to familiar monasteries, closer to the hearth of one's family and friends. A missionary assignment undertaken with zeal or "holy obedience" might become unbearable, despite one's determination to follow convent rule. In 1884 Sister St. Gertrude of the Brown County, Ohio, Ursulines arrived in Montana to assist the small group of Toledo Ursulines staffing two Indian schools and a private academy. By March 1885, the "borrowed" nun had assumed a range of duties—sewing, preparing altar laces, and working with the children at St. Peter's mission—all of which she performed with notable diligence. The superior at St. Peter's, Mother Amadeus, however, perceived that all was not well and hoped that "we may coalesce," for Sister St. Gertrude "remains very reserved."[103] Seven months later, before the next hard Montana winter locked in on St. Peter's, Mother Amadeus reported to Toledo that Sister St. Gertrude, "a most faithful worker[,] . . . has lost courage and will return to her home in Brown Co[unty]. She really is not to blame. She truly is not able to bear the strain of missionary life."[104] The cloistered convent of urban Cincinnati welcomed Sister St. Gertrude home, and she left the isolation of St. Peter's, as well as its public duties, behind.

Given such episodes and the financial and emotional expense they entailed, within motherhouses there was some growing apprehension about the liabilities of releasing members for the West. In 1885 the Sisters of St. Francis of Philadelphia sent their first missionaries to Baker City, Oregon, over strong opposition from the community. Some members felt the distances too great and the conditions in the West too precarious for eastern sisters. Finally, when a charter band of five left for the West, the congregation agreed to the election of Sister Stanislaus as superior because she had "frontier experience," having lived at St. Clair, a town somewhat west of Allentown, Pennsylvania.

A year after the new foundation, Mother Agnes visited Baker City, where she "discerned the great possibilities for the growth of Catholicism in the West," and upon her return to Pennsylvania, she advocated for a new school to be located at Pendleton, Oregon. For a second time, the mother superior encountered "great opposition to the proposed mission in the West by conservative members of the Order who believed . . . [in] opening institutions nearer home where success was more certain."[105] Among senior convent administrators, that "success" was almost surely phrased in terms of financial stability and control of congregational personnel.

Mother Agnes prevailed, and by fall, four untried sisters joined Sister Stanislaus at a Pendleton mission that became infamous for its privations. The fortunes of the area depended on sheep raising, rail transport of wool, and a nascent milling industry. In this unpromising economy, the sisters drummed up support and recruited students by walking from one sheep ranch to the next, convincing families to enroll their children in the new boarding school, St. Joseph's Academy. Failure loomed, but the nuns persevered, raising money, gathering local support, and expanding their property as commerce improved, eventually coming to include the Pendleton Woolen Mill, destined for national success. When the local economy benefited from the rise of the mill, the sisters built a school addition and a chapel, and in 1902 they opened a hospital at a cost of $65,000. Twenty years later, that structure was improved with a $300,000 wing.[106] Central to these Oregon advances were the efforts of Sister Kilian, one of the original band to join Stanislaus at Pendleton. Sister Kilian took on a host of jobs but gained special acclaim for her ability to raise money through the music department. Working as the portress at the mission, she honed her leadership skills by directing the business affairs of the academy. After sixteen years in the "pioneer mission of the West," Sister Kilian became provincial of the western district of the Philadelphia Franciscans. Then, thirty-three years after she had left Pennsylvania untested and inexperienced, she returned to her motherhouse as the elected superior general of the Sisters of St. Francis.[107] Three decades after a congregation fretted about the impact of the West on its isolated missionaries, its voting members turned to a woman educated in many arenas by the demands of her religious career in eastern Oregon.[108] In Mother Kilian, a dynamic expansionist, the sisters found a "renewal of energy" and, swayed by the romantic language of western writing, they responded to her "progressive spirit," which they thought "an inheritance from the great West where are bred the initiative and self-reliance . . . which have transformed barren deserts."[109]

There was much to question about the so-called initiative and self-reliance cultivated in a West so carefully aligned with the social and economic interests of European and American families. Within that family culture, significant differences existed for unattached males and single women. The West with its out-of-doors industry catered to the labor of men and with ease welcomed bachelors, who enjoyed the freedom of remaining and establishing families or returning to their original home locations to do so. On the other hand, young women in the West—whether American-born or immigrants—had limited employment opportunities, but for a few exceptions. Such choices as schoolteacher, prostitute, waitress, or domestic worker appealed to only some unattached women. Each of these careers offered western employment, but the benefits came with very real liabilities.[110] Overall, the secular West generally lacked a comfortable or profitable place for a woman to spend a lifetime as a single person.

Convent life, on the other hand, presented a wide range of travel options and work possibilities for unmarried Catholic women.[111] Although they might encounter religious prejudice and extreme hardship, the nuns could do so in community, their convent lifestyle affording them companionship and its many assists. Loneliness and poverty assaulted unmarried sisters as surely as the secular schoolteacher, but shared experiences, common goals, and the mantle of the religious congregation helped to undercut discouraging circumstances inside remote and shabby convents. This support network aided young women in forming their intellectual identity as members of a religious congregation in a western world.

As sisters confronted odd circumstances and new peoples, they did so backed not just by the spiritual and temporal network of the Roman Catholic Church but, in a more intimate, womanly way, by their religious congregation as well. The culture of the cloister and the specifics of a congregation carried the force of family. The language of the convent world reminded sisters of such ties and built in them bonds to other members of the order. Superiors were known as "Mother," and their words to "my dear and beloved daughters" reflected the depth with which these feelings were cultivated across congregations.[112] Within this constructed family infrastructure, sisters immersed themselves in an intellectual environment that not only permitted but also vigorously encouraged the execution of strategies for a productive life as unmarried women in western communities.

Clashes between Old and New

At the same time, the western experience generated episodes in convent life that brought impossible clashes between old forms and new demands. Trained in a life that idealized obedience in the smallest matters, nuns quickly learned that the West had little patience for such a constraint. Western travel forced nuns to act on their own agency, and increasingly they were not shy about doing so. The exigencies at hand, some involving life-threatening circumstances, meant that sisters, separated from their authorities, acted on the call of necessity. The choices and how to make them were not always immediately clear to some, especially those in the first groups of a congregation traveling into the West. With no previous experience in which to place these western emergencies, the women scrambled for decisions they hoped to reconcile with the convent rule and mission plan of the leaders who sent them to the West.

Actions, especially those undertaken without express permission, created friction with superiors who remained in the motherhouse and did not understand or accept the explanations they read in letters from the West. For example, the sisters stranded in Colorado by the Pullman strike expressed dismay when their Pennsylvania motherhouse wired a rebuke, causing one to reply: "Your . . . telegram . . . was a puzzle to us . . . as . . . we were most explicit in giving all the details of our present situation."[113] Only four months after her arrival in Montana, Mother Amadeus of the Ursulines wrote in annoyance to her Toledo motherhouse: "You cannot conceive how we are placed out here *sometimes*."[114] Others referred to the demands of work, one Montana missionary noting: "I have been so busy that it was impossible for me to write." Another, Sister St. Francis, apologized for her long silence to the motherhouse, asserting that she "had no idea it was over six months."[115]

Missioned sisters slipped easily into an attitude that those who did not live in the West could not possibly understand western circumstances. It only required a slight adjustment for sisters in the West, like many Anglo-Europeans, to see their experiences, and consequently themselves, as "unique" and set apart from nonwesterners. Mother Amadeus suggested to her former companions in Toledo: "If I could properly portray . . . the vicissitude of our missionary life here you would instantly forgive all."[116] It would not be long before such attitudes strained the bonds between many distant motherhouses and western missions.

Separation sown with the seeds of distance and poor communication foreshadowed erosion between houses of some congregations. Yet some who remained in the East regarded the West as a catalyst for change at the motherhouse, encouraging those on the missions to exploit the world before them. An Ursuline in Kentucky wrote to nuns who had left the motherhouse to begin a school in Kansas: "This move seems . . . bound to bring the desired changes *here* and if these do not come, I, myself, may be with you yet."[117]

These dynamics of western mission building placed burdens and risks on migrant nuns quite different from those of other travelers. For nuns, independent decisions could shake the chain of congregational command, rattling issues of spiritual and financial support as well as long-standing loyalties. The journey into the West forced sisters and nuns into an active engagement of the region and its inhabitants. Stepping beyond the walls of their monasteries and convents, nuns and sisters, often painfully uniformed about the way ahead, became part of a vast migration, dominated by Anglo-Europeans, that moved relentlessly into and through the American West. Ultimately, the upheaval caused by these waves of intrusion forced Catholic nuns to question the legitimacy of power structures, including their own. These were years that tested the women and revealed to them a region embroiled in many kinds of social, economic, and political rancor, producing egregious confrontations for all concerned. What had appeared a simple trip by ship and stagecoach mutated into a classic tale of human complexity fueled by physical, cultural, and intellectual ramifications.

In 1870 Sister Monica Corrigan and her companions from the motherhouse of the Sisters of St. Joseph immersed themselves in the diversity of the American West. On 26 May, the seven missionaries from St. Louis, under escort of Natives, priests, and soldiers, arrived in Tucson, Arizona. Three thousand wildly cheering residents greeted the exhausted sisters with lighted torches and exploding fireballs, as the sounds of cracking rifles and ringing bells filled the night air.[118] In a joyous midnight celebration, Tucson's men, women, and children, long intertwined with Catholicism and wondering about the fate of the missionaries, acknowledged the remarkable overland accomplishment of the seven sisters.

Nothing in the travels of the nuns had been as they expected, including their own reactions to the crooked road. Repeatedly, they smothered

Nineteenth-century convent life meant that young sisters, like these
Daughters of Charity, expected foreign assignments, especially in the highly
advertised missions of the American West. Many knew that they might never
see their mother country or family members again, a reality that increased
internal congregational bonds. (Author's collection)

fear, looked forward, accepted novelty, laughed together, and concentrated
on the daily rigors. The trip from St. Louis to Tucson cut off all communication with their Missouri superiors for weeks. It required the sisters
to compromise several long-standing regulations of convent life and reassess themselves and their immediate choices. Then, with no leisure for
reflection, the cultural world of Tucson, their new home, utterly enfolded
them, and the Sisters of St. Joseph had to choose how they, in turn, would
fit into that life. Sister Monica and her companions, ensconced in a one-
story adobe convent quite unlike their St. Louis brick edifice, appeared to
sense the changes that had occurred and those ahead, as they cautiously
expressed hope for "the success of . . . our schools" but also for "our own
spiritual welfare."[119]

For religious women, journeys such as this one revealed the West as a
natural environment, a social force, and a place for self-illuminating perception. As a result, sisters realized they must grapple with the physical,
cultural, and intellectual power of the American West and do so with de-
cisiveness. Some did so with determination but trepidation, others with a

light heart and a sense of adventure; still others saw the road as too rugged, the destination too uncertain. For those who stayed the course, the dangers and delights, insights and astonishments, human cruelty and compassionate moments in the West descended on them with life-changing velocity. These convoluted western experiences for nuns represented more than anecdotes for building congregational heroines and lore.

Rather, from those happenings emerged influences that touched the way Catholic religious women viewed themselves, the world they had come to inhabit, and the way they would choose to practice professed life under a Catholic mantle in the West. These proved not to be subtle matters for quiet debate. On a daily basis, what it meant to be an unmarried woman living by religious vows of the Catholic Church and the authority of a congregation's rule faced considerable revaluation through the emergence of the sisters' West.

Each aspect of the trip into the West shifted the ground beneath the once-sandaled feet of formerly strictly cloistered women. Disruption flooded into religious life with the first step the women took toward the American West; those forces inflated as the women endured public travel and looked into the homes of unfamiliar cultures; they solidified in the ways the West changed the thinking about person and profession for migrant nuns. Opportunity tempered obedience, spontaneity undercut tradition, and womanhood threatened patriarchy, as these unlikely pioneer migrants, carrying sharply defined religious and gender identities, joined a region complicated by a multiplicity of visions and goals from its many intersecting ethnicities. Nowhere would these conflicting forces be more evident than when nuns and sisters in the West turned to earning a livelihood in new environments with new peoples.

*She wanted us to be women
of strength. . . . [To] stand on
your feet and do your work and
help one another.*

—Memories of Mother
Baptista Bowen by Sister
M. Immaculata Pawluch,
Mother M. Baptista Bowen
File, Archives of the Sisters of
the Presentation of the Blessed
Virgin Mary, Fargo,
North Dakota

The Labor

The expectation of Mother Baptista
Bowen that her North Dakota Sisters
of the Presentation exercise fortitude
in their labors as individuals and as a
community resonated throughout western convents. Nuns, like other newcomers, moved into the West in search
of a livelihood, on which survival itself
depended. Perhaps that quest seemed
misguided, as solid opportunities for
paid employment in the West appeared
to bypass women and particularly nuns.

Industries driven by the extraction
of natural resources and dependent on
the labor of men undergirded the economic West. Work tilted toward life in
the out-of-doors, making it the place
for brawling, tough-minded, masculine
roustabouts. Industrial development

called out to cowboys, freighters, soldiers, and railroaders as the muscle of the West.

Actually, no shortage of physical labor existed for women. Typically, such endeavor fell into the category of unpaid household work, augmented by generous doses of farm chores—tilling fields, harvesting crops, tending livestock. In combination, these domestic and agricultural labors made women substantial, if undercompensated, contributors to western economies.

Granted, gender boundaries caved in some locales and women secured paid work.[1] Yet jobs, employment venues, local demographics, and social dictates emphasizing childbearing biology cast females as temporary employees awaiting maternity rather than desirable candidates for the local workforce or ambitious career builders. Anglo-European society designated western labor, with its ancillary wage-earning capabilities, the provenance of men.

Women religious turned all elements of this gender equation on its head. Nuns and sisters defied economic constraints, defining a womanhood (often intensely maternal but without childbirth); constructing multifaceted, labor-centered lives over many decades; and constructing their own employment history in the West. For nuns, work and leisure overlapped, as the congregation urged useful productivity at all times. With the West upon them, sisters combined domesticity of the household economy with professionalism in the formal economy, fashioning dual sources of convent income and refining definitions of western women's work.

The purpose of this western work—grounded in female communal cooperation—was to generate self-sustaining income for the mission house, support the temporal and spiritual goals of the religious congregation, and extend the influence of the American Catholic Church. Nuns focused on those intentions with resolve, producing results that propelled these women toward a broad range of work adaptations that ultimately influenced the patterns of religious life.

No congregation demonstrated these forces more clearly than the Presentation Sisters of North Dakota. In 1882 a few Irish sisters agreed to open a Fargo school, anticipating that an influx of postulants from Ireland and New York would shore up the faculty. Their poverty, exacerbated by the Dakota climate, dashed these hopes, as one by one postulants and novices, overwhelmed by religious life in the West, withdrew.[2] The congregation limped on, even when church authorities, spurred by the federal organization of North and South Dakota, formed two parallel Catholic dioceses, separating the Fargo sisters from their Aberdeen affiliates, dividing personnel, splintering resources, closing down friendships, and plunging both convents deeper into various kinds of adversity.[3]

In this year of civic and religious cleavage, a young Annie Bowen entered the floundering Presentation Sisters at Fargo; twenty-one years later, as mother superior, she moved to overcome the lingering deficits inflicted by the diocesan split, promoting a "North Dakota mentality" for the congregation. A shrewd expansionist and financial strategist, Bowen, now known as Mother Baptista, viewed North Dakota as a work opportunity for the small order of Presentation sisters. She strengthened her core personnel by persuading young women to enter the motherhouse, nurtured them through her maternal instincts, oversaw their development as professional educators, cultivated congregational loyalty, accepted missions in previously rejected locations, and launched a building program, supervising her business associates.[4]

Mother Baptista relied on her philosophy that "it is not necessary for every woman to be a sister, but it is necessary for every sister to be a woman." When dispatching nuns to distant and dangerous assignments in North Dakota, she was renowned for advising, "Now, sisters, don't come back with N.G. [No Good] written all over you. Be women!"[5] For Mother Baptista, with her strong sense of gender confidence, a public label of "no good" threatened the expansion of Presentation sisters into North Dakota Catholicism. This western woman guided her congregation—which climbed to approximately seventy, many from Ireland—to accept North Dakota in its geographic realities, capitalize on the region's employment needs, and shape a Presentation identity attractive to local communities.[6]

Across the urban and rural West, nuns thus assessed societal conditions and exploited the occupational constraints implied by gender. Building staff, they used the shortage of employable females to their advantage, dispersing service-minded employees among the public and creating a legacy of religious women as western workers.

The Call to Work

This initiative to define work arenas in America emerged from a legacy of European power struggles between nuns and the church that ranged over several hundred years. Since the Middle Ages, Catholic reform appeared to enhance male congregations while devising new regulations for the suppression of cloistered women.[7] Invariably, the outcome of the theological and political sparring of men resulted in more seclusion for women and a reduction in the spiritual and monetary power of their monasteries. In the thirteenth century, the rise of the Beguines, who eschewed convent life but practiced personal piety in their homes and community charity in their parishes, foreshadowed the way Catholic women would push back against a marginal religious status.[8]

The successful melding of public works with a nonenclosed women's community gained traction through Louise de Marrillac and Vincent de Paul of France. In the 1620s, the two used a crisis of poverty sweeping Paris to nudge the church into accepting a new institute known as the Daughters of Charity. Sidestepping the formal perpetual vows that dictated enclosure, the institute called on the Daughters to renew a simple annual promise and to dedicate themselves to mingling among the poor.[9] Both conditions struck a heavy blow to the masculine vision of cloister and suggested a fresh wave of organization for women. Still, a church authority besieged by the pleas of the poor, but wedded to control of vowed females, kept a taut line between the male hierarchy and the women seeking active missions as professed religious.

In America, Catholic sisterhoods broke through the cloister with government service during the Civil War of 1861–65. Nuns leaving monasteries and ministering on European plains of war had some precedent, but in the United States, Catholic sisters did not compile a vivid history on battlegrounds. With the onset of the war, women of nearly two dozen different congregations, totaling over 600 strong, labored in tent hospitals, nursed in trenches, transformed private infirmaries for army personnel, or tended the injured and fevered in prison camps. Sisters of Mercy, Sisters of the Holy Cross, Sisters of Saint Dominic, Daughters of Charity, Sisters of Saint Ursula, and other nuns who climbed into military ambulances and onto floating river hospitals did not always have medical training, nor were they seasoned in the bloody scenes of armed conflict.[10]

The nuns volunteered, trading quiet chapel for thundering warfare, wading through muck-covered fields, assisting at stomach-churning amputations, bathing infection-filled wounds, moping up vomit, closing the eyes of the dead without regard for Blue or Gray loyalties. No sanitized storybook war for these women, among whom several died from infectious diseases. Those who survived did so after experiencing the danger, hunger, exhaustion, and grief of a campaign; the curses of the wounded and screams of the dying; and the vile stench of war—choking gunpowder, decaying animals, putrefying humans.

Other than in St. Louis, Missouri, and Galveston, Texas, their battlefront nursing occurred principally in the eastern locations of Civil War engagement, but the nuns created an American profile out of their four years amid the rancor of brotherly strife.[11] Beyond convent gates, the Civil War revealed nuns as steely, tough workers, a fact that won the attention of Catholics and Protestants, officers and enlisted men, civil servants, and families and gained for the sisters congressional recognition.[12] Their distinctive religious habits, incongruous in the slop, blood, and mud, symbolized a womanhood willing to set aside an identity shaped by privacy and assume uncommon duties in unlikely places.[13]

Inside convents, the sister veterans of the Civil War gave witness to the way nuns, with the approval of mother superiors, could and would weaken boundaries that dictated spheres of work and a rigid definition of sisterhood. Their war nursing established that in times of pestilence and plague, societal needs superseded gender constraints, human suffering canceled monastic rules, and government service in Protestant-dominated America had room for Catholic nuns.[14] These were lessons not to be forgotten among sisters.

With the Civil War service of nuns as a template, Catholic bishops charged with the spiritual care of the West saw a chance to stabilize the western church infrastructure. Easterners and European immigrants crowding into the homelands of the North American indigenous communities piled problem upon problem, while bishops puzzled over the spiritual quandaries of the first-time circumstances. Western bishoprics stretched across thousands of square miles; within these, Catholicism counted an array of native tongues among its communicants; financial resources did not flow freely from the church coffers or the western parishes; and an effective ministry for the regular churching of these diverse peoples throughout many Wests called for a hefty troop of volunteers.[15] Yet among the ordained, men eager to undertake the poverty and singularity of the western priesthood remained few.

Even bishops faltered under expectations so different from the ways of European Catholicism. Louis A. Lootens of Belgium, after six years as the vicar apostolic of Idaho, wrote to a priest friend: "I have no one here to whom I can unbosom myself. . . . I am about to send my resignation to Rome."[16] An embittered missionary fleeing the West captured the sentiments of those who came ill-prepared for the environment and its folk, explaining to his bishop that he found it disagreeable to travel by horseback, could not find a cook, feared for the salvation of his own soul, and, summing up his complaints, remarked: "I hate the long dreary winters of Iowa."[17]

The Catholic labor for these vineyards appeared to rest with the religious congregations of women, whose mission bands had a communal advantage over the solitary priest toiling alone in the West.[18] In this moment of good fortune, nuns turned to the American West, building community for themselves and the surrounding society. In doing so, sisters managed responsibilities that wove together secular jobs and religious duties into seamless days of work.

In Texas, an elderly nun remembered that when she was a sixteen-year-old postulant, "all the floors of the convent had to be scrubbed on our knees with brush and soap. . . . We helped to clear the . . . brushwood . . . to reap the sugar-cane and to press our own molasses."[19] Another Texas sister reminisced about her place in a human chain passing water buckets from a hand pump to the kitchen window, where a novice perched on a chair hoisted the pails through to those filling a huge heating tank.[20] On washday at a Minnesota hospital, the sisters and postulants started the fire for the laundry water at 2:00 or 3:00 in the morning. On other days, the convent residents "languished" abed until 4:00 or 5:00 A.M. With morning devotions finished and a skimpy breakfast hastily consumed, the sisters went to the hospital, where "manual labor occupied the entire day." In the evenings, after night prayer, the nuns gathered for study hour and recitations from 9:00 until 10:00. This demanding regimen, with limited sleep, heavy labor, meager diet, prayer routines, and academic studies, led the annalist to the comment: "Candidates . . . flabby in muscle or in character were more or less out of place."[21]

Other congregations did not offer postulants and novices a softer introduction to the work of religious life. At the novitiate of the Sisters of Mercy, located three miles outside of Eureka, Missouri, the young women maintained a large convent farm known as Josephville. On occasion, men performed some chores, but poverty ruled out regular employed hands; early on, the postulants learned not to expect male assistance. The women answered a 5:00 A.M. call to begin a day of fieldwork—feeding, herding, and milking cattle, as well as the bloody and smelly slaughtering of pigs. With exhausting hours given to the livestock, gardens, and orchards, the postulants and novices were not entirely delighted when a new superior added a daily communal recitation of the divine office and directed that the cumbersome formal habit replace dresses and bonnets for farm labor.[22]

At the refectory table, the diet, reduced during fast periods such as Lent and Advent, was not the best for youthful appetites fresh from the fields: dry bread and coffee at breakfast; a noon meal of vegetables, occasionally with meat; and for supper, cooked fruit and bread, seldom with butter. Operating a productive farm for the Mercy community and adhering to the rules of novitiate formation kept the work hours lengthy at the rural

Setting aside Minnesota classroom duties and administrative responsibilities, School Sisters of Notre Dame, wearing long aprons over formal habits, went into the fields, working as a team to harvest green beans that could be canned and stockpiled for convent pantries. (Courtesy School Sisters of Notre Dame, Mankato, Minn.)

convent. Like the young sisters in other western convents, those in Missouri filled each day with physical and mental exertion—spiritual exercises, academic lessons, and secular work that frequently stepped around gender barriers of the era.

In such circumstances, congregations sending their members to western service looked for candidates with good health. Work—whether temporal or spiritual—meant bone-crunching hardship for substantial periods of time. To be retained, postulants and novices had to demonstrate they could keep pace with the extreme demands and do so without complaint. Women with chronic illness or physical disability threatened to drain the personnel and monetary resources of financially strapped congregations. Should such a sister reach her final profession of vows, she became a permanent burden, a congregational liability rather than a productive worker.

Accordingly, mother superiors diligently canvassed for women suitable to all aspects of congregation life, but a strong constitution and a sound work ethic ranked as high priorities. Certainly, religious orders highlighted piety, but work trumped rosary beads. An enthusiastic immersion into daily labor was essential, as one Texas woman discerned when informed that her daughter would be denied permanent vows since the young nun "doesn't work—only prays."[23] A Kansas priest also valued the sturdy, advising the superior of a new foundation: "In case you get any sisters, . . . no cranks or hysterics."[24]

Consequently, many novitiates applied a standard comparable to that of the superior who rejected one candidate with a limp and would not admit any who wore glasses.[25] Another congregation stipulated in the rules and constitution that prospective postulants should have "no falling sickness, contagion, [or] infirmity."[26] At an Iowa motherhouse, the superior released a novice because of deafness and chronic kidney problems, noting in the convent diary: "The duties of our vocations require that only persons in health should be retained in the Community. . . . It is wise to dismiss from the novitiate persons suffering from incurable diseases."[27]

With work as their training, professed sisters applied the toughness of formation, overcoming obstacles as they reached for ways to aid the larger congregational good. For example, in 1874 the Sisters of the Holy Cross relied on the work ideals of their novitiate to survive the varied hardships of a new bigendered congregational endeavor in Austin, Texas.

Two sisters, led by their ecclesiastical superior, Edward Sorin—who was carrying out bequest instructions of a wealthy Texas widow, Mary Doyle— left Indiana to organize a school destined to become St. Mary's Academy. Sorin, founder of the University of Notre Dame and a congregational expansionist, assigned the sisters a two-room cabin on Doyle's property. Here, the women divided the space: one room for the parlor, classroom, study hall, recitations, music hall, general assembly, and sewing room, and the other for a storeroom; a second-floor garret served as a dormitory for children and nuns. In these woeful quarters, the Holy Cross sisters began their school with eighty students.[28]

The two women assumed all classroom and domestic work, certain they were participating in a potentially profitable operation for the Holy Cross priests, brothers, and sisters. By 1875 the school spread over six widely spaced buildings, including a stable the nuns "converted" into a kitchen and refectory. The sisters, their number increased from Indiana, moved back and forth nonstop over the ramshackle estate and continued to live in the leaky, bat-filled garret, which they "affectionately" called "the Ark." The sprawling campus taxed the sisters physically, with its far-flung boarding children—all in want for clothing, food, schooling, and familial care. The sisters, however, managed, anticipating their share in the benefits to the Holy Cross order from the Doyle legacy.

Most immediately, the sisters expected nutritional support from the crops raised at a 400-acre site included in Mary Doyle's estate. By harvest time, those thoughts were dashed. The Holy Cross brother supervising the farm at the property, now called St. Edward's, informed the sisters they could purchase vegetables at a cheap price, but it would not be possible for the convent and school to receive produce free of charge.[29]

Further, the men at St. Edward's, located an inconvenient three miles outside the city, missed the domestic service so common at Notre Dame, and in 1875 three Holy Cross sisters arrived from Indiana to do the household work. These daily duties included the usual labor-intensive chores: scrubbing, cleaning, cooking, washing, ironing, and sewing. By the time St. Edward's College opened, the number of Holy Cross sisters working for the men had risen to twelve, none of whom received compensation, other than food and clothing—both of which they prepared themselves. The sisters at St. Mary's Academy presumably continued to purchase their fresh vegetables at the "discounted" rate. This mélange of exploitation— sisters teaching and living in questionable quarters, exhausting themselves across a huge, battered physical plant, nurturing increasing numbers of resident students, struggling through loans and debt to construct a more suitable residence and academy, buying food from their own religious compatriots while others of their congregation provided free domestic labor for the men—continued for seventeen years.

Still, the sisters as religious women in Austin moved ahead, always enlarging the Holy Cross reputation through the city. They engaged the lay community, encouraged displays of art and music, acquired more lots, strengthened the academy, and by 1888 had twenty-five sisters promoting the Holy Cross name in Austin. In 1892 the mother general from Indiana, convinced the hard work of missioned women had advanced all branches of the congregation, visited Texas and insisted the men at St. Edward's compensate the sister domestics at the rate paid to nuns at the Holy Cross headquarters, the male-run Notre Dame University.[30]

The history of the Holy Cross men and women in Texas underscored some of the gender inequities that fueled western Catholicism and the management of work. Religious women invested heartily in Catholic work opportunities, determined to prove their temporal and spiritual worth. In response, bishops and priests, anxious to secure the work of the women, frequently interpreted a willing commitment to mean that no boundaries curtailed the duty demanded of nuns and sisters.

Responding to the Call

The clergy translated the notion of "service without limits" into an insistent chorus that nuns take up the mantle of the western church. Given the paucity of personnel and pocketbooks, the women's congregations accumulated a solid record for answering the calls. For example, between 1866 and 1900, the Divine Providence sisters, responding to pleas, opened fifty-five missions in Texas and fourteen in Louisiana and Oklahoma. Between 1900 and 1920, the sisters established another thirty-four Texas houses and thirty-four others in Louisiana, Oklahoma, Missouri, and New Mexico.[31] The Sisters of Loretto, in Santa Fe by 1853, took on at least thirty-seven new posts between 1865 and 1890, choices that spread them through New Mexico, Texas, California, Missouri, Colorado, and Kansas.[32] A small group of Mercy sisters in Omaha supervised twenty-six schools, orphanages, and homes between 1864 and 1920 throughout Nebraska.[33] In 1872 the School Sisters of Notre Dame accepted thirty mission requests in Minnesota and two in Canada. By 1878, they had added another twenty-five houses in Minnesota.[34] Between October 1903 and September 1906, the same sisters in St. Louis, separated from the Milwaukee motherhouse for only a few years, received twenty-one requests to staff schools in Texas, Missouri, Arkansas, Illinois, Kansas, Nebraska, and Iowa, as well as one supplication from Saskatchewan, Canada, to manage an orphanage.[35]

The tally proved remarkable given that annually, each religious order had a finite group of newly professed sisters ready for mission assignments. The small number each year intensified the competition between bishops and priests for available workers. Each uncorked all his persuasive skills to convince a mother superior that spiritual urgency drove every request.

First, a supplicant assured the superior that all the locals—whether European, Mexican, Anglo, or Native American—anxiously awaited sisters to staff a school or hospital. Second, he raised the specter of "the Protestants," suggesting that the likes of the Baptists or Presbyterians would "steal" Catholics by opening a rival facility. Third, he addressed financial stability, calling a new mission part of a boom area, where property values would escalate quickly, adding to the congregation's wealth. Fourth, the cleric promised—regardless of the western location—nothing but a salubrious climate all year. And finally, he stroked the nuns' desire to participate in the promotion of Catholicism.

The missionary priest Lambert L. Conrardy unleashed all those strategies when he tried to convince Minnesota Benedictines to come to Oregon in the 1880s. He described with alarm the "great efforts . . . to put the boarding school in the hands of the Methodists," telling the sisters that, with a Catholic mission, "you will have more children than you can accommodate." The area, he stated, "[is] growing fast. . . . Land outside of the reservation will be valuable in a few years," and he urged the nuns to invest in real estate. A month later, at the end of December, he wrote again, boasting about the balmy Oregon weather but moaning that the "mission will fall to another denomination" and concluding with a promise that the nuns would have German priests from Minnesota for spiritual care.[36] On such turned recruitment letters, flattering epistles to assure sisters that deep wilderness locations could yield professional, financial, and religious rewards.

In his promising description, Father Conrardy avoided discussing the Sisters of the Holy Names of Portland, Oregon, who previously staffed the Grand Ronde mission for several clans of Native peoples confined to the reservation as early as the 1850s.[37] The ensuing years had brought the usual reservation decline, as whites crowded in around the Willamette valley lands and the Natives fended off hunger, disease, and cultural disorganization. Three or four Holy Names sisters worked at Grand Ronde deep in Yamhill County from April 1874 until October 1880, each day confronting the disastrous economic and social conditions of the resident Natives.[38] Information from the Holy Names sisters might have given the Minnesota Benedictines pause.

Upon their 1874 arrival, the Holy Names sisters commented on the prevalence of English, French, Latin, and Chinook but made no mention of German, common to the Benedictine sisters. When hosting clergy visitors, the Canadian-based Holy Names sisters noted conversing with others in French, but they never spoke of socializing with any German priests. Indeed, Father Conrardy himself was a French-speaking Belgian who abandoned his Oregon work and moved far from these German-speaking Benedictines he wooed.[39]

Still, Father Conrardy's promise that a new congregation would have more than enough children than could be comfortably taught hit the mark; the Holy Names school began with forty boys and girls crammed into one room. The sisters found that in their two-story building, "the joists are rotten, as well as part of the floor, a few rooms are lined with printed cotton covered with whitewash. . . . Soiled cotton makes the ceiling of our parlor, which is also our refectory."[40] There was no local prosperity, so sisters took on all the domestic work, providing basic clothing and food for the emaciated children, nursing the sick, cleaning the church, washing linens, restoring straw mattresses, and doing continuous battle with an army of rodents.

Perhaps in no area was Father Conrardy more dissembling than that of weather. Contradicting Conrardy's pleasant winter descriptions, the sisters of the Holy Names wrote of January: "The cold is so severe that we do not know what means to take to protect us or our pupils. The children cry from cold. . . . The snow falls abundantly. The violent wind causes a drift which recalls the winters of Canada. . . . We place some blankets in the windows of the dormitory and on the floor."[41] Nor was it only winter that assaulted the Grand Ronde Reservation, a geographic area noted for its heavy rainfall. One October a sister wrote that "the autumn wind blows furiously turning over everything in its path; the gigantic trees of our forest bend[;] . . . the rain falls with such force that we expect . . . to see our windows broken in a thousand pieces. . . . The doleful and mournful whistling of the wind sporting furiously around our poor reservation seems to warn us that it sweeps all in its path." The sister did not appear comforted that, of the convent, she could say, "our old shaky hovel rocks us."[42]

The Holy Names left an occupational vacancy for the Benedictines, but not a life as described by Conrardy. In fact, after a harrowing trip that included wagon, steamer, and train, the Benedictines stayed only briefly at the Grand Ronde in Oregon, conducting school from April 1881 to January 1882.[43] Like the Sisters of the Holy Names, the Benedictine nuns refused to teach and board older boys. In consequence, the U.S. government withheld contract payments for three months because of low enrollments, so the convent received no income.

Ensconced at the uninviting mission, the nuns—denied a government salary and an alternate source of earnings—pondered how to support themselves. They had no money for the purchase of real estate, as suggested by Conrardy, nor any interest in agricultural lands outside the reservation. In addition, once their monk escort left for Minnesota, the isolated women realized there would be no German-speaking priests. Regular opportunities for spiritual exercises—especially confession—in German had been a fantasy. In the management of the mission, the nuns faced a population fluent in almost every language but theirs.

Nor were the sisters satisfied with the poor health conditions, worsened by the swampy land on the reservation, a place the displeased missionaries labeled "unfit." By early December, the weather displayed a full array of wintery ways, contradicting Conrardy's cheery climate prognostications and replicating the bitter days of the Holy Names sisters. Although these nuns may have desired to stave off Protestant schools as much as any other Catholic congregation, the Benedictines judged this mission an untenable work environment. With two years already invested at another desperate mission, visiting leaders doubted the wisdom of taking a second inaccessible spot devoid of economic promise or spiritual support. The succinct comment "Things here are not rosy" summed up the reaction of the Benedictines to the Grand Ronde.[44]

For the second time in two years, a congregation of women decided the work demands at Grand Ronde were incompatible with their requirements for employment. The Indian Catholic bureau had paid for the Benedictine sisters' trip to the mission, but facing the loss of another faculty, the central office waspishly declined to send the return tickets to Minnesota. The Benedictine sisters appealed to their own parents for the train fare, packed their bags, and headed for their motherhouse. Given the many requests for their sisters, they knew they could staff other missions with a better return to the convent and more tolerable living conditions for their workers.[45]

Expanding the Call to Work

An energetic and forward-looking businesswoman, the superior Mother Scholastica Kerst shook off the ill-fated excursion to Grand Ronde, not permitting those events to slow her initiatives. Kerst had other ventures in mind, deciding that hospital management was the way for the sisters to reach beyond their pedagogy in parish schools and academies. In health care, the Benedictines could pursue an employment agenda involving an entirely different set of professionals and businessmen. Hospital design, medical equipment, patient management, legal issues, nursing certification, health insurance, and scientific advances all promised to broaden and deepen the work experiences of the entire community. Mother Scholastica turned to Bismarck, Dakota Territory, where she calculated that changing resident populations and shifting economies—railroading, ranching, and tourism—melded her sisters' needs with opportunity.[46]

In 1885 voting members of her chapter approved an arrangement whereby the St. John's Abbey abbot, legal clergy overseer of the sisters, purchased the Bismarck Lamborn Hotel, which he turned over to the nuns to "conduct the hospital at their own expense and risk."[47] In vague terms, the abbot promised that, if the abbey loan was repaid in "due time," the building would revert to the nuns. In the meantime, the abbot, who was closely aligned with the Kerst family and had elevated Scholastica to superior despite some objection among the nuns, asserted his right to maintain "full control" of the facility, converting it to a male monastery if he deemed necessary.[48] Despite the monk's stranglehold, the women leveraged their situation through their on-site hospital management, admitting their first patients in May 1885. They continued forging a local nursing presence, even as the debt grew to include furnishings, equipment, and medicines, raising to approximately $30,000 the sum due to St. John's Abbey.

Mother Scholastica had no desire to default on this loan—now a debt on land and goods—or hand to the abbot, friend or not, the Lamborn Hospital, a building whose Bismarck identity had been reinvented by the sweat and toil of the nuns. To prevent such an outcome, Scholastica selected Sister Alexia Kerst, her biological sister, as superior for the Dakota hospital. Under Scholastica and Alexia, the sum owed the abbey was reduced to less than $10,000 by 1887, and the abbot, as religious patriarch and family adviser, forgave the remainder. He released the facility to the Benedictine sisters, who promptly renamed the property St. Alexius Hospital.[49]

Mother Scholastica made a sound choice in the woman she delegated to protect Benedictine, as well as her own, interests in the Dakota Territory. Alexia took full charge of the hospital for Scholastica, contracting with the county for indigent patient care, organizing begging tours, supervising the staff, and finally taking on the delicate task of anesthesiologist for the surgical patients.[50] From Minnesota, Mother Scholastica manipulated her personal connections to a powerful authority figure, negotiated a real-estate transaction that enlarged the assets and regional influence of female Benedictines, reduced the abbot's influence in Bismarck, eliminated abbey control over the hospital, and avoided financial penalties written to benefit the male Benedictines at the expense of the women's labor.[51]

In 1892 Sister Boniface Tummins assumed charge of Bismarck's St. Alexius Hospital. She devoted forty-two years to the institution, converting it from a simple medical facility into a prestigious and modern operation. Under her direction, physicians of reputation affiliated with St. Alexius, nursing training was professionalized, equipment and bedding for patients was standardized, and plumbing and electrical systems were improved. Her attention to detail ranged from selecting the hospital heat ducts and sink fixtures to escorting a Boy Scout troop through the patients' rooms as the youngsters distributed Christmas gifts.[52] In her efforts to upgrade the hospital, Sister Boniface purchased the first six telephones in Bismarck, keeping one at the hospital and distributing the others to physicians and pharmacists. She essentially strong-armed them, over their reluctance, into recognizing the efficiency and speed of the new technology.[53] In every aspect of hospital administration and personnel management, Sister Boniface tightly supervised St. Alexius, further marketing the regional stature of the motherhouse in Minnesota.

Like Mother Scholastica and Sister Boniface of the Benedictines, Mother Alfred Moes of the Franciscans seized on the twin forces of need and opportunity to advance her congregation. She used a cataclysm of nature to facilitate her plan.

In 1883, following a tornado that flattened a quarter of Rochester, Minnesota, Mother Alfred, whose teaching sisters assisted the maimed and dying, proposed a hospital project to a local physician, Dr. William W. Mayo. The nun argued that injuries had been increased and the death toll heightened because Rochester had no medical facility. A solution, she suggested, could be found if the doctor wedded his medical skills to the domestic and nursing services of the Franciscan sisters. The result, she insisted, especially once the nuns acquired health certification, would be a quality hospital in Rochester and employment for her congregation.

Dr. Mayo reportedly declined, fearing Rochester too isolated and he too elderly to oversee an ambitious new medical program. Mother Alfred, a thirty-year veteran of convent life in three different religious congregations, did not yield easily to objection and obstacle.[54] She responded that with Mayo's two sons, William and Charles, currently in medical school, and the nursing, administration, and housekeeping assumed by her congregation, a thriving partnership could emerge.

The scheme, which required four years to reach fruition, succeeded because Mother Alfred diversified her financial backing through patient fees, charity events, individual donations, and the support of the local Catholic church, patching together enough money. Mother Alfred took her medical proposal beyond Catholic interests and directly to public and private agencies. In turn, the Freemasons pledged an annual contribution of $150, and the same amount came from county officers—insurance that guaranteed a bed for lodge members or county residents.[55]

The original plan called for patients to see the physicians at a secular diagnostic clinic in the morning and the surgeons to operate in the afternoon at St. Mary's Hospital of the Franciscans. At the start, things wobbled a bit unevenly, given the distance between the two sites, and as the sisters relied on personal know-how and common sense for hospital procedures. In the early years, a young sister did not take formal academic courses but acquired her first nursing skills through the mentoring of a more-seasoned nun who taught the basic routines.

Such was the case for Sister Sylvester, who recalled that on her second day in the Franciscans' hospital, an older nun "took me up to the ward on the second floor and showed me how to make beds and other things about the work."[56] From linens in the ward, Sister Sylvester went to her first observation in the operating room, remembering of the young Mayos: "Dr. Charly [*sic*] did the operation of resection of the ribs. Dr. Will was the first assistant and Sister Joseph the second and Sister M. Sienna the nurse. . . . The patient got on fine and developed a hearty appetite."[57] Out of this unusual collaboration between Protestant doctors and Catholic nuns came a merger of the diagnostic facility and the surgical hospital into the renowned Mayo Clinic, formally organized in 1912.[58]

Along with business acumen and astute partnerships, congregations drew on the difficult toil of their earliest days to strengthen their employment circumstances as the nineteenth century advanced. For example, in the 1840s the Sisters of Charity of the Blessed Virgin Mary arrived in Dubuque, Iowa, after a rambling trip that had taken them from Philadelphia to Pittsburgh, Louisville, St. Louis, and Dubuque by means of rail, canal, and river. About two dozen strong and unknown in Iowa, the sisters strained to secure an economic footing in the young Catholic see along the Mississippi River.[59] They confronted a variety of obstacles: "On account of the poverty of the Community . . . the Sisters were obliged for years to go into the fields and perform the ordinary work of day laborers. . . . They made their own shoes, performed the dairy and laundry work."[60] Further, early in the Dubuque days, a fire destroyed their buildings, but the nuns gamely rebuilt and in three years reopened the academy. Still, financial shortages continued, and they reluctantly bowed to the bishop that they try a hospital; but to their relief, a priest friend intervened, convincing the prelate that the sisters had "banded together for school work, not for hospital duty."[61]

Released from nursing, the sisters concentrated on their pedagogical efforts. By the 1890s, the strengthened congregation flourished in the region, boasting more than fifty houses throughout Iowa, Illinois, Kansas, and Colorado. By the early years of the 1900s, nearly 1,500 young women had entered the motherhouse at Dubuque to test the waters of a religious life dedicated to advancing Catholic education.[62]

Growing size and ascending reputation gave the administrators in Dubuque the confidence to manage the give-and-take of their dealings with western pastors and parishes. When a priest in Kansas declared that if the sisters did not attend evening benediction in his church, "scandal" would arise among parishioners, the stage was set for a clash between the distant clergyman and the motherhouse. Fortified by a retreat master who had warned the congregation, "The rule which says that you are not to go out before daylight and . . . must be at home before dark . . . is a rule for all occasions,"[63] the council united in its opposition to the implied charge that staying at home in the convent equaled a moral indiscretion. In reply, the sisters at Dubuque stated the congregation's rule had been approved by the church, "a sufficient guarantee that we are safe in following it." The sisters declared that "no dispensation was to be granted, no matter what might be the consequence of a refusal."[64]

A speedy consequence came in a pronouncement from the Kansas pastor that he would dismiss the Sisters of Charity of the BVM from his school. Cheered by his earlier success to force the sisters into domestic work and laundry, the priest insisted on the benediction matter, demanding that a nun play the organ and conduct the choir; this lack of music constituted his "scandal." To hasten the firing of the sisters, the confident cleric dispatched a flurry of telegrams, canvassing other congregations for replacement staff. These "secret" solicitations were shortly known by the Dubuque council, news undoubtedly conveyed by mother superiors of other congregations. His failure to hire a new faculty then prompted the pastor to announce that the BVM teachers must vacate the parish-owned convent, live with their sisters at a crosstown academy, and commute each day to the parochial school.

In Dubuque, the mother general and her council considered these various declarations and determined that the "long ride back and forth[,] . . . the cold dinner[,] . . . and other inconveniences connected to such an arrangement" created "hardships" the council was loathe to inflict on sisters who were simply observing their congregational rule.[65] Under their language lay the unequivocal surety that, while priests wielded substantial power, a distant one connected to the sisters only by a work contract did not have the authority to override the women's more-binding constitution and rule. The sisters in Dubuque understood that principle, guarded the legitimacy of their rule, and refused to capitulate to clerical pressure.

At a meeting of 29 October 1896, the council "decided to insist on rigorous observance and to vacate the house in Wichita by recalling our Sisters to Dubuque." The mother general so informed the priest and with her councillors settled in to "await his answer." A plan for withdrawing sisters from a mission house had been written into the BVM's policy almost twenty-five years earlier. A previous council had stipulated that if a parish owned its school and convent, the resident priest must supply all furnishings for the missioned teachers, "so that the Sisters, if they should leave, would have nothing to take but their trunks."[66]

The Sisters of Charity of the BVM prepared for an overnight departure from the Wichita school and, given their strong name in Catholic education, could expect that a replacement offer would be forthcoming shortly. Within eight days, the priest, his requests for teachers rebuffed by other congregations, confronted the futility of crossing the sisters on a point of their constitution. He no doubt surveyed the upheaval of his own creation: faculty dusting off the convent trunks, pending closure of his school, mounting ire among parish families, growing public attention to a religious spat, and almost certainly accelerating displeasure at the residence of the local bishop. Swallowing his loss of face, the priest asked the mother general to cancel the recall to Dubuque, the council secretary laconically noting: "The sisters will be allowed to observe their rule."[67]

As communities and businesses proliferated in the West and the requests for mission sisters grew, administrators such as Mother Scholastica Kerst, Mother Alfred Moes, and the BVM leadership perceived unique opportunities for their sisters. The widespread social, economic, and political deficits of the West increasingly allowed women's congregations to bargain from a position of strength with various officials. Institutional voids led to fresh venues of work, where nuns planted the name and influence of the congregation. Granted, in some cases, church or civil authorities forced concessions, and sister administrators did not soar forward on some unfaltering trajectory of female victory. There were disputes and setbacks; in these treacherous male-dominated waters, efforts to maintain cordial relationships with power brokers, whether from Caesar or God, required women's congregations to stay vigilant and assertive.

Carving out New Venues

In 1872, when Mother Mary Odilia Berger and four sisters left Germany and traveled to St. Louis, they, like the sisters in Dubuque, built a professional identity from scratch, one that eventually sustained them as a religious community. Anxious to find an accommodating political and religious environment, the five immigrants hoped their background of caring for the sick and injured in Europe would translate into a program of home nursing in Missouri.

A brief survey of St. Louis indicated the sisters found a fertile ground in which to pursue their congregational mission and support themselves. St. Louis, with its strategic river location, diverse citizenry, and population in excess of 300,000, pulsated with several youthful economies. Manufacturing and commerce, supported by the abundant agricultural yields beyond the city, fueled transportation and freighting businesses, each sustained by railroads and river boat traffic. These same factors, however, also produced the difficulties of an urban area that grew too rapidly, suffered from economic immaturity, and lacked a hefty infrastructure to manage the ecological and human problems that resulted. Foreign workers, including thousands of German Catholics, flowed into the city, taking up the waiting jobs, but the city could not produce at a rapid pace the housing, schools, government oversight, and medical facilities needed to absorb the newcomers, whose numbers nearly doubled between 1860 and 1870.[68] Immigrants, holding to their own language, religious practices, and social customs, crowded around their workplaces, throwing up a warren of shanties amid the warehouses and factories in several sections of St. Louis. Municipal systems without enough resources or leadership more or less defaulted, resulting in the unregulated, nonhygienic slums darkened by violence and death so endemic to nineteenth-century American cities.

Neither could the few private asylums and orphanages address all the health issues of the working poor. In this scenario, it was the marginal communities of St. Louis that lacked medical services, as the single city-operated dispensary for diagnosis and medicine distribution to the indigent did not open until 1874 and a visiting nurse program until 1895. By 1872 disease held the upper hand among the economically depressed immigrants of St. Louis.

The Sisters of St. Mary, themselves as destitute as their fellow immigrants, arrived in St. Louis at exactly the right moment to add their brand of home health care to the needy Germans. Perhaps these virulent and deadly health conditions convinced Archbishop Peter R. Kenrick to permit Mother Odilia to take up nursing outside of a traditional hospital setting.[69] Kendrick had before him German women ready to devote their energies to the Germans of St. Louis; allowing them to do so promised a modicum of relief to his desperate flock and reduced his concerns about the well-being of a new congregation of women.

It was to these immigrant families and working poor that Mother Odilia directed her four companions. Here, within the community of the indigent, Odilia began her operation of a home nursing service. Mother Odilia's program clashed directly with Old World notions of enclosure and brought into question convoluted regulations about interactions with laypeople, conditions for conducting business in the secular world, and matters of travel and escorts. With this public nursing service, Mother Odilia and her sisters answered those questions through community activism that struck at an earlier style of convent life and its validity for the nineteenth-century West.

The five women moved into a stricken neighborhood, renting a small, unappealing house located a short distance from the wharves along the Mississippi River. The free nursing service was publicized by the proximity of the sisters' home to St. Mary of Victories Church, a parish devoted to German immigrants. It was easy for the priest to announce the sisters' charitable work from the pulpit or direct a family to the nearby "convent." In addition, walking the streets to and from the convent, the sisters often rang a handbell to advertise their available nursing services, as well as give warning that they had been among the contagious.[70] It did not take long for news of the in-home medical care to spread through the immigrant dwellings packed along the waterfront.

By the time a volunteer nurse reached the sick, the primary patient was often moribund and other family members soon prostrate on their pallets. Consequently, a single sister stayed for weeks in a household, care for one patient turning into support for the entire family, all of it carried out with the comforting German language of home. A sister, completing her duties for one family, returned to the convent, typically finding the house deserted, her companions working in other homes in the German neighborhood. Picking up a note with directions to the next household, a sister took a bit of nourishment, a short rest, and left for the new post.[71]

Mother Odilia expended her energies in keeping the tiny sisterhood unified and sustained. She assumed the role of messenger, booster, supply clerk, spiritual director, and relief nurse. She begged for money wherever she could and for food at a city market. She did laundry and brought clean linens to the nurses on duty, relieving the sisters for a few hours at a time. She kept the congregational spirit enlivened by moving from one work assignment to the next, relaying anecdotes of the day's nursing events and exhorting the sisters in special prayer devotions that added to a bond of unity. Remarkably, two young German women applied for admission to the order of paupers and were immediately sent, without religious formation, to do home nursing.[72] By the end of 1873, the sisters had nursed 298 patients from among 173 families for a total of 2,090 days and nights. In 1874, now known as the Sisters of St. Mary, the congregation, with twenty members, nursed 266 patients for a total of 2,725 days and nights.[73]

The Sisters of St. Mary, a title grafted onto them because of their location next to the German parish of the same name, literally stepped outside the comfortable patterns of convent life, especially as practiced in the European monastic model. The sisters were immigrants, exceedingly poor, and both hindered and helped by their German-speaking ways. Set directly inside a problematic neighborhood, their tiny house, with its barren attic dormitory, could hardly be dignified with the label "convent," and by the time their number reached eleven, there was hardly room for the whole congregation to fit inside the seedy waterfront building.[74]

Further, in contravention to the rules regulating women's enclosure, each Sister of St. Mary worked alone for many days in the homes of secular families. These sisters, although not professionally trained, bathed and nursed men and women, assisting in their most intimate bodily functions. They fed infants and cooked for small children. Over time, the sisters started bringing youngsters—some orphans, some half-orphans—into the convent.

How this child care evolved remained unclear, but the sisters certainly often looked into the faces of infants and youngsters robbed of kith and kin. In the dank hovels of those children, the sisters stood over mothers, fathers, and siblings in their death throes, covered corpses and guided in the removal of bodies, and arranged funerals. With no responsible adult in residence, the sisters took small hands in theirs, leading the children back to a congregation that folded the orphaned and the abandoned into its mission.

Mother Odilia's sisters took on every labor in situations of filth and poverty, where their ministrations ameliorated but could not eliminate the climate of deprivation. They traveled, without a sister companion, through the streets of a stressed neighborhood within the commercial district bordering on the riverfront. They witnessed all the turbulence of industrial commerce and human competition along the St. Louis wharves. They heard abrasive vulgarities and crude chants sometimes directed at them, as all persons were not favorably moved by the presence of immigrant Catholics—nuns or no.

Still, they hammered out their place among the Germans. They brought friendless children into the private rooms of their house, further reducing the conventional guidelines for cloistered life. They answered to any knock at the convent door, suspended the daily hours of grand silence, kept no enclosure, and rarely enjoyed the luxury of regularized community life—rising at a common bell, reciting morning devotions together, gathering for meals eaten to the sound of inspirational readings, and lightening their workday with community prayer in the chapel and evening recreation in the parlor. Instead, their convent, set in the shadow of St. Mary of Victories Parish, reflected the bread-and-butter challenges of all immigrant communities and pulsated with the rhythms of urban life in a river city of the West. The Sisters of St. Mary were, like other immigrants, a force on the streets of St. Louis, a force they built by conducting noncloistered work, even as they committed to fostering a private religious life as professed women.

Overall, the Sisters of St. Mary used the medical exigencies of St. Louis to create a professional role for the congregation, one that led them to advance nursing care in America. They built their reputation among indigent people by carrying into their homes relief services that questioned how Catholic nuns might legitimately use the hours of each day. From their first week in St. Louis, the sisters made themselves visible as medical providers and, in doing so, revised acceptable work arenas for nuns.

They not only developed an active noncloistered ministry far afield from standards upheld for hundreds of years in Europe, but they also undertook a type of nursing largely denied to American secular women during the same time period. While middle-class laywomen might have endangered their "reputations" by circulating day and night through the riverfront, the sisters called on their status as nuns, the charity of their work, and the response to the religious habit to silence criticisms. The ringing of the handbell through darkened streets did more than advertise their nursing; it declared and warned that the unescorted woman should be recognized as a religious sister, entitled to deference and protection—regardless of the hour, the vulnerability of the lone veiled figure, or the hostility to followers of Rome. Having immersed themselves in the German community, the Sisters of St. Mary benefited from growing approval, appreciation for their rescue work among children, and an American clerical endorsement that allowed them to build permanent institutions in St. Louis.

Other congregations, some who had arrived in St. Louis at an earlier date, also tackled groundbreaking work that rubbed against nun stereotypes. For example, the Sisters of Mercy, formed in 1831 by the Irish Catherine McAuley, emphasized ways to serve the poor and consistently searched out new opportunities for social service. By 1856 the Mercy sisters took that search to St. Louis, where they faced a mountain of financial obstacles.

Despite a fragile start, the sisters pursued work among the poor and with prison inmates. Schools, however, promised regular income as well as contact with poor families, and the sisters gladly took a number of teaching assignments in St. Louis. Relying on the widely accepted educational work of nuns, the congregation was free to explore nontraditional employment that connected with the ideals of their founding mother.[75]

For example, the Sisters of Mercy Industrial School in St. Louis ripened into something richer than its original plan. In the 1850s, the sisters had come to St. Louis specifically to open this establishment, proposed to them as a school where "the children come in the morning and return to their homes after school and . . . we give them something to eat for their dinners."[76] Under the direction of the Mercy sisters, the industrial school began combining social-service initiatives with vocational training, an orphanage, and a protective shelter. Rather than managing a typical day school, the sisters offered long-term living accommodations for girls left at the home by their families, the courts, or other religious institutes.

With the exception of an occasional elderly woman, most of the residents fell between the ages of five and fifteen. The youngest girls lived at the home for an average of six to eight years, during which time they received, along with the usual school subjects and religious studies, occupational training in domestic service or sewing. The majority of residents identified themselves as Catholic, using their baptismal record as proof, but religious affiliation was not a requirement for the free care. In exchange, the residents participated in the cleaning, cooking, sewing, and laundry of the house. Eventually, the sisters added a small charge, which by 1905 had climbed to $2.50 a week, with a trunk-storage fee of $1.00 per month.[77] These monies permitted the Mercy sisters to upgrade the school, adding steam heat and electricity and supplying each child with an iron bed, chair, and table.

At the industrial school, the nuns took on multiple roles, acting as educators, confidants, surrogate parents, and guardians of teenage girls. Under the Mercy umbrella, a child could grow to young adulthood in a protected environment and, upon departure, exit with job training that emphasized domestic labor and sewing. The program did not stress advanced academic studies or upward class mobility, but it equipped young women to avoid the unemployment and homelessness associated with unmitigated poverty. Using an in-house employment office, the sisters carefully monitored each job placement if a biological family did not reclaim a grown daughter.[78] Through the industrial school, the Mercy sisters molded a safe haven for urban women and children, defining service work according to existing societal conditions, a characteristic of this congregation.

For example, in 1884, when five Mercy nuns left Illinois to operate a boarding school at the Sacred Heart mission of Indian Territory, they shortly enlarged their local involvement and sources of income. After launching the Indian academy for girls, the Mercy superior, Mother Mary Joseph, accepted another school for a new parish in the nearby community of Krebs, where most families, drawn from a variety of European locations, depended on the coal mine for work. This mine, the sisters quickly realized, kept adolescents who should be in school toiling for the coal industry rather than over their lessons.

In response, the nuns began evening classes for the boys and young men who labored in the mines. The Krebs night school attained considerable status, with the scholars—some not yet in their teens—pursuing their academics after their daily mining shift. This evening school was a unique project, as most sisters, by congregational rule, confined their activities to daylight hours. In addition, the teaching of older males could be problematic and raised the hackles of mother generals for many congregations. In Krebs, the sisters decided the needs of children overrode such conventions.

With the school operating both day and night, the sisters then added to their outreach, offering religion classes for surrounding communities and going into residences to visit the sick. In and around Krebs, the Mercy nuns, in addition to providing classroom instruction, socialized inside the homes of working-class people, encouraging participation in the parish, promoting religious education, caring for a family's personal needs, and dispensing free medical attention to the indigent.[79]

In January 1892, with the evening school a popular town resource and the home visits of the sisters regular events, all of Krebs was overtaken by a massive explosion in Mine Number 11 of the Osage Coal and Mining Company. In small-town Krebs, where no resident physician practiced for another two years, the underground inferno decimated nearly every family. At least 100 men and boys died or were buried in the initial blast; their bodies, when recovered, were literally in pieces—a torso, a head, a foot, an arm, or a leg. Another 150 to 200 workers caught in the mine fire sustained equally grisly injuries, such that "it was almost impossible to recognize any resemblance to human form."[80] Chaos marked the entrance to the mine, with several thousand persons shoving and screaming as grotesque corpses and body parts were brought to the surface and panicked wives and mothers tried to locate relatives or their remains. In this grief and anger, further ugliness erupted when Europeans objected to the presence of African American relief workers, who were driven from the site by U.S. marshals brandishing weapons.[81]

The Sisters of Mercy may have missed this explosive racist scene near the perimeter; they had pushed through the screaming crowds to the temporary morgue in the company blacksmith shop, where the sickening odors of burned flesh greeted them. There, they separated the living from the dead, treating the victims, most of whom had lost limbs or were charred beyond recognition. On this night of horror, each Mercy sister suspended her role as teacher and took on that of nurse, offering care in the latter identity to the very boys educated by the former. Then, as the death toll mounted, the sisters prepared the corpses burned beyond identification for burial, a common grave serving as the final resting place for some of their evening-school students.

These Mercy sisters organized their initial mission around the profession of teaching, a reliable if negligible source of income. They employed themselves with Native students at Sacred Heart and subsequently with children at the St. Joseph parish. But they also devised an imaginative way in which to keep youthful miners at their books, doing so by making an exception to practices about nuns teaching teenage boys or restricting work to daytime hours. Over several years, they furthered their acceptance in all the small towns around them, moving among Italian, Polish, Irish, Welsh, Russian, and Swedish mining families with a variety of services. Then, when disaster struck, the sisters, without waiting for the customary authorization from an ecclesiastical superior, suspended their educational work to respond as medical caregivers to the workers and families of the mining community.

Drawing on the original principles of their congregation, the Sisters of Mercy ignored the darkness of the hour, the baseness of the situation, and the bald rawness of death and waded into the drastic rescue operation around them. They immersed themselves in a highly charged secular space dominated by secular men—miners and marshals, reporters and responders—to assist the families and students with whom they had worked for six years.[82] Such behaviors by sisters eroded the perception of nuns as easily shocked and excessively sheltered, unable and unwilling to confront the realities of life, the coarseness of humanity, or the harshness of the West.

This continual rearranging of work and duty in secular arenas set the pace for innovation within many sisterhoods in the West. For example, in Missouri early in the 1870s, the Daughters of the Sacred Hearts of Jesus and Mary, Franciscan German immigrants, shaking off several financial false starts, rented the extra rooms of their convent to unskilled women workers, eventually convincing their boarders to train as nurses with the sisters.[83] In the 1880s, different German Franciscans, working in Indiana before moving to Nebraska, supported themselves with home-care nursing and cooking that included hauling water and wood, as well as shoveling snow—typical compensation possibly bringing fifty cents per day.[84] In Montana, after Ursulines took out homestead papers, they secured their claim by camping at the site with several Native children.[85] When the Sisters of Charity of Cincinnati decided to build a three-story trade school in

Santa Fe, they assigned Sister Blandina Segale, a well-known missionary of the Southwest, as construction manager and site supervisor. She recruited volunteer backers, acted as timekeeper for the Mexican day laborers, procured quarried rock, contracted with Native Americans for timber, oversaw the manufacture of bricks, negotiated credit, and gave private music lessons on the side.[86] Ten years later, Oregon Benedictine sisters, living inside the unfinished walls of a new monastery, limited construction costs by removing dirt, rocks, and trash in a horse-drawn lorry or one dragged by their own muscle; during the day, the sisters cooked for the carpenters, and in the evening, they hoisted timbers by a hand pulley to the upper floors to further reduce fees.[87] Struggling Franciscans in Minnesota designed and published a monthly magazine, *Annals of Our Lady of the Angels*; through subscriptions and advertisers, the nuns realized more than $10,000 per annum in less than fifteen years and created a worldwide network among Third Order Franciscans.[88] Poverty and the demands of the moment impelled sisters, fueled by their mission as a congregation, to think of creative solutions, assume new responsibilities, and diversify their ways to earn a living.

Urban Challenges

In various western locations, nuns and sisters with ingenuity devised strategies to support themselves, often using income from one endeavor to support charitable works in another. In doing so, they heightened the place of religious women and promoted reliance on nuns as workers and community builders. It was not surprising, then, that an American sisterhood predicated on the growing principles of secular social work and devoted exclusively to urban problems emerged in a major city of the West.

In San Francisco, these Sisters of the Holy Family evolved over several years, as the founder, Elizabeth Armer, tailored the scope of her interest and gathered together other women of common purpose. Early on, Armer, later known as Mother Mary Dolores, and a companion began their ministry with the enthusiastic backing of their friend Father John J. Prendergast.

Disturbed by unstable economic conditions exacerbated by the depression of 1873 and convinced that "secular ladies, however pious and charitabl[e] . . . have their own domestic duties to attend to," the priest endorsed the birth of a congregation to work among the poor of San Francisco.[89] With zesty enthusiasm, he and several of his colleagues practically drove the fledgling sisterhood into the streets of the city. The insistent messages from Prendergast motivated the women, who listened to his advice to "give the poor *as much as they actually need*. . . . Give rather too much than too little."[90]

Mother Dolores formulated proactive responses to this charge. As her work took shape, she circulated leaflets among church members begging for "the poor of the parish," whose "cause is placed in your keeping." Once the Holy Family Sisters accumulated a record, Mother Dolores promoted the congregation through more brochures, informing the parishioners: "We have given to the poor . . . $3,583.65. . . . We have, besides, distributed a large quantity of clothing . . . found employment for some persons . . . [and] endeavored to rescue the children of careless parents."[91] Thus, the sisters advertised that they acted as charitable surrogates for the parishioners, disbursing their donations among the poor whom wealthier Catholics avoided.

Priests further approved of the Sisters of the Holy Family as activists, calling on them to be messengers for and agents of the diocese. These assignments added legitimacy to the work of the women as religious sisters and as representatives of male clergy. For example, Joseph Sadoc Alemany, the archbishop of San Francisco, routinely asked the Holy Family Sisters, whose labors not only mitigated against but eschewed European enclosure, to intervene in the lives of the poor and homeless.

On one occasion, Alemany, without regard for the hour, requested that Mother Dolores immediately escort three youngsters whose parents were in the city jail to the Daughters of Charity orphanage, saying that "the children cannot remain with Mrs. Stevens longer than this evening."[92] Requests also came from other clergy, prominent laypersons, and sisters of religious congregations: "One of the children is dead in the Bassity family on Jones Street. . . . Send two of the sisters there, and also . . . bury the child nicely"; "The family . . . father and mother and at least four children really deserve aid and support"; "The bearer of this is known by me to be poor and destitute of a home or means"; "If you can . . . place her in some employment as a servant. . . . Her husband is lying paralyzed"; "She has not a dollar to pay rent or purchase food for her husband, two children, and herself."[93] Neither death nor disease, alcoholism nor violence, time of day nor city location inhibited the Sisters of the Holy Family, who alone and in pairs advised and assisted the most destitute among the San Francisco poor.

In keeping with their frequent presence among people found on the streets and in the tenements, the Holy Family nuns rejected the common nineteenth-century religious habit. Seeking to "fit" with the secular world, the women favored a long black dress with a matching three-quarter-length cloak and a black straw hat, a plain design that blended with voguish styles of the day. Once the order formalized in 1878, the sisters kept to an unadorned attire, adding a plain white collar, a short cape, and a simple white linen coif with a black veil. Even after agreeing to wear the veil inside the convent, the sisters retained the original secular-like dress with its distinctive straw hat for their outside assignments.[94]

Along with clothing that suggested assimilation into the lay community, the Sisters of the Holy Family waived many of the usual strict requirements for admission, applying a generous standard for those seeking to join the new congregation. Mother Dolores, who experienced difficulty convincing aspirants to stay in the austere circumstances, more than once accepted an aged or widowed applicant if she showed an aptitude for the civic nature and grinding poverty of the work. Archbishop Alemany recommended at least nine recruits, backing the unorthodox procedures for formation by saying of one: "If necessary or considered advantageous afterwards, she may spend a little time in a religious convent."[95]

Yet one of the archbishop's other directions underscored even more thoroughly that the Sisters of the Holy Family adjusted rules for nuns in the West. In January 1875, as Mother Dolores searched for members, the archbishop advised admitting a widow with two minor children, suggesting the recruit could leave the sisters at six o'clock each evening, attend to her maternal duties, and return to the convent by eight in the morning. Novitiate and profession, he recommended, should be delayed until the sons had become independent of their mother's care and support. In the meantime, the congregation would benefit from the added labor.

This extraordinary clerical approbation for mixing religious women with a widow bound to responsibilities that restricted her convent residence highlighted the radical transformations implicit in the organization of the Sisters of the Holy Family. Although some orders might have paused over a candidate with significant age, sexual identity, and maternal ties—both legal and emotional—the San Francisco convent apparently successfully weathered the secular and religious blending. The widowed mother became Sister Mary Magdalen Javete, one of the original five nuns pronouncing vows. Sister Magdalen, who already had balanced family responsibility and convent affiliation for five years, continued in a range of domestic chores for the Holy Family congregation until her death in 1886.[96]

The Sisters of the Holy Family defined urban San Francisco as their mission. As providers of social services, they acquired a record that included keeping death vigil in homes, preparing bodies for burial, and arranging

In California, the Sisters of the Holy Family adopted a secular fashion for the habit, a symbol of their willingness to travel into the neighborhoods of the poor, directly addressing problems of housing, hunger, unemployment, and disrupted family life. (Courtesy Sisters of the Holy Family, Fremont, Calif.)

funerals; administering the donations of parishioners; circulating among lay- and religious people with tickets for a fund-raising event that netted $16,000; conducting a sewing school for adolescent girls in a parish basement; rescuing children of deceased or incarcerated parents; and transporting youngsters to public and private orphanages. By 1878 the sisters had distributed almost $14,000 in rent, food, clothing, medicine, furniture, and funeral expenses.[97]

The Holy Family sisters, however, did not envision charitable goods and money as the full measure of their congregation. Rather, they aggressively pursued the growing professional aspects of social work, providing scaffolding that supported the efforts of poor people, especially women. The original constitutions of the sisterhood recognized the day-to-day urban economy for women, declaring a charge of care for small children "whose mothers have to leave home to go out to work during the day."[98]

To that end, the sisters opened neighborhood centers designed to nurture infants, toddlers, and preschoolers in a family atmosphere. "Homes," complete with ornate carpets and white curtains, fresh floral arrangements, large paintings, American flags, children's art, religious statues, and cages with canaries, set the centers—buildings independent from the convent residence—apart from drab state institutions. The nursery gave a light and sunny effect. The dining hall doubled as a chore area for children, who, after a hot midday meal cooked by the sisters, straightened the chairs, refolded their cloth napkins, brushed the table linens, and swept the floor. In the playroom, well-groomed youngsters sat at child-sized tables and chairs with books and toy blocks, painted at easels, and amused themselves with rocking horses, scooters, games, or dollhouses. The schedule incorporated free play with lessons, music, and catechism, the latter for the older siblings who came to the home before and after school hours. Eventually, the sisters operated four day homes in the area, accommodating over 1,000 families a year.[99]

Furthermore, the sisters participated in the burgeoning kindergarten movement, studying practical and theoretical models that stressed observation and reasoning as tools for teaching. In 1884 four sisters certified as "kindergarteners" with a German woman who operated a private secular school in San Francisco using the Froebel method, which stated that "the mother shall become the teacher, and the teacher the mother."[100] The sisters, whose kindergarten expertise was sought by other religious congregations, applied this motherly philosophy in their day homes, where they reinforced working families and prepared children for elementary school.[101]

In these initiatives, the Sisters of the Holy Family enlarged the changing work traditions that influenced nuns in the West. They concentrated on the needs of San Francisco residents and, in doing so, widened acceptance of what constituted appropriate work venues for Catholic nuns. These sisters, organized under the conditions of the West, never wrestled with the binding rules of monastic life or the torn emotions of congregational loyalty rooted in European origins. Instead, these California sisters adjusted their conduct as religious women to fit the surrounding city, carried the interests of the Catholic hierarchy into needy neighborhoods on a daily basis, recognized the legitimacy of womanhood in the "working mother," heightened the professionalism of church charities, and pioneered in social work and progressive education, providing reliable, safe environments for prekindergarten and school-age children decades before these notions achieved currency throughout America.

Rural Challenges

Nineteenth-century urban conditions in the West led sisters into work that addressed the problems attached to commerce and industrial development. This pursuit took them into many rural areas in the West. Whatever, whenever, and wherever their assignments, sisters strove to reconcile western work and their training as religious women.

In November 1878 two nuns, Sisters Philomene Ketten and Lioba Braun, leaving St. Benedict's monastery for White Earth, Minnesota, saw the ideals of their motherhouse regulations slide away with each passing mile. Great distance, diminished communication, and new associates did not permit consultation with St. Benedict's monastic superiors, none of whom had significant knowledge of the cultural and physical complexities at White Earth. Life in the far reaches of Minnesota promised to change Philomene and Lioba.

The two nuns found not only that mission days clashed with motherhouse routines, but also that the fundamentals of Native life differed from the teleology of white Christianity and the assumptions of a convent general council. The Ojibwa people at White Earth, among whom there was considerable diversity and varying political views, had been battered by the bickering between secular agencies and religious denominations for years. Federal government agents, usually practitioners of a Protestant faith, openly fought with the local Catholic missionary to White Earth, Father Ignatius Tomazin. The irrepressible Tomazin, with his fierce advocacy of Native people, so offended all authorities that he was removed from White Earth. For those Ojibwas who had accepted Catholicism through early French Canadian contacts, their one supporter was silenced, replaced by two untested women, coming to a mission where coercion and suppression systematically led to mounting social, economic, and political deprivation.[102]

The dreary scene that greeted the young nuns as their wagon rattled into the mission laid before them the results of draconian policy badly implemented by whites of every persuasion. Before the nuns lay a mission compound with dilapidated buildings, a parish cabin stripped of Tomazin's every belonging, a neglected garden, and a poorly situated well — all indicative of the decades of havoc that had left the Ojibwas handicapped before the white agents who oversaw their space.[103] Beyond the reservation, the Ojibwas were reviled by encroaching white settlers; inside the reservation, although endorsed by Protestant and Catholic missionaries alike, the Native people existed on the barest of material goods, allocated on the basis of favoritism and religious allegiance. The White Earth mission threw the sisters, well accustomed to physical labor, into human maelstroms, moral dilemmas, and theological contradictions greater than they could have anticipated.

As this alien world and gloomy landscape unfolded before them, the nuns, without furnishings or bedding, moved into the so-called convent — the ill-built log parish house with a leaky roof. The abbot father who escorted them departed in the morning, leaving the pair with a few dollars, a barrel of flour, a keg of lard, and a handful of frozen potatoes. The nuns surveyed a mission remarkable in its bleakness and poverty, a place where they had virtually no food and little idea how they would survive the winter.[104]

Standing at White Earth the day after their arrival, the untried missionaries had to figure out the nature of the work they would undertake and how they would fit that labor into the scheme of Benedictine sisterhood. Perhaps not fully recognizing the isolation to come, the two young women — one twenty-three, the other twenty-five — applied themselves and within six days opened the school, which after a month had an enrollment of thirty-five pupils, including two orphan girls who moved into the squalid convent.[105]

Almost immediately, the work brought unexpected and crippling disasters. Sister Philomene, for example, suffered a severe case of pleurisy that did not yield in the bitterly cold days and nights. Then the school burned to the ground, the smoke further endangering her health as she dove into the flames to retrieve the pathetic supply of books and furniture. Her sorry condition led the new mission priest to write: "Sisters cannot endure this weather much longer"; "[they] are still ill from the fire of New Year's."[106]

Little slowed Philomene, however, and despite her illness, she partnered with a carpenter to renovate the barn sufficiently and make a temporary classroom. In the warm months, she pumped water by hand, but when the well froze in the winter, she dragged ice and snow indoors and melted it for laundry water. She fed and watered the livestock, managed the barn chores, taught the students to raise crops, and painted the mission buildings. There was no labor that she avoided; her companions remembered that she hired oxen and cleared away stumps, was known to herd and kill cattle, and at one harvest reportedly cut ten tons of hay.

A sister from the mission in later years recalled that Philomene was "rough and ready," and one of the priests boasted that the sturdy nun "hoed like a man."[107] Indeed, in 1888, when the Drexel sisters of Philadelphia came to White Earth to assess reservation conditions, Elizabeth, the oldest, called Philomene "the Wild Sister." She road a horse with abandon, showing a demeanor hardened by years as a nun-teacher-farmer.[108]

The two missionaries, in opposition to monastery rule, also regularly circulated inside the Native community, attending events and mingling at local gatherings, where they conversed with parents and children. When Buffalo Creek Indians questioned why their youngsters should not have access to the same Catholic instruction as White Earth, especially since the priest had promised them a school, Philomene responded—as was her custom—with action. After the Natives constructed a small school building, she volunteered to teach at Buffalo Creek.

To do so, she rose each morning at three, fed the stock, cooked the day's food for her students and orphans, completed her morning devotions, and then rode by horseback to Buffalo Creek, a distance of seven or eight miles. There, for three years during April to October, she conducted a school, regularly taking her noon meal with a nearby Irishman and his Native wife.[109] The Buffalo Creek venture succeeded in several ways: it deflected a potential argument between the priest and the disappointed Indian families, it softened jealousies between two neighboring groups of Natives, it furthered the goodwill of the Catholic mission among local residents, it provided an on-site solution without wading through the channels of "permission sought and denied" at the motherhouse, and it cost the congregational administrators neither teachers nor supplies from their mission budget.

For seven months each year, Sister Philomene was apart from White Earth for many hours of the day, another irregularity that cut into the formal schedules of nuns. The travel through wilderness and in the dark, the "unladylike" ride by horseback, the school at Buffalo Creek, and the daily meal in the home of secular people immersed Philomene in nontraditional practices that lay outside a cloistered community. At the same time, her absence laid on Sister Lioba another set of unusual demands: managing all aspects of the mission, caring for orphans and students, leading religious exercises, supervising Native laborers, and dealing with the sick or the injured.

In addition, the mission priest traveled frequently and was away from White Earth for lengthy periods, leaving the sisters responsible for all temporal and spiritual activities. Work divisions and decisions fell to the sisters, whether alone or together, on a daily basis. The sisters at White Earth oversaw convent regulations, spiritual ritual, classroom education, orphan care, reservation employees, and the needs of the people. They dealt with emergencies of the moment, whether connected to the livestock, physical plant, or mission family.

Over time, these circumstances of western living conditions exerted a subtle influence over the White Earth convent. These scenes of life became the usual, and their rhythms beat into the routines of religious life. The irregular communication between the monastery and the mission, caused by inaccessible roads, wretched travel, and formidable weather, facilitated the emergence of behaviors that conflicted with earlier models for Catholic nuns. Such circumstances might be considered "exceptional" by the congregational administration, but these procedures ordered the hours of each day for the two nuns.

White Earth was not a romantic dream in which "happy" Natives flocked to Christianity. Rather, these two sisters placed themselves inside the home environs of an alien culture, where Natives died of starvation and their orphaned children had few advocates. The sisters knew that they lived in a real place with real people; nothing bonded together the structured life of St. Benedict's monastery and the daily horrors of White Earth. It was not possible for these European-centered nuns to recreate a miniature version of the Catholic world they left. At White Earth, adaptability in all things meant survival.

Not until 1885 did White Earth enjoy even the whisper of a guaranteed income—1,000 government dollars to cover the expenses of but ten of their fifteen orphans.[110] The White Earth mission never transformed into a station of comfort and prosperity. Rather, it remained a regional symbol of the grinding deprivation of the rural missions across the West. As well, it symbolized how nuns chose to work through and around that deprivation, even as in a dawn of understanding they recognized the broadly negative policies of church and state that crushed many aspects of Native American life.[111]

In 1922 nuns of St. Benedict's monastery honored those professed sisters marking a special anniversary in religious life. Among the celebrants were two nuns long far from the priory. Side by side in the formal photograph stood Sister Boniface, the urban hospital administrator from Bismarck, and Sister Philomene, the rural mission educator from White Earth.

Each, called home for the festivities, had labored for the Benedictine community for fifty years, always removed from the corridors of the motherhouse. One, elegant and tall, implemented progressive business procedures at a Benedictine hospital and left her print on the medical community of an entire city. The other, gnarled and worn, created a legacy of rugged athletic toughness and entered into cross-cultural relationships with generations of Native families. One stressed the intellectual in her work, the other the physical; both pursued the practical. Neither received personal remuneration or ascended to the inner political circle at St. Benedict's. Yet each contributed to the regional economic and social power of the Benedictine congregation, extending its reach and its name. Each lived according to the rule of the Benedictines but applied it in ways that, although deviating from a monastic model, generated congregation income, advanced the ideals of the order, heightened the visibility of the Catholic Church, informed their own thinking, and enlarged the work performed by Catholic nuns across the American West.

Seeing Results

The Benedictine sisters and their counterparts had taken up an "obedience," an assignment given by congregational superiors or clerical authorities, and they pursued that assignment with vigor and commitment. Confronted by urban and rural worlds, nuns in the West suspended conventions that limited the initiative of sisters or the conditions under which they could operate. Nuns adopted new visible roles, showing themselves, church authorities, and secular people that religious women could contribute to the working West in sophisticated, critical, and innovative ways.

The sisterhoods in the West, most with limited financial resources, searched out sources of support from the region. Upon arriving in a new location, they began some form of work within days, placing their meager earnings into a common convent fund. Sisters suspended the dictates of enclosure and moved among the people of a community, identifying the obvious social deficits and devising ways to convert them into convent livelihood.

With ease, teaching and nursing drew nuns into rural and urban settings. A school could be opened with a few writing tablets, some sticks of chalk, and no capital. A hospital required only a shack, an assortment of beds, and the daily attention of the "nursing" nuns. Frequently, nuns took the homeless, the needy, the sick, and the orphan into their own cramped living quarters, utilizing their convents as personal and professional spaces. Nuns in many locales excelled at responding to the social, economic, and political elements of the cultures around them, using female work—domestic and professional, structured and leisure—as their admission ticket to western society.

In all places, the sisters declined to separate themselves from the men and women of the West. Indeed, they assumed an active, highly personal role in connecting to western people of every culture. Sisters exploited their European languages as a way to circulate among an immigrant constituency, but they also developed other language competency to work more broadly in their adopted country. In this, sisters further refused to limit their labor to the inner sanctums of their convents. Nuns aggressively sought and entered the byways of secular life—many of them unattractive and dangerous—for work.

Sisters took on domestic and nursing chores in the homes of the ill, often living with a collection of sick folks for many weeks at a time. Lacking the protection of some sentimental shield that existed only in the popular imagination, nuns went into the most filthy and hazardous locations, bringing nourishment and consolation to working families. They provided safe shelter for children and single women. They stepped into Native lives hoping to halt the downward spiral of poverty. They nursed the cruelly injured, and they prepared the dead for burial—tasks often done under gruesome circumstances and without compensation. As nuns, they felt the warmth of appreciation but also the scorn of distaste.

No other group managed to navigate the dual roles of public caregiver and spiritual symbol quite so successfully. As workers in the West, nuns and sisters, in opposition to age-old images of cloistered women, reached to the secular populations around them, using service as a means to build steady employment, public identity, and congregational reputation.

In all western locations, sisters relied on traditional institutions to segue into more unusual workplaces, calling on the sisters' individual talents to broaden a venture. A day school evolved into a residential home for young women; a single orphanage mutated into daycare centers for the children

Although western work meant labor-intensive days, it also introduced nuns to innovative art forms, such as the culturally mingled designs produced by this Arizona rug- and lace-making class of Pima students at a school of the Sisters of St. Joseph. (Courtesy Congregation of St. Joseph of Carondelet, Los Angeles, Calif.)

of working mothers; a teacher at one Indian mission added on the role of itinerant educator for another. Wisely, these nuns largely kept to the ecumenical, accepting students and patients without a religious requirement. In doing so, they widened their customer base, expanded their own intellectual horizons, and aided efforts to build a favorable reputation for Catholicism.

Nuns and sisters, in addition to their professional occupations and social service, scrubbed clothes, chopped wood, slaughtered livestock, plowed fields, raised crops, and built convents. They stitched altar linens, made shoes, hauled rocks, spun wool, kept orchards, harvested wheat, and pressed cider. They milked cows, herded goats, and churned butter. While many women, both indigenous and immigrant, labored mightily under exacting emotional conditions, not so many combined their physical endeavors with separation from all biological family, formation in religious life, or the establishment of numerous institutions of social service. Not so many undertook rigorous academic studies combined with endless hours of drudgery and structured daily communal prayer. Fewer yet, as single women, answered to such a complicated and rigid male hierarchy that relied on religious authoritarianism to justify a lifetime of unquestioned loyalty, excruciating work, and skimpy remuneration. And still a smaller number of females accepted all of these constraints while contributing paid and unpaid labor over many decades for the common purpose of strengthening a specific organization of women.

Having discovered western work, nuns were not inclined to relinquish their changed roles or bow to the many obstacles attached to life as professed women in the West. Rather, many relished the changes and challenges that came with transformation; those who lacked relish depended on personal endurance—another theme in convent life.

Perceiving how well they could do in a region of many surprises and even more adversity, rather than staying behind locked convent doors, the nuns searched the secular community for new sources of income. With these, they looked to extract fair compensation for labor given, construct financial stability for their sisterhoods, and protect their congregational rights. These elements would solidify as sisters harnessed, developed, and formalized their initial inroads into western work.

Mother Baptista Bowen would have applauded the varied initiatives, gritty efforts, and personal tenacity in each congregation, as the women entered the gathering places of the American West. Mother Baptista never met all of those nuns, but she would have recognized their common zeal for work in many forms. Few returned to any motherhouse with "No Good" written on their backs.

*I hope you understand very
clearly that you can expect
no financial help from
San Antonio.*

—J. W. Shaw to Mother
Maria-Teresa of the Heart of
Jesus, 23 August 1913,
Carmelite Sisters of the
Divine Heart of Jesus,
Religious Orders of
Women, Archives of
the Archdiocese
of San Antonio

The Finances

In 1913 Mother Maria-Teresa of St.
Joseph, seeking employment for her
handful of Carmelites, contacted the
bishop of San Antonio about a placement in his diocese. Encouraged by the
endorsement of the Carmelites' European director, who remarked that "by
penetrating into the family circle . . .
they have rendered the most salutary
services . . . to . . . the entire civil community," Bishop John William Shaw
entered into protracted negotiations to
bring these semicloistered Carmelites
to Texas.[1] Anxious to improve services
in poverty-ridden Mexican neighborhoods, where he envisioned Mother
Maria-Teresa's nuns might have "some
clubs in the evening for the young
people . . . [and] later . . . [a] day clinic

for the poor sick," Shaw nonetheless distanced himself from financial obligations for the immigrant congregation, remaining stubborn about his funding or that of other diocesan agencies.[2]

The bishop squelched hopes that the nuns harbored about aid for purchasing property or building a novitiate for the Carmelites. Shaw did suggest he might lease the sisters an inconveniently situated piece of his land, but he hedged on Mother Maria-Teresa's request for train tickets to bring the nuns from Milwaukee.[3] Immediate or projected financial commitments constricted his enthusiasm, for as Shaw mentioned in an inquiry for references and confidential information about the sisterhood, "I should especially like to know if they would . . . put up with very simple quarters."[4] Shaw surely wanted workers for his understaffed diocese, but not if they came with moving fees, living costs, and expectations of improving their circumstances.

Deep in south Texas, Bishop Shaw captured the broad church policy among clerical administrators concerning finances and women's congregations. The widespread belief circulating among Catholics and non-Catholics that the Vatican-centered European and then American church supported and sustained women's religious orders was not only completely inaccurate but also possibly amusing to strapped congregations and destitute sisters in the field. Religious women never received a regular, automatic infusion of money into convent coffers. Rather than basking in church largesse, a congregation, embracing the motherhouse and all daughter convents, shouldered responsibility to generate the income for its own shelter, food, clothing, education, religious ceremonies, medical care, and travel and work initiatives, as well as church-mandated charities, miscellaneous expenses, and long-term debts. In short, the women pursued internal and external streams of funding to meet their many obligations because the institutional church, in its religious and secular membership, did not give operating costs to convents.

Confronting their many expenses in the American West, nuns identified regular income as an essential priority. However, in regional markets notable for dispersed human communities, rural economies, and male-dominated Anglo-European industry, clusters of unmarried white women bound by a church appeared to be disadvantaged. In this environment, both secular and religious barriers hindered nuns and sisters seeking paid work. Nevertheless, there was no escaping that earning a living fell to the professed women themselves, who depended on multiple ways to raise funds.

First, early émigrés, leaving their European monasteries, often held tightly to their economic centers, drawing income, however sporadic, from their homelands. Nuns who moved into the West carried financial baggage from a complicated Old World legacy closely tied to competition between powerful families and princely lords. Political patronage, local economic privilege, or a generous dowry from relatives elevated one priory above another in the prickly religious history of Catholic Europe.[5] With America attracting scores of zealous missionaries, some European benefactors were willing to extend that hand of patronage—and their own political reach— across the Atlantic Ocean.

For example, King Ludwig I of Bavaria, a promoter of all things Germanic and a booster for the Catholicism of his countrymen in America, acquired a reputation as European royalty with florins for women's congregations. During the 1840s and 1850s, German-speaking nuns agreeing to ventures in America courted the royal rogue and fancier of Germanism for funds to assist their missions. He responded favorably, for he asserted that "religious and school instruction in the German language will always be needed for the continuance of the German spirit."[6]

The prestige and coin of the king declined, however, when he abandoned an early interest in broad liberal reform, distracted as he was by a sensational affair with the Irish-born and decidedly non-German dancer Lola Montez. Burdened politically and socially by a backlash from the boulevard, Ludwig abdicated in 1848 but retained his interest in Catholicism for German émigrés.[7] Missioned nuns requesting donations never enjoyed the cascading wealth that King Ludwig showered on Lola Montez, but neither did the royal benefactor leave them empty-handed. Their persistence, undeterred by the king's reversal of fortune, prompted the deposed Ludwig to grumble, "I am besieged by the needy, just as if I were still king, although my revenues were decreased considerably at my resignation," but complaints notwithstanding, he continued sending money to German Catholics in America.[8]

In one community, nearly fifteen years after she led the School Sisters of Notre Dame from their native Bavaria, Mother Caroline Friess maintained contact with the Louis Mission Society. This association, under Ludwig's benevolence, often defrayed travel expenses, construction costs, and missionary wages. Indeed, sisters insisted that on the day of their 1847 departure, King Ludwig himself had come to the motherhouse to bid them farewell, promising: "I shall not forget you in America. I shall not forsake you."[9]

Mother Caroline, through her detailed letters home, made certain the king's reassuring words—whether echoing truth or imagination—stayed vibrant on both sides of the Atlantic Ocean. Her epistles to Bavaria described every event, mission request, and encounter of the sisters to document their service on behalf of German immigrants. Mother Caroline made certain that thousands of miles away, a small mission board in Bavaria would know her sisters guarded the interests of German Catholics in America.

In her colorful accounts of American life, Mother Caroline began with flattering words of gratitude, such as, "during all these years we have received the generous help of our noble benefactors in the beloved fatherland," and concluded with an almost offhand plea: "I would again beg of your charity a donation."[10] In between, she painted the German scene in America for Europe. In one letter alone she wrote: "The colonists here are healthy German people"; "agree . . . our first obligation is to provide for the German poor"; and "the German parents, who cannot forget their dear fatherland, are glad to . . . rouse the consciences of their children." She then signed the letter as "Maria Caroline Friess, German-American School Sister."[11] A Bavarian panel reading her words approved the cultural outreach and rewarded Mother Caroline, sending, among its donations, 15,000 florins on one occasion and 12,000 florins for an orphanage for German children.[12]

Still, the fundamental preference for priests over nuns influenced how much money a woman's congregation could collect. For example, power struggles between Benedictine men and women in America shaped their relationships, especially the use of funds from Europe. For the women, their initial difficulty lay with Boniface Wimmer, a European abbot who staked a claim for control of the Benedictines in America.[13] In the 1850s, Wimmer appropriated Ludwig's florins, intended for construction of a convent, and used the cash for the construction of two saw mills, expanding employment for the Benedictine priests and brothers. A few years later, he took Ludwig's donation to Minnesota sisters, using the nearly $1,500 to purchase land for the men's monastery, which he offered to name in honor of the former king because "this is of much greater importance than a convent of sisters."[14]

Regardless of such gender conflicts, foreign contributors, even the most faithful, could not sustain the day-to-day operations of the growing mission enterprise. In America, goals for expansion increasingly guided congregational decisions and surpassed the vision of grandiose royal patrons. To implement their burgeoning work, congregational leaders perceived that sturdy structures for permanent income should be closer to their new home, where the women themselves controlled the money. Women of several congregations shuttered their European windows and opened the portals of the American West, moving to put their members on a more solid financial foundation.

Personal Wealth of Nuns

As European support faded, religious women relied, as much as possible, on funding drawn from inside their congregations. Claims to cash, real estate, family heirlooms, commercial establishments, and land represented critical income for American motherhouses. A vow of personal poverty did not invalidate secular citizenship, nor make convent administrators indifferent to exercising the property rights of nuns. Congregations, therefore, focused on fundamental financial and legal rights of members to protect convent monies and advance goals.

The personal wealth of founding mothers, their biological families, or other community members provided capital for more than one religious order. Congregations fortunate enough to have such resources enjoyed flexibility and independence that promoted a degree of financial autonomy within the institutional church. The American West contributed to that flexibility and independence, its relentless call for nuns heightening their bargaining strength in work arrangements and introducing the means for regular livelihoods.

For example, Peter J. and Anna M. Kerst, parents of Mother Scholastica and Mother Alexia of Benedictines in Minnesota, cultivated circumstances that positioned them to monitor the business interests of their two daughters, advancing the religious careers of both. While the parents of a young family, the elder Kersts had migrated from Prussia to Minnesota, where the father pursued interests in business. Directing his attention to America's most valuable resource — land — Peter Kerst worked the soil, not as a poor immigrant farmer but as a real estate entrepreneur and financial investor of means.

Acquiring wealth in Minnesota, Kerst harbored reservations about convent life, chosen by two of his daughters when they reached adulthood. Despite his own attachment to Catholicism, Kerst resisted surrendering his children to monastic anonymity inside the excruciating poverty of the Benedictine cloister. Those feelings solidified following a visit to Mother

Scholastica's first religious residence at Shakopee, Minnesota, where the shoddily clad and poorly fed nuns greeted him in a room blackened by smoke from a broken stove.[15]

This experience appeared to galvanize Kerst, who used a two-pronged strategy for educating Scholastica and Alexia in the ways of the emerging business world of the West. Over the next several years, he assumed the role of economic adviser and personal financier to his daughters, instructing them in the commercial skills that had made him successful. From him, Mother Scholastica, described by some as a born leader but one who "courted opposition for the sake of overcoming it," learned about property values, business alliances, and corporate expansion.[16] Additionally, Peter Kerst insinuated himself into the politics of the male and female Benedictine houses in Minnesota and invested his money to alter the convent destitution he viewed as unsuitable for his children.

In 1877 Mother Scholastica, dissatisfied with monastic life at Shakopee, transferred, with the endorsement of her parents and the father abbot at St. John's Abbey, to St. Benedict's. Less than three years after entering St. Benedict's, and over the displeasure of some nuns who thought the election was "conducted . . . to sidetrack all opposition," Scholastica was elevated by the father abbot of St. John's Abbey to head the women's priory.[17] With Scholastica as mother superior, the Kersts, who lubricated their friendship with the monks through generous donations, increased their monetary contributions to St. Benedict's monastery.[18] Between 1881 and 1890, the years during which Mother Scholastica led St. Benedict's, Peter Kerst poured more than $22,000 into the convent and continued his counsel in financial and legal matters.

In 1892 Mother Scholastica and Mother Alexia, unhappy with an administrative decision that removed the former from office, separated from the motherhouse and established their own priory in Duluth, Minnesota. No doubt they felt the confidence to do so because they enjoyed the financial backing of their parents. To reinforce that confidence, the Kerst parents decamped from St. Paul and joined their daughters in Duluth, beginning an acrimonious but ultimately successful legal action for the return of thousands of dollars and real estate holdings they claimed as the rightful property of their daughters and not the St. Benedict's monastery.

Although Kerst's secular input into the business affairs of his daughters' convents appeared to violate the traditional separation of biological family and cloistered daughters, it rather pointed to one avenue by which nuns gained expertise in financial transactions and experience in business management under safe tutelage. Nuns from well-placed families benefited within a congregation as their status and money positioned them for promotion and leadership. With business knowledge and family backing, these sisters assumed crucial roles in advancing fledgling congregations in religious and secular matters.[19]

Of course, when the founding mother of a congregation possessed the wealth herself, the lines of authority dictating management of family money simplified. In San Antonio, Texas, Margaret Mary Healy Murphy, a well-to-do widow and social activist of the 1880s, focused her energies on projects for the spiritual and educational well-being of African Americans and Mexicans. Murphy, who invested more than $20,000 of her personal funds in the building of St. Peter Claver parish and school for African Americans, buttressed her legal knowledge with money to counter the hostile reactions of city residents, as well as church members, who considered her little more than a loose racial cannon.[20] Murphy admired but could not match the immense fortune and business accomplishments of Katharine Drexel, who also channeled her money into minority education. Drexel effectively became the banker and headmistress of Catholic education for persons of color in the South and West, establishing her own sisterhood as a personnel resource. These two women illuminated the way Catholic nuns with personal bank accounts could define their own sphere of influence, living and working with, as well as resisting interference from, male administrators.[21]

Although a wealthy founder gave a congregation of nuns a financial and management edge, only a few orders enjoyed that circumstance.[22] Most congregations organized in spare beginnings and so welcomed the personal property an individual sister contributed to the convent finances. Given the wrenching process inside the church to establish congregational autonomy and identity, it behooved a sisterhood to have property rights as carefully and clearly defined as possible. Sworn profession statements—such as "I have no claim on property nor money I have paid for the expenses of my . . . taking the habit" or there is "no pay on departure"—and congregational by-laws that declared "all property now owned by . . . any of its members shall belong to said corporation . . . [and] no heir of any member shall have any right, title, claim whatsoever to the property" were hoped to be a blanket protection for the congregation.[23]

Detailed records of the cash and property contributed by young women when they entered the convent were designed as buffers against inflated claims in the future. Dowries might include mattresses and bedding, summer and winter undergarments, and dresses and shawls, as well as cash ranging from fifty to two hundred dollars. Better still was a donation large enough to serve as a down payment on property or construction of a new motherhouse, such as the $5,000 Mary Griffin presented to the Dominicans in Benicia, California, on the day of her 1887 profession as Sister Mary Regina. Not only did this money push the building program forward and better the congregation's credit, but Mary Regina's family also continued to endow the Dominicans, never raising legal challenges to these contributions.[24]

Still, enough years of confusion and disagreement in these matters in part led to the publication of a canon law for women's congregations, which included rules about sisters and personal wealth. To standardize religious life across congregations, the 1909 law attempted to detail every possible convent circumstance concerning wealth and property. For example, a woman could donate to her religious order any personal holdings she wished, but this presumed the obligations of a binding contract, so she could not reclaim—unlike her dowry—the property should she one day leave the congregation.[25] Total renunciation of property by a novice was frowned on by Vatican advisers, and they recommended that such designations be made on condition of a woman's continued membership in a sisterhood. Sisters, nonetheless, were entitled to name the congregation as the sole heir to their personal property. The Catholic Church, its many gender restrictions notwithstanding, acknowledged that enclosure aside, nuns retained their fiduciary rights and obligations; they could inherit and dispose of personal property from benefactors and through family lines.

Convent residence did not necessarily deflect family property squabbles nor mean that every relative would release legacies to congregations.[26] Indeed, an unscrupulous relative could perceive the convent as a convenient cover for questionable business dealings. In 1898 a Sister of Charity of the BVM in Iowa was astonished to learn that her recently deceased brother had legally encumbered her Illinois property, valued at $2,500. Apparently, the brother had surmised that his nun sibling would never know he guaranteed his mortgage with a lien against her land. No doubt he thought to clear the matter without the nun in a far-off Iowa convent ever learning of his chicanery. Alas, his unexpected death revealed his secret dealings. In this case, the congregational council backed the nun, voting to honor the unpaid loan and its accumulated interest out of the central treasury. The aggrieved nun traveled to Illinois, settled the entire obligation of $1,740.62, and entered a claim for her money against her brother's estate.[27] Presumably the settlement would return the sum to the nun, who in turn would pay her debt to the congregation—reminded that for her "family" meant more than biological kin.

Entry to religious life did not eradicate the legal rights of nuns and sisters. Congregations permitted and expected sisters to participate in the necessary action to protect their property, which they hoped would benefit the treasury of the sisterhood. Mother superiors wanted to avoid public clashes with family, which were guaranteed to stimulate secular curiosity about the lives of the sisters and deplete convent bank accounts because of legal fees. Disputes with former members called for speedy resolution so that they did not become sensational stories, drain money, and distract other sisters.

Inheritances stimulated convent treasuries, allowing congregational leaders to contemplate improvements on a motherhouse, reduction of debt, or expansion into new territories. Money matters might open family wounds, but they gave sisters an opportunity to understand the legal system, pursue their rights, and settle their responsibilities through the courts. Perhaps most important, a family inheritance and its adjudication showed that the legal system recognized the right of cloistered women to name their own heirs, whether those be the religious congregation or biological relations. Personal funding, formal business skills, control of wealth, and application of legal rights all emerged as important tools for congregations seeking fiscal stability in the West.

Financial Growth and Legal Protection

To strengthen their finances and reduce exploitation, congregations turned to the law, using formal structures to define a legitimate place in the business world and to protect their members at the motherhouse or on the missions. The West trained congregations to be alert to those circumstances that hindered an economic return and a positive reputation for working sisters. It required many years and varied experiences for congregations to develop the legal and business expertise that made them stronger participants in community building.

In 1868, after years of poverty and erratic employment, the Sisters of Charity of Leavenworth successfully incorporated their organization under the laws of Kansas. Among the provisions secured, the Sisters of Charity could "buy, sell, lease, rent, hold, exchange and dispose of real and personal property."[28] The articles of incorporation, with legally designated officers and perpetual life, gave order to the business activities of a congregation, regardless of personnel rotations common to mother superiors and their councils.[29] This state-mandated directive guided congregations into the business community, offering tangible benefits. It created a formal entity empowered to conduct a broad range of commercial transactions, established legal protections for individuals acting for the corporation, and demonstrated compliance with the statutes that regulated government contracts. The state-defined articles of incorporation placed nuns under a secular umbrella, granting them recognition and authority outside their religious community.

Further, incorporation underscored yet another way in which congregations advertised their proactive relationship with secular society, giving nuns credibility as executive leaders for local service initiatives. They showed the women's institutions — schools, hospitals, asylums, orphanages, academies — as extensions of and endorsed by the mechanisms of the state. This implied entrepreneurial expertise, articulated through articles of incorporation, suggested a weakening in the dominant caretaker role of clergy managers. Thus, in a subtle way, as sisters legitimated their employment plans, incorporation drove a wedge between the nuns and those priests who controlled their every financial move.

On occasion such control subtly vanished, if an astute mother superior saw an opportunity to sever finances from the ruling authority of a priest and did so. For more than twenty-six years, the priest superior Terence J. Donaghoe dominated the "financial and human" resources of the Sisters of Charity of the BVM in Dubuque. Although she cooperated with her mentor for nearly thirty years, Mother Mary Frances Clarke, setting aside grief, looked on Father Donaghoe's death as the moment to extricate the congregation from priestly financial domination. Reluctantly, the dying priest, pressured by Clarke and the local bishop, signed over title to the lands and property of members of the congregation.

Following Donaghoe's demise, Clarke speedily filed articles of incorporation for the BVM, assumed the presidency of the corporation, and recalled her strongest congregational ally to Dubuque to serve as vice president.[30] Operating under those articles granted in 1870, the newly formed general council mapped out conditions for sisters' employment, decreeing that each nun receive a salary of $30 a month, that missions have a furnished house, and that pastors provide heat to the convent.[31] These events represented only the beginning of a forceful program by the Sisters of Charity of the BVM to self-direct their religious and business identity.

The independence intrinsic to articles of incorporation helped congregations managing remote missions in the American West. The corporate regulations established a baseline by which motherhouse leaders debated and explored the desirability of proposed missions in unfamiliar locations. In 1877 administrators of the St. Louis Sisters of St. Joseph, anticipating congregational growth in Colorado and assessing the obstacles in long-distance management, formed a corporation among their missions in Central City, Georgetown, and Denver. This transferred some authority to the missioned sisters, giving the board of directors in Denver "full control of the management of all schools . . . founded or to be founded by the Order in Colorado."[32] In planning for their future, sisters, both at the motherhouse and on the missions, relied on civil business practices, in conjunction with their community rule, to oversee their far-flung western investments.

A formal business organization proved to be but the first step in gaining recognition as effective western workers for sisters. Enforceable work contracts that complemented the acts of incorporation were critical for sisters in the field. Without them, missioned sisters stumbled along in dangerous or unjust work environments.

For example, in 1869, a year after they incorporated, the Sisters of Charity of Leavenworth, persuaded by the entreaties of the renowned Jesuit Pierre De Smet, considered sending six nuns to a new mission in Montana. The sisters finally accepted the assignment, expecting to support themselves by teaching. In return, they believed, a convent and assistance from priests awaited them in Helena. Throughout, De Smet's contractual arrangements had been a verbal blur, and the personable Jesuit not only kept details vague for the sisters but also neglected to notify his colleagues in Helena about the plan.[33] Only after his return to St. Louis, a journey of more than 250 miles, did De Smet write to the Montana Jesuits that the nuns were en route and would need a school and a convent.[34]

When the women arrived ahead of De Smet's letter, they discovered the priests stunned to see them, no rooms available for the school, and the convent residence nonexistent.[35] The priests moved into the church and the six sisters lived from October until January in the "rectory," an unheated shanty roofed with boards and sod. To raise capital, the women begged among the citizens and cooked hot meals for passing workmen, opening their school at the beginning of 1870.[36] While the nuns lived in this dank and snow-filled shack, scrambling for their lives, De Smet cheerily wrote to the Leavenworth motherhouse: "I hope the good sisters are all doing well."[37]

The predicament of the Sisters of Charity highlighted the turmoil that resulted when nuns relied on informal agreements sealed by a friendly smile and religious reassurances.[38] Not only did these situations stir chaos for the missioned sisters, but they also threw economic embarrassment into the mix. Three or four women with no shelter and less money had few choices in poorly developed western towns. Their training told them to accept the circumstances at hand and to cooperate with the local clergy, themselves baffled by the needs of women. For sisters, compliance produced uneven results, threatened the well-being of those at the mission, and derailed the congregation's plans for employment and expansion.

This problem intensified for nuns when mother superiors made only their councils privy to the business arrangements. The superiors, overseeing large congregations with many houses, frequently doled out funds to missions without explaining details to distant sisters.[39] The complicated chain of authority, privileged information, and poor communication were especially detrimental for sisters in the West, who had limited knowledge about their own wages. The arrangements tilted toward a two-tiered sisterhood—those with access to funds and financial plans and those divorced from the fiscal aspects of a congregation.

For their part, many pastors and priests for long years showed themselves notoriously willing to take advantage of sisters' work, withhold compensation, and overlook the desperate living conditions of the nuns. For example, in Oregon, the Sisters of the Holy Names, directed by their Canadian bishop to funnel their mission solely toward teaching, got snared into doing the wash for the Portland cathedral and rectory.[40] This labor, required by Bishop François Norbert Blanchet, included heating water; beating, scrubbing, and rinsing fabrics over washtubs; boiling starch; hand wringing all items; and ironing altar laces and cloths, as well as household linens and laundry for the rectory. In 1894 the mother provincial, thirty-five years after the first sisters from Canada accepted the duty, finally stopped the gratis work. She declined to continue the domestic services, noting the sisters had done the labor-intensive laundry for twenty-eight years without any payment. A recent stipend of $700, offered for the previous seven years, did not ameliorate her annoyance. She tartly recommended the nuns of another congregation to the cathedral priests and withdrew the Holy Names sisters from the grueling situation.[41]

Apparently, the inclination to use "courtesy" services from sisters ran deeply in the Blanchet family tree. In 1880, when the successor to Archbishop Blanchet, Charles John Seghers, visited the Sisters of the Holy Names in Jacksonville, Oregon, he noticed that the pastor relied on their labor "without remuneration." According to the sister superior, the new archbishop chided her for having "too much charity" and said "it is time our clergy . . . acknowledge your devotedness. . . . I shall ask the pastor how much he pays for his board."[42] Within days, that pastor, the nephew of Archbishop F. N. Blanchet, presented himself at the convent with $150, effusive thanks, and a promise to pay his future expenses.[43] Without the intervention from a ranking male authority, the Holy Names sisters, in isolated Jacksonville, could have expected to continue feeding their priest, washing his laundry, and preparing all church linens without payment.[44]

This gender-based, superior-driven control of cash encouraged dishonesty and financial sleight of hand at the missions. In some situations, financial inequity mingled with personal discrimination directed toward a congregation. In Ft. Madison, Iowa, the School Sisters of Notre Dame, after years of successful teaching, bumped up against the ill will of a new pastor, who openly conveyed disdain for the congregation. Even an 1865 visit from Mother Caroline, a major personality in western parochial education, did not settle the issues, and the superior departed feeling "things were not according to her taste."[45]

Three years later, the awkward conflict intensified when the pastor complained to the parish trustees about the mission nuns. He grumbled that they did not use all of their salary allotments, sending what they saved to their Milwaukee motherhouse; he asserted he "would not allow that any longer," for "what the sisters have left over they should always give to him."[46] Taking his grievances to the Sunday pulpit, the pastor announced to the assembly that "he is the number one head of the parish, without him nothing, not the least thing dare be done; all must bend themselves under him and fully have approval from him."[47]

When dealing with such autocratic persons, mother superiors employed as much persuasion as possible before raising formal objections or sending protests to the presiding bishop. Years of underpayments, however, had a way of institutionalizing themselves. Accordingly, they required Herculean efforts by women administrators to collect the deficits, an activity to which Mother Caroline lent her energies on more than one occasion.

For example, in 1858 the School Sisters of Notre Dame assumed responsibility for the school of the St. Joseph parish, a church supporting the rapidly growing number of German immigrants in St. Louis. By 1865 construction began on a new building for the overcrowded parish; later, in 1880, the facade was replaced, including the addition of twin towers for the church, which accommodated 2,600 people.[48] Despite the relative affluence suggested by such enhancements, it was not until twenty-six years after the SSND began teaching at St. Joseph that the current pastor agreed to a stated salary for the faculty. Previously, the nuns at the thriving St. Joseph parish lived on whatever the pastor declared he received in the school fund.

These School Sisters of Notre Dame, like their colleagues in Iowa, had a long history of struggling for their income from the rectory. At least until

1879, each pastor had required the sisters to organize needlework exhibitions twice a year, the proceeds of which went to the parish and none to the convent.[49] The preparation of the fancy sewing represented an increase of work but not of income for the convent and created a burden for the sisters, one of whom remarked: "We entertained the fond hope that this would no longer be expected."[50]

During an 1884 visit to address the compensation matter, Mother Caroline, threatening to withdraw her congregation, stipulated that the sisters could no longer survive on the pittance and insisted each missioned sister would receive an annual salary of $300. Caroline agreed that the pastor should continue to collect the student book money, which he promised to divide evenly between parish and convent. Given the long-standing coercion to supply items for the church bazaars, the lack of payment for the needlework, and the secretive school-fund records, it must have seemed doubtful that these nuns could expect a fair share of the book money, the total of which was likely to remain a mystery.

In St. Cloud, Minnesota, Benedictine sisters contended with similar issues. In 1884 the Benedictines petitioned for St. Benedict's Orphanage to be incorporated under state law, a move intended to steady the struggling home and give the sisters a stronger hand in its finances. In response to pleas from families of German railroading and freighting laborers, the Benedictines, a St. Cloud presence for twenty years, had informally run the orphanage since the mid-1870s. Finally, with seven children living in their private space, the Benedictine nuns decided to make the orphanage an official agency of their congregation and began the application for incorporation.[51]

Despite their reputation for service on behalf of St. Cloud workers, the nuns found stabilizing the income to be frustrating. Their funding sources—surviving parents, diocesan contributions, and begging tours by the nuns—never adequately met the orphanage expenses. Only the nuns' house-to-house supplications produced income. The other contributors sent their payments sporadically, with poor parents inevitably falling on yet harder times and the diocese routinely delinquent on its commitments.[52]

In 1894 Otto Zardetti, the bishop of St. Cloud, a patrician-minded European conservative who argued more than once with the Benedictine women, ordered the orphanage relinquished to a congregation of destitute Franciscan sisters.[53] Zardetti, who rarely explained himself, justified his decision by saying the new caregivers for the asylum "needed an activity" but lacked teaching credentials for America.[54] Otto Zardetti congratulated himself for his management of these nearly collapsed Franciscans of the Immaculate Conception, dragooned by him into becoming a diocesan institute over which, unlike the Benedictines, he could exercise ecclesiastical control.[55] Pointing out that as he wanted a *"regular Orphan asylum* for the diocese, I entered with them into a very favorable contract according to which they will for 25 *years* provide *for all the orphans."* Zardetti looked forward to a future where the Franciscans, in return for their exhausting and long-term work, could claim a diocesan collection but once a year and would receive only $2,000 toward construction of their new orphanage—to be named St. Otto's, no doubt another factor in the bishop's satisfaction.[56] These beneficial monetary conditions and guarantees for two decades of work for all diocesan waifs must have more than satisfied Zardetti's desire to oversee a "regular orphan asylum" as well as reduce the Benedictine presence in his diocese.

As for the Benedictine women, a sour relationship with the bishop worsened when the Swiss-born Zardetti, rumored among the nuns as determined to break the local power of the German Benedictines, refused to pay the diocesan account due the orphanage.[57] With little grace, Zardetti sent the Benedictines $300 for their care of the St. Cloud orphans. As for the balance, Zardetti, who returned to Europe for a post in Bucharest, suggested that Mother Aloysia might ask for three or four hundred more dollars at a "more prosperous time" in the diocese's fortunes, a request unlikely to be satisfied but no longer his concern.

In this era of work exploitation, clergy privilege and power, and restricted access to cash, well-drawn contracts became increasingly important to nuns. They had only to review the litany of work abuses for congregations around the West to realize that missioned sisters needed employment protection: in 1864 Sisters of Loretto in New Mexico lived on bread and beans in a convent memorable for the rain that leaked through the walls and roof; in 1867 the Oregon bishop, looking to reduce his debt, pressured Sisters of the Holy Names to conduct a begging tour for his accounts through the Idaho gold fields; in 1875 a Missouri pastor insisted that each day his noon meal be cooked in the rectory, a lengthy distance from the parish school, so one teaching nun made the trek, prepared the hot food, and carried the priest's leftovers back to the convent as dinner for the sisters; in 1881 a pastor in California installed four Dominican sisters in a vacated county courthouse surrounded by tall weeds and furnished with a table and an old sofa; in 1884 a priest at Baker City, Oregon, launched an inflammatory regional campaign against a principal who refused to change her school's curriculum without permission from her mother provincial; in 1885 Sisters of Divine Providence in Texas, with only a one-room shack and no chaplain for months, taught under a tree draped with a wagon cloth and moss to block the sun; the Sisters of Charity of the BVM closed one Iowa mission because the pastor added on church cleaning and another because of a refusal to improve an unheated, dilapidated convent; in Kansas, the Adorers of the Blood of Christ relied on neighbors to transport them by wagon ten miles to the parish for mass, while the Ursulines received $71.55, a portion of the salary due them, after their pastor argued over contract stipulations and claimed "reverses"; in 1900 an Oregon priest "suggested" that sisters organize a "paying entertainment" for "his personal benefit"; in 1910 two Mercy sisters arrived in Kalispell, Montana, to reopen an abandoned hospital, but the cavernous, drafty building had neither water nor electricity; at the start of the twentieth century, all School Sisters of Notre Dame were forbidden to prepare or conduct parish entertainments, the mother superior writing to pastors: "We beg you not to be difficult in these matters."[58]

By 1920 the bitter, often humiliating earlier years led congregation leaders to insist on explicit terms for sisters working in the West. Gone were the days when superiors assumed missions came with decent circumstances, as had the Sisters of the Incarnate Word who in 1888 wrote to a Texas pastor: "With regard to furnishing the house . . . whatever you choose and arrange will be pleasing."[59] Guided by earlier debacles, sisters backed off from such assumptions and revamped the contracts that represented their livelihood, showing they had learned what could happen at remote western missions.

In Pennsylvania, the Sisters of St. Francis—led by Mother Kilian, who first worked in Oregon and knew about shortcomings at western missions—endorsed a twelve-point contract for their missionaries, who had been working in the parish since 1912.[60] The Franciscans consented to supply no fewer than four nuns, including one for the domestic department. The remaining eleven stipulations addressed conditions required of Tacoma, each point reflecting the nuns' determination to prevent sisters from becoming the common laborers for a parish while compensation remained negligible or nonexistent.

To secure the work of the Franciscan sisters, the Washington parish accepted the following conditions: each nun, including the domestic sister, would receive a salary of $250 a year, the salaries due each month to the local superior and to be monies independent of any other endeavors by the sisters; the nuns would live in a rent-free, furnished convent, including specific kitchen, parlor, recreation, and bedroom facilities with light, fuel, and water provisions detailed; the Franciscan superior refused to supply an

Mother Kilian—here pictured with a Wyoming Native couple employed by the entertainment industry—led the eastern Sisters of St. Francis of Philadelphia, drawing on her decades-long experience at western missions to pursue expansion while protecting the rights of missioned nuns.
(Courtesy Sisters of St. Francis of Philadelphia, Aston, Pa.)

organist for public worship services; the pedagogy of the school, especially textbook selection, remained the domain of the sister principal; the faculty rejected teaching boys over fourteen or conducting a night school; the sisters organized only one school entertainment per year, to be held during day hours; sisters declined to supply items for a bazaar table or participate in public festivals; the sisters expected access to regular religious services without "inconvenient journeys"; the sisters required four months' written notice before dismissal and would grant the same if leaving the mission by their own choice; and the right to transfer sisters inside the mission or to another was reserved for the mother general and her council.[61]

This contract addressed in clear terms all the problem areas of the previous six decades of western work for nuns of all congregations. Since the middle of the nineteenth century, repeatedly, and despite promises and agreements, male administrators denied nuns a reasonable income, assigned them to unfit residences without access to religious rituals, ignored the basics of a decent diet, increased mission labors but not salaries, and violated community rule. In these lopsided church negotiations, contentious pastors and careless bishops inadvertently sharpened the business wit of sisters.[62] Over several years, the nuns at a motherhouse refined their contracts with church agencies, learning from earlier disasters, strengthening their demands, improving their compensation, avoiding pitfalls and arguments, and preparing missioned sisters more fully for life in the American West.

The lessons of those battles honed the skills of sisters and readied them for drafting more successful legal agreements in commercial and government spheres. Here, they were able to cast off the disadvantage of "nun versus priest" that dogged them through the West. In the secular community, sisters entered work areas that promised steadier income for the congregation—but also a new set of problems, as they dealt with non-Catholic organizations.

For example, since their hospital work during the Civil War, the Sisters of Charity of Leavenworth had shown themselves equally willing to nurse the poor or the prosperous, resulting in numerous health-care requests from emerging western business regions.[63] By 1870 the sisters were in Helena, Montana, where they added a small hospital to their school efforts. The call for additional beds continually rose, although the sisters' treasury did not.[64] To halt their deficits, the sisters augmented their income through agreements to care for the indigent sick from three different counties. A contract to house mentally ill patients at the hospital increased the sisters' publicly generated income again and made available another service the Montana Territory could not yet provide.

Although their nursing was generally appreciated in the area, the sisters ran into difficulties over hospital admission policies. County officers argued that only the indigent with written permits should be treated, while the sisters preferred to accept any who sought assistance. The dispute over who had authority to admit patients irked the county, which feared it paid for many more sick people than enumerated in the original contract. At least one county physician entered the fray, declaring the sisters' care more pious than medical, an attack the nuns found particularly offensive.[65] Eventually, the contracts for the indigent and the mentally ill were withdrawn, and dependency on the sisters' hospital shifted to public agencies. Criticisms about professionalism may have stung the sisters, but they served as a catalyst, and within a few years, congregations throughout the West pushed to upgrade their efforts in primitive work environments.

Despite the county problems, by now the Sisters of Charity had a firmer western footing and better strategies for building resources. They began to understand that by melding public contracts with private corporations, the congregation could diversify and stabilize income. Such a move could carry the congregation away from the economic margins and constant financial uncertainty. Acting on this thinking, in 1880 the Sisters of Charity simply renovated the old county hospital in Helena and reopened the building as St. Jerome's Orphan Asylum, which they operated through private donations.[66]

In this manner, nuns looked to multilayered sources of income. No longer did they rely on one parish contract or one county agreement to keep congregation operations solvent. Rather, they exploited all available business connections to produce the operating capital and marketing accounts they needed. Many lines of funding not only kept existing missions functioning but also gave ballast to plans for congregational expansion.

Cooperating with Western Industry

Nuns also partnered with entrepreneurial ventures that brought modern industrial development to many western regions. Sisters worked with and in the quintessential western industry—the railroads—to strengthen their finances. As the spiderlike network of tracks crept across every geographic area of the West, congregations of nuns made their health-care services available for workers through contracts with the railroad companies. The Union Pacific; Montana Central; Anaconda, Butte & Pacific; Missouri, Kansas & Texas; Missouri Pacific; Denver and Colorado; Texas Pacific; Santa Fe; and Great Northern were only some of the lines to negotiate with sisters for railroad hospitals.[67] The railroad company often constructed the first building for the facility, supplied medical and surgical supplies, and paid a flat daily rate to the sisters for each railroad patient or charged workers a small monthly insurance fee. The sisters, who did all the nursing, food preparation, household cleaning, and property maintenance, guaranteed hospital admission to those injured on the cars and in the yards.[68] With these contracts, sisters kept annual expenses stable and typically admitted 300 to 500 patients for treatment per year.[69]

There were ancillary benefits that came from business dealings with railroads. One type of agreement could lead sisters into another area of economic opportunity. In the 1890s, the Sisters of the Good Shepherd at St. Paul, Minnesota, sinking under a debt of nearly $50,000 and limited by the rules of their congregation in their public work choices, found relief in the Great Northern and Pacific Railroad of James J. Hill. Not only did Hill take over the note due on the convent, but he also supplied the means for the Good Shepherd sisters to make regular payments on the debt. Hill hired the convent to do the washing for the workers of the Great Northern, each week delivering wagons heaped with soiled linens to the sisters' laundry building, an arrangement that brought income to help pay the heavy debt and employment for the young women assigned by the courts to the sisters' care.[70] The Sisters of the Good Shepherd, despite enclosure rules, attached themselves to the railroad experiments of other congregations who had pursued the enthusiasm of companies for business arrangements with nuns.

Railroads energized the corporate industrial transformation of the American West, and sisters expressed their appreciation for the diverse possibilities the completion of a line, a productive mine, or aggressive lumbering meant for them and the region around them.[71] In 1878 the Sisters of St. Joseph agreed to operate a hospital for miners in Prescott, Arizona. During slow stretches in ore extraction, as admissions dropped, the sisters used the hospital space for a school for local families. In 1880 the same congregation opened a miners' hospital in Georgetown, Colorado, but branched out to the surrounding towns of Silver Plume and Lawson, advertising care for these communities' injured at St. Joseph's Hospital. The miners supported the facility through a subscription of fifty cents a month, available because company owners underwrote the hospital with a sizeable donation, by which the nuns guaranteed hospital beds or medical care at employees' homes. Miners without the company-backed plan paid an annual fee of ten dollars for health insurance. A third category for those without any insurance asked for eight dollars a week for hospital services, with additional payment to the doctor.[72]

The vigorous mining in Colorado brought other congregations with nurses into the region. In 1882 the Sisters of Mercy opened Mercy Hospital of San Juan at Durango. The nuns drew money from several sources, not hesitating to ask the mine owners for large donations. They, too, used a subscription service, charging a dollar a month for a health-insurance card an injured or sick worker produced when in need of treatment. In 1887 the Mercy sisters used the same plan for a hospital in Ouray, Colorado, where they built a two-story facility with sun porches. The sisters broadcast the name of their hospital by carrying medical care into several small mining camps in the surrounding mountains, asking for contributions as they nursed. In 1894, even before the arrival of the railroad, the Sisters of Mercy opened another miners' hospital in Cripple Creek, Colorado. Within two years, the nuns were treating more than 300 patients annually, which led them to build a larger, more modern facility, convincing local businessmen to furnish the patient rooms.[73]

Every undertaking was not a financial success for congregations, for as with any business venture, risks often outweighed potential returns. In the nineteenth-century West, proximity to industrial districts meant everything; the sisters' fortunes rose and fell along with those of railroading and mining. By 1886, with ore production in decline, admissions to the Prescott, Arizona, hospital of the Sisters of St. Joseph had stagnated. With just one visit to the site, the supervising bishop determined that the hospital had outlived its usefulness and proclaimed his preference for a school in Prescott, commenting: "The best opportunities are often lost here in this country by inopportune delay."[74] The sisters understood the lack of "suggestion" in the bishop's July letter, immediately converting the miners' hospital into a boarding academy that opened in September.

Business competition also played a role in the outcomes of the sisters' work contracts. Over nearly two decades, Mary Judge, the Catholic widow of a successful mine owner, hoped to establish a retirement home for elderly miners in Salt Lake City, Utah. The local bishop, Lawrence Scanlan, encouraged Judge, aided her with financial investments, convinced her to broaden the design to be a full medical-service facility, and secured a hospital staff, lobbying a longtime and well-to-do friend to bring her Sisters of Mercy to Salt Lake City.[75]

The plans dragged along for several years, complicated by the murkiness of the hospital mission, the slowness of construction, the fragility of the Mercy foundation, and Bishop Scanlan's changing moods. Matters were further confused because in 1875, Scanlan had recruited the Sisters of the Holy Cross from Indiana to open a Salt Lake City school and hospital. The Holy Cross sisters made an impressive show of their endeavor—not the easiest accomplishment inside the heartland of the Church of Jesus Christ of Latter-day Saints—launching in the same year the prestigious St. Mary's Academy, attended largely by Mormon children, and Holy Cross Hospital, operated with the customary laborer subscription services. With crucial support from the dominant culture of Salt Lake City, the Holy Cross sisters branched out to other industrial Utah towns, notably in 1887 to Ogden, where they signed a hospital contract with the Union Pacific Railroad.[76] Scanlan, however, like Bishop Otto Zardetti with the Benedictines in St. Cloud, indulged in rancor against the flourishing Holy Cross sisters and apparently chafed before the independence of a congregation outside his direct diocesan control. Perhaps Scanlan thought the Mercy sisters he invited to Salt Lake City would manage a hospital that he could administer more fully, so he could distance diocesan institutions from the Indiana-based Holy Cross sisters.

Against this background of Holy Cross prominence, the few Mercy sisters had slim prospects for their hospital, always burdened as it was with cultural, administrative, and personnel problems. The seriously ill mother superior funneled her own family wealth into the facility, trying to eliminate its many flaws. She appeared to have gained momentum for the hospital, but after brief railroad patronage, physicians and patients swung back to the better-managed operation of the Sisters of the Holy Cross. The Mercy sisters struggled along for five years, but the initial endowment from the widow Judge could not counter the deteriorating health of the mother superior, the complications of solidifying a new Mercy foundation, the defection of the bishop who returned to the Sisters of the Holy Cross for medical care, and the competition with a better-positioned congregation running a quality medical facility and a well-regarded academy. In 1916 the small band of Mercy sisters, decimated by death, illness, church politics, and poverty, closed the Salt Lake City hospital and relocated to Pocatello, Idaho.[77]

Thus, sisters and nuns for good and for ill immersed themselves in the industries most commonly identified as those that recast the rural West as a region of capitalist venture. As ancillary participants, sisters made a significant contribution to the impact of these businesses on a changing West—impacts that meant work for western newcomers but also upheaval and destruction of every part of the western environment. In this multi-faceted turbulence, the early hospitals undergirded railroading, mining, and logging, supporting companies as they pushed deeper into the remotest West. At the same time, the hospitals, part of the corporate invasion, introduced structured medical care—particularly after industrial accidents—for workers.

Sisters thus promoted regional commercial growth, molded some parts of the alterations of the western environment, and established partnerships with company owners, even as they focused on social-service institutions, early forms of health insurance, and medical attention for western workers. Alert to the income potential of an insurance plan, nuns enlarged these programs independent of company sponsorship, such as the Benedictine sisters in Arkansas who toured the logging camps, selling their own nine-dollar "hospital ticket," good for one year of care.[78] As business managers, nuns valued cooperative relationships at the public level, saw opportunity in the commercial growth of the West, and seized on congregational economic initiative for themselves.

As women, they added an off-type gender component to western industrialism, one that gave them a dual role as administrative agents for management and as care providers of workers. At the same time, having experience at circumventing male authority, nuns did not permit regulations of governments and businesses to create barriers to their service, finding ways to bind their charitable interests to their paid labor and coercing owners to upgrade philanthropic efforts.[79] As western forces of capitalism advanced, sisters exulted in knowing that "our city has a grand display of state and world industries. . . . [And] we, too, have contributed our share."[80]

Public Blackboards and Chalk

Nothing spoke to common visions of Catholic sisterhoods more than the parochial school system. Catholics and non-Catholics alike viewed parish schools as undisputed nun territory, where women in religious habits ruled; by the mid-nineteenth century, the hierarchy vociferously insisted that every church build its own classrooms for general education, increasing the call for teaching nuns. Citizens agreed that here, beneath the gaze of a church spire, nuns supervised Catholic education and Catholic children. Further, it appeared that in this single arena, sisters worked for religious hegemony, wielded unchallenged authority, and laid their brand of instruction and faith before youngsters of every background.

Like all simplistic explanations, this skewed notion overlooked the intensely complicated way that teaching sisterhoods interacted with and worked for the community at large. Just as they exploited corporate venues, nuns saw the merit in diversifying their teaching choices and professional exposure. Their little-understood arrangements with civil officials offered employment opportunities outside the obvious parish school provenance, significantly broadening the teaching careers of Catholic sisters and adding a nonreligious dimension to their western lives. In many rural areas, sisters, literally stepping beyond their church-sponsored parochial education system, earned income with public school districts hampered by a shortage of teachers and salary monies.

These arrangements required sisters to qualify for a certificate through the same examination given to public schoolteachers. In the nineteenth century, some counties considered one certified teacher among the sisters adequate for a district contract.[81] The certificates were county specific, so passage of the examination in one district did not permit sisters to teach in another. In Texas, the Sisters of the Divine Providence for forty years operated dozens of these schools, each teacher earning between thirty and seventy-five dollars a month, depending on the grade of the certificate.[82] The county limited the school year, and consequently the sisters' salary, to four months rather than ten. After depletion of county funds, the parish school often rebounded, filling out the remainder of the academic calendar. Those parents who did not withdraw their children for seasonal farm chores were obligated from fifty cents to a dollar a month for each family scholar, bringing the nuns' annual salary to a total that did not compromise their vow of poverty.[83]

Several variations on these "free public schools," attended mainly by white or Mexican children, existed around the West; contracts for the education of Native Americans occurred under a different government umbrella. The county system, for example, led the Sisters of Loretto to staff their own academies as well as public schools in Bernalillo and Santa Fe, New Mexico. After more than thirty years in St. Paul, Oregon, the Sisters of the Holy Names accepted a public school in addition to their private academy, operative since 1861. In 1891 the Dominicans signed a public school contract in Faribault, Minnesota. With these contracts came income for the congregation as well as other financial assistance. For example, the Faribault school board furnished blackboards and the geography and social-studies books for the Dominicans, a more political than generous gesture—a move to ensure that Catholic texts stayed out of the classroom.[84]

Association with the public schools offered an obvious way for sisters, many from teaching congregations, to earn crucial income and address the educational needs of isolated western communities. The boards leased the classrooms from the parish during school hours, and it was only then that sisters came under the authority of the local district. Inevitably, however, the mixing of secular and religious education led to differences, especially in areas with Protestant families, some of whom expressed uneasiness about sending their children to a parish school named for a Catholic saint. One school board took a pointed stand after examining the sisters' credentials and textbooks, announcing to the convent superior: "Mother, we don't want a novitiate here!"[85]

They insisted the sisters conduct religious instruction only before or after regular school hours and omit classroom prayer, but they suspected these restraints were ignored.[86] Nuns grieved that citizens—whether out of differing religious persuasion, anti-Vatican sentiment, or concerns about separation of church and state—demanded the removal from classrooms of crucifixes and religious pictures, educational fixtures for Catholic sisters.[87]

Even armed with the information of predecessors, some missioned sisters could not conquer the school tensions between Catholics and Protestants. In 1902, eleven years after the Catholic parish began elementary classes, the School Sisters of Notre Dame followed Benedictines and Sisters of Divine Providence to Gainesville, Texas, where an excellent public-education system was in place.[88] Perhaps that well-functioning district explained why citizens remained "opposed and bitter" to the Catholic nuns, although when the parish school opened, more than half of the thirty-two students were Protestants.[89]

Ultimately, in many western areas, powerful emotions surfaced over the right of Catholic sisters to wear their religious habit while teaching in publicly subsidized schools.[90] Despite these conflicts with congregational religious goals and the increasingly hurt feelings of the nuns as restrictive public laws evolved over several decades, the employment of sisters by county school boards delivered basic education to remote, underpopulated western areas, prodded sisters to upgrade teaching credentials to meet the county standard, and deposited important income in convent treasuries.

Making Money inside the Convent

Sisters directed intense efforts toward the economic gain to be realized from within their own organizations. To that end, they geared their convent lives toward the paying talents of individual members and permanent frugality by everyone to build congregational coffers.

Congregations excelled at identifying the moneymaking abilities of individual members and exploiting those talents for the good of the congregation. Many mission reports sent to the congregation's general chapter might have duplicated the one that laid out a stark reality: "The temporal resources come from the sisters' salaries."[91] In the western missions, where three or four sisters earned meager dollars, every convent member used her personal abilities to supplement the small group salary earned by the work contract.

Among teaching congregations, no sister on the faculty was of greater importance for adding to the financial accounts than the music teacher. Accomplishment on an instrument or in voice meshed with convent rituals of prayer and song, making nuns attentive to music in many forms. This translated well into secular society, where in the last half of the nineteenth century, training in graciousness, defined by "ladylike" arts, focused on music, needlework, and foreign-language fluency.[92] Even in rural North Dakota, a superior explained to the motherhouse in France: "To complete the cycle of studies, we must add a music department to satisfy the demand. . . . Everywhere, up and down, in rooms and lobbies, pianos and violins are never silent. From morning till night, teachers have their ears filled with melody."[93]

Likewise, from the early days of St. Clara's Academy, operated by the Dominican sisters at Sinsinawa, the catalog advertised the availability of music instruction. Beyond the basic charges of annual tuition of $175 with a $12 fee for washing and $3 for bedding, the nuns highlighted the elective subjects of lessons in guitar, piano, or harp for $24, $48, and $80 per year, respectively. Voice and cultivation of voice were available for quarter fees of $5 and $10. By the 1880s, St. Clara's Academy added zither, organ, and violin instruction as more choices for students and as additional income for the motherhouse.[94]

As the Dominicans spread into mission schools, they took their music teaching with them. When sisters wrote of those missions, success or failure was often explained in the numbers taking private music classes. In Iowa, the Dominican annalist at one struggling school noted that the music students did not exceed fifteen, while at another, the annalist welcomed the arrival of Sister Mary James, who would "take charge of music."[95] These Dominicans had been in Denver less than a year when a fire caused them to suspend their parish school for several weeks. The sisters regrouped, using the time to collect alms, but the failing health of the music teacher limited the income to be made from private lessons. The dying sister returned to the motherhouse, and with her went the music

In Iowa, a Dominican sister, standing amid her musical instruments, gave lessons before and after school hours to earn convent income, promote the pedagogical standards of the congregation, and meet parental expectations that daughters acquire voice training and performance proficiency. (Courtesy Dominican Sisters of Sinsinawa, Wisc.)

department, the annalist shortly remarking that "the income was small."[96] In Missouri, when the music class closed, the financial difficulties of the school prompted the Dominicans to "pack their belongings." When the bishop objected to the closure, the sisters returned, but they remembered "much difficulty was felt at this time, . . . owing to the fact of having no music teacher."[97]

Musical instruments that belonged to the nuns were critical for even the poorest convent. In 1884 four Ursulines, the first nuns to settle in Miles City, Montana, wrote to their Toledo motherhouse: "It would do us a great deal of good if we had a piano." They had combed the town for one to rent by the month, as they found that "everyone wants to hear the sisters sing and play."[98] By March the sisters in Ohio succeeded in shipping a piano and an organ to Miles City, causing the Montana superior to enthuse: "You should have seen the embrace the piano received!!!" Now fortified with two basic instruments, the Montana Ursulines looked to brighter income prospects, as they were certain that "now . . . we will be able to get some good music pupils."[99]

Other congregations relied on their music teachers in a similar fashion, later remembering that these instructors generated much-appreciated income. Between 1871 and 1881, the Sisters of St. Joseph in St. Paul, Minnesota, established three new convents, each equipped with departments for vocal and instrumental classes. This emphasis on music led the St. Joseph sisters to a series of summer institutes, where they studied the newest methods for piano and violin instruction. Fretted instruments—mandolin, guitar, and zither—required extra preparation, as the sisters strove for proficiency that would qualify them as instructors and, consequently, income producers for the convent.[100]

When the Sisters of Charity of the BVM opened a school in Fort Dodge, Iowa, they had three teachers, one housekeeper, and a music teacher. The school enrolled 112 students, twenty-nine of whom became music pupils paying $10 a quarter for twenty-four lessons and "providing a principal source of income for the sisters."[101] For the music teacher, the responsibility to shore up convent income often meant longer teaching hours than the other faculty, with lessons for children taking the hours before and after school, as well as through the dinner hour.[102] Even tightfisted pastors recognized the income value, one writing to Ursulines in Kansas "The sister that teaches music makes what she can out of it."[103]

Recognizing the importance of music, the Servants of Mary had stipulated in one parish contract that "sisters turn over to the treasury all moneys received from school or private lessons" and were pleased that "the number of pupils for music promises to double, provided the same teacher remains—at least until the class is well established." This plan gave the congregation cause for fiscal cheer, for in the previous year, the "good teacher of music" brought in sufficient tuition to support the mission community "without touching the salary which could be entirely devoted to paying off the debt" on the motherhouse.[104] Aware of the importance of a healthy return from music instruction, in 1911 an Iowa band of the Servants of Mary entered a contest at a local store and won the grand prize of a piano—adding a touch of flair to a program they offered for fifty students.[105]

While the music teachers produced steady income, other sisters did their share, individually and collectively. In one year, twenty-seven Franciscan missions shipped to the motherhouse earnings from crafts and fancywork for a total of $1,090.99—the congregation treasurer carefully recording the highest amount of $244 and the lowest of $.25.[106] In the motherhouse of these Franciscans, the nearly fifty sisters passed many hours each day filling orders for needlework, fine embroidery, rosaries, and flowers. During their only daily recreation, the nuns assembled in the stitching room, where, working in pairs, they applied their talents to piano covers, religious items, and footstools, one for a customer who requested an intricate white beaver design in satin stitch.

Nobody was excused, regardless of position in the community. An older sister and candidates worked through the day, with the classroom teachers joining them after school dismissal. The sister in charge of the labor-intensive, time-consuming laundry also squeezed in time for the sought-after needlework. Even one sister described as "sickly" was "active in embroidery as much as her strength allows." This unwell nun was shortly joined by Sister Mechtilidis, removed from hospital duty because of ill health but expected to spend her days in the stitching room. Sister Mechtilidis, sick or not, arrived in time to assist with the extra fancywork orders submitted by families with children preparing for first communion.[107]

In some congregations, the meticulous and artistic needlework that sisters produced emerged as more than supplemental income. For example, the Sisters of the Precious Blood of O'Fallon settled in Missouri at a time when many congregations were competing for the available educational and hospital work. As they hunted teaching vacancies in the Catholic schools of Missouri and Nebraska, these German sisters, known for designing embroidered religious vestments of exceptional beauty, fell back on their knowledge of fabric for their initial support. Ultimately, the O'Fallon sisters added a favorable American reputation to their German one and developed a prosperous art department noted for its colorful silks, weblike laces, and delicate threads used in the elaborate vestment making.[108]

Using less-ornate needle skills, the Servants of Mary earned money by sewing shrouds for deceased parish members. For each death garment, they received two dollars and connected themselves more personally to the spiritual life of their neighbors. In one case, following the funeral, the widower presented the sisters with a gift of his wife's pump organ—the work of needle and thread boosting the income possibilities from the music teachers.[109]

Donations, such as the much-welcomed pump organ, became another means by which sisters added income to their convent treasuries. Given the widespread public social service that sisters contributed to communities, the needy women did not hesitate to appeal to the generosity of local citizens for support. In Virginia City, Nevada, where the Daughters of Charity ran the orphanage, the sisters used local newspapers to advertise their gratitude for favors. On occasion, the sisters published precise lists of donations, a way to highlight their needs and to prod the less giving to match the spirit of neighbors and business competitors. Fourteen sacks of potatoes, a dress pattern and some calico, two heavy cloaks, a little pig—the presenters of each found an elegantly phrased "thank you" in the *Territorial Enterprise* newspaper.

These messages carried an explicit reminder to all citizens of the sisters' most powerful weapon on behalf of the public: their assurance that the "prayers of the orphans will ascend on high for him and his that they may ever enjoy those blessings . . . beneficial to them in this life and assist in procuring for them above all the blessings and happiness of the world to come."[110] Who among Virginia City's citizenry, where life often came to a sudden and violent end, would not want to feel comforted by the sisters' promise of some assistance in the afterlife? Which business wanted to see a competitor act more generously toward the orphans and that generosity publicized for all to know? Use of the newspaper as a forum for the orphanage helped keep the work and the poverty of the Daughters of Charity before the public eye.

Donations may have served as an unreliable source of income, but they often brought in odd assortments of goods that helped the daily life of women running a variety of public institutions. Fruit and vegetables fed boarders but also improved the sisters' paltry table. Furniture for new convents, beds and mattresses for dormitories, landscaping of the convent grounds, five gallons of cider, pro bono legal services, medical equipment for a surgical suite, a wagon of firewood, the complete works of Dickens—all of these represented very real dollars the sisters would not have to spend. Priests, despite the shoddy employment contracts of some pastors, also gave regularly to congregations they befriended. Visiting a convent for a cornerstone dedication or an investiture of sisters, priests and bishops often bestowed some extra gift from their personal pocketbook—$100 for a new chapel, a religious statue for the convent, money for the electric bill.[111]

Finally, in the most destitute of situations, sisters turned to public begging to raise funds. This was another uneven amount of income, but it increased nuns' travel through western locations, exposing the women to many cultural circumstances—an experience some found exhilarating. Begging in mining and logging camps and among railroad workers became another way in which nuns interacted with the secular community and observed the conditions of western life.

For some sisters, however, begging assignments reeked of onerous and deflating characteristics. The sisters' bishop often imposed harsh conditions for granting the required begging permission letters, expecting a share of what the sisters collected. In 1867 the two Sisters of the Holy Names who left Portland for begging in Idaho had been required to do so

Members of the first congregation to the Pacific Northwest, these Canadian Sisters of Providence prepared for a possible begging tour, an experience that, depending on location, could subject nuns to extreme hardship and public hostility with only a small monetary return. (Courtesy Sisters of Providence, Sacred Heart Province, Seattle, Wash.)

by their archbishop, who then confiscated one half of their $648, collected on a trip so unpleasant that it was mentioned twice in the congregation's annals.[112] The Holy Names sisters may have been dispirited, but they were not surprised by the bishop's tax on their labor; Mother Joseph of the Sisters of Providence in Vancouver, a close confidante of the Sisters of the Holy Names, at least five years earlier had grumbled that Archbishop Blanchet claimed two-thirds of the money collected during her nuns' begging missions through his territory.[113]

Once on the road, many sisters met a local bishop who, displeased at the prospect of money drawn from his own strapped territory, denied nuns the right to canvass. In addition, sisters encountered unvarnished anti-Catholic hostility, and some sisters regarded the entire process as humiliating beyond the expectations of the vows of poverty and obedience.[114] One professed sister transferred to a Presentation convent in the East, saying of the hardships around Fargo in the Dakota Territory: "I could not bring myself to go on a begging tour."[115] In 1871 the mother superior of a debt-burdened Dominican convent assigned herself the begging mission in San Francisco and wrote about the discouraging effort: "We have been out all the time we could for the purpose . . . but [have collected] only a little over one hundred dollars in cash."[116]

With creativity, sisters explored many possible avenues for earning income, and each member of the community focused on the various efforts. That so many succeeded against the bleak odds of a convent that began with a nearly empty treasury spoke to the industriousness that attended the undertakings. A central ingredient that may account for the number of successful congregational narratives lay in the overall frugality of daily life practiced by nuns. This willingness, even eagerness, to live in simplicity reflected the poverty the women expected. Some appeared to prepare themselves in advance for the hardships of convent life. One woman recalled of her biological sister who died at the age of eighty after sixty-three years as a Daughter of Charity, "When our dear Johanna had made up her mind to enter your community, I noticed that she was using a nightgown made of gunny cloth and . . . slept on a hard board."[117] In support of the ideal of the poverty vow, nuns excelled at finding innovative ways to condition themselves for a lifetime of penuriousness.

In Oregon, Sisters of the Holy Names, "for the sake of economy," dared not "squander" their wood for a fire, so they huddled in two rooms with twenty-five boarders during a January freeze.[118] Franciscan Sisters of Perpetual Adoration at a rural mission used the natural resources around them, picking and canning fresh strawberries, plums, and raspberries and turning out batches of twenty-five to fifty quarts of fruit at a time, building their food storage for Native children. Other days, they baked pies and bread, using free time for making or mending clothes for the boarding students.[119] In California, a Dominican sister, who made her own religious clothing by piecing together the discarded habits of her colleagues, turned used envelopes inside out and reused them, and made "stationery" out of butcher's paper or old tissue.[120] In 1873 the Sisters of St. Mary limited their celebration of the mother superior's feast day to a "few verses and songs of congratulation."[121] In 1890 four Franciscan sisters at the Umatilla Reservation searched the barren countryside to gather straw to make into beds.[122] In 1912 a St. Louis Sister of Mercy listed the uncompensated jobs of twenty-five hospital nuns, calculating the savings in annual salaries, if paid to secular employees, at nearly $15,000.[123] A Sister of Divine Providence from Texas recalled sloshing to the train depot with rainwater gushing through her shoes. After she and the flowers she carried fell into the mud, her unsympathetic superior ordered her to retrieve the soggy, mud-drenched flowers, declaring: "Sister Barnabas, this is mission life!"[124]

That sister summarized the parsimonious nature of mission life well. For example, Mother Emily Power of the Sinsinawa Dominicans sent all in her congregation an exhortation that, because of debt, she "look[ed] to the missions for help," and she directed all the sisters to "be economical and restrict expenses in every way." Mother Emily continued: "If only five cents is saved each day for 365 days for a number of persons, how much would this add to the general fund?"[125] In Texas, Mother St. Pierre Cinquin, nervous about the financial implications of a priest's "request" to make decorative banners for a parish procession, ordered: "If . . . something [is] costly to furnish at our expense . . . we should not do so." She added that "the Blessed Virgin . . . knows our financial difficulties."[126] In Missouri, Mother Petra of the School Sisters of Notre Dame asked each sister to raise eight dollars by selling 1,000 bricks for a motherhouse expansion. With that a success, Mother Petra proposed that the nuns sell souvenir cards of the new building and chapel for ten cents each, a profit, she said, of nine cents per card for the congregation. Well acquainted with the callousness with which parish priests claimed a percentage of sisters' moneymaking, she cautioned" "If you think it more prudent . . . say nothing to your pastor."[127]

Mother superiors like Emily, Pierre, and Petra did not ask economy of only the rank-and-file members. Provincials and mother generals, too, practiced the scrimping they demanded of the mission sisters. Mary Frances Clarke of the Sisters of Charity of the BVM refused to replace her worn habit and was known among the congregation for using bits of paper and salvaging even the shortest thread.[128] Mother Caroline Friess of the School Sisters of Notre Dame often remarked, "Do we not all stand on the same platform?" She was encouraging her teaching nuns, who drafted their own maps and charts for the classrooms, used homemade blackboards, and cut pictures from donated pamphlets and magazines.[129] Sisters of Mercy who made their novitiate with Mother Katharine Drexel, herself a woman of great family wealth, remembered the heiress darning the edges of her dinner napkin.[130] Mother Madeline of the Sisters of St. Joseph introduced fiscal conservatism through a conventwide purchasing policy based on economy and durability, her nuns joking that previously, their serge habits wore out before the fabric bill had been paid.[131] Such anecdotes about superiors, whether actual or imagined, inspired those living rigorous days at the missions to sustain the financial goals of the congregation through extreme personal poverty.

Accordingly, it was this stark mission life that made financial stability a possibility. Those Servants of Mary who sent their entire annual salary of $4,300 toward the payment of the motherhouse debt had made careful use of the small monies that came into their mission. They reported an income of $547.95 from music instruction, another $93.80 from other private lessons, $356.28 from boarders' fees, $49 from their kindergarten, $5.27 from miscellaneous work, and interest on their bank account of $31.80. They added this to their starting balance of $259.60, plus $433.50 from the motherhouse for travels and a $2 donation, to show a total of $6,079.20. However, after subtracting salary income, the small convent was left with operating money of $1,779.20.[132] From this, depending on their parish contract, they paid convent operating costs and repairs, grocery bills, hired help, clothing, medical care, transportation, postage, and educational supplies. Perhaps as Mother Emily had suggested to her Dominicans, the Servants of Mary could find more ways to practice frugality, saving an extra nickel a day. Overall, it seemed that, year in and year out, they lived their mission life close to the bone, adding a significant dimension to the manner in which sisters took responsibility for their own financial support.

The Road to Fiscal Stability

Many sisters, as recent immigrants, identified and pursued various lines of funding, turning from their European homes in favor of their American foundations. The florins of a European benefactor simply could not sustain the dramatic proliferation and expansion of sisterhoods in America. As nuns weakened their links to the past, they did so with a clear view of the economic imperatives before them.

The sisters came to understand the power of congregational wealth in American society and its importance in giving them a measure of independence. They saw the way that solvency could loosen the grip of a male superior, leading the women toward greater autonomy in a hierarchal church. Through wrenching heartache and numerous hazards, they learned about the very real peril of placing their well-being—economic and otherwise—exclusively in the hands of male administrators. Looking about their new Catholic world, sisters had to acknowledge that no person or agency within the church intended to support and protect professed women in America.

The West, with its changing economy, demographic challenges, and human traumas, unfolded as the perfect location for shaping the economic fortunes of nuns, who seized the corporate opportunities that revamped an entire region. Pointing to the aid they could bring to upended western environments, the sisters capitalized on their abilities to offer unique, if often primitive, services in time of great urgency. They prepared themselves for economic self-determination by following the path that gave them legiti-

In this building, St. Mary's Hospital, the Daughters of Charity brought health care
to Virginia City, Nevada, where they also operated a school and an orphanage for
the isolated multinational mining community, much in need of social services.
(Courtesy Daughters of Charity, Los Altos, Calif.)

macy under American law and credibility within communities. Armed
with validation as legal entities, they courted secular communities through
public contracts that bolstered annual income for the congregation.

Energized by the possibilities for building solid institutions in the West,
the sisters welcomed donations of money and material goods, quick to re-
mind local citizens of the important, largely ecumenical work they performed. They exploited the talented within a sisterhood, such as the music
teacher, to earn mission salary; they encouraged the less gifted to reach
deep inside, find hidden abilities, and achieve. Busy schedules excused
none, including the sick; every sister expected to work hard at all times
for the congregation. In their most difficult financial times, nuns turned to

public begging, again employing the rhetoric of "community good" to appeal to donors. Above all, these sisters, as individuals and as congregations, lived by a code of frugality. Their decades of personal economic restraint created a culture within convents that made the saving of goods and money a way of life and was measured in the substantial growth of congregational bank accounts.

The accomplishment of these congregations rested in the way they pieced together functioning financial identities out of many segments, often doing so in the face of opposition from their own church. Developing negotiating abilities in the secular world, although sometimes discordant, improved associations inside church circles, as sisters framed a clearer sense of appropriate work conditions and fair remuneration. By accumulating income from several sources, congregations relied on multiple strategies for the construction of financial strength through economic diversity. For nuns, fiscal grounding handed them one more important lesson about survival in the American West. One thing was certain: nobody paid their way. The sisters and nuns earned their own living from Oregon to Texas, from Missouri to California, from Arizona to Montana.

*A religious must respect and
obey ecclesiastical authority to
deserve the name of "religious."*

—Generosa Callahan CDP,
*The History of the Sisters
of Divine Providence:
San Antonio, Texas* (1955)

Contests for Control

If size, change, and competition
marked the history of the American
West, so did these factors influence the
administration of the Catholic Church,
with its desire to lay its spiritual mark
over a large and diverse landscape. That
holy dominance included a large dose
of earthly rule and regulation for the
very missionaries hoisting the pope's
banner. Church bureaucrats, especially
through the Society for the Propagation
of the Faith, plotting a Catholic course
in America did so from the distance of
crowded European centers or within
the corridors of the Vatican and with
an authoritarian, sadly uninformed air.
Infrequently did these administrators,
who rarely set foot on North American

soil, grasp the magnitude of what they asked of church workers in the West.[1]

California, named a diocese after the withdrawal of the Mexican government and the 1849 discovery of gold, epitomized how size and competition collided with the traditions of convent women. In 1851 a Spanish Dominican priest, José Sadoc Alemany, accepted the new bishopric that stretched over upper and lower California, Nevada, a chunk of Utah, and parts of Arizona and Oregon, a pastoral area of more than 300,000 square miles.[2] It was an unrealistic assignment, but with a blossoming California economy, one Dominican observed, "Alemany will find many willing to go for the gold either of this or of the next world."[3]

Traveling from Europe to his American duties, the thirty-seven-year-old Alemany sensed finding those willing workers a task best not left to chance and charm. Among his companions, Alemany counted a brother priest, Francis Sadoc Vilarrasa, and several sisters, including a French nun and two postulants bound for a Dominican convent and boarding school in Somerset, Ohio. Vilarrasa, who for years opposed Alemany as a leader for the American Dominicans, was now attached as assistant to the California endeavor, a circumstance that did nothing to smother the rivalry between the two men or ease their vicelike demands on mission nuns.[4] Youthful, inexperienced prelate for America though he was, Alemany lost neither time nor pleasantries when it came to commands. His actions over the next several years routinely infuriated the Dominican men and posted a warning to women religious that bishops came with many faces, not all of them wreathed in friendship and empathy.

Bishops and Challenges

At Somerset, Alemany, fluent in French, ordered the nun to abandon her Ohio teaching plans and continue with him and Vilarrasa to California, where he directed she would establish a Dominican community of women.[5] Rounding out his scheme for Catholic teachers in California, Alemany "swapped" the two French-speaking postulants for American-born Dominicans, who after their novitiate were to relocate in California. Thus it occurred that a single nun, Mother Mary of the Cross Goemaere, arrived in San Francisco obedient to José Alemany, whose threefold authority over her emanated from his status as priest, bishop, and Dominican provincial in the United States.[6] Destitute, alone, hindered by language, and charged with a surprising administrative role, Mother Mary, then over forty, wrote that she "willingly" remained with Alemany, "thinking that by doing all that he told me I could not fail to do the Holy Will of God."[7]

Accordingly, when Alemany made his residence at Monterey, California, Mother Mary left San Francisco to follow the bishop, as did Father Vilarrasa and a few Dominican friars. In Monterey, Goemaere relied on donations from her French convent, opened a school, and accepted into the new Dominican foundation the aspirants that Alemany sent her way. By 1854 Mother Mary of the Cross, with her limited Spanish and English, managed a multicultural convent of ten—in addition to herself, the two American Dominicans from Ohio, one Mexican, and six Spanish nuns. Only Mother Mary spoke French.

When church authorities divided the California diocese between Monterey and San Francisco, Alemany relinquished the former and returned to the latter. The Dominican monks in Monterey, intent on remaining close to their confrere, recently promoted to archbishop, joined him in northern California. As the friars prepared to leave, Vilarrasa informed Mother Mary that her convent, operating under his supervision, had been transferred to Benicia, the former capital. Hastily, the nun, her Monterey patronage lost, rented a schooner, packed up the sisters, school materials, and furnishings, and set out on a costly voyage north along the Pacific coast, across San Francisco Bay, into San Pablo Bay, and through the Carquinez Strait to Benicia.

Starting from scratch, the nuns opened St. Catherine's Convent and Academy, situated on undesirable land and housed in a rough wooden structure so common to the early days of sisters in the West. The sisters commenced instruction in the European classics, fine arts, and needlework and began to stabilize, but Alemany raided the small faculty, seeking teachers for a parish in San Francisco. One "request" came upon the previous, and each time, the Dominican sisters depleted their convent and novitiate, even sending personnel for a boys' orphanage.

Although the Dominican nuns, given their California contributions and common congregational heritage, had reason to feel that they enjoyed a special place with Alemany, the archbishop did not limit his attention to their convent. Desperate for workers, he aggressively pursued other religious women for California. Often described as an "amiable" leader, Alemany resorted to nongentle, even callous tactics to corral religious teachers and nurses.

In the early 1850s, he privately negotiated with the superior of Notre Dame de Namur nuns in Oregon, offering California allurements if she withdrew her sisters from the jurisdiction of Archbishop François N. Blanchet. With the surreptitious arrangements—which blindsided the unsuspecting Blanchet—concluded, Alemany watched for Notre Dame de Namur reinforcements coming to San Francisco. Determined to intercept the sisters before they communicated with their motherhouse or Blanchet, Alemany boarded a small boat, crossing to a ship anchored in the bay. There, he staged a hearty welcome for the four nuns, blessing them and announcing to the stunned women that their travels to Oregon had ended, as he and Sister Loyola had transferred the Notre Dame foundation to California. Confident that the exhausted and foreign nuns had no way to oppose him, the archbishop personally escorted the women to his residence for dinner, later quartering them in the home of a local Catholic. Sequestered in a strange city, denied contact with the Oregon archbishop, and fearful they disobeyed their French mother general, the nuns, three days later, and despite their reservations, joined with the charismatic Sister Loyola.[8]

The archbishop further cut off the Oregon nuns, sending them fifty miles away to the less-prosperous San Jose, then a hamlet of about thirty Spanish-speaking people. In this unpromising quarter, the French nuns started with little. They began a long association with Italian Jesuit priests of Santa Clara College but lived in a hovel the sisters described as "materially in ruin" and that Alemany himself had earlier called "wretched."[9]

By 1860 a handful of the Daughters of Charity, Sisters of the Presentation, Mercy, and Notre Dame de Namur—their congregations each somewhat bullied to the missions—added to the Benicia Dominicans in the needy vineyards around San Francisco. Hailed as "kind" and "beloved," Archbishop Alemany was rather more the despot. By pressure and deception, he increased the size of his workforce, even threatening sisters with heavenly retribution if they obstructed his wishes.[10] Once nuns entered into his jurisdiction, he tightened his hand over them, placing them in remote California towns, bonding them to his administration through debt, and forbidding travel that would take a nun back to her birth country or original motherhouse.[11]

With plenty of religious distractions, the feisty Alemany did not want for entanglements in San Francisco's public life.[12] Still, he did not hesitate to take on more and engaged in an unpleasant, protracted feud with his former friends the Jesuits over property titles. His relationships inside the Dominican order and with Vilarrasa deteriorated, the rancor escalating until the friars complained to the Vatican: "Tyrannical have been these actions in the extreme."[13]

Perhaps these many pressures kept Alemany off center and ill-humored as woes piled onto the Benicia convent's already overloaded finances. The Dominican nuns, whose tuition from St. Catherine's could not reduce the debts caused by the new missions, defaulted on their notes, held by none other than Alemany.[14] The insouciant archbishop seemed disinclined to forgive the obligations. He appeared to forget that the nuns acquired the debts through his insistence they relocate, build a novitiate, establish an academy, expand their holdings, incur travel costs, and maintain faculties many miles from the Benicia motherhouse.

Given their years of cooperation, it must have startled the compliant sisterhood when in 1867 the archbishop invited Dominican sisters in Ireland to assume the financial notes of St. Catherine's. Implicit in his invitation was future control of Benicia for the Dublin Dominicans. The Irish Dominicans declined, but the California nuns, appalled by an assault on their congregation, argued for an extension while they worked to pay the interest on the loans.

Their reprieve was short-lived and their efforts to reduce the loans unsuccessful. In 1872 Alemany proposed to advertise widely that the congregation's property was available to any other female order willing to contract for the debts. This plan, endorsed by Father Vilarrasa of the Dominican men, also barred the admission of new postulants for the St. Catherine's community at Benicia and ordered a gradual absorption of the professed members into other area convents.

Thus, twenty years after Alemany pressured a single nun to put aside her teaching plans, assist him in establishing Catholic schools in California, and bring Dominican women to the state, the archbishop prepared to wrench away the property of the sisters and eliminate the very congregation he had insisted be opened.[15] In addition, disagreement swirled between the nuns and Alemany about past transactions. A bank statement intended to sort out the payment history included a column headed "the following monies the sisters claim to have paid the Archbishop, but they are not in the Archbishop's books," and a second column headed "the following items are found in the Archbishop's books to credit the sisters, but they are not found in the sisters' books."[16] If the archbishop's office had not recorded monies received but had placed hidden charges against the sisters' account, as this entry suggested possible, an amicable resolution seemed questionable. For the immediate future, the lopsided finances between the Dominican archbishop and the Dominican nuns represented an issue of poisonous disagreement.

With controversies rippling through many circles, in 1887 the leaders at Benicia, where completion of the railroad sucked away local prosperity, agreed that a motherhouse closer to the economic and cultural life of San Francisco better suited their interests. They moved to San Rafael, a more-accessible three miles to San Francisco, and initiated plans to branch into higher education. Well versed in archdiocesan politics, the unhappy finances of the past, and the creep of a bishop's control, the sisters protected the new operation by incorporating their College of the Rosary under the laws of the state of California.[17]

Mother Mary of the Cross, approaching eighty, remained at the St. Catherine's convent. She objected to moving the motherhouse and siphoning off the youngest and most active sisters to San Rafael; perhaps in reality, she did not desire greater proximity to the residence of any archbishop. Certainly, the former archbishop of San Francisco, José Alemany, with a capricious wave of authority, had sent her hither and yon on the American landscape.

In 1885 Alemany returned to Europe, his retirement enhanced by a purse of $18,000, a gift from clergy and citizens.[18] Alemany left behind the French nun whose life he frequently and impulsively altered. At her death in 1891, Mother Mary of the Cross—separated from her native country, biological family, and original religious congregation and never the recipient of diocesan title or a large monetary purse—had spent forty years accommodating Archbishop José Sadoc Alemany, Father Vilarrasa, and the male-dominated industry for which she worked in the American West.

To the north in Oregon, Francis N. Blanchet showed that other bishops also were willing to build a diocese by imposing on the individual and collective lives of nuns. Indeed, Blanchet must have been caught off guard by Alemany hijacking the Notre Dame sisters and rued a welcoming letter he had written years earlier in which he told the Dominican archbishop, "Allow me to offer my felicitations . . . at your happy arrival."[19] Blanchet, having lost the Sisters of Notre Dame de Namur to Alemany and California, did not want workers stolen away again. In 1859, when the Canadian Sisters of the Holy Names came to Oregon, Blanchet moved to block strikes on his personnel by brother bishops and looked to reenergize his vicariate with these nuns.

Blanchet watched closely the Portland sisters, directing them, contrary to their rule, to admit boys into their classrooms. He then insisted an Oregon City school formerly operated by the Notre Dame de Namur sisters be reopened. For the Holy Names, "one consideration was paramount—His Grace . . . wished it and it was impossible to refuse the request."[20]

Two ill-at-ease Holy Names sisters moved the fifteen miles and began classes for only six children, the real purpose of their presence in Oregon City surfacing quickly. Within weeks, the archbishop and his priests moved into the convent, adding their domestic service and the washing of church linens to the sisters' daily schedule. The two, in addition to teaching duties and spiritual obligations, started laundry by four in the morning and prepared three meals each day, using their evening recreation hour to wash the pots and dishes. As the priests continued their meal during the kitchen cleanup, the archbishop ordered that silence for meditation be maintained in the house. When one sister objected that by congregational rule, this was the women's recreation hour—one that, with its dirty crockery, few would have described as frivolous—the archbishop ordered the outspoken nun to keep silence and listen to the other sister talk.[21] Two years later, the archbishop, disgusted with the black-market economy and disastrous flooding in Oregon City, returned to Portland, allowing the relieved sisters to close their miserable house, escape his daily mandates, and return to their Holy Names convent.[22]

Likewise, in 1881 in the Dakota Territory, Bishop Martin Marty adopted a less-than-kind attitude toward nuns, initially advising a priest to encourage Presentation sisters to move to Deadwood, saying, "I would have no objection to your corresponding with Mother John Hughes . . . on the subject."[23] But almost immediately, Bishop Marty, annoyed by Mother Hughes's independence, railed against her and regretted the $600 he expended for the trip to Deadwood, a placement the nun refused due to the haphazard spiritual arrangements for the convent.[24]

While it may not have comforted Mother John Hughes, others endured troubles with Bishop Marty. The hard-charging bishop meddled freely in the internal affairs of religious congregations, precipitously removing the Benedictine superior at a Yankton convent and dissolving a Mercy community in the same town.[25] Indifferent to the havoc he wrought inside convents, Marty indulged in considerable self-promotion, once demurring that he did "not wish to put a letter in the papers" himself, but hoped someone would write to the editor "that they found Bp. Marty at Standing Rock doing all in his power to recommend the project."[26]

The church power by which a bishop could dismiss a nun from office within her congregation or disband a community of sisters represented a substantial threat to women religious, who would be left adrift in every way. Institutional legitimacy, access to church sacraments, and day-to-day survival rested on episcopal approval. Bishops built public stature in a secular community and held church authority in a diocese, making sure that sisters, with their lives modeled on cloister privacy, recognized the very real dangers of opposition.

In Texas in 1886, four priests, confident of masculine supremacy in church politics, objected to the manner in which Mother St. Andrew Feltin managed the schools of the Congregation of Divine Providence. Leveling manufactured charges of gossip and slander, they, undoubtedly piqued because Mother St. Andrew stood up to them, took their complaints directly to Bishop John C. Néraz. The four demanded a new mother superior, asked greater control in parish schools, and—with the sweep of a punitive brush—refused to hear confessions of any Divine Providence sister if Mother St. Andrew remained in office.[27]

Néraz, smelling a chance to wrest the nuns away from their motherhouse in France and transform the sisterhood into a diocesan institute under his control, instantly authorized an "investigation" of Mother St. Andrew. Summoned, she appeared before a committee (of its three male members, one was her main accuser) to a long list of charges, including whether she warned her sisters "to beware of priests,"[28] which ensuing events made a legitimate caution.

Within two months, Bishop Néraz traveled the twenty-five miles to Castroville for the election of the next superior. Despite an earlier letter declaring that the superior must resign, two ballots upheld the reelection of Mother St. Andrew. Faced with defiance, the bishop announced he would appoint a superior from another community—a thinly veiled notice he would absorb the property of the Divine Providence sisters and suppress their identity as a congregation.[29]

Néraz earned a harsh reputation among religious women. Some Texas nuns regarded the bishop as "macho" and a "tyrant," his condescending paternalism evident when in the Mother St. Andrew debacle, one of her allies begged a transfer to Galveston. The bishop sent her a cool "refusal of the favor," for she had "disobeyed" and "must bear the consequences."[30]

Nor was the vindictive Néraz satisfied to remove Mother St. Andrew from office. He hounded her for years, suspending her rights to the sacraments, denouncing her to bishops in other dioceses, warning them against giving her sanctuary, undercutting her efforts to relocate to California, and advocating for her deportation to Europe. With Néraz obstructing her on every front, Mother St. Andrew could not find refuge in any diocese or support from any bishop. Finally, she put aside her religious habit, returned to secular clothing, and moved to California to care for her brother's children following the death of her sister-in-law.

In 1900, six years after Néraz died, Mother St. Andrew petitioned the Sisters of Divine Providence to readmit her. Now in her midsixties, Mother St. Andrew received permission to return, although she was not allowed to live at the motherhouse. Donning her habit, she renewed her vows and headed for a convent home at Castroville, amid an enthusiastic welcome from the sisters. They acknowledged what she endured, retained their affection for her, grieved over her exile, and admired her efforts to shield the sisterhood from ecclesiastical assault, but they recognized their vulnerability if they openly supported her, even after the death of her nemesis, Archbishop Néraz.

Acceptance of masculine domination and its legalized place within the Catholic Church represented crucial factors for convent viability. The failure to yield before a bishop or priest promised a church answer that could mean individual censure, separation from the sacraments of faith, and collapse for a congregation. Wary of the thin religious ice under their feet, sisters stifled their grievances, only confiding to each other, "he understands to a high degree how to test the patience of defenseless religious and . . . many ways to torment."[31]

In addition to orchestrating convent affairs and commanding obedience, bishops also cared greatly about the deference and childishness the women displayed. In Oregon, Archbishop Francis N. Blanchet—chuckling at the sight and pointing to one then the other—required the sisters, who apparently dreaded the performance, to kneel in front of him for a recitation of the day's events.[32] Bishop J. W. Shaw of San Antonio, the referee in a dispute between two houses of a congregation, reprimanded one superior, telling her, "[I] advise you for your own good to be careful how you express yourself in your letters."[33] When Mother Amadeus wished to shop in public stores, she asked permission with such deference that her new bishop responded, "I will say 'Yes' to everything, as long as you are good children."[34]

Predicaments and crises taught religious women—many, like Mother Amadeus, most unchildlike—to stay watchful, anticipate dangerous topics, and fend off autocratic masculine controls when they could. Though the contest could be fatiguing and the outcomes demoralizing, sisters learned to better their place in these gender matches.

Besting the Bishops

Mother Amadeus Dunne, who outflanked the bishop without his realizing it, adapted easily to her life in Montana only weeks after leaving behind twenty years of formal cloister in the Ursuline convent of Toledo, Ohio. The thirty-eight-year-old nun, cursed by arthritis and problematic health, brought talents as an educator and convent administrator, which she applied to energizing the Ursuline community in the West. In Miles City, she abandoned her private life for a public career, where she exercised new dimensions of personal agency that resulted in a complex western presence for herself and her companions.[35] Much of her success rested on the fact that she regarded relationships with priests and bishops as tools for Ursuline advantage.

In January 1884 Mother Amadeus stepped onto the Miles City railroad platform and presented herself, still subject to the bishop of Toledo and her mother superior in that city, to John Baptist Brondel, a portly Belgian only recently named the Montana bishop. Brondel, having no convent prepared, transported Mother Amadeus and her five companions to the home of a local Catholic woman, the proprietor of a rundown boarding establishment for transient laborers.[36] After a raucous evening and a nearly inedible meal, the sisters climbed to a public loft, devoid of heat but decorated with drifting snow. They shivered on the floor through the bitter night and Mother Amadeus, her arthritis aching anew, reported to her Toledo superior: "Says I to myself, 'this will be our last night at Bridget McCanna's.'"[37]

In the morning, Mother Amadeus set out for the bishop's more comfortable lodgings. She had not served two terms as the elected head of the Toledo convent and several years as the mistress of novices for naught. She approached the bishop with an administrative background that prepared her for exchanges with a newly elevated church superior of European lineage.

In the end, this accomplished businesswoman, declaring Bridget McCanna's household with its open dormitory for cowboys and bartenders as "too promiscuous," extracted precisely the terms she wanted from the bishop: permission to engage the Miles City business district on her own. By nightfall, Amadeus had leased, for twenty-five dollars a month, a modest, five-room house; bought stoves and installed them; and purchased coal. Mother Amadeus infused the humble rental with new dignity, naming the shabby building the "Ursuline Convent of the Sacred Heart." Although the dwelling, furnished with a couple of boxes and a makeshift table covered by newspapers, hardly resembled a dignified convent, the superior, in a brisk move, transformed an empty property into a respectable church icon. Satisfied that the sisters had decent shelter, Mother Amadeus wrote to Toledo: "We had no assistance from anyone—happier to do it alone."[38]

Now nearly penniless, Amadeus remembered asking how she was to fund the Miles City mission. Her Toledo bishop, Richard Gilmour, lightly dismissed her inquiry about finances, scolding her to display no concern for earthly matters but to look for supernatural protections.[39] Mother Amadeus, while guided by spiritual conviction, was much too practical to wait quietly for divine intervention or the generosity of parsimonious bishops to fill her purse. In Montana, Mother Amadeus enjoyed the freedom to find employment and make choices without a major superior or watchful priest adviser present to criticize or endorse her actions.

Asserting the authority invested in her by her Ohio superiors, Mother Amadeus used the first months to push the Ursulines deeper into Montana society. She led three sisters to Otter Creek, where she left the nuns to mission work among the Cheyenne Indians, who, only five years earlier, had been driven onto this unappealing space.[40] By the fall of 1884, Amadeus had traveled seventy miles beyond Helena for a visit to St. Peter's mission, operated by the Jesuit fathers. Mother Amadeus decided this spot was exactly the place to open an Ursuline novitiate and undertook the organization immediately.[41] Within a year, the former Ohioan had inflated her Montana governance by increasing the number of Ursuline missions and consequently her own role as mother superior. As a result, the original administrative separation from Toledo widened.

Mother Amadeus arrived in Montana wearing a somewhat complicated mantle of authority, one woven by the weft of independence and the warp of attachment, which invariably rubbed against one another. While the Miles City convent was freestanding from Toledo and Amadeus was its superior, the Montana nuns remained tethered to the house of Mother Stanislaus by the possibility of reunion, either as individual sisters or as a community.[42] Nonetheless, Amadeus never permitted these details to inhibit her and operated from a well-formed definition of personal responsibility, one that drove her to promote the Ursulines in Montana.

A decisive thinker with expansionist sentiments, Amadeus trusted her own judgment as she made choices designed to give her sisters greater visibility in the territory. Using the novitiate at St. Peter's as her base, she eventually placed Ursuline teachers among the Blackfeet, Assiniboine and Gros Ventres, and Cheyenne and Crow people.[43] Despite her place as superior at St. Peter's, she worked with the other sisters, doing the heavy labor of the required domestic service for the Jesuits. Never one to conceal her annoyance, she complained publicly and bitterly that the priests selfishly never promoted the Ursulines during their fund-raising tours in the East.[44]

As her obligations rose, Mother Amadeus intensified her insistence that Toledo release more nuns for Montana.[45] When Mother Stanislaus denied the petition, Amadeus redirected her request, funneling it through Bishop Gilmour. She flattered him, saying that she had told her Montana bishop that the Ohio prelate was "almost all powerful" in the city of Toledo.[46] She knew, of course, that her letter bypassed Mother Stanislaus, risking the irritation of the Toledo superior. Stanislaus recognized the ploy and her displeasure flared, as she resented the strategy of Mother Amadeus.[47] To minimize the affront, Amadeus placed the onus on Bishop Brondel and described herself as merely acquiescing to his instruction that she write to his Toledo counterpart.[48]

Now adopting a more aggressive stance, Amadeus sent a letter in which she listed items immediately needed from the motherhouse. She ignored the contradictions of being a supplicant and a rebel at the same time and again defended herself for writing to Gilmour. She declared: "You mistake Mother, when you suppose I thought episcopal authority would be necessary to wrest assistance from our Toledo nuns." Again, she insisted, she only "followed the injunctions of our present bishop who ordered me to proceed in the manner in which I made the application."[49] Where once she had lobbied for personal autonomy with Bishop Brondel during her first days in Montana, now she acted the subservient nun, required to obey; she never acknowledged that she played one superior against another.

The quarrels between Ohio and Montana centered on competing authorities—bishop against bishop, nun challenging nun. Mother Amadeus adopted a variety of postures in this contest, each to advance her Montana agenda. Her descriptive letters to old friends in Toledo excited their curiosity about the West and the ways of missionary life. Ultimately, Bishop Gilmour exercised power where he could—inside his own diocese—rebuking the Toledo Ursulines who had a "spirit of restlessness" and a "feverish desire" to join Amadeus. Gilmour trounced those dreams, announcing to the Toledo nuns he would no longer permit conversations about their longing to teach among the Indians, for "hereafter, Montana must depend on itself."[50]

That pronouncement suited Mother Amadeus Dunne. She devoted herself to the Ursuline missions, accepting young women into the St. Peter's novitiate and welcoming professed nuns from the Ohio towns of Toledo, Cleveland, and Tiffin. In the 1890s, she sparked a disastrous episode with Canadian Ursulines who volunteered for temporary service in the Montana missions. Abruptly reversing agreements with Canadian superiors, Amadeus declared the six visitors to be permanent members of the Montana foundation. Incensed, the overworked nuns, despite the obstinate refusal of Mother Amadeus to pay for their travel, returned home.[51] Amadeus rued the lost personnel, but even with this heavy-handed error, she strengthened Montana Catholicism. Bishop Brondel acknowledged that to Bishop Gilmour, perhaps rubbing in the earlier moratorium on behalf of Mother Scholastica, thanking the Ohio prelate for "the Toledo Ursulines . . . six in number . . . [now] increased to about forty . . . [with] seven schools . . . [and] over 700 boarders."[52]

By 1900 the empire-building nun was keenly interested in a Vatican conference expected to affiliate all Ursulines in an international union. An advocate of amalgamation, Amadeus developed alliances within the European clergy and assumed a prominent role in the discussions in Rome.[53] When the ballots were counted, the sisters under her supervision had voted for union, although later, some Montana nuns disavowed their consent.[54]

Over the next few years, illnesses and a near-fatal injury sustained during a fiery train accident eroded Amadeus's already bad health, and she moved about with difficulty. In 1903 the sudden death of Bishop Brondel, who for twenty years kept a benign eye on her expansionist nature, taxed her declining stamina. Brondel's replacement, Mathias Lenihan, a paternalistic bishop who preferred docile nuns, took an instant dislike to Mother Amadeus. Harsh exchanges marked their first meeting, prompting Amadeus to write: "He thinks because he is a bishop, he has unlimited power over us. . . . I am not going to give in to these bishops."[55]

When Lenihan vetoed plans for Ursulines in his diocese to accept a mission in Alaska, Mother Amadeus resurrected her combative ways and earlier style of bypassing one authority to secure ecclesiastical endorsement from another. Confident that she could rely on the Ursuline Union, powerfully housed in Rome, to back her, Mother Amadeus ignored Lenihan. She selected three Montana nuns living outside of Lenihan's jurisdiction and sent them to Akulurak, Alaska.

Enraged by the hierarchal insult, Lenihan censured Mother Amadeus to the motherhouse and novitiate at St. Peter's mission and wrote rather grandly to the defiant nun, "You have acted contrary to my personal orders in regard to the best interests of religion in Montana." Her long absence in Seattle permitted the bishop to exploit the ambitions of sisters housed at St. Peter's, splitting the Ursuline ranks. By the time Amadeus returned from Washington, where she had seen the Alaskan missionaries set sail, gloom enveloped the convent, much of it fueled by fear of reprisals from the bishop and the growing rift among the sisters in the motherhouse.[56]

Emboldened, her opponents petitioned the mother general, charging Amadeus conducted an invalid election to win earlier approval of union. In a diplomatic move that acknowledged the worldwide impact of the great missionary of the Rockies, the Ursuline Union divided the United States into two provinces and named Amadeus the first provincial of the North. It was a promotion that granted her the autonomy she sought when separation from Toledo began in the 1880s. With a prestigious title that honored her stature and headquartered in an obscure New York town, Amadeus sidestepped further clashes with Bishop Lenihan. The weary mother general in Rome confided to a friend about Amadeus: "I have tried to make her understand that bishops are necessary . . . and that we have to work to make them our kind friends."[57]

Mother Amadeus Dunne hardly agreed with that sentiment. For over twenty years, she viewed the bishops as oppressive obstacles to her ambitions for the Ursulines and herself. Montana released her from convent enclosure and inflamed the most active aspects of her personality; she responded with her own spiritual vision. She favored the grand plan, disliked the tedium of details, and resented obstruction. Finally, late in her life, restless under the dulling bureaucratic routines and fired by her old quest for adventure, she joined the small convent of Ursulines she had missioned to Alaska five years earlier.

Despite this bold move, painful days filled Amadeus's last decade, as did flashes of the pioneer administrator who maneuvered her way through church protocols with personal determination. Once the Ursulines had three small Alaska missions under way, Amadeus envisioned launching a novitiate in Seattle. From this base, she planned to train young missionaries and send them to the scattered villages of the Inuit.

In her typical fashion, Amadeus moved forward with more confidence than permission, convinced she would win over the Seattle bishop, Edward O'Dea.[58] Again, though, careless about interpersonal relationships, she stumbled at the local level. The Jesuit pastor at Valdez, Alaska, wrote to O'Dea that Mother Amadeus and her assistant were "entirely and totally unfit" to carry out the novitiate plan. The mother general in Rome, bombarded with complaints from Alaska, informed the bishop she had instructed Amadeus to leave Seattle. The aging missionary suffered a final indignity when young sisters in Alaska begged the bishop for transfers to any other Ursuline house, because "the religious life is impossible under her."[59]

As her support collapsed, Mother Amadeus reverted to past behaviors. The novitiate defeated and her exile ordered, Mother Amadeus did as she had done many years before in Miles City: she parsed a request for something she knew no bishop or priest could refuse. In this case, she unexpectedly asked for her convent to be permitted eight hours of adoration before the Blessed Sacrament, a practice gaining popularity in larger religious houses.[60]

Adoration required a major adjustment in the schedule of the convent, necessitating that each day at least two sisters be present in the chapel during the eight-hour period. The obligations involved consent from the mother general in Rome and the bishop in Seattle, which they gave, no doubt with reluctance. Their denial would have been awkward, since many spiritual directors actively encouraged release time to free sisters for adoration. For Amadeus, acquainted with that trend, the petition allowed her one last chance to knock her religious superiors off balance.

Stymied by superiors at every level and with her newest scheme in ruins, Amadeus took refuge in her congregation, trying to bolster the few Alaska missionaries with visits and enthusiasm. By now, however, her intellectual and physical resources had faded. She could not ward off the bitter cold of Alaska, chronic pain, infirmities of age, or merciless onset of dementia. No longer able to stand on her frostbitten feet and fatigued by illness and injury, Amadeus returned to Seattle. There, at the age of seventy-three, she died on 10 November 1919.

Mother Amadeus Dunne of the Ursulines reconfigured the profile of the nineteenth-century nun. Initially, she chose a convent lifestyle of security, framed by academic and religious calendars. Within that context, she accumulated considerable reputation and had every reason to expect she would conclude her life among the ranking teachers and administrators of the Ursulines in Toledo. On the cusp of middle age, however, she tried the alien world of the pioneer, where the greatest revelations concerned insights about herself and her ambitions.

This western world, with its stunning beauty, ferocious hardship, and great diversity, overtook Mother Amadeus; she adored the spaces and vistas and never seemed comfortable in the East again. In the West, she used her quick mind to shape Ursuline identity and her own power, reveling in the diverse world around her. In the ways she chose to exercise authority, willing to be direct and abrasive, she placed herself on a collision course with superiors, especially those bishops who expected subservience. Their objections, anger, and threats did not intimidate her but only caused a momentary pause while she plotted a route through the burrs and thistles of permitted nun behaviors. Over the years, she appeared less wedded to the rigid religious rule and more interested in unfettered action on behalf of Ursuline prominence. With her singular career, Mother Amadeus added texture to the place for sisters in the West; appropriately, the Ursuline sisters buried this assertive and unflinching nun where she honed her agency and independence—at St. Peter's mission, in the shadow of Montana's Rocky Mountains.

Controls inside Convents

"Don't do as you *think*, Sister; do as you are told," Mother Mary Magdalen de Pazzi Bentley, superior of the St. Louis Sisters of Mercy from 1856 to 1909, allegedly barked at a nun under her supervision.[61] Whether an incident in convent life or a fancy of convent legend, the remark aligned with much public impression about the fiercely oppressive and highly directive nature of a nunnery. Like most opinions, it contained elements of both veracity and falseness.

It appeared indisputable that Mother de Pazzi ruled with an inflexible discipline that suffered no contradiction.[62] Her selection as leader for a St. Louis foundation guaranteed rigor at the new mission and relief for her New York convent, where she became assistant only three years after her profession.[63] Prior to de Pazzi's arrival, St. Louis archbishop Peter Richard Kenrick warned Mother Agnes, the superior in New York, that "the house is not . . . such a house as would be deemed suitable for a convent," adding that, because of the planned $800 annual stipend, "no doubt . . . small as is this sum, the sisters will have no reason to complain of insufficient support."[64] In reply, Mother Agnes warned the archbishop "not to cross the new superior."[65]

Educated in France, the daughter of an Irish judge who presided over a district wherein lived Archbishop Kenrick's father, and the sister of a Vatican-connected priest, Mother de Pazzi, described by other nuns as a "czar," imposed a stern European monastic flavor on her St. Louis convent for over fifty years. Known for traveling about the city with her carriage windows swathed in black curtains, extending convent prayer hours, adding days of fast, and restoring grates to the parlor, Mother de Pazzi earned respect and enmity. Her affection for time-consuming community devotional recitations and near enclosure strained the people-centered activism for which the Mercy sisters gained fame in the American West. She took the selfless charge of her religious institute literally, agreeing with one of her Mercy contemporaries in California, "we never undertake any duty however meritorious . . . for the purpose of supporting the Community."[66] Mother de Pazzi's resistance to tuition at a Mercy school prompted the underfunded St. Louis archbishop to reply that "almost everywhere . . . where endowments are rare, candidates for the religious life almost without dowry, and public charity not always an available resource, . . . the [pay] school is a necessary adjunct to religious institutes."[67]

Mother de Pazzi finally yielded on that point; the first Mercy pay school in St. Louis asked its twenty-six students for a weekly fee of twenty-five cents.[68] This changed Mother de Pazzi not at all, and she continued a convent life of severity, promoting such a strict interpretation of the congregation's public-service traditions that several sisters abandoned St. Louis and formed new Mercy foundations in California, Colorado, Arkansas, Louisiana, Kentucky, and Missouri. Late in life, still anxious to direct these branch houses, Mother de Pazzi, an expansionist by accident of her rigid leadership, requested and received an ecclesiastical declaration that new foundations must remain dependent on the St. Louis motherhouse.[69] Such moves added to her autocratic legacy among the Mercy sisters, one associate writing about "our dear Rev. Mother never having been very popular . . . being considered too great a stickler for the Holy Rule."[70]

Despite the turmoil of Missouri border politics, the violence in race relations, and the intense poverty of her sisters, the "queenly" Mother de Pazzi unflinchingly pursued groundbreaking social-service initiatives, especially for indigent women and girls.[71] Without sentiment, however, she demanded unconditional obedience, immediate acquiescence to every plan, and adherence to increasingly cumbersome, old-style regulations. She effectively squashed the leadership interests of other sisters through curtness, intimidation, and punishment. As a result, potential candidates for profession in the Mercy congregation withdrew, sisters in the St. Louis convent feared her, and some of her nuns chose to escape by volunteering for distant posts.

Mother de Pazzi's tenure, interwoven with family, clerical, and political power, demonstrated the professional and personal tensions percolating through American convents in the second half of the nineteenth century. The American West fanned the flames of these stresses. In western regions, overlapping ecclesiastical authorities, manipulative clergy, competing personal ambitions, frustrating rules, and the fluidity of regional conditions coalesced to effect change. American transformations strained the European roots of women's congregations, triggered confrontations, challenged traditional hierarchies, encouraged individual decision making, and forced new elements into convent governance.

The internal world of the convent operated just as surely on a system of hierarchal control as the male cohort. The foundation of that control lay with the vows of poverty, chastity, and obedience women recited upon profession in a religious congregation. For those outside the convent, the vows somehow turned a woman away from the human world and kept her perpetually entranced by the supernatural, which she proved by the many extremes of denial that appeared repugnant to secular society.[72] In actuality, within the vows, nuns perceived the means to deflating gender rules that burdened laywomen, blocking their intellectual and spiritual lives.

The vows grew out of a European tradition that encouraged self-imposed disciplines intended to emulate the life of Christ and restore the earliest forms of Christian living.[73] They declared that one chose to cast aside the "lesser" behaviors of the world; the promise to abide by them announced to the world the pursuit of a "higher" life course. Over time, the Vatican wrote and rewrote regulations for religious vows until canon law systematized every nuance of their observance.[74] At the center of the vows, however, lay more than simplistic secular perceptions and complicated rationales spelled out in Latin. Rather than enthralled in a spiritual universe at every moment, women understood that their vows defined both the essence of religious life and, of equal importance, the source of its many tensions.

Beyond the spiritual ideals they might inspire in individual nuns, the vows functioned as the signposts for guiding a common life among a collection of unrelated people, setting the broad outlines for convent environment. When a woman swore allegiance to a particular congregation, she did so with an affirmation of her intention to abandon ownership of material goods, the intimate company of men, and self-direction. Observance of the vows, most particularly obedience, was not optional, one annalist noting about the annual assignments and transfers: "Sisters . . . are called to Mother's room—some leave it with satisfaction beaming on their countenances, others unable to repress an abundant flow of tears."[75] Seen as the universal element in Catholic religious life, the vows undergirded the general behaviors of convent life, where the unique rule and constitution of each congregation provided diversity.

The profession of vows led a woman deeper into the rule and constitution of the congregation. For example, in 1878 the Sisters of Charity of Nazareth acknowledged their connection to the French institute of the same name but expanded the ministry from poor orphan girls to "all female children in whatever station in life they may be," setting the objectives to work to honor Jesus Christ, care for the poor, and educate "young persons of their sex."[76] The constitution delineated the workings of the congregation, its ministry, conditions for admission and program of study to profession, explicit authority of the mother superior and her council, procedures for chapter meetings, voting eligibility, and conduct during an election.

Testing their European attachments, Sisters of the Holy Family of Nazareth
left their motherhouse in Poland, emigrated to Chicago, served among immigrant
Poles, and further stretched their Old World congregational allegiance with a
mission to yet further New Mexico. (Author's collection)

The "holy rule" functioned as a blueprint for the constitution and furthered the practice of the three vows. Here, the directives tried to cover
every exigency in which a sister might find herself: "abhor the maxims of
the world"; "no attachment to anything earthly, particularly places, em-
ployments, or persons"; "shall never deviate in their dress, food, furniture
from the strictest simplicity"; "in time of sickness . . . never fretting or
murmuring at not being treated according to their fancy"; "avoid precipi-
tancy in their walking."[77] Nothing was left to chance; even exceptions were
outlined in the constitution and practical advice given about the rule.[78]

The organized rule required approval of a clergy adviser, who guided its
acceptance through the final arbitrator: the Vatican. The lengthy process,
which included editing from many clerical pens, did not always reach for
the pinnacle of womanly potential. The Sisters of Charity of the BVM in
Dubuque protested that their priest superior supplied the nuns "without
more than the most primitive rule, and with no clear effort manifest on his
part to see them established along canonical lines and free to expand beyond the domination of a single bishop."[79] Further, the sisters came to feel
"the inhibiting spirit of the times was concerned only with the vows. . . .
What was then only an imitation for . . . the feminine psychology, all the
spirit, the charisma of a mother foundress was sacrificed to the masculine

mentality."[80] Even without male input, perfection in the rule presented a formation hardship for candidates, one nun remembering of her fledgling sisterhood: "It was difficult. We were to train ourselves according to the rule and at the same time we still engaged in criticism, gossiping, suspicion, and the like."[81]

Thus, enforcing the rule for a few sisters dispersed from the motherhouse represented a major challenge to congregational leaders, who knew how easily violations occurred. In many motherhouses, superiors thinking about mission stations they could not reach with ease must have worried over the aphorism "out of sight, out of mind." Their vast numbers of passionate letters about observing the rule suggested that this uneasiness existed at more than one motherhouse.

In 1872 Mother Caroline Friess wrote Lenten instructions to her sisters, including dozens in Missouri, Iowa, and Minnesota: "There are . . . truths which . . . urge us to bind our stubborn will by the holy rules of the Order. . . . [For] the transgression of the rule in trifling matters is no small evil."[82] From Iowa, Mother Mary Francis Clarke reminded a young missioned sister renewing her vows: "Unless we keep rule, we will neither be good nor happy religious."[83] In 1889 Mother St. Pierre Cinquin of San Antonio exhorted sisters she had not seen for months, including those in Sequin, San Angelo, Tyler, and Fort Worth, as well as New Mexico and Mexico: "Be faithful to your religious duties, prayer, mortification, observe silence . . . be humble."[84] On the other side of separation, Mother Cabrini, leader of the Italian Missionary Sisters of the Sacred Heart, warned sisters during her two-year absence: "Only in obedience will you recognize the safety of your steps. . . . Submit your will to that of the superior."[85]

These letters of spiritual encouragement connected authorities to missioned sisters and, coupled with formal motherhouse declarations, produced a steady stream of reminders. At one motherhouse, the council reviewed mission regulations, deciding "no sister should travel or go shopping without a sister companion and that no unnecessary visits may be made to relatives or others."[86] Apparently still dissatisfied by accounts of lax mission behavior, the council shortly voted to examine "matters tending to a more exact observance of the rule."[87]

The offbeat circumstances at western missions—nuns walking miles to reach their classrooms, riding in wagons along mountain trails, taking meals in public restaurants, or living in a loft with twenty orphans— forced superiors and councils to reexamine the rule, define extenuating circumstances, and amend or retain regulations. For example, the Sisters of Charity gathered all superiors to Dubuque for a conference about one point because "the real meaning of the rule in question has been a subject of dispute and . . . that lack of uniformity . . . has been a cause of no small amount of trouble to the community."[88] Although this discussion concerned whether sisters could direct choirs or play the organ in a public church, the real decision restricted autonomy at missions, with the pronouncement, "let the superior understand . . . she cannot grant dispensations from the rule without sufficient cause."[89] Refining the rule quickened as a council issue, when the central leadership recognized that western missions blunted the traditional schedule for nuns. Superiors hoped for absolute conformity throughout a congregation but increasingly watched the West loosen their controls.

One quandary facing a council lay with finding an effective means for informing all branch houses simultaneously of the latest interpretation of the rule. Circular letters issued by the superior emerged as the preferred device, albeit a slow one, for spreading information. These directives to the mission houses created a congregational network to reinforce regulations or announce new ones to those far from the order of home. Circular letters covered a range of subjects: transfers, changes in superiors, a death, a jubilee, or spiritual directives that asked an entire congregation to "join in a novena in honor of St. Joseph to obtain assistance in the affairs of the community."[90] Mother Emily Power of Dominicans isolated in a southwest corner of Wisconsin, close along the Mississippi River, used her circular letters for religious and practical purposes, in one asking "to have your community make a novena . . . [for] the health of the sisters, the railroad from Dubuque, and the means to pay our bonded debts."[91] Spiritual rights of the nuns were also advertised through the circular letter, Mother Mary Ernesta of the School Sisters of Notre Dame directing missions in Minnesota, Iowa, and Missouri that "rules for reception of the Eucharist must be read aloud to the community once and then annually each September."[92]

Mother Mary Florence Walter, propelled into the office of superior general of the Sisters of Divine Providence after the bishop's forced expulsion of Mother St. Andrew, relied on circular letters to recharge the emotionally shattered congregation and kindle a motherhouse presence in convents across Texas. She wrote frequently on every subject, sending consolation, comfort, encouragement, and inspiration, always promoting congregational loyalty and unity. As leader, she advocated a philosophy of "a strong hand, laid on lovingly," telling the nuns that "a good superioress governs her religious as she would wish to be governed," but, with a touch of the enforcer from afar, she added that subordinates should "give me a direct account of . . . non-professed or professed not living up to profession."[93]

That instruction showed the corrective nature of the circular letter, the authoritarian voice of the mother general dispatched in response to, not in anticipation of, unacceptable conduct reported from the missions. Mother Innocentia, in a long memo intended to quell some practices, reminded the sisters that "only with special permission may married women be accepted for private music instructions"; and further closing out secular contacts, she added: "with traveling salesmen, sisters are not to engage in conversations that have no connection to their business."[94] Mother Mary Cecilia, with her sisters cast through Iowa, Kansas, Missouri, and Montana, complained that "in spite of . . . my admonitions to superiors, the sisters have been in streetcars and on the streets after dark. Nothing can justify this." This was not her only objection to behaviors in western missions. One time, she commented acidly, "When the sisters travel in the day time, they should not take off their bonnets and sit in the trains with their face veils thrown over their heads."[95] Mother Emily also scolded sisters about public laxness, commenting: "I trust that the sisters will adhere to the custom of not going out on Sundays, except in cases of urgent necessity." Then, perhaps in a move to keep spirits raised at poor missions, she mentioned: "I hope, too, that the sisters who have charge of the cooking will provide good meals. There is much toward a good health in . . . palatable food."[96]

The circular letter addressed the rule violations in missions, but not as a confidential instrument. The circular letters notified sisters at one mission how miscreants at another circumvented the rule, an unfortunate additive to convent gossip. These episodes amused missioned sisters, gave them ideas about skirting regulations, and made their own transgressions appear minor in comparison. With mission stations springing up in many corners of the West, enforcing universal behavior promised to become more, not less, difficult.

The manner in which the rule ordered life in small mission houses hundreds of miles from a motherhouse thus continued to fluctuate, sometimes wildly. Local superiors tended to ignore the tiresome routines of requests and permissions, taking on decision making for themselves. These superiors and their sisters glided along with comfortable practices that meshed with the community around them. If the nuns could only attend a church service in the evening and return home after dark, they began to do so. If the sticky heat on a train in Montana or a streetcar in Kansas became insufferable, sisters removed bonnets and flipped their veils. In Montana, Mother Amadeus set the low standard for this attitude, brushing aside the fact that she opened a mail pouch intended for the superior in Toledo, saying blandly, "I knew you would approve."[97]

When a motherhouse received a letter such as the one from a priest who, observing "irregularities" in one convent, wrote to "inform you about a few things that are going on in your vast and fervent order without you perhaps being aware of them," administrators chose action beyond the circular letter.[98] Direct supervision entailed a practice known as "the visitation," a reference to the journey of the biblical Elizabeth to see her cousin Mary before the births of John the Baptist and Jesus. In modern visitations, a mother general and one councillor traveled to a mission, stayed a few days, assessed the circumstances at the mission, interviewed the sisters individually, and wrote a report of the house for the congregational records. Like the visit of Elizabeth to Mary, a spirit of joyful family reunion was intended to prevail, but at mission convents, correction and discipline also played a role.

In the West, these visits jolted missioned sisters into recalling the world of the motherhouse, so utterly removed from their daily circumstances. The presence of the mother general reminded them of their spiritual allegiances, gave them personal moments with leaders, revealed failures in adherence to the rule and constitution, and generally reaffirmed bonds stretched thin by absence. The missioned sisters hoped for a favorable evaluation, such as "the rule, it is our pleasure to say it is punctually obeyed and the sisters are attentive to the duties of their state," or "punctual observance of the rule is the aim of every sister here."[99]

Generally, a mother general did not mince words if she felt dissatisfied with either the performance or the attitude of the sisters. At several Oregon and Washington missions, Mother Mary Agnes, the superior general of Franciscans from Philadelphia, repeatedly noted, "Our holy rule is punctually observed," but she appeared equally pleased that "cleanliness is very noticeable" or "the house is a model of neatness." When housekeeping fell below her standard, she recorded her disappointment, commenting on one school that "cleanliness in the classrooms might be observed much better than it is. . . . I called . . . attention . . . to this matter."[100] As for the straightforward Mother Caroline of the School Sisters of Notre Dame, she sharply reprimanded some of her St. Louis sisters for their "lack of religious discipline and infringement of the daily convent order."[101]

The visitations thrust the congregational leaders and the missioned sisters into a sudden and artificial closeness. Seventy-two hours hardly allowed either to talk deeply about the way "old" life and "new" life collided in the West. The dangerous and extended travel to reach a St. Stephen's in Wyoming exposed the breadth of the gulf between home and mission. The pinched and weary faces of the sisters documented the differences in safer

At a small boarding academy in rural anti-Catholic Oregon, the pensiveness of
Mollie Britt and the solemnity of Holy Names Sister Fibronia, a Canadian immigrant,
underscored the cultural loneliness that some women experienced at western missions.
(Southern Oregon Historical Society, print no. 7988, Medford, Ore.)

housing, better diets, and reasonable workloads at a larger, better-situated convent. The bravado of cheerful letters dimmed when a mother general looked on the physically worn sisters who greeted her.

Mother Agnes, far from her residence in Pennsylvania, blanched at western conditions, writing of an Oregon school: "The sisters . . . practice in its fullness the poverty . . . recommended by our holy founder St. Francis. There is here not only the spirit but the reality."[102] Even Mother Agnes, who for forty-three years pushed for western missions and placed her personality on them through a constant round of visitations, finally, with age upon her, canceled one more winter trip by rail and carriage deep into Wyoming.

The physical and emotional toll of mission life could not be denied when congregational leaders visited in the small convents and recorded their findings. In the Oklahoma Territory, the visiting superior noted: "Though the rule is obeyed here, yet one of the sisters proved unfaithful to her vocation. Investigation shows she lacks . . . confidence in her superiors. . . . The other sisters make good her deficiency."[103] At Rawlins, Wyoming, one sister had been "faulty" and, although she "promised to do better," "should never be a superior."[104] In a Washington hospital with fifty patients, eighteen students in nursing training, and an additional thirty orphans, the superior general commented: "Sister Mary Elizabeth . . . is not happy." Of the harried local superior of this mélange, the visitor wrote that "Sister Helena . . . is rather quick and abrupt to the sisters."[105] In Iowa, at a parish with the pastor leading a public "wrathful" assault on the sisters, a young nun, teaching ninety-six pupils and then denied profession of her vows, sank into a "prolonged dejection" and for some months "sought brutal revenge on her companion sisters."[106]

Overall, the goal of the visitation was to collect firsthand information about the mission and its staff and reaffirm their place within the congregation at large.[107] Where sisters drifted from the rule, a conference with the leadership was intended to prevent further erosion. Through conversation, common prayer, and shared meals, the administrators hoped sisters would recommit themselves to a motherhouse, its rules and constitution. The premise of the visitations acknowledged the ease with which those assigned to remote areas could lose their congregational focus and slip away from central controls. The missions in the West delivered a sobering message on that subject; administrators in distant motherhouses worried correctly about retaining oversight and keeping sisters loyal in the West.

Clashes inside Convents

In 1888 Bishop Nicholas Gallagher of Galveston, Texas, counted ten Sisters of St. Agnes teaching under his jurisdiction in Texarkana and Jefferson. He did not know the women well, as both towns were more than 300 miles from the bishop's Galveston residence, a fact that limited his personal interaction with the sisters. The nuns had come to Texas from a small congregation with a motherhouse in Fond du Lac, Wisconsin, nearly ten years earlier.

Deep in the cotton fields of east Texas, the Sisters of St. Agnes had inherited two unappealing missions from the Daughters of Charity. The Daughters began inauspiciously in 1869, and when they withdrew in 1875, they reported "the school is still small and not very remunerative; the Catholics are few in number and unable to get bread enough to eat." The Daughters attributed their problems to the fact that "the Protestants are the prevailing portion of the inhabitants, and they are all anxious to put obstacles in the way of our success."[108]

After the unhappy days of the Daughters of Charity, the Wisconsin sisters must have satisfied in some manner, for other northern nuns coming into Texas usually found they were unwelcome "Yankee sisters."[109] Apparently, the Sisters of St. Agnes endured the hostility and kept their toehold in the two Protestant communities. By the summer of 1888, the group, led by Sister Thomasine, questioned its allegiance to the motherhouse and nuns with whom they no longer felt a sisterly bond. With lives focused on families in Texarkana and Jefferson, the nuns agreed to sever ties with the Wisconsin congregation, located almost 1,500 miles to the north.

Bishop Gallagher of Galveston, their local clergy superior—only recently forced to yield to Bishop John C. Néraz in the matter of Mother St. Andrew of the Divine Providence Sisters—cooperated with this defiance. Gallagher, who lost a chance to increase his cadre of teaching sisters with the exile of Mother St. Andrew, feigned distress that the Sisters of St. Agnes wanted to break with Wisconsin and form a diocesan congregation under his protection. Vaguely asserting that there was "so much disaffection" between Texas and the northern motherhouse, he suggested he could restore "obedience and respect to authority" by backing the separatists.[110] Gallagher omitted identifying the nature of the disaffection or the ways in which the nuns had shown a lack of respect for authority. Convinced he could organize a new sisterhood and retain Catholic teachers for two Texas towns, Gallagher traveled more than 1,000 miles to Wisconsin to negotiate a separation that would save his schools in Texarkana and Jefferson.

Mother Agnes, the Wisconsin superior general, must have felt curiosity and suspicion when Bishop Gallagher undertook the inconvenient travel from Galveston to Fond du Lac to visit with her. Five years earlier, Mother Agnes had spent time in the Texarkana convent recuperating from illness, writing to her Wisconsin councillors: "I do wish Father Francis could come here to give the sisters a good retreat. It is really necessary."[111] All had not gone smoothly during her stay with Sister Thomasine, and Mother Agnes heard the rumblings of dissatisfaction, now manifest in the person of Bishop Gallagher seated in her parlor.

Mother Agnes told the bishop that the constitution of her congregation did not allow her to grant a separation, a permission that must come from Rome. She stood her ground with Gallagher, who held no local power over her, refusing to surrender her ten sisters in Texas to his jurisdiction. Finally, the superior indicated she had little choice but to recall the sisters to Wisconsin and terminate the Texas missions.

Gallagher, who arrived in Wisconsin confident he could broker a deal to keep his schools and enlarge his diocesan oversight, faced a hollow return to Texas, defeated by a nun. Not only would he lose authority over a newly defined congregation, but also the schools, for which Catholic families clamored, would close. Ultimately, the Texas bishop and the Wisconsin superior agreed that Mother Agnes order the dissident sisters to the motherhouse and replace them with ten others from Fond du Lac. It was not the outcome Gallagher planned, but he would rid himself of the rebels, expel them from Texas, and keep his schools in Texarkana and Jefferson.

In Texas, however, Sister Thomasine and her associates resisted the motherhouse. Instead, she informed the bishop that if replacements came to Texas, her group would not return to Wisconsin but would "set up their own school." Now the bishop faced the public embarrassment of endorsing a new community of teachers while the resident faculty began a counter-school. Gallagher explained to Mother Agnes that in the face of the sisters' adamancy, it would be pointless to deploy a fresh team, as the Texas nuns enjoyed strong support from the local priest and the parish families. His about-face struck an out-of-character conciliatory note from a bishop to any subordinates. Only a few years later, in an effort to quiet a troubled convent, another Texas bishop told nuns from Chicago that "the people have nothing to say . . . for it rests entirely with the bishop . . . to decide what sisters shall teach the parish schools of the diocese."[112]

If Gallagher enjoyed a momentary flash where he thought he could exercise his powers as bishop, recoup the situation, and keep the Sisters of St. Agnes for Texas, his advantage quickly slipped through his fingers.

Confronted by his ecclesiastical superiors about the controversial events, he could not mount a canonical legal argument for overruling Mother Agnes and protecting the dissident sisters. Further, Sister Thomasine's sharp rejection of a compromise may have been off-putting to him, hinting the nun harbored a more independent spirit than he cared to engage. Challenged publicly by the parish priest, his chance to organize a diocesan sisterhood blocked, questioned by his superiors, and confronted with the destitution of the ten nuns, Gallagher withdrew his endorsement and joined those ordering the sisters back to Wisconsin.[113]

The Texas congregation that the sisters envisioned did not materialize. Of the ten nuns, six eventually returned to Fond du Lac humiliated and penniless, chaperoned by one of Mother Agnes's allies. The remaining four, abandoned by the parish priest and the bishop, requested secularization and left religious life. Lack of funding, collapse of clerical support, small numbers, and poor location in Texas combined to make their plans unattainable.

Ten years removed from their congregation, the Sisters of St. Agnes in Texas lost their sense of attachment to Wisconsin. In the Lone Star State, the ten sisters found professional success and their own religious identity but nothing that fired their feelings for home. As the ten nuns began to see in each other a possible new congregational validation, their alienation from the motherhouse mounted. Their home congregation, never destined to be widely known, counted just over a hundred, not enough to build a strong network between Wisconsin and Texas. An extended visit from their mother general did nothing to reconnect the Texas sisters to their Wisconsin home, refresh their loyalty to the congregation, or dampen the ambitions they developed. The nearly 1,500 miles between the central administration and the small missions effectively destroyed the congregational bonds of the Texarkana and Jefferson sisters, sent some home in disgrace, left others to terminate their lives in religion, and generated sorrowful memories among those who kept their loyalty to Fond du Lac.[114]

Other dissenters broke from their motherhouses with greater success. Perhaps nobody did so with more flair than Mother Scholastica Kerst of the Minnesota Benedictines, who established a powerful presence for her congregation in several western areas. The unswerving force with which she, always a controversial superior, oversaw the priory at St. Joseph, Minnesota, divided the sisters, the annalist commenting of her tenure that "the last two years of Mother Scholastica's reign form the darkest period in the history of St. Benedict's Convent."[115] By the time of the next vote for mother superior, tensions at St. Benedict's smoldered between those who

Building community identity, memory, and loyalty, Mother Scholastica Kerst
(in hammock), a powerful congregational leader, incorporated spiritual reading into a
fresh-air excursion, giving these Benedictine sisters a change from their indoor convent
routines of work and prayer. (Courtesy Sisters of St. Benedict, Duluth, Minn.)

wanted Mother Scholastica eligible for reelection and those who wished
her deposed. Two years later, when a chance occurred to effect a separation
between the Benedictines at St. Joseph and a daughter house in Duluth,
Mother Scholastica stepped forward to assume the superiorship. In forming this independent priory, Scholastica recruited among the sisters,
gathering thirty-one women who chose to divorce themselves from their
St. Benedict's motherhouse. Known as a "born leader," Mother Scholastica wounded many, and her raid on the personnel at St. Benedict's unleashed bitter legal and personal fights between the two houses, as former
friends and coworkers quarreled over material property and spiritual obligations.

In Duluth, Mother Scholastica looked for ways to distance her burgeoning priory from the St. Joseph Benedictines working in the area, settling on Canadian missions as one solution.[116] When Mother Scholastica died in 1911, her biological sister Mother Alexia became superior in

Duluth, which included responsibility for the houses across the border in Canada. Within months, Mother Alexia confronted a situation identical to the earlier split between the Benedictines who remained at St. Joseph and those who chose Duluth and Mother Scholastica.

With the small convent strained to meet all its Minnesota teaching commitments, Mother Alexia, pressured by her local bishop to staff his schools, recalled the sisters from Winnipeg, Canada. The Canadian archbishop, left without Catholic faculty, resisted this departure. It was a battle largely argued in the official correspondence of the clergy, but in Winnipeg, Sister Veronica Zygmanski, one of the nuns missioned from Duluth, saw an opening for her future. Veronica responded with interest when the bishop suggested the formation of a Canadian Benedictine priory, under his protection. Assured that she would be named superior, Sister Veronica refused to return to Duluth and, with the backing of her high-ranking patron, organized three of the other four nuns into a Benedictine foundation for Canada.

Such ruptures cut deeply into convent relationships, flooding the involved convents with confusion, shock, and recriminations. One Winnipeg companion, close to Sister Veronica but distraught by the sudden events and loyal to Duluth, asked the defector how "she could ever take such a step?" The reply must have echoed in the memory of Mother Alexia as the voice of her sibling, Mother Scholastica, for Sister Veronica commented: "We are doing nothing different from what our present community did at its separation from St. Joseph's."[117]

Sister Veronica spoke honestly about what she had witnessed in two priories. She perceived that inside a congregation, when rivalries solidified, distant employment openings could silence arguments and offer solutions for everyone. Factions could leave, alliances could be preserved — separation and the establishment of new houses proved a useful mechanism for resolving convent conflicts. Once again, however, many miles between motherhouse and mission allowed a bishop to exploit the aspirations of local sisters, encouraged missioned nuns to choose innovation over tradition, led to personal decision making and congregational separation, and further spread the presence and influence of Catholic sisters in the West.

Within a year, the now Mother Veronica reached out a hand of friendship to her former superior, Mother Alexia, writing: "If there is still any difference between us, we ask your pardon." Not all rejections are easily forgiven, even among nuns. Mother Alexia's reply not only withheld the blessing the Winnipeg sisters requested but hardened feelings by declaring, "We shall never . . . acknowledge you as a foundation originating from our motherhouse . . . for you separated yourselves . . . without regard to the obedience and stability that your vows imposed on you."[118]

These divisions of convents stirred anger and resentments, some occasions taking decades for reconciliation. The individual ambition of one or two sisters, sparked by the many possibilities in the West, marked the lives of many. Long years assigned to the outpost stations diluted loyalty to a motherhouse. The mission world emerged as the place of interest, the zone where a sister might rearrange her vision of how religious life should be followed.

Nuns nursing anger over a slight, stifled by an oppressive mother superior, or driven by a strong sense of self saw advantage in leaving one congregation and forming another. Bishops fueled these personal competitions to further diocesan development. As a result, religious organizations multiplied, as women cultivated a firmer sense of agency, grew impatient under the yoke of some administrators, crafted their own designs for a congregation, and recognized their importance in the grand plan of the Catholic Church to evangelize the American West.

Such situations dramatized the impact of disagreements and ambition and the way in which they enlarged the Catholic presence in the West. Yet not every disagreement led to a wholesale reorganization or a new congregation. Lesser differences, with smaller results, showed that individual sisters found the means to resolve their personal conflicts inside a convent.

Some nuns did not wish to leave religious life, but in the West, their extreme living circumstances added to the difficulty of executing the vows in a manner of "perfection." One sister might find a companion "domineering and censorious," but the two actually shared those traits, making it impossible for them to "work harmoniously together."[119] In one parish, a priest complained that one of the nuns "terrorizes" the others and demanded that the bishop "put this sister . . . in her place, which is certainly not under the protection of a religious habit."[120]

And sisters were not above an open verbal battle with each other. In Nebraska, a former academy student of the Mercy sisters recalled that witnessing two teachers in a loud exchange so shocked her that she entered the Franciscans instead, where, she laughingly admitted, plenty of pitched fights occurred.[121] A nun in Minnesota, reminiscing about the excruciating labor of her early convent life, remarked, "Amid such harsh conditions, angelic tempers did not always prevail among the sisters."[122] When these clashes could not be lightly dismissed and caused insurmountable stumbling blocks, one solution was to seek a transfer to another house of the same congregation or a different one.

In 1863 seven nuns from St. Benedict's monastery in Minnesota left to form a foundation in Kansas. Twenty years later, Sister Magdalen Euste received permission to join the group in Atchison because, her Minnesota superiors noted, "she had always been dissatisfied."[123] When Dominicans from Sinsinawa took over a faltering school in Rockwell, Iowa, the five Holy Ghost sisters stationed there asked for admission to the incoming congregation.[124] Not all mother superiors greeted transfer requests with equanimity. Mother Caroline Friess of the German-centered School Sisters of Notre Dame sniffed, "Sister Tita has decided to enter the Polish sisters, for love of their despised nation. God grant that she may change her mind for the better."[125]

Although obedience to superiors ruled convent life, sisters with complaints did not always withdraw, especially if they felt they could evade congregational administrators and lay their grievances before the bishop. The male clergy compiled a dubious record for their attitudes about and treatment of women religious in the West, but in the face of conflicts, sisters used the higher authority of the bishop for personal ends. Bishops may have been exceedingly difficult in their approaches to women religious and as biased as their priests, but they owned the authority to intervene inside a congregation and override a mother superior or a powerful faction.

In 1917 a representative for Archbishop Edward J. Hanna of San Francisco, visiting several area congregations, encountered a range of problems, especially frictions between conservatives and progressives. In one convent, he reported a sister "came to me in tears, lamenting that after thirty years faithful service she had been passed over." Another he described as "particularly bitter. . . . She wished to . . . revive past memories, and to tell me, what . . . was wrong with the house." At a second congregation, he noted, "all the sisters welcomed [me] and talked freely. . . . The visit of the mother general a few years ago was disastrous." He thought the superior in one convent to be the source of widespread unrest because "the good mother believes that the only kind of prayer that is worthwhile is . . . said on bended knee."[126]

If, among these disagreements, an individual nun felt she could no longer tolerate her living circumstances, church procedures permitted her to formally withdraw from the sisterhood. Even the profession of final vows could be excused and women could leave the congregation as Catholics in full favor.[127] The process was lengthy but provided sisters with an authorized way in which to be released from vows. Mother Caroline expressed that since a sister had written "an admission of her own conscience;

then it is a *duty* to let her go," for "it certainly means that obedience is . . . renounced."[128]

The official paperwork traveled slowly, however, adding stress to those sisters anxious to end their convent commitment. In small missions, the wait could seem interminable and created awkwardness for the one wishing to leave and those expecting to remain. In those close quarters, differences and disagreements inflated quickly. In some locations, the sister waiting for secularization papers might act on her own to speed the process. If a sister could reach a train depot, river dock, or carriage, a quick departure without explanations or recriminations proved attractive. Flight represented one way in which the vow of obedience collapsed and gave women an avenue, albeit unauthorized, to resolve conflicts within convents.

If the flight of a sister revolved around a rumored or actual involvement with a man, the departure took on exaggerated proportions. When a sister left to join a male companion, all vestiges of the three vows imploded. For those choosing the convent, these occasions sundered the veil between the lay and religious worlds and exposed the sisters to public speculation—the very antithesis of the purpose of the vows.

These events provoked intense distress among convent residents, the sadness of which was little understood by the outside world. In 1886, two years after the Ursulines opened their mission in Montana, one of Mother Amadeus's closest associates, Sister Sacred Heart of Jesus Meilink, laid aside her religious habit and slipped away in the middle of the night. Part of the original group from Toledo, Sister Sacred Heart had moved from Miles City to open the convent among the Cheyenne Indians at St. Labre's. Her letters occasionally suggested she found the isolation overwhelming, writing from the reservation: "I do not see how we can get along." Returning to Miles City, she had been overheard singing an old tune to herself, "O, that I never more might see the smile that hides a sorrow." While the melancholy might have caused some uneasiness, Mother Amadeus wrote, "her voice gives new life to our little convent and everybody is rejoiced to have her back." Her companions did not hear in the poignant words a warning that one day, Sister of the Sacred Heart would abandon them without a word of explanation.[129]

After leaving Miles City, the former sister, who had been a professed nun for ten years, traveled to Spokane Falls, Washington, from whence she refused a meeting with the grieving Mother Amadeus and made formal application for dispensation from her vows. In time, she married a David

Toner, a widower she had met in Montana. They moved farther west and raised four children together.[130] The abrupt separation hurt and confused the remaining sisters; four months later, one of the younger nuns, still hearing the melodies that drifted from the parlor, confessed: "I cannot speak of our lost member; it only recalls the bitter past."[131]

Others nuns pursued a more conservative route for leaving and took advantage of the impending vows ceremony as the best time to extricate themselves. Early in July 1885, less than a month before her first vows expired, Sister Emmanuel asked for traveling money to return to her family. A successful music teacher for the congregation, she went to her convent cell, dressed in street clothes, laid aside her instruction books for the nun who would replace her, and headed to the family home. About two months later, her father ordered the former Sister Emmanuel to retrieve her dowry and a bed she had brought when she entered the convent. The former she received, but the latter could not be located, the two sisters who helped in the search telling others that she "looked anxious and ashamed."[132]

Surely, all three women felt "anxious" as a they climbed among the trunks and furniture in the convent attic for an old bed. How did one woman justify to her former sisters in religion why she rejected the authorities of professed life? How did women in their habits reconcile their own attachment to that same rule? The language of the laywoman and that of the nun diverged along the fault line of religious vows, leaving only a tense atmosphere in the high garret. Caroline Claus, once known as Sister Emmanuel, took her dowry and left St. Rose Convent.

Unsettling forces lurked in convent life, compelling some to rethink the choices between secular and religious community. The exhausting work, grimy poverty, frustration of personal relationships, miserable and meager diet, anger over a transfer denied or a transfer ordered, relentless prayer obligations, fear in dangerous situations, overbearing superiors, boredom with routines, disheartening cross-cultural experiences, loneliness of a single life, attractions of an intimate physical relationship, or desire to birth children—any of these assaulted the ideals of poverty, chastity, and obedience that defined the way convent life functioned. When one of those factors or any combination coalesced in a sister's mind, she might sprint from her congregation, leave her closest friends, and return to society. Such appeared to be the case of a School Sister of Notre Dame, described as "never discontent," "very merry," and "never sick," who left "without saying goodbye," finding work in St. Louis as a maid and declaring that "she could not stand the confinement of the convent, . . . longed for more freedom, and the place was too dirty, sooty, and smokey."[133] Other nuns suppressed those feelings when they boiled over or never noticed them at all, as they held to their choice of religious life despite its many convoluted rules.

Professed women confronted layers of controls, and, as with any persons regulated by an institutionalized system of authority, they surprised themselves by exerting their own energy against complete domination—whether from the highest levels of the church, local bishops, priestly spiritual directors, congregational leaders, local superiors, or each other. The West, with its oddly different environment, offered nuns, many raised or trained in a European religious tradition, a chance to think about submission, its benefits, and its costs.

Nuns, surrounded by unorthodox circumstances, recognized that regulations oppressed agency. In the West, long-cherished convent practices simply made no sense—sisters could not always travel in tandem; they chose to accompany the Indian child who came after dark pleading for a dying parent; they thought it foolish to leave worthy parishioners without organ music for evening services; they hurried to bloodied workers when a mine explosion killed some of their students; they questioned the wisdom of closing classrooms to little boys who had no other educators.

The sisters trod on prohibited ground, generally expecting a brief interruption and a speedy return to the old routines. Disruptions proved, however, to be the new tradition, not the exception to the old ones. Skirting the rules subtly altered the way religious women expected themselves to behave, making them less willing to fit arbitrary regulations into daily demands.

At the same time, the West prodded sisters to discover more about themselves as religious women. The once-typical life of monastic stability was more or less useless in the nineteenth-century West. Formal contact with a bishop or priestly director dissipated for many western sisters who spent months without access to male clergy. Gone were the days when the bishop traveled across town by carriage for weekly consultations, admonitions, or blessings; in the West, he lived 300 miles away and would not be seen for two years. No longer were priests ensconced in comfortable apartments attached to a large motherhouse, available for access to the sacraments or consolation when a nun sickened and died in the night. In the West, sisters lived for lengthy periods without priestly ministrations and lessened their dependence on clergymen as the exclusive route to meaningful spiritual exercises.

That thinning dependence applied to the congregation's leadership, as well. The early, well-appointed motherhouses of St. Louis, New York, or Philadelphia still stood, but their missions crisscrossed many western landscapes. Proximity to the motherhouse, a constant in the East, vanished in the West. For example, the Baltimore School Sisters of Notre Dame sponsored dozens of schools and convents, many of them less than two miles from the motherhouse and within easy reach of the superiors. In Baltimore, a mother general could attend a graduation and be home for dinner; a sister could be summoned from a parish and dismissed by evening prayer.

In St. Louis, the same congregation papered the city and state with its schools but also supported missions in Minnesota, Iowa, and Canada, resulting in a second motherhouse because "the . . . tremendously wide expansion . . . [made] it difficult to give necessary assistance and to make visitation journeys."[134] Even this division did not settle the separation problems; in 1898 the mother general stayed three months in St. Louis, visiting all but sixteen of the missions as they were "too widely scattered and remote from the railroad."[135] Increasingly, motherhouse councils acknowledged the impracticality of long-distance supervision and the breakdown of daily regulations. In this tug-of-war, sisters in western missions pulled away from central control, and administrators yanked them back in the direction of authority.

Many saw in the West an interesting chance, one that permitted their religious profession but also advancement in personal power. This was no easy thing to justify in a lifestyle that highlighted the former and eschewed the latter for women. The juggling act required managing the church controls while bargaining for adjustments. Over time, sisters became more canny and adept at balancing irascible bishops, their imperial style, the hopes of a congregation, and personal ambition. Sisters looked for ways to fulfill themselves as women and as congregation members while avoiding the censure always threatening in the conversation with male superiors.

Most sisters worked within the existing system, cooperating, at least outwardly, with the male hierarchy to pursue opportunities for themselves or their congregations. They paid for their deference, like Mother Mary Goemaere, unable to satisfy her archbishop even as she nurtured a Dominican presence in California for him. Others, like Mother St. Andrew in Texas and Mother Amadeus in Montana, governed by challenge to the establishment. This demeanor carried real risks, as Mother St. Andrew learned when she lost everything after her defiance of local priests. Mother Amadeus triumphed frequently over similar foes, but ultimately age and illness defeated her within religious circles. Still, the individual characteristics and broad accomplishments of nuns like Mother Mary Goemaere, Mother Scholastica Kerst, Mother St. Andrew, and Mother Amadeus left indelible marks on their congregations, creating a convent legacy of fortitude that reinforced other sisters who faced their own foibles and endured their own controversies.

Controls brought contests—institutional, congregational, and personal. From those contests, sometimes won and sometimes lost, nuns and sisters broadened their life selections, enlarged their expectations, and found ways to forge a convent life that complemented the realities of the American West. In 1912 in Winnipeg, Canada, a troubled sister contemplating the break with the Duluth Benedictines had chided her friend, "Is it not evident that you are acting contrary to our holy rule, which speaks so strongly of obedience to our superiors?" The woman who became Mother Veronica of the Canadian Benedictines replied with defiant words that neatly unraveled the Gordian knot of convent regulations: "There are exceptions to every rule."[136] For nuns and sisters, sorting out the exceptions to rules, even when chancing risk, laid the groundwork for far-reaching choices. Individual women and congregations pursued those choices, as they continued to engage new situations and new cultures in the West.

*The white man's conduct . . .
in . . . dealing with the Indians
has never been such as could make
them fall in love with
our ways and our manners.*

—L. B. Palladino, *Indian and
White in the Northwest: Or
a History of Catholicity in
Montana* (1894)

A Woman for the West
Mother Katharine Drexel

On 3 March 1955 a ninety-six-year-old
nun, Mother Katharine Drexel, died
in her convent infirmary at Bensalem,
Pennsylvania. Laid to rest far from
mountain, prairie, or desert, this private woman from the cloister seemed
an unlikely figure to have shaped entire
segments of Catholic education in the
American South and the American
West. Katharine Drexel, through her
religious zeal, immense wealth, business
acumen, and organizational skill did
exactly that and in the process transformed herself into one of the most unusual adopted daughters of the West.

The Drexel biography diverged from
the narrative of western nuns, but it
illuminated the lived experience of

thousands of sisters. Her influence touched so many women, men, and children that the personal history of Katharine Drexel invaded all aspects of the Catholic West. Drexel's close association with the West began in the 1880s; across decades, it remained an important lens through which to view the evolving complexity Catholic religious women experienced in Native American, African American, Mexican, and Anglo relationships.

Further, the religious community founded by Katharine Drexel, the Sisters of the Blessed Sacrament for Indians and Colored People, demonstrated that Catholic women who wished to escape the confines of their own culture discovered in religious identity and social service the means to do so. In the process, the Sisters of the Blessed Sacrament, in concert with nuns from other congregations, established uncommon contacts among people of color, especially inside the West and the South. For their part, Native American and African American communities granted these professed religious women rare opportunities to cross cultural thresholds, immerse themselves in the lives of others, and rearrange the contours of their racial vision.

Early Life

Little in Katharine Drexel's early years in Philadelphia, Pennsylvania, suggested her future as an influential figure in the women's West or within an American Catholic pantheon. Born 26 November 1858 to a wealthy banking family, Katharine grew up surrounded by boundless family privilege. Her parents, Francis and Emma Drexel, lived out the extravagant rituals of the nineteenth-century rich. In keeping with America's Gilded Age, they owned multiple residences, lived fashionably, traveled extensively, and presented their daughters to Philadelphia society.[1]

Actually, Katharine's biological mother had died from complications of childbirth when the infant was five weeks old. Sixteen months later, Emma Bouvier, the new bride of Francis Drexel, assumed maternal care for Katharine and her older sister, Elizabeth, and by all accounts treated the girls as her own. The arrival of a third Drexel child, Louise, in 1863 enlarged the family. For many years, the older daughters remained unaware that Emma was, in fact, their stepmother. When revealed, the news stunned Elizabeth and Katharine but did not weaken their attachments to Emma, who was always "Mamma," nor estrange the older girls from the younger half sister, Louise. Social engagements, intellectual interests, religious fervor, and business dealings marked the daughters' lives, bonding the siblings into an unusually close threesome.

Both Francis and Emma Drexel exerted a powerful presence over this family, stressing a vigorous and highly visible commitment to the Roman Catholic Church. In particular, Emma Drexel closely monitored the educational and social lives of the three sisters. By their teen years, her daughters had vacationed at most of the fashionable resorts of Upstate New York, explored several European countries, and, after 1870, spent time at a nearly 100-acre property christened "St. Michel."[2] Here, the Drexels renovated the summer house for year-long comfort, incorporating Catholic art and statuary. Each daughter oversaw a segment of the estate, with the adolescent Katharine assigned as manager of the housekeeping activities and the staff of servants. In addition to adult chores, the girls conducted a religious vacation school for disadvantaged Catholic youngsters in the area, and the family distributed food and goods at holidays.[3]

Despite this training in domestic discipline and community outreach, the Drexels mixed with an aristocratic, international set and commonly entertained high-ranking Catholic clergy or met in private audience with the pope when abroad. The girls knew singular opulence, were privately tutored by a governess, and received music and language instruction from specialists and religious training from the French-speaking Madames of the Sacred Heart. The Drexel parents generously endowed numerous Catholic institutions, and their homes contained chapels for individual and group prayer; family recitation of the rosary was common. Of her formative years, Katharine Drexel remembered: "Prayer was like breathing. . . . There was no compulsion, no obligation. . . . It was natural to pray."[4] In this rarefied high-society and Catholic atmosphere, Emma Drexel imbued her daughter and step-daughters with a philosophy, expressed in intensely religious terms, that emphasized the privilege and responsibility of the wealthy.[5]

The premature demise of Emma Bouvier Drexel in 1883 and Francis Anthony Drexel in 1885 left the three daughters devastated but heirs to a highly publicized fortune. Katharine and her sisters shared an estate rumored to range between $14 million and $20 million, estimated in modern values to be at least $250 million. Francis Drexel bequeathed a separate million and a half dollars to Catholic institutions and religious orders in the area. Given the Drexels' well-known generosity, those excluded from the will longed for the sisters — each estimated to receive, in a pre–income tax era, an annual income in excess of $350,000 — to expand the family tradition of beneficence.[6] Elizabeth, Katharine, and Louise did not disappoint.

With her background calling and church agents petitioning, Katharine

Drexel cemented her connection to the American West through two distinct factors. The first involved the impressions made on her by two tours: one through the Dakotas and the other in Minnesota. The second element drawing Drexel to the West came from her struggle for a direction in life.

In the first instance, the attractions of the American West made their way into the mind of Katharine Drexel shortly after the loss of her parents. In 1887 Katharine, Louise, and Elizabeth, unmarried heiresses to one of the greatest banking fortunes in the country, stepped onto the Rosebud Reservation in the Dakota Territory.[7] Although they once took a sightseeing excursion across the West with their widowed father, this time, the Drexel sisters eschewed the touring railroad car and came into the homeland and living places of western people.

Well educated, sophisticated, and witty, the sisters insisted on firsthand information about the Catholic mission work among African Americans and Native Americans that others asked of them. Under the escort of two advisers keenly interested in the outcome of the trip—Father Joseph Stephan, director of the Bureau of Catholic Indian Missions (BCIM), and Bishop James O'Connor of Omaha, Nebraska—these elite eastern women sought to assess the isolated reserves mapped out by the U.S. government for Native habitation. The sisters, careful stewards of their father's wealth, wanted specific examples of how and where Drexel charitable monies landed. Katharine Drexel had already invested $15,000 for a Rosebud building named in honor of her father, but the sisters looked about for additional ways to offset the enforced privations on reservation lands and encourage the spread of Catholicism.[8]

After the Rosebud, the travelers continued across the Dakotas, stopping at one after another of the Catholic missions and entering Native communities they had never even imagined. For example, after hours crossing prairie bare but for occasional livestock herds, the party was unexpectedly surrounded by six mounted Indian policemen, silent guides and honor escorts during the final four miles to the mission.[9] These unprecedented contacts with people from a world completely alien to effete Philadelphia society occurred at each stop. Everywhere, the three Drexels came forward to shake hands with Native men, eat food cooked by Native women, experiment with Native vocabulary, and observe the overlap of Indian and white customs, whether for feast, dance, or worship. One Drexel, struck by the array of Native styles at Sunday mass, described the "squaws in bright colored shawls and dresses—some with faces painted red, some yellow, some with paint down the hair part, some with papooses held onto their backs."[10]

At each mission, as they watched and participated in these events, the Drexels critically evaluated and found wanting the Catholic institutions in place for Native Americans. Overall, as the small troupe moved deeper into the hinterlands, it realized that the poverty of the Indians and the handful of missionaries worsened. A scenic ride along the "wooded banks of White Clay Creek" or the sweeping vistas of the Missouri River from atop a bluff did not diminish the thirty-, forty-, or sixty-mile distances from one lonely sod house to the next sorry mission.[11] Colorful attire for Sunday worship did not hide the threadbare clothing of men, women, and children. The meals, provided by slaughtering one among precious few oxen, did not fend off the universal hunger, felt even by the Drexels, who knew the pinch of the "slim" breakfast and "lard can lunch."[12]

Their clergy escorts on this journey into poverty, as well as others responsible for Native missions, coveted the Drexel fortune. In search of revenues to alleviate reservation conditions, the bishops competed among themselves for donations from the wealthiest eastern members of the lay church and lamented the indifference of affluent Catholics for the Indian mission work in the West. Well-to-do Catholics in the East showed little inclination to relieve the fiscal burdens of bishops in such "exotic" and distant places as Montana, Idaho, or Arizona. In 1885 Bishop Martin Marty of the Dakotas complained: "While the Protestant missionary in the West are [sic] amply and gloriously supported by their concligiancate [comrades] in the East, we . . . cannot even get the surplus of our rich Catholics."[13] In the same year, Marty's ecclesiastical neighbor, Maurice Burke of Cheyenne, Wyoming, groaned of his poor prospects: "If I had the zeal and ability of St. Paul, I could accomplish nothing here. I am without people, without priests, without any means whatever of living or staying here."[14]

In the meantime, the missionaries in the field—both men and women— that the Drexels met clung to a stark existence. They threw together rough chapels, lived in shacks, and tried to survive on meager diets. They hoped that through example, self-denial, proselytism, and their few material goods, they could bring Native Americans to the Catholic faith. Realistically, they increasingly faltered under the inadequacy of their resources, long months of isolation, collapsing personal health, and mounting casualties among their mission constituents. Politics and economics smothered faith and zeal for some, one desperate missionary writing in an open letter to Bishop Marty: "I have . . . spent here . . . forty-five days, busy . . . at the bedside of the dying and burying . . . the dead, of whom in one day, I buried three, who died of no disease other than hunger."[15]

The Drexels had arrived at a defining moment in the political, cultural,

In this photograph, artistically posed over a dirt floor—numerous craft materials and elaborate Native dress notwithstanding—constant deprivation and near starvation showed in the faces of Gros Ventre and Piegan students and Montana Ursulines, including Mother Amadeus Dunne (left). (Courtesy Jesuit Oregon Province Archives, Gonzaga University, 106-01d)

and economic deconstruction of Native societies, whose prospects remained far less than those of the white missionaries. The deadliest Indian wars lay behind, the full disaster of severalty ahead—bookends in the cataclysms that left Natives reeling from losses of life and land.[16] No matter how supportive the whites of any religion entering this disheartening milieu, they could retreat—albeit personally defeated—from this crumbling world to their own cultural centers.[17]

Unlike their missionaries, Indian people remained locked on circumscribed terrain, closed out of a mainstream economy, and blocked from opportunities for escape. Assessing their few choices, some Indians gravitated to the missions, little more than outposts of white paupers, as possible sources of sustenance. Already well versed in the ways and wiles of white society, Indian families cautiously brought what remained of their culture, religion, and politics into the mission. Recognizing the brutality of the past, clinging to the frayed lifelines of the present, and evaluating the choices for the future, especially for their children, many Indians aggressively pleaded for white schools and legal protections.[18] The missionaries in place—a single priest or a handful of nuns—had little to offer. From these poverty-driven interactions came murky relationships, wherein participants clashed and accommodated, liked and disliked each other.

Katharine Drexel looked about the Dakotas and saw a different dynamic moving events. In her view, the reservations held a simpler meaning. In a world invented by a neglectful government, disadvantaged Indians had been abandoned to poverty, ignorance, and ultimately death. Without Anglo schooling, the Indians had no chance to extricate themselves from the dreary arrangements imposed by a disdainful white society nor, by her thinking, to enjoy Christianity. The reservations doomed Native people to prejudice, illiteracy, unemployment, and godlessness.

The situation existed, Drexel believed, because most priests and nuns refused the extreme austerity of the Indian mission call. The few congregations willing to try the reservation missions lacked the personnel or monetary resources to maintain themselves or reverse conditions for Indians. Only a year after Drexel aided a school in the Dakotas, a distraught priest begged anew to Bishop Marty: "The population of the reservation being largely Catholics, through me, as a last resort, turn their eyes and stretch their hands towards you . . . their only hope of success."[19]

Early Initiatives

Western bishops, with impassioned pleas, turned to Katharine Drexel for help. With assertions that hundreds of thousands of Native Americans lacked Catholic spiritual care because too few missionaries went to the West, the bishops begged Katharine to shore up the mission effort. Without the Catholic missionary, they argued, the church lost its central hope for bringing destitute Native Americans into the Roman fold while training them for jobs in white society.

Drexel's vision took on its own hues, some of which would not have colored the perspective of the Indians, the government, or the missionaries of other denominations. Nonetheless, for Katharine Drexel, in whom personal privilege demanded social responsibility guided by Catholicism, the Dakota trip fixed her determination. She decided to use her fortune as an educational lever for those who had no money, no champion, and no opportunity in white society.

In keeping with an American view, Drexel trusted the force of the classroom, especially when managed through a Catholic prism, to elevate humankind. In the Dakotas, she applied that vision. Witnessing the reservation life that Native people revealed to her, she bonded two important forces of her life: belief in the value of Catholic education and the moral obligation to make institutions of learning available to Native Americans.

Katharine Drexel, no ordinary sheltered, charity-minded young woman, returned to the East and set into motion the first phase of her plan to enhance the education of Native Americans. Her strategy superimposed eastern business tactics and pedagogical thinking onto a western stage. That stage, however, represented Indian space about to be altered yet again by the tangible and visual products of white society. Buildings and compounds would rise on Native landscapes, a process that Drexel assumed indigenous people welcomed.

Dipping into her considerable monies, Drexel purchased land along the perimeters of several different Indian reservations. With bases secured, she hired architects to design school buildings and paid construction costs, which included hauling lumber and supplies over rough miles to the work sites.[20] At these locations, the employees, for whom Drexel paid the salaries, were Native brick makers, lumber workers, and carpenters.

Despite her infusion of money into reservation economies, Drexel realized she could not alone staff the completed campuses. She had some concerns about the efficiency of the BCIM, but given her personnel limitations, she kept herself connected to this church office for Natives. She deeded her facilities to the BCIM for administration, that agency securing its operating capital through government contracts for boarding schools.[21] The sheer magnitude of the undertaking, although not necessarily the most appropriate for the West or for Indian people, reflected the scope of Drexel's imagination, thinking, energy, and determination.

Philanthropy for Drexel appeared not to be driven solely by personal piety but also fueled by direct action. In 1888 Katharine, with Elizabeth and Louise, gave the Sisters of St. Francis of Philadelphia a purse of $30,000 in exchange for their commitment to maintain ten Native missions in the Oklahoma Territory.[22] From such pragmatic decisions, Drexel drew energy, relishing the confidence born of success and wealth, as two Catholic sisters from Oregon on an eastern begging tour observed. They reported that Katharine received them in the magnificent Drexel family home, where she "served us in grand style."[23] Delighted the nuns had recently met Joseph Cataldo, the well-known Jesuit missionary to the Nez Percés (Nimíipuu), and hopeful for their future work among Oregon Natives, Drexel saw them off with a $300 donation.

Drexel felt she had more to do, however, than simply entertain begging western missionaries or dole out funds. She herself wanted to return to the homeland of the western tribes and to decide how her wealth could best assist people of color. In 1888, with various ambitious projects under way, Drexel agreed to another trip into the West. Again, she, Elizabeth, and Louise set forth with a clerical escort, heading for the White Earth and Red Lake Reservations in Minnesota. For a second time, the three sisters entered into Native communities.

A week on the road brought the Drexels to Odanah, Wisconsin, an exquisitely beautiful wooded area with a small convent staffed by Franciscan Sisters of Perpetual Adoration. The missionaries patched together the usual welcoming dinner, and Natives who had closely watched over the handful of nuns in the remote area provided a rich rendering of music for the mass.[24] Katharine summed up the situation with dispatch: a few sisters, little money, overcrowded building, and an involved Native population, many of them practicing Catholics. Before departing on the next leg of the journey, Drexel bargained to secure a nearby Presbyterian mission of 160 acres and a twenty-room schoolhouse. Within a year, Drexel concluded the transaction for $8,000, and the Franciscans undertook an expansion that enlarged their boarding facility, strengthened academic offerings, increased an agricultural program, and upgraded the laundry.[25]

The sisters' arrival in Minnesota showed conditions no more encouraging than a year earlier in the Dakotas. Once again, the three visited inside homes, attended chapel services, and watched elaborate dances. Once again, Indian men—White Cloud, Little Feather, Hole in Sky, Clouds Drifting Along, Leading Thunder—pleaded with the women to improve the reservations, especially their schools.[26] The trek, which included "corduroy partially rotted," roads, beds of "ticks filled with fresh hay," morning ablutions from a "tin pudding dish," and "horrible discomfort," convinced the Drexels anew that life for Native peoples begged for corrective action.[27]

What the Drexel sisters understood less well concerned the Natives themselves and their perceptions of how relief action should proceed. The Drexels interpreted the long speeches begging for schools as pleas for Christianity, particularly Catholicism. It perhaps did not occur to them that with the press of a changed West on them, Indians tried for any advantage a receptive listener might provide. For Indians mired in the misfortunes of the reservation, the proximity of white visitors offered a chance of reaching absent administrators, whether of church or state.

Despite any naïveté they may have shown in this morass, the young women from the wealthy Drexel family acquitted themselves well. Hazardous terrain, unpolished huts, humble meals—these nor any combination thereof elicited the pinched comments of the idle rich. Although they mentioned "half-breeds" and "squaws," their diaries remained largely free of racist slurs and cultural judgments. One dance, performed in a round-house by the light of a log fire, Louise labeled as "very weird," but in general the theme of poverty dominated her comments.[28]

That poverty, they thought, accounted for the uninhibited and driven personality of the stalwart Sister Philomene, the Benedictine sister from White Earth who accompanied the Drexels for part of the journey. Elizabeth Drexel labeled her the "Wild Sister," with her frenzied accounts of mission deprivation told while racing the horses through miles of burned forest to a stop at the Thompson ranch. Elizabeth Drexel confided to her diary of the excursion that "the Wild Sister [was] bent on hunting up a new field of savage labor."[29] Drexel appeared to employ the word "savage" as reference to the unyielding aggressiveness and furious intensity with which Philomene attacked life, a manner the heiress seemed to find unnerving in a nun.

The encounter made its impact on Katharine Drexel, as well. She returned to Philadelphia and focused her attention on the school-building program. She named among her beneficiaries the Benedictine sisters at White Earth, whose tenacity, even if unorthodox, struck the Drexels. After so many years of isolation, the two lonely nuns had not hesitated to let the Drexels know what the more-than-humble existence had cost them and the Indian families around the mission.

The Benedictine teachers witnessed the remarkable changes that a startling infusion of $40,000 could make for their outpost.[30] A new three-story brick school that accommodated 150 children opened in 1890. In a short time, the mission was strengthened, both internally and externally. With tangible improvements changing the face of the mission, White Earth Indian families could only look back on their earlier negotiations with the Drexel sisters as at least a modest success. Native parents showed themselves more willing to support the upgraded facility, where student enrollment rose from the usual fewer than three dozen children to over 100 by 1891.[31]

White Earth, Minnesota, was only one of many missions to receive assistance under Katharine Drexel's determination to raise the standard of living for Native people. Between 1888 and 1893, as acreage was acquired and buildings rose at distant sites, Drexel continued deeding the finished products—lands and physical plants—in Wyoming, New Mexico, Idaho, Montana, California, Oklahoma, and Washington to the BCIM. That agency held to its policy of funding the schools through federal contracts and hiring nuns from religious congregations as teachers. Within five years, Drexel organized and oversaw the completion of mission schools for several prominent tribes, including Cheyennes (Dz?'ts??stäs), Sioux (Ogalala Lakota), Nez Percés (Nimmíípuu), Cherokees (Tsalagi), Comanches (Numunuh), Osages (Wah-Zha-Zhe), Crows (Absaroka), Blackfeet (Aamsskáápipikani), and Pueblos (Taos, Acoma, Cochiti, Isleta, Hopi, Zuni). Her efforts made it possible for missionaries from numerous congregations—among them Franciscans, Dominicans, Benedictines, Ursulines, Jesuits, Grey Nuns, and Daughters of Charity—to have sufficient income to remain as workers in the West.[32]

Thus, this nontypical socialite from the East channeled her business interests in ways that changed the economic and educational face of the American West. The construction of mission dormitories, barns, shops, laundries, convents, and schools stimulated the local economy and planted small enterprises across reservation lands. Sisters and priests held onto employment at the missions, as did Natives who worked as farmers, cooks, housekeepers, drivers, carpenters, herders, and interpreters.[33]

The clusters of buildings became magnets for Natives with few Anglo institutions from which to extract jobs, schooling, or economic growth. The decision to become mission employees allowed Indian families to move as units across the reservation, the children attending school and the parents working nearby for the sisters. In Montana, Cheyenne mothers came to the fields to harvest crops with their children and the Ursuline teachers.[34] Families camped on the grounds for the first weeks of a term, shadowed the children during the daily schedule, and left only after satisfied with school conditions and treatment of scholars by the nuns.[35]

The interactions were not seamless. Indian parents resisted culture losses even as they lobbied for a better standard of living for their children. Adults and children alike entered into Catholicism with varying degrees of enthusiasm. Native leaders worked hard to secure a school, but confronting three or four white women—alone and inexperienced in western conditions—questioned the commitment and ability of the nuns.[36] Some missionary sisters who launched schools with Drexel support misread these Native concerns, one of them advocating for a school location "not so convenient for the parents to take them [the students] to their homes."[37]

Despite these areas of poor communication, both Native adults and children expected the missionaries to deliver spiritual ritual, secular learning, and daily healthfulness. While the boarding arrangements were not ideal for Native parents, they outweighed the coerced government enrollments in schools hundreds of miles away. The academic calendar of the Anglos gave Native children fairly regular meals and some heated dor-

Even at a poor reservation school, a puppy sporting a hat and a playful
kitten exerted universal animal appeal for these Native children and two Sisters
of Providence, allowing a light moment across cultures. (Northwest Museum
of Art and Culture, no. L97-24-42, Spokane, Wash.)

mitories during the months of bitter weather when illness and starvation
stalked the reservation camps. Most important, regardless of the disapproval of some mission faculty, Drexel's schools allowed Native families
a place in education, as parents moved into school zones and cautiously
watched the temporal and spiritual well-being of their children sheltered
inside the residential schools of white teachers.

Katharine Drexel, operating from her home in Pennsylvania, most certainly did not fully appreciate these complicated dynamics that pitted
Natives against sisters, even as the unlikely groups became collaborators.
Drexel saw only the potential benefits to Native communities if they had
ongoing access to the white educational system, guided by Catholic principles. So, in a decision of importance, Drexel did not limit her support to
the construction of mission sites but continued to cover the expenses that
guaranteed missionaries could keep a school in operation.

Drexel diversified her efforts and engaged many different religious congregations to structure a multilayered approach for enhancing Native life.
She paid tuition and board fees for indigent children, monthly salaries for
priests and nuns, insurance on mission buildings, grocery bills, and travel
expenses.[38] Ultimately, she served as a conduit for rising post-nineteenth-

century Native agency, organizing modern landscapes inside ancient spaces where Indian peoples once again claimed identity, gathered to reassert voice, and planned political strategies.

As she undertook these monetary responsibilities, Drexel cultivated an air of "financial vagueness" for the world. Perhaps the unending appeals for money, uncertainty over the management of the BCIM, distaste for publicity, or recognition that few shared her passion for changing lives in minority America influenced her. She never relinquished her suspicions about openness with funding, whether in dealings with government officials, religious congregations, or the BCIM. Sometimes she sent a stipend directly to an Indian or African American school. At other times, she funneled her money through the BCIM, with a blurry paper trail and a touch of anonymity. Her charities eventually became so extensive and mysterious that a complete recording of them proved impossible, even by members of the religious congregation she founded.[39] Katharine Drexel relied on regular inspection tours, explicit instructions for loans, strict and prompt accountability, and immediate suspension of funding when misappropriations were detected as her constants for developing integrity as a benefactor.

Choosing a Convent

Growing comfortable with her plan for the disposition of her fortune, Katharine Drexel devoted more time to the matter of her personal goals. This determining factor in her life grew from the Drexel family's highly spirited Catholicism. The element of inner spirituality, like her wealth, tied Katharine Drexel permanently to the American West.

For several years, Katharine increasingly felt drawn to religious life as a sister. Following the death of Emma Drexel in 1883, this second daughter spoke more openly about joining a convent, but in her search for a religious home, she decided against an order of nuns with solemn perpetual vows, daily Divine Office chants, and European enclosure rules. She turned aside a suggestion that she join the Ursuline nuns in Philadelphia, saying, "I do not know the . . . order, but I am under the impression that they do not change from house to house. . . . It does not attract me."[40]

Drexel's interest lay with a congregation dedicated to an active apostolate—those sisters who renewed simple vows annually and developed a public ministry outside the cloister. Drexel sought a woman's congregation with rules in place for complementing America's social organization, which she saw in need of a Catholic voice. She admired the Franciscans of Philadelphia and the Benedictines because they sent missionaries among Native peoples, but she determined to scrutinize the congregational regulations of each. Showing considerable self-understanding, she asserted her next step would be "to see whether these orders are too strict for me."[41] To find the best choice among the religious congregations available in America, the twenty-five-year-old Katharine turned for advice to James O'Connor, the bishop of Omaha.

Generally, the Catholic male clergy gave enthusiastic encouragement to nineteenth-century women who yearned for convent life. Katharine Drexel received a different response. For the next five years, O'Connor— who, before moving to the West, had been the pastor of a Pennsylvania church frequented by the Drexel family—opposed Katharine's desire to enter religion.

Early in their conversations, he declared: "The conclusion to which I have come in your case is that your vocation is not to enter a religious order."[42] He suggested the change from a home of opulence to the "cell of a nun" would be too drastic for Katharine; he questioned the stability of her health; he insisted that her good works depended on her complete freedom; he fretted about what would happen to her contributions to the poor; and he assured Drexel that if God had other plans for her, God would so inform the bishop.[43] Despite the rising crescendo of these manufactured excuses, O'Connor's real worry came from the monetary policies guiding most religious congregations.

If Katharine Drexel entered an established religious congregation such as one she admired, the Sisters of St. Francis of Philadelphia, her wealth would go to the community. Thereafter, a mother general and her advisory board would decide on its uses, directing it exclusively to the projects of their own sisterhood. Drexel, as a junior professed sister in a congregation, would have surrendered her right to allocate the funds or be consulted for her opinion in the matter. At risk in this scenario was the influence of the western bishops over the orphaned Drexel sisters, whose money flowed so regularly from East to West and aided many congregations of men and women working in poverty-stricken missions.

The advice of O'Connor, who knew that this one woman endowed the western missions more generously than the entire American Catholic community, also appeared to be tied to his knowledge of the will of Francis A. Drexel.[44] According to provisions in that document, the three daughters received equal shares of the $14 million family allocations, but at marriage, no new in-law could inherit Drexel money. Only the future children of Elizabeth, Katharine, and Louise were eligible heirs to the trust.

On the death of a Drexel daughter, her full inheritance passed to her children, bypassing the widowed husband. If the deceased left no children, the surviving sisters divided that portion of the trust income. Should Elizabeth, Katharine, and Louise all die without offspring, the estate reverted to those Philadelphia-based Catholic institutions endowed at the time of Francis Drexel's death in 1885.[45] The will reflected the intense Catholicism of Francis Drexel but also his business-minded determination to shield his daughters from the enticements of fortune hunters. He failed to foresee that fortune hunters were not all bachelor rascals; some came with other identities, their designs on the Drexel money just as calculating.

Any life-changing decision of Katharine Drexel, the reluctant heiress, to relinquish control of her trust—either through marriage or membership in a religious community—threatened the mission enterprise in the West. The bishops had only recently secured a linchpin for Catholic education among Native Americans, and vows, whether for marriage or for religious profession, would end their growing plans. The influence of a husband or a mother general was certain to distract Katharine from her single-minded commitment to Native causes. Faced with these unappealing possibilities, O'Connor intensified his efforts to direct Katharine's religious future.

On the one hand, O'Connor wanted Drexel to remain in secular society, where she would manage her trust without the restrictions of a congregation's financial regulations. On the other hand, if she continued to circulate in Philadelphia society, the chances of her marriage to a person of means increased. Such an individual would almost certainly be of an educational and social status sufficient to handle marrying into such extraordinary wealth, able to check the influence of the bishop in far-off Omaha, and inclined to limit the charitable inclinations of his bride.

Not only did O'Connor insist that Drexel belonged "in the world," but he also tried to manipulate the conditions of that worldliness. He suggested that Katharine take a vow, renewed each year, to follow a celibate life.[46] He thought she could try the arrangement and then decide if she wanted to make the vow a perpetual one. He suggested a form of prayer she might use and cautioned she would not be obligated to mention the vow to anyone, even her regular priestly confessor. Thus, O'Connor sought a creative way to assure that Drexel's money remained accessible to the missions, assuage her interest in religious life, and block objections from any other priestly confidant. This secret celibacy in the world was a clever ploy to bond Drexel only to O'Connor for consultation should she find herself pursued by an insistent suitor. Although not an absolute guarantee, the constraint of the vow for a woman with the intense Catholic sensibilities of Katharine Drexel would have slowed courtship, delayed marriage, prevented new heirs, and closed out the possible persuasions of a less-charity-inclined husband.

Perhaps at no other moment in her life did Katharine Drexel demonstrate the strength of her own intellect more than in her refusal to yield to O'Connor's arguments. Reared in a religious tradition that taught women to honor male clergy and defer to priestly authority, Drexel held her ground. On 26 November 1888, Katharine wrote to O'Connor: "It appears to me, Reverend Father, that I am not obligated to *submit* my judgment to yours, as I have been doing for two years, for I feel so sad in doing it, because the world cannot give me peace."[47] Katharine Drexel had resolved to remove herself from the management of her money, leave it in the care of Elizabeth and Louise to benefit people of color, and join a religious congregation of women. A careful and informed thinker who depended deeply on her spiritual instincts, Drexel would not be dissuaded, even by a bishop.

O'Connor accepted defeat with thin grace, suggesting that he merely "tested" Katharine's vocation to religious life, which was now, five years later, "sufficiently manifest."[48] Beneath his acquiescence no doubt lay the troubling gossip he had heard of "the well meant *plans* made by those of your own flesh and blood to *entangle* you and Lizzie in mere worldly alliances."[49] The secular and religious competition for the Drexel daughters' assets appeared to be escalating, and O'Connor decided the time had come to reverse his earlier objections. Katharine Drexel's profession as a nun, despite its drawbacks, gave administrators of the western church a better chance for fiscal influence than leaving the heiress within the circle of her marriage-minded family. O'Connor, who had lobbied against a nunnery for five years, immediately listed three religious orders—two of which practiced enclosure—that he thought appropriate. Although Katharine had written to O'Connor of the Sisters of St. Francis of Philadelphia, saying, "I admire what I see of their character," the Franciscans, with their convent spirit based on American democratic values, were not among O'Connor's recommended congregations.[50]

Mother Katharine Drexel Emerges

On 6 May 1889 Katharine Drexel, in a crowded Pittsburgh church, exchanged a silken gown for a black veil and, after a luncheon for 300 people, entered the novitiate of the Sisters of Mercy, escorted by her two sisters and her new brother-in-law, the husband of Louise.[51] Within four days, she wrote to O'Connor: "I have reached this Harbor of Peace!"[52] Here, in this enclosed "harbor," Drexel, as a Mercy postulant, was to explore the rigors of the convent to see if they suited her and she them. She devoted the summer months to learning the tenets of religious life, and on 7 November 1889, she received the habit and white veil of a Mercy novice.[53]

This introduction to the convent proved somewhat taxing for Katharine Drexel. Obeisance and obedience replaced self-sufficiency and personal decision making. While most young women signed on for the training program of a cloister between the formative ages of fifteen and twenty, Katharine approached her thirty-first birthday as she crossed the threshold of the Mercy Convent of St. Mary's. Already a mature woman who routinely made professional business decisions; consulted with bankers, engineers, and architects; employed workers with a broad range of skills; and set complicated plans into motion across thousands of miles, Katharine faced the challenge of allowing others to mold her words and actions.

In her first days with the Mercy sisters, she enthused: "This convent life is full of joy for me."[54] Reared in the worship practices of her family, she responded easily to the regimented prayer routines and was permitted extra hours for extended spiritual reading. She liked less some of the work assignments, especially with young children in the classroom.[55] In addition, she took on this world of rule and ritual separated from Elizabeth and Louise, with whom she had shared everything. No matter how much Katharine Drexel sought religious life and argued for her right to choose it, the novitiate required that this exceedingly privileged and independent woman yield to new patterns and new behaviors.

Besides the opulence of her May reception, at no time did Drexel's early training as a sister adhere to the strict regulations for postulants and novices. Postulants did not visit at the family home, entertain in the convent parlor, follow world events, or set off on shopping trips. Indeed, even within the walls of the motherhouse, postulants did not mingle freely with novices, and neither group exchanged casual conversation with the professed sisters.

In contrast to these long-standing practices, the Mercy sisters designed a strikingly different novitiate for Katharine Drexel, one that altered the usual regimen of prayer and work and even enhanced her breakfast menu to include fresh fruit. Most significantly, Drexel did not surrender control of her money, although she briefly considered making her two sisters trustees of the income.[56] During her postulancy, Drexel stayed connected to her Indian projects with a massive correspondence to missions throughout the West. She continued to receive requests, sorted them, decided which to endow, and set the size and conditions of the bequeaths. Not only did she use part of her day for her business interests, but she also left the convent on certain occasions to conduct transactions with her financial advisers. Along with other disciplinary exemptions, she received intense instruction from the Sisters of Mercy in convent administration and spiritual oversight of nuns—not among the usual lessons for postulants and novices.[57]

The explanation for these exceptions lay in the future planned for Drexel by Bishop O'Connor and other priests associated with missions for people of color. With Drexel's intention to enter the convent unshakeable, O'Connor launched a campaign to persuade Katharine to establish her own religious congregation of women rather than profess in one of the older orders. Drawing on Katharine's desire to provide education for people of color, O'Connor warned the reluctant Drexel: "If you do not establish the order . . . you will allow to pass an opportunity of doing immense service to the church, which may not occur again."[58] When Katharine, now a postulant, vacillated, O'Connor shot back abruptly: "I beg you not to consider . . . the proposed foundation an open question." And apparently wearying of her hesitation, he added: "If you expect an angel to be sent to enlighten you in regard to this matter, you may be looking for a little too much."[59] Nevertheless, Drexel was not easily wooed, and she considered staying among the Mercy women she knew and respected to be more attractive than her agreement with O'Connor.

When Bishop O'Connor died in 1890, one year after Katharine joined the Sisters of Mercy, the Philadelphia archbishop Patrick J. Ryan assumed the role of her spiritual and business adviser. Although not of the western diocese, Archbishop Ryan was well acquainted with the Drexel heritage and the family personalities. He was privy to the plans for the new religious community and hoped to keep it centered in Philadelphia. Within two days of O'Connor's death, Archbishop Ryan reiterated the late bishop's theme about the crucial nature of Katharine Drexel's specialized work. He deflected any thoughts of her continuing with the Sisters of Mercy and emphasized his willingness to confer about the new sisterhood before Drexel relocated to another diocese.[60]

Confronted with intense clerical lobbying and faced with a series of difficult decisions, Katharine was ill prepared for the sudden death of her older sister at the age of thirty-five. Elizabeth, who had married only the previous January, passed away during childbirth in September 1890. The premature infant died as well; no offspring survived Elizabeth to inherit her portion of the Drexel estate. According to the will of Francis Drexel, Elizabeth's share of the trust was to be divided between Katharine and her younger sister, Louise Drexel Morrell. Following the death of Elizabeth, Katharine Drexel focused more purposefully on the formation of her own order of religious women. She may have finally accepted the argument that no other congregation would devote itself so exclusively to her mission interests for people of color. She, vowed to poverty, may have conceded the administrative and emotional difficulties of disengaging from a fortune just increased by half in dollars and responsibility, both of which bound her to her deceased parents. She, vowed to chastity, may have chosen the personal stability of remaining with kinfolk—the much-cherished Louise; the loved brother-in-law, Colonel Edward "Ned" Morrell; and Elizabeth's respected widower, Walter George Smith, who never remarried and at his death in 1924 was buried in the Drexel family crypt next to his wife.[61] She, vowed to obedience, may have conceded that as the decision-making mother superior of her own congregation, she retained control over her money, which suited her temperament better than the deferential junior professed sister in any religious order.

Whatever forces impelled her, Drexel thought in terms of how to implement the plan and sought a location for a new convent. Despite appeals to move to her beloved West, Drexel chose to remain close to Archbishop Ryan, her few relations, and the familiar sights of home. She settled on a pastoral location near Philadelphia for a novitiate and motherhouse. Thus, Katharine Drexel organized this distinctly western-oriented congregation around a fixed eastern base.

In February 1891 Katharine Drexel, in the presence of most of those she counted as family and before Archbishop Ryan, pronounced her religious vows as the first Sister of the Blessed Sacrament for Indians and Colored People. She adopted a religious habit that honored the various congregations she long admired—habit and coif closely detailed after that of the Mercy sisters, a full-length scapular such as that of the Benedictines, and a three-knot white cord about the waist that called to mind the Franciscans. In this unspoken but visual way, Katharine acknowledged the formative influences of the congregations that attracted her missionary zeal.

Now known as Mother Katharine Drexel, she withdrew from the sisters in Pittsburgh. Accompanied by Mother Inez, a novice director on loan from the Mercy convent to further the religious decorum of the new sisterhood, Mother Katharine led a small band of thirteen to St. Michel, the Pennsylvania summer residence of the Drexel family.[62] At St. Michel, a comfortable and familiar haven, under the direction of Mother Inez, the first Sisters of the Blessed Sacrament for Indians and Colored People immersed themselves in building a community identity.

For those young women who chose to pursue their religious life with Mother Katharine Drexel, the new congregation offered an exceptional, fresh opportunity in religious life. By standing with her, these new Sisters of the Blessed Sacrament bonded with the most powerful, and certainly the richest, woman in the American Catholic Church, she who held the attention and respect of priest and pope. Drexel, as a well-placed, wealthy woman inside the Catholic Church, was secure, but as a professed religious, she needed these women to execute her larger design.

In addition, by its very title, the Sisters of the Blessed Sacrament for Indians and Colored People captured the impulses of reform that swept across America in the early twentieth century. Although much of that reform resonated within secular groups, it intensified when reinforced by religious philosophy. The civic duty to eradicate national social ills took on moral obligation and spiritual redemption under a denominational rubric.

For Catholic women, Mother Katharine Drexel—with her firm personality, clear social message, established philanthropy, unswerving faith, and vast fortune—emerged as an attractive leader. Demanding and exacting, she radiated a confidence in her position that complied with Catholic notions of leadership and authoritarianism. Mother Katharine embodied the traits of the traditional mother superior, calmly overseeing the temporal and spiritual well-being of sisters and charges alike, all the while holding steady to a personal course of integrity and prayer. Drexel expanded that imagery of the competent mother superior and offered young would-be nuns additional chances for exciting work and new horizons.

Katharine Drexel avoided vague idealism and concentrated on practical plans, devising a Catholic agenda for women reformers. She did not just talk about improving society but aggressively undertook the projects she thought would bring important positive changes—and she was not dissuaded by naysayers, regardless of their rank and prestige. Drexel reached out to the humanity of the American West—Native peoples—and she made it possible for eastern and European women to enter their world. With this combination of characteristics, Mother Katharine Drexel had no problem convincing her new sisters that she would lead them to the West.

The Nun as Benefactor

Although seemingly pleased that the congregation was finally under way, Drexel refused to allow its business to divert her from her first passion: building and fortifying Native American missions. Armed now with money and the authority of her place as a Catholic religious, Mother Katharine took direct action. In June 1891, leaving those at the Drexel summer home under the supervision of Mercy assistant Mother Inez, Mother Katharine journeyed to St. Stephen's mission, deep in the Wind River Reservation of Wyoming.

An Arapaho/Shoshone mission with a troubled administrative history, St. Stephen's had received Drexel money since 1885; despite many contributions for building construction and local salaries, however, improvements at St. Stephen's had not materialized. Business dishonesty, faulty workmanship, poor administration, continuous feuding, erratic mission personnel, missionary illness, extreme isolation—all resulted in chaos for St. Stephen's and misuse of Drexel money.

In 1888 the Sisters of Charity of Leavenworth sent missionaries, but they arrived in Wyoming to find matters less acceptable than had been described by the resident priest. The six nuns, led by the sixty-eight-year-old Sister Joanna Bruner, first sought refuge in a dilapidated cabin, gathering nuts and berries to supplement their meager pantry.[63] Learning that after three years, these sturdy missionaries announced they must withdraw, a dismayed Mother Katharine proposed to investigate conditions at St. Stephen's. Mother Katharine, distracted during events that included her admission to the convent and the death of her sister, now desired to correct the problems at St. Stephen's. She planned that, after an on-site inspection, she would resupply the mission and staff it with her own Sisters of the Blessed Sacrament.[64]

Traveling under the escort of the bishop of Cheyenne, Mother Katharine and her companion, Sister Patrick, recaptured the zest of the 1888 western trip of the three Drexel sisters. Filled with enthusiasm for the landscape, the adventure, the welcome of the Indians, and the needs of the school, Mother Katharine wrote effusive descriptions of her travels to Mother Inez, the Mercy nun overseeing daily events at St. Michel in Pennsylvania. Before Mother Katharine arrived back home in Philadelphia, however, both the mother superior of the Mercy sisters in Pittsburgh and Archbishop Ryan blocked her plan to staff St. Stephen's with members of the new congregation. They greeted with coolness the exuberant and detailed letter that described two newly minted sisters taking public meals at stage stops, crossing the Wind River on a small ferry, or walking down Beaver Canyon at four o'clock in the morning.[65] Mother Katharine failed to perceive that more-senior church leaders looked on the Sisters of the Blessed Sacrament as something of an experiment, a collection of unseasoned recruits lacking maturity in their religious vocations.

In the archbishop's assessment, temporal and spiritual influences, exacerbated by distance from Philadelphia, might lead to any number of disagreeable situations. Appropriate convent decorum might falter among the ill trained, especially inside Mother Katharine's group, where she was the only professed sister. More than one band at a mission outpost had set aside congregational conventions. More than one had fallen into bickering. More than one, citing poor communication and mistreatment, had tried to separate itself from an eastern motherhouse.[66]

Just as dangerous, from the archbishop's perspective, were the western bishops who might declare jurisdiction over the Blessed Sacrament sisters, leading to a clerical fight. After all, Ryan had only recently overcome suggestions that Katharine Drexel locate her motherhouse in California or Nebraska, a move that would have taken her beyond the influence of her many Philadelphia associates. Now he confronted the reality that Maurice Burke, the bishop of Cheyenne—who flattered the western benefactress with lavish praise, saying, "Your work among the Indians has been and is indeed a charity so great that words cannot express it"—had served as the eager guide for Mother Katharine and Sister Patrick on the moonlit road to St. Stephen's.[67]

Archbishop Ryan ordered Drexel to see to the formation of her nascent sisterhood in a convent accessible from his residence. The archbishop reportedly declared: "Mother Katharine needs me, she needs my supervision and counsel in the most minute details, for she is now planning for the future, and that future must rest on very secure foundations."[68] Whether the new foundress needed quite as much oversight as the archbishop envisioned, the selection of members, the organization of policies, the construction of a motherhouse, and the Catholic Church's requirements for official approval from the Vatican were expected to be Drexel's priorities.

Mother Katharine recognized the discretion in conformity and suspended her intent to send Blessed Sacrament sisters to the West. St. Stephen's went to the care of Mother Katharine's highly regarded friends, the Sisters of St. Francis of Philadelphia, who stabilized the school and worked there from 1892 until 1984.[69] Mother Katharine concentrated on the required administrative tasks. The refusal to do so would have invited defeat for her grand plan. If the archbishop publicly withdrew approval of the Sisters of the Blessed Sacrament, suppressed their rule, and directed them to disperse, Katharine Drexel knew her congregation could not function under the mantle of the Catholic Church. Should the edict include excommunication, even Drexel's champions among the western bishops would not be sympathetic to receiving the sisters in their dioceses. In her enthusiasm, Mother Katharine may have overstepped, but, after years of wrangling with priests over her convent desires, she was not inclined to threaten her new life.

Expanding the Work

Although Drexel yielded on the immediate activities of her new sisterhood, she did not suspend funding for the missions of other congregations. For example, her affection for the Sisters of St. Francis held fast, and she continued to support them in various locations. Her earliest impressions of these women stayed with her, as she recalled about a band she financed for an Oklahoma mission: "I remember when I was a secular I went to the Convent of St. Francis . . . to see the five sisters who were to found the school. . . . The five stood around me in the little parlor there and I looked at them as heroines, in wonder."[70]

Mother Katharine saw in those five faces the Catholic activism of the missionary, to which she herself aspired. She especially valued the Franciscan tradition of hospitality, which made these missionary sisters welcoming to the Apaches, Kiowas, and Comanches who came to their convent door. The sisters at St. Patrick's in the Oklahoma Territory reported to Drexel: "We have visits paid us every day. . . . One chief comes to see us. . . . He asks for something to eat then sits down . . . for a little talk in Kiowa and English."[71]

Encouraged, the Franciscans expanded their food distribution and provided a dinner of meat, bread, and coffee for those who came for Sunday church services. Natives and missionaries worked out a weekly arrangement whereby the sisters batched out food from their kitchen and Indians waited in family groups until summoned in shifts of forty for the meal.[72] Some of the Native people had accepted Christian baptism, and among the Sunday visitors were adult Mexicans captured by Indian raiders many decades before; these reveled in the renewal of Catholic devotions, one walking on his knees to the altar rail to receive the Eucharist.[73] Although the sisters tied the Sunday repast to attendance at mass and Sunday school, they did not demand a profession of Catholic faith in return for food. To do so would have violated the Franciscan concept of the missionary as one directed to move among non-Christian cultures, winning converts through longtime local interaction.

These assemblies around the convent and school gave form to new social behaviors between disparate groups and facilitated the sisters' entrance to camps in the distant parts of the reservation. There, the sisters offered some basic medical care—placing a salve-soaked cloth around a child's stiff neck, washing and dressing the sores of a baby. The Franciscans assured Mother Katharine that by building relationships through assistance, "It is the wish of the families that their children should go to our school." Still, these little advances did not disguise the overall desperate circumstances of the Indian community. After a year at St. Patrick's, the superior wrote to Drexel: "It is not as easy to work among the Indians as it is to read about them."[74]

Nonetheless, the Franciscans knew that their philosophy of mission service appealed to Mother Katharine, who expected a full accounting of their work. They relied on a regular correspondence to keep her assured that they remained committed to the advancement of Indian people. Mother Katharine, with her executive vision, wanted results for her monetary investment of more than $6,000 a year. A superior writing of her Oklahoma visit—"The Indian children are all making rapid progress in music, sewing, and learning. An entertainment . . . displayed the pupils' proficiency"— addressed the core issues about which Mother Katharine cared.[75]

While the letters stressed accomplishments with the schoolchildren and the adults, each included the inevitable plea for more money. The extreme poverty of these missions placed the sisters in the role of lifetime beggars before Mother Katharine. The requests were for simple necessities— money for an overdue grocery bill, an increase in the annual allotment for each child in the school, fifty dollars for a door to enclose the clothes wardrobe, window screens, material for bed comforters to replace the ones purchased when the mission had opened thirty years earlier.[76]

No matter how often Mother Katharine tried to improve a physical plant or clothe and feed its residents, the want at the missions remained endless. In 1909, almost twenty years after the opening of St. Patrick's in the Oklahoma Territory, the roof and stairs of the school building had fallen into near collapse. Workmen estimated that the repairs would cost $12,000. Even if that renovation took place, the school still needed a new building, furniture, coal, and firewood. The Franciscans regretted that without the repairs, St. Patrick's would not open for the fall term.[77]

The plight of the Franciscans in Oklahoma did not stem from occupational malaise on their part. Sisters at the Indian missions tried to supplement their stipends in a number of ways. Like other members of their congregations stationed in more urban settings, they valiantly sold their preserves and needlework, gave music lessons, made rosaries, charged tuition to day students, organized bazaars, and begged through the Anglo community. The nuns did not lack initiative and schemes, but a poor location and fiscal void could lead a visiting mother general to comment, "The Sisters find it a very difficult task to carry on the work of the mission."[78]

A further impediment rested in Drexel's policy of sending the sisters' stipends to the mission priest. It was not rare for a pastor to use the convent check for his own overdue grocery bill or church repairs. In 1910 the superior of the Franciscans at St. Patrick's Indian mission discreetly inquired as to the whereabouts of Drexel's allotment for coal and wood, a check that would have been mailed to the Benedictine pastor. A week later, the sister wrote again, saying there appeared to be "some confusion" over the money, which had been received at the mission. Hastening to add she wanted to "avoid any misunderstanding" with the priest, the Franciscan sister could not resist a jibe about Benedictines wishing all the money, but none of the work.[79]

For the most part, Mother Katharine remained aloof from these personality differences at the missions and concentrated on the use of the funds. Drexel subsidized certain projects through friendly loans but outlined a regular schedule of repayment. Ever courteous, even deprecating in her business letters, Drexel did not hesitate to press for an overdue account. She acknowledged each installment on a debt with long prayerful letters, always reminding the sender that other equally desperate missionaries awaited the money. As Drexel sifted through the hundreds of requests, she kept meticulous records of all donations and loans. She compiled a massive file of correspondence and amassed a collection of nearly 20,000 business letters, which she used as a database for keeping abreast of her commitments. Determined to dispose of her wealth in a purposeful manner, she remained cautious and private about disbursements.[80]

Over the years, Drexel routinely rejected the many requests that did not fit her criteria for the education of Indians and African Americans. Appeals from Catholic charities directed at other than children of color did not move her, no matter how worthy the cause. A Mercy sister building an Omaha orphanage felt, as many did, that the famous fortune was limitless and suggested approaching the Drexels and "Sister Kate," as "they would never miss $30,000." The confidant Omaha sister even promised to name the refuge the "Drexel Orphanage and Protectory," but the offer did not produce the hoped-for dollars from Philadelphia.[81]

Mother Katharine had developed explicit guidelines for her contributions, and she maintained an inflexible policy in that regard. She permitted her funds to be expended only for the education of Native Americans as she defined such a program. If a mission suspended its Indian education efforts, Drexel expected her payments for insurance and interest on debts to be returned.[82] The money was never to underwrite the schooling of white children who lived in mission areas or for expenses Drexel thought extravagant or superfluous. The argument that the enrollment of white students brought tuition money to a small mission meant nothing to her. and she dropped her support accordingly.

When a bishop in Oklahoma assured a mission superior that she could use a donation for furniture rather than for tuition and board for students, Drexel disallowed the purchase. She declared the new furnishing outside the benefit of Indian children, refused to replace the amount in the tuition fund, and withdrew her pledge for that school term. The bishop himself restored the $1,890 to the Pottawatomie school fund, thus deflecting the rancor of the mission sisters for his bad advice and of Mother Katharine for his presumptuous action.[83]

Through this watchfulness and singleness of purpose, Drexel maintained sufficient funds to continue allocations. As her own community grew, she reduced her dollars to other congregations but never entirely terminated her friendly assistance. Using careful business strategies, she stretched her donations to approximately $70,000 a year to the mission schools of the West. By the early 1920s, Drexel supported in some form more than 100 missions and schools for children of color on a trust income of less than $220,000.[84]

Blessed Sacrament Sisters Head West

Archbishop Ryan did not lift his travel ban on the Sisters of the Blessed Sacrament until 1893, when he allowed members to accept western missions. Drexel cast her gaze toward Santa Fe, New Mexico. She selected nine sisters to staff St. Catherine's, named in her honor as the one whose money built the school when it first opened in 1886.

With the arrival of these sisters at Santa Fe, another phase of the impact of Mother Katharine Drexel on the West began. For the previous ten years, her endeavors on behalf of Native Americans sprang from her individual actions. Her wealth permitted her to give shape to her inner convictions in a tangible manner. Yet the continued scarcity of mission personnel in several congregations restricted her efforts; schools opened and closed as missionaries in twos and threes came and went. Further, without local representatives to protect Drexel's interests, her control over the schools, and ultimately her money, remained limited. Planting her own sisters in the West promised to broaden her influence and to steady its direction.

The Sisters of the Blessed Sacrament sent to the West brought with them the philosophy of Mother Katharine. They cared about protecting her monetary investment and promoting her values among Native students. With lively letters to Pennsylvania, the western sisters fueled the zeal and resolve of those at the motherhouse, one sister writing: "Now all you future Navajo missionaries, listen to my tale."[85] The sisters on the mission were perfectly willing to spark the curiosity at the novitiate with humor-filled, self-deprecating anecdotes that might begin, "At last I have had the pleasure of gazing upon a real live Indian, but let me tell you how I acted and you will doubt my saying it was a pleasure at first."[86]

The sisters who transferred to western missions linked the social-justice concepts of Mother Katharine Drexel, the world of the West, and the imaginations of young nuns in the East. Their western presence allowed Mother Katharine to monitor the tone of mission management as well as the conduct of the nuns who directly represented her. With these developments, Mother Katharine's western focus shifted to the sisters of her own congregation, and in her position as their undisputed leader, she lengthened her shadow across western education.

In addition, these sisters learned how to be women of the West. Their experiences as travelers and workers exposed them to the personal growth and change that marked the western newcomer. Once the Sisters of the Blessed Sacrament opened St. Catherine's in Santa Fe, all of them undertook the work of the mission as a community ministry. The first sisters to arrive, disappointed by the low school enrollment, attended Indian festivals and began a Franciscan-style hospitality program to advertise their work among Natives. Usually ten or twelve Native families stopped for supper and slept on the grounds each night.[87] Finally, Mother Katharine had placed her own among Native Americans on a daily basis, the very essence of her congregation calling for a sisterhood that routinely passed its time in the midst of its constituency.

Mother Katharine's expectations for Native Americans prodded single young women in her congregation to make a place for themselves in western society. The sisters were required to build meaningful relationships with each other and the members of the Native American community within the context of the West. These Sisters of the Blessed Sacrament lost no time in carving such a place for themselves, doing so with a relish for Indian culture not often expressed by white society. Describing the beauty of a dance in which their students "wore belts of small bells which kept time with their feet," one sister wrote to Mother Katharine: "I never saw anything in my life as graceful as their movements. . . . Oh, if . . . the sisters

After their 1890s arrival in New Mexico, the Sisters of the Blessed Sacrament
learned to guide beast and wagon along dangerous mountain trails, staying
in the homes of Mexican and Native families and returning with boarders
for St. Catherine's School, named for Mother Katharine Drexel.
(Courtesy Sisters of the Blessed Sacrament, Bensalem, Pa.)

could only see this dance."[88] In these moments of western life, the sisters
helped to enlarge the definition of the woman's West and to bend further
the meaning of convent life.

Only a year after their arrival in New Mexico, the sisters pursued new
ways to live out the Drexel charge, traveling at the invitation of local Indians to pueblos for celebrations. For one such event, the nuns rose at four
in the morning to fulfill their prayer duties, after which they traveled by
wagon to the Cochiti pueblo, where the Indians rang the church bell to
announce their arrival and "all the Indians in the Pueblo were out to meet
us and we never got such a warm welcome."[89] While one sister rehearsed
the choir for vespers, the others walked about the pueblo, talked with residents, and made visits inside the homes of the sick.

Over a two-day period, pueblo residents performed an elaborate set of
Catholic rituals, more ornate than the sisters had ever seen. At the Indians'
insistence, the sisters led the choir and attended an evening vespers and a
public feast. They participated in a lengthy torchlight procession in which
a statue of St. Bonaventure, under a large canopy, was paraded about the

grounds with all residents of the pueblo singing a Catholic litany. The sisters witnessed a wedding, entered an Indian home for the community celebration, and conveyed their good wishes to the bridal couple.[90] These kinds of social events fell beyond the usual allowed to professed sisters. They reflected the rising insistence in the West that traditional roles for sisters change and the willing way in which sisters adapted to regional circumstances.

Natives and the Drexel Vision

The sisters' interaction, however, turned on more than one element. The New Mexico tribes, unlike Native Americans in some areas, came from a long tradition of Catholicism. They knew Catholic missionaries and how to define relationships with them. Ceremonial practices differed between Natives and whites, but there was an underlying spirit that provided a unifying sense of Catholicism. The sisters felt reasonably at ease with the Catholic life at the pueblos. They did not perceive, however, how much Native Americans directed the course of the associations, and the women tended to see themselves as the leaders in the relationships.

For Indians, advantages for families inclined them to form an alliance with the sisters. Although children from the pueblos had to leave home to attend St. Catherine's, they did not always travel the vast distances that some Indian schools required. San Juan Pueblo, for example, was only a few hours from Santa Fe along a well-known Indian roadway, making access to the children a reasonable possibility.

Through sojourns on the convent grounds, parents came to know the sisters personally and watched the operations carefully. Some adults were comfortable with the religious training for their children, as Christianity had become part of their faith practices and the patterns of Catholicism were familiar. Some hoped that Anglo education might mean future jobs for children locked inside the Native economy. Perhaps most important, Indians and nuns exchanged conversation and hospitality within each other's domestic provenance.

The New Mexico Indians also knew how to bring more than a dash of cultural·selectivity to their Anglo associations. During her second visit to St. Catherine's, Drexel, ignoring the advice of government officials, charged out to the San Domingo Pueblo during an epidemic. Burning for direct action, she misread the tone of the pueblo and tried to force her way inside.

When the Indians flatly refused her admittance, Drexel explained away the rejection as an example of Native concern for her personal health and well-being.[91] It more likely reflected the political sentiment and religious feeling of those inside the pueblo, who may have been using healing traditions they did not want disrupted by a white presence. In addition, Drexel was not a regular visitor to the pueblo or a familiar figure among the sisters working in New Mexico.

Six years later, at another pueblo, the residents sent for two Sisters of the Blessed Sacrament to nurse, cook, and clean in their homes during a malaria epidemic. The nuns stayed with a Mexican family, traveling by hired wagon to the sick, but shortly, the two nuns moved into the pueblo, assisting the priest, the government teacher, and the doctor when they visited. What started as routine nursing care with the distribution of milk and oatmeal gruel, beef extract, and quinine with daily prayer turned into excruciating weeks of watching whole families sicken, counting the dead, and preparing bodies for burial.[92] After weeks, the two sisters, their own health weakening, were anxious to return to Santa Fe, but neither the government employees nor the Indians wanted them to leave.[93] If Katharine Drexel had not won access to the private areas and intimate experiences of New Mexico Indians, some of her sisters did so—and with appreciation.

By 1900, with St. Catherine's on a firm footing, Mother Katharine wanted to increase her mission houses among Native Americans. She restructured an existing arrangement she had with Franciscan fathers in Arizona among the Navajos and drew up plans for a convent and school.[94] Again, she absorbed construction costs, bought furniture, and paid salaries. On this occasion, she moved to the mission location, spending several weeks reviewing and approving the work.

St. Michael's felt the presence of the strong-willed Katharine, for she pushed and badgered the work to completion.[95] By the fall 1902, despite several setbacks, she had the school ready for occupancy. The reception, however, of her missionary sisters among the Arizona Navajos proved different from the New Mexico pueblos.

In 1900 the Franciscan fathers and Mother Katharine conferred with Navajo leaders to convince them to send some children to St. Catherine's in New Mexico and to support the new St. Michael's when it opened. The Arizona Indians vehemently rejected these suggestions. They denounced separation from their children, questioned the benefits of Anglo education, and doubted the healthfulness of living among the sisters. Although the Franciscan fathers had pioneered in learning the Navajo language, the sisters had no such skill, adding another layer to the distance between themselves and the students. Only five children went to St. Catherine's from Arizona, and enrollment lagged at St. Michael's for the first year.[96]

Eventually, St. Michael's flourished, and in 1925 a Navajo tribal committee requested that it be enlarged or perhaps a second school be constructed in the area. Yet, at the outset of this mission, Mother Katharine again misread important cultural indicators of Native feeling. She who instructed her sisters to be sensitive to Indian parents, who wrote about the loving bonds between Native American children and their fathers, allowed her goals to blind her to the repugnance of family divisions for the Navajos. She failed to see that absorption into the conventions of Anglo Christianity had limited appeal for Native people determined to retain their own cultural identity.

Drexel may have lapsed because she blurred the distinctions between her two ministries. Eastern and southern African American families did not share with western Indians the same cultural response to the presence of Anglo schools in their communities. The benefits perceived to exist in Anglo schools differed for African Americans and Native Americans. While the former used schools in the struggle for economic and political parity in mainstream society, the latter generally preferred to resist the white-dominated curriculum in an effort to hold to traditional cultural patterns. With the administrative center of the Sisters of the Blessed Sacrament in the East and closer to the philosophical underpinnings of its African American constituency, Drexel, despite her great love for the West, lacked a regional compass to keep her grounded in western local cultures.

Mother Katharine's western experiences, always limited to tours of the mission houses, cast her as a visitor to the West. In contrast, many of her Blessed Sacrament sisters spent their professional lives as western residents. For example, the German-born Sister Liguori worked for almost forty-five years at missions in Arizona, New Mexico, and Nebraska.[97] Although Mother Katharine knew many Indians, she seldom remained long enough to cultivate the relationships that marked those who lived at the missions.

Distance and romantic feeling undercut Drexel's understanding of the West, particularly as its character changed across time. In 1902 Drexel grasped some insight into this reality about herself. Her enlightenment occurred because of a tour she made to the Indian Territory.

After years of relying on missionary letters for information, Mother Katharine wanted to see for herself the results of her donations to other congregations. She set out with her young cousin Josephine Drexel to survey the results of nearly fifteen years of mission building. Her itinerary took her to mission sites she had endowed for years, based on the pleading letters of desperate missionaries. At mission after mission, she barely concealed her shock at the appearance of the student population: in all places, she saw the children as Caucasian rather than Native American. She found it hard to believe that many youngsters with fair complexions could truly be Native Americans, and she referred to them as "bleached Indians."[98]

Mother Katharine did not consider a single Indian grandparent to be a sufficient bloodline for enrollment in her schools. Her distress mounted in those classrooms where she could not identify a single Indian child. She described herself as "surprised" and "horrified" by the light hair and blue-eyed appearance of students who told her "my mother was a Creek half breed, or my father is a Chickasaw, not full blood, or my grandfather was a Choctaw."[99]

That mixed-blood children seemed oblivious to the hatred of their full-blood classmates further disturbed Drexel. She saw that these intense reactions grew out of political and economic differences among adult Indians. At issue was the distribution of land in the Indian Territory. Even those with a small fraction of Indian ancestry could claim 360 acres under the severalty provisions and would benefit further when sale profits from the surplus lands were divided. Full-blood Indians would lose as mixed-blood and near-white families claimed the limited acreage.

The Indian Territory trip renewed Mother Katharine's fervor to save the full-blood Indians so "that they may not be cheated out of their land by the teeming population of whites."[100] If no one would make this effort, she felt the full-bloods destined to become "paupers and die out." Drexel reiterated her belief that through education, Indians could be made ready to marry among white people, leading to a dissolution of racial divisions.[101] She repeated these exhortations over the years, calling for a society in which Native Americans, African Americans, and Caucasians melded into one race. Although hers was a demographic picture that led all people into whiteness, it emphasized societal unity through marriage and procreation across races—a sexual notion abhorrent to most white Americans of the early twentieth century.

Paradoxically, Mother Katharine did not celebrate the evidence of marriage between Native Americans and whites that she saw on her tour. Perhaps her displeasure lay in her assessment that those unions had not been "with good Catholic whites" but rather with "the worst white element."[102] She remained, after all, a privileged product of Victorian America, raised with the class biases of the wealthy and her family's religious prejudices. The astonishing dimension of her life concerned the extent to which she set these hindrances aside and immersed herself and the women around her in an exceptional effort in American education.

Above all, the 1902 trip through Indian Territory convinced Mother Katharine that over the years, the intent of her donations had been diluted. It galled her that, even under the guidance of religious congregations, whites usurped the Indian right to education. She felt those bonded to the white community, mixed-bloods among them, forced Indian boys and girls out of their own institutions and off their own land. As a result, full-blood Indian families retreated deeper and deeper into reservation backlands, having even less chance to secure an education for their children. Ultimately, that meant a speedy death knell for Native Americans as their access to all mainstream economic opportunity collapsed.

Drexel reiterated that an absolute commitment to Indian peoples depended on the Sisters of the Blessed Sacrament. Mother Katharine warned her mission sisters to seek "true" Indian children for their schools. She expected the sisters to conduct recruitment trips into the Indian camps, for the purpose of finding full-blood children and convincing their parents to send them for an education. Although these sisters, traveling into backcountry and mountain towns by horse and wagon, listened to the pleadings of many Mexican families for school enrollment, Mother Katharine's requirements prohibited such arrangements.

Disturbed by what she had witnessed for Native Americans, Mother Katharine returned to the East and church bureaucracy. She recognized that the administrative procedures for securing formal papal recognition required her close attention. In 1908, with preliminary Vatican approval in hand, Mother Katharine, formerly the mother superior of the Sisters of the Blessed Sacrament, was elected as the first superior general of the congregation.

Free to refocus on the mission work, Drexel returned to the pleasure of her annual inspections to the West. In 1911 the death of Archbishop Patrick Ryan sank her into a paroxysm of grief. The following year, while in Santa Fe, she fell dangerously ill with a lung infection, compounded by a heart problem. Both her physical and mental state teetered at the edge of collapse. Accustomed to long years of authority, Drexel ordered the sisters to make nothing of her condition; the nuns had no context for knowing how to challenge her. As Drexel weakened, her brother-in-law overrode the convent indecision and arranged for her return to Philadelphia.

Now fifty-five and exhausted from years of travel and administration,

Mother Katharine recovered slowly over the next year. Her congregation, never destined to attract large numbers, had grown somewhat, and she placed part of the management into the hands of the more-experienced sisters. Finally restored, Drexel made a lengthy trip abroad, during which she sought European volunteers for the Blessed Sacrament congregation.

Finally, in 1916, Drexel returned to the West, traveling to San Antonio to visit with the Sisters Servants of the Holy Ghost and Mary Immaculate, a small congregation dedicated exclusively to the education of African Americans, Mexicans, and Mexican Americans. She left San Antonio for New Orleans, where she wanted a new project. There, her interest lay with the transformation of an old school into what became Xavier University, the first and only Catholic institution of higher education for African Americans in the United States.

From its genesis, Mother Katharine's work with African Americans and Native Americans met with mixed reactions in U.S. society. In 1891, the very day of its consecration, the St. Elizabeth's motherhouse outside Philadelphia had been the object of bomb threats. In the West, Anglos had shown themselves unsympathetic to Indian land claims, economic needs, or political parity. In all areas, African Americans had faced suspicion, hostility, and violence.

East or West, not everyone looked on the Sisters of the Blessed Sacrament for Indians and Colored People as noble humanitarians. Many saw them as radicals, misguided at best and dangerous at worst. The institutional church showed little inclination to endow the parishes and schools of African Americans and Native Americans. According to her friend Monsignor Stephen, the bishops "treated the Indian missions indifferently," saying: "Don't bother. Mother Katharine will take care of the . . . [Indian] schools."[103]

Into her seventies, and despite the dislike of some and the apathy of others, Mother Katharine continued funding schools for Native Americans and African Americans. She maintained her vagueness about exact tallies, and the amount given to the Indian missions remained shrouded in mystery; over fifty years, she invested approximately $11 million in schools for African Americans. As an elderly woman, she found satisfaction in managing these diverse charities and traveling to the mission houses for visits. At age seventy-seven, she was again taken ill while at St. Catherine's in New Mexico.

Drexel pushed on to South Dakota, where she wanted to explore a novitiate for Native American women who wished to enter the convent. She was keenly aware that religious vocations from among Native Americans had been scarce for all sisterhoods. Then, in 1935, a priest at Marty, South Dakota, wrote to Mother Katharine about seven Sioux women interested in forming a congregation for work among their own tribe. Perhaps still regretting an earlier failed effort for Native women that had been the subject of bitter infighting at the BCIM, Drexel agreed to assist this new project with money and training personnel.[104]

Drexel left South Dakota exhausted and unwell, suffering a serious heart attack in Chicago. She managed to return to the motherhouse, but she never again visited her beloved West. She lived out her long life on the infirmary floor at St. Elizabeth's. In 1937, at age seventy-nine, Mother Katharine stepped aside for a new superior general, her close friend Mother Mercedes.

Still, Katharine Drexel never lost interest in the financial affairs of the community. The terms of the Drexel will remained in place, and Mother Katharine refused to challenge them. Neither she nor Louise had any children, so upon their deaths, the fortune would return to Francis Drexel's original Philadelphia charities. Mother Katharine set up a small endowment for the congregation and encouraged the sisters to develop ideas for self-sufficiency.

The sisters already had branched out into many areas of work. They ran industrial schools and orphanages, conducted a prison ministry, did settlement work, and opened health centers. These occupations, however, would not be adequate to meet the expenses of the entire congregation once it was cut off from the Drexel money. The clouded financial future for the Sisters of the Blessed Sacrament remained unresolved as Mother Katharine approached her eighties.

In 1941 the Sisters of the Blessed Sacrament celebrated their fiftieth anniversary. It was a massive liturgical event, one that the infirm foundress managed to attend. Student talent—poetry, choral singing, Native dances, sand painting, crafts, plays, artwork—formed the centerpiece of the celebratory event. The scene moved a former student from St. Catherine's to remark of Mother Katharine: "Hers was a flaming desire to dream lofty dreams . . . a vision that promised what you and I should be."[105]

These words captured the fundamental spirit of Katharine Drexel. Raised to be an independent woman capable of executive decision making, she disliked obstacles and rarely yielded to them. Patrician by birth, she considered wealth cumbersome, a hindrance to the person she wished to become, and she determined to divest herself of material trappings. At the same time, Drexel refused to ignore her vision of the responsibility that money and status imposed. The image of Drexel swathed in a sweeping ivory silk gown and veil for her convent reception actually did not clash with her religious ideal of poverty. Rather, it spoke to how Katharine intended to transform the accidental privilege of birth into a resource for the poor while she allowed herself few comforts.

For Drexel, an intense sense of family bonding and Catholic philanthropy originated with her parents and Elizabeth and Louise. Later in life, she shifted this allegiance to her sisters in religion, with whom she developed a maternal identity and crafted an outlet for her business acumen, organizational skills, and executive leadership compatible with her faith beliefs.

Drexel valued personal relationships, whether family member or old friend, Philadelphia archbishop or Navajo chauffeur. At the intersection of her secular and religious lives, she chose to stay in Philadelphia with the biological sisters she cherished. Separations by death caused her exceptional pain, each one reviving the grief of earlier losses. The passing of Mother Mercedes took away a Drexel friend from the first days, and the ailing foundress felt this loss deeply.

The sudden death of Louise in 1943, fifteen years after that of her husband, Edward Morrell, brought Mother Katharine a wave of nearly unbearable sorrow. The prospect of life without Louise seemed unthinkable to the eighty-five-year-old, who smothered her agony in terms of religious acceptance.[106] Now the sole Drexel heir, she would not challenge her father's will. At her death in 1955, this less-than-sound business decision left her Blessed Sacrament sisters vulnerable, a situation rumored to have been partially rectified by the archbishop and the cooperation of the other beneficiaries.

The fortune of Katharine Drexel aside, the importance of relationships, which began in the Drexel family, in part explained her passion for reaching to others. Her respect for enduring human closeness perhaps led to her refusal to tamper with her father's financial choices and her willingness to host Indian parents at reservation boarding schools. She held to a code of conduct that she deemed appropriate and was loathe to violate it at any time in her life.

That code ignored racial boundaries in ways uncommon to the society around Mother Drexel and prompted her to think about divisive elements in American society. During years when white America, by custom and law, violently opposed any integration, she introduced a measure of it, gave it a springboard from which to take form. She did not, in the internal management of her congregation, strike down racial segregation—white sisters did not recruit and live with Native Americans and African Americans in the convents of the Sisters of the Blessed Sacrament.

This policy stemmed from the explicit and implied racism that tainted the minds of white Americans and invaded the thinking of the institutional Catholic Church in Drexel's era. In 1899 Monsignor Stephen, writing to thank Mother Katharine for a donation of $83,000 to finance government contract schools, remained pessimistic about the "dark future of the Indian work of the Church." Not only did Stephen bemoan the unyielding refusal of American Catholics to respond to the needs of minority groups, but he also worried about sustaining the future membership of the Sisters of the Blessed Sacrament. Unlike other religious congregations who "have in charge only white children" and thus have a source for religious vocations, "your subjects are Indians and Negroes, from whom you cannot receive postulants," he wrote to Mother Katharine.[107] Stephen, who had lobbied for many years on behalf of persons of color, recognized the real dangers associated with a white society that prided itself on its barriers to "race mixing" of any kind. He envisioned that in the segregated areas of the West and the South, a tiny, unprotected convent housing women of different races risked life-threatening assault. His fears were not exaggerated or misplaced.[108]

Even with these limitations, Mother Katharine sponsored interaction between and among hundreds of western "culture brokers"—those separated by cultural fences but willing to cross boundaries and exchange ideas, experiences, custom, and feeling. Such people constituted the messengers for societies locked in conflict, for they were the curious, interested in the "other side" and anxious to know something of its mechanics, mysteries, and people. Their efforts to relate to one another rested on an avalanche of cultural imperatives and economic factors that necessarily included the positive and negative. Nonetheless, Native Americans, African Americans, and Sisters of the Blessed Sacrament reached for an ideal of cultural understanding and human decency that might guide American society in its quest for a realized democracy.

Katharine Drexel wanted her ideas and her money to hone Catholic education into an upward-mobility tool for Native Americans and African Americans. The entrenched social and economic conditions that stymied her vision drove her to a moral philosophy about U.S. race relations that influenced American church thinking. Although it took many decades, the American clergy could not indefinitely ignore her voice, her constituency, or her money. Katharine Drexel embodied the potential of American Catholic women to widen gender constraints within the church and to shape the direction of Catholic thought.

Above all, Mother Katharine's work focused on promoting others, and she did so in the spirit of social justice. Her missions gave Native Americans community centers and reinforced their convictions not to tolerate the neglect of their rights as citizens. Her congregation offered young Anglo women a context for understanding regional and cultural differences as they committed themselves to societal betterment. Her early insistence on justice, regardless of flaws, prepared both her students and her sisters to respond to the changing meaning and practice of equality and dignity through the twentieth century.

As ethnic Americans redefined their place on the national stage and voiced their cultural expectations, the Sisters of the Blessed Sacrament responded with a Drexel-like spirit of action grounded in justice. In the 1960s, fueled by the Vatican II call for modern adjustments to religious life, the sisters reexamined their purpose and goals. They dropped the racial designation in the congregation's title. Still cherishing their historical mission, they embraced a ministry for people from all national and ethnic backgrounds. In an era when many religious congregations lost members, some African American and Native American women saw personal opportunity with the Sisters of the Blessed Sacrament and joined their ranks. By the 1980s, the members had elected Sister Juliana Hayes, an African American woman, as president of the congregation.

In November 1988 the Sisters of the Blessed Sacrament and their friends gathered in St. Peter's Basilica in Rome for a beatification ceremony for Katharine Drexel. This procedure, a step leading to a pontifical declaration of sainthood, gave Vatican recognition to the major impact of this one woman on the church in the United States. Although the Sisters of the Blessed Sacrament, led by Sister Juliana, played a prominent role in the ceremony, it was those served by Mother Katharine who dominated.

Eagle Dancers from the Laguna Pueblo in New Mexico swirled about the altar, Victor Bull Bear from South Dakota offered the "Prayer of the Four Directions," and Marie Tso Allen spoke the first Navajo ever used in a Vatican liturgy. Native American culture and faith mingled with church ritual and theology in unprecedented ways at the very center of Catholicity. Far from little mission schools in Wyoming, Montana, Arizona, Oklahoma, and New Mexico, Native Americans gave witness to the enduring strength of their own heritage and the legacy of Katharine Drexel. The originality of this celebration exceeded even the splendor of her 2000 ceremony of canonization, for this first event laid bare the lasting temporal and spiritual partnership between one white woman and countless peoples of color.

Many Native Americans and African Americans agreed that Mother Katharine Drexel, in her way and her manner, loved people far outside her life circle, acting over decades to raise whole communities out of the mire of poverty, discrimination, and disadvantage. She lacked a sophisticated understanding of cultural diversity, and she appeared to see all Native people through a generic lens. Yet she did not presume personal perfection, just a simply defined commitment to decency. From this, Katharine Drexel relentlessly linked variant cultures, insisting on the reality of a common humanity and leading many nuns to the inner heritage and personal heartland of peoples of color.

*Oh, dear sister, this afternoon,
I got a letter . . . that my beloved
sister Blanche . . . died Friday
night and was buried yesterday.
I can't write any more.*

—Agnes Jeager to Sister Mary
Joseph, 6 April 1902, St. John's,
Komatke, Arizona Missions,
Archives of the Sisters of St.
Joseph of Carondelet,
St. Louis

Ethnic Intersections

In March 1902 Agnes Jeager, a Yuma
(Quechan) teenager at the Phoenix
Indian Industrial School—a large government institution boarding students
from nearly two dozen Southwest
tribes—wrote to her former teacher, Sister Mary Joseph Franco: "All of us Yuma
children of this school are doing nicely
with our studies and work. . . . I am
very glad to tell you that we Yuma girls
never get into trouble."[1] Reports of her
parents and siblings at Fort Yuma were
less happy, for Agnes told Sister Joseph
that "Blanche has been sick ever since
I left her. . . . Joseph was sick for many
months too; and baby brother was lame,
so they are not feeling comfortable at
home."[2] A week later, a deeply saddened
Agnes wrote the news of Blanche's
death.

One year later, grief continued to haunt the Jeager family, as Agnes told Sister Joseph that her father "never writes to me so often since the loss of my sister and my two brothers. Most of the letters that I get from Yuma telling me that my father has a heart broke but he bravely bore it."[3] Further, Agnes confided that she pondered leaving the Phoenix school to escort Joseph, her surviving brother, to a blind asylum in Oakland, California, on the chance that his sight could be restored. Agnes had to set the plan aside, however, because "my father and mother do not want to part with him as he is the only one at home."[4] With an assurance that "all the rest of the girls [Yuma] are just as fat as usually [sic] and tall, except me," Agnes ended her letter: "I am your loving girl."[5]

In the West of popular imagination, Native Americans and white westerners traveled over parallel roads, jogging along shoulder to shoulder, casting furtive, sideway glances at each other but separated by insurmountable political and cultural divides. In this view of the West, Indians and whites saw each other, but as through a glass wall, their faces expressionless—no word, no sound, no gesture of one acknowledging life in the other. In this construction, both groups had western identity but no common humanity, no shared moments of joy, sorrow, hope, anger, or laughter, nothing that wove them together into the warp and woof of mankind.

Historians, however, have searched for more complex relationships between and among the many peoples of the West. Their inquiries reveal that interactions across race involved tightly woven intimacies and intensely voiced emotions, occurring as they did within the cradle of American imperialism and colonialism.[6] In such an environment, Indian boarding schools, the locus of fluid community—children and adults, Natives and whites, seculars and religious, non-Christians and Christians, families and single persons, employees and transients—set the stage for complicated, varied, or misunderstood associations.

Given that reality, easy depictions of perpetual adversaries driven by distaste and disinterest ignored the stubbornness with which human relationships simply refuse to follow a mandated script. Instead, the intersection of cultures always produced, along with broad general results, the singular, the unusual, and the untidy. In the American West, as elsewhere, circumstances and individual personalities stirred this lesser-noticed, random dust within cosmic encounters.

In addition to the tidbit that Native people corresponded with one another through the regular mail, the poignant letters of Agnes Jeager to Sister Mary Joseph implied that relationships between nuns and people of color followed more than one trajectory. This chapter argues that as Catholic sisters moved into worlds of color, the responses of ethnic communities to the presence of nuns shuffled some of the broader assumptions about the interracial narrative of the West.

Native Americans

Catholic missionary initiatives contributed to the earliest European incursions into North America. Franciscan friars hiked through Mexico and the Southwest in the sixteenth century, and Jesuit missionaries canoed along the St. Lawrence River in the seventeenth century. By the nineteenth century, several religions had jumped into the fray, so that coerced conversions and deadly encounters with Christianity had scarred personal and tribal histories from the Atlantic to the Pacific.[7] For good and ill, this religious jousting accommodated a Catholic disposition to sacrifice oneself for the church and partially explained the persistence with which missionaries pursued converts in every sandy desert and on every rocky mount.

In addition, for Catholics, convinced of the exclusivity of their theology, the proselyting activity of competitors further fueled their enthusiasm. Exhortations to deliver the "true" faith to the unchurched, thwart the efforts of rivals, and advance one's own sanctity were irresistible and ignited much of the motivation of nuns who ventured into Native American communities.[8] Fired as crusaders with spiritual ideals, Catholic religious women assumed teaching, nursing, and farming duties on reservations, engaging the controversial dynamics of Indian/white relations. As a result, the impact of these previously underestimated actors—indigenous peoples and white nuns—on the formation of western Catholic history calls for reassessment.[9]

The odious events, embroiled as they were in denominational, political, and military interests, roiled along from one generation to the next, leaving Native women and men constantly adjusting their strategies with religious and secular contacts. Across the West, the 1860s and 1870s, with their steady drumbeat of American expansionism and empire building, saw tribes assessing their imploding situations. Blistering armed conflicts and legalized land grabs, fueled by the continuous streams of white groups, dimmed the future for traditional Indian lifestyles in all corners of the West.[10] Advancing waves of farmers, soldiers, mercantilists, and industrialists—essentially the ground troops of the U.S. government—invaded tribal lands, confiscated hunting and fishing areas, and restricted water access, pushing Native people to rearrange their military, economic, and political conduct.

Depleted by violence and disease, Indian people regrouped, using the government-measured reservations—the spaces intended to strangle traditional life—as centers to reassemble their lives and identities. In actions frequently overlooked by whites, tribal members asserted the legitimacy of Indian rights and made choices connected to forced residency on reservations.[11] The responses of tribes varied widely: the Pueblos ejected white poachers from their federal game reserve; the Poncas (Dhegiha), "in the midst of severe privations," were "unwavering in their fidelity to their treaty"; the Yankton Sioux addressed the new government agricultural expectations by "planting nearly 600 acres of corn, potatoes, pumpkins, and squash."[12]

These efforts early in the 1860s to adhere to treaty agreements and define a changed but viable lifestyle from the Native side slammed into indifference or hostility on the other side. As if uneven governance by the United States was not sufficient for disruptions, the infamous weather of the plains inflicted scorching drought and swarms of grasshoppers that destroyed Indian crops.[13] By 1894 one agency farmer for the Arizona Pima [Akimel O'odham], after five years of frustration, complained to Washington: "I have sent in list after list of farming implements required. . . . [I] have received one farm wagon." He concluded, "When I stated . . . that these Indians had always been treated by the government like neglected stepchildren, I stated but the bare truth."[14]

All tribes knew that the farmer spoke correctly about the niggardly federal policies, and some reasoned that nuns' schools would increase government stipends and medical supplies, opening a chance for meals, health care, and clothing.[15] Despite conflicting opinions among tribal members about white education, some Indians thought it might serve as one component in battling white expansionism and worked to bring nuns to their reservations. In 1866 Lake Huron Ojibwas, disinterested in a boarding facility that would separate children and parents, agreed instead to offer six acres of land to any nuns willing to manage a day school.[16] Nine Coeur d'Alene Indians (Schitsu'umsh), acquainted with Jesuit missionaries, made an 1870 visit to the Sisters of Providence in their Walla Walla, Washington, convent to query the nuns about teaching the girls at their northern Idaho reservation, telling them: "You made [us] so welcome that [we] could see how well you like the Indians."[17] In 1881, when four Benedictine nuns arrived at Standing Rock Reservation in Dakota Territory, some of the more than 3,000 Sioux (Dakota and Lakota) Indians commented drily that the women were overdue, noting they had been hearing promises about a permanent faculty since the 1848 mission tours of the itinerant Jesuit Father Pierre De Smet.[18]

In 1874, when the Sisters of the Holy Names from Portland arrived at the Grand Ronde Reservation, their carriage was met by several hundred Chinook (Tsinúk) people on foot and horseback, as well as by a booming cannon salute. Once the large celebratory crowd escorted the sisters to the agent's home, two Chinook leaders, one using French and the other English, stepped forward to welcome the nuns. The French-speaking Indian told them, "All our hearts rejoice now because we have the sisters whom we desired for so long. For ten years we asked for you and today you come."[19] He was followed by another leader, who was said to enthuse in English: "We feel proud now, we have the good sisters to teach our children."[20]

Thus, the work of the French-speaking Holy Names sisters among these multilingual Natives started through Indian initiative. The sisters were the neophytes; the Indians drew on many years of white behaviors, dealt with strangers regularly, knew Catholicism intimately, and were well prepared to introduce the nuns to a new worldview.

In these encounters, Catholic missionaries initially saw themselves as the proactive parties, but it was Indians who defined the internal politics of a reservation, lobbied for sister-teachers, and protected Native family interests.[21] For new missionaries, the huge public displays of welcome appeared to be indicators of burgeoning Christian fervor and the desire for religious conversion. Yet within the reservations, motivation generally lay more closely to the hopes of parents for the futures of their children—futures that embraced their own traditions and culture. As these attitudes surfaced for sisters, one spoke for many about the force of Indian society, writing to her motherhouse: "Admiration and astonishment succeed one another."[22]

The possible advantages of schooling prompted more than words of welcome from interested Indians but included a sense of responsibility for the few white women among them. In 1883 Lake Superior Ojibwas built a log dwelling with kitchen, sitting room, chapel, loft sleeping apartments, and a large classroom in preparation for teachers from the Franciscan Sisters of Perpetual Adoration. In March, when the changing season called the men back to their hunting and fishing camps, Ojibwa women completed the construction before the arrival of two nuns.

Once the duo reached their transfer point, an Ojibwa escort met them and cautiously guided their heavily laden bobsled across the remaining solid ice on Lake Superior.[23] Fourteen miles later, the sisters climbed from the sled and viewed the convent, which was a tad rough but still a better residence than many offered by parish priests around the West. Here, too, the Natives supporting the school greeted the nuns, closely examined the two women—known to eschew the married state expected in Indian society—and carried the cumbersome baggage to the log house. Within a few weeks, parents of school attendees brought the sisters a half barrel of sugar, such an ample amount that the nuns shipped it to the motherhouse.[24] In this community, the sisters did not quite understand that school advocates took responsibility for their housing, safety, food, and reception.[25]

Although forty students immediately enrolled in the school, it did not mean that the nuns and the Native families, supportive as they were, agreed with or understood each other's educational philosophy. Despite the enthusiasm of families and teachers, the students disliked white classroom styles of group recitation, conducted in English. The children found the regimen of silently sitting along benches to be stifling and textbooks about penmanship or geography to be obtuse.[26] An academic calendar, designed from August to May, had no relevance to the Natives. Even the clock that ticked away the lesson hours meant nothing to Indian youngsters, and at recess, some ran for home while others went to the kitchen side of the building, ringing the bell for food. The nuns really had no effective way to enforce attendance or transform behaviors; any subtle changes hinted at the disciplinary hand of Indian mothers and fathers.

Progress in the alien subjects of arithmetic and catechism, and less restlessness among the scholars, appeared to impress some Indian families from a nearby Protestant school, and these parents transferred their children to the Franciscan sisters. If the sisters thought this meant harmony had developed concerning their Catholic presence, they were mistaken. The Ojibwas—Catholic, Protestant, and non-Christian—remained divided, and the nuns served as a subject for Indian factionalism, a problem exacerbated by the sisters' weaknesses in the Objibwa language. When the nuns, confused by a conversation about vegetables, told a non-Christian Ojibwa woman that they had no turnips, word spread among the Native camps that Catholic Indians failed to care for the sisters. Among the Ojibwas, the antischool group widely "rebuked" those who supported the mission for allowing the nuns to starve, insisting "they were not worthy to have the sisters, since they neglected to provide for them."[27] With this embarrassing censure from the non-Christians (a taunt that touched on Ojibwa communal traditions), the Catholic Indians increased their insistence that the sisters make known their every need.

More watchful than ever, the Ojibwa men intensified their role as protectors to the sisters living far from their own society. When the sisters decided that an excursion would be better in a boat than in a wagon through a "lumpy forest" where the "ride would have been a terrible hippedihopp [*sic*]," two men volunteered for the rowing. A pleasant afternoon outing vanished as soon as the small craft hit turbulent water in Lake Superior and all "seemed dangerous and gloomy."

Sister Cunigunda remembered their Indian escorts "rowed steadfastly forward into the stormy water [where] the waves rose like towers and hills and . . . knocked against the sides of our boat." Certain that the boat would capsize, Sister Cunigunda and her companion, Sister Catherine, who ultimately worked for thirty-five years at the Odanah mission, implored their guides to put to the shore, which the oarsmen refused to do.[28] Finally, the Indians, against their better judgment, yielded and turned toward land. As soon as they reached the shallows, the nuns jumped from the boat and onto the marshy bank, immediately realizing why the Natives had warned against a landing. As the sisters attempted to wade through the muck, the sand gave way, sucking them down until they could not move in any direction. The boatmen extricated the floundering women, who rushed into the dense forest, either to push on in their travels or escape the embarrassment of a "quicksand" rescue at the hands of Native men.

In the brambles and vines, the two became separated, and later, Sister Cunigunda recalled: "The twigs and shrubbery so tormented my eyes that at last I fell over a fallen tree. I had no relish to go onwards. . . . She [Sister Catherine] came up to me, and delivered an eloquent sermon, whose tenor was my clumsy and silly behavior."[29] The two soaked and muddy nuns, one less distraught than the other, limped back to the clearing, where they found the waiting Natives beside the boat. Unimpressed by the lake winds as well as by the total disconnect of communication, the Indians helped the nuns aboard, headed onto the open waters, and delivered the pair to their destination.[30]

Other Natives who did not know Catholic nuns also raced to the aid of women in danger. In New Mexico, when two sisters and their driver could not ford a wide river, a passing Native man climbed into the wagon, leading the way to a possible crossing. In the fast-moving stream, the wagon sank deeply into the sand, so that the straining horses lost their footing and fell sideways into the raging river. In the midst of panic and danger, the Indian jumped into the water, alone throwing his weight against the current and the lodged wagon wheel. On the far bank, two other Indian men, coming on the watery drama, plunged into the river and, joining with the Good Samaritan, released the wheel, pushing the wagon, the animals, and the nuns to the bank. The trio of soaking wet strangers then left the sisters to continue to a pueblo, which awaited a church celebration.[31]

Here were situations that reversed the perceptions of the missionary priests and nuns, who viewed themselves as the caregivers. In return for protection of a few women thrust into a strange environment and allegiance to their values, Indians asked for spiritual ministry, but most commonly for their children to access white society through its brand of schooling. Such sentiments failed to resonate with all Native people, many of whom considered the white schools—whether distant boarding facilities or nearby missions—as literal and figurative deathtraps. These many conflicting feelings added to the forces that pushed sisters toward cultural perceptions they had not anticipated.

Issues of family unity, protection of the young, and the power of destructive influences underscored Native reactions, for, as a Benedictine sister realized of children in her many years at the White Earth, Minnesota, mission: "It is heartbreaking for them to leave their homes, even though it might be a poor hut."[32] Her long life at White Earth led her to say of Native parents, "If they had nothing to eat themselves, . . . [they] always provided for their children," and "to ease the hunger pangs, the adult Indians would tighten their belts and then go without food."[33] An emotional Ursuline in Montana described returning fifty cents to a destitute Gros Ventre mother who had brought a starving daughter to the mission and begged the Catholic sister to take the coin and "to love her child."[34] A Sister of the Blessed Sacrament, working among various Arizona pueblos, spoke of the tenderness and sensitivity of Native mothers and fathers, saying: "That is why I would tremble to disregard their rights as parents."[35] A nun at a New Mexico pueblo, returning a small boarding student to his family, cringed at a poignant scene when the child stood silently before his mother "because he could not understand her Indian, and answered her in English; she felt it 'keenly.'"[36] Indeed, during her 1902 tour of the Oklahoma Territory, Mother Katharine Drexel seemed to gain greater empathy for the reluctance of Native parents and children to separate and to perceive more deeply their bonding, recalling a pleasant scene of families gathered together eating watermelon; perhaps her most powerful memory, though, was the defiant farewell of an Indian boy who called after her entourage, "You'll not get me."[37]

Despite such scenes, many Native families did not reject Anglo pedagogy out of hand, and many persisted in sending their children for instruction. Indian children—white misjudgments and dismissive epithets aside—showed themselves adept at advancing in the new curriculum.

Chinook children at the Grand Ronde Reservation made rapid progress in writing skills, memorization, and various manual arts but found arithmetic challenging.[38] The Ursuline sisters in Montana reported that the

Blackfeet (Aamsskáápipikani) children were "getting along nicely in school," and that the "little ones have written letters to their Indian parents."[39] Of Arapaho (Iñunaina) students in Wyoming, the sisters recalled that "in teaching them there was no trouble, so great is their power . . . in the line of drawing."[40] A Sister of St. Joseph remembered of the Papagos (Tohono O'odham) that the "children are . . . a pleasure to teach. . . . [And] for the most part, they are gifted, often remarkably so."[41] After the Native chief of police from Fort Belknap brought his son to an Ursuline school, one nun wrote: "He is a very promising lad . . . never saw a letter . . . and now reads well in the first reader. . . . Will make a good writer and understands his numbers well."[42] By 1902, the Franciscan sisters in Oklahoma had graduated students who qualified in algebra, bookkeeping, shorthand, geometry, rhetoric, and literature.[43] Impressed by the "spirit of the people" at Purcell, the visiting Mother Katharine Drexel appeared to question an exclusive industrial-arts curriculum for Indian students, declaring: "Higher education is a necessity here."[44]

If Mother Katharine and other sisters applauded the tangible advancement in English composition and mathematics, they questioned less the depth of understanding for children forced out of their own language and into another. In that violent linguistic world, a smoother bridge between cultures materialized in the cadence of music. When academic subjects and domestic skills of the white world left teachers and students wearied and frustrated with each other, group singing represented a happier meeting ground. While among some, debates intensified about the comprehension of Euro-Anglo lyrics or Latin chants, the common pleasures of music appealed to both faculty and pupils. Many different languages—Latin, Native, English, French, German, and Italian—rose and blended in the harmonies of song.

One sister in Minnesota recalled: "The Indians are very fond of music . . . and dancing."[45] Only shortly after their arrival at White Earth, two Benedictine sisters organized a choir able to perform the difficult notes of the high mass.[46] In Montana in 1888, an Ursuline sister remarked about the Latin skills of the choir: "It was very touching to hear the children singing the *Laudate*." Six years later, she continued to find solace in bicultural music as she enthused about being awakened by the boys' brass band, declaring: "The *Adeste Fidelis* sounded heavenly at that midnight hour in the lonely and peaceful mountains of the Rockies."[47] In 1899 in the Dakota Territory, a sister touched by the universal balm of music noted of the Christmas singing: "The Indians looked upon their clever children with true pride and a great deal of joy, although they did not understand a word

In 1935, at a South Dakota ceremony where a photographer possibly captured the last image of Mother Katharine in the West, seven Sioux women established a Catholic sisterhood dedicated to Native Americans, part of the Drexel vision from nearly fifty years earlier. (Author's collection)

of it."[48] As much as ten years earlier, these Franciscan sisters led prayer and song in the Lakota language at the Sunday masses, a local Catholic tradition the nuns had not sought to terminate.[49] In Arizona in 1907, when many families flocked to the mission for Christmas, a nun wrote about the music: "The old Indians . . . around the door, on the porch and in the courtyard too seemed much pleased." Nodding to the cultural exchanges that drift back and forth across artificial societal divisions, she added: "The girls then sang the *Hail Mary* in Navajo, at which everyone was *more* pleased, and if I ever see you again, I'll sing it for you."[50]

Some Indians with long ties to Catholicism developed their own imperatives about how church music fulfilled religious exercises. Like the Lakota in the Dakota Territory, Native people in the Southwest had formulated their Catholic spirituality over generations and demanded that nuns conform to those practices. In Arizona, adult Native speakers came to the classrooms after Sunday church to learn the next set of prayers and hymns in Spanish, thus keeping their control over local worship services.[51] Over time, nuns missioned among Native peoples appeared to accept more fully the legitimacy of Catholic ritual as defined by Indian traditions.

For example, in 1895 Sister Liguori left Santa Fe with the popular boys' choir, invited to the Cochiti pueblo for a celebration. When the nun and her singers reached the mountain town of Peña Blanca, they were informed that in one hour, the nearby pueblo residents expected vespers for the opening of the festival. The choir had not practiced this chant, and the organ, critical for the musical phrasing, was at the pueblo. Organ or not, the Indian organizers, having set the agenda, made clear that cancellation of vespers would be unacceptable to the Cochiti Catholics.

The situation caused considerable anxiety for Sister Liguori, deeply invested as she was in local communities. Summoning the parish priest and his violin, the nun gave the boys some speedy instruction, took advantage of an hour delay for more rehearsal, and led the children in a performance that blended with the rituals at the Cochiti church. The outcome was a vespers service that one nun reported had "impressed me very much."[52]

What impressed this nun was the intense expression of Catholicism adapted to and imbedded in the culture of Indian peoples. High in the New Mexico mountains, white nuns deferred to Catholic rubric fashioned by Native people. The frequent repetition of gunshots in threes, though startling to the sisters, resonated with their Christian belief in a holy Trinity. The combination of bell ringing, rifles firing, and drums beating during the mass; solemn processions through the streets; and reverence for the statue of St. Bonaventure further layered the sisters' European Catholicism and that of Native Americans.[53] At Cochiti, the rituals of faith overlapped in ways that suggested to these nuns the best of spiritual commonality crossing cultures.

Less than a year after the Chochiti event, Sister Liguori and the choir had achieved such regional renown that "their presence is regarded as almost indispensable for some of the Indian feasts."[54] Among the requests, the governor of the Tesuque pueblo, a place of sunken poverty, sent his personal delegate to ask with futile hope whether the sisters would make a ten-mile trip for a celebration for San Diego. After the nuns agreed to bring the choir with its sacred songs, the astonished Indian reciprocated with a dance of thanks he performed in the sisters' kitchen. Once at Tesuque, the choir added interest and liveliness to the proceedings, which drew Indians from surrounding pueblos as well as a large crowd of Mexican faithful.

Thus for some Indians, the music diluted the tedium of difficult lives, centered them in the rituals, and gave them a communal role in a religion that typically spotlighted performance by a single priest. In Arizona, Teresa Tash-quin and Juanita Antone, writing "thank you" letters to the mother general in St. Louis in what was certainly a class assignment, chose to tell her: "My oldest sister and I sing in the choir. We have a nice choir about fifty girls and boys sing"; and "I sing in the choir and every morning we sing."[55] Rhythms of joy, sorrow, faith, and memory pulsated through cross-cultural experiences in all parts of the sisters' West.

Along with the bonds forged through music, students taught nuns about another factor that could enhance mission life for everyone. Native children convinced their white teachers that for homesick, school-bound boarders, the out-of-doors world brought a happy release and a return to comforting environs. The sisters' immediate reaction to the "wildness" of Indian children for escaping the classroom altered over time. In Oregon, the Sisters of the Holy Names, at first critical of the students' efforts to get outside of school buildings, came to "make these days of freedom as agreeable as possible."

Although the nuns, older than students and dressed in lead-heavy habits, described the outings for themselves as "compelled exercise," they yielded to the realization that "the greatest amusement that we can procure . . . is to let them run in the woods."[56] In Montana, when rain and hail forced the postponement of a picnic dinner, Sister Mary of the Angels expressed her disappointment for the children because they "have a walk to the mountains every pleasant day to pick flowers and camp."[57] Three months later, her companion, Sister Francis, wrote of these children: "They love to roam over the hills and climb rocks, that is their greatest delight," and she joined the students, boasting that she, cumbersome habit notwithstanding, had scaled an exceptionally high boulder the previous week.[58] Three years later, Sister Francis admitted that an outing could burden the cook, who spent days preparing meals with treats, but she said, "I have promised the children a picnic tomorrow; they are nearly wild talking about it."[59]

As sisters learned from students more of the natural world, they also branched out from their missions for community events. When Chippewa leaders announced that a parade route would not pass the convent, the nuns walked to the Native settlement for the Fourth of July celebrations. They socialized among Indian families, watched the Bear and Moccasin games, shared the ice cream, saw the girls play croquet, and enjoyed the evening fireworks.[60] Returning to the convent long after dark, these sisters carried with them the imprint of Indian culture, some of which reflected white influences but with the strong flavors of Native traditions.

Despite damaging missteps, regular use of racist language such as "savages" or "little pagans," abetting forced acculturation, and conceit of "saving the heathen," many sisters accepted symbols of Indian Catholicity, learned and used Native language, came as guests to gatherings designed by Indian communities, and intensely embraced duties as teachers and surrogate parents for Native children. They did these things, of course, while still holding deeply to their own cultural beliefs and often overlooking the long-range, disastrous changes resulting from a national policy of forced Americanization.

Still, many sisters actively cultivated personal relationships with Indian peoples and attempted to be advocates for a better daily life on the reservations. At small missions, such as White Earth in Minnesota or Komatke in Arizona, a tiny faculty of two to four sisters, living on limited financial and physical resources, staggered under the effort to supply every necessity. A Benedictine sister, describing how the children stayed with the nuns "day and night," had written: "It takes quite a bit to provide for them all."[61] A Sister of St. Joseph pleaded for another mission nun: "We have 90 children right here in the house: you know what that means."[62] In all departments—classroom and kitchen, church and fields—sisters pushed their skills to the limit or learned new ones as need arose. One nun, over thirty years among the Chippewas, recalled that in the absence of a cobbler, she voluntarily mended 3,000 shoes for Indian families. As holidays approached, and in addition to her assigned duties, she sewed until two in the morning, turning out as many as seventy-five dresses for the boarders.[63] In Arizona, calico, flannel, buttons, and ribbons donated by the St. Louis motherhouse became dresses, pants, and shirts through the stitching of just one sister, who remarked, "How many poor little children they will cover this winter."[64] For special events, such as the first communion of a chief and his wife, the nun wanted "something very nice" and requested a "few yards of brown silk braid [and] a very pretty piece of watered silk, either white or cream." For the chief, she ordered "a pair of gentleman's riding gloves, [for] I promised them to him."[65]

These many different interactions took place by means of garbled language, making the West a regional "Tower of Babel." In a system of coerced Americanization, it would seem that "English only" prevailed at all times, for an inflexible language mandate applied to schools receiving government funds. Missionaries in the field, however, often ignored the rule. They acquired Native language skills to support that Americanization and facilitate proselyting, but their own linguistic interests and a desire for cross-cultural conversation often won the day.

Accordingly, some nuns made studious efforts to gain proficiency in the language of the Indians around them. Kansas Jesuits remembered of the mid-nineteenth-century death of a Sister of the Sacred Heart who had worked among the Pottawatomie Indians for more than twenty years that "she had a ready command of their language."[66] The first Sisters of Providence in Montana from Canada began immediately to study Indian language under the tutelage of a Jesuit priest.[67] One sister eschewed English completely, becoming fluent in the Native tongue, which she used exclusively.[68] In 1884 Indians at St. Labre's recited a Christmas Eve rosary in the Cheyenne language. During the next few months, one of the Ursuline sisters pushed for better skills, writing to her superior: "Mother, you know how *hard* it is for me to learn anything; and such a language as the Cheyennes have, takes up all my spare time."[69] One of her companions explained that farm labor kept the sisters in the fields during the warmer months, so that, presently, "We are trying to accomplish something with the *language* this winter."[70] Twenty years later, a sister missioned to Arizona reported that with the help of a student, she was "learning the Maricopa language," which she found much like the Yuma that she already spoke.[71] In the 1890s, one Jesuit missionary acknowledged that among the approximately 1,000 Montana Native children in sisters' schools, "besides English, many of the teachers speak also the Indian languages of the pupils under their charge," suggesting that more than one sister sidestepped federal policy.[72]

In part, the sisters recognized that to retain their government contracts, they had to maintain the residential conditions, advance the students in academics, and demonstrate that they taught the Indian children "how to work."[73] After years on Indian reservations, nuns in many western regions had witnessed enough fraud directed at Indian peoples to have developed some skepticism toward federal investigators and agents. Although nuns expected their own lives to be grounded in poverty, the depth and breadth of Native indigence, tied directly to disastrous government policies, appalled them. Further, the nuns did not act from a position of strength with the government, as contentious relationships between Catholic sisters and Protestant agents and supervisors dominated at many agencies.

For example, even before the Ursuline nuns from Toledo arrived among the Cheyenne people in Montana, local stockmen harassed the Indians there, objected to a plan for more families, and lobbied for the removal of all Natives from the potential grazing acres.[74] Within a few months of moving into their leaky cabin, the walls of which were decorated with old pages from the *Police Gazette*, the Ursulines were detailing pitiful accounts of "our poor and half-starved Indians."[75] In January 1885 Sister Ignatius wrote to her superior that a band of starving Tongue River Indians, disgusted by the lack of food, had walked back to the Pine Ridge Reservation in the Dakota Territory when the agent, cooperating with the cattlemen, refused to release rations.[76] Two years later, matters were no better in Dakota, where the biweekly supplies distributed on "beef-days" at the Rosebud Agency were so shorted that Natives had no food for four and five days before the next allotment. By 1894, missionaries visiting barren campsites encountered families starving en masse, the adults so weakened that they could barely stand and children chewing a few green berries or a dry bone.[77]

Such deliberate murderous tactics were not abstracts for the nuns living among Indians; they accentuated the realities caused by inhumanity and corruption. Direct appeals to agents, among whom turnover was rampant, further convinced nuns of the intractable policies of the government. Even an apparent generosity could hinge on greed, as when an agent gave two bolts of printed fabric and two of unbleached muslin to the nuns at the St. Ignatius mission. Approximately three years later, the Montana missionaries, entirely by chance, learned that the agent's financial report had claimed "by domestics furnished the sisters' school at St. Ignatius, $1,600.66." Stunned at the fraudulent charge for a few yards of material, the sisters "felt loath to ask for any assistance from such a quarter, lest . . . we should become accessory to the dishonesty of those gentlemen and give them an occasion to exercise their thieving propensities."[78]

Catholic sisters lived as both friend and foe of Indians. For nearly a century, the general population of nuns agreed with prevailing ideas that Indians should forget their history, language, culture, and spirituality. The women endorsed a dominating Christianity and the layering of one culture over another until the latter became invisible. The widespread racist language of the late nineteenth and early twentieth centuries permeated convent reports and letters. Boarding schools, by design, contributed to the dissolution of Indian family life and the fraying of traditional practices. Shorn long hair, often described as necessary hygiene or benevolent punishment, wounded Native selfness. Even the intended good spirit of a school Christmas tree or an Easter-egg hunt overlooked the cruelty of traditions ignored. The collective impact of such attitudes drained away large portions of Indian identity and led to disaffection among Native peoples for many generations.

As individuals, however, nuns compiled a more complicated legacy within Indian communities. In Arizona, they recalled the pleasure in "[the] little ones teasing . . . half English, half Navajo," but whose suffering led to anger that "Washington will have a . . . problem . . . to keep these poor people from starving if the Whites come in and get the best of their land and . . . everything else worth having."[79] In California, sisters could laugh when one student wrote about the religious laxness of another: "He had no brains in his constitution, so what can anyone do?"[80] In Wyoming, nuns explored friendships with Native women of several ages.[81] At all missions, nuns nursed Indian families through epidemics and grieved that "most of the Indians die of consumption."[82] In the Dakotas, Minnesota, Oregon, and New Mexico, sisters entered into intimate spaces within Native cultures, among the few whites permitted to see rituals of illness, birth, marriage, and death.[83] Above all, sisters invested in cultures beyond their own and discovered themselves transformed, so that after ten years in Montana, one nun, apologizing for her awkward correspondence to an eastern motherhouse, wrote: "I know you will pardon me because I am much like an Indian myself."[84]

Such feelings would not extricate the nuns and Natives from the impossible world situation that battered indigenous cultures. Uncertainty, loneliness, and poignancy filled the letters of Agnes Jeager, the Yuma girl who wrote to her nun friend, "Your dear little welcome letter was handed me Saturday evening."[85] Two years later, she ended a letter "my love to all the sisters" after confiding about her troubled life: "Today I am all alone here in the room thinking of my hard future days to come which I have to struggle through, in order to graduate this coming spring."[86] Hard days they must have been, for by January 1906, Agnes Jaeger had completed her examinations at the Phoenix Industrial School, returned briefly to the poverty surrounding her grieving parents at Yuma, and moved away. Without success, Sister Mary Joseph anxiously queried nuns and Indians, trying to confirm if Agnes "had gone to Los Angeles to work"[87] or perhaps had connected with the Sisters of St. Joseph at San Diego or Banning, California.[88] The friendship between one nun and one Yuma girl disappeared into the scrim-draped narrative of Catholic sisters and Native Americans.

African Americans

In December 1890, after weeks of rumor and uncertainty, ten German Franciscan nuns—defying the bishop, a mother superior in New York, and Katharine Drexel, their mission sponsor—chose to remain in their Pine Ridge convent, situated between rallying Natives and massing army troops along Wounded Knee Creek. At one point in the hostilities, when it appeared that the Lakota forces would prevail, "another black cavalry regiment came charging in support, and the Indians had to give way."[89] Remembered as the Massacre of Wounded Knee—in which young and old, women and children were slaughtered and most of their frozen bodies thrown into a common grave—this disaster closed one phase of Native resistance.[90] It also brought to the warfare between whites and Indians the deciding presence of the Buffalo Soldiers, mounted African American troops of the U.S. Army. This occasion, in which peoples of color warred against each other in the interests of white hegemony, reeked with irony, for in the American West, these ethnic groups faced systematic and institutionalized discrimination. As that unsavory account ground forward, Catholic nuns, as they had with Native Americans, sought their own role with and as African Americans.

In May 1865, a month after the conclusion of the Civil War, the bishop of Natchez wrote to the archbishop of New Orleans: "Would it not be a good thing now to establish in the South . . . those colored Sisters of Baltimore?" The bishop looked ahead to changing schools for African Americans, whom he thought "have no great inclination toward the Church— but . . . the Sisters' teaching and training would soon please them." Most important, the bishop suggested, along with the channeling of black family discretionary income into education, was that "the very nature of the community would flatter them—Sisters of Charity of their own color."[91]

Bishop William Henry mused about the Oblate Sisters of Providence, an order of African American women. In 1828—impervious to the legality of black slavery in Maryland, a general American distaste for Roman Catholicism, and the tepid endorsement of their own church leaders— four women formed a religious congregation for women of color. Émigrés from the French-held Caribbean island of St. Domingue, they persevered under exasperating or openly hostile conditions, building a reputation as religious educators of black children.

The Oblates' identity—influenced by a mixed ethnic ancestry among the founders, a political climate where both enslaved and free blacks circulated on the boulevard, and the inherent contradictions within a church that more than tolerated the suppression of Africans and women—apparently seasoned the sisters for their challenging life in Baltimore, heralded as the "cradle of Catholicity" in America.[92] By 1865, as literacy for former slaves and their children gained attention, the Oblate Sisters of Providence stood poised to further their teaching and social-services ministry. They understood that African American Catholic education carried with it personal threat and deprivation, but they aimed to do everything "with all the smiling grace of the French and the Negro's admirable endurance of wrongs."[93]

Prepared to move beyond their eastern motherhouse, the sisters in 1880 entertained a request to staff St. Elizabeth's in St. Louis. Organized by Archbishop Peter Richard Kenrick, this church, the single one for African Americans, replaced the worship space of a segregated loft at St. Louis University, whose Jesuit priests lobbied for the new parish. As a young administrator before the Civil War, Kenrick, according to legend, traveled throughout Missouri accompanied by a free black servant as the two searched for needy Catholics and possible converts.[94] Whether those outings, coupled with the petitions of black Catholics and Jesuits, inspired the archbishop to form an African American church or not, his city had compiled a less-than-attractive record with persons of color—free or slave.

During the slavery era, St. Louis had not shown itself receptive to the few white sisterhoods operating schools for children of color. After their arrival in St. Louis, the Sisters of St. Joseph, with the approval of Kenrick, opened a school for African American girls from free homes. At this location, the sisters added a ministry to instruct slaves, but only for the reception of the sacraments of the church. But one sister remembered general teaching for "some of the Catholic slaves of the French families," and that, in the school, "the slave occasionally mixed with the free Negro."[95] Learning among free and enslaved blacks, especially in the same classrooms, frenzied the surrounding Anglo-European community; one young nun explained to the French motherhouse: "This displeased the whites very much. They threatened to drive us out by main force. The threats came every day."[96] Once the ugly climate escalated to open hostilities, with cursing men hurling themselves against the front door of the convent throughout one night, the St. Louis mayor intervened on behalf of the white protesters, demanding that the school be closed.

Religious congregations like the Sisters of St. Joseph and the Sisters of Mercy, who had opened small segregated schools staffed by two or three nuns, caved before the violent intimidations and lack of government protection.[97] After the Civil War, Kenrick, perhaps wishing to discourage a fresh excuse for confrontations, decreed that whites could not fulfill their religious obligations at the African American St. Elizabeth's. Blacks, in theory if not reality, could worship in any St. Louis church.[98]

It was to this tumultuous racial history that three Baltimore Oblate nuns came in October 1880, locating in a renovated building used previously by Baptist and Presbyterian churches. By March 1881, African American families—Catholic and non-Catholic—swamped the school with student applications, despite its unappealing rooms in the basement at St. Elizabeth's. In 1883 the Oblates, after outgrowing another inadequate space, relocated for the third time since coming to St. Louis.[99] Demands on the Oblates still outpaced their space as they struggled to accommodate boarders, day scholars, and a growing number of orphans.

By 1888, at least nine orphaned girls lived with the sisters, a crowded arrangement that impeded convent life and confused classroom routines. The nuns, in a move to protect the integrity of each operation, divided the orphanage and the school, opening a separate facility for the parentless children. The orphanage fit with the congregational goals to undertake "ministrations to the intellectual, spiritual, and social nature of black children."[100] At St. Frances Orphan Asylum, the sisters pledged "to shelter, feed, clothe, and educate colored orphans and neglected and abandoned colored children irrespective of religious creed."[101]

St. Louis had welcomed the Baltimore sisters, but apparently, in keeping with its earlier racial record, the city excluded "equality" from the greeting. Efforts by the Oblates to purchase a property for the orphanage met with obstacles on several fronts. Barriers and conflicts mounted to such a degree that later, the nuns mentioned discreetly that "their trials were so many and so great that had they not been actuated by high motives . . . they would have become disheartened."[102]

Financial want, as well as social bias, impeded progress. The archbishop aided the initiative with $1,000, but the orphanage had no regular endowment to provide operating monies. Remarkably, over the years, the African American nuns received no portion of the money gathered in the annual collection for the orphans of the archdiocese.[103]

In addition, no provision was made for the sisters to have mass said in their orphanage chapel. Instead, they walked many blocks to a white church. Risky it was for black nuns to take to public streets and a time-consuming activity they only rarely reconciled with their many obligations to the children inside the orphanage. St. Frances Orphan Asylum came into existence with fiscal, equity, and spiritual handicaps for the Oblate sisters, indicators of the low priority given to these African American nuns and their charges.

By 1895, the orphanage again needed larger quarters, and the Oblates purchased an eight-acre tract of land in Normandy, Missouri; ample funding did not materialize, however. Some families paid board for orphan relatives, and the sisters accepted donations of food, money, and furnishings; sold votive lamps, fruit, and vegetables; or sent two nuns to beg in the streets. In 1902 the overcrowding demanded substantial relief, so the sisters laid their plight before the archbishop—the first time in twenty years that the nuns sounded a public appeal for the orphans.

In response, the St. Louis pastors agreed that through their parishes, the Oblates' white chaplain could issue coupon books, each containing 100 tickets. Pastors could sell as many books as they wished, distributing them through the Sodality or the Knights of Columbus, hosting parish parties, or designating a special "orphans' collection" at Sunday services. With the purchase of a ten-cent ticket, a subscriber "bought" one brick for the orphanage. Through this project, which kept the African American nuns and their dark-hued wards invisible to white congregants, the Oblate sisters raised almost $2,250 for the building fund.

One force—not so invisible for the orphans—came in the person of Sister Petra Boston of Baltimore, who, by the early 1900s, had been named superior.[104] Sister Petra, undeterred by the many slights of discrimination, excelled as an administrator and enjoyed a personal style that brought benefits to the orphans. She welcomed assistance from wealthy benefactors and nurtured relationships with Catholic auxiliary associations from white parishes. She built networks with the Jesuits, the Christian Brothers, the Queens' Daughters, the Passionist Fathers, the St. Vincent de Paul Society, the St. Bridget's Lyceum, the Western Catholic Union, and the *St. Louis Star* newspaper. One afternoon, 125 members of St. Agnes' Church appeared with their parish orchestra, supplying plenty of music and handing out boxes of candy. The parishioners left 300 yards of calico with the nuns, enough fabric for each child to have a new dress—undoubtedly sewn into that single institutional pattern so popular among nun caregivers in many facilities.

On the occasion of the 1904 World's Fair in St. Louis, Sister Petra's charges joined 300 white orphans on a special car provided by the Suburban Railroad Company for an outing to the Belgian building. At the fairgrounds, the orphans toured the rooms, heard speeches from dignitaries, dined in the administration restaurant, and gave loud cheers for the local benefactors who had underwritten the event. Sister Petra headed an institution disadvantaged by various discriminations, but she cultivated ways to keep the African American orphans before the St. Louis philanthropic community, and the nun employed those strategies freely and often.

In keeping with their pedagogical goals, the nuns at St. Frances Asylum instituted a detailed program of development for the orphans and the half-orphan girls admitted for care. Regardless of religious affiliation, once the girls—eligible between the ages of two and twelve—entered the asylum, they remained "under the exclusive management and control of the Sisters until discharged." While residents of the orphanage, the girls received instruction in a common school education and the domestic arts—cooking, cleaning, washing, ironing, sewing—to "fit them for such useful and practical careers as domestic servants or housekeepers."[105]

When girls reached the age of fourteen or fifteen, the Oblates expected them to return to society as servants in white homes, but they retained oversight for an individual student until she reached her legal majority. The nuns personally reviewed each placement in a "good Catholic home," and the girl's tenure there was monitored by a nun who made regular visits to the residence. During these inspections, sisters reiterated that they accepted no less than "fair wages" and a "safe" moral environment for each of their graduates.[106]

In the racially hostile post–Civil War years, the Oblate Sisters of Providence, well cognizant of the charges of lax "virtue" hurled at black women—including themselves—conducted an orphanage where they functioned as classroom teachers, moral guardians, legal advisers, and surrogate parents, protecting and directing the formative years of the children in their care. The standards that the nuns required for domestic placements, as well as their visits into the homes of white Catholics, demanded respect and countered prevailing attitudes that African Americans lacked intelligence, humanity, and community. In effect, the Oblate Sisters of Providence challenged the racism of whites by entering their private space with a black womanhood that was authoritarian, professional, maternal, and spiritual. That the nuns devised such a sophisticated response to the societal assaults of every kind on African Americans might be found in the morning prayer recited by the Oblate sisters, which asked: "Let me be a woman of wide sympathy, of broad view, patient, unprejudiced, forgiving and thoroughly in earnest. For, as a teacher, I have a high . . . vocation."[107]

Responding to the changing economic climate, in 1912 the nuns opened St. Rita's Academy. A residential campus with a finishing-school atmosphere, it promised to draw students throughout the Midwest. With it, the Oblates replicated the 1871 expansion of their highly prestigious St. Frances Academy in Baltimore, which claimed distinction as the first secondary school for black females in the United States. The decision for St. Rita's in Missouri showed that the Oblates recognized that their position as Catholic educators for African Americans had spread beyond their Baltimore roots. They acted to broaden their appeal within the African American community by meeting the changes of the twentieth century, wherein more affluent parents wanted a college preparatory education for their daughters, along with social preparation as potential brides for a rising cadre of black professionals.

Further, in 1906 the Oblate Sisters of Providence had altered their original habit, which included a bouffant white bonnet—striking in design but reminiscent of servants—to the more stereotypical black veil and white guimpe common among European nuns.[108] With traditional habits and traditional academies, the Oblates moved their African American sisterhood closer to the image of women religious as advocates of middle-class values. Still, the Oblate Sisters of Providence, regardless of attire or trends, never abandoned their work among poor blacks.[109] The calls were many from African Americans in the West, but the Oblates simply did not have enough professed sisters to support more missions.

Other than the Oblates of Providence and Katharine Drexel, few nuns committed exclusively to the education of African Americans. Drexel counted few allies among the white members of the Catholic community. Thus, when other sisterhoods wanted to address the inequities in education for African Americans, Drexel applauded their participation. Such a person was Mother Margaret Mary Murphy, a Texas counterpart to Drexel, founding her own congregation for the education of persons of color.

In racially divided municipalities like San Antonio, the general public militantly opposed schools for black children. On 4 September 1888, at the city council, an alderman airily declared that only fifty blacks expressed an interest in public classrooms and laughed off the request for a minority school allocation, pushing his colleagues to move to other business.[110] Despite the councilman's pronouncement, less than two weeks later, crowds of black and white San Antonians paraded to the elaborate dedication of St. Peter Claver Church and Free School for African Americans.[111] San Antonio, a coven of virulent racism, had encountered the energy and determination of Margaret Mary Healy Murphy, who alone donated the money for a 500-seat church, a rectory, and a school.

A fifty-four-year-old widow of affluence and social prestige, the Irish-born Murphy came to the city with a solid reputation as a Catholic philanthropist, honed through years of civic service undertaken with her late attorney husband. Approaching the age when she might have retired to her nearby ranch, Murphy launched a new career along the Rio Grande. It was one that promoted social justice for persons of color and wedded that cause to the religious activism of young Catholic women. In so doing, Margaret Murphy confronted nineteenth-century race, class, and gender constraints, planning to reorder the dynamics of equality in the Lone Star State.

In San Antonio, Murphy looked around at a white community largely determined that minority people should remain bound to the soil as a cheap agricultural labor force and a black community largely loyal to Protestant churches and wary of Catholic institutions. For Murphy, that San Antonio, with its Mexican, African American, and Anglo-European divisions, hosted exactly the sort of racial climate that whetted her sense of social-service responsibility.[112]

The African American church galled many San Antonians—even more so because Murphy built her school in a white neighborhood. With confidence, she placed learning for black scholars at the center of the city's attention and forced San Antonians, their indifference to ethnic schooling a matter of public record, to reckon with its presence. By stint of her assertiveness and legal knowledge, one day after the dedication of St. Peter Claver Church, Margaret Mary Murphy opened the school with 120 students, putting a lie to the councilman's estimates.

Immediately, however, her volunteer teachers—threatened and harassed on a daily basis—began to disappear, and Murphy decided to resolve faculty weaknesses by organizing her own religious congregation. In 1890 she wrote to a Baltimore priest friend that the local bishop had approved the community for which she had five potential candidates.[113] In the end, three women joined the now Mother Margaret in what was known as the Congregation of the Sisters Servants of the Holy Ghost and Mary Immaculate. This first congregation of Catholic women organized in Texas expressed its vision in its constitution, which stated that the sisters' labors would be directed to the "spiritual and temporal good of the Dark Races."[114]

Murphy then acted to cement the financial base of the school, placing an advertisement for assistance in the Catholic periodical the *Southern Messenger*. For the next year and a half, she juggled the demands of the religious training of the new congregation with those required by the education of the now approximately 200 students at St. Peter Claver. At the same time, she warded off the ongoing public ill will and efforts within the Catholic clergy to gain control of her property and oversight for the new sisterhood.[115] To sharpen her wit in church affairs, she often invited sisters from other congregations to her San Patricio ranch, which she had transformed into a religious retreat, complete with a chapel. There, on the veranda during long summer chats almost certainly punctuated by many knowing chuckles, Murphy learned from more-seasoned religious women strategies for reckoning with a male-controlled hierarchy.[116]

Despite the advice, Murphy faced the reality that admissions to the Sisters of the Holy Ghost continued at a desultory pace. Young sisters, pressured by outsiders, withdrew to enter other local convents such as the Ursuline, Incarnate Word, or Good Shepherd sisters.[117] Murphy scored some successes, one sister recalling: "I was present in the classroom when she talked to the children, so . . . I packed my bag and came right away to San Antonio with Mother Margaret."[118]

Generally, however, white women living in America regarded the work of educating blacks as too lowly or its hardships as too overwhelming, prompting Murphy to search beyond Texas for applicants, her eye falling on Ireland, her country of birth. Inspired, Mother Margaret set sail for the Emerald Isle on what proved to be the first of many recruitment trips.[119] Not every Irish postulant remained with Mother Margaret—some left for the secular world, some died, and some continued the pattern of withdrawal to other religious congregations. Nonetheless, the Irish candidates infused the small congregation with vibrant workers and softened the personnel problems that had so hampered the first years. The importance of the Irish contingent to Mother Margaret's plan could be seen in the fact that not until 1919 did an American-born woman, Emma Short of Philadelphia, enter and remain with the Sisters of the Holy Ghost.[120]

Once the Irish postulants arrived, Mother Margaret sequestered them at the San Patricio ranch for their religious formation. At this location, safely insulated from the racial volatility of San Antonio, Mother Margaret Mary had time to solidify purpose in the new sisters before they encountered the inflammatory scorn of white society. The added numbers among the nuns meant that more requests from education-deprived parishes could be accepted, spreading the influence of the Holy Ghost sisters and schooling to hundreds of African American children. Schools translated into income for the congregation, which, despite the founder's real estate and money, never enjoyed financial ease. Indeed, in 1908, several years into its existence, the congregation listed a cash balance on hand of $139.33.[121] Most important, as a congregation with a religious and familial identity, the sisters showed unswerving loyalty to the racial vision of Mother Margaret.

Although the Sisters of the Holy Ghost worked for educational advancement grounded in tenets of intellectual equality, their record was not unblemished. Differences with priests, who objected to the independent streak and a lack of tradition among Mother Margaret's nuns, plagued the congregation. Mother Margaret embarked on religious life when she was over fifty years of age—perhaps too advanced to tolerate the myriad dictates from male authorities. The two categories of responsibility—organization of a religious house that could earn canonical approval and management of an enterprise that incited hatred from every corner of society—pressed on her. Her successor, Mother Evangelist, dealt with peevish complaints from the archbishop concerning "the discipline of the house" or the sisters' poor attention to the children during church services.[122] More disquieting, disputes with the African American community were not unknown for the little sisterhood, numbering only thirteen professed nuns on the death of the foundress in 1907.

For example, the sisters apparently never established smooth relationships with the black parishioners at Holy Redeemer Church. In 1901 an African American parishioner wrote to a priest complaining that in a church he believed to have been reserved for his own race, white people filled the pews. He ventured that if Mother Margaret wanted to do well, she should turn the church over to a black congregation, the Holy Family sisters.[123] Less than a month later, another church member recommended that the priest be removed, as he gave a third of his time to the Mexican missions instead of Holy Redeemer's African Americans.[124]

As late as 1912, matters had not improved, although details of the conflict remained sketchy. Part of the coolness may have stemmed from abrasive feelings between the Catholic sisters and the Protestant Baptists in the area, or, as one sister suggested, from "the lingering bitter residue of slavery."[125] On one occasion, the priest publicly embarrassed the sisters, asking them to leave the church during his sermon, presumably so that he could speak openly against their presence in the parish.[126] By 1914, the Sisters of the Holy Family from Louisiana had taken the school, a change that placed black educators in the classrooms of black students. That same year, Bishop John W. Shaw wrote to the national administrator of the Catholic Indian and Negro fund and asked that $750 targeted for the black missions of the Holy Ghost sisters be diverted to Mexican missions in Texas. Bishop Shaw reasoned that Mexicans were "almost" Indians, were already Catholics, and had greater economic need than African Americans.[127]

Mexican Americans

Bishop Shaw's letter, with all of its convoluted cultural notions, reflected the magnitude of the poverty faced by people of color, as well as the scant religious resources available for their relief. Further, Shaw appeared oblivious to the deadly combination of forces that accounted for the indigent hovels of the people around him. The military aggression, land thievery, changing demographics, and legal chicanery on which Anglo society soared as it overtook sovereign Mexican regions did not inform Shaw's understanding of the destitute Spanish-speaking population. He commented not at all on the deeply entrenched, many-faceted racial hatred that haunted Mexicans and Mexican Americans of every economic strata as an invading Anglo government wrenched away their social, economic, and political traditions.[128] Few employment options for men or women;

In 1905 the overcrowded school of the Sisters of the Holy Ghost
in Laredo, Texas, demonstrated the enthusiasm of the Mexican American
community for education but also the limited number of teachers.
(Courtesy Sisters of the Holy Spirit, San Antonio, Tex.)

rising death from disease, accident, and murder; social scorn; ineffective
institutions of church and state—all of these exacerbated disruption and
confusion within Mexican families.[129] Shaw, who came to Texas in 1910,
did not know the people in and about San Antonio, but he identified one
irrefutable fact: worn by exploitation at every level and by every agency,
Mexicans, whom he numbered at approximately 70,000, received little or
nothing from their church in return for generations of religious loyalty to
Catholic forms.

Mother Margaret considered this reality from a different angle. She
saw matters in terms of social justice—an entitlement rather than a gift—
and that ideal guided the Sisters of the Holy Ghost from their incep-
tion. Her vision of an active ministry for "the spiritual and temporal good
of the 'Dark Races'" included Mexican and Mexican American women
becoming congregation members and subsequently pursuing a rich involvement with their community. The original constitution and rule for
the sisterhood—two handwritten documents, one in English and one in
Spanish—indicated that Mother Margaret expected the membership to be

racially diverse.[130] Profession registers suggested that by 1911, perhaps half a dozen Mexican women had entered the Sisters of the Holy Ghost.[131] At least one, born in Puebla, Mexico, persevered as Sister Michael, who at her final vows in 1911 was one in a congregation that numbered only thirty members.[132]

To attract more Spanish-speaking women, Mother Margaret Mary wanted to open mission houses deeper in Mexico. The San Antonio bishop, no doubt loathe to share one of the few congregations available for San Antonio's Catholics of color, thwarted her request. Finally, he relented, and at the beginning of 1902, five Holy Ghost sisters, all of Irish background, arrived in Oaxaca, Mexico, to operate an orphanage for poor and abandoned children.[133] With this facility, housed in an old monastery located deep among those she hoped to recruit for religious vocations, Mother Margaret Mary visited Casa de Cuna frequently. She used her considerable networking skills to raise money and to attract Mexican women to the new congregation.

In 1904 Sister Michael, one of the Mexican applicants and at the time still a novice, joined two other Holy Ghost sisters in the opening of Our Lady of Guadalupe school in Laredo, Texas. Laredo was a natural venue for Mother Margaret, as she had lived in the area when married to her late husband, with whom she had built a reputation for hospitality and philanthropy. Although her return generated a social flurry among her former friends—Mother Margaret was entertained by well-to-do acquaintances—the deteriorating circumstances of Mexicans left the nun aghast.

Sister Michael was the lone Spanish speaker among the faculty, but families still enrolled 135 students by the first day. The three sisters lived in poverty, dependent on the meager food and livestock offered by the destitute parents of their students. Enrollments continued to climb, and by the following year, the people had managed to erect a better building, though one still inadequate for the growing size of the school population. Two more Holy Ghost sisters joined the staff, and the nuns worked there until 1912, when oblique references to "difficulties" caused the congregation to withdraw, transferring the school to the Ursuline sisters.[134]

The shabby living conditions, the social and political hindrances, and the low admission rate for women of color did not dissuade the small congregation. In 1911, despite the anti-Catholic policies of the Mexican government, which disallowed the wearing of a religious habit in public, four sisters left San Antonio for Tabasco, Mexico. At the American border, they removed their rosaries and crucifixes, substituting mantillas for their religious veils. The anti-Catholic rumbling aside, the sisters received a tumultuous welcome in the streets of Tabasco, where they opened a boarding school named the Academy of the Holy Spirit.[135]

The academy, conducted in Spanish, did not want for an abundance of scholars and benefited from the presence of Sister Michael Ballesteros and Sister Soledad Crespo, each returning to the country of her birth. The secular authorities imposed a number of oversight regulations, requiring the nuns to incorporate themselves through the district school board. Every weekend, the sisters sent their lesson-plan books to a local official, who stamped the state approval and returned them on Monday. Finally, four examiners came to the school, testing students and teachers with verbal and written exams, pleasing the nuns with a high rating.

In Tabasco, the sisters, regardless of the constraints imposed by the government, adopted a visible public role. They went walking with the women who worked in the convent; shopped daily in the nearby open-air market; traveled by mule-drawn cart; attended a bullfight; and during Holy Week sat, according to local custom, among the worshippers on the floor of the cathedral. The Academy of the Holy Spirit appeared to be one of the sisters' best missions, one where they became comfortable, engaging in cultural exchange with their neighbors.

In Tabasco, four sisters—two Mexican and Spanish speaking, two Irish and English speaking—lived out the ideal of racial exchange envisioned by their foundress. They made education accessible for children of color, but they also attached themselves to the residents in various ways that brought personal satisfaction and friendship. One recalled, "Life in . . . Tabasco was too good to last."[136] The general council of the Sisters of the Holy Ghost, uneasy about shifting political conditions in Mexico, "suppressed" the academy by majority vote.[137]

The sisters in Tabasco, grieving their departure, returned to the United States, where the matters of Catholicism and Mexican Americans stretched across a textured terrain.[138] Not only were there few workers for these Catholics, but also the Mexican community itself was no monolith. A common language did not guarantee unity, even if Anglos with disdain lumped all Spanish speakers into one despised group. Political loyalties, class differences, partisan debates, economic issues, and religious practices frequently kept Mexican immigrants separated from Mexican Americans, Tejanos estranged from Californios, and the urban barrio distanced from the rural rancho. Bogus borders snaked over ancient lands, producing complicated identities, distorting family connections, compounding responses to America's many aggressions, and molding local expressions of Catholicism.[139] Here were not people to be converted to the Roman Catholic Church; here were western peoples who owned Catholicism, had shaped its expressions in their homes, designed its celebrations, absorbed its essence and breathed it back onto the West with a dynamic and animated spirituality that escaped the casual European observer.[140] The West intended to ask much of Anglo-European nuns who walked into this religious sanctuary.

As the sisters tried to do so, the barriers of language and poverty intensified the discrimination encountered by Spanish speakers in their own homeland, constraining the sisters as well. In Durango, Colorado, Mexican Catholics living across the Animas River from the town center stayed attached to their faith without a church or parish school, although white residents had both. On the "Mexican" side of the river, the people, accustomed to the lack of a resident pastor, undoubtedly continued in their faith tradition as secular activists, setting up small home altars and holding prayer services among themselves.[141]

Yet when Protestants in the area discovered an interest in converting these families, Catholic authorities suddenly took notice. To offset the incursions, church officials assigned Father Munoz, a returned missionary from Guatemala, as chaplain to the Durango hospital of the Mercy sisters. With anemic results, the sisters had operated the facility, as well as an academy and a free school for the poor. Father Munoz, however, found the nuns in disarray, devastated by the gruesome death of their superior, Mother Mary Baptist Meyers, who had been dragged and nearly decapitated when she was thrown through a passenger-car window during a train wreck.[142]

Munoz appealed to the Mercy sisters, floundering from the loss of their strong leader, to cooperate with him in starting a church, Sacred Heart parish, inside the Mexican community. Two nuns agreed and initially taught catechism after the Sunday services. In 1903 they began a small school, but it closed in a few months, and Father Munoz left for other assignments. The Mercy sisters, still feeling the loss of Mother Baptist, lacked the congregational leadership that might have kept them at Sacred Heart, and they retreated from the Mexican side of Durango.

In the years that followed, a priest passed through occasionally, but there were no regular Spanish services available. In 1907 an order of priests, the Theatine Fathers, active among Mexican missions, attempted to reenergize the parish, and the Mercy sisters returned to the Sacred Heart classrooms. Two nuns taught all eight grades, worked in deplorable conditions with the children, and received no salary.[143]

The sorry tale of Sacred Heart school and church as outreach efforts to the large Catholic Mexican population duplicated itself in many areas. A lack of appreciation for Spanish faith traditions, Eurocentric elitism, and faulty language skills tainted nineteenth-century and early twentieth-century contacts with the indigenous Catholics of the West. Burdened by the great distances and the scant personnel, the institutional church could not counter its own neglect.

Effective relationships between the people of color laity and a European church called for workers drawn from within the community itself, a concept grasped by Mother Margaret Mary Murphy when she produced her first congregational constitution in Spanish and English. Many years after Murphy's attempts to create a bicultural congregation, a nun in the Congregation of Divine Providence, also headquartered in San Antonio, sensed the social and religious spirit pulsating among Mexican Americans. Her vision and labors no doubt sprang out of her early life experiences, from which she found relief among poor neighborhoods in Mexican towns.

In 1895 fifteen-year-old Elizabeth Vermeersch, an orphan raised since the age of three by the San Antonio Sisters of the Incarnate Word, arrived in Mexico, assigned to the nuns' schools in Monterrey, Saltillo, and Lampasos. Although principally charged with domestic work for the Incarnate Word sisters, the orphaned Vermeersch also attended classes, studying, among other subjects, Spanish, English, and music during her three-year Mexican sojourn. Beyond the classroom, the young woman immersed herself in the poor-driven daily life of the communities outside the privileged campus atmosphere of the academy.

Further, at least once a year and by entreaty of the sisters, parents from the academy prepared a large dinner for the free school, also operated by the Sisters of the Incarnate Word. Outdoor tables covered with white linens sat about the academy grounds for the guests, while a harp-and-violin duo supplied the musical entertainment. For this event, the nuns chose their best academy students and domestic workers to serve food to the poor, symbolism with clear messages about the social responsibility of the privileged and the respect due the disadvantaged.

During these years in Mexico, Vermeersch broadened her perception of Mexican people, nurtured her devotion to service, and absorbed Catholic ritual as shaped within a culture of common people.[144] She was already poor with few relatives, dependent nearly her entire life on the charity of the orphanage and its nuns. In Mexico, she had social and educational opportunities that made her comfortable in poverty and freed her from notions of white supremacy.

On her return to Texas in 1898, Vermeersch decided to enter the convent but did not choose the sisterhood where she had lived since she was a toddler, instead making her religious home the Congregation of Divine Providence. After the completion of her novitiate, she assumed the name Sister Mary Benitia and, for the next several years, lived the typical life of a teaching sister assigned to poor missions.[145]

In 1915 Sister Benitia joined the faculty of the Immaculate Conception School in Houston, Texas, a facility opened three years earlier that boasted an enrollment of at least 100 Anglo scholars. Here, Sister Benitia began in a systematic manner to act on her long attachment to Mexican and Mexican American Catholics.

Each day, Sister Benitia and one other nun left the more-affluent Immaculate Conception parish and commuted to Our Lady of Guadalupe Church and School. This Catholic facility, the only one for Mexicans and Mexican Americans in Houston, had opened at the same time as Immaculate Conception. Although in the 1912 opening year, the Mexican school began with a high enrollment, the poor conditions, a lack of resources, and employment demands on children had caused the student roll to dwindle from over 100 to 23.[146] As principal of the school and a committed educator, Sister Benitia looked to restore student numbers, or she would not be able to justify to the leadership the assignment of two nuns to the barrio operation.

Drawing on her earlier life in Mexico, Sister Benitia took herself into the streets and homes around the school, reaching across the Texas cultural divide. Equipped with her fluent Spanish, she walked along miserable roadways and alleys, stepping over rotted-out stoops and knocking at hovels, where she counted and collected the school-age children. Once inside these homes, she immersed herself in the many layers of want for the Mexican immigrants and Mexican Americans of Houston.[147] Whole families lacked home furnishings, bedding, household supplies, clothing, and food while living in vile shacks without even the vestiges of sanitation.

Securing obligatory permission for begging, Sister Benitia set out to form a public program that would force Houston to recognize conditions in the Mexican community and draw students back to Our Lady of Guadalupe School. She made regular rounds to merchants, grocers, bakeries, and dry-goods stores, accepting any and all donated supplies. At the school, she began food distribution with bread and coffee, but increased donations of meats and vegetables allowed her to better the food service. Assisting the nun, the mothers and young girls in the parish formed into a women's auxiliary that prepared meals and distributed clothing to the children attending classes. At the end of the day, each schoolchild received a loaf of bread for younger siblings at home, and by the 1913–14 academic year, Sister Benitia had recouped the enrollment losses.

Spurred by this success and backed by enthusiastic women from the parish, Sister Benitia asked the priests for the use of a back lot on church property. This she turned over to the parish men and boys, who parceled off the land into several gardens and raised crops to distribute among the poor.[148] Despite the organizational developments, the duties of the classroom, and the daily physical exertions of collections and distributions, the sisters at Our Lady of Guadalupe did not have their own convent home in the parish until 1921, until that year continuing their commute between the white and Mexican churches.

The hearty response of the Mexican community to Sister Benitia's efforts to upgrade the school pointed to the strong Catholic identity and the desire for education that the people possessed. Still, two nuns working without remuneration could hardly sustain the entire neighborhood. Even with the spirited input from the parents at Our Lady of Guadalupe, evident gaps, especially spiritual ones, plagued the effort.

From among Sister Benitia's older students emerged a desire to assist in the religious instruction of illiterate children and adults, especially those who had no access to the parish school. Strengthened by the endorsement of Sister Benitia, who assumed responsibility for their catechetical and pedagogical training, these young women formed a nascent group of Catholic educators and fanned out through the community, taking religious education into the homes of Mexicans. They targeted public-school children who had no regular religious instruction and took on the serious task of preparing youngsters to receive their first Communion.

The Catechists, as they were called, continued to live with their families, wore a simple uniform, and made, with a few basic promises about their religious conduct, a six-month pledge to the program. As they gained momentum, the women organized centers for study and instruction, using old buildings or open-air spaces. Over time, more women expressed an interest in the work and in a more-structured communal life, shared together. Not surprisingly, solid financial support from the hierarchy and local Catholics eluded the women of color, and not until 1935 did the Catechists have their own residence, Providence Home in Houston.

On the surface, this movement appeared to be an inspiring effort by Mexican women and their nun advocate to eradicate ignorance and improve the lives of a population mired in poverty. The women evinced an admirable willingness to enter the poorest districts, live under the most im-

Fired with zeal for work inside their own community in Texas,
the Missionary Catechists of Divine Providence struggled for decades against
civic and church discrimination before gaining ecclesiastical recognition as
an independent congregation of Mexican American women. (Courtesy
Missionary Catechists of Divine Providence, San Antonio, Tex.)

poverished personal conditions, emulate the patterns of professed religious
life, and submit to the rubric of the Catholic Church. Several women who
worked as Catechists chose to enter the convent and joined the Divine
Providence congregation or other Texas orders. Overall, however, the institutional response to these sacrifices often seemed more obstructionist than
supportive, perhaps explained by several factors.

First, Sister Benitia sidestepped the traditional anonymity of nuns and
in fact crafted a highly public profile. She reached deep into the Houston
business and social community for fiscal support and counted important
laypeople among her friends. Within the Mexican and Mexican American barrio of Houston, she acquired devoted followers and friends, more
than 700 of whom signed a petition requesting that she, after twenty-
three years of service, not be withdrawn from Our Lady of Guadalupe.
She supervised a large school, personally trained the Catechists, worked
closely with a Spanish priest of the parish, raised great sums of money, influenced a number of religious vocations to her order, oversaw much of the
construction of Providence Home, and, above all, strove to use all of her
energies and contacts to strengthen the voices of the Mexican and Mexican American poor.

Some in the Congregation of Divine Providence seemed cool to Sister
Benitia, perhaps feeling jealousy at her success and the single-mindedness
of her dedication or harboring reservations about the desirability of a
strong Mexican membership inside the order.[149] Recurring threats to re-

move Sister Benitia from Our Lady of Guadalupe hung over her, and the Houston bishop possessed the greatest weapon with rumors that he would suppress the Catechists, snuffing out their legitimacy within the offices of the Catholic Church.[150] The young women with whom Sister Benitia associated took responsibility for the religious instruction of their own community, always looking for ways to further define themselves as daughters of their church. The racist skepticism emanating from that very church hampered their advance.

During the 1940s, the Catechists continued their work in Houston, but they now centered their operation in San Antonio, close to Sister Benitia and the motherhouse of the Divine Providence congregation. The Catechists lived in great poverty, surviving on beans, cream of wheat, or corn meal until they received the leftovers of the nearby Our Lady of the Lake College.[151] Dietary poverty aside, the women suffered from an organizational split personality: they were neither a completely lay nor a completely religious organization. The blurriness in their definition threatened them with instability, what with lukewarm ecclesiastical endorsement and young women joining and leaving the house; but through all, the Catechists retained the support of Sister Benitia and other Divine Providence sisters who moved into the Catechist house.

It took many decades for these sisters to acquire formal status as an independent religious congregation that was no longer an adjunct affiliation of the Divine Providence sisters. Not until 1989 did the Catechists achieve Vatican approval as a fully independent women's religious congregation; Sister Benitia, who championed the material rights of Mexican immigrants and Mexican Americans and the spiritual integrity of women of color, had died in 1975 at age ninety-five.

As for the Catechists, who had confronted many obstacles on their way to independence, their congregation addressed the most basic human and spiritual needs among the poorest of Mexican immigrants and Mexican Americans. Many of the members of the congregation had themselves risen from such poverty. Through the Missionary Catechists of Divine Providence, the women had found an avenue to self-improvement, education, professionalism, social service, and religious life while always keeping their labors sharply focused on the communities from which they came.

Catholic nuns and the people of color in the West wove a unique legacy out of their parallel cultures. In many places, the institutional story emerged as the brutal account of coerced religion and suppressed tradition. But beside that narrative ran another, one in which white women pushed themselves to build harmonious relationships with strangers and did so by entering the cultural space of others. Among the Daughters of Charity in El Paso, one was remembered as a nurse who "never kept a poor person waiting"; another oversaw a soup line and free clinic only for Mexicans; and a third "trudged in all kinds of weather, up and down the hills of the Mexican settlement, carrying food and remedies to those whose age and infirmities rendered a visit to the asylum impossible."[152]

The peoples of the West often demonstrated in response that they wanted to understand these unusual women, so set apart from the usual representatives of white society. Certainly, in the nineteenth century, religious women and the Catholics of color lacked the temporal and spiritual power to reshape the administrative bureaucracy of a European church or an American government. At the same time, cultural borders, even those that seemed impenetrable, shifted. By plan and by chance, remarkably dissimilar people exchanged rituals and memories, encountering each other's humanity.

In 1906 three Sisters of the Blessed Sacrament left Santa Fe, traveling by wagon into the mountains to recruit Indian children for the coming academic year.[153] After a rough and perilous trip of nearly twelve hours, they reached Abiquiú. Surrounded by the sounds of four different languages, taken by the distinctive architecture of the hacienda, and surprised that clothing styles blurred between Mexicans and Indians, these three sisters stepped into a more-intimate world of even greater cultural plurality than they witnessed in Santa Fe. They found ethnic segregation weaker here, with Mexican and Indian families working and worshipping together across their seeming divides. The Mexican community, employers of the Indians, held the economic advantage, with large, well-furnished homes, many trained servants from the pueblo, and perhaps a child or two enrolled at the Santa Fe academy of the Sisters of Loretto. Nonetheless, Indians controlled access to the highly prized religious space inside the pueblo, granting Mexican families the right to join in music, festivals, and worship.

An informal encounter during the visit, however, made plain the mixing of cultures for the three nuns. Ameliana Chavez, Santa Fe–educated daughter of a wealthy Mexican family, secured permission for the Blessed Sacrament nuns to enter the *morada*, a locked building of the local brotherhood of Penitentes.[154] Although the priest had cautioned the sisters that the Penitentes were "ignorant" and had been ordered to cease their rituals of blood penance, such as having "bundles of cactus tied to their naked backs," the sisters themselves reacted somewhat differently to the brotherhood. The sisters, despite nervousness at entering the darkened *morada*, saw not ignorance but a religious space, one they did not fully understand but nevertheless perceived as sacred. The chapel-like aura, wooden altar, figures of the Mother of Sorrows and Doña Sebastiana, skeleton of death, huge crosses, and instruments of penance—including a wide "leather belt, thickly studded with wire points"—struck them as unusual but powerful indicators of personal faith.

This was not Catholicism as the nuns practiced it, nor did they endorse the extreme flagellations and bloodletting, especially severe during Holy Week. But neither did they patronize, scorn, or ridicule. It seemed that as Catholic women, often challenged for seeking their own agency inside the church, they identified with the brotherhood's difficult position with clerical authorities. Regardless, that somewhat unorthodox moment—a young Mexican woman and three Anglo-European nuns, by silent invitation, entering into the shrouded holy place of Native men and finding mutual spirituality—suggested the best that the cultural diversity of western religion might, and sometimes did, produce.

In western places, Catholic nuns and sisters stood amid the crossing of religious faiths and confronted the differences between and among traditions. Repeatedly, sisters found themselves in unknown environments where they interacted with persons who defined fellowship and friendship according to local culture, where they learned as often as they taught, where custom wooed them as skillfully as they courted converts. The women thought to bring immutable religious and cultural values to a region that responded by demonstrating the breadth and depth of its own.

They had planned to plant a faith, but faith surrounded them; to shape the people, but the people shaped them. They arrived in the West certain of their cultural and religious superiority. Once inside that varied West, young Anglo-European nuns began to see that families from every strata cherished their own lives and beliefs and did not require "approval" from outside cultures. Increasingly, more sisters understood the West not as home to "savages" and "coloreds" who needed "civilizing," but as a cauldron of grave injustice, perpetual struggle, and unmitigated poverty for peoples of color—elements that drove their own sisterly lives as well. Some lowered but did not abolish their wall of cultural certainty as they struggled to reconcile the concepts of their society with the lived realities around them. Nuns and sisters, especially those who worked long years in the West, let a different cultural foreground wash over them. In the aftermath, they pondered the futures of western people, embraced the expectations of others, and rethought their own personal goals as they continued to sort out a transformed religious life in a changing American West.

*[She] was a woman of
remarkable qualities—with an
enlightened mind, and a strong
will. . . . [W]hen we take [her]
circumstances into account . . . on
the barren plains [we are] filled
with . . . astonishment. . . . Such
women are the salt of the earth.*

—Funeral eulogy for Mother
Josephine Cantwell by Rev.
Thomas F. Kinsella, in Mary
Buckner SCL, *History of the
Sisters of Charity of Leaven-
worth, Kansas* (1898)

Nuns of the West

Warm words for Mother Xavier Ross
during the funeral of Mother Josephine
Cantwell—herself a pioneer who oversaw convents in Montana, Missouri,
Kansas, and Colorado—captured the
way many described the nuns who called
the nineteenth-century West "home."
If asked, sisters would have dismissed
funeral orations that trumpeted nunly
tenacity across a range of western experiences and pious descriptions of inborn
virtue. Nuns tended to wave off applause
and accentuate matter-of-factness, saying, as did Blandina Segale, a Sister of
Charity of Cincinnati who spent over
twenty years in the Southwest as a fierce
advocate for the poor: "It is difficult to
understand anyone putting his hand to
the plow and then looking back."[1]

Sister Blandina put her hand to the plow with thousands of other nuns. The labor of nuns in the American West blazed a trail with schools and hospitals, adult homes and orphanages that spoke to the dogged productivity of sisters. From leaky shacks rose prestigious academies, and out of canvas tents grew modern hospitals. Congregations in many locations received praise as heartfelt as that for Mother Josephine.

Sisters and their congregations looked far beyond mortar-and-stone achievements. A ministry among people also guided their western lives. With widening regional exposure and deeper immersions into the cultures of the West, nuns emerged as strong-minded friends of the oppressed, denouncing discrimination, supporting the working class, speaking up to public officials, and squeezing from the institutional church more monetary and spiritual assistance.

For such hard work, admirable at the very least for the womanly grit displayed, sisters more than earned the glowing funeral eulogy that celebrates the individual. Yet effusive phrases from visiting dignitaries ignored the harsher aspects of how and at what costs sisters compiled their accomplishments. The real lives of nuns remained hidden from those who viewed sisters as adorable religious icons rather than as complicated women traveling a complicated western path.

The American West rarely treated its peoples gently. More typically, it tormented its residents, crazed with desert heat and paralyzed with mountain cold, while heaping onto these assaults of nature the indignity and pain designed by warring humans. Too easily, raconteurs gazing back on these sisters' life narratives tinted them with a rosy glow of nostalgia that glossed over the hard-core baseline of history. "Salt of the earth" hardly described the wrenching processes required when risking a known personal identity for a physical, intellectual, and spiritual self in a region of intense human suffering and major political contests.

The crosscurrents of western contest did not waft only through Native lands, wagon trains, urban barrios, mining camps, or cattle ranges. They seeped under convent thresholds, drifted through kitchens, and worried their way into chapels, parlors, and refectories, bearing a real West, not a fictional one, to alter the patterns of American religious life for women. The West wrapped nuns in conflicting situations and priorities, and the sisters, like westerners on all landscapes, responded in ways that enhanced and damaged the many faces of the region. One sister, on hearing plans to extend a railroad line to a remote town, captured the western perplexity by responding, "Progress is in sight—so is disaster . . . to our native population."[2]

Essential transformations in religious expectations, choices that defied long-held practices, or decisions that set nuns against church or government or each other exploded in a region already engaged in dramatic and profound change. Through individual and collective experience, professed women confronted the fact that, for good and ill, pressured by ethnic cultures and regional demands, the pulse of religious life changed in the American West. The nuns who left the monasteries of Europe, inundated by western life and western place, had emerged as the sisters in the convents of America.

Voices of Opposition

Not all westerners greeted Catholic nuns with friendship or tolerance. In many western areas, sisters encountered a virulent rhetoric from other Anglo-Europeans, revealing the deeply held objections of neighbors. Some detested the national allegiances of nuns who came to work in their communities, preferring sisters from their own European countries. Others defined all sisters as agents of anti-Americanism, a theme of the nativist sentiment sweeping the nation. Some westerners vigorously endorsed the governing principles of separation of church and state and questioned a Catholic nun dressed in a religious habit as a teacher in a public school.

These impulses had the muscle to drive sisters out of western communities, turning little missions into failed catastrophes. "Anti-Catholic sentiment" explained the sisters, who did not take the threats lightly. Nuns legitimately feared anti-Catholicism when Protestant nativists stoked their election campaigns with slander; published slurs against nunneries; and, in 1844 Philadelphia, left dead and wounded among the smoldering ruins of several Catholic churches.[3]

To deflect hostile jeers from strangers or fury from nativists, nuns frequently resorted to wearing secular clothing for public business or travel. Prior to 1850, when Mother Caroline Friess toured the United States looking for promising mission locations, one stop took her to the Mercy sisters in western Pennsylvania. Caroline, who made her trip in dark street clothes, noted that she was not alone, describing the Mercy "black habit with wide sleeves and a long train worn" by her hosts and commenting: "They must go out in secular garb. . . . And every sister . . . has a black dress, black shawl, and black hat lying in her cell."[4] In 1866 two Dominicans traveling from the Midwest to the East for music training dressed in secular clothing for their trip and the duration of their studies.[5] Some attitudes that greeted sisters in the West warranted these precautions.

When the Canadian Sisters of the Holy Names, daughters of a city of Catholic ways and Catholic voices, settled in Portland, they steeled themselves to tread carefully under a new flag and among other religions. On their arrival in 1859, the twelve sisters felt the first sneer when a snappish newspaper reported that "six priests and fourteen nuns have just arrived in Portland! What a foothold romanism is gaining in our state!"[6]

Within a month, the sisters opened a school for girls, its students including three Catholics, three Jews, and one Episcopalian. They followed this with classrooms for little boys and accepted an orphan girl as a boarder at the convent. As the sisters' English skills and pocketbooks were slight, lay families in the neighborhood interpreted during transactions with merchants, provided meals, and donated goods for the convent. One shop of six bakers sent a large cake with a note that said, "Please accept this gift as a testimony of the high esteem which we entertain for the noble work that brought you to this distant world." Gratified, the sisters remarked: "These children are, for the most part Protestant, and . . . so devoted to us."[7]

The Portland newspapers, however, continued their public disapproval of Catholic nuns. Almost two years after their arrival, the sisters bemoaned that "some of the daily papers . . . desire to vilify the name of the Catholic sisterhood," apparently hoping "to prevent children from attending our school." The nuns stated firmly that they ignored the articles, "convinced that our safest reliance is in proving . . . that our lives are in direct opposition to what they are represented to be," but they installed locks on all the convent doors.[8]

While expressions of anti-Catholic bias left them unsettled, the nuns clung to their own negative ideas about other groups. When the priest arrived to bless a new convent purchased from a Protestant association, the sisters asked for extra holy water on the "profane walls" as they cared not to "inherit any of the Freemasons' dust." The obliging priest assured them that "the devil had that day danced his last polka in the building."[9]

The humor of such comments trivialized the episodes as fastidious prejudice on both sides of the religious fence. In reality, the Sisters of the Holy Names came from a foreign country, dressed in a foreign manner, spoke a foreign language, and worshipped in a foreign church. Suspicions popularized by newspapers, in benevolent associations, and from pulpits made for uneasiness among the young, single women from Canada. Less than ten years before, a government surveyor had written: "The French are not liked at all by the other citizens of Oregon. They speak their own language . . . and are kept in ignorance by their Romish priesthood."[10] The fact that by the end of the 1864 school year, the nuns counted 132 students on the rolls did little to assuage their discomfort in this atmosphere. Among the pupils, only two practiced the Catholic faith, a matter of discouragement for the faculty. The sisters described the situation as "a great trial," for they felt "totally isolated in a Protestant land, where the spirit of criticism and censuriousness [sic] is so prevalent."[11]

Given their cautions to avoid secular attention, sisters stifled responses to hostility aimed at Catholicism. Still, open rudeness violated ideals of courtesy, causing some nuns to show their verbal mettle. In 1881, at the request of managers, the Sisters of Charity conducted a hospital collection among New Mexico workers laying railroad track. Subscription cards supplemented the company contract with the nuns and guaranteed care for injured employees. Sister Blandina Segale, approaching one Kansan laborer whom she judged "one who had read plenty against nuns," asked if he wanted the hospital insurance plan. He cut off her inquiry with an abrupt, "No, ma'am. I never get sick." Sister Blandina, a voice for the poor who refused to be intimidated by anyone—merchant, bishop, or politician—turned away, shouting back, "Should you need our services, do not hesitate to come. The surest admittance card is sick and moneyless."[12]

The quick retort, however, remained the public weapon of only a few sisters. Most nuns chose cautious ways to address opposition. Sisters, relying on public funds for schools, hospitals, orphanages, and Native missions, tread a narrow line with state officials. While certainly not every objection to the sisters stemmed from religious bias, the nuns felt criticism to be such and worried how organized anti-Catholicism curtailed their employment in western areas.

Professionalism

The funding contracts that congregations negotiated with government agencies provided the money to keep institutions operational and sisters employed. With the dollars came the authority of federal, state, or county officials—usually practitioners in a Protestant denomination—to hold the sisters accountable to secular regulations. Overall, nuns and sisters agonized over their vulnerability in these arrangements, which they often dismissed as tainted by anti-Catholic sentiment. Yet in the long term, the formal demands of state agencies, however acrimonious or religiously charged, benefitted Catholic sisters, motivating them to raise their professional standards and ultimately enlarging their remuneration and acclaim. Chided for European allegiances, accused of inferior training, and scrutinized for management policy in public institutions, congregations responded with herculean efforts to fend off critics, strengthen their credibility in a number of fields, raise the quality of their schools and hospitals, and elevate the intellectual achievement of the sisterhood.

As an initial step, sisters addressed the issue of their teaching credentials. The press on congregations to staff western parochial schools exceeded the available professed sisters. In response, some congregations assigned teaching duties to a young woman after she donned her postulant's clothing, sending her to a post within days of entering the convent.[13] According to one congregational legend, the mother general took a train to a mission, escorted a sick teacher to the motherhouse, at the vestibule whipped off the sister's black veil, pinned it on a novice, and whisked the stunned young nun back to the depot, filling the faculty vacancy by nightfall.[14] Freshly minted novices, just invested with the habit, suddenly found themselves at a mission. There, more experienced sisters were to instruct the untrained in professional duties, as well as weave those lessons into the charism of the congregation and the routines of religious life.[15]

This professionalization by apprenticeship posed multilayered problems for congregations. First, it violated church law that required novices to pass one full year of uninterrupted study in religious and spiritual formation. Breeches that shortened the canonical year, even by an hour, or permitted a novice to leave the novitiate house nullified profession.[16] The final permission for profession rested with the bishop, who could declare a novitiate year invalid; congregations bypassed the novitiate rule because the same bishop often hounded congregations for teachers.[17] Once again, the politics of church management snagged sisterhoods trying to obey canon law and their local clergy.

The second problem stemmed from the civic regulations for public schools that took on more formality as western institutions matured. When sisters entered into contracts with school districts and drew salaries from the public treasury, administrators increasingly expected them to qualify for the same certificates mandated for lay employees. Certificates not only required a qualifying examination but also often called for license renewal every two to five years and an annual credentials status report to the district. Sisters, without higher education and living at small, isolated missions, scrambled to operate the schools, satisfy the inspectors, and secure their certificates.[18]

Driven by an intense commitment to education, assertive leaders such as Mother Caroline Friess of the School Sisters of Notre Dame, Mother Emily Power of the Sinsinawa Dominicans, and Mother Cecilia Dougherty of the Sisters of Charity of the BVM moved to eradicate these professional problems. They designed programs to meet state standards and improve the overall credentials of the congregation. Since withdrawal of all faculty in need of higher education would have imploded the network of Catholic schools, educational projects started in stages at the missions.

Mother Caroline called on head sisters to review and enforce daily lesson plans, conduct biweekly observations in classrooms, and disseminate a wide range of professional reading materials to faculty.[19] A constant attention to better pedagogy meshed with the early thinking of Mother Caroline, who declared: "Sisters should study, and not wash or do laundry or clean."[20] Another School Sisters of Notre Dame mother general, Mother Mary Marianne Haas, introduced a more systematic approach, forming a school commission "for the improvement of our teachers" that prepared a course of study aimed for success with government and diocesan examinations in all locations.[21]

In 1894 Mother Cecilia convened a six-day congregational conference that, through panels, committees, and group discussion, addressed classroom issues and teaching expertise. More than 100 BVM sisters drafted a three-year course of study plan for mission teachers. To launch the program, home-study packets, tailored for individual faculty, arrived at schools early in summer, with sealed examinations following at the end of the vacation period.[22] To strengthen her nuns, Mother Emily assigned each teaching sister one subject—English, mathematics, Greek, or Latin—for personal intensive study. In another variation of the project, the Sinsinawa Dominicans as a community concentrated on a single discipline, such as grammar or American history, for a full year. At the conclusion of the spring term, sisters traveled to the motherhouse for written tests, the regulations for which had been explained in circular letters to the missions.[23] In 1896 the Dominicans reaped the rewards of study when University of Wisconsin examiners gave state accreditation to the Sinsinawa flagship academy, St. Clara's.[24]

Pleased with the success, Mother Emily in 1903 reminded her sisters that "vacations should be spent quietly in study."[25] This represented no small directive. Most schools remained in session until the last week of July, and sisters departed for new missions in mid-August. All nuns made a mandatory eight-to-ten-day summer retreat, and missioned novices were supposed to return to the motherhouse during the vacation months. Other available days sisters devoted to mending or making habits, as well as to thoroughly cleaning the convent and the school. The last included more than shaking a dry mop; it meant scrubbing classroom floors and cloakrooms, washing cupboards and windows, cleaning kitchen appliances, scraping paint, slating blackboards, polishing fixtures, ironing linens, starching curtains, airing drapes, varnishing desks, and beating carpets and upholstery.[26] All these activities, compressed into a six-week period — along with planning the coming school year, interviewing parents, and maintaining daily prayer schedules — limited individual academic study. Apparently, the mountain of tasks prompted some discontent among Dominicans, for Mother Emily conceded: "At the almost universal request of the missions, I have decided to defer the sisters' examinations until some later date." Though she yielded on the test date, Mother Emily added pointedly: "You all must see the need of . . . perfecting our methods and personal equipment . . . to keep up with the march of progress."[27]

The "march of progress" invaded religious sisterhoods throughout the West. Once again, great distances between missions and limited resources posed major problems, as congregations grappled with the logistics and finances of educating sisters. Self-study projects with monitored motherhouse examinations or summer institutes with learned speakers created an uneven system for professionalizing that could not educate large groups of nuns quickly enough to satisfy state regulators or counter the competition from better-staffed public schools.

Catholic colleges refused to admit nuns, and secular normal schools remained an unacceptable option for some religious congregations. In 1905 one mother general wrote to sisters at the western missions they would "never be permitted to attend public places for instruction of any kind . . . pertaining to school work."[28] As sisters formed interests in degree programs and professional certification, this inferior and piecemeal approach to higher education offered a tedious ten or fifteen years of part-time matriculation before graduation and burdened an already overextended community of women across the West.

Conservative views and practical obstacles failed to deter sisters, for, like their counterparts in the lay world, many nuns understood that a better future awaited the educated professional woman.[29] Further, sisters began to see the common benefits in sharing information across congregational boundaries. In 1910, during the school break between Christmas and New Year's, teaching sisters in Galveston, Texas, gathered for the first diocesan institute. Members of the Dominican, Incarnate Word, Holy Cross, Divine Providence, and Ursuline sisterhoods presented papers to the assembly and, enthusiastic about the event, scheduled a second cross-congregational event for the following August.[30] Cooperation between and among congregations promised sisters a stronger voice in demanding access to higher education, a demand they argued would prepare Catholic schools for the inevitable day when state certification only came to those with a four-year degree.[31] Impelled by the intellectual liveliness they carried with them into the West, sisters from many areas broke through decades of congregation isolation and convent seclusion, acting across religious orders to promote their own education. The strength to be gained when women set aside differences and organized under a common goal began to influence the thinking of western sisters.

With their sights set on academics, sisters might have turned to the Catholic college system as their entrée into higher education. Early attempts, however, to affiliate with men's universities met with icy resistance. Priest professors made no effort to hide their discomfort when women came to campus, even for abbreviated vacation sessions. In some cases, uneasiness spilled over into overt hostility. In 1911 a priest in San Antonio complained to the bishop that among the Sisters of Divine Providence, "there is a tendency to cater too much to the worldly spirit . . . manifested in the fact that . . . a summer school has been established for the sisters."[32]

In the same year, The Catholic University of America opened the Sisters' College, allowing nuns from the United States and Canada to gather at one accredited institution to matriculate for undergraduate and graduate degrees. Twenty-three women's congregations sent sisters, so many nuns that some spilled out of four campus dormitories and into nearby schools and convents for shelter. Among them were nineteen Texas nuns, undoubtedly anxious to escape further priestly complaints about their academic leanings.[33] Mother Agnes Gonzaga Ryan of the Sisters of St. Joseph of Carondelet in St. Louis managed to enroll seventeen nuns in the first Catholic University term and sent two others to Italy to study art. Mother Pauline of the Dominicans approved two of her Galveston sisters for the 1913 session in Washington, and the following year, she allowed another two to study china painting and tapestry in New York.[34]

Travel costs and tuition fees aside, the enthusiasm for advanced education permeated the sisterhoods. Sisters set about to validate their academic credits from their years of part-time workshops and seminars. Those attending Catholic University submitted personal résumés that detailed summer sessions, studies at normal schools, university correspondence courses, state examinations, and grades for evaluation of their accumulated credits. Some nuns documented more than ten years of pursuing a degree, elusive for lack of a matriculating institution. In June 1912, in a ceremony replete with meaning, The Catholic University of America bestowed the bachelor of arts degree on eighteen religious women, several of whom immediately began graduate studies.[35] With the doors opened at Catholic

University, sisters—those who attended the Washington campus and those who did not—looked on a new era of intellectual empowerment.

In 1914 the Sisters of Charity of the BVM in Dubuque, enlarged on their contacts with Catholic University to offer accredited courses for nuns across the West. The BVM sisters hosted a summer session, drawing nuns from Texas, Canada, Missouri, and the Dakotas, as well as forty-nine Sisters of St. Francis of the Holy Family who traveled across town to the event.[36] In doing this, the BVM sisters identified the regional needs of sisters living in the West and attracted many without the funds or congregational permission to travel as far as Washington, D.C.

Even before these national developments, several women's congregations explored the feasibility of opening their own colleges. Congregations centered in the American West tallied several reasons why such an initiative would benefit them. After reviewing expensive and lengthy journeys from remote locations, costs of supporting sisters at degree-granting institutions, protracted part-time study to degree completion, perceived drawbacks of public colleges, and the fierce antieducation sentiment of many clergymen, nuns determined that bringing accredited higher learning inside their own sphere promised to resolve these problems.

The Benedictine sisters of St. Joseph, Minnesota, launched their experiment in 1905 by sending a handful of nuns to the University of Minnesota, opening their college in 1913 with the congregation's postulants as the students. Lay women gradually enrolled, and within two years, the sisters expanded to a four-year curriculum and graduated the first class in 1918.[37] The Benedictine nuns, who had bowed to monks at nearby St. John's abbey for fifty years, had identified a powerful antidote to male oversight and infused women's intellectual autonomy.

The local monks and bishop may have thought the college would serve to contain Benedictine women, keeping them close to home, but the men miscalculated. By 1912, six Benedictine sisters headed for Catholic University to begin graduate work and later returned to further upgrade the college faculty.[38] The Sisters of St. Benedict designed an entirely new phase as educators, one that, although they lived in a remote western setting, inexorably propelled them forward as informed intellectuals and trained professionals.

In addition, their college increasingly appealed to female students drawn by the rising gender trends in higher education. At St. Benedict's, young women from the spacious states of Minnesota and the Dakotas chose Catholic education, living and studying in what their families endorsed as a "safe" convent environment. Some graduates chose to enter the Bene-dictine congregation, but others formed the nucleus of an active alumnae association, cherishing their bond with the college for a lifetime.[39]

The Benedictine network added another link with this relationship be-tween sisters and laywomen, the alumnae association extending a female source of friendship and financial support for the priory. In turn, St. Benedict's represented an emotional attachment and a gathering place for graduates, Catholic laywomen dispersed across wide, lonely spaces. As the nineteenth-century nuns had done with the college and its students, the sisters strengthened the congregation internally and reinforced the Benedictine presence in the region, as graduates carved out careers, at-tended universities, and built families. Thus, the Benedictine community of women—religious and lay—deepened and broadened female power in western locations.

The college of the Benedictine sisters was but one in a number of con-gregational institutions that looked to educate sisters and reach out to secular students. In 1920, thirty-eight years after a small group of Sisters of St. Joseph came to Kansas in abject poverty, they watched a cornerstone-laying ceremony for their Marymount College. Perhaps more amazing than their success, they heard the presiding bishop Francis Tief enthuse, "We must be abreast of the times. . . . Education is carried on . . . by these women and it is through their efforts that Catholic educational institutions are built and maintained."[40] The mantle of church and civic duty had re-placed the skepticism that had hampered the intellectual advancement of sisters.

Liberal-arts education for nuns and their female students headed for classrooms proved to be only one area of professional training affected by the rising expectations about credentials. Sisters faced the serious issue of appropriate licensing for the many hospitals and care facilities they staffed in the West. Their first efforts in such places as Billings, Montana, and Aberdeen, Washington, relied on the skills of amateur nurses or those with limited practical care training.[41] Although the experiences made for "heroic" narratives later, in reality the life was grueling, intensified by the sisters' nursing limitations.

In 1892 the Daughters of Charity collected tubercular patients from the tents and shacks around El Paso and opened the Hotel Dieu under the leadership of an experienced institutional administrator for the congrega-tion. El Paso surpassed even her abilities, though, and the sisters struggled with financing, staffing, isolation, and local flooding. Their requests for

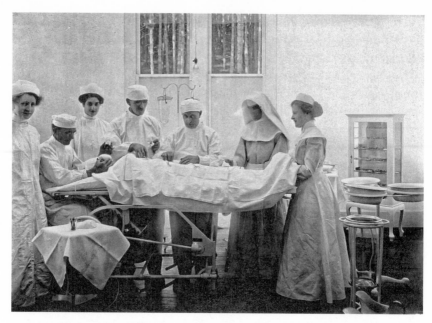

By the early twentieth century, nursing congregations advertised the scientific training, professional staff, modern equipment, and state-of-the-art procedures of their medical facilities, as seen by the Dominican sisters, whose first Washington hospital opened in a shack on stilts. (Author's collection)

relief brought letters from the motherhouse that counseled, "Do the best you can. . . . Keep the expenses . . . low," and the discouraging news that "I can't promise you a sister who understands medicine."[42]

Such limitations overwhelmed nurses, who tried to make a clean space with iron cots and fresh linens, a washstand, decent nourishment, and a kindly bedside attention that encouraged the ill to seek spiritual solace. In this role, sisters acted out, within a Catholic setting, the traditional "woman as caregiver and nurturer" identity generally acceptable to nineteenth-century America. With the rise of national educational standards, the nuns, already painfully shorthanded, knew that a lack of training made their hospitals targets for criticism, both valid and manufactured.

Even the Franciscan sisters of Rochester, Minnesota—architects, under the leadership of Mother M. Alfred Moes, the mind behind the original Mayo Clinic—came to their new nursing vocation as classroom teachers, not students of medicine. Situated a remote half mile beyond the center of town, the first hospital lacked electricity, modern plumbing, and telephone service. The "nursing" sisters lived at the barren hospital, but others, formerly accustomed to classroom duties, walked from the motherhouse to oversee patient care and domestic chores, including hand pumping water from the basement to the upper floors. The few kerosene lanterns cast an uninviting gloominess throughout the hospital, and the nuns summoned a physician by sending a sister on foot to the doctor's home or the clinic.[43] All in all, the original St. Mary's Hospital represented a spirited but amateur medical setting, its scientific authenticity stemming from an intense association with the Mayo siblings and their father, all of whom found in the arrangement an exceptional career opportunity. The brothers, Protestants and neither having completed the standard medical residency of the day, understood the unusual nature of the effort and referred to themselves among the sisters as "the greenest of the green crew."[44]

By 1893, the Mayo doctors by formal contract agreed to refuse privilege invitations from other hospitals, limiting themselves to diagnosis at the clinic and surgery at St. Mary's. "Dr. Will" and "Dr. Charlie," as the nuns called them, assumed an aggressive policy of professionalization for St. Mary's, advancing the hospital over local competitors, backing campaigns for expansion, inventing improved surgical equipment, strengthening the building's infrastructure, and launching a two-year nurse-training program centered on clinical lectures.[45] The Mayo family, always intensely loyal to and appreciative of the Franciscans—Dr. Will once declared, "We are but the sisters' agents"—invented a unique environment for doctors, one destined to ascend to power across international borders.[46]

These arrangements gave the Franciscan sisters an exclusive and original place in the regional medical community, one with which other hospitals could not compete. The nuns enjoyed an uncommonly close relationship with talented doctors willing to work cooperatively with women at a time when resistance to scientific education for females hardened. Despite the general bias, the immersion in hospital management and broad schooling improved the quality of the sisters' nursing knowledge and reinforced their medical confidence.

These advantages did not, however, free the nuns from the financial obligations of improving and enlarging the physical plant. Their responsibilities extended beyond sick patients to negotiating land boundaries, assuming construction loans, and overseeing the facility.[47] The same sisters might also assist in surgery, administer medications, give bedside care, cook and distribute meals, and do all the laundry, including a nightly exhausting preparation of operating-room linens. As convent restrictions concerning intimate contact with men remained in place, the nursing sisters relied on Dr. Will and Dr. Charlie for answering the daily physical needs of male patients. The growth of the hospital made these many duties within a complicated and grueling schedule impractical for all concerned, limiting time for the sisters' formal education and threatening the institution's growing reputation.

Through a series of changes, the Franciscans moved to correct these problems. In 1906 the training school for nurses introduced a more structured curriculum, offering classes in anatomy, physiology, sanitation, and hygiene as well as practical nursing courses for a total of 142 hours of instruction.[48] By this time, a trained nurse directed the school, and in 1914 its program, now affiliated with a larger secular hospital, was expanded to three years and state accreditation was secured in 1915.[49] Steadily, the Franciscan sisters added requirements that improved their preparation as medical caregivers and aligned their facility with state regulations.

The Franciscan nuns, whether reassigned from teaching duties or sent directly for health-care work, studied medicine at the St. Mary's Hospital Training School for Nurses. Within this Catholic educational enclave, they developed some academic privacy, especially avoiding censure from clergy who questioned medical education for religious women. At the same time, the sister students gained from the growing celebrity of the Mayo Clinic, its international clientele and the prominent medical visitors drawn to Rochester from the secular scientific world. Taking advantage of this sophisticated and unusual opportunity for nuns, the Franciscans focused on studying the latest medical advances, learning the complexities of an emerging health-care profession, training members in hospital administration, sending promising candidates for graduate work at universities, and in 1927—in cooperation with the Mayo Clinic—offering a four-year bachelor of science degree in nursing through their own College of Saint Teresa, which had awarded diplomas to sisters since 1911.[50]

The Franciscans, who started their western work as untrained amateurs, successfully blended their teaching and nursing ministries, simultaneously enhancing the academic quality of each, raising the professional stature of the congregation, and showing that Catholic sisters could build powerful lasting relationships with Protestant associates. A symbol of those melded ministries and broadened credentials emerged in the person of Sister M. Domatilla DuRocher, who in 1915 entered the Franciscan nursing program after three years as a classroom teacher. Completing her RN training, Domatilla pursued a bachelor's degree in science and certified in teaching and supervision at Columbia University, returning to Rochester as the educational director and later the superintendent of nurses at Saint Mary's Hospital. Her appointment to the Minnesota State Board of Examiners of Nurses and her ten-year tenure on a committee of the National League of Nursing Education reflected the changing relationship between western sisterhoods and state regulators, with nuns determined to meet secular requirements. Further, Domatilla's combined church and state résumé demonstrated that by the 1920s nuns increasingly perceived, regardless of church impediments and gender discrimination, employment survival demanded sisters seek academic achievement and professional credibility.[51]

Perhaps no congregation captured the transformation of nursing sisters into educated professionals better than the German immigrant Sisters of St. Mary. When the six sisters arrived in St. Louis in 1872, their leader, Mother Mary Odilia, sought work for the impoverished newcomers, whose employment hope rested on their ability to convince German immigrants of their talents as home nurses.[52] By 1880 the congregation paired inexperienced postulants with more-knowledgeable sisters, who gave instruction at the bedside of the sick. In 1893, when a large group of foreign candidates arrived in St. Louis, administrators introduced regular language classes, outfitting each postulant with an English/German pocket dictionary.[53] Once a young women mastered sufficient English, she attended medical lectures and laboratory demonstrations taught by staff doctors and one sister. In 1907 the Sisters of St. Mary formalized medical training for their nuns, with a school of nursing at the St. Mary's Infirmary location. In 1910, when the first class graduated, the nuns began a rotation system, recalling noncertified nurses from their hospital posts and enrolling them in the formal training at the infirmary. The selection of five or six sisters each year revealed the hindrances of educating in a timely fashion some 200 members of the congregation.[54] By 1912, the superior general hired a trained lay nurse, who delegated hospital assignments and supervised bedside care given by the nuns. Despite these efforts, trained nurses remained underrepresented in the congregation, and it was not unheard of for a housekeeping sister to work the night shift, give patient injections, and fill in with other nursing chores.[55]

In 1915 the nursing sisters took the Missouri state boards for the first time, and the state board of examiners accredited the nursing school at St. Mary's Infirmary. By the 1920s, the nurses of the Sisters of St. Mary, like nuns in many other congregations, enrolled in university degree programs, building their credentials in hospital administration, X-ray technology, medical records, and pharmaceutical preparation.[56] At the motherhouse, the sisters began a small high school operation for the youngest postulants who lacked the certification to enter the nursing program. A piecemeal academic operation that relied on adjunct faculty and relocated several

In Missouri, the Sisters of St. Mary upgraded patient nutrition at their infirmary through the formal study of home economics, food science, and agricultural chemistry, and their first nun pharmacists used the kitchen to prepare medical syrups and glucose solution. (Courtesy Franciscan Sisters of Mary, St. Louis, Mo.)

times, it secured accreditation in 1949, and when closed fourteen years later, it boasted 256 sister-nurse graduates, a nod to the creative ways the congregation educated its professional staff.[57]

The possible western anti-Catholicism and secular development of standards that fueled demands for certified teachers and trained nurses privileged nuns in ways their detractors had not anticipated. These elements forced sisters to demonstrate their professionalism and to qualify for secular examiners. The study assignments, mostly begun as a response to congregational obedience, unleashed the academic interests of sisters, driving them to seek the highest possible training in their respective fields. Across congregations, the names of sisters earning undergraduate and advanced degrees rose dramatically and showed no evidence of slowing.[58]

Mother generals appreciated the prestigious boost that degreed sisters gave to congregation schools and hospitals. University programs, progressive teaching methodology, and modern scientific advances became part of the thinking of nuns, as they committed themselves to being the best possible professionals in their chosen fields. They accepted the drudgery of part-time study, abandoned their slim chance for summer vacations, traveled great distances to renowned eastern and European universities, returned to the West with impressive degrees, and emerged as academic role models, encouraging young western women into teaching and nursing programs with the possibility of graduate study ahead. All of these conditions intensified for sisters of color, whose original missions had taken them to the streets and barrios of their constituencies. Their immersion in physical labor, coupled with the segregation that they themselves faced in colleges and universities, conspired to make their professional development a monument to tenacity and dedication.[59] In these movements, all sisterhoods, guided by gender-focused goals, reduced their pedagogical dependence on the male clergy, leaned against the boundaries of educational discrimination in their church, altered the intellectual profile of their congregations, drew laywomen into a female college community, built that community into a permanent source of allied supporters, and improved the quality of Catholic schools and hospitals across the West.

Americanization

Professionalization, coupled with the social demographics changing the country, produced yet another adjustment for western sisters. Although in many early western convents, immigrant voices dominated philosophy and policy, that supremacy weakened over time. Intentionally and accidentally, sisterhoods put down American roots.

In 1856, only eight years after her arrival in America, Mother Caroline Friess, an enthusiastic and loyal patron of Germanic culture, applied for and received U.S. citizenship.[60] Mother M. De Pazzi Bentley, founding superior of the Sisters of Mercy in St. Louis, relinquished her Irish citizenship in favor of fealty to the United States.[61] Mother Gertrude Guinaw of Omaha, Nebraska, received her U.S. naturalization papers in 1921, just months after she celebrated her golden jubilee among the Servants of Mary and five years before she unexpectedly returned to England for her retirement.[62] These immigrant sisters looked to strengthen the American aspects of their work and demonstrate their personal commitment to a new society. Broad forces for Americanization surrounded congregations for decades, and the West appeared to energize these influences among nuns.

When the Sisters of Providence and the Sisters of the Holy Names began their 1850s ministries in the Pacific Northwest, they arrived cognizant of the complicated language dynamic in a region where many dialects colored daily life. To help themselves when they left Canada, the nuns selected among their Irish-born, English-speaking Montreal sisters when organizing their first mission groups.[63] Yet, with the sounds of English rising throughout Washington and Oregon, the attendant issues of Americanization moved directly into both cloisters.

In 1858 patients at the St. Joseph Hospital of the Sisters of Providence came from more than a dozen homelands, including the English-speaking worlds of New York, Ireland, Scotland, and England. With each passing year, the names of more English speakers appeared in the hospital register, intensifying the language pressure faced by the sister nurses.[64] By 1865, only limited English progress had been made among the Sisters of Providence, and their local superior, Mother Joseph, for the second time rejected a school staffing request from Idaho because "[you know] how short we are of English teachers."[65]

A single incident did not evoke language decisions, but English as a force managed to inject itself into convent life. In 1891, when the Sisters of Providence established a provincial house in Montana, they conducted their first retreat in French. The following year, twenty-four sisters made the annual retreat in English.[66] Although this appeared to indicate a march toward Anglo domination, only three years later, a Spokane priest was unable to hear the confessions of all the sisters at the Holy Names Academy because he lacked enough fluency in French.[67]

In addition to these language issues, the sisters missioned to the Pacific Northwest began to feel the long miles and inevitable separations from Montreal, which led them closer to American connections. Most important, these French/English–speaking sisters watched other religious congregations of women—several of them spawned in America—move into the area. These incoming mission groups tailored their work to the interests of American settlers, more than 600,000 of whom traversed the Oregon Trail as early as 1860.

For example, one American-founded congregation, the Franciscan Sisters of Philadelphia, appeared as a new educational presence at Indian reservation schools in Washington and Oregon. Their teaching goals emerged out of their Philadelphia origins and their financial and philosophical association with Mother Katharine Drexel. Drexel made no secret of her conviction that the essentials of western education rested on the Catholic faith and American democracy. Likewise, the Sisters of St. Joseph promoted an "American curriculum," laid out in a 300-page course of study written for use in all U.S. foundations of the congregation.[68] The French-Canadian sisters could not have missed the thrust of these other sisterhoods.[69]

At their missions, American ways drifted into unlikely venues. Sister Perpetua of the Holy Names sisters liked to recall the festivities at the Grand Ronde Reservation for the Fourth of July, where for several years the French-speaking nuns had forsaken French and Chinook conversations for English usage. Counting Sister Perpetua, four French-Canadian sisters celebrated the most important national holiday of the United States of America and commented with pleasure when Native people raised the Stars and Stripes to honor the nuns as they entered the reservation.[70]

These immigrant nuns watched their mission region stamped with a U.S. identity, reinforced by government affiliation, cultural impulses, and American Catholic sentiment. In this fast-paced transformation, they began to see themselves no longer as missionaries in a foreign port but as residents of an American society. In 1872, less than twenty years after the Sisters of the Holy Names arrived in Oregon, their superior resigned her right to a seat at a motherhouse chapter to be held in Canada. The sisters recognized the conflicts "between duty and duty," the pull to see old friends, "a country which she reluctantly left, . . . [and] an aged father."[71] Those factors aside, the weight of new responsibilities in a new environment kept Sister Mary of the Sacred Heart in Oregon. The sisters, despite deep regard for their Montreal motherhouse and much as they treasured their Canadian associations and their French origins, embraced their American lives in the Pacific Northwest.

In other congregations, the pull toward Americanization also gained strength. The desire to counter charges of a pro-Vatican loyalty dominating the Catholic immigrant world, the persuasiveness of the "national church" movement led by Archbishop John Ireland of St. Paul, and the numbers of American-born postulants entering the convent explained the swell. Many priests and nuns with European loyalties quarreled with Ireland's views and objected to his determination that the "foreign" tone of the American Catholic Church be eliminated. The fight went straight to the Vatican, and ultimately Ireland and his forces for Americanization of the church fell before conservative opponents, among them, in convents, Mother Caroline Friess and Mother Frances X. Cabrini, both intense national advocates.[72]

Despite the squelching of John Ireland, Americanization moved onward. On 4 July 1876 the Sisters of the Holy Names noted that with "the loud thunder of the booming cannon and joyful peals of church bells," all "Portland is in holiday attire" for the "glorious centennial of our independence." The sisters watched the parade, more than a mile long, with an estimated 20,000 participants from the portico of their community room and enjoyed the close of an "eventful day" with its "pyrotechnic display of fireworks." For the Fourth of July celebrations in 1894, these same sisters in Seattle marked the "country's true holiday" by decorating the front entrance to their academy with fifty-seven U.S. flags, pleased to note that "passers-by marvel to find so much national pride within convent walls." In 1908 the nuns parlayed the opening of a Marylhurst, Oregon, orphanage into a two-day event that included a religious dedication and a chartered steamboat excursion to the new building, where the sisters served a luncheon to Portland residents who made the trek.[73]

In the twentieth century, as Europe fell into World War I and then America joined, congregations appeared particularly anxious to display their national patriotism. In 1918, at the Queen of Angels monastery in Oregon, an increasing number of sisters, mostly of German origins, began the naturalization process. On the Fourth of July, the monastery took on a festive air, the ban of silence lifted, even for mealtime. The nuns enjoyed picnic fare of hot dogs and homemade ice cream in an atmosphere that clearly defined the monastery as American turf.[74]

Congregations also responded to U.S. domestic politics. Mother Caroline Friess, only five years a naturalized citizen, wrote to her friends in Munich: "I have still to express my sorrow on account of the Civil War in which our America is involved."[75] The Sisters of Mercy often encountered armed soldiers on the streets of St. Louis, and the superior Mother M. De Pazzi volunteered the convent as a holding area for wounded soldiers awaiting hospital treatment.[76] The Sisters of the Holy Names rejoiced when the Civil War ended in 1865 and expressed horror only days later that Abraham Lincoln had been assassinated, "the tidings that awoke today a pang of deep regret in every heart loyal to the Union cause."[77]

Even though western nuns lived far from the centers of American political activity, they showed an interest in civic matters and, given their compliance to a masculine hierarchy, considerable respect for U.S. presidents. In September 1901 the Sisters of St. Mary, responding to a request from the mayor of St. Louis, "profusely draped" St. Mary's Infirmary with mourning bunting in honor of the assassinated president William McKinley.[78] On a happier occasion, the Sisters of the Holy Names welcomed President William Howard Taft to a gala reception at their Portland academy. After welcoming speeches and the presentation of a bouquet of flowers, the gathered Catholic children from many schools "raised their voices in the patriotic anthem, 'America.'" The president responded with an address that praised "our church's teaching that loyalty to God is the same as the fidelity to country and reverence for constituted authority."[79] The Sisters of the Holy Names, who had negotiated the uncertain waters of the Pacific

Northwest during some of its most anti-Catholic days, could feel that their American credentials had just been authenticated from the country's highest elected official.

The congregation kept a steady pace in its move toward Americanization. The sisters' academy in Spokane established an annual tradition of celebrating Arbor Day with festivities that one year included the planting of twenty-six trees and the next sixty-two. By 1906, the elaborate event meant that classes donated trees, filling the campus with western spruce, white oak, maple, and weeping willows.[80] Attention to these secular occasions paved the way for reaction to the onset of World War I, which prompted one sister to write, "May the God of Nations preserve our land in peace and prosperity!"[81] By February 1918 the Holy Names sisters were besieged with requests for war relief work. Their efforts, which they undertook with the students at the academy, ranged from knitting sweaters and socks to constructing posters advertising food conservation.[82]

Loyalties to the homeland of a congregation had not evaporated, and internal disputes about heritage hung over most congregations. But Catholic sisters felt the sweep of Americanization and encouraged its presence in their convents. Faced with political foes regarding school regulations and the right to wear habits when teaching in a publicly funded school, sisters came to rely on rhetoric grounded in democratic principles. They wove secular language into arguments for their schools, saying "that these children may . . . receive in their civic training a perfect preparation for the duties and responsibilities of American citizenship."[83] In 1912, with the school debates still unresolved, Sister M. Angeliqua in the Oklahoma Territory received word that all Catholic pictures and statues should be removed from public walls, which "should be adorned with the flag and patriotic pictures." Sister Angeliqua hoped that the motherhouse would "free us from the slavery of Uncle Sam," but her battle was being waged in secular language.[84]

It was no surprise that in 1924, during school controversies in Washington, the Sisters of the Holy Names looked to the ballot box for vindication, using organized political action to defeat the bill. They urged family involvement and sent their students on two-hour shifts as poll workers, handing out "Anti-Bill 49" pamphlets. At midnight, contacted by an ally, they rejoiced at the defeat of what they considered a discriminatory bill against private Catholic education.[85]

The speed with which sisters used American elections did not stem entirely from their immersion in the political culture around them. Oddly, their own governance system, generated within a rigid gender structure, furthered their adoption of an American life. The congregational constitution, even though the ratification of that document depended on masculine approval all the way to the Vatican, set sisters toward democracy, an outcome surely not intended in Rome.

Carefully drawn rules for the election of a superior—for example, that the candidate must be at least thirty years of age, have five years of profession, and be limited to two three-year terms—laid out procedures that gave sisters practice in democratic ways.[86] True, meddling bishops frequently circumvented the procedures for counting secret ballots and skewed election results for their own purposes, but the sisters knew the spirit and the intent of the rule.[87] In 1887 the annalist for the Benedictines at St. Joseph declared that in the motherhouse, the air was "tense" as the election approached because of the lobbying efforts of the existing superior. Sisters on the missions were said to be "aroused" because they could not attend the voting nor choose their own proxies.[88] In 1889 Franciscans in Rochester were uneasy when, after two ballots, the votes remained "confused and scattered," and in 1900, many among the Sisters of Charity of the BVM doubted the results when the archbishop announced the defeat of the popular Mother Cecilia and a winning vote for a seventy-three-year-old former superior general.[89]

More and more sisters accumulated direct experience with democratic governance. They sat on congregation councils, met in general chapter, and served on appointed committees. The sisters participated in decisions concerning congregational expansion, financial management, and daily life. They nominated each other for treasurer, secretary, or education director. The nuns voted on a regular basis, shaping the very policy that guided their lives in the congregation.[90] Fair elections that saw sisters elevated to administrative posts gave a moral imperative to the process, and sisters turned restive when bishops and superiors tampered with voting rights.

This method of congregational governance placed nineteenth-century and early twentieth-century nuns in a position quite distinct from their secular counterparts. Years before laywomen secured voting rights in national elections, nuns and sisters exercised the franchise as a routine part of convent life, making political choices as individuals and groups. They lobbied for favored candidates, rejected rigged elections, and protected their suffrage. Dictatorial cloister management not only evolved in America but also brought nuns and sisters closer to the political and cultural expressions associated with a republic, even as the women developed a gender autonomy unique within the nation's conventions of the day.

Nuns, like these Denver Sisters of Charity of Leavenworth escorting well-turned-out orphans on a visit to a donor, showcased their ability to raise well-educated, hard-working American citizens as a response to political or religious critics. (Denver Public Library, Western History Collection, May 1980, X-29156, Denver, Colo.)

Sisters in several western locations had reshaped major parts of their original identity. Individually and collectively, they narrowed the gap between the Catholic institution and the American world. It behooved them in their work initiatives to reconcile themselves to American custom and manner, but often they did so without an overt intent to change themselves or rearrange local custom. Rather, they thought to protect Catholic tradition even as they undermined it, and they promoted conservative standards for womanhood even as they countermanded them.

Through this process of Americanization, the ideals and goals of nuns slid as on ice, producing a new generation of religious women. Over sixty years and across two continents, changes diluted the traditions of the European monastery for enclosed nuns, producing a cohort of noncloistered sisters comfortably aligned with American democratic values.

In 1911 a group of Dominican nuns newly arrived from Portugal regarded Chicago as a "pioneer" city, and the mother superior, accustomed to lengthy rituals with elaborate musical orchestrations, wrote of her astonishment that only the priest and a one-woman choir sang a requiem mass. She described the liturgy as "simply awful . . . as I had never . . . assisted at a similar function." Further, she was flabbergasted to make her confession to an elderly priest in the "quick American fashion" in "a funny kind of box beside the altar."[91] Forty years later, this congregation—with sisters missioned to Oregon, California, and New Mexico—acknowledged that "it was inevitable . . . working in a country with other traditions . . . [we] develop in other directions," that "it took weeks or months to receive an answer from the motherhouse," and "there were no longer any sisters who had been trained in the Portuguese novitiate or were of Portuguese nationality."[92] Thus, the American sisters, once thinking themselves pioneers in the Windy City, made formal application to separate from the Lisbon motherhouse, adding their congregation to the many reconfigured by experiences in the American West.

Shifting Traditions

This dilution of European traditions and the ascendancy of American political and social values created responses within convent life. In the American West, these shifting dynamics resonated with regional impact. The western experiences of many congregations fostered deep-seated revisions in convent objectives.

From the outset of European missionary work, nuns who came to America encountered mounting problems with a distant European motherhouse. Issues of the dominant authority, priestly oversight, financial management, loyalty to motherhouse, and national commitments plagued everyone, as the story repeated itself across congregations. Often the first correspondence about sending missionaries to the West revealed the poor understanding of American realities common among European monastic leaders.

In 1878 Mother de Sales Garrick of Ireland wrote to Bishop Martin Marty in the Dakota Territory that his directive that the "houses of these poor people be visited" was disappointing, as, she explained, "we cannot, under any circumstances, relinquish our *vow of enclosure*." She concluded emphatically, "We do not go to secular houses, even of the poor."[93] By the time the Irish Presentation sisters boarded a ship, crossed the ocean, and arrived at a dilapidated Indian mission north of Yankton, weeks of compromise to seclusion undercut their enclosure. Discouraged, the recently uncloistered nuns settled in Fargo, opening an academy for girls. Within a few years, the high fence they built surrounding the convent and school—an attempt to reinstate strict enclosure—provoked complaints from students' parents. By 1897, the pressures of sustaining an academy among irate parents of several nationalities in economically depressed Fargo wore on the nuns. A controlling local bishop who opposed cloister and disliked the Presentations quite possibly instigated the problems, but the mother superior agreed to remove the fence. Her decision represented the literal and figurative acknowledgment that in western settings, many forces conspired to make enclosure undesirable and impractical.[94]

Enclosure surfaced quickly as a dilemma for other congregations as well. The Benedictines in Minnesota not only tried to keep a strict house closure, but their rule also required nuns to rotate out of the classroom each hour to limit secular contacts and to give time for prayer. These revolving teachers did not intend to create problems, but their enclosure rules disrupted lessons, encouraged student misbehavior, and inhibited meditation periods for nuns, altogether a chaotic scenario for the inexperienced German immigrants.[95]

In 1850 Mother Caroline Friess, who aggressively pushed her congregation into the American West, journeyed to her European motherhouse to argue against enclosure for the mission sisters. The ideal of the rule required nuns to live and teach inside a convent physically attached to a church and prohibited teachers from speaking to students outside of the classroom or conversing within the private cloister about school matters. After only three years touring the outreaches of several states and viewing the primitive conditions of western settlements, Mother Caroline regarded enclosure unrealistic and incompatible with the development of Catholic schools for American children. At the conclusion of a somewhat testy meeting with her superiors, Mother Caroline left Europe with the begrudging agreement that when "there will be no other alternative than to cross your threshold," such was permitted for the purpose of attending church services.[96]

These few words guaranteed the collapse of enclosure in the West. One after another, congregations found ways to justify, when "no other alternative" existed, crossing thresholds for many reasons other than attending parish prayer events. In 1884, when Mother Amadeus Dunne made her way through Miles City, establishing an Ursuline convent in the crude town, the Montana bishop John Baptist Brondel advised her: "Go everywhere for a few weeks and after that keep [your] enclosure as strictly as possible."[97] Bishop Brondel must have laughed at his advice later, as Mother Amadeus, who transferred from an enclosed house in Toledo, Ohio, traveled extensively through Montana and to Europe, New York, Washington, and Alaska, dealing with priests, businessmen, and nuns in many locations.

Enclosure created difficulties for many convents in the West. In Texas as late as 1916, the superior at Hallettsville requested a cloister dispensation for the Sisters of the Incarnate Word, as "many parents do not want to send their children because of the strict enclosure." In Sister Magdalene's assessment, the physical restriction led to a more significant matter, since the low attendance at the school made it "hard to get new subjects for the order." Enclosure, she also noted, prevented the sisters, missioned approximately 100 miles from San Antonio, Houston, or Corpus Christi, from taking "advantage of the normal schools and . . . professional training to keep up with the modern methods of teaching."[98] After nearly thirty years in Minnesota, the Benedictine sisters adopted some adjustments for their monastery, once said to be run by "arbitrary discipline." Inside the convent, although dietary allowances remained stringent, the superior eliminated the iron grates separating public spaces from the cloister and permitted nuns to enter the parlor when visitors were present. The sisters considered themselves obedient to enclosure but acknowledged they left the monastery only with "special permission," "chiefly when sent out to collect."[99] Enclosure became a spiritual albatross for nuns, making their lives untenable, alienating them from target groups for recruitment, and retarding congregational advancement.

Inside monastic communities, the American West challenged other arrangements of convent life. The European practice of a division between choir and lay sisters did not travel well into the West. In small convents scattered across rural towns and Indian reservations, a separation between the "teaching" sisters and the "domestic" sisters quickly became irrelevant, as every nun worked furiously for survival. Even in urban areas, relations between the choir and lay sisters could be tense; a pastoral visitor in San Antonio urged the mother superior to "treat the lay sisters with more kindness," suggesting she "get them some relief for all the work they do."[100] By 1881, one house of Benedictines adopted a common black veil for lay and choir sisters, who then received identical embossed gold rings. At the same time, prayer schedules relaxed, and the congregation substituted the English-spoken Little Office of the Virgin Mary for the public recitation of the Latin-based Divine Office, which had excluded the lay sisters. The change, a nod to the diminishing number of illiterate sisters, wiped away one more barrier that separated convent classes.[101] Emboldened, the lay sisters argued for complete equality with the choir sisters when the congregation adopted a new constitution in 1888. Not until 1894 was all resolved; at that time, the lay sisters took their "rank according to their age in religion with equality to the choir sisters."[102]

Dominican sisters in Texas—where, at least until 1877, lay sisters wore a distinguishing black scapular—also wrestled with regulations that imposed class division inside the convent. In 1909 the mother general and her council decided that perpetually professed lay sisters could take recreation time with the choir nuns, the first casual contact allowed between the two groups. Still, the Dominicans struggled over several years to find a fair balance, yielding through several constitutions and chapter votes to the opinion that lay sisters remained ineligible for election to congregational office. Ultimately, elections of new administrations, significant revisions in the constitution, breakdowns of distinctions in small mission convents, and protests from both lay and choir sisters led the Dominicans to eliminate their class structure.[103]

Congregations could not but notice that with each passing year, the young women seeking admission for the lay-sister class declined. In 1885 Mother Emily Power of the Sinsinawa Dominicans, a relentless worker for the professional education of nuns, challenged the efficacy of the lay category, writing to Rome: "This country is so different from Europe, so new, the spirit of equality is so prevalent, that it is difficult to have . . . two elements in a religious community." She concluded that "the community would be better, more prosperous without this distinction."[104] She sensed, as did the St. Louis–based Sisters of St. Joseph of Carondelet in 1908, that the lay-sister category "should be abolished as being incompatible with American ideals." For Sister Leonie Forrest, head laundress at St. Catherine's College in St. Paul, the decision meant that after nearly thirty years of domestic labor for her congregation, she was a fully vested, voting member of the Congregation of St. Joseph, which had inexorably moved toward integration with American custom.[105] Visual distinctions and prayer obligations dividing the "learned" and the "laborer" of convent life, so handy in a European world dependent on silent communication and family prestige, faded in the West.

The West also caused sisters to rethink the confinement and inconvenience of their attire. The traditionally white-clad Dominican nuns, defending their use of a black dress, successfully explained to a European superior that "the cold region . . . scarcity of water in winter, the high price of fuel . . . the great work of teaching and other duties render it very difficult—and we could say impossible—for several months in the year to wash white woolen habits, besides the two or three days' time to dry them."[106] Veils shortened, cuffs reduced, and guimpes simplified as sisters decided the labor-intensive, time-consuming production of habits cost money, drew sisters from their duties, and interfered with necessity in demanding western missions.[107] In 1895 the Franciscan Sisters of Perpetual Adoration separated their one-piece headgear into an easier-to-launder, round guimpe and coif and finally removed the stiff white lining of the veil—alterations to a habit worn since 1862.[108] In the West, elaborate religious dress that required yards of expensive serge, heavy starch, and intricate ironing lost appeal, as nuns reworked their clothing to better accommodate their active lives.

Nursing sisters also developed concerns over appropriate clothing for hospital settings while retaining religious identity with congregational garb. Their efforts to respond to the demands of their western lives and modern medical standards met with a storm of protest. The controversy turned on a complicated axis, as it involved canon law regarding the religious habit, questions of competing bishop authority over nuns, medical demands of secular physicians, and issues of modernity and secularization. By 1920, nursing sisters, vexed that they performed all types of hospital labor while doctors and priests controlled the conversation about nuns' clothing, expressed their objections, noting that the men had been dithering about the subject for years. The nuns understood the ease of wearing washable white habits when working on hospital wards and in operating rooms, a sensible improvement that spoke to comfort, practicality, and sanitation.[109]

Nothing reflected the changing world for nuns more than language, which consistently fueled the shifting regional complexion of convent life. Regardless of nationality, sisters confronted an American West where English as the language of the boulevard ultimately dominated. In Washington and Oregon, both the Sisters of Providence and the Sisters of the Holy Names relied on one or two English-speaking nuns who came to the first missions in the 1850s. In this way, inside the convent, the sisters conversed, prayed, wrote letters, and kept records in French; when secular business took them to the outside world, they turned to their English speaker.[110] In 1874 Mother Caroline Friess instructed the School Sisters of Notre Dame that classroom lessons must offer geography, natural history, and science in the German and English languages. Despite this direction, by 1889, after reviewing her mission schools, Mother Caroline complained that overall the "sisters constantly speak English among themselves."[111] The Franciscan Sisters of Perpetual Adoration by the 1880s offered both confession and the homily at mass in German or English.[112] In 1909 Mother Matilda Wagner, superior of a Franciscan congregation with a membership dominated by German and Polish sisters, declined to send only German-speaking teachers to a Minnesota parish, for she told the pastor that to do so would undercut the sisters' competitiveness with the nearby all-English public school.[113] Yet as late as 1909, Benziger Brothers published an illustrated German/English reader for Catholic schools, indicating that the debate about language instruction in parochial schools had not ended.[114]

The language struggle continued within congregations. At the turn of the century, Mother Mary Concordia, a national advocate for the education of nursing sisters, was influenced by her own efforts to translate teaching notes from her native German into English days before each lecture.[115] Within her own congregation, a German/English dispute had been brewing, with the mistress of novices replaced by someone "more sympathetic with German-born girls."[116] Although Mother Concordia stayed with the American-minded segment, a German contingent separated and moved deeper into Missouri, only translating the prayer book into English in 1921, at the same time the sisters applied for naturalization.[117] The Maryville sisters, originally of the St. Louis congregation of Mother Odilia Berger, divorced themselves from St. Louis in part over national issues, but they finally capitulated to an American identity.

Other congregations struggled with similar issues. Between 1911 and 1914, the Franciscan Sisters of Chicago strove unsuccessfully to conduct a Polish school in Falls City, Texas. Although Polish- and English-speaking sisters came to Texas understanding that they would teach the language and culture of their homeland, the school community divided into opposing constituencies. National loyalists threatened to fall away, but the bishop countered their inclinations, asserting that "our Polish people understand very well the importance of having their children learn English."[118] The Franciscan Sisters of Chicago left Texas, but more and more they found that even in "Polish" parishes, English prevailed. As sisters absorbed Americanization, the impact of English altered classroom management, influenced congregational leaders of education, invaded convent routines, and tainted relationships with pastors and parishioners.

Attachment to language required decades of transition, and every debate did not resolve easily. As late as 1904, a Sister of Providence, whose congregation had been in Washington since the 1850s, wrote to the Montreal archbishop that those nuns who were not French or French-Canadian suffered discrimination. She charged that although the congregation's constitution stated "the spirit of nationality must be banished," such had not occurred. The displeased nun complained that all positions of authority went to the French sisters, who were not "suitable to govern in an English-speaking province, as they neither understood the ways of the people nor even of the sisters not French."[119] Her comments reflected the sort of awkward but insightful difference sure to surface among sisters split by international boundaries and increasingly by language. The Vancouver sister probably felt little surprise when the archbishop, affronted by her discontent, sent a sharp rebuke—which was, of course, written in French.[120]

Traditional ritual and the use of national languages collapsed before the rapid pace of change that came to the Catholic Church in the West. Less clear were the changes that came to convents as English replaced those languages that some sisters thought they had come to the West to preserve. The unexpected complicated language choices for nuns. The peoples of the West—indigenous and newcomer—made clear the place of English; it ranked behind Native dialects and Spanish, although it had its place. Sisters accommodated those interests or moved on. They saw, however, that within convent spaces, and as their chapels filled more and more with young women born in the American West, many traditions—once thought unalterable—shifted to new ground.

Spiritual Discretion

Perhaps the most dramatic issue for nuns concerned a subject that nuns kept more veiled than any other in their cloistered lives. The American West created moments that thrust sisters across spiritual boundaries, when circumstances asked of them actions outside their expressly defined church role. Rigidly prohibited from fulfilling spiritual rituals designated for priests only, nuns complied willingly with this restriction. Their letters and diaries did not reveal a community of women seething to assume the sacred privileges of the priest. In the West, however, expectations that nuns perform spiritual ritual devolved on them without warning.

Sisters expected to assume duties connected to religious instruction among those with whom they lived and worked. Their charges, beyond the classroom subjects, included the preparation of children and adults for reception of the sacraments. They gave lessons in church music, led the way in worship behaviors, introduced the lives of the saints, encouraged the artistic decoration of chapels, explained the recitation of the rosary, and taught the steps of a novena. They organized the parish Sodality and the Children of Mary. In the absence of the priest, nuns were known to lead the congregation with prayers and hymns in place of the Sunday mass.[121]

The peoples of the West did not hold with separation of spiritual authority so assumed within the Catholic Church. Committing to the practice of Catholicism and failing to see any clear pastoral difference between a black-robed priest or a nun, many westerners insisted on receiving the rituals of the faith, regardless of the gender of the minister. In 1888, when Franciscan sisters first moved among the Lakota people in South Dakota, the Natives questioned them closely about their lives and declared them "holy women."[122]

Because nuns worked in mission situations where priests were more often absent than present, the laity viewed the women as the representatives of the church. Indigenous and immigrant alike expected to call on the spiritual authority of nuns. Over time, the women became accustomed to practicing those legitimate services allowed to them.

For example, in her 1883 report from Texas, Mother St. Pierre noted with enthusiasm that she and another sister personally baptized three different dying patients, each given the name "Joseph."[123] At about the same time, Franciscan sisters at Odanah near Lake Superior visited many Indian homes during a deadly measles epidemic, baptizing dying children or blessing the sick with holy water.[124] The sisters recalled that "since Father could not easily come for a while," "we had the happiness to baptize in urgent cases of death."[125]

The administering of sacraments, of course, fell exclusively within the provenance of male priests, with the exception of baptism. Thus these sisters, moving among the pallets of moribund children, acted within the dictates of the church, which allowed for persons other than priests to perform baptisms in cases of urgency. That rule, however, was typically observed in the exception. For nuns such as the Sisters of St. Mary in St. Louis, with their urban location close to a parish church, access to a priest for sacraments of baptism and extreme unction posed only a small problem.[126] For sisters and nuns in many western locations, however, the "emergency" baptism became a routine of frontier life. In the absence of the priest and with the dying before them, sisters exercised their permitted spiritual duties, which they often noted in an oblique fashion in their records.[127]

At the White Earth Reservation, a Native man came seeking help for a sick relative, but he arrived to find an empty rectory. Turning to the nuns, the distraught man begged for assistance. Although dark had fallen, the pair of Benedictine sisters packed up two small children left in their care, hoisted them onto their backs, and made the two-mile hike through snow-drifts and over icy trails. When the sisters reached the home of the dying man, they found him collapsed on the floor, begging them to hear his confession. The nuns recited appropriate prayers and led him in the act of contrition.

Weeks later, when the sick man died, his Native relations, undeterred by the absence of the priest yet again and reassured of the prayer abilities of the nuns, asked the women to conduct the funeral. The sisters arranged the funereal appointments — securing a coffin from the government, preparing the body for burial, sewing the shroud, and making paper flowers. With the deceased laid out in the church, the sisters repeated the prayers for the dead, blessed the body with holy water, and accompanied the coffin to the cemetery. There, the two sisters stood while family dug a grave through nearly frozen ground and then recited the prayers for internment.[128]

This cross-culture religious event spoke to the spiritual communication that passed between the nuns and the Native family. Although the sisters would not have used the sacred words of formal absolution given by a priest, it remained unlikely that they turned a cold ear to the dying man's plea to confess. Further, their conduct during the man's illness satisfied the family sufficiently that the grieving members had religious confidence in the sisters to prepare the body for burial and conduct the funeral, even if it deviated from their oldest custom.

Similarly, in New Mexico, a dying man at a tuberculosis hospital called out to the sisters praying at his bedside to hear his confession. One of the sisters jumped to her feet to run for the priest, but the young immigrant, fearful that death was upon him, stopped the sister, exclaiming that the nuns must at least allow him to confess in Italian so he would be sure to rid himself of his spiritual burdens.[129] Apparently the dying youth felt it better to have spoken the words, even in a foreign language to a woman, than to have missed the chance to repent and receive comfort before one of God's professed.

But it was not only laypeople in the West who accepted a porous spiritual identity for nuns. In times of religious crisis, priests could adjust their canonical compass as well. In 1871, as a fierce fire swept through the mining town of Virginia City, Nevada, the parish pastor rushed into the convent and pressed the Eucharist into the hands of a startled sister. He ordered her to deliver her package to the Gold Hill camp, a walk of ten miles over a rocky mountainside, through smoke-dense air and in the dark.[130] This woman, so strictly enjoined from touching a consecrated host, except as a communicant—this nun, so forcefully restricted to daylight travel with a companion—in the emergency of the moment saw her spiritual boundaries not only erased but done so emphatically by a priest of her church.

Across congregations, sisters had no unified understanding of how they assumed spiritual place with the people of the West. They generally minimized their role in religious situations that infringed on priestly functions. Over time, however, the spiritual role of sisters meshed with the larger western reality that the faithful of the church took responsibility for their worship outside of the domain of priests. Catholic sisters, however, geared to avoid offense to male clergy and sensitive to issues of spiritual confidentiality, suppressed their place in an active ministry in circumstances designated as a priestly right. They were reluctant to admit that dying people confessed to them and begged for absolution and that families expected them to deliver spiritual ceremony. Regardless of their reasoning, the sisters of the nineteenth-century West overlooked the growing view of Catholics in many areas that the gender of the spiritual provider mattered less than the religious comfort delivered.

Homes in the West

The Catholic Church in the American West gained its regional foothold from the labor of nuns and sisters. Many of those women entered into the places of the West convinced they brought religious salvation to the inhabitants, whether indigenous or immigrant peoples. As the story of the region unfolded, however, quite a different scenario encompassed the sisters, who thought they were visitors. Circumstances reversed, and sister newcomers became sister residents.

By 1872, the Sisters of the Holy Names and the Sisters of Providence, living in the Pacific Northwest from Canada since the 1850s, opened novitiates in Portland and Vancouver. In so doing, these French sisterhoods crossed a cultural fault line. The novitiate training centers gave the congregations increased local visibility, suggested residential permanence in the United States, altered the immigrant profile of the sisters, distanced the missioned nuns from their Canadian motherhouses, enhanced their place as workers for the American Catholic Church, and underlined the autonomy of the Oregon and Washington houses. The French-Canadian sisters hoped for vocations among the American students they educated. They were not disappointed.

Increasingly, young Catholic women born in the American West, whose national loyalties rested with the United States and whose cultural identity emerged from Anglo institutions, entered the welcoming convent portals at Portland and Vancouver. Between 1871 and 1909, the Sisters of the Holy Names admitted 200 postulants and professed 126 at the Portland novitiate.[131] The Sisters of the Holy Names, lovingly attached to their Canadian roots, nonetheless began to perceive the geographic differences between Oregon and the Montreal motherhouse as a threat to recruiting postulants. In 1909 the community historian, defending the opening of an American novitiate, wrote: "Would not these candidates for the novitiate falter in their holy purpose when the necessity of going to distant Montreal was made plain? Would not the question of a change of language, climate, and customs, materially influence their decisions?"[132] Apparently, this congregation did not entirely agree with the bishop of Montreal who earlier had written to the Sisters of Providence, "The distance that separates us is nothing, nor can it prevent . . . our hearts from strengthening the bonds that unite us."[133]

In 1917 several sisters of Notre Dame de Namur living in San Francisco, San Jose, and Alameda expressed strong opposition to the central government in Belgium, believing "that the future of the community in California depends upon breaking loose entirely from the motherhouse."[134] Although the archbishop's delegate making the visitation to the Notre Dame de Namur convent declined to endorse that suggestion, he called the visit of the European mother general "disastrous," as "she wished to place our California girls under the full rigidity of the Belgian Rule." He particularly voiced astonishment that during vacation, the sisters still rose at five in the morning, just as during the school term, and he concluded that "very little joy has come into their lives."[135] The Notre Dame de Namur sisters kept their international attachment, but increasingly, the European administration yielded authority and financial control to the American province.

As bonds between sisters and eastern or European houses frayed, not every severed connection unraveled in the West. In 1890 the administration of Dominican sisters in Brooklyn, New York, sent seven nuns to Aberdeen, Washington, where they established a school and hospital for those connected to forestry. The separation from the Brooklyn motherhouse raised numerous hardships for the missioned group, which faced excruciating poverty and more than one personality conflict. In the spring of 1919, Mother Emmanuel arrived from Brooklyn, interviewed each of the nuns, changed the local leadership, and gave the sisters permission for a vacation at the seashore.[136] Four years later, it stunned the Edmonds sisters during a closed retreat to learn that a few weeks earlier, Mother Emmanuel, writing from Brooklyn, had informed the archbishop that "it is utterly impossible for us to continue sending sisters to St. Rose province," arguing that "the distance between New York and Seattle would be justifiable reason for us to ask to be relieved."[137] Mother Emmanuel recommended that the Washington sisters should merge with other Dominicans in the West. Debt, distance, and misunderstandings between New York and Washington collapsed the East/West alliance. Cut asunder, the small congregation elected Sister Guilelma, a native Washingtonian, as mother superior. Although Guilelma, the westerner, served only one year as mother superior, she influenced the Dominicans until 1934, strengthening finances, building membership, and deepening their Washington identity.[138]

Catholic nuns and sisters surveyed the American West and realized they were no longer newcomers. Over seventy-five years, the women, once transients, had become residents with ties to many locations within the nation's most diverse region. They had managed the natural world and engaged its inhabitants. They had confronted themselves and adjusted their vision.

The horizon had changed because of their labors. Substantial institutions, designed to serve the needs of a community, arose in every part of the West. The architecture of Catholicism rose on many landscapes because of the labor of sisters. A hospital in Colorado, a novitiate in Montana, a residence for working women in Iowa, a college in California, an orphanage in Minnesota, a free kitchen in Kansas, a monastery in Idaho, a night refuge for girls in Missouri, a boarding academy in Utah, a free school in Arkansas—across the West, the visible signs of a Catholic presence appeared through the initiative and determination of Catholic sisters.

The adobe and brick, the schools and hospitals that sisters tirelessly built for their church and not for their own gain, represented only one aspect of their western imprint. They nursed the sick and comforted the dying. They educated the children of the West, accepted many of its daughters into their congregations, and returned them to the western world as workers in many regions. The strongest influence of Catholic sisters, however, stemmed from their enormous personal and professional impact on the women's West. Their lives underscored the originality, power, and endurance of institution building by women. Nuns and sisters earned their stature as participants in the long process of defining a women's West.

SISTER HELEN KYLE SSM
(Courtesy Franciscan Sisters
of Mary, St. Louis, Mo.)

*Our field of labor . . . is
reached. . . . We are all in the
best of spirits and at once
undertake the work.*

—Oregon Chronicles, Baker
City, 28 and 29 April 1875,
Archives of the Sisters of the
Holy Names of Jesus and
Mary, Portland, Oregon

Nuns and Wests
Melding

In the American West, nuns confronted circumstances that led them to reshape two components of sisterhood. That these components frequently collided added complexity but also vitality to the experiences, as nuns and sisters mapped out life within a West of many parts. The first factor centered on defining a religious identity that accommodated the ideals nuns cherished from a European monastic tradition and the fresh opportunities for professed women that arose in America. The second element called for crafting a regional identity that reconfigured religious behaviors to fit changing expectations for nuns and those they held for themselves. In both of these areas, new forms won over old ways.

Nuns and sisters first entered into western regions as European immigrants, like thousands of others displaced by economic and political turmoil that made resettlement in America a reasonable and desirable decision. Religious women thus faced the same life-changing dramas as secular migrants. They turned away from their known world, leaving the ground of home and the familiar folk who tread it. With but a few coins in their pockets, nuns boarded wretched ships and spent weeks in miserable steerage, smothered by the unvarnished humanity surrounding them. On occasion, they traveled under the protection of priests and bishops, but such arrangements did not enhance their accommodations or their diet; everyone was poor. On these chaotic voyages, nuns tried to concentrate on prayer and missionary goals, but homesickness and uncertainty made these journeys unsettling for women only recently accustomed to a closed monastery.

Once in America, the sisters gambled on finding refuge and employment among some needy group, especially their own countrymen who had preceded them. The quest for paid work brought sisters into many corners of the American West, their hazardous journeys replicating those of other migrants. The nuns searched for place, but their experiences as western travelers never folded into the usual white pioneer epic for which America maintains such a fondness. The uniqueness of Catholic nuns, single women of mixed ages living and working for a lifetime in all-female community, has been overlooked in the Anglo-European pantheon of western journeys.

Unlike Anglo-European females around them, nuns chose purposefully to enter into western landscapes committed to a status of unwed womanhood. They traveled, lived, prayed, worked, and died together in same-gender clusters, offsetting the "Madonna of the Prairie" ideal of an American West dominated by white families whose wives and mothers achieved mythic celebration. Accordingly, Catholic nuns, who focused on their own concept of a Madonna, remained marginal, their role in western narratives reduced to stereotype and caricature.

Ventures across plains, through deserts, and along rivers introduced nuns to a physical environment that broadened their knowledge of the natural world. They learned about topography and weather, danger and beauty. The sisters, ill prepared for the trails they crossed, felt the sting of searing heat, sub-zero temperatures, and terrifying winds. They climbed mountains and forded rushing rivers. They lived through blizzards, earthquakes, and tornadoes. They bounced over corduroy roads in stagecoaches and wagons; they traveled in leaky skiffs and small canoes. They rode horses and mules and walked hundreds of miles on blistered feet. This immersion into a mercurial climate and brusque landscape seasoned the nuns and released in them an appreciation for the grandeur of the West, whether in the Willamette Valley, the Mojave Desert, or the Rocky Mountains. With that environmental awakening came another for themselves—the realization that, single women though they were, the physical intensity of the American West not only failed to defeat them but also often elated them.

Once located in western places, immigrant nuns, increasingly joined by sisters from newly formed American congregations, aggressively sought the employment that would sustain them. They connected their work to notions of social service and looked for ways to support themselves by introducing educational and medical facilities to communities in need. Guided by their Catholic religious ethic, the sisters generally established ecumenical policies, welcoming persons of all persuasions to their schools, hospitals, and orphanages.

Encouragement for nuns to move into the West came from bishops overseeing the religious care of Catholics spread across seemingly limitless acres of space. Although the bishops wanted a cadre of priests for the West, it proved difficult to find enough ordained men to sign on for long periods at remote parishes. With a widespread flock and but a handful of priests, the bishops cultivated women's congregations as missionaries, enticing them with images of Christian conversions or berating them with accusations of timidity and selfishness.

Many congregations in Europe and the American East succumbed to these pressures and sent small groups of sisters to urban and rural western locations. Early schools and hospitals represented a dismal assortment of ramshackle buildings, with one congregation after another realizing the haphazard nature of the western mission program. With no ordered life plan for the women, bishops virtually abandoned the temporal and spiritual needs of missioned sisters. These missions, contrary to commonly held notions by Catholics and non-Catholics, did not come with gratis financial support from the local community, pastor, bishop, or the Vatican. Even a motherhouse, itself burdened with debts, provided negligible monetary assistance. A truism of considerable import escaped most people: nuns and sisters supported themselves.

Generally starting from extreme poverty, Catholic sisters assumed responsibility for their own livelihood and managed under grueling circumstances to survive. Like other western newcomers around them, the nuns scrambled in a fluctuating and unpredictable economic infrastructure. Anxious to capitalize on local need, the sisters willingly closed one operation and launched another—a school for a hospital, a hospital for an orphanage. When the economy weakened or collapsed, sisters followed the working population, relocating to more-promising venues. Thus, they showed themselves to be part of the mobile Anglo-European population attracted by the potentials of western employment and determined to make themselves available to fill a service vacuum.

The sisters earned salaries through school tuition, hospital insurance services, and contracts with public authorities. They sold their own produce and fancy needlework; organized bazaars; accepted donations of materiel and money; depended on the generosity of biological family; and begged in business, military, and parish districts. As individuals, they lived for decades in unmitigated poverty, any extra mission dollars going to the congregation's coffers. Elite boarding academies gave the mistaken impression of luxury for nuns, when in fact the income from such operations frequently supported free schools operated for the poor and children of color. As their sisterhoods stabilized, the nuns purchased land and built facilities, typically negotiating with banks or bishops for huge loans, which they retired over many years of congregational scrimping.

Those who employed the nuns did so in a manner that could only be described as miserly. Agreed-upon wages, set by western priests and bishops with the congregational leadership, often failed to materialize. Bishops also endured severely constrained budgets and struggled with diocesan finances, but they allowed the superior ranking of men in the church to color their actions toward nuns. In more than one western location, pastors refused to release wages, used convent stipends to cover parish expenses, or withheld salaries unless the nuns assumed domestic duties for the church and rectory. When frictions escalated or national rivalries dominated, some pastors did not hesitate to attack the sisters verbally from the pulpit, further disadvantaging nuns, who were obliged to adhere to public silence about church matters. Regardless of the reasons, missioned sisters across the West lived in drafty, unheated, dimly lit convents, faced empty pantries, and were at times abandoned by their pastoral leaders and embarrassed before their creditors.

Sisters responded to these difficulties with thought, spirit, and anger. For relief, missioned nuns appealed to their administrative leaders, who in turn relied on the constitution and rule of the congregation to counter unreasonable male oversight. Although nuns began western mission work guided by high ideals and verbal promises, with the passing of each decade, they grew more astute about the drawbacks to running isolated convents. Mother superiors and their councils became less willing to act on the glib assurances of a visiting frontier priest, sending sisters to be blindsided by unlivable conditions and utter poverty. By the 1900s, congregational leaders toughened the terms, insisting on legally sound contracts designed to protect those sisters on the missions and avoid problems before they materialized. Given a stalemate, a mother general was not opposed to circumventing an obstinate priest or bishop by appealing to a higher ecclesiastical power. Thus, through the realities of lived western experiences, nuns honed strategies for making their way through the financial and managerial levels of a church structured on the authority of men.

During the last half of the nineteenth century, the West, with its boom-or-bust extremes, saw no lack of deprivation in every corner and for all its peoples. One did not look far to find people, especially those of color, living in grueling want. Yet as industry and its attendant labor unrest stabilized, the West swung toward more even economies. Highs and lows still occurred, but the concept of a living wage worked its way into the conversations of rich and poor. In this evolving perception of decent compensation and appropriate housing, society deserted Catholic sisters.

As the West inched toward a better standard of life for some of its peoples, the nuns remained on the lowest rung of the economic ladder. Overall, an attitude emerged among clergymen and lay Catholics that permanent poverty represented an acceptable, even preferred, existence for sisters and nuns. With sisters set apart by religious attire and fenced convents, the public, relying on a distorted perception of the poverty vow, believed that nuns sought, or even insisted on, the privations detrimental to health and well-being. This assumption, virtually unchallenged, hung as a dark cloud over the church collective—clergy and laity—which burdened its most diligent workers with a cruel poverty that far exceeded the intent of a religious vow. By 1920, new churches and rectories dotted much of the Catholic West, replacing the wooden huts of the early years for a parish. Not so for the domestic quarters of nuns. Sisters, with barely enough to eat, continued to follow strict laws of fast and abstinence, abide by inflexible prayer schedules, work unreasonable hours, and live in shabby convents that had not been improved for thirty years. The dismal residences provided a visual reminder of how religious women workers were excluded from all aspects of a decent standard of living.

Despite the harshness of convent life, sisters intentionally sought centers of social and economic upheaval, where immigrants and indigenous peoples lived surrounded by an almost relentless violence, both regional and personal. In these environments, nuns immersed themselves in the public worlds of the peoples for whom they worked. They embraced communities of Native Americans, Mexicans, African Americans, and Anglos mired in the most taxing arenas of western life.

At the same time, sisters and nuns, impelled by an interest in working for people in need, actively engaged the middle and upper classes of western society. They acquainted themselves with shop owners and skilled artisans, business leaders and elected officials, Catholics and non-Catholics. Even where they lived within the shadow of anti-Catholicism, the sisters prodded citizens to support public institutions, their own lives offering a reminder about working for a common good. With ease, the sisters moved back and forth between rich and poor, their religious habits serving as a badge of admission to any quarter. Many well-positioned persons found it difficult to deny nuns living on the margins and caring for the people of the same. Sisters performed the actual philanthropy of wealthier people, freeing them from personal contact with the poor. Those in want welcomed nuns when they brought the gestures of interest and assistance in an ungenerous western world. Thus, nuns built an important societal bridge— real and emotional—across class divisions, connecting politicians, executives, managers, laborers, journeymen, and transients. Catholic sisters inexorably facilitated the process of community building in the West.

Although in their conduct, sisters chose a sedate and quiet demeanor, this personal decision did not deter them from engaging the fullness of the society around them. Sisters, from their first days in a convent, actively cultivated the ability to balance public and private lives, a circumstance that made them calming figures in a western world of human chaos. Undaunted by corruption, criminality, depravity, and illness, nuns showed resilience before the baseness that marked lives in crisis. The disasters of humanity drew sisters by virtue of their self-imposed professional and spiritual duty. They courted those at the edges of society, entered their spaces, and offered their services as a deterrent to a careening world. The stereotype of nuns as "shocked" by profanity, "embarrassed" by worldliness, or "ignorant" of sexuality was ludicrous in the nineteenth century and remains a patronizing, even silly, representation of Catholic sisters.

Their many western experiences did not induce nuns to alter their own worldview. Sisters clung to their faith and belief in its authenticity over all others. They actively promoted the Catholic religion and frequently denounced indigenous cultures for "superstition" and "paganism." They built hospitals, schools, and convents in Native spaces and without insight into the losses those cultures endured. Accordingly, they participated in the suppression of western cultures and the advancement of white hegemony.

This, however, produced some unexpected results. Because nuns placed themselves inside the worlds of peoples of color, they developed a keen ear for the dispossessed and disadvantaged. Thirty- and forty-year assignments to missions for people of color produced changes in the nuns who had first arrived at those stations. In the West, Catholic sisters initiated regular contact with peoples of color long before other Americans even thought about the impact of racism and discrimination. Most particularly, religious women and indigenous peoples were thrown together in ways that neither anticipated.

These two unlikely groups—peoples of color and white women—found themselves alone, removed from state and church authorities. Disparate neighbors of disparate heritage lived together and depended on each other in unprecedented intimacy. The proximity of sisters to the peoples of the West, although it did not free the nuns of every early prejudice, gave both groups an opportunity to learn about unfamiliar cultures, explore friendship, and broaden cross-cultural relationships. These intimacies weakened the hold of distant Catholic centers for western nuns. In the mountains of New Mexico, a coastal bay in Washington, or the plains of Kansas, the vision, philosophy, and policy of an eastern or European motherhouse diluted before the power of cultural interaction.

Granted, the sisters moved forcefully to establish classrooms where they introduced the principles of American education and the rituals of the Catholic faith, holding high their own culture. African Americans, Mexicans, and Native Americans were equally determined to do the same for their traditions—and they did. The lived interactions did not follow precisely the design of either group but demonstrated the fundamental courage and curiosity of those who dared to reach across the barriers of race when to do so prompted considerable scorn and ridicule. Over time, the rigidity that marked early contacts softened, paving the way for sisters to emerge as staunch allies of indigenous peoples in both civic and religious circles.

Perhaps the greatest challenge to nuns and sisters in the West came not from an overwhelmingly powerful physical environment or the richly diverse cultures that drove its great span but from within their own world. The major obstacle for nuns seeking a new religious identity in the West stemmed from the warp and woof of their church. Sisters in the West grappled with ways to adjust their traditional behaviors, earn a living, promote their faith, and remain within the strictly defined gender boundaries of the Catholic Church. The long record of contests between professed women and the male hierarchy of their church attested to the nearly insurmountable difficulty the sisters faced.

The very essence of Catholic practice celebrated a lesser role for women under a rubric that justified itself by a male priesthood. Nuns understood this spiritual and practical reality and often championed it themselves. At the same time, they chafed against the restrictions and commands that emanated from male superiors. Their complaints, however, centered on a disagreeable personality with whom they clashed rather than as a rallying call against the discrimination of women in their church.

Overall, the Catholic bishops of the American West compiled a stunningly autocratic record when dealing with women's congregations. They acted within the framework of their own training and spiritual understanding, often impelled by competing ambitions with brother bishops. Their dictates extended well beyond the realm of spirituality and intruded on practical management of convent affairs, especially concerning congregational finances.

Their attitudes and behaviors meshed with a worldview that delegated women to secondary roles, and the male hierarchy lived confidently with that designation. With the infrastructure of their faith so tightly wedded to notions of female inferiority, nuns and sisters could not fully extricate themselves without facing expulsion from the very universe they wished to inhabit.

In no way could it be argued that all priests and bishops treated sisters badly, as the assistance and generosity of many uplifted and encouraged nuns living under difficult circumstances. Many sisters recounted the affection and concern of priest friends or relatives, and several clergymen devoted many years to guiding a fledgling congregation toward full Vatican approval. Others, concerned about overzealous practices of self-denial in convents, suspended fasting regulations or granted a holiday to the nuns. Yet so powerful was the network of male supremacy that even those priests who reached out to nuns with honest friendship, spiritual justice, professional appreciation, and human equality could not sway the institutional commitment to gender discrimination.

The West, with its many areas of human need, had little time for a sluggish male mentality, whether applied to temporal or spiritual life. All its mountains and valleys presented landscapes of human want and struggle. Sisters entered into those landscapes as both participants in the adversity and activists to undo it.

This dual role was further complicated by association with priests and bishops who, on the one hand, insisted on the radical suspension of monastic patterns but, on the other hand, required childlike submission to masculine spiritual power. Sisters juggling these life elements risked both success in the secular world and approval within their church world as they searched for strategies of compromise. Accommodation to the human, natural, and spiritual worlds of the West threw down a life-changing gauntlet to nuns.

Occasionally, the women tried direct confrontation with priest superiors, but the dangers of censure or excommunication were painfully real. Nuns and sisters preferred drawing plans privately, within the cloistered space of their all-women world, finding ways to deflect criticism or worse. Although in their public utterances, nuns curbed the way they spoke, within the privacy of their convents, no such restrictions checked their tongues.

The nearly insatiable needs of the western church, with its healthy dose of regional anti-Catholic sentiment, galvanized nuns to solidify their position in the secular and religious worlds. Among themselves, sisters explored the possibilities, encouraging each other to strive for educational, scientific, and artistic achievement. This impulse increased their desire for formal learning, producing a corps of highly trained educators, improving Catholic institutions, and broadening the academic opportunities for young women across the West.

In a geography that stretched the imagination, convents, missions, and monasteries found themselves detached from the strongest tethers of authority. Unpredictable travel along perilous routes and erratic, slow communications aided nuns in building autonomy. An old observation about colonies at the borders of empire held for the nuns: too much time elapsed between an inquiry to superiors and the response from the home base. In the interim, sisters in all western locations simply moved ahead, adjusted their rules, and hoped to offer an acceptable excuse later. The tendency to improvise or even challenge motherhouse dictates increased over time, as western sisters gained confidence in their ability to finance their mission institutions and manage their own spiritual lives.

The Catholic work of the West transformed once-sedentary women into professional migrants often living on their own and for whom traditional restrictions became annoying or obsolete. Sisters came and went from one mission assignment to the next, never expecting to stay in a house permanently. With each change of "obedience," a sister inflated her worldview, learned more about western living, and considered again how to make her religious identity mesh with the West where she currently lived.

Not every western initiative succeeded, but generally, imperatives of the moment led to greater independence in convents, even as they nurtured separation from a distant motherhouse. Just as nuns diluted their reliance on male overseers, so did they fiercely disagree among themselves, seek fresh alliances, and open branch houses. No congregation escaped the tensions of conflicting ambition among members, a rise of dissident factions, or friendship-ending quarrels. Out of distance and disputes, however, came congregational growth and individual authority. Those who remained in a foundation regrouped and reassessed goals, drawing on what they had already accomplished for an infusion of strength. Those who broke away defined fresh agendas, outlined a new ministry for recruits, and literally expanded the horizons of sisters' work. Through individual and group power, nuns spread the influence of religious women in the American West, even as they stabilized the presence of their existing institutions.

For all this inner-convent decision making, an unfortunate truth remained: sisters and nuns of the American West lacked the spiritual and temporal power to remake their place within the worldwide Roman Catholic Church. Instead, they made the most of each opportunity for taking control of their lives in the West. They forced adjustments within religious life, the impact of which reverberated through American convents everywhere. European traditions of the supposedly immutable monastery crumbled before the lived realities in western convents. Through daily life within the communities of the West, cultural borders, even those that seemed impenetrable, weakened and shifted.

Enclosure and the divisions between choir and lay sisters fell first. These were not insignificant changes. The customs hindered work in western locations, where a few religious women engaged a demanding world. Walled-off convents and class exclusion resonated poorly within the societies the sisters began to call "home."

This does not suggest that an "egalitarian" West won over the European nuns, conquering the traditions of their ancient church and making them instant equality-minded American women. With its long history of imperialism, nationalism, and racism, an egalitarian West did not exist. No romantic transformation overtook nuns and sisters who moved into the many lands of many cultures.

Rather, the nuns thought to remain just that—nuns of the Catholic Church. Class distinctions and male dominance guided the infrastructure of their monasteries. They were not members of a democratic church; they did not set out to usurp male authority. They came to the West to endorse and build that church. When they faced change, nuns thought to alter their behaviors temporarily, intending to retain the traditions of professed life as they understood it. In the West, nuns expected to preserve traditions, and they partially succeeded, even as they diverted from the past.

At the same time, nuns saw the West through a female prism, one refracting life as professed religious. No other group of women looked across western landscapes with that lens or with the determination to advance a gendered community as a temporal and spiritual whole. The West, with its vibrant cultures and lifestyles, validated nuns and sisters as women capable of innovation and achievement. With its spaces of diversity, the West led them, for good and ill, into the humanities of others. There, nuns appreciated the ways that regional life beckoned specifically to them, and they organized a western persona that allowed them extensive participation as contributors in the building of community.

Their West was not the West of anybody else, nor did they think it should be. For sisters, the West was a region largely filled with chances to better varied aspects of life for many kinds of people, including their congregations. In settings of jagged cliffs, prairie grasslands, towering pines, and sandy flats, under skies tinted by lavender and blackened by storm, beside rivers and through thickets, sisters, listening to the narratives of place, reconfigured religious and regional identity for professed women. By happenstance and by intent, Catholic nuns and sisters rearranged professional, intellectual, emotional, and spiritual components of convent life, changing western womanhood, themselves, and their church as they journeyed across God's frontiers.

Glossary

Abstinence. Day on which meat and soup or gravy made from meat may not be eaten.

Adoration. Acts of worship when the sacrament is displayed in the monstrance on the altar.

Archbishop. A bishop of an archdiocese who has a limited canonical role over the bishops of the province. The latter are known as suffragan bishops.

Archdiocese. A diocese presided over by an archbishop and one of several dioceses within a province.

Begging tour. A trip through the secular world by two or more sisters for the purpose of soliciting money for support of the congregation. Permission is required from the bishop where the sisters live and those prelates whose jurisdictions they visit.

Benediction. A worship service, with incense, when the sacrament is removed from the tabernacle and displayed in a monstrance for a time of prayer, singing, and blessing.

Branch house. A group of women religious living apart from the motherhouse of the congregation but under its jurisdiction and general supervision.

Candidate. A woman admitted to the first probationary training of a congregation and frequently called a "postulant." She is not typically clothed in the official habit of the congregation but in some simple dark garb.

Canon. Usually refers to the body of church law; can also be a portion of the mass or a member of the clergy.

Cape. Part of a nun's habit over the upper arms and shoulders.

Chapter. Official governing body of a congregation, consisting of elected delegates; also a meeting of a congregation for the purpose of altering governance, conducting general business, or holding elections.

Cloister. Enclosed building or set of buildings or part of a building in which only members of a religious community may enter.

Coif. Hoodlike cap usually white and worn under the veil; interchangeable with "wimple," a linen cloth arranged in folds over the head.

Confessor. A priest who hears confessions and administers the sacrament of penance. In the nineteenth century, nuns and sisters typically had a regular confessor assigned to a convent, so that priest "heard" all the confessions for that convent.

Congregation. Community of women religious with simple vows.

Convent. Residence where a group of religious women share community life.

Council. Leadership group within a congregation.

Diocese. Territory designated by the Vatican that embraces all the parishes and peoples within the given area.

Divine Office. Public liturgical prayer of the church, distinct from the liturgies; it is intended to sanctify the day through formal prayer at stated hours. Women who have taken solemn vows incur an obligation to recite the Divine Office each day.

Entrance. Date on which a woman enters a convent with the intention of determining if she has a religious vocation.

Eucharist. The sacrament of the Catholic Church, defined by the Council of Trent (1545–63), that through the transformation of bread and wine, the body and blood of Christ become present, although the original appearances remain; the consecrated host and wine may also be called communion.

Excommunication. Censure within the Catholic Church whereby a person is deprived of reception of the sacrament of communion.

Friar. A professed religious male, usually a priest, working under a father general or central director.

Generalate. Central administrative offices of a congregation that has subordinate, provincial, or regional administrations.

Grille. Wooden or metal grating that separates the private enclosure of cloistered nuns from the visiting room used by the public.

Habit. The special dress or attire for the members of a religious order or group; each group has its own regulation habit, approval for which comes from the Holy See.

Holy See. The term includes the pope and the various congregations, offices, and tribunals that aid him in governing the Catholic Church. The Holy See is located in the Vatican.

Institute. A religious society of women living together in a motherhouse or at mission stations but all under a common rule, observing the vows of poverty, chastity, and obedience and having approval by ecclesiastical authority.

Mission. Each sister's assignment for the following year.

Monastery. Autonomous religious house of a community, usually with a contemplative rule; the term is often broadly applied to a residence for nuns and monks.

Motherhouse. The first religious house of an order or society from which other foundations develop; the usual residence of the mother general.

Novena. Devotion, usually directed to the Blessed Virgin Mary or a particular saint, that requires nine consecutive days of recitation of a set group of prayers.

Novice. A woman received into the novitiate, passed the period of candidature and with the profession of first vows, who is eligible for full membership in the congregation; usually distinguished by clothing in the habit of the order, but with a white veil.

Novitiate. Place of habitation for postulants and novices or the period of training that precedes the taking of vows necessary to be a professed member of a congregation.

Nun. Used in the vernacular to mean any woman religious, but in its strict meaning, it refers to a woman of a cloistered order with solemn vows whose chief purpose is to worship with a number of devotionals; thus, although most nuns are addressed as "sister," all sisters are not nuns.

Order. In popular usage, any religious community; strictly, a community professing a religious life in accordance with a rule approved by the church and having solemn vows for its members.

Ordinary. The bishop of a diocese.

Pope. Called the "Holy Father," the supreme ruler of the Roman Catholic Church as well as the bishop of Rome.

Postulant. A woman who has been received as a candidate for membership in a religious community; the stage previous to receiving the habit of a novice.

Priory. A religious house of men or women ruled by a prior or prioress; some are independent (conventual), while others are dependent on another house (obedientiary). Used interchangeably with "monastery."

Professed. Sister or nun who has taken either temporary or final vows and entered into full membership in a congregation.

Province. Administrative subdivision of a large congregation with a generalate as its headquarters.

Refectory. A dining hall where meals are generally taken in silence while one member provides a reading for meditation.

Religious. Popularly used as a noun to refer to a person who has taken the three vows of religion and lives according to the rule of a congregation in a shared community.

Religious life. Refers to living as a member of a religious community.

Retreat. A spiritual exercise varying from a few days to a month, during which the participant withdraws from usual activities to meditate, pray, and carry on other devotions aimed at advancing the spiritual life; silence is generally observed.

Rosary. A series of prayers, counted as they are repeated, on a string of beads; or the string of beads on which the prayers are counted. The prayers recited are the Lord's Prayer, the Hail Mary, and the Glory Be to the Father; each section of the rosary is called a "decade."

Secularization. Permission for a professed religious to leave her institute permanently with a corresponding dispensation from the religious vows.

Sister. Member of a sisterhood usually living in community and bound by the simple religious vows of poverty, chastity, and obedience and practicing a mixed life of contemplation and active service.

Sister, extern. A member of a contemplative or cloistered community who performs
duties outside the monastery.

Vatican. The residence of the pope in Rome, Italy; the papacy or papal authorities.

Vicariate. The territory administered by a vicar apostolic and divided into various
missions.

Vows. Public promises made to live according to the evangelical counsels of poverty,
chastity, and obedience; these promises are accepted in the name of the Catholic
Church by a lawful superior.

Sources: These definitions have been taken in whole or in part from Albert J.
Nevins MM, *The Maryknoll Catholic Dictionary* (New York: Grosset & Dunlap,
1965); George C. Stewart Jr., *Marvels of Charity: History of American Sisters and
Nuns* (Huntington, Ind.: *Our Sunday Visitor* Publishing Division, 1994); and Karen
Marie Franks OP, ed., *Strength of Our Roots, Faith in Our Vision: Dominican Sisters
of San Rafael, 1850–2000* (San Rafael, Calif.: Dominican Sisters, 2000).

Notes

Abbreviations

AAD	Archives of the Archdiocese of Dubuque
AAP	Archives of the Archdiocese of Portland
AASA	Archives of the Archdiocese of San Antonio
AASC	Archives of the Adorers of the Blood of Christ
AASF	Archives of the Archdiocese of San Francisco
ABVM	Archives of the Sisters of Charity of the Blessed Virgin Mary
ACAS	Archives of the Archdiocese of Seattle
ACAT	Catholic Archives of Texas
ACCVI	Archives of the Sisters of Charity of the Incarnate Word
ACDP	Archives of the Sisters of Divine Providence
ACSJ	Archives of the Sisters of St. Joseph of Carondelet
ADC	Archives of the Daughters of Charity
AFSM	Archives of the Franciscan Sisters of Mary
AFSPA	Archives of the Sisters of St. Francis of Perpetual Adoration
AJF	Archives of the Josephite Fathers
AOP	Archives of the Sisters of St. Dominic
AOSB	Archives of the Sisters of St. Benedict
AOSF	Archives of the Sisters of St. Francis
AOSM	Archives of the Servants of Mary
AOSU	Archives of the Ursuline Sisters
APBVM	Archives of the Sisters of the Presentation of the Blessed Virgin Mary
ARSM	Archives of the Sisters of Mercy
ASBS	Archives of the Sisters of the Blessed Sacrament
ASCL	Archives of the Sisters of Charity of Leavenworth
ASHF	Archives of the Sisters of the Holy Family
ASHSp	Archives of the Sisters of the Holy Spirit and Mary Immaculate
ASMM	Archives of St. Mary of the Mountains Church
ASMP	Archives of the Sisters of Mary of the Presentation

ASNJM   Archives of the Sisters of the Holy Names of Jesus and Mary
ASP   Archives of the Sisters of Providence
ASSND   Archives of the School Sisters of Notre Dame
ASSSF   Archives of the School Sisters of St. Francis
AUND   Archives of the University of Notre Dame

Preface

1. Guide, Roll Notes, Etc., Danville, Peoria, Woodstock, Bexley, Microfilm Reel No. 1, author's possession.
2. Ibid.

Introduction

1. McNamara, *Sisters in Arms*, 62–63.
2. Rosa Bruno-Jofré poignantly detailed the disagreement and pain that could invade a congregation intent on reexamining its foundation, identity, and development. For a moving and scholarly assessment of one Canadian sisterhood, see Bruno-Jofré, *The Missionary Oblate Sisters.*
3. Thompson, "The Context," 25.
4. Ibid.
5. Hawaii, with the recent attention to its history as part of the American West, represents a legitimate subject in this study about western nuns. In 1883 Mother Marianne Kopp OSF of the Franciscans in Syracuse, New York, traveled to Honolulu to begin medical assistance to those with Hansen's disease, living under the care of Father Damien De Veuster, renowned missionary on Moloka'i. Despite this appropriate link, Hawaii remains outside the considerations of this manuscript. Engh, "The Pacific Slope—'When Others Rushed In,'" 144, 164–67; Dehey, *Religious Orders of Women in the United States*, 426–28.

Chapter 1

1. In 1762 John Martin Moye founded the Sisters of Divine Providence in Lorraine, France. Following a period of instability, the congregation was reorganized in the early 1800s. Callahan, *The History of the Sisters of Divine Providence*, 19–30; Dehey, *Religious Orders of Women in the United States*, 599.
2. Henninger, *Sisters of Saint Mary*, 1.
3. Mother Mary Odilia to Wegman, 11 August 1872, in Henninger, *Sisters of Saint Mary*, 4.
4. Chronicles, 1, 1–3, AFSM, St. Louis; Henninger, *Sisters of Saint Mary*, 1–6.
5. Duratschek, *Under the Shadow of His Wings*, 37–60.
6. Notebook, Mt. Vernon, Indiana File, AOSM, Omaha; Watson, "No Land Too Far," 7–19.

7. *Registre des Soeurs de la Maison Notre Dame du Sacre Coeur*, 1–47, misc. 52–76; *Registre du Personal Maison de Wild Rice*; *Liste du Personnal Foundation de Collegeville, Minnesota*, ASMP, Valley City.

8. Historical Sketch of the Congregation of the Sisters of Mary, 23 April 1902, 3:106, ASMP, Valley City.

9. Ibid.

10. Mother Francesca Saverio Xavier Cabrini to My dearest daughters, 18 November 1902, in Provenzano, *To the Ends of the Earth*, 246; Stewart, *Marvels of Charity*, 275–83.

11. Sisters also remained in the East; nascent groups of the Daughters of Charity, founded by Elizabeth Ann Seton, were in Baltimore by 1808, in Philadelphia by 1814, and in New York City by 1817. Dehey, *Religious Orders of Women in the United States*, 69–85.

12. Figures are from a comprehensive calculation in Barkan, *From All Points*, 463.

13. Nugent, *Into the West*, 54–65; Rohrbough, *Days of Gold*.

14. Nugent, *Into the West*, 46–45, 77–78, 116.

15. Mother St. Pierre to Beloved Sisters, 1 October 1883; Sr. St. Pierre, to Dear Sisters, 1 February 1885; St. Pierre to My dear Child, 12 November 1885; St. Pierre to My good Mother, 18 November 1885, Letters of Mother St. Pierre Cinquin, ACCVI, San Antonio.

16. Sr. St. Pierre to Dear Sisters, 14 September 1889, ACCVI, San Antonio.

17. McCarthy, *Guide to the Catholic Sisterhoods in the United States*, 60.

18. Dehey, *Religious Orders of Women in the United States*, 816.

19. Register figures are rarely precise. Withdrawals, dismissals, or inaccuracies in recopying registers can account for discrepancies. In these registers of overlapping dates, there were no duplicate entries. Register and Necrology, Bk. 1, 1852–1887, Bk. 2, 1886–1949, ACSJ, St. Paul.

20. Choosing a congregation based on its European origins was a common pattern. Mercy Sisters, founded in Ireland, established a small convent in Dubuque, Iowa, in 1867. By 1915, the group numbered 138. Of the first 120 receptions, Irish surnames—such as Hogan, O'Shea, McNally, Casey, McNamara, Maloney, Duffy, and Ryan—dominated the entrance register. Another Mercy foundation in Cedar Rapids, Iowa, replicated the Irish ethnicity of the Dubuque group. Of sixty-five women entering the Cedar Rapids novitiate between 1885 and 1910, there were three foreign-born applicants—two from Ireland and one from Austria. The remaining names—such as Hurley, Curran, Reilly, and Connelly—in the assignment ledger appeared to be of Irish ancestry. Early Years: Dubuque; Dubuque and St. Joseph Hospital Statistics, ARSM, Farmington; Record of Assignments, ARSM, Cedar Rapids.

21. Entrance Records, Applicant numbers 1–95, 1852–79, AOSB, St. Joseph.

22. Curry Statistical Report, in Stewart, *Marvels of Charity*, table 13, 564.

23. *Sadlier's Catholic Almanac, 1865*, 160–61.

24. Thurston and Meehan, "Catholic Directories," *The Catholic Encyclopedia*.

25. Congregations by Alphabetical Order, *Hoffman's Official Directory, 1900*, 714.

26. Franks, *Strength of Our Roots*, 1–140, 465; *In Harvest Fields*, appendix 6; *Gleanings of Fifty Years*, 136; Barnaba, *A Diamond Crown*, 102, 283; O'Brien, *Journeys*, 77, 173, 637; Holland, *Lengthened Shadows*, 70–84; Duratschek, *Under the Shadow of His Wings*, 343; Thomas, *Footprints on the Frontier*, 124, 222, 237; Callahan, *The History of the Sisters of Divine Providence*, 191.

27. Thomas, *Footprints on the Frontier*, 363.

28. All Received, from Books of Entry, AOP, Sinsinawa; O'Connor, *Five Decades*, 338–48.

29. Mary Caroline, Report to the Central Council, 31 May 1859, "Mother Mary Caroline Friess," 1:95; Faherty, *The St. Louis German Catholics*, 26.

30. In the St. Louis house, among European SSND members born before 1900, the date of birth for 127 women fell between 1821 and 1864. Another 132 born between 1864 and the end of the century added to immigrant statistics in the St. Louis congregation (birth dates of two European sisters were unknown). For the same periods, Americans entering the St. Louis province demonstrated the eventual U.S. domination of the congregation, with 228 born between 1821 and 1864 and 809 between 1865 and 1900. Sisters of St. Louis Province Born before 1900, comp. Mary Ann Kuttner, 28 July 1995, ASSND, St. Louis.

31. Ibid.

32. Mother Caroline to My very dear Sisters, [26 December] 1880, "Mother Mary Caroline Friess," 1:280.

33. Mother M. Caroline to [Sisters], 15 December 1882, "Mother Mary Caroline Friess," 1:314.

34. Register of Deaths: West Central Province, Cagley-Welty; Collected Notes: Lives/Notes, Bowling-Schiefer, ADC, St. Louis. Ninety appears low. In 1885 a priest responding specifically about the Daughters of Charity from Emmitsburg, Maryland, noted "with regard to the number of Sisters of Charity in this country . . . as accurately as could be ascertained is 1307. But I don't think this includes the novices and postulants . . . probably 50 or 60." H. F. White to Peter Baart, 12 March 1885, Peter A. Baart Papers, Correspondence, AUND, Notre Dame.

35. Reception Records, 1900–1910, and All Received from Books of Original Entry, AOP, Sinsinawa.

36. Community Register, 1863–1910, 1–7, AOSF, Rochester.

37. Cott, "Giving Character to Our Whole Civil Polity," 107–21.

38. Turbin, "'And Are We Nothing but Women,'" 28–29; Simmons, "Companionate Marriage and the Lesbian Threat," 185–86.

39. Marsh, "Motherhood Denied," 216–23.

40. Riley, *The Female Frontier*, 80.

41. Elizabeth Ballingal to Sister Vincent Marie, 13 October 1933, Sister Mary Buckner Personal File, ASCL, Leavenworth.

42. Eulogy by Father Thomas Kinsella, April 1915, Sister Mary Buckner, Personal File, ASCL, Leavenworth.

43. Hackett, *Dominican Women in Texas*, 126, 591.

44. Register, Entry Records, 1899–1912, Julia Jennings/Sister M. Evangelist-Brigid Hanly/Sister M. Paschal, ASHSp, San Antonio.

45. M. Caroline to Our Pater Spiritual, 7 January 1887, "Mother Mary Caroline Friess," 2:413.

46. McDonald, *With Lamps Burning*, 3–49. For Riepp's impact on Benedictine women through the West, see Dieker, *A Tree Rooted in Faith*; Hockle, *On High Ground*; Boo, *House of Stone*; George, *Mother Paula O'Reilly OSB*; Voth, *Green Olive Branch*; Schuster, *The Meaning of the Mountain*; and Bower, "'The Women in White' March across the North Dakota Prairies," 3. See also Annals, "Previous to Foundation in Texas in June 1919," AOSB, Boerne.

47. Hegarty, *Serving with Gladness*, 205–17.

48. Callahan, *The History of the Sisters of Divine Providence*, 128, 143–44.

49. *Regulations for the Society of the Sisters of Charity, 1877*, 9, Religious Orders of Women, Charity Sisters of Nazareth, Kentucky, AUND, Notre Dame.

50. Markey Diary, 15 November 1894, ABVM, Dubuque.

51. Diary, St. Rose, 24, 25 December 1884 and 19, 25 December 1885, AFSPA, La Crosse.

52. Sister Mary of the Angels to My dear Mother, Mothers and Sisters, 28 December 1885, St. Peter's Mission, Letters, 1884–1906, AOSU, Toledo.

53. Chronicles, 1: 61, 107, AFSM, St. Louis.

54. Abbelen, *Venerable Mother Caroline*, 130–31.

55. Gilmore, *Come North!*, 220–21.

56. Ibid.

57. Sister Florence Cloonan, in Gilmore, *Come North!*, 230.

58. Daily Record, Odanah, 22 February 1906, AFSPA, La Crosse.

59. The feast of the Epiphany (6 January) is commonly called "Little Christmas" and celebrates the arrival of the Three Kings to Bethlehem; Daily Record, Odanah, 6 January 1909, AFSPA, La Crosse.

60. Oregon Chronicles, St. Mary's, Portland, 1860, 1861, 22, 25, ASNJM, Portland.

61. Sister Evangelista, 15 November 1888, letter fragment, Red Lake, Memoirs of Missionaries, AOSB, St. Joseph.

62. Sister Ladislaus Twardowski, White Earth, Memoirs of Missionaries, AOSB, St. Joseph.

63. Annals, Sister M. Scholastica to Mother Mercedes, [1905], ASBS, Cornwells Heights.

64. Annals, Sister M. Evangelista to My very dear Sister Margaret Mary, 17 October 1894, ASBS, Cornwells Heights.

65. Annals, Sister Miriam to My dear Mother and all at St. Elizabeth's, 21 December 1908, ASBS, Cornwells Heights.

66. Annals, Sister M. Mercedes to Dear Mother, 1 July 1894, ASBS, Cornwells Heights.

67. Annals, Sister M. Evangelista to My dear Mother, 7 March 1906[?], ASBS, Cornwells Heights.

68. All details about the visit of Cardinal Gibbons, Annals, Sister M. Evangelista to My dear Mother, 17 October 1895, ASBS, Cornwells Heights.

69. Memoir, Sister Sylvester, ca. 1950, St. Mary's Hospital File, AOSF, Rochester.

70. Hackett, *Dominican Women in Texas*, 105–6 (quote on 106).

71. Memoir, Sister Pancratia Studer, 1–4, AASC, Wichita.

72. Knawa, *As God Shall Ordain*, 150; Meyers, *The Education of Sisters*, 6–7. Some European nuns lacked schooling. Thus, reading the congregational rule aloud during meals encouraged illiterate nuns to learn by memorizing regulations. Mullay, *A Place of Springs*, 24.

73. Meyers, *The Education of Sisters*, 8; Coogan, *The Price of Our Heritage*, 2:455–58.

74. Meyers, *The Education of Sisters*, 9.

75. Contract between Father Mathias . . . and Maria Caroline Friess, "Mother Mary Caroline Friess," 1:134–35. See also Father Joseph LaSage to Sisters of St. Joseph from Kansas, that the "sisters must speak and be able to teach both languages, French and English," in Thomas, *Footprints on the Frontier*, 180.

76. Coogan, *The Price of Our Heritage*, 2:72.

77. Ibid., 74.

78. Ibid., 74, 75.

79. For another school that stressed academics, see the curriculum at St. Clara's, as the sisters pursued a college ranking in 1901. Synon, *Mother Emily of Sinsinawa*, 214–15.

80. All details from Sister Wilfrida Hogan, My Reminiscences, I and II, ca. 1920, ACSJ, St. Paul.

81. Mother M. Caroline to Dear Sisters, 15 October 1891, "Mother Mary Caroline Friess," 1:480.

82. Synon, *Mother Emily of Sinsinawa*, 238.

83. Biography for the Annals, Sister Mary Buckner, Personal File, ASCL, Leavenworth.

84. Callahan, *Mother Angelique Ayres*.

85. Sister Mary Assumpta Friesenhahn, Memoirs of Pioneer Sisters, ACDP, San Antonio; Chronicle, vol. 1, 1833–76, 86, ASSND, Milwaukee.

86. Patient Ledger: St. Joseph's Hosp., 1890–1913, Mission Records, Colorado, ACSJ, St. Louis.

87. Davis and Phelps, "*Stamped with the Image of God*," 6–12.

88. Clark, *Voices from an Early American Convent*, 11–12, 16–18 (footnote 15).

89. Doyle, *Pioneer Spirit*, 121–25.

90. Supan, "Dangerous Memory," 31–67; Morrow, "*Persons of Color and Religious at the Same Time*," 186–92.

91. Morris, *American Catholic*, 78.

92. Pastoral Letter of Monsignor the Bishop of Natchitoches . . . , 1861, in Davis and Phelps, "*Stamped with the Image of God*," 36.

93. Bonner, "Extern Sisters in Monasteries of Nuns," 6–50.

94. Ibid., 46–47.

95. Oregon Chronicles, St. Mary's, Portland, 13 August 1859, ASNJM, Portland; *Gleanings of Fifty Years*, 60–61.

96. Foundresses and St. Paul Sisters, Summary, ASNJM, Portland.

97. M. Caroline to Mother Superior General, 22 September 1882, "Mother Mary Caroline Friess," 1:308.

98. Kane, *Gender Identities in American Catholicism*, xxiv.

99. For women's Catholic identity when confronted by shifting gender roles in the early twentieth century, see Cummings, *New Women of the Old Faith*.

100. Caroline Friess to the Propagation of the Faith, 12 November 1853, "Mother Mary Caroline Friess," 1:54.

Chapter 2

1. Journal of the Sisters of St. Joseph en Route to Arizona, 1870, ACSJ, St. Louis.

2. The Sisters of St. Joseph knew about difficult travel, having journeyed from Lyons, France, to St. Louis in 1836 and expanded their mission to St. Paul, Minnesota, in 1851. See Dougherty, *Sisters of St. Joseph of Carondelet*, 51–56, 139–40.

3. An extensive literature supports these assertions about the systemic changes in the West. For a comprehensive account, see Nugent, *Into the West*.

4. For the evolution of women's religious life, see McNamara, *Sisters in Arms*, especially parts 2, 3, and 4.

5. For comments about the rigors of western travel and personal responses, see examples in Riley, *Frontierswomen*, 13–28, and *Women and Indians on the Frontier*; Myres, *Westering Women*, 98–139; Schlissel, *Women's Diaries of the Westward Journey*, 132–35, 173–74; Poling-Kempes, *The Harvey Girls*, 30–32; and Abrams, *Jewish Women Pioneering the Frontier Trail*, 21–37.

6. Sister St. Ignatius to Dear Mother, 28 January 1884; Sister Sacred Heart to My dear Mother, 2 February 1884, Miles City, Letters, January 1884–May 1884, AOSU, Toledo.

7. Annals, 28 October 1880, ASHF, Fremont.

8. Journal of the Sisters of St. Joseph en Route to Arizona, 1870, ACSJ, St. Louis.

9. Mother Mary of the Cross Goemaere to Father Vincent Jandel, January 1889, in Franks, *Strength of Our Roots*, 1.

10. For the history and uses of the rule and the constitution, see Geser, *The Canon Law Governing Communities of Sisters*, 33–39.

11. Two freshly minted Dominicans traveling by train from New York to Washington could not bring themselves to use their emergency cash when their food basket completely spoiled. They both served many years in the West, developing leading positions in the congregation. Annals, 1890–1923, 46, AOP, Edmonds; Buerge and Murray, *Evergreen Land*, 86–87.

12. Annals, Sister M. Mercedes to Dear Mother, June 1894, ASBS, Cornwells Heights.

13. Journal of the Sisters of St. Joseph en Route to Arizona, 1870, ACSJ, St. Louis; and Dougherty, *Sisters of St. Joseph of Carondelet*, 73–74, 427.

14. Journal of the Sisters of St. Joseph en Route to Arizona, 1870, ACSJ, St. Louis.

15. Ibid.; O'Brien, *Journeys*, 72–81.

16. *Life of Mother Mary Monholland*, 38–40.

17. Sister Joseph of the Sacred Heart to Father J. B. A. Brouillet, 5 August 1859, ASP, Seattle.

18. When nuns seeking hospitality received a cool welcome, it could mean the host sisters feared sheltering imposters who used convents to hide from law enforcement, enjoy free room and board, or launch a bogus begging tour. In 1872 Sister Blandina Segale of the Sisters of Charity charged that a convent, suspicious of a late-night arrival, denied her access to the superior and confined her to a convent room until her train left the following evening. Segale expressed displeasure about the incident, although she had once kept guard over two nun impersonators who stopped at her Ohio motherhouse. Segale, *At the End of the Santa Fe Trail*, 13–18.

19. Oregon Chronicles, Sister Edwardine Mary, 21, ASNJM, Portland.

20. Mother Philomene to Mother Joseph of the Sacred Heart, 12 September 1859, ASP, Seattle.

21. Chronicles, Arkansas, Morrilton, Mission Records, 1899–1966; Chronological Sketches, Reports not in vol. 1. Also see Chronicles, Fort Madison, Book 2, 5, ASSND, St. Louis.

22. Buckner, *History of the Sisters of Charity*, 125; and Sister Mary Amadeus to My dear Mother, 29 October 1884, St. Peter's Mission, Letters, 1884–1906, AOSU, Toledo.

23. Diary, Motherhouse, Cherokee, 12 February and 8 May 1909; 30 March, 12 May, and 21 July 1910; 2 January, 21–22 February, and 15 August 1911; 16 March 1912; 24 January, 11 March 1913, Mother Mary Gertrude Papers, AOSM, Omaha. For other examples, see Annals, 1, 5, APBVM, Fargo; Recollections of Sister M. Scholastica, Annals, Anaconda, 5, 7, and Recollections of Sister Albert, Annals, Denver, 6, AOP, Sinsinawa; and Diary, St. Rose, 14, 15 July 1883, 21–22 July 1884, and 20 August and 5–7, 9–11 September 1885, AFSPA, La Crosse.

24. In 1877 one nun wrote to the motherhouse: "Please let the Sisters bring some little gifts to the Loretto Sisters, we have been here so long." Sister M. Perpetua to Mother M. Julia, 1 May 1877, Letters of Sister M. Perpetua, Colorado Missions, ACSJ, St. Louis. For other examples, see Annals, 9 July 1896, ASHF, Fremont; Annals, Austin, 1910–11 entry for Sister Engelbert, 1914–15 entry for Sister Maria Pieta, Sisters of the Holy Cross, Microfilm Records, Roll 45, author's possession; Finck, *The Congregation of the Sisters of Charity of the Incarnate Word*, 50; and Schoenberg, *These Valiant Women*, 107.

25. In December 1875, two Sisters of Charity of Leavenworth left Denver for Laramie, passing through Sherman, where they noted the bitter winds each time a car door opened. These sisters also felt fear crossing the Dale Creek Bridge, the location

of the earlier anxiety among the Sisters of St. Joseph. Buckner, *History of the Sisters of Charity of Leavenworth*, 260–61.

26. Journal of the Sisters of St. Joseph en Route to Arizona, 1870, ACSJ, St. Louis.

27. Russell, *The Three Sisters of Lord Russell*, 27, 34–43, 72. For an explanation that sorts out the differences between the California Sisters of Mercy in San Francisco and those in Grass Valley, including the duplicate religious names, see O'Brien, *Journeys*, 13–55.

28. Journal of the Sisters of St. Joseph en Route to Arizona, 1870, ACSJ, St. Louis.

29. Ibid.

30. Ibid.

31. An early narrative of the Sisters of Loretto, sanctioned by the congregation, relates this episode by largely quoting Archbishop J. B. Salpointe's description of the storm and omitting the response of the stranded sisters. Minogue, *Loretto*, 148–52.

32. Ibid., 150–52.

33. Sister Hildegarde Soethe, Memoirs of Pioneer CDP Sisters, ACDP, San Antonio.

34. Sister Mary Bona Reiff, Memoirs of Pioneer CDP Sisters, ACDP, San Antonio.

35. Oregon Chronicles, Jacksonville, 1877, 138, ASNJM, Portland.

36. Annals, 5, APBVM, Fargo.

37. Mary Caroline to My dear Sisters, 17 June 1858, "Mother Mary Caroline Friess," 1:91.

38. Sister Sacred Heart to Dear Mother, 27 April 1884, Miles City, Letters, January 1884–May 1884, AOSU, Toledo.

39. The two wanderers did find a homestead, where Sister Clare declined an invitation to stay the night and insisted the owner get a lantern and walk them to town. Chronicles, Sister Mary Clare Letter, 5 November 1909, 68–72, ASCL, Leavenworth.

40. Sister M. Perpetua to Dearest Mother, March 1877, Letters of Sister Perpetua, Colorado Missions, ACSJ, St. Louis.

41. Ibid.

42. Annals, Sister M. Ignatius to My dear Mother, 22 August 1895, ASBS, Cornwells Heights.

43. Sister Mary Amadeus to My dear Mother, 29 March 1884, Miles City, Letters, January 1884–May 1884, AOSU, Toledo.

44. Sister Mary Amadeus to My dear Mother, 29 October 1884, St. Peter's Mission, Letters, 1884–1906, AOSU, Toledo.

45. Sister Angela Lincoln in "Mother Mary Amadeus of the Heart of Jesus," in Code, *Great American Foundresses*, 454–55.

46. Sister Martha to Dear Sisters at Home, 2 January 1876, in Buckner, *History of the Sisters of Charity of Leavenworth*, 267.

47. Oregon Chronicles, The Dalles, 1864, 114, ASNJM, Portland.

48. Oregon Chronicles, Baker City, 26 April 1875, 172, ASNJM, Portland.

49. Oregon Chronicles, Baker City, 28 April 1875, 173, ASNJM, Portland.

50. Journal of the Sisters of St. Joseph en Route to Arizona, 1870, ACSJ, St. Louis.

51. Ibid.

52. Sister Gabriel to Very dear Sisters, 6 January 1885, Letters of Mother St. Pierre Cinquin, 149–50, ACCVI, San Antonio; Memoirs of Mother Wilhelmina, in Schoenberg, *These Valiant Women*, 149; McCrosson, *The Bell and the River*, 192–93; Sister Gustave to the Motherhouse, 1906, in Historical Sketch of the Congregation of the Sisters of St. Mary, 3:150, ASMP, Valley City; Sister M. Catherine May in Franks, *Strength of Our Roots*, 25; Maria Willibalda Scherbauer de Mater Dolorosa to Gracious Lord and King, 4 December 1864, in Girgen, *Behind the Beginnings*, 179; Paavola, *Upon the Rock*, 35.

53. Duratschek, *Under the Shadow of His Wings*, 93–94, 99–114, 121–22, 135–36.

54. Hackett, *Dominican Women in Texas*, 108–14.

55. "Convent a Haven of Refuge," *New York Times*, 17 September 1900.

56. Moore, *Acts of Faith*, 21–25.

57. *In Harvest Fields*, 247–50.

58. Kavanagh, *The Holy Family Sisters of San Francisco*, 154–58.

59. In December 1906, the Sisters of the Holy Family received $5,000.00 in earthquake damage compensation from the San Francisco Relief and Red Cross Fund. Ibid., 158.

60. Ibid., 151–62.

61. The narrative of western sisters is also tied to peoples of color. See chapters 6 and 7.

62. Oregon Chronicles, 5, ASNJM, Portland. Mother Cabrini sailing from Italy wrote of the ship's "complicated and marvelous apparatus," saying: "I wish I knew the science of navigation well so I could explain well the structure of this beautiful steamer that transports thousands of persons from the old to the new continent." Provenzano, *To the Ends of the Earth*, 88.

63. An Account of the Journey . . . for . . . Founding Houses, "Mother Mary Caroline Friess," 1:14.

64. Ibid.

65. "Mother Mary Caroline Friess," 1:47.

66. "Mother Mary Caroline Friess," 1:38, 40, 41.

67. Barnaba, *A Diamond Crown for Christ the King*, 225–30 (quote on 230).

68. M. Evangelista to Respected Committee, 4 April 1875, in Schuster, *The Meaning of the Mountain*, 57.

69. Sister Ambrosia Layer, Sister Barnabas Siebenhor, Sister Brigid Beier, Memoirs of Pioneer CDP Sisters, ACDP, San Antonio.

70. Sister Adorers of the Blood of Christ came to Immaculate Heart of Mary Parish in 1910. Until 1913, only two sisters were assigned to the school. Parish of the Immaculate Heart of Mary: Windthorst, Kansas, 23–33; Annals, Windthorst; Annals, Wichita Province, vol. 1, AASC, Wichita.

71. Sister Blandine, in McCrosson, *The Bell and the River*, 228.

72. Book of Foundations, vol. 3, Recollections of Sister M. Scholastica, Annals, Anaconda, 5, AOP, Sinsinawa.

73. Sister Baptista to My very dear Mother, 18 November 1894, DC File, ASMM, Virginia City.

74. Annals, St. Rose Academy, 59, AOP, Edmonds.

75. Annals, St. Rose Academy, 44–48, AOP, Edmonds. There are some differences between the Annals and *Evergreen Land*, 84–99, concerning the sequence of events, especially begging, at Aberdeen and Chehalis. Regardless, the Dominicans immersed themselves in deeply forested logging locations in both places and the experiences closely replicated one another.

76. Annals, St. Rose Academy, 91–93, AOP, Edmonds.

77. Annals, 43, 44, 48, AOP, Edmonds.

78. For the impact of the Pullman Strike on California and the Southwest, see Howes, "Three Weeks That Shook the Nation and California's Capital."

79. Annals, Sister M. Mercedes to Dear Mother, 28, 29 June 1894, ASBS, Cornwells Heights.

80. Annals, Sister M. Mercedes to Dear Mother, 30 June 1894, ASBS, Cornwells Heights.

81. For the 1880s Harvey House chain, see Poling-Kempes, *The Harvey Girls* (for menu descriptions, 41–42).

82. Annals, Your devoted and exiled sisters to Dear Mother, 1 July 1894, ASBS, Cornwells Heights.

83. Annals, Sister M. Mercedes to Dear Mother, 28 June 1894, 29 and 30 June 1894, 1 July 1894, quotes on 38 and 43, ASBS, Cornwells Heights.

84. Annals, Your devoted and exiled sisters to Dear Mother, 30 June 1894, ASBS, Cornwells Heights.

85. Annals, Sister M. Mercedes to Dear Mother and Sisters, 4 July 1894, ASBS, Cornwells Heights.

86. Ibid.

87. The cars passed Raton without incident, but in the mountains, a storm enveloped the train and the winds jettisoned a bridge just ahead into the gorge below. This natural disaster prompted one sister to remark wryly, "It seems when the strikers didn't kill us, God Almighty Himself seem[ed] bound to do it." Annals, 49, ASBS, Cornwells Heights.

88. Annals, Sister Mary Mercedes to My dear Mother and Sisters, 8 July 1894, ASBS, Cornwells Heights.

89. Mother Frances X. Cabrini to My dearest Daughters, 18 November 1902, in Provenzano, *To the Ends of the Earth*, 249–50. Also see details of nuns and labor violence in a 1900 St. Louis streetcar strike in Chronicles, 1, 102, AFSM, St. Louis.

90. Mary Caroline Friess to the Louis Mission Society, April 1862, "Mother Mary Caroline Friess," 1:115.

91. Ibid.

92. Oregon Chronicles, Holy Names Academy, Seattle, 5 May 1903, ASNJM, Portland.

93. Mother Francesca Saverio Cabrini to My dearest young ladies, 31 May 1904, in Provenzano, *To the Ends of the Earth*, 257–58.

94. "Spreading the Truth: From El Paso to Paris—From Dallas to Tascosa," unidentified newspaper clipping, 9 April 1892; History of Hotel Dieu; Emerson and Berrien to Rev. Mother, 1 October 1901, El Paso, Hotel Dieu, Correspondence, ADC, St. Louis.

95. Sister Jane Frances, in Buckner, *History of the Sisters of Charity of Leavenworth*, 279.

96. Buckner, *History of the Sisters of Charity of Leavenworth*, 328–29.

97. Ibid., 330.

98. Ibid., 306.

99. For other examples of sisters left alone following decisions by male clergy, see Annals, 2–3, APBVM, Fargo; Gloden, *Sisters of St. Francis of the Holy Family*, 43.

100. Sister of the Sacred Heart to Dear Mother, 8 June 1884, Miles City, Letters, June 1884–December 1885, AOSU, Toledo.

101. Mother Amadeus Dunne, in Mahoney, *Lady Blackrobes*, 30.

102. In Galvin, *From Acorn to Oak*, 59.

103. Sister M. Amadeus to My dear Mother, 29 March 1885, St. Peter's Mission, Letters, 1884–1906, AOSU, Toledo.

104. Sister M. Amadeus to My dearest Mother, 26 October 1885, Miles City, Letters, June 1884–December 1885, AOSU, Toledo.

105. Barnaba, *A Diamond Crown for Christ the King*, 205–14 (quotes on 223).

106. Ibid., 228, 236.

107. Ibid., 225–39.

108. Mother Mary Stanislaus, who led the first band to Oregon, was elected general superior in 1918 but died unexpectedly in 1920, before she could build a strong record as leader of the entire congregation. "The Sisters of St. Francis, 1855–1928," 51–54.

109. Ibid., 291.

110. Myres, *Westering Women*, 248–52; Kaufman, *Women Teachers on the Frontier*; Butler, *Daughters of Joy, Sisters of Misery*; Poling-Kempes, *The Harvey Girls*, 60–1, 52–6, 78–81; Riley, "Gainfully Employed," in *A Place to Grow*, 164–76; Cordier, *Schoolwomen of the Prairies and Plains*, 294.

111. Life as a western missionary, especially in terms of proselytizing among Native people, drew a number of Protestant women. Generally, non-Catholic groups required women volunteers to be married, partnered with a like-minded male spouse. The iconic figures of this genre, Narcissa and Marcus Whitman of the American Board of Commissioners for Foreign Missions, wed as total strangers so that she might pursue her religious interests in the West.

112. For examples, see "Mother Mary Caroline Friess"; Provenzano, *To the Ends of the Earth*; and Letters of Mother St. Pierre Cinquin, ACCVI, San Antonio.

113. Annals, Sister M. Mercedes to Dear Mother, 4 July 1894, ASBS, Cornwells Heights.

114. Sister M. Amadeus to My very dear Mother, 29 May 1884, Miles City, Letters, January 1884–May 1884, AOSU, Toledo.

115. Sr. of the Sacred Heart to My ever dear Mother, 2 February 1885, Miles City, Letters, June 1885–December 1885; St. Francis to Dearly loved Sister, 14 June [year?], St. Paul's Mission, Letters, 1888–1889, AOSU, Toledo.

116. Sr. Mary Amadeus to My dear Mother, 29 March 1884, Miles City, Letters, January 1884–May 1884, AOSU, Toledo.

117. Italics added. M. Jerome Schaub and M. Thomas Reichert File, 1894–1942, Mother Leander quote in handwritten, undated account by Mother Thomas, AOSU, Paola.

118. Journal of the Sisters of St. Joseph en Route to Arizona, 1870, ACSJ, St. Louis.

119. Ibid.

Chapter 3

1. Secular females did push back constricting economic barriers. Among studies that demonstrate women enhancing employment, see Passet, *Cultural Crusaders*; Riley, *A Place to Grow*; Armitage and Jameson, *The Women's West*; Butler, *Daughters of Joy, Sisters of Misery*.

2. Annals, 1–6, APBVM, Fargo.

3. Peterson and Vaughn-Roberson, *Women with Vision*, 169–70; Karolevitz, *With Faith, Hope, and Tenacity*, 60–61.

4. Memories of Mother Baptista Bowen by Sister M. Immaculata Pawluch, Mother M. Baptista Bowen File, APBVM, Fargo.

5. Quotes, Mooney, "Sisters of the Presentation of Fargo," 33; Galvin, *From Acorn to Oak*, 78.

6. Kardong, *Beyond the Red River*, 59, 86.

7. Lawrence, *Medieval Monasticism*, 218.

8. Ibid., 231–35.

9. Ibid., 216–37, 264–65; McNamara, *Sisters in Arms*, 482–84.

10. Metz, "In Times of War," in *Pioneer Healers*, 39–57.

11. For an account of the war for one congregation, see McGill, *The Sisters of Charity of Nazareth*, 148–63. For the Sisters of Mercy in several dioceses, see Herron, *The Sisters of Mercy in the United States*, 13–16, 35–38, 61–62, 82, 134–36, 228–29, 245–46.

12. Barton, *Angels of the Battlefield*, and Jolly, *Nuns of the Battlefield*, treat the congregations and the individuals who participated in the Civil War but are written with piety. More scholarly are Maher, *To Bind up the Wounds*; and Coburn and Smith, *Spirited Lives*, 192–94.

13. For the impact of the nuns' dress in secular war zones, see Kuhns, *The Habit*, 121–24.

14. For an overview of sisters during the war, see Kauffman, *Ministry and Meaning*, 82–95.

15. In 1889 twenty-six priests, most clustered in Helena or at Jesuit missions, attended to approximately 25,000 Catholics at more than 100 missions or outposts in Montana Territory; by 1914 the number of priests in Montana had risen to seventy but the number of Catholics to approximately 95,000. *Sadlier's Catholic Directory, 1889*, 256–59; *Kenedy's Official Catholic Directory, 1914*, general summary page.

16. Louis A. Lootens to Toussaint Mesplie, 10 March 1874, in Bradley and Kelly, *History of the Diocese of Boise*, vol. 1, 96.

17. Jean C. Perrodin to Mathias Loras, 10 April 1851, Jean C. Perrodin Papers, AAD, Dubuque.

18. Ursulines said of a priest but three weeks at their mission: "he looks quite sad and discouraged at times; he is astonished at our courage and cheerfulness." Sister St. Ignatius to Dear Mother, 27 April 1884, Miles City, Letters, January 1884–May 1884, AOSU, Toledo.

19. Sister Antoinette Loth, Memoirs of Pioneer CDP Sisters, ACDP, San Antonio.

20. Sister Colubkille McEnery, Memoirs of Pioneer CDP Sisters, ACDP, San Antonio.

21. Annals, St. Mary's Hospital, Mother M. Alfred Moes, Papers, AOSF, Rochester.

22. Impressions of Life in Novitiate, Sister M. De Pazzi Specking, Houses and Ministries, ARSM, St. Louis.

23. Mother Agnes to Mrs. Emily Foster, 29 August 1914, Incarnate Word and Blessed Sacrament, Religious Orders of Women, AASA, San Antonio.

24. L. M. Fink to Mother Jerome, 12 August 1895, Bishop Fink Letters, M. Jerome Schaub and M. Thomas Reichert File, AOSU, Paola.

25. Peters, "History of the Poor Sisters of St. Francis Seraph," 72.

26. *Rules and Constitutions*, 21, APBVM, Fargo.

27. Markey Diary, 41, ABVM, Dubuque. See, also Chronicles, 1, 8, AFSM, St. Louis; Annals, 19 July 1885, ASHF, Fremont; Chronicles, 9 December 1904, ASCL, Leavenworth.

28. History of Saint Mary's Academy, Austin, Texas, Sister Ignatius Gutherie, and Annals, Austin, Sisters of the Holy Cross, microfilm roll 44, author's possession.

29. Annals, Austin, "The Farm," Sisters of the Holy Cross, microfilm roll 44, author's possession.

30. Ibid.

31. Table of Foundations: Opening Dates, ACDP, San Antonio.

32. Another six assignments took the Sisters of Loretto into Illinois and Alabama during the same time period. Minogue, *Loretto*, 148–61, 175–92.

33. O'Brien, *Journeys*, 643, 644, 648–50, 655–57.

34. Chronological Sketches, vol. 1, 20, 25, 30, 32, ASSND, St. Louis.

35. Applications of Priests for Sisters, 1904–43, ASSND, St. Louis.

36. L. L. Conrardy to Mother Scholastica, 1, 18, 31 December 1881, Records of Scholastica Kerst, Grand Ronde, Oregon, 1881–82, AOSB, St. Joseph. McDonald, *With Lamps Burning*, 123–26.

37. This Willamette valley area reservation should not be confused with Grande Ronde valley in Union County in eastern Oregon, home to Cayuse, Nez Perce, Umatilla, Shoshone, and Walla Walla tribes.

38. Details of this mission in Oregon Chronicles, Grand Ronde, 159–70, ASNJM, Portland.

39. Conrardy went to Hawaii, where he worked on Moloka'i with the famous Father Damien De Veuster, who championed care for those with Hansen's disease. Dissatisfied on Moloka'i, Conrardy purchased an Asian island, where he established his own colony for Chinese with the then-incurable disease. Conrardy died in China in 1915. "Sisters of St. Francis, 1855–1928," 238.

40. Oregon Chronicles, Grand Ronde, 160, ASNJM, Portland.

41. Oregon Chronicles, Grand Ronde, 166, ASNJM, Portland.

42. Oregon Chronicles, Grand Ronde, 167, ASNJM, Portland.

43. Chronicle, 60–61, AOSB, St. Joseph.

44. Oregon Chronicles, Grand Ronde, 170, ASNJM, Portland; Alexius Edelbrock to Norb. Hofbauer, 9 December 1881, Records of Scholastica Kerst, Grand Ronde, Oregon, 1881–82, AOSB, St. Joseph; McDonald, *With Lamps Burning*, 123–26.

45. Chronicle, 60, AOSB, St. Joseph.

46. In 1882 Scholastica proposed to the city council that Benedictines, with "some substantial encouragement" from the town, should open a professional hospital, as "the sick must now be sent far away or lodged in miserable hovels not calculated to benefit . . . soul or body." Scholastica failed to negotiate all the terms she wanted, but the project moved forward; in 1886 four sisters from St. Benedict's priory began hospital duties in St. Cloud. McDonald, *With Lamps Burning*, 252–54.

47. Ibid., 129; Chronicle, 81–83, and Minutes of Chapters, 10 April 1885, AOSB, St. Joseph.

48. McDonald, *With Lamps Burning*, 93–95, 252–54.

49. Sister Boniface Timmins, File of Sister Boniface Timmins and Bishop Wehrle, AOSB, Bismarck.

50. McDonald, *With Lamps Burning*, 128–33.

51. Scholastica's action did not release the Benedictine women from their complicated relationship with the abbots, nor was the intent to sever those connections. Over many years, the St. Joseph priory of women faced an ongoing struggle to define itself within the arena of church politics. Ibid., 211–23.

52. *Bismarck Tribune*, 23 October 1937, Miscellaneous hospital clippings, AOSB, Bismarck.

53. St. Alexius Hospital to Buechner and Orth, 12 March 1914; "Saint Alexius Hospital," *History of North Dakota*, 2:533; "A Fitting Tribute," *Bismarck Tribune*, 8 February 1922, 4, St. Alexius Hospital, AOSB, Bismarck; McDonald, *With Lamps Burning*, 134–37.

54. Kauffman, *Ministry and Meaning*, 131–33.

55. In the first month, the hospital intake of $295 barely covered the expenses of $244, which included wages for secular staff. The sisters' cows and chickens, along with their vegetable gardens, boosted the hospital kitchen, but fruits and meats added to the operating costs. Despite the rough start, within a few years, the Franciscan sisters had negotiated a series of complicated real estate transactions that enlarged and enhanced St. Mary's Hospital. Earliest Account Book, St. Mary's Hospital; Annals, Land Acquired for and by St. Mary's Hospital, 1887–1889, AOSF, Rochester.

56. Sister Sylvester, When I Came to the Hospital, AOSF, Rochester.

57. Ibid.

58. Many were unaware of the link between Mother Alfred and the Mayos. The brothers always acknowledged their debt to the Franciscans, and the sisters spoke of the two doctors with affection and loyalty. *Post Bulletin*, 26, 30 May 1939; *Alumnae Quarterly*: Dedicated to William James Mayo, 6–10; *St. Paul Dispatch*, 28 July 1939, 2; The Mayo Pioneers in Medicine File; Story of Mother Alfred, Mother M. Alfred Moes Papers; Annals, Land Acquired for and by St. Mary's Hospital; Haun, "Mercy Rides the Clouds," *Commonweal* 12 February 1937: 435–73, AOSF, Rochester.

59. Markey Diary, 10, 176, ABVM, Dubuque.

60. Sister M. Pulcheria McGuire's Annals, 149; Markey Diary, 10, ABVM, Dubuque.

61. Mission Data I, St. Joseph's Academy and Novitiate and 1855 Dubuque Hospital, 74, ABVM, Dubuque.

62. Markey Diary, 78, Journal of Statistics, 10–73, ABVM, Dubuque.

63. Markey Diary, 4 April 1896, 81, ABVM, Dubuque.

64. Council Meetings, 2 February 1894–2 February 1900, 73, ABVM, Dubuque.

65. Ibid., 73–75. The Sisters of Charity of BVM had a substantial record of teaching in Kansas. In 1887 they expanded into Wichita and purchased a property there for $3,000. Council Meetings, Articles of Incorporation, Special Meeting, 1 March, 29 April 1887, 54, ABVM, Dubuque.

66. Council Meetings, Articles of Incorporation, Special Meeting, 1 March, 29 April 1887, 9, ABVM, Dubuque.

67. Council Meetings, Articles of Incorporation, Special Meeting, 1 March, 29 April 1887, 75, ABVM, Dubuque.

68. Reavis, *St. Louis*, 42, 44.

69. Faherty, *The St. Louis German Catholics*, 9–13, 42–43.

70. *A Century of Caring: Sisters of Saint Mary*, 4, pamphlet, AFSM, St. Louis.

71. Chronicles, 1, 1–9, AFSM, St. Louis; Henninger, *Sisters of Saint Mary*, 5–10.

72. Chronicles, 1, 3, AFSM, St. Louis.

73. Chronicles, 1, 6, 9, AFSM, St. Louis.

74. Not every woman could endure the public conditions, extreme work, and lack of convent routines. Sister Marianna Herker, of the original group but older than her companions, found the transition to America with its English unbearable; she with-

drew from the congregation and returned to Germany. Chronicles, 1, 10, AFSM, St. Louis.

75. Lennon, *Milestones of Mercy*, 24–26.

76. A. Damen SJ to Sister Agnes, 19 May 1856, in Lennon, *Milestones of Mercy*, 12–13.

77. Ledger, Industrial School, 1899–1904; Ledger, St. Catherine's and "The Home," November 1904–October 1909, Houses and Ministries, Homes for Women, ARSM, St. Louis.

78. Smith, *A Sheaf of Golden Years*, 42–44.

79. Herron, *The Sisters of Mercy in the United States*, 355–56.

80. *New York Times*, 10 January 1912.

81. Ibid.

82. The Sisters of Mercy in Oklahoma, 54–55, Houses and Ministries, Oklahoma Missions, ARSM, St. Louis. Two sisters from Illinois never left the West; Mother Aloysius Lonergan and Mother Catherine Troy developed leadership roles that expanded the number of Mercy nuns in Oklahoma to more than 100 women by the first third of the twentieth century. Dehey, *Religious Orders of Women in the United States*, 357–59.

83. *History of the Franciscan Sisters of the Province of St. Clara, 1873–1915*, 26; Religious Orders of Women, Franciscan Sisters, Daughters of the Sacred Hearts of Jesus and Mary, AUND, Notre Dame.

84. Peters, "History of the Poor Sisters of St. Francis Seraph," 19; *Community of the Sisters of the Sorrowful Mother*, 40, Religious Orders of Women, Community of the Sisters of the Sorrowful Mother, AUND, Notre Dame.

85. Sister Eustella to Reverend Mother, 26 January 1958, 7, Gertrude Bush Papers, ASSSF, Milwaukee.

86. Segale, *At the End of the Santa Fe Trail*, 123–28, 189, 191–94.

87. Dieker, *A Tree Rooted in Faith*, 54.

88. Ahles, *In the Shadow of His Wings*, 79–86, 155–57. Other Franciscans sent two sisters to typography classes and purchased a printing press, using it for their materials and to increase students in vocational classes. Gloden, *Sisters of St. Francis of the Holy Family*, 268.

89. Kavanagh, *The Sisters of the Holy Family of San Francisco*, 28, 27–36.

90. J. J. Prendergast to Dear Sister Mary, 1873[?], Folder, J. J. Prendergast to Sister Dolores, ASHF, Fremont.

91. Notice to Friends and Benefactors of the Poor, 16 October 1876, Book 24: 32; Notice to the Friends and Benefactors of the Poor, 18 September 1878, Book 32: 31, Published Letters and Notices, 1860–1885, ASHF, Fremont.

92. J. S. Alemany to Miss Armer, 26 February 1874, Book 24: 61, Published Letters and Notices, 1860–1885, ASHF, Fremont. Although the Holy Family sisters did not pronounce religious vows until the late 1870s, the congregation traces its origins to Armer's organizational work and lifestyle as early as 1872. Kavanagh, *The Holy Family Sisters of San Francisco*, 27–50, 53.

93. Jn. E. Cottle to Dear Sister Dolores, 21 February 1884; M. D. Slattery to Miss Armer, 9 August 1875; J. Sullivan SJ to Miss Armer, 12 August 1875; F. F. H (?)araher to Miss Armer, 29 September 1875; J. S. Alemany to Dear in Christ Sister, 14 June 1876; Book 24: 56, 110, 60, Published Letters and Notices, 1860–85, ASHF, Fremont.

94. Kavanagh, *The Holy Family Sisters of San Francisco*, 55.

95. 29 April 1880, 28 February 1881, 18 November 1881, 6 December 1882, 14 October 1884, and 26 December 1884, Book 23: 23, 26, 42, Alemany Letters, ASHF, Fremont.

96. J. S. Alemany to Dear in Christ Mary Armer, 14 January 1875. In 1878 Alemany again gave support for a widow with older children to enter the congregation but counseled that the woman should have regular opportunities to "give them good advice and direction." J. Flood to Dear Sister in Christ, 9 January 1875, Book 23: 24, 25, Published Letters and Notices, 1860–1885, ASHF, Fremont; Kavanagh, *The Holy Family Sisters of San Francisco*, 258, 324.

97. Response of J. S. Alemany's Request for Letter, 23 November 1877, Alemany Letters, ASHF, Fremont.

98. Day Care Ministry in San Francisco, unbound xerox typescript, n.p., ASHF, Fremont.

99. Kavanagh, *The Holy Family Sisters of San Francisco*, 129–42.

100. Flora S. Boyd to Emma Marmedel, 24 August 1884, Book 24: 48; Day Care Ministry in San Francisco, Early Kindergarten Training in San Francisco, ASHF, Fremont. The Servants of Mary who began missions in Indiana before moving to Nebraska advertised that their kindergarten "taught according to the renown Froebel system by (non-sectarian) teachers from Europe." Souvenir of the Ladies' Fair at St. Matthew's Hall: Mt. Vernon, Ind. 26, 27, 28 Nov. 1901, Mt. Vernon File, AOSM, Omaha.

101. Sisters of Notre Dame to Dear Sisters, 27 May 1886, Book 24: 48, Published Letters and Notices, 1860–1885. In 1894 the Sisters of the Holy Family, rejecting an identity as a "teaching order," declined to attend a meeting of nuns from San Francisco Catholic schools. Subsequently, a Sister of Mercy requested on behalf of all the congregations "anxious to have ideas on kindergarten and child study" that Mother Dolores reconsider, as "yours is the most important of all teaching, the foundation." Day Care Ministries in San Francisco, 5, see 6 for 1898 kindergarten training provided to the Sisters of the Holy Names from Portland and Seattle, ASHF, Fremont.

102. McDonald, *With Lamps Burning*, 227–31; Berg, "Agents of Cultural Change"; Vecsey, *Traditional Ojibwa Religion*, 29, 37. In 1916 a seventy-year-old priest, Ignatius Tomazin, after disputes with parishioners in Minnesota, jumped from a Chicago hotel window and committed suicide. *New York Times*, 27 August 1916.

103. Chronicle, 36–37, AOSB, St. Joseph.

104. Chronicle, 34–38, AOSB, St. Joseph.

105. Chronicle, 33–38, AOSB, St. Joseph; and McDonald, *With Lamps Burning*, 232–34.

106. Father Aloysius to the Abbot, 19 January 1879, in McDonald, *With Lamps Burning*, 235.

107. Chronicle, 42–43; Sister Corbinian, interview, 5 December 1941; Sister Thea to Sister Carol Berg, 12 August 1980; Father Benno Watrin to Sister Carol Berg, 18 September 1980, Indian Mission Records, White Earth, Interviews, AOSB, St. Joseph.

108. Diary, 26, 28 September 1888, Travel Diaries, 1870–1887; Drexel Girls, Elizabeth and Louise, ASBS, Bensalem.

109. Chronicle, 42, Indian Mission Records, White Earth, AOSB, St. Joseph.

110. McDonald, *With Lamps Burning*, 240.

111. In 1888 a mission priest in the Dakotas wrote to the Catholic Indian bureau: "One's blood runs cold to think of all the schemes invented by some white people . . . to deprive these . . . Indians . . . of their first home on earth." "A Letter to Bishop Marty," 31 May 1888. Untitled newspaper clipping, Peter Rosen Papers, Letters Received, AUND, Notre Dame. An Ursuline nun in Montana said of the Cheyennes: "their situation becomes worse. . . . [T]he whites seem determined on their removal. . . . [N]o more rations until Congress appropriates a fund for their relief." Sister of the Sacred Heart to Dear Mother, 8 June 1884, Miles City, Letters, June 1884–December 1885, AOSU, Toledo.

Chapter 4

1. Carl Emanuel Csáky, Credentials for the Carmelite Sisters, 7 May 1908, Carmelite Sisters of the Divine Heart of Jesus, Religious Orders of Women, AASA, San Antonio.

2. J. W. Shaw to Mother Maria-Teresa, 12 July 1913, Carmelite Sisters of the Divine Heart of Jesus, Religious Orders of Women, AASA, San Antonio.

3. J. W. Shaw to Mother Maria-Teresa, 30 July, 17 December 1913, Carmelite Sisters of the Divine Heart of Jesus, Religious Orders of Women, AASA, San Antonio.

4. J. W. Shaw to S. G. Messmer, 8 May 1913, Carmelite Sisters of the Divine Heart of Jesus, Religious Orders of Women, AASA, San Antonio.

5. For developments and changes in finances of European monasteries, see McNamara, *Sisters in Arms*, especially chapters 6 and 7.

6. Ludwig I to Boniface Wimmer, 30 August 1849, in Girgen, *Behind the Beginnings*, 10.

7. Ludwig, *A Chapter of Franciscan History*, 23.

8. Ibid.

9. *Mother Caroline and the School Sisters of Notre Dame*, 1:26.

10. Mother Caroline to Mueller, 18 June 1850, 12 November 1853, 15 March 1856, 19 March 1857, April 1858, 31 May 1859, April 1862, "Mother Mary Caroline Friess," 1:28–50, 52–58, 60–66, 68–79, 80–89, 95–105, 112–19 (quotes on 112 and 118).

11. Mother Caroline to Mueller, 18 June 1850, "Mother Mary Caroline Friess," 28–50 (quotes on 36, 44, 47, 48).

12. "Mother Mary Caroline Friess," 35, 40. For other German foundations in America supported by Ludwig I, see Murray, *Other Waters*, 29–31; and Kohler, *Rooted in Hope*, 4, 7.

13. For the struggles of the Benedictine women to define their own monastic identity and the nuances of the relationship between Benedicta and Wimmer, see Hollermann, "The Reshaping of a Tradition"; and McDonald, *With Lamps Burning*, 3–49.

14. Mueller to Wimmer, March 1859, and Wimmer to Ludwig, 9 April 1859, in McDonald, *With Lamps Burning*, 45–46, 48.

15. Kerst reportedly stormed away from the convent, returning several hours later with clothing, groceries, and a stove. Boo, *House Made of Stone*, 11.

16. Chronicle, 53, AOSB, St. Joseph.

17. Chronicle, 16 August 1880, 55, AOSB, St. Joseph.

18. Chronicle, 55–60; Mother Aloysia Autobiography, handwritten, 30 July 1895, AOSB, St. Joseph.

19. For example, see the biography of Mother M. DeSales Kirk, who was named mother general of the Dominicans of San Rafael only two years after she pronounced vows and held high administrative positions for more than fifty years. Mother DeSales, a member of a California family with real estate and legal connections, frequently relied on her attorney brother for professional advice. In the same congregation, see Sister M. De Chantal Enright, a "valuable executive member of the community" who "held positions of importance" and whose family paid for a new building by contributing the nun's share of a real estate sale to the Dominicans; also see the generosity of the family of Sister M. Clarita Duran. Franks, *Strength of Our Roots*, 65, 131, 154.

20. M. M. Murphy to Slattery, 8 October 1888; M. M. Murphy to Slattery, 13 September 1890, Letters, Margaret Mary Murphy, AJF, Baltimore.

21. For Mother Katharine Drexel, see chapter 6.

22. Personal wealth could facilitate the plans of a founder and also reveal clerical cynicism. Mother Paula led Benedictines to Iowa and Oklahoma, but her relationships with the hierarchy were testy. In 1901 a Kansas bishop wrote of the sixty-one-year-old nun: "As she is advanced in years, she may not be of much service to the community; unless she has something which outbalances this. I heard she has money." Fink to Mother Aloysia, 9 May 1901, in George, *Mother Paula O'Reilly*, 96.

23. Feast of St. Joseph, 1879, Formula of Simple Profession, Register of First Vows, Receptions and Profession File, 1878–1915, AOSF, Rochester; Legal Agreements, Profession, 1901–9, Sisters of Divine Providence, ACDP, San Antonio; Coogan, *The Price of Our Heritage*, 2:4.

24. Franks, *Strength of Our Roots*, 94.

25. Lanslots, *Handbook of Canon Law*, 60–61. The Franciscan Sisters of Perpetual Adoration kept inherited monies listed in the account book. In 1910, after the latest regulations announced in canon law, they dedicated a separate ledger to inheritances and wills. Account Book B, 1885–92, St. Rose Convent, Sisters' Inheritance Ledger, 1910–34, AFSPA, La Crosse.

26. See the cases of Sister Juliana Will OSB and Sister Jubelline Hopfer SSND, Chronicle, 115, AOSB, St. Joseph; and M. Ernesta [Funke] to Dear Sister Magdalen, 21 April 1887, "Mother Mary Caroline Friess," 2:422, 425.

27. Council Meetings, 21, 22 January 1898, ABVM, Dubuque.

28. Buckner, *History of the Sisters of Charity of Leavenworth*, 78–81.

29. For examples, see Council Meetings, 43-101, ABVM, Dubuque; Corporation Record, Articles of Incorporation of St. Rose Convent, Minutes of Meetings, 24 July 1883-22 July 1907, AFSPA, La Crosse.

30. For differing assessments of these events, see Coogan, *The Price of Our Heritage*, 2:21–33; and *In the Early Days*, 275–79.

31. Council Meetings, 9-10; "Mother Clarke's Feast Day and Our Hundred Fortieth Anniversary," 4 October 1873, typescript, 3, ABVM, Dubuque.

32. Articles of Incorporation, 11 March 1887, Folder 2; Records of the Corporation Meetings of the Academy of Sisters of St. Joseph, Denver, 16 May 1887–October 1915, Colorado Missions, ACSJ, St. Louis. Quote in Dougherty, *The Sisters of St. Joseph of Carondelet*, 77.

33. De Smet to [Father Van Gorp], 24 September 1869, in Gilmore, *Come North!*, 280.

34. Buckner, *History of the Sisters of Charity of Leavenworth*, 121–23. De Smet, famed as an irrepressible missionary, tended to overlook the details of mission building, a trait for which he received criticism, even from his Jesuit colleagues. *In Harvest Fields*, 38–39; Carriker, *Father Peter John De Smet*, 108–10.

35. Buckner, *History of the Sisters of Charity of Leavenworth*, 121–23.

36. Ibid., 134–35.

37. Gilmore, *Come North!*, 182–87 (quote on 187). For another example of verbal contracts and problems, see Holland, *Lengthened Shadows*, 201–4. Although pastors frequently made no adequate housing provisions for sisters at new missions, some gave up their own space for nuns. See Chronicle, Geneva, 5 September 1912, ASSND, St. Louis.

38. For another example of contract problems, see the 1869 arrival of the Daughters of Charity in Jefferson City, Texas, and the quote: "As we had been under the impression that a house already furnished was *in waiting* for us, this was quite a damper . . . but nothing was to be done . . . but made the best of a disagreeable beginning; so we jogged on." Annals, Jefferson City, typescript, Daughters of Charity of St. Vincent de Paul, Religious Orders, Women, ACAT, Austin.

39. Thomas, *Footprints on the Frontier*, 169.

40. *Gleanings of Fifty Years*, 119–20.

41. Oregon Chronicles, St. Mary's Academy, Portland, 55, ASNJM, Portland. In 1876, when the Sisters of St. Joseph replaced the Sisters of Charity of Leavenworth at a Colorado parish, the former congregation noted church records that showed the departing nuns had been paid nothing for the previous four years. Typescript, Miscellaneous File, Colorado Missions, ACSJ, St. Louis. At one mission, sisters performed all labor for a priest, his mother, and a family servant when their superior

contracted for the convent to give the three room and board, as well as do all the cleaning, washing, and mending, for an annual salary of one dollar. O'Brien, *Journeys*, 260–69.

42. At the end of 1883, Seghers, who earlier had traveled extensively in Alaska, successfully petitioned the Vatican to be named bishop of Vancouver Island. He returned to Alaska for a fifth time to take up his bishopric and establish missions among Native people. On 28 November 1886, on a reconnaissance that took him beyond Juneau and Skagway, Seghers died, the victim of a random homicide, inexplicably shot by one of his escorts. "Archbishop John Charles Seghers," in Renner, *Alaskana Catholica*, 577–9.

43. Oregon Chronicles, Jacksonville, 27 May 1880, ASNJM, Portland.

44. Without question, priests in western mission areas confronted daunting financial pressures. Father Joseph Perrier, who served as the first resident pastor of Concordia, Kansas, wrote of his life in 1883: "I came here three years ago. I was then proprietor of a house, I had a little money, two horses and a buggy. Now my house is gone, I had to sell my horses and buggy, my organ. . . . My traveling expenses amount to $200 a year. I never had a full salary." Perrier to Fink, 7 December 1883, in Thomas, *Footprints on the Frontier*, 141.

45. Chronicle, Fort Madison, Book I, 8 June 1865, 19, ASSND, St. Louis.

46. Chronicle, Fort Madison, Book I, 8 June 1865, 28, ASSND, St. Louis.

47. Chronicle, Fort Madison, Book I, 8 June 1865, 30, ASSND, St. Louis.

48. Faherty, *The St. Louis German Catholics*, 26, 35–36.

49. Chronicle, St. Joseph Mission, St. Louis, 1857–1915, 17, 19, ASSND, St. Louis.

50. Ibid.

51. Chronicle, 12 September 1881, AOSB, St. Joseph.

52. Chronicle, 29 April 1884, 78, AOSB, St. Joseph; McDonald, *With Lamps Burning*, 122–23.

53. Chronicle, 29 April 1884, 78, AOSB, St. Joseph; and McDonald, *With Lamps Burning*, 149–52.

54. Chronicle, 29 April 1884, 78–9, AOSB, St. Joseph.

55. These Franciscans have a rich history, including the conversion of their founder, Mother Ignatius Hayes, from the Anglican Church; her travels to Italy, Jamaica, and the United States; and her social justice initiatives. Reversals left the Minnesota sisters on the brink of closing when they came to the attention of Zardetti, who is credited with saving the group from extinction. The fact remains that he forced the Minnesota branch to separate from Mother Ignatius and submit to diocesan oversight. Ahles, *In the Shadow of His Wings*, 222–48.

56. Zardetti, Summary Report: 21 November 1889–1 May 1894, in Ahles, *In the Shadow of His Wings*, 274. Emphasis in original.

57. Chronicle, 104, 107, AOSB, St. Joseph.

58. Minogue, *Loretto*, 148–49; *History of the Franciscan Sisters of the Province of St. Clara*, 12; Religious Orders of Women, Franciscan Sisters, Daughters of the Sacred Hearts of Jesus and Mary, AUND, Notre Dame; *Dominicans of San Rafael*, 52–53.

Oregon Chronicles, Jacksonville, 25 March 1900, 152; Idaho City Mission, 156; Baker City Mission, 2, 13, 15, 20 August, 26 September, 9 December 1884, 180–82, ASNJM, Portland. Sister Adeline Jonas, Memoirs of Pioneer CDP Sisters, ACDP, San Antonio; Markey Diary, 31 July, 9 August 1897, 220, 226, ABVM, Dubuque; Annals, Cunningham, Kansas, 23 October 1908, AASC, Wichita; A. M. Jennings to Mother Jerome, 1 August 1899, 7 June 1903, 28 August 1894, 3 June 1905, Mother Jerome Correspondence, AOSU, Paola; History of Mercy Hospital, 6, Local House Minutes, Kalispell, Montana, ARSM, Cedar Rapids; Mother Ernesta Funke, Circular Letters, 13 April, 15 May 1900, ASSND, Milwaukee.

59. Sister St. Gabriel to Lawrence Murphy, July 1888, Letters of Mother St. Pierre Cinquin, 285, ACCVI, San Antonio.

60. Apostolic Missions, Tacoma, Washington, 17 September 1912, typescript, 4, AOSF, Aston; "Mother Mary Kilian," *Records of the American Catholic Historical Society* 41: 56.

61. Mother Solano, provincial of the West, signed the document. Contract of the Sisters of St. Francis (Philadelphia Foundation) with Geo. F. Weibel, Director, St. Leo School, Tacoma, 3 September 1920, Religious Orders of Women, Sisters of St. Francis of Philadelphia, Correspondence (1889–1957), ACAS, Seattle. For other contracts, see A. M. Jennings to Mother Jerome, 1 August 1899, Mother Jerome, Correspondence, AOSU, Paola; and Circular to Pastors, 2 February 1907, Mother M. Marianne Haas, Circular Letters, 1906–17, ASSND, Milwaukee.

62. For example, in July 1897, before the start of school, the Servants of Mary stamped out an agreement whereby the sisters received a raise from $250 to $300 for the first teacher in the mission band and $200 for each succeeding one. In August 1907, with another parish, Mother Gertrude signed a contract that brought an annual salary of $900 for the teaching sisters and an additional twenty dollars for the laundress when she was washing and ironing for the rectory and church. The pastor claimed money from book and holy-items sales and, in a rare agreement, kept the tuition from the music lessons given by the nuns. This Document, 30 September 1893; and Indenture, 14 July 1897; This Agreement, 31 August 1907, Mother Mary Gertrude, Letters, AOSM, Omaha.

63. Buckner, *History of the Sisters of Charity of Leavenworth*, 87–100.

64. Biographical, Mother Josephine File, Mother Superiors, ASCL, Leavenworth.

65. Buckner, *History of the Sisters of Charity of Leavenworth*, 471.

66. Ibid., 468–74.

67. In a railroad hospital, a substantial number of nuns could find employment. See Sister St. Gabriel to Dear and Beloved Sisters, 8 April 1885, Letters of Mother St. Pierre Cinquin, 161–62, ACCVI, San Antonio. Some Franciscans, exiled by the German *Kulturkampf*, strengthened their foundation through hospital work in Kansas, Nebraska, and Colorado with the Santa Fe and Union Pacific Railroads. Peters, "The History of the Poor Sisters of St. Francis Seraph," 73–75.

68. For the Missouri Pacific Railroad facility in Ft. Worth, Texas, see Sister St.

Gabriel to Dear and Beloved Sisters, 8 April 1885, Letters of Mother St .Pierre Cinquin, 162, ACCVI, San Antonio. For other hospital details, see Kauffman, *Ministry and Meaning*, 113.

69. Chronicles, 1, 48, 50, AFSM, St. Louis; Buerge and Murray, *Evergreen Land*, 120, 15; O'Brien, *Journeys*, 137–40; Finck, "The Congregation of the Sisters of Charity of the Incarnate Word," 88–90.

70. Forliti, "The First Thirty Years of the Sisters of the Good Shepherd," 43.

71. Oregon Chronicles, 104, 181, 238–39, Sacred Heart Academy, Salem, 10 October 1870; Baker City Mission, 3 September 1884; Astoria Mission, 16 May 1898, ASNJM, Portland.

72. For a yearly contract, see Agreement between the Sisters of St. Joseph and the Seventhirty, Stevens, or Burleigh Mines, 18 March 1889, Georgetown/Silver Plume, Colorado Missions, ACSJ, St. Louis; additional support came to the nuns when they inherited all rights to the title and interest of mine holdings from one Jeremiah O'Brien. Dougherty, *Sisters of St. Joseph of Carondelet*, 296, 322–23; Kauffman, *Ministry and Meaning*, 110–11. In 1879 the Sisters of St. Joseph in Minnesota charged ninety-five cents a day for a ward bed, seven to nine dollars a week for a private room, and twenty to eighty cents for charges for medicines. Register: Bills, St. Joseph's Hospital, 16 May 1879, ACSJ, St. Paul. By the 1890s, the Sisters of Mercy in Des Moines and Davenport charged eight dollars a week for ward care, with the scale for private rooms starting at ten dollars. O'Brien, *Journeys*, 443. In 1907 the Dominicans in Chehalis, Washington, charged two dollars a day for a private room and one dollar for ward accommodations, which included all medications. Buerge and Murray, *Evergreen Land*, 121.

73. O'Brien, *Journeys*, 237, 239, 245–50.

74. Bourgarde to Mother Asst. Julia Littenecker, 13 July 1886, in Dougherty, *Sisters of St. Joseph of Carondelet*, 323.

75. O'Brien, *Journeys*, 575–77.

76. Kauffman, *Ministry and Meaning*, 113.

77. O'Brien, *Journeys*, 574–87.

78. Hockle, *On High Ground*, 83.

79. For example, of ten patients admitted to St. Alexius Hospital in May 1885, seven were listed as "pauper," whereas in June two of six were designated thus. Ledger of Patients, St. Alexius Hospital, May 1885–December 1897, AOSB, Bismarck; in 1879 the Sisters of St. Mary accepted 117 sick persons to the infirmary, 52 of whom were poverty cases; in 1880, 30 of 106 admissions went to charity wards; in 1881, 60 of 185 were poverty admissions; by 1900, 660 of 1,505 were "entire charity ward" cases. Chronicles, 1, 31, 36, 41, AFSM, St. Louis.

80. Oregon Chronicles, St. Rose's Academy, Seattle, 248, ASNJM, Portland.

81. Allhoff, "The School Sisters of Notre Dame in Osage County, Missouri," 23.

82. Untitled typescript, n.p., Religious Orders, Women, ACAT, Austin.

83. Callahan, *The History of the Sisters of Divine Providence*, 164–66.

84. Minogue, *Loretto*, 158–60; O'Connor, *Five Decades*, 153; Oregon Chronicles, St. Paul's Academy, 22 October 1906, 74, 86, ASNJM, Portland.

85. Our Missions, Saint Gabriel's School, 63, AFSPA, La Crosse.

86. Oregon Chronicles, St. Paul's Academy, St. Paul, 22 October 1906, 86, ASNJM, Portland. Opinions about civic contracts differed, and there was disagreement about whether sisters should conduct the schools. O'Connor, *Five Decades*, 250–53.

87. O'Connor, *Five Decades*, 153–54.

88. St. Mary, Gainesville, Texas, 1895–1899, Table of Foundations, typescript, 2, ACDP, San Antonio. The Sisters of St. Joseph of Concordia, Kansas, also recorded a brief tenure in Gainesville around 1896. Thomas, *Footprints on the Frontier*, 195.

89. St. Mary, Gainesville, 1902–54, typescript, ca. 1927, Mission Records, ASSND, St. Louis.

90. In 1923 Oregon passed a law known as the "Garb Bill," which prohibited anyone from wearing a religious habit while teaching in a public school. Gloden, *Sisters of St. Francis of the Holy Family*, 174–75.

91. Statement to the General Chapter, July 1894, n.p., Notebook, 1891–1925, St. Matthew's, Mt. Vernon, Indiana, AOSM, Omaha.

92. O'Connor, *Five Decades*, 297.

93. Historical Sketch of the Congregation of the Sisters of Mary, 3:153, ASMP, Valley City.

94. Annual Catalogue of St. Clara Academy, 1867, AOP, Sinsinawa. The Dominicans at St. Clara had always advertised the music opportunities, in 1854 offering piano or guitar "by a most accomplished teacher" for $8.00 per quarter. O'Connor, *Five Decades*, 51.

95. Annals, Rockwell, Iowa, 1901, 1 and 2; Annals, St. Michael's (formerly St. Joseph's), Sioux Falls, Iowa, December 1905, 6, AOP, Sinsinawa.

96. Annals, Denver, Colorado, 1894, 6, AOP, Sinsinawa.

97. Annals, Kansas City, Missouri, 1892 and 1893, AOP, Sinsinawa.

98. Sr. Amadeus to My dear Mother, 18 January 1884, Miles City, Letters, January 1884–May 1884, AOSU, Toledo.

99. Sr. Mary Amadeus to My dear Mother, 29 March 1884, Miles City, Letters, January 1884–May 1884, AOSU, Toledo. For another example, see the importance of a music teacher for the Sisters of St. Joseph opening a school in Central City, Colorado. S. M. Perpetua to Dearest Mother, 3, 12 April, 2 May 1877, Letters of Sister M. Perpetua, Colorado Missions, ACSJ, St. Louis.

100. Hogan, Review of Music Teaching, typescript, 1–6, Personal Papers, ACSJ, St. Paul.

101. Coogan, *The Price of Our Heritage*, 2:288 and 312 (note 16).

102. In a group that became the Sisters of St. Francis of Rochester, Minnesota, "One sister was occupied all day giving music lessons." Hayes, "Years of Beginning," 10. In Iowa, a Franciscan annalist reported, "the sisters had much to do . . . with

music going from early morning until night." Our Missions, Lansing, Iowa, AFSPA, La Crosse.

103. Jennings to Mother Jerome, 1 August 1899, Mother Jerome, Correspondence, AOSU, Paola. The evident demands of doing so showed for a Franciscan Sister of Perpetual Adoration occupied all day with music or designing art objects, or for a novice from the same congregation sent from formation at the motherhouse to be the third helper in a music program of fifty pupils. Diary, St. Rose, 29 March 1883, 30 September 1884, AFSPA, La Crosse.

104. This Agreement, 30 September 1893, Mother Mary Gertrude, Letters; Statement to General Chapter, July 1900, Notebook: 1891–1925, Mt. Vernon, Indiana, File, AOSM, Omaha.

105. Sister M. Julianna, Reminiscences of Pioneer Days in America, 196–99, AOSM, Omaha.

106. September 1886–September 1887, Mission Accounts, 1886–90, AFSPA, La Crosse.

107. Diary, St. Rose, 13, 16 March, 1 April, 7–9, 24 June, 3 September 1883; 31 December 1884; 13, 17, 30 January, 12 March 1885, AFSPA, La Crosse.

108. The Ecclesiastical Art Department, Publications, Religious Orders of Women, Precious Blood Sisters, O'Fallon, Missouri, AUND, Notre Dame.

109. Mother Mary Gertrude, Diaries, 4, 12, 21, 24 February 1909, 9 May 1910, AOSM, Omaha.

110. For examples, see *Virginia City Territorial Enterprise*, 1 January, 12 and 27 February, and 1 March 1867; 27 December 1870; and 3 January 1873.

111. For a summary list of donations, see Ave Maria: List of Benefactors, 1907–25, Mother Mary Gertrude, Mt. St. Mary's, Cherokee, Iowa, AOSM, Omaha.

112. Oregon Chronicles, St. Mary's Academy, Portland, and Mission of Idaho City, Idaho, 1867, 38, 156, ASNJM, Portland.

113. Kauffman, *Ministry and Meaning*, 103.

114. For an account of the best and the worst of begging, see the diary of Sister Pius, in Buckner, *History of the Sisters of Charity of Leavenworth*, 178–204. Convent differences also influenced attitudes. One sister who did not wish to collect for a facility said she accepted the duty "in obedience," but, "I cannot begin to define to you the unconquerable repugnance I feel to collect for the hospital." S. Perpetua to Dear Mother, 17 May 1877, Letters of Sister M. Perpetua, Colorado Missions, ACSJ, St. Louis.

115. Quoted in Peterson and Vaughn-Roberson, *Women with Vision*, 64.

116. *Dominicans of San Rafael*, 47–48.

117. Sister M. Joseph Holly, 1824–1924, Collected Notes: Copy of Lives/Notes, ADC, St. Louis.

118. Oregon Chronicles, St. Paul's Academy, St. Paul, 13 January 1862, 77, ASNJM, Portland.

119. Daily Record, Odanah, 10, 16, 18, 22 July, 1, 3, 9, 13, 30 September, 28, 29 October, 4, 11, 21 November 1908, AFSPA, La Crosse.

120. Franks, *Strength of Our Roots*, 52.

121. Chronicles, 1, 6, AFSM, St. Louis.

122. Barnaba, *A Diamond Crown for Christ the King*, 266.

123. Highlights: St. John's Hospital, 1912–66, binder, ARSM, St. John's Hospital, St. Louis.

124. Sister Barnabas Siebenhor, Memoirs of Pioneer CDP Sisters, ACDP, San Antonio.

125. Mother Emily to the Missions, 7 December 1899, Mother Emily Power, Mission Letters, 1891–99, AOP, Sinsinawa.

126. St. Pierre to My dear Sister, 5 October 1879, Letters of Mother St. Pierre Cinquin, 15, ACCVI, San Antonio.

127. 18 April, 2 November 1908, Papers of Provincials, Mother M. Petra Claver, Circular Letters, 1901–11, ASSND, St. Louis.

128. Coogan, *The Price of Our Heritage*, 2:190.

129. *Mother Caroline and the School Sisters of Notre Dame*, 1:287, 292.

130. Duffy, *Katharine Drexel*, 142.

131. St. John's Hospital, Fargo, 10, Personal Papers: Sr. Helen Angela Hurley, ACSJ, St. Paul.

132. Statement to General Chapter, July 1900, St. Matthew's, Notebook, AOSM, Omaha.

Chapter 5

1. This translated into unfortunate selections of bishops for administrative duty in America. They exhibited European sentiments about the relationship between the clergy and the laity that led to conflict. When the French Jean-Baptiste Lamy and Joseph P. Machebeuf arrived in Santa Fe in 1851, they mistakenly believed that the public welcome heralded a citizenry anxious to yield to the religious authority of outsiders. Bridger, *Death's Deceiver*, esp. 81, 108. John B. McGloin wrote about the Diocese of Monterey: it "was far distant from Rome and only vague notions were had concerning it." *California's First Archbishop*, 116 (footnote 2); also 126.

2. For the complicated demographics concerning the California church jurisdictions and their division, see Engh, *Frontier Faiths*, 6–12.

3. Mazzuchelli to Loras, 26 September 1850, in McGloin, *California's First Archbishop*, 103.

4. McGloin, *California's First Archbishop*, 52–58.

5. Mother Mary of the Cross to Jandel, January 1889, in Franks, *Strength of Our Roots*, 1.

6. Dominicans questioned that Alemany could serve in any position of authority within the order once he was elevated to a larger church assignment. Indeed, Alemany himself may have been the only one to think that he could. Vilarrasa headed the California foundation of Dominicans, men and women. McGloin, *California's First Archbishop*, 110–11, 128–29.

7. Mother Mary of the Cross to Jandel, January 1889, in Franks, *Strength of Our Roots*, 1.

8. McNamee, *Willamette Interlude*, 231–73; *In Harvest Fields*, 102–4, 130, 135–55.

9. *In Harvest Fields*, 143; McKevitt, *Brokers of Culture*, 226.

10. When Mercy Sisters in Ireland refused to send missionaries for California, Alemany dispatched a personal emissary to Kinsale, where after many attempts to secure a mission band, he told the mother superior she risked heavenly wrath for interfering with evangelizing work. Russell, *The Three Sisters of Lord Russell*, 39–40; O'Brien, *Journeys*, 17; Herron, *The Sisters of Mercy in the United States*, 149–50. For another congregation pressured to expand western missions before the sisters felt prepared for a new venture, see Hockle, *On High Ground*, 31–32.

11. Russell, *The Three Sisters of Lord Russell*, 72, 78.

12. In a city of more than 150,000 people that was burdened with employment, educational, and religious issues pressing on European and Mexican immigrants, Alemany actually found time to worry about conversions among the non-Christian, non-English-speaking Chinese. His Herculean proposal for the Chinese district was doomed by a lack of missionaries. Paddison, "Anti-Catholicism and Race in Post–Civil War San Francisco," 512–13, 520. Concerning sisters and Chinese conversion, see Herron, *The Sisters of Mercy in the United States*, 160.

13. McGloin, *California's First Archbishop*, 192–226, 253–78 (quote on 269).

14. The archbishop apparently pursued several business interests. In the early 1880s, he wrote a long newspaper advertisement endorsing the purity of the communion wines and olive oils produced at his diocesan vineyards in San Jose. *Salt Lake Herald*, 23 May 1882, 3.

15. For a summary of these events, see *The Dominicans of San Rafael*, 26–48.

16. Statement, Office of the Hibernia Savings and Loan Society of San Francisco, 6 December 1883, Bernicia, St. Catherine's Convent Folder, Dominican Sisters, Up to and Including 1903, Religious Orders of Women, AASF, Menlo Park.

17. *The Dominicans of San Rafael*, 81–84; Franks, *Strength of Our Roots*, xi, 45.

18. By modern calculations, the gift approximated $400,000. *Salt Lake Herald*, 21 May 1885, 1.

19. F. Blanchet to Alemany, 14 February 1851, in McGloin, *California's First Archbishop*, 119.

20. Oregon Chronicles, Oregon City, 72, ASNJM, Portland.

21. Oregon Chronicles, Oregon City, 73, ASNJM, Portland.

22. *Gleanings of Fifty Years*, 78–83.

23. Marty to Rosen, 21 July 1881, Peter Rosen Papers, Letters Received, AUND, Notre Dame.

24. Marty to Dear Sir, 28 October 1881; Marty to Gleeson, 5 December 1881; James Gleeson Papers, AUND, Notre Dame; Annals, 1880–1938, 4–6, APBVM, Fargo.

25. Duratschek, *Under the Shadow of His Wings*, 129; O'Brien, *Journeys*, 476–91.

26. Marty to Rosen, 18 September 1883, Peter Rosen Papers, Letters Received, AUND, Notre Dame.

27. Pefferkorn to J. C. Néraz, 29 June 1886, Sisters of Divine Providence, 1878–1910, Religious Orders of Women, AASA, San Antonio.

28. Callahan, *The History of the Sisters of Divine Providence*, 140. Other congregations had international administrative problems with the bishop. Two years earlier, Mother St. Pierre of the Incarnate Word Sisters wrote to her motherhouse in Lyons, France, about Néraz: "He doesn't want to hear about union." Sister St. Pierre to My good and patient Mother, 19 June 1884, Letters of Mother St. Pierre Cinquin, ACCVI, San Antonio.

29. Callahan, *The History of the Sisters of Divine Providence*, 141–44.

30. Notes for Biography of Mother Margaret Healy-Murphy, compiled by Turley, ASHSp, San Antonio; Moore, *Through Fire and Flood*, 177–79; Sister St. Arsene to Néraz, 17 September 1886; Néraz to Sister St. Arsene, 20 September 1886, Sisters of Divine Providence, 1878–1910, Religious Orders of Women, AASA, San Antonio.

31. Chronicle, Fort Madison, Book 1, 20, ASSND, St. Louis.

32. Oregon Chronicles, Oregon City, 73, ASNJM, Portland.

33. Shaw to Mother Augustine, 22 July 1913, Incarnate Word and Blessed Sacrament Sisters, Religious Orders of Women, AASA, San Antonio. Men religious also faced censure if their tone was perceived as disrespectful to a church superior. In 1880 Alemany complained about a letter from a prior, of which the archbishop said, "what is altogether very wrong . . . is the insulting manner in which a bishop is addressed." Alemany to Vilarrasa, in McGloin, *California's First Archbishop*, 271.

34. Sister Amadeus to My Dear Mother, 18 January 1884, Miles City, Letters, January 1884–May 1884, AOSU, Toledo.

35. For the Ursulines in Montana, see Palladino, *Indian and White in the Northwest*, 132–256.

36. For Amadeus's first year in Montana, see Butler, "'We Had No Assistance from Anyone,'" 91–119.

37. Sister Amadeus to My Dear Mother, 18 January 1884, Miles City, Letters, January 1884–May 1884, AOSU, Toledo.

38. Sister St. Angela to My very dear Mother, 27 January 1884; Sister Amadeus to My dear Mother, 18 January 1884, Miles City, Letters, January 1884–May 1884, AOSU, Toledo.

39. Code, *Great American Foundresses*, 440.

40. West, "Called Out People: The Cheyennes and the Central Plains," 2–15.

41. Your Sister Amadeus to My beloved Mother and Sisters, 1 November 1884; Sister Amadeus to My very dear Mother, 8 December 1884; Your Sister Amadeus to My very dear Mother, 14 December 1884; Sister Amadeus to My very dear Mother, 19 December 1884, St. Peter's Mission, Letters, 1884–1906, AOSU, Toledo.

42. Apparently, a newspaper article that identified the Miles City group as part of a New Orleans Ursuline motherhouse offended Mother Stanislaus, which showed that bishops were not the only administrators to demonstrate territorial rivalries. Sister of the Sacred Heart of Jesus to My ever dear Mother, 2 February 1885; Sister Francis

to My ever dear Mother, 8 February 1885, Miles City, Letters, June 1884-December 1885, AOSU, Toledo.

43. McBride, *The Bird Trail*, 74.

44. McKevitt, *Brokers of Culture*, 163.

45. Mahoney, *Lady Blackrobes*, 28.

46. Sister Amadeus to R. Gilmour, My Lord, dearest Father and Bishop, 22 July 1884, Miles City, Letters, June 1884–December 1885, AOSU, Toledo.

47. Gilmour to Dear Child, 17 June, 28 July 1884; Gilmour to Mother Stanislaus, 14 February 1885; Gilmour to Dear Child, 19, 28 February, 5 March 1885, Richard Gilmour, Letters, 1884–1890, AOSU, Toledo.

48. Sister Amadeus to My dear Mother, 29 July 1884, Miles City, Letters, June 1884–December 1885, AOSU, Toledo.

49. Sister Amadeus to My dear Mother, 31 August 1884, Miles City, Letters, June 1884–December 1885, AOSU, Toledo.

50. Gilmour to the Religious of the Ursuline Convent, 28 February 1886, Richard Gilmour, Letters, 1884–1890, AOSU, Toledo.

51. Mahoney, *Lady Blackrobes*, 135–64.

52. Ibid., 134 (quote).

53. The decision to join the Ursuline Roman congregation or remain a diocesan institute cast a long shadow for several years. For example, see the 1916 through 1926 correspondence between and among Sister Carmel, Sister Agatha, Sister Monica, and Archbishop Edward J. Hanna, Ursuline Sisters, Religious Orders of Women, AASF, Menlo Park.

54. Mahoney, *Lady Blackrobes*, 224–26.

55. Ibid., 204–13 (quote on 207).

56. Ibid., 218–20 (quote on 218).

57. Ibid., 228.

58. Sister Amadeus to Edward O'Dea, 24 October 1912, Religious Women, Ursuline Nuns of the Roman Union, Correspondence, vol. 1, (1912–31), ACAS, Seattle.

59. Vander Pol to the Bishop of Seattle, 2 January 1913; Mother Angela Lorenzutti to Rt. Rev. Bishop, 27 September 1915; The Novices, per Sister Evangelist, 11 August 1917, Religious Women, Ursuline Nuns of the Roman Union, Correspondence, vol. 1 (1912–31), ACAS, Seattle.

60. Mother Angela Lorenzutti to Rt. Rev. Bishop, 27 September 1915, Religious Women, Ursuline Nuns of the Roman Union, Correspondence, vol. 1 (1912–31), ACAS, Seattle.

61. O'Brien, *Journeys*, 343. Mother de Pazzi acted as mother superior from 1856 to 1868. Sister Ignatius Walker held the office during 1868–69, but the strong-minded de Pazzi served as the assistant mother for that year. In 1869 she resumed her place as mother superior until 1909. Lennon, *Milestones of Mercy*, 279.

62. O'Brien, *Journeys*, 229–30.

63. History: St. Louis Foundation, vol. 1: loose leaf binder, ARSM, St. John's Hospital, St. Louis.

64. Peter Richard to Rev. Mother, 19 May 1856, in Herron, *The Sisters of Mercy in the United States*, 179.

65. O'Brien, *Journeys*, 342.

66. Mother Baptist Russell to Bishop Eugene O'Connell, ca. 1862, quoted in O'Brien, *Journeys*, 24.

67. Peter Richard to Dear Madam, 7 May 1860, in Lennon, *Milestones of Mercy*, 28.

68. Lennon, *Milestones of Mercy*, 29.

69. Decree from Diomedes Falconio, 12 November 1907, Sister de Pazzi Bentley, Legal Documents; Falconio to de Pazzi, 12 November 1907, [?] to Mother de Pazzi, n.d., Mother de Pazzi Bentley, Letters, ARSM, St. Louis.

70. O'Brien, *Journeys*, 343.

71. Ledger: Industrial School, 1899–1944; Ledger: St. Catherine's and "The Home," November 1904–October 1909; Ledger: Sick Calls, 1904–6; Early Prison Ministry, 1856–1955, Statistics of St. Joseph's Convent, 7, Houses and Ministries, ARSM, St. Louis.

72. Scott, *Convent Life*, 66–67, 95–106.

73. McNamara, *Sisters in Arms*, 245.

74. Lanslots, *Handbook of Canon Law for Congregations of Women Under Simple Vows*, 71–116; Geser, *The Canon Law Governing Communities of Sisters*, 272–91; Rocca, *Manual of Canon Law*, 146.

75. Chronicles, 17 August 1904, Notebook: 20 July 1904–12 December 1904, ASCL, Leavenworth.

76. Constitution of the Sisters of Charity, 1877–78, 3, 4, Religious Orders of Women, Sisters of Charity of Nazareth, Kentucky, Constitutions and Regulations, AUND, Notre Dame.

77. Regulations for the Society of the Sisters of Charity . . . for the Motherhouse of Nazareth, Kentucky, 1877, 5, 6, 7, 8, 9, Religious Orders of Women, Sisters of Charity of Nazareth, Kentucky, Constitutions and Regulations, AUND, Notre Dame. For another example, see Rules and Constitutions of the Institute of the Religious Sisterhood . . . , APBVM, Fargo.

78. The constitution required that an applicant be examined by the mother superior, but western congregations could not afford losses because a candidate lived far from the motherhouse. Mother St. Pierre Cinquin of Texas asked for local interviews to be conducted with extra vigor—"No flattering, no flattering, no foolishness about vocation. . . . Be smart for God." Sr. St. Pierre to Dear Sister, 25 April 1884, Letters of Mother St. Pierre Cinquin, ACCVI, San Antonio.

79. Mother Clarke's Feast Day and Our Hundred Fortieth Anniversary, Message to the Community, 4 October 1973, 3 inserted, Council Meetings: Articles of Incorporation, 11 August 1870–31 October 1892, ABVM, Dubuque.

80. Ibid.

81. Knawa, *As God Shall Ordain*, 113.

82. Mother Caroline to My dear Sisters, 7 February 1872, "Mother Mary Caroline Friess," 1:139.

83. Mary F. Clarke to My dear Sister, 3 July 1887, in Coogan, *The Price of Our Heritage*: Mary Frances Clarke, Foundress, 1977 Special BVM edition, 203.

84. General Letter of Encouragement, Sr. St. Pierre to Dear Sisters, 14 September 1889; Sr. St. Pierre to My loved child, 17 September 1889, Letters of Mother St. Pierre Cinquin, ACCVI, San Antonio.

85. M. Francesca Saverio Cabrini to My beloved daughters, 20 October 1895, in Provenzano, *To the Ends of the Earth*, 134.

86. Council Meetings, 22 March 1894, ABVM, Dubuque.

87. Council Meetings, 7 May 1894, ABVM, Dubuque.

88. Markey Diary, 4 April 1896, 79, ABVM, Dubuque.

89. Markey Diary, 4 April 1896, 80, 83, ABVM, Dubuque.

90. Markey Diary, 7 November 1895, 31, ABVM, Dubuque.

91. Mother Emily to the Community, 4 March 1904, Mother Emily Power, Mission Letters, AOP, Sinsinawa.

92. Mother Ernesta, [?], [?] 1896, Mother Ernesta Funke, Circular Letters, ASSND, Milwaukee.

93. Mother Mary Florence, Circulars, 1890–1925, esp. 22 April 1890, 19 April 1891, ACDP, San Antonio.

94. Mother Innocentia to the Community, 29 July 1900, Catalog, Generalate and Commissariat Correspondence, 1879–1915, ASSND, St. Louis.

95. Mother Cecilia Daugherty, 1 October 1907, 30 October 1899, Circular Letters, ABVM, Dubuque.

96. Mother Emily to the Community, 6 September 1904, Mother Emily Power, Mission Letters, AOP, Sinsinawa.

97. Sr. Amadeus to My dear Mother, 29 March 1885, St. Peter's Mission, Letters, 1884–1906, AOSU, Toledo.

98. Lambert to Mother Superior, 21 May 1879, in Coogan, *The Price of Our Heritage*: Mary Frances Clarke, Foundress, 1977 Special BVM edition 118.

99. Chickasha, second visit, 29 September 1903, 28; Pawhuska, first visit, 1901, 40, Superior General Visits to Indian and Oklahoma Territory, AOSF, Aston.

100. St. Joseph's Academy and St. Anthony's Hospital, Pendleton, second visitation, 28 February 1906, 50; Mt. St. Joseph Academy, Tekoa, second visit, 7 March 1906, 55; St. Joseph's Orphanage, Spokane, second visit, 14 March 1906, 59, Superior General Visits, AOSF, Aston.

101. St Mary of Victory, August 1895, typescript, Missions, St. Louis, ASSND, St. Louis.

102. St. Francis Academy, Baker City, second visit, 18 February 1906, 75, Superior General Visits, AOSF, Aston.

103. Anadarka, second visit, 27 September 1903, 33, Superior General Visits, AOSF, Aston.

104. St. Joseph's School, Rawlins, first visit, 5 April 1902, 86, Superior General Visits, AOSF, Aston.

105. St. Joseph's Hospital, Tacoma, second visit, [March 1906?], [?], Superior General Visits, AOSF, Aston.

106. Mother Caroline visited in June 1865 and conditions apparently led her to deny profession the following year. Chronicle, Fort Madison, Book I, September 1866, 26, ASSND, St. Louis.

107. For other examples, see the Servants of Mary, whose records started in Illinois but included Cherokee, Iowa. Register of Visitations, Enfield, Illinois, 4 May 1902–1924; first visit to Cherokee, 25 July 1911, AOSM, Omaha.

108. Annals, St. Mary's School, Jefferson City, Texas, n.p., partial typescript, Daughters of Charity of St. Vincent de Paul, Religious Orders of Women, ACAT, Austin.

109. Dominican Motherhouse, Sacred Heart Convent, typescript, 4, Dominican Sisters of Columbus, Ohio, Religious Orders of Women, ACAT, Austin.

110. Gallagher to Cardinal Simeoni, 2 January 1889, partial letter, Sisters of St. Agnes, Religious Orders of Women, ACAT, Austin.

111. Naber, *With All Devotedness*, 116.

112. Shaw to Dear Sisters in Christ, 29 September 1913, in Knawa, *As God Shall Ordain*, 280.

113. Gallagher to Cardinal Simeoni, 2 January 1889, partial letter, Sisters of St. Agnes, Religious Orders of Women, ACAT, Austin.

114. Naber, *With All Devotedness*, 116–17.

115. Chronicle, 91–95, AOSB, St. Joseph.

116. For details and letters concerning the Benedictines' arrival in Duluth, decision to accept the Canadian missions, and subsequent controversies, see Boo, *House of Stone*, 45–68.

117. Sister Jerome, Recollections, in Boo, *House of Stone*, 62, 63.

118. Boo, *House of Stone*, 68 (quotes).

119. Caroline to My dear Sister Theophila, 24 January 1883, "Mother Mary Caroline Friess," 1:315.

120. Shaw to Mother Evangelist, 6 February 1915; O'Neal to Shaw, 28 June 1916, Sisters of the Holy Ghost and Mary Immaculate, Religious Orders of Women, AASA, San Antonio.

121. O'Brien, *Journeys*, 124.

122. Annals, St. Mary's Hospital, 1889–1935, n.p., Mother Alfred Moes Papers, AOSF, Rochester.

123. Chronicle, 8 November 1863, 7, and 4 February 1883, 21, AOSB, St. Joseph.

124. Annals, Rockwell, 21 August 1901, AOP, Sinsinawa.

125. M. Caroline to [P. M. Abbelen], 2 January 1880, "Mother Mary Caroline Friess," 1:262.

126. Vicar General to Hanna, 16 October 1917, 2–4, partial report filed under one congregation but including others, Ursuline Sisters, Religious Orders of Women, AASF, Menlo Park.

127. For example, see the file Presentations Sisters, Personal, Religious Orders of Women, AASF, Menlo Park.

128. M. Caroline to [Sister Theophila Bauer], [ca. Fall 1879], "Mother Mary Caroline Friess," 1:123.

129. Sr. of the Sacred Heart to Dearest Mother, 14 June 1884, St. Labre's Mission, Letters, 1884–85; Sr. Amadeus to My dear Mother, 31 August 1884, Miles City, Letters, June 1884–December 1885, AOSU, Toledo.

130. For complete details of this episode, see Mahoney, *Lady Blackrobes*, 64–73.

131. Sr. St. Francis to My own dear Sisters, 21 July 1886, St. Peter's Mission, Letters, 1884–1906, AOSU, Toledo. Also, see notations for Annette Martin, dismissed when she received letters from a man who had escorted her to the convent on entrance day and corresponded with her by pretending to be her mother. Journal of Statistics, #992, 49, ABVM, Dubuque. In Nebraska, a Mercy sister left to join a janitor from a school where she had once been a teacher. O'Brien, *Journeys*, 172.

132. Diary, St. Rose, 10 July 1885, AFSPA, La Crosse.

133. Chronicle, St. Mary and Clara at St. Mary's School, August 1876, ASSND, St. Louis.

134. Chronological Sketches, 1858–1916, 1:24, ASSND, St. Louis.

135. Chronicle, Sancta Maria Ripa, 12 January 1898, ASSND, St. Louis.

136. Boo, *House of Stone*, 63.

Chapter 6

1. For details of Drexel's early life, see Duffy, *Katharine Drexel*, 15–49.

2. Annual Travel List, Elizabeth Drexel, Travel Diaries, 1870–1887: Drexel Girls: Elizabeth and Louise, ASBS, Bensalem.

3. Baldwin, *A Call to Sanctity*, 16–18.

4. Oral Memoir, Mother Katharine Drexel, 29 November 1935, in Baldwin, *A Call to Sanctity*, 14.

5. Baldwin, *A Call to Sanctity*, 20–23.

6. Duffy, *Katharine Drexel*, 73–75.

7. Annual Travel List, Elizabeth Drexel, Travel Diaries, 1870–1887; Drexel Girls: Elizabeth and Louise, ASBS, Bensalem.

8. Karolevitz, *With Faith, Hope, and Tenacity*, 185.

9. 25 September 1887, Travel Diaries, 1870–1887, Drexel Girls: Elizabeth and Louise, ASBS, Bensalem. It is unclear which sister wrote the 1887 travel diary.

10. 25 September 1887, Travel Diaries, 1870–1887, Drexel Girls: Elizabeth and Louise, ASBS, Bensalem.

11. 25, 26, 29 September and 4, 6 October 1887, Travel Diaries, 1870–1887, Drexel Girls: Elizabeth and Louise, ASBS, Bensalem.

12. 25 September and 1, 6 October 1887, Travel Diaries, 1870–1887, Drexel Girls: Elizabeth and Louise, ASBS, Bensalem.

13. Marty to Dear Father, 11 March 1885, Peter Rosen Papers, Letters Received,

AUND, Notre Dame. Nearly thirty years later, a Catholic layman, speaking about the desperate conditions of western missions, echoed the complaint, noting the wastefulness of a $100,000 mausoleum in New York City when the donor might have constructed a "hundred little churches in churchless communities." Kelley, *The Great American Catholic Missionary Congresses*, 435–36.

14. Burke to Drexel, [1885?], in Duffy, *Katharine Drexel*, 174.

15. Genin, A Letter to Bishop Marty, 31 May 1888, Untitled newspaper clipping, Peter Rosen Papers, Letters Received, AUND, Notre Dame.

16. By 1860, white intrusions sparked Native resistance in many locations. After 1865, the U.S. government increased military force against Indian activists. Aside from the 1876 rout of George A. Custer, most battles favored the larger armies and firing power of white society. By the 1880s, the Sioux, Cheyennes and Arapahos, Crows, Apaches, and Navajos, wearied from attack and starvation, were herded onto gerrymandered reservations that stifled Native participation in the emerging industrial economy of the West. The 1887 Dawes Severalty Act placed into motion federal policies that further isolated Natives and curtailed their control over tribal land. For an overview and readings, see White, *"It's Your Misfortune and None of My Own,"* 85–118.

17. Ethelbert Talbot, Episcopalian bishop of Idaho and Wyoming, said of retaining missionaries: "If a zealous and gifted young man is moved in his heart to go West, his success soon makes him a shining-mark for some comfortable Eastern parish, and he is lost to the missionary field." Talbot, *My People of the Plains*, 116–17. At the Turtle Mountain Reservation, the Mercy sisters tried to operate an industrial boarding school, but, nearing starvation, the nuns withdrew to Devils Lake to open a hospital. Kardong, *Beyond Red River*, 232.

18. 23 September 1888, Elizabeth, Travel Diaries, 1870–1887, Drexel Girls: Elizabeth and Louise, ASBS, Bensalem.

19. Genin, A Letter to Bishop Marty, 31 May 1888, Untitled newspaper clipping, Peter Rosen Papers, Letters Received, AUND, Notre Dame.

20. Annals, February 1901, 4–5, ASBS, Bensalem.

21. Duffy, *Katharine Drexel*, 170–71.

22. Fossy and Morris, "St. Katharine Drexel and St. Patrick's Mission," 66–67.

23. Schoenberg, *These Valiant Women*, 125.

24. 23 September 1888, Louise; 23 September 1888, Elizabeth, in Travel Diaries, 1870–1887, Drexel Girls: Elizabeth and Louise, ASBS, Bensalem.

25. Our Missions, Odanah, 1883, 170, AFSPA, La Crosse; Ludwig, *A Chapter of Franciscan History*, 243–48.

26. 27, 30 September and 4 October 1888, Louise; 23, 27 September 1888, Elizabeth, Travel Diaries, 1870–1887, Drexel Girls: Elizabeth and Louise, ASBS, Bensalem.

27. L. B. Drexel to Dear Melon, 1 October 1888; 23 September 1888, Louise, Travel Diaries, 1870–1887, Drexel Girls: Elizabeth and Louise, ASBS, Bensalem.

28. 1 October 1888, Louise, Travel Diaries, 1870–1887, Drexel Girls: Elizabeth and Louise, ASBS, Bensalem.

29. 28 September 1888, Elizabeth, Travel Diaries, 1870–1887, Drexel Girls: Elizabeth and Louise, ASBS, Bensalem.

30. Chronicles: White Earth, 1888, 44, AOSB, St. Joseph.

31. White Earth, Quarterly Reports, 3 March 1890–30 September 1891, Indian Mission Records, AOSB, St. Joseph.

32. Deutsch to Mother Agatha, 17 March 1901; Deutsch to Sr. Julia, 13 April 1901, St. John's, Komatke, Arizona Missions, ACSJ, St. Louis. Sister Aemiliana to Katharine Drexel, 25 October 1892, St. Patrick's, Anadarko, Correspondence, AOSF, Aston. Payments, 8 January 1900, $250; 11 March 1900, $100 per year for interpreter; 23 May 1900, $250 priest salaries, $50 interpreter, Mother Katharine to Franciscan Fathers, 1900–1925, ASBS, Bensalem. *Records of the American Catholic Historical Society of Philadelphia* 40: 235–37, 364–66, 371–72; Duffy, *Katharine Drexel*, 106–7.

33. Duffy, *Katharine Drexel*, 218, 219, 225.

34. Sister Amadeus to My very dear Mother, 10 October 1884, Miles City, Letters, June 1884–December 1885, AOSU, Toledo.

35. Your Ignatius to My dear Mother, 10 January 1885, St. Labre's Mission, Letters, 1884–1885, AOSU, Toledo; Duffy, *Katharine Drexel*, 235.

36. Sister of the Sacred Heart to Dearest Mother, 14 June 1884, St. Labre's Mission, Letters, 1884–1885, AOSU, Toledo.

37. Sister Paul to Edward Morrell, 18 May 1891, Gray Horse, Oklahoma, Correspondence, AOSF, Aston.

38. St. Patrick's, Anadarka, Indian Territory, 1901; St. Elizabeth's, Purcell, Indian Territory, 1901, 1903; St. Andrew's, Umatilla, Oregon, 1906; St. George's, Blanchet, Washington, 1906, Visitations Made by the Superior General, 1900–1906, AOSF, Aston.

39. Duffy, *Katharine Drexel*, 268–73.

40. K. M. D. to Dear Father, 15 December 1885, Writings of Katharine Drexel, 1:1–89, no. 55, ASBS, Bensalem.

41. Ibid.

42. O'Connor to Katharine Drexel, 29 August 1885, in Baldwin, *A Call to Sanctity*, 33.

43. Drexel's letters about convent life spanned several years. By April 1889 she had informed her uncle Anthony Drexel of her intent, despite the convoluted objections of O'Connor. K. M. Drexel to Dear Father, 6 April 1889, Writings of Katharine Drexel, 1:1–89, no. 62, ASBS, Bensalem. For the ongoing debate with O'Connor, see Duffy, *Katharine Drexel*, 112–28.

44. In 1930 the Catholic sociologist John O'Grady argued that American Catholics did not coordinate organized charitable work before 1890 and that programs struggled to identify resources and policy. O'Grady, *Catholic Charities in the United States*, esp. 416–49.

45. Duffy, *Katharine Drexel*, 73–75; Baldwin, *A Call to Sanctity*, 28–29.

46. Baldwin, *A Call to Sanctity*, 34. O'Connor first proposed this in 1883 but continued his vehement insistence that the heiress remain in secular society until 1888.

O'Connor to Katharine Drexel, 25 October 1883, in Duffy, *Katharine Drexel*, 118–33 (quote on 118).

47. Katharine M. Drexel to O'Connor, 26 November 1888, in Duffy, *Katharine Drexel*, 129.

48. O'Connor to Katharine M. Drexel, 30 November 1888, in Duffy, *Katharine Drexel*, 130.

49. Ibid. Emphasis in original.

50. K. M. D. to Dear Father, 15 December 1885, Writings of Katharine Drexel, 1:1–89, no. 55, ASBS, Bensalem.

51. Herron, *The Sisters of Mercy in the United States*, 20; *New York Times*, 8 May 1889.

52. K. M. Drexel to Dear Father, 12 May 1889, Writings of Katharine Drexel, 1:1–89, no. 65, ASBS, Bensalem.

53. Herron, *The Sisters of Mercy in the United States*, 20.

54. K. M. Drexel to Dear Father, 12 May 1889, Writings of Katharine Drexel, 1:1–89, no. 65, ASBS, Bensalem.

55. Duffy, *Katharine Drexel*, 147, 154–56.

56. K. M. Drexel to Dear Father, 12 February 1889, Writings of Katharine Drexel, 1:1–89, no. 57, ASBS, Bensalem.

57. Duffy, *Katharine Drexel*, 141–47.

58. O'Connor to Katharine Drexel, 28 February 1889, in Duffy, *Katharine Drexel*, 136.

59. O'Connor to Katharine Drexel, 16 May 1889, in Duffy, *Katharine Drexel*, 144.

60. Ryan to Katharine Drexel, 29 May 1890, in Duffy, *Katharine Drexel*, 159–60.

61. Duffy, *Katharine Drexel*, 44, 82.

62. Herron, *The Sisters of Mercy in the United States*, 20. The identity of the original associates remained unclear, but they were likely postulants and novices of the Mercy sisters who had met Drexel in the novitiate.

63. Sister Joanna Bruner, Personal File; Sister Leo Gonzaga Erbacher, Personal File, ASCL, Leavenworth.

64. Duffy, *Katharine Drexel*, 175.

65. Mother Mary Katharine to Mother Inez, 22 June 1891, Writings of Mother Katharine Drexel, 2:90–168, no. 91, ASBS, Bensalem.

66. For events influencing Wisconsin sisters sent to Texas, see unsigned letter fragment to Simeoni, 2 January 1889, Sisters of St. Agnes, Religious Orders of Women, ACAT, Austin.

67. Burke to Mother Katharine, in Duffy, *Katharine Drexel*, 174.

68. M. Georgiana Rockwell, History of Community Rules, 1985, 8, ASBS, Bensalem.

69. Book of Foundations, 176, St. Stephen's Indian Mission, Correspondence, AOSF, Aston. According to Evangeline Thomas, Mother Katharine also briefly supported in Wyoming the St. Stephen's Boarding School for Indians conducted by the Sisters of St. Joseph of Concordia, Kansas. Thomas, *Footprints on the Frontier*, 186–87.

70. Mother to My dear Daughters, [?] November 1902, Writings of Mother Katharine Drexel, 2:90–168, no. 133, Archives, ASBS, Bensalem.

71. Sister Aemiliana to Katharine Drexel, 25 October 1892, Correspondence, Anadarko, AOSF, Aston.

72. Sister Aemiliana to Katharine Drexel, 1 May 1893, Correspondence, Anadarko, AOSF, Aston.

73. Ibid.

74. Sister Aemiliana to Katharine Drexel, 30 November 1893, Correspondence, Anadarko, AOSF, Aston.

75. Visit, 4 October 1903, Purcell, Indian Territory, Visitations Made by the Superior General, AOSF, Aston.

76. Sister Aemiliana to Katharine Drexel, 25 October 1892, 1 May 1893, 13 March 1894, 26 August 1926, Correspondence, Anadarko, AOSF, Aston; Deutsch to Mother Gonzaga, 7 June 1907, Komatke, Arizona Missions, ACSJ, St. Louis.

77. Sister Paul to Katharine Drexel, 23 August 1909, Correspondence, Anadarko, AOSF, Aston.

78. Gray Horse, Oklahoma Territory, vol. 2, 5 October 1903, Visitations Made by the Superior General, AOSF, Aston.

79. Sister Paul to Katharine Drexel, 5, 13 April 1910, Correspondence, Anadarko, AOSF, Aston.

80. Fossey and Morris, "St. Katharine Drexel and St. Patrick's Mission," 63.

81. Sister Pierre Jones to O'Connor, 7 October 1889, in O'Brien, *Journeys*, 154.

82. Drexel to Meerschaeert, 3 December 1912; M. M. Katharine to Dear Mother, 12 February 1913; Drexel to My Dear Sister, 1 July 1921; M. M. Katharine to My Dear Sister, 30 July 1921, Letters of Mother Katharine Drexel, Oklahoma, Houses and Ministries, ARSM, St. Louis.

83. [?] to Katharine Drexel, 23 October 1899; Katharine Drexel to Dear Mother, 1900, Letters of Mother Katharine Drexel, Oklahoma, Houses and Ministries, ARSM, St. Louis.

84. Fossey and Morris, "St. Katharine Drexel and St. Patrick's Mission," 76.

85. Annals, Mother M. Ignatius, To my very dear Sisters, 27 May 1902, ASBS, Bensalem.

86. Annals, Sister M. Ignatius to My dear Sisters, September 1895, ASBS, Bensalem.

87. Annals, Sister Evangelist to Dear Mother & Sisters, 12 August 1894; Sister Evangelist to Sister Margaret Mary, 17 October 1894; [?] to My dear Mother and Sisters, 10 February 1895, ASBS, Bensalem.

88. Annals, Sister Evangelist to My dear Mother, 7 March 1896, ASBS, Bensalem.

89. Annals, Sister Evangelist to My dear Mother, 15 July 1895, ASBS, Bensalem.

90. Ibid.

91. Duffy, *Katharine Drexel*, 194–95.

92. Annals, 1901, 22–37, descriptions of the annalist and letters from Cochiti Pueblo, New Mexico, ASBS, Bensalem.

93. Annals, 1901, 28, ASBS, Bensalem.

94. Katharine Drexel to My dear Sisters, Writings of Mother Katharine Drexel, 2:90–168, no. 128, ASBS, Bensalem.

95. Annals, Sister Agatha to My dear Sisters at St. Catherine's, St. Elizabeth's, and St. Francis de Sales, October 1902, St. Michael's, Arizona, ASBS, Bensalem.

96. Wilken, *Anselm Weber*, 80.

97. Memoirs of Sister M. Liguori, St. Catherine's, Santa Fe, New Mexico, ASBS, Bensalem.

98. Your Mother to My dear Daughters, [?] October 1902, Writings of Mother Katharine Drexel, 2:90–168, no., 133, ASBS, Bensalem.

99. Ibid.

100. Mother [K. D.] to My very dear Daughters, 15 October 1902, Writings of Mother Katharine Drexel, 2:90–168, no. 144, ASBS, Bensalem.

101. Ibid.

102. Ibid.

103. Annals, 1901, ASBS, Bensalem.

104. Foley, *Father Francis M. Craft*; Duffy, *Katharine Drexel*, 345–46.

105. Duffy, *Katharine Drexel*, 361.

106. Ibid., 374–75.

107. Annals, Stephen to Dear Mother, 29 September 1899, ASBS, Bensalem.

108. In 1878 Bishop William H. Gross agreed that Mother Ignatius Hayes could establish a foundation of white Franciscan sisters in Savannah, Georgia, with one of the conditions being that "they are in no manner whatever to work for the white population." When one African American student at the boarding school wished to enter the congregation, a local race crisis was averted by sending the applicant to Rome, Italy, where Mother Ignatius had been living since 1881. There, Frederica Law received the habit at Assisi, the birthplace of Franciscan life, but she died while still a novice. Ahles, *In the Shadow of His Wings*, 141, 152–53, 182.

Chapter 7

1. Agnes Jeager to Sister Mary Joseph, 31 March 1902, St. John's, Komatke, Arizona Missions, ACSJ, St. Louis.

2. Ibid.

3. Agnes R. Jeager to My very dear sister, 8 March 1903, St. John's, Komatke, Arizona Missions, ACSJ, St. Louis.

4. Ibid.

5. Ibid.

6. Among several works that address these issues are Abbott, *How Cities Won the West*; Klingle, *Emerald City*; Thrush, *Native Seattle*; Barkan, *From All Points*; Igler, "Engineering the Elephant," 93–111; Nugent, *Into the West*; Milner, *The Oxford History of the American West*, 155–93; and Limerick, *Legacy of Conquest*.

7. Weber, *The Spanish Frontier in North America*, 92–121.

8. McKevitt, *Brokers of Culture*, 106–11, 120.

9. Jacqueline Peterson, who wrote about the sensitivities and sadness within Native/Catholic history and the resulting spiritual legacies in the Northwest, created a model for reassessment. Many of her observations can be applied generally to the West. Peterson, "Sacred Encounters in the Northwest: A Persistent Dialogue," 37–48.

10. White, *"It's Your Misfortune and None of My Own,"* 85–118.

11. For an example of the actions taken by one tribe, see Heaton, *The Shoshone-Bannocks.*

12. *Report of the Commissioner of Indian Affairs, 1864,* 14, 18, 157.

13. Ibid., 154, 157, 159–61; *Report of the Commissioner of Indian Affairs, 1867,* 15.

14. Berger, Farmer, 28 August 1894, *Report of the Commissioner of Indian Affairs, 1894,* 110.

15. In 1881 the Bureau of Catholic Indian Missions assured the Benedictines that federal agents were required to provide schools with medicines and medical stores. Brouillet to Sister Scholastica, 25 August 1881, and Price to Brouillet, 24 August 1881, Office of the Prioress, Sister Scholastica Kerst, Records, Grand Ronde, Oregon, 1881–1882, AOSB, St. Joseph.

16. Dougherty, *Sisters of St. Joseph of Carondelet,* 124.

17. Selstice, Chief of the Coeur d'Alenes, in McCrosson, *The Bell and the River,* 210.

18. Carriker, *Father Peter John De Smet,* 114–19; Duratschek, *Under the Shadow of His Wings,* 90–91. Also see the 1877 requests of Lakota Sioux to Rutherford B. Hayes for nun teachers in Archambault, Thiel, and Vecsey, *The Crossing of Two Roads,* 118.

19. Oregon Chronicles, quoted from "Beautiful Reception of the Sisters at the Indian Mission of Grand Ronde," in the *Catholic Sentinel* (1875), 159, ASNJM, Portland.

20. Oregon Chronicles, *Catholic Sentinel* (1875), 160, ASNJM, Portland.

21. For example, hardly had the 1868 Ft. Sumner Treaty been executed than Navajo (Diné) leaders challenged the land reduction and attendant hunting and grazing restrictions. The Navajo refused to yield, despite a 300-mile death march from Arizona to New Mexico and years of imprisonment at Fort Sumner. By the twentieth century, stock growers and homesteaders collaborating with railroads to further disadvantage the Indians through land surveys were startled by the persistence and cogency with which Navajos objected to reservation boundaries, track construction, and diverted rivers, as they argued for legal enforcement that would restore original borders and prompt payment of land leases. Wilken, *Anselm Weber,* 199–206.

22. Oregon Chronicles, 163, ASNJM, Portland.

23. Our Missions, Odanah, 158–59, AFSPA, La Crosse.

24. Diary, St Rose, 7–9 June 1883, AFSPA, La Crosse.

25. For a similar Native welcome to the Sisters of St. Joseph in the Southwest, see St. John's School at Komatke via Phoenix, Ariz. mss., 3, Komatke, Arizona Missions, ACSJ, St. Louis.

26. Other texts included O'Shea's reader, Wilson's speller, and Kearney's arith-

metic; School Records and Monthly Reports, White Earth, 31 July 1886, Indian Missions, AOSB, St. Joseph.

27. Our Missions, Odanah, 160-61, AFSPA, La Crosse.

28. A teacher at Odanah, Sister Catherine, wrote: "I am now at my last station with the poor Indians, where I have been for the past twenty-five years. I hope to end my days here." Ten years later, at age eighty-two, on an errand to retrieve butter for the sisters, she fell going into the cellar and died about three weeks later. Sister Catherine Buckley, #94, Sisters' Personnel Files, AFSPA, La Crosse.

29. Our Missions, Odanah, 163-64, AFSPA, La Crosse.

30. Ibid. For other Natives protecting Catholic sisters during dangerous mountain travel, and even intervening when confronted by members of an unknown tribe, see Mother Joseph's 1863 three-week trek from Washington to Montana and back in McCrosson, *The Bell and the River*, 190-94.

31. Annals, Sister Evangelist to My dear Mother, 15 July 1895, ASBS, Bensalem.

32. Sister Ladislaus Twardowski, Memoirs, White Earth, Indian Missions, AOSB, St. Joseph.

33. Ibid.

34. Sr. Francis to My darling Sister, 3 June 1891, St. Paul's Mission, Letters, 1888-94, AOSU, Toledo.

35. Annals, Sister Evangelist to My dear Sisters [?], [?] October 1897, ASBS, Bensalem.

36. Annals, Sister Ignatius to My dear Sisters, September 1895, ASBS, Bensalem.

37. Your Mother to My very dear daughters, 15 October 1902, Writings of Katharine Drexel, 2:90-168, no. 144, ASBS, Bensalem.

38. Oregon Chronicles, 164, ASNJM, Portland.

39. Sister Francis to Dear Mother, 5 November 1886, St. Peter's Mission, Letters, 1884-1906, AOSU, Toledo.

40. Buckner, *History of the Sisters of Charity of Leavenworth*, 417.

41. Sister Marsina Powers, Reminiscences, Arizona Missions, ACSJ, St. Louis.

42. Sister Francis to My own dear Sister, 7 February 1888, St. Paul's Mission, Letters, 1888-94, AOSU, Toledo.

43. Your mother to My dear daughters, [?] October 1902, Writings of Katharine Drexel, 2:90-168, no. 133, ASBS, Bensalem.

44. Your Mother to My very dear daughters, 12 October 1902, Writings of Katharine Drexel, 2:90-168, no. 143, ASBS, Bensalem.

45. Sister Ladislaus Twardowski, Memoirs, White Earth, Indian Missions, AOSB, St. Joseph.

46. McDonald, *With Lamps Burning*, 241. For other examples, see Annals, Sister Evangelist to My dear Mother and Sisters, 4 November 1894; Mother to My dear Daughters, [?] October 1902, Writings of Mother Katharine Drexel, 2:90-168, no. 133, ASBS, Bensalem.

47. Sr. Francis to My very dear Sister, 15 July 1888, Sister Francis to Dearly loved Sister, 27 December 1894, St. Paul's Mission, Letters, 1888-1894, AOSU, Toledo.

48. Sister M. N[orberta Howard] to Dear Mother, 7 February 1899, in Kreis, *Lakotas, Black Robes, and Holy Women*, 107.

49. Kreis, *Lakotas, Black Robes, and Holy Women*, 75.

50. Annals, Sister Miriam [?] to My dear Mother, [?] December 1907, ASBS, Bensalem.

51. Sister Mary Joseph to Dear Mother Julia, [between 1903 and 1904], Komatke, Arizona Missions, ACSJ, St. Louis.

52. Annals, Sister Evangelist to My dear Mother, 15 July 1895, ASBS, Bensalem.

53. Ibid.

54. Annals, Sister M. Ignatius to My own dear Sisters, July 1896, ASBS, Bensalem.

55. You [*sic*] loving child, Childis [*sic*] Teresa Tash-quin to My Dear Mother Julia, n.d.; You [*sic*] loving little girl, Juanita Antone to Dear Mother Julia, n.d., Komatke, Arizona Missions, ACSJ, St. Louis.

56. Oregon Chronicles, Grand Ronde, 26 December 1879, 169, ASNJM, Portland.

57. Sister Mary of the Angels to dear Mother, Feast of the Ascension 1885, St. Peter's Mission, Letters, 1884–1906, AOSU, Toledo.

58. Sister Francis to My own dear Sister, 4 August 1885, St. Peter's Mission, Letters, 1884–1906, AOSU, Toledo.

59. Your own Sister Francis to My dearly loved sister, 30 May 1888, St. Paul's Mission, Letters, 1888–1889, AOSU, Toledo.

60. Our Missions, Odanah, 5 July 1909, AFSPA, La Crosse.

61. Sister Claudina to Dear Brother, 21 August 1910, Memoirs, Red Lake, Indian Missions, AOSB, St. Joseph.

62. Sr. Joseph to My dearest Sister, 30 April 1905, Komatke, Arizona Missions, ACSJ, St. Louis.

63. Sister Ladislaus Twardiwski, Memoirs, White Earth, Indian Missions, AOSB, St. Joseph.

64. Sister De Sales to Dear Mother, 29 March 1903; Sister Joseph to My dear Sister; and Sister Joseph to My dear Mother Julia, 1 January 1904, Komatke, Arizona Missions, ACSJ, St. Louis.

65. Sister Joseph to My dear Sister Alphonse, 13 April 1904, Komatke, Arizona Missions, ACSJ, St. Louis.

66. Wand, "The Jesuits in Territorial Kansas, 1827–1861," pamphlet, 27, Religious Orders Men, Jesuits in Territorial Kansas, AUND, Notre Dame.

67. Jesuits were particularly committed to the proselyting benefits gained through acquisition of Native languages. They pursued fluency with vigor and encouraged sisters to follow their example. For linguistic approach and pedagogy of the Jesuits, see McKevitt, *Brokers of Culture*, 125–30.

68. McCrosson, *The Bell and the River*, 209.

69. Srs. Holy Angels, St. Angela, and Ignatius to My dear Mother and Sisters, 23 December 1884; Sr. St. Angela to My beloved Mother, 11 January 1885, St. Labre's Mission, Letters, 1884–1885, AOSU, Toledo.

70. I am your Ignatius to My dear Mother, 10 January 1885, St. Labre's Mission,

Letters, 1884–85, AOSU, Toledo. For the Indian language studies of another congregation, see Annals, 5, APBVM, Fargo.

71. Sr. Joseph to Dear Mother Julia, July 1905, Komatke, Arizona Missions, ACSJ, St. Louis.

72. Palladino, *Indian and White in the Northwest*, 248.

73. Buckner, *History of the Sisters of Charity of Leavenworth*, 418.

74. Sr. Amadeus to My dear Mother, 17 June 1884; Sr. Amadeus to Dearest Father and Bishop, 22 July 1884, Miles City, Letters, June 1884–December 1885, AOSU, Toledo.

75. Srs. Holy Angels, St. Angela, and Ignatius to My dear Mother and Sisters, 23 December 1884, St. Labre's Mission, Letters, 1884–85, AOSU, Toledo.

76. Your Ignatius to My dear Mother, 10 January 1885, St. Labre's Mission, Letters, 1884–85, AOSU, Toledo; Palladino, *Indian and White in the Northwest*, 208.

77. Kreis, *Lakotas, Black Robes, and Holy Women*, 133, 195.

78. Palladino, *Indian and White in the Northwest*, 131.

79. Annals, Mother Agatha to My Mothers and Sisters, [?] 1905, 34; S. M. B. to [Mother Katharine Drexel?], letter fragment, n.d., St. Michael's, Arizona, ASBS, Bensalem.

80. Sister Anna Francis Stack, 4, Reminiscences, Arizona Missions, ACSJ, St. Louis.

81. Buckner, *History of the Sisters of Charity of Leavenworth*, 412–13.

82. Annals, Mother Loyola to Dear Mother and Sisters, 21 August 1901, ASBS, Bensalem; and Kreis, *Lakotas, Black Robes, and Holy Women*, 83.

83. Annals, Sister Evangelist to Dear Mother, 15 July 1895; Sister Ignatius to Dear Sisters, [?] July 1896; Mother Loyola to Dear Mother and Sisters, 21 August 1901; Sister Perpetua to Dear Mother and Sisters, 10 September 1901, ASBS, Bensalem; Chronicle, 38–39, AOSB, St. Joseph; Our Missions, Odanah, 165–66, AFSPA, La Crosse; Kreis, *Lakotas, Black Robes, and Holy Women*, 76–77, 88–90.

84. Sister St. Francis to Sister Assumption, 19 April 1894, St. Paul's Mission, Letters, 1888–94, AOSU, Toledo.

85. Agnes Jeager to Dear Sister, 31 March 1902, Komatke, Arizona Missions, ACSJ, St. Louis.

86. Agnes R. Jeager to My dear Sister, 11 September 1904, Komatke, Arizona Missions, ACSJ, St. Louis.

87. Sister Joseph to My dearest Mother Julia, 10 January 1906, Komatke, Arizona Missions, ACSJ, St. Louis.

88. McNeil, "St. Anthony's Indian School in San Diego, 1886–1907."

89. Kreis, *Lakotas, Black Robes, and Holy Women*, 169–71 (quote on 168).

90. Although the essay deals with Protestants, for the competitions across and within cultures fueling events surrounding Wounded Knee, see Kerstetter, "Spin Doctors at Santee," 45–67.

91. Henry to Odin, 6 May 1865, Religious Orders of Women, Oblate Sisters of Providence, AUND, Notre Dame.

92. For the definitive scholarship on the formation of the OSP, see Morrow, *"Persons of Color and Religious at the Same Time."*

93. Golden Jubilee of the Oblate Sisters of Providence in St. Louis, Missouri: October 1880–October 1930, 9, Religious Orders of Women, Oblate Sisters of Providence, AUND, Notre Dame.

94. Faherty, *The St. Louis Irish*, 29.

95. Sister Francis Joseph to Sister Monica, 10 September 1890, Personal Files, Sister Francis Joseph Ivory, ACSJ, St. Paul.

96. Sister St. John Fournier, in Thomas, *Footprints on the Frontier*, 53.

97. Morrow, *"Persons of Color and Religious at the Same Time,"* 172; Educational Efforts of the First Sisters of Mercy, Schools, 1856–60: St. Francis Xavier School for Girls, Night School for Colored Children, History of St. Louis Sisters, vol. 1, ARSM, St. Louis.

98. Faherty, *The St. Louis Irish*, 132.

99. Silver Jubilee of the Oblate Sisters of Providence in Saint Louis: A Brief History of the Order and the Sixteenth Annual Report of St. Frances' Orphan Asylum, Religious Orders of Women, Oblate Sisters of Providence, AUND, Notre Dame.

100. Morrow, *"Persons of Color and Religious at the Same Time,"* 36.

101. "Saint Frances Orphan Asylum, Aim and Purpose," Silver Jubilee of the Oblate Sisters of Providence in Saint Louis: A Brief History of the Order and the Sixteenth Annual Report of St. Frances' Orphan Asylum, Religious Orders of Women, Oblate Sisters of Providence, AUND, Notre Dame.

102. Ibid.

103. Ibid.

104. Knecht, *Oblate Sisters of Providence*, 22.

105. "Saint Frances Orphan Asylum, Aim and Purpose," Silver Jubilee of the Oblate Sisters of Providence in Saint Louis: A Brief History of the Order and the Sixteenth Annual Report of St. Frances' Orphan Asylum, Religious Orders of Women, Oblate Sisters of Providence, AUND, Notre Dame.

106. The St. Louis Mercy sisters had a parallel program for House of Mercy residents. Although the sisters did not visit in the placement homes, they encouraged girls with serving positions "to return frequently for advice and parental sympathy." Smith, *A Sheaf of Golden Years*, 42.

107. Souvenir Booklet, "Golden Jubilee of the Oblate Sisters of Providence in St. Louis," 27, Religious Orders of Women, Oblate Sisters of Providence, AUND, Notre Dame.

108. Knecht, *Oblate Sisters of Providence*, 44–45, 29.

109. Ibid., 47–51.

110. For details of the city council meeting, see *San Antonio Daily Express*, 4 September 1888.

111. Ibid., 18 September 1888.

112. Certainly Murphy knew that the Sisters of the Incarnate Word and the Sisters of Divine Providence made significant contributions to ethnic education. Their

work, however, usually took shape as an auxiliary to other initiatives. Sister St. Pierre to Beloved Sisters, 1 October 1883, 19 April 1884, 12 October 1884, Letters of Mother St. Pierre Cinquin, 83, 86, 105, 132, ACCVI, San Antonio; Sister Assumpta Friesenhahn, Sister Benedict Fenelon, Sister Boniface Koenig, Memoirs of Pioneer Sisters, ACDP, San Antonio.

113. M. M. Murphy to Slattery, 13 September 1890, Correspondence with Margaret Mary Murphy, AJF, Baltimore.

114. Constitution and Rule, 1896, ASHSp, San Antonio. The ecclesiastical authority by which Murphy established her congregation is not clear in community records or her biography. Turley, *Mother Margaret Mary Healy-Murphy*, 67–84. After Vatican II, the congregation name changed to the Sisters of the Holy Spirit and Mary Immaculate. The original title is used in this work.

115. Mother Margaret to Néraz, 9 March 1894, Box 17, Mother Margaret to Néraz, 12 May 1894, Box 10, ASHSp, San Antonio; Turley, *Mother Margaret Mary Healy-Murphy*, 81–87.

116. Bishop Néraz did not always interact successfully with the local congregations of women; Moore, *Through Fire and Flood*, 177–79.

117. See Annie McNally, Katie Dignan, Mary O'Brian, List, Sisters' Entry, 1893–1933, Box 23; Sister Laurence SSU to Sister Mary Immaculata Turley, Notes for the Biography of Mother Margaret Healy-Murphy; Kilroy, "History of Catholic Education of the Negro in Texas, 1886-1934," handwritten, partial copy, 71–72, Box 11, ASHSp, San Antonio.

118. Sister M. Michael, Reminiscence, Laredo, Texas, Box 4, ASHSp, San Antonio.

119. Extant letters to the Irish clergy, Box 16, Envelope 5-C and Box 17, Envelope 3-A.2, ASHSp, San Antonio.

120. Entry for Emma Short, b. 22 May 1897, entered 6 November 1919, Community Register, 1899–1947, Box 14, ASHSp, San Antonio.

121. Statement: Financial Condition of the Congregation, 24 June 1908–24 June 1911, Balance on Hand, 24 June 1908, Governance of the Congregation, 1911, Box 9, ASHSp, San Antonio.

122. Shaw to Mother Evangelist, 28 January 1915; "Items to Discuss with the Holy Ghost Sisters," n.d., handwritten on diocesan chancery stationery, Sisters of the Holy Ghost and Mary Immaculate, Religious Orders of Women, AASA, San Antonio.

123. Jeremiah Dixon A.[?] to Father Slattery, 17 October 1901, Letters between Josephites and Mother Margaret, Box 11, ASHSp, San Antonio.

124. Francis J. Tobin to Father Slattery, 10 November 1901, Letters between the Josephites and Mother Margaret, Box 11, ASHSp, San Antonio.

125. The sisters' school for girls also encountered resistance from African American Baptists in Dallas, Texas. Kilroy, "History of the Catholic Education of the Negro in Texas, 1886-1934," handwritten partial copy, 92–94, 119, Box 11, ASHSp, San Antonio.

126. Sister Evangelist, Diary, 3 March 1912, Box 7, ASHSp, San Antonio.

127. Shaw to Dyer, 16 March 1914, Sisters of the Holy Ghost and Mary Immaculate, Religious Orders of Women, AASA, San Antonio.

128. DeLeon, *They Called Them Greasers.*

129. González, "The Widowed Women of Santa Fe," 34–50.

130. There is no evidence that Mother Margaret intended to receive African American women into the congregation. She appeared to regard conversion to Catholicism the first order of business with Protestant-minded African Americans, but there is no indication she would have denied an applicant. Constitutions and Rule, 1896, Box 8, Box 23, ASHSp, San Antonio.

131. Profession registers are uneven and overlap. It appears registers were added and/or edited. Registration, 1893–1933; Community Register, 1899–1947; Profession Register, 1909–1973, Box 14; Chronological Death List, Box 23, ASHSp, San Antonio.

132. Bertha Ballesteros, perpetual vows, 24 June 1911, Community Register, 1899–1947, Box 14, ASHSp, San Antonio.

133. Other Texas sisterhoods explored vocations from Mexico. Mother St. Pierre of the Congregation of the Incarnate Word dispatched missionaries into Mexico by the mid-1880s. The sisters opened academies, encouraged students to enter the convent, and tried to restore their own health. St. Pierre to My loved Mother, 12 January 1886; S. Gabriel to Dear Father, July 1888; Sister St. Pierre to Sisters, 25 October 1888; St. Pierre to My dear child, 6 June 1889; St. Pierre to My Gabbie, 3 May 1890, Letters of Mother St. Pierre Cinquin, ACCVI, San Antonio.

134. Finnerty, Historical Report, typescript; Sister M. Michael Reminiscence, typescript, Handwritten Notes, Our Lady of Guadalupe School, Box 4, ASHSp, San Antonio.

135. Information about the Tabasco, Mexico, mission from Sister M. Vincent Murray, Reminiscence, 8 November 1978, Mexico, Short-Term Ministries, Box 5, ASHSp, San Antonio.

136. Ibid.

137. L'Academia del Espiritu Sancto, San Juan Bautista, Tabasco, Mexico, undated, Box 5, ASHSp, San Antonio.

138. Other congregations with Spanish-speaking members sought refuge or accepted placements in the Southwest, where they hoped to work among Mexican communities. The California Institute of the Sisters of the Immaculate Heart came from Olot, Spain, to Los Angeles, California, in 1871, and a separate group from the European motherhouse went to Tucson, Arizona, in 1915. Due to political events, some members of the Society of St. Teresa of Jesus left Barcelona, Spain, and relocated to San Antonio, Texas, in 1910. The Sisters, Servants of Mary were formed in Spain and by the 1900s had opened twenty-two houses in Mexico; during political unrest, the nuns traveled with U.S. Army troops from Vera Cruz, Mexico, to Galveston, Texas, settling in New Orleans, Louisiana, and Kansas City, Kansas. Mexican congregations immigrating to the United States over several years included

Carmelite Sisters of the Third Order, Daughters of the Purity of Mary, and Cordi-Marian Missionary Sisters. Dehey, *Religious Orders of Women*, 617, 859, 798, 815–17; McCarthy, *Guide to the Catholic Sisterhoods*, 21, 60, 148, 151, 259.

139. Matovina, "Enduring Communities of Faith in the Southwest," in Matovina and Poyo, *Presente!*, 45–58.

140. Treviño, *The Church in the Barrio*, 23–25.

141. Timothy M. Matovina argued that the absence of priests in the Southwest gave rise to an activist laity, including women, accustomed to taking responsibility for worship services. Matovina, "Lay Initiatives on the Texas *Frontera*," 107–20.

142. O'Brien, *Journeys*, 269–71.

143. Ibid., 280–81.

144. Valdez, *History of the Missionary Catechists of Divine Providence*, 180–81.

145. Benitia Vermeersch, 1898, Alsatian, German, and Other European Members of the Congregation, compiled April 1955, 3, ACDP, San Antonio.

146. Valdez, *History of the Missionary Catechists of Divine Providence*, 5.

147. For Our Lady of Guadalupe Church, see Treviño, *The Church in the Barrio*, 103–9.

148. Valdez, *History of the Missionary Catechists of Divine Providence*, 5–8.

149. An early history appeared to sidestep the breadth and theological importance of Sister Benitia or the Catechists. Callahan, *The History of the Sisters of Divine Providence*, 266–67. The account by Sister Mary Paul Valdez, a Cathechist, is informative and pious.

150. Callahan, *The History of the Sisters of Divine Providence*, 19–48.

151. Sister Consuelo, in Callahan, *The History of the Sisters of Divine Providence*, 53.

152. Sister Camilla Broden, Sister Brenden O'Beirne, Sister Leonide Bowling, Collected Notes, Necrology Records, ADC, St. Louis.

153. Details about the trip to Abiquiú are drawn from one twelve-page letter. Annals, Sister Evangelist to My dear Mother, 7 March 1906[?], ASBS, Bensalem.

154. The brotherhood, formally the Hermandad de Nuestro Padre Jesús Nazareno, is a subject of scholarly attention. One interpretation argues that the organization traces its roots to the early Christian missionaries and builds on themes of mysticism and social service found in medieval Franciscan life. See Steele, *Folk and Church in New Mexico*, 9. Another view holds that the Penitentes emerged out of modern circumstances that prompted Hispano action responding to various forms of dispossession. Carroll, *The Penitente Brotherhood*. In Abiquiú there were two *moradas*, apparently the result of a fracture within the brotherhood.

Chapter 8

1. Segale, *At the End of the Santa Fe Trail*, 200.

2. Ibid., 161.

3. Mannard, "The Escaped Nun Phenomenon in Antebellum America."

4. Chronicle of the Congregation of the S.S.N.D, 1833–1876, 1:26, ASSND, Milwaukee; Account of the Journey of Mary Caroline Friess, after 29 June 1859, "Mother Mary Caroline Friess," 1:11–12.

5. O'Connor, *Five Decades*, 116.

6. Oregon Chronicles, St. Mary's Academy, Portland, 21 October 1859, ASNJM, Portland.

7. Oregon Chronicles, St. Mary's Academy, Portland, 21 October–22 November 1859 (quote, 22 November), ASNJM, Portland; sisters tended to use the word "Protestant" generically to mean all non-Catholic Christians. Douglas Firth Anderson demonstrated that Anglo-Protestant identity in the West was complicated, using the term "a divided collective mind." "We Have Here a Different Civilization," 199–221 (quote on 201).

8. Oregon Chronicles, St. Mary's Academy, Portland, 18 January, 24 May 1861, ASNJM, Portland.

9. Oregon Chronicles, Sacred Heart Academy, Salem, 29 August 1863, 91, ASNJM, Portland.

10. Major N. A. Armstrong, in Buerge and Murray, *Evergreen Land*, 70.

11. Oregon Chronicles, Sacred Heart Academy, Salem, 1 May 1864, 95, ASNJM, Portland.

12. Segale, *At the End of the Santa Fe Trail*, 203–4.

13. A representative of the San Francisco archbishop, inspecting several convents, found that in one congregation, second-year novices were "sent to schools in the neighborhood to teach for a few hours, to gradually break them in to their work." J. N. [?] Vicar General to Hanna, 16 October 1917, Ursuline Sisters, Religious Orders of Women, AASF, Menlo Park. See also Sister Ambrosia Layer, Sister Antoinette Loth, Sister M. Assumpta Friesenhahn, Sister Mary Borgia, Sister Mary Chantal Bastien, Memoirs of Pioneer CDP Sisters, ACDP, San Antonio. The Sisters of the Holy Ghost were nearly denied a profession ceremony when "the night before profession of the sisters the bishop discovered that four novices had been teaching school five hours daily, five days a week." Undated, unsigned, Sisters of the Holy Ghost and Mary Immaculate, Religious Orders of Women, AASA, San Antonio.

14. Coogan, *The Price of Our Heritage*, 2:235–36.

15. Meyers, *The Education of Sisters*, 5–6.

16. Lanslots, *Handbook of Canon Law for Congregations of Women under Simple Vows*, 61–63.

17. For the Sisters of the Holy Ghost, the bishop invalidated the novitiate but allowed profession to "avoid scandal," ordering the novices to repeat the canonical year. A priest denied he pressured the superior for novices to teach. However, with fewer than two dozen in the congregation and the paucity of teachers for children of color, the sisters were caught between the demands of a local pastor and expectations of the bishop. Typescript, undated, unsigned, Sisters of the Holy Ghost and Mary Immaculate, Religious Orders of Women, AASA, San Antonio.

18. Annals, St. Mark's, 1898–1954, Kansas, typescript 1, AASC, Wichita; Sister

Gustave to Motherhouse, in Historical Sketch of the Congregation of the Sisters of Mary of the Presentation, 3:153, ASMP, Valley City.

19. Mother Caroline to the Teachers of our Day and High School, [between June 1881 and May 1889, precise date missing], "Mother Mary Caroline Friess," 1:290–91.

20. M. Caroline to Dear Dionysia, [after 5 September 1874], "Mother Mary Caroline Friess," 1:159.

21. Mother M. Marianne Haas, Circular Letters, 4, 21 January 1907, ASSND, Milwaukee.

22. Coogan, *The Price of Our Heritage*, 2:249–50, 322.

23. Mother Emily Power, Mission Letters, January 1900, January 1902, AOP, Sinsinawa; Synon, *Mother Emily of Sinsinawa*, 178. In 1893 the Sisters of St. Francis in Rochester, Minnesota, opened a school at the motherhouse, "placed under the direction of an experienced and competent teacher," and began a vacation rotation system to continue "until all have had that help they so much need," with the goal that "the sisters are better prepared to work." Hayes, "Years of Beginning," 58.

24. Kennelly, "Faculties and What They Taught," 101; Synon, *Mother Emily of Sinsinawa*, 167–68. Dominican rigor in teacher training was also demonstrated by California sisters, who in 1902 earned state accreditation for their San Rafael academy. *Dominicans of San Rafael*, 85–86.

25. Mother Emily Power, Mission Letters, 30 May 1903, AOP, Sinsinawa.

26. Coogan, *The Price of Our Heritage*, 2:256–57.

27. Mother Emily Power, Mission Letters, Undated [ca. 1904?], AOP, Sinsinawa.

28. Coogan, *The Price of Our Heritage*, 2:308.

29. For the positive and negative responses of religious and secular Catholic women to the goals of the "New Woman" in the Progressive Era, see Cummings, *New Women of the Old Faith*.

30. Hackett, *Dominican Women in Texas*, 174.

31. Ibid., 177. In 1921 Minnesota eliminated examinations, requiring that certified teachers hold a degree earned at a college or university. McDonald, *With Lamps Burning*, 189.

32. Callahan, *Mother Angelique Ayres*, 67.

33. Ibid., 68.

34. Dougherty, *Sisters of St. Joseph of Carondelet*, 78, 369; Hackett, *Dominican Women in Texas*, 176.

35. Callahan, *Mother Angelique Ayres*, 70–71.

36. Coogan, *The Price of Our Heritage*, 2:369; Gloden, *Sisters of St. Francis of the Holy Family*, 268.

37. McDonald, *With Lamps Burning*, 189–92.

38. Ibid., 190–91. For the SCL sending several nuns to Catholic University, see Sister Vincent Marie Berry (Bridget Berry), Personal File, ASCL, Leavenworth.

39. McDonald, *With Lamps Burning*, 192–93, 195, 199–200; Blatz and Zimmer, *Threads from Our Tapestry*, 46–50, 57–59, 60–61, 63–65.

40. Remarks of Francis J. Tief, in Thomas, *Footprints on the Frontier*, 267.

41. A major health epidemic that swept through a secular community often brought aid from sisters, whether they had medical training or not. See Kalmer, "Pages of Heroism: The Franciscan Sisters of Joliet," *Franciscan Herald* 16, no. 8 (August 1928): 374–78, Mother Mary Augustine Fricker Box, AOSF, Rochester; Chronicles, Notebook, 1898–1903, Notes taken Regarding the Scarlet Fever Quarantine, 17 October–8 December 1903, 1:27–42, ASCL, Leavenworth. For hospitals opened by sisters with more teacher than nurse training, see examples in Buerge and Murray, *Evergreen Land*, 81–82, 85–86; and O'Brien, *Journeys*, 142, 356–57.

42. Sister Marianna to Sister Stella, 10 May 1892, 20 May 1893, and 4, 25 January 1894; Unidentified El Paso newspaper clipping, 29 September 1897, Hotel Dieu, Correspondence, El Paso Records. Sister Mary Stella Dempsey, Personnel Files: Deceased Sisters, ADC, St. Louis.

43. Hayes, "Years of Beginning," 40–41, 48, 50–51.

44. St Mary's Alumnae Quarterly: Dedicated to William James Mayo, 6, quote on 10, The Mayos: Pioneers in Medicine Box, AOSF, Rochester.

45. Obituary, Dr. Charles H. Mayo, *Post Bulletin*, 26, 27 May 1939, The Mayos: Pioneers in Medicine Box, AOSF, Rochester.

46. Address, Dr. Will. Mayo, in Memorial of St. Mary's Hospital, 1894, pamphlet, 20, St. Mary's Hospital File, AOSF, Rochester.

47. St. Mary's Earliest Account Book, Land Acquired for and by St. Mary's Hospital, Report made by Register of Deeds, AOSF, Rochester. For an example of protracted legal negotiations that stymied the Daughters of Charity, who spent years trying to pacify a fickle benefactress and secure her funding for a sisters' residence at their hospital, see Records of St. Joseph, Missouri, St. Joseph Hospital, Correspondence, Box 2, Folders 1 and 3 (especially Folder 3), Sister Agatha to Sister M. Barbara, 24 July 1919, ADC, St. Louis.

48. In 1905 the Franciscan leaders met to "formulate a definite educational system for the community." Chapter Meetings, Minutes, 9, 15 August 1905, AOSF, Rochester.

49. Homan, "Years of Vision," 106–8.

50. Ibid., 77–78, 109–10.

51. Ibid., 113–14.

52. Although Catholic social service efforts through sisters' hospitals appeared directed mainly to German and Italian immigrants, other nationalities benefitted, as well. See Cetina, "In Times of Immigration," 86–115.

53. Chronicles, 1, 69, 71–72, 74, 78, AFSM, St. Louis; Henninger, *Sisters of Saint Mary*, 291.

54. Henninger, *Sisters of Saint Mary*, 116–17.

55. Ibid., 291.

56. Ibid., 31–32.

57. The SSM also developed an African American ministry in the 1930s. They renovated St. Mary's Infirmary as a hospital for patients and physicians with a training school for black nurses attached. In 1946 they opened a novitiate for African American women, intending to build a daughter province for women of color. With the rise

of the civil rights movement, these plans collapsed; in 1950 the novitiate closed, and the Sisters of St. Mary integrated the congregation. On 10 March 1965, one of the African American sisters was the only woman religious of color to march at Selma, Alabama, in the historic civil rights event. Henninger, *Sisters of Saint Mary*, 292, 41, 43, 45–48; Stepsis and Liptak, *Pioneer Healers*, 210.

58. For examples, see Henninger, *Sisters of Saint Mary*, 347–49, 429, 461–65; and *Historical Sketch of the Congregation of the Sisters of Mary of the Presentation*, 3:149, 153, ASMP, Valley City. The struggle to educate an entire congregation continued, with problems exacerbated by local bishops. The School Sisters of St. Francis, with a charism focused on education, encountered many stumbling blocks in their efforts to acquire degrees, even into the 1940s. Stiefermann, *Stanislaus . . . With Feet in the World*, 205–31.

59. See the educational history of Mexican American sisters in Valdez, *History of the Missionary Catechists of Divine Providence*, 120–24. In the 1940s, two Oblates of Providence registered all summer school applicants at a local Catholic college to draw attention away from the number of sisters of color coming to the campus. Author's notes.

60. Certificate of Naturalization, 9 January 1856, copy, "Mother Mary Caroline Friess," 1:59.

61. Lennon, *Milestones of Mercy*, 272.

62. Naturalization Papers, Johanna Guinaw, 24 September 1921, Mother Gertrude Guinaw Letters, AOSM, Omaha; Watson, "No Land Too Far," 27, 29.

63. Biographical sketches, Sisters Francis of Assisi O'Neil, Mary Simon Drew, Norbert Drew, Foundresses and St. Paul Sisters, typescript, and Oregon Chronicles, 2, ASNJM, Portland; McCrosson, *The Bell and the River*, 119.

64. St Joseph Hospital, Vancouver, Washington, Patient Ledger, 1858–1911, ASP, Seattle.

65. Mother Joseph to Poulin at Idaho City, 24 April 1865, Mother Joseph, Correspondence, English translations, Box 9, ASP, Seattle.

66. Mason, *History of Saint Ignatius Province*, 14–15, ASP, Seattle.

67. Oregon Chronicles, Holy Names Academy, Spokane, 3 August 1895, ASNJM, Portland.

68. Thomas, *Footprints on the Frontier*, 58–59.

69. *Records of the American Catholic Historical Society of Philadelphia* 40 (1929): 235–48.

70. Oregon Chronicles, Grand Ronde Mission, 17 April 1874, 159, ASNJM, Portland.

71. Oregon Chronicles, Sacred Heart Academy, Salem, 15 May 1872, 106, ASNJM, Portland.

72. For the life and Americanization views of John Ireland, including the way foreign-leaning congregations opposed him, see O'Connell, *John Ireland and the American Catholic Church*.

73. Oregon Chronicles, 48, 195, 244, ASNJM, Portland.

74. Dieker, *A Tree Rooted in Faith*, 97.

75. M. Caroline Friess to Louis Mission Society, April 1862, "Mother Mary Caroline Friess," 1:117.

76. Lennon, *Milestones of Mercy*, 21–22.

77. Oregon Chronicles, St. Mary's Academy, Portland, 9, 14 April 1865, ASNJM, Portland.

78. Chronicles, 1, 6 September 1901, AFSM, St. Louis.

79. Oregon Chronicles, St. Mary's Academy, Portland, 3 October 1909, ASNJM, Portland.

80. Oregon Chronicles, Holy Names Academy, Spokane, 26 April 1895, 24 April 1896, 31 March 1906, 221, 222, ASNJM, Portland.

81. Oregon Chronicles, Holy Names Academy, Spokane, 27 July 1914, 223, ASNJM, Portland.

82. Oregon Chronicles, Holy Names Academy, Seattle, 4 February 1918, 212, ASNJM, Portland.

83. James J. Conry in O'Connor, *Five Decades*, 152–53; Father Conry made these remarks in defense of closing his parish classrooms and placing students in the public school, a proposal that earned the displeasure of the archbishop.

84. Ketchum to Sister M. Angeliqua, 7 February 1912; Mother Angeliqua to Mother Aloysius, January 1912, Mother Aloysius Letters, Correspondence to and from Anadarka, AOSF, Aston.

85. Oregon Chronicles, St. James Cathedral School, Seattle, 4 November 1924, ASNJM, Portland.

86. For an example of the way a constitution evolved for a congregation, see Coogan, *The Price of Our Heritage*, 2:31–61.

87. For examples, see the 1866 removal of Mother Willibalda of the Minnesota Benedictines by Abbot Seidenbush and the 1887 questionable election of Mother Scholastica Kerst, Chronicle, 12 December 1866, 21 April 1887, AOSB, St. Joseph; and the 1886 removal of Mother St. Andrew Feltin by Bishop John C. Néraz, in Neeb, *Memoirs of Fifty Years*, 46–47.

88. Chronicle, 21 April 1887, AOSB, St. Joseph.

89. Canonical Appointment, 16 July 1889, Chapter Book, 1882–1905, AOSF, Rochester; Coogan, *The Price of Our Heritage*, 2:275.

90. For examples, see 8 August 1882; 16 July 1889; 4 August 1890; 16 July 1892; 16 July 1896; 15 July 1900; 5 July 1902; and 16 July and 9, 15 August 1905, Chapter Minutes, 1882–1905, AOSF, Rochester. See also Minutes of Chapters, 16 October 1876–3 July 1885, St. Benedict's Convent, AOSB, St. Joseph; and Matters Treated of in Chapter, loose pages, inserted in "Be It Known" Book, 15 December 1908–7 July 1991, APBVM, Fargo.

91. Thomas, *The Lord May Be in a Hurry*, 83.

92. Ibid., 202.

93. Mother de Sales Garrick to Marty, 11 March 1878, Letters: Early Foundation, APBVM, Fargo.

94. Annals, Presentation Nuns in North Dakota, 1–8, APBVM, Fargo; Kardong, *Beyond Red River*, 58–59.

95. McDonald, *With Lamps Burning*, 60.

96. *Mother Caroline and the School Sisters of Notre Dame in North America*, 1:48–49.

97. Sister M. Amadeus to Dear Mother, 29 January 1884, Miles City, Letters, January 1884–May 1884, AOSU, Toledo.

98. Sister M. Magdalene to Shaw, 13 June 1916. The sisters at Hallettsville lived through several contentious years in which a series of prickly letters, some involving enclosure, were exchanged between Sister M. Augustine and Shaw. Incarnate Word, Victoria and Shiner, [1911–12], [1914], [1915–June 1918], Religious Orders of Women, AASA, San Antonio.

99. Chronicle, (ca. 1945), typescript from handwritten account, 52–54, AOSB, St. Joseph.

100. Pastoral Visitation Report and Ursuline Monastery Votum, [ca. 1904], Ursulines, (1851, 1870–), Religious Orders of Women, AASA, San Antonio.

101. Chronicle, 23 July 1881, 62; Minutes of Chapters, 23 July 1881, AOSB, St. Joseph.

102. Chronicle, 91–93, AOSB, St. Joseph.

103. The internal process by which the Texas Dominicans decided to embrace their congregational goals with a single category membership required nearly 100 years. For an explanation of the complicated events, see Hackett, *Dominican Women in Texas*, 200–208.

104. Mother Emily Power to Father Bianchi, 12 March 1885, in O'Connor, *Five Decades*, 245.

105. Dougherty, *Sisters of St. Joseph of Carondelet*, 369, 198.

106. Mother Joanna Clark to Jandel, (ca. 1858), in O'Connor, *Five Decades*, 79.

107. For example, Dominicans in the humid Northwest used an impractical starched guimpe until 1904. Each guimpe took twenty to thirty minutes of hand pleating and one or two days to dry. Wishing to "devote this time to something more profitable," the nuns changed to a plain soft guimpe, so large it covered the habit's shoulder seams. Later the starched guimpe returned, as labors had eased and a lay sister had more laundry time. Annals, 54, 72, AOP, Edmonds.

108. Ludwig, *A Chapter of Franciscan History*, appendix B.

109. Kauffman, *Ministry and Meaning*, 181–83.

110. The Sisters of Providence at Providence Academy kept their local annals in French until 1938. Providence Academy, House Chronicles, ASP, Seattle.

111. Regulations and Conditions for the Introduction of the School Sisters d. N.D., [ca. 1874], and M. Caroline to Superior General, 26 February 1889, "Mother Mary Caroline Friess," 2:447, 536.

112. For examples, see diary entries for 23 February 1884–1 June 1885, AFSPA, La Crosse.

113. Mother Matilda to Schels, 20 August 1909, Mother M Matilda Wagner, General Correspondence, AOSF, Rochester.

114. *German English Reader for Catholic Schools*. Author's possession.

115. *A Century of Caring: Sisters of Saint Mary*, 1872–1972, 15, pamphlet, AFSM, St. Louis.

116. Hirner, *Called to Be Faithful*, 12.

117. Ibid., 14.

118. Shaw to Spetz, 17 July 1914, in Knawa, *As God Shall Ordain*, 281.

119. Sister Paul to Proper Ecclesiastical Authorities, 15 September 1904, Religious Orders of Women, Sisters of Providence, Correspondence (1852–1918), ACAS, Seattle.

120. Paul, arch. De Montreal to Ma Chere Soeur, 30 September 1904, Religious Orders of Women, Sisters of Providence, Correspondence (1852–1918), ACAS, Seattle.

121. Voth, *Green Olive Branch*, 78.

122. Kreis, *Lakotas, Black Robes, and Holy Women*, 86.

123. Mother St. Pierre to My dear Mother, unfinished letter [May 1883], Letters of Mother St. Pierre Cinquin, ACCVI, San Antonio.

124. These Christian actions led to vehement objection among non-Catholic Natives, who used their own care and prayer for the dying. Our Missions, Odanah, 166, 169, AFSPA, La Crosse.

125. Ibid.

126. Patient Ledger, St. Mary's Infirmary, 1877–89, Births, 1880–81, AFSM, St. Louis.

127. See St. Francis mission in South Dakota. It is clear the priest oversaw confession, communion, and confirmation at religious events; it is less certain who baptized perhaps as many as 2,000 Natives. Kreis, *Lakotas, Black Robes, and Holy Women*, 77–90.

128. Chronicle, 38–39, AOSB, St. Joseph.

129. Segale, *At the End of the Santa Fe Trail*, 154–55.

130. The sister said she left Virginia City in 1874, thus eliminating the superior Sister Frederica as the one charged with the duty. Annals, Daughters of Charity File, ASMM, Virginia City.

131. *Gleanings of Fifty Years*, 136.

132. Ibid., 130.

133. Bourget to the Sisters of Vancouver, 30 January 1880, Mother Joseph Collection, Correspondence, Translations, vol. 2, ASP, Seattle.

134. J. N. [?], Vicar General to Hanna, 16 October 1917, Ursuline Sisters, Religious Orders of Women, AASF, Menlo Park.

135. Ibid.

136. Annals, 105–6, 129, AOP, Edmonds.

137. Mother M. Emmanuel to O'Dea, 12 April 1923, Religious Orders of Women, Dominican Sisters of Edmonds, Correspondence, 1897–1934, vol. 1, ACAS, Seattle.

138. Buerge and Murray, *Evergreen Land*, 177–235.

Bibliography

Primary Sources

Archival Sources

Aston, Pa.
    Archives of the Sisters of St. Francis of Philadelphia
        Indian Schools
        Register, 1855–1906
        Superior Generals: Visitations to the Northwest
Austin, Tex.
    Catholic Archives of Texas
        Religious Orders of Women
Baltimore, Md.
    Archives of the Josephite Fathers
        Correspondence with Margaret Mary Murphy
Bensalem, Pa.
    Archives of the Sisters of the Blessed Sacrament
        Annals, 1894–1908
        Annals from the Missions
        Community Rules, History
        Correspondence: Contract Schools
        Drexel Files: Elizabeth and Louise
        Drexel Files: Mother M. Katharine
        Franciscan Fathers, 1909–26
        Writings, vols. 1 and 2
        Memoirs: Sister Mary Liguori
Bismarck, N.Dak.
    Archives of the Sisters of St. Benedict
        Lambron Hospital, 2 vols., 1885–97
        Ledger of Expenses, 1910–36
        Miscellaneous Papers

Mothers' Statements and Miscellaneous Reports, 1893–1934
Patients: Accounts Book, 2 vol., 1906–14
Press Clippings
St. Alexius Hospital
Boerne, Tex.
  Archives of the Sisters of St. Benedict
    Correspondence Files, 1911–15
    Journals, 1911–19
    Personnel Register
    Profession Register
Cedar Rapids, Iowa
  Archives of the Sisters of Mercy
    Customs and Minor Regulations
    History of Mercy Hospital, Kalispell, Montana
    Personal Essays of Sister M. Agatha
    Record of Assignments
    Records of Missions, 1875–1919
Dubuque, Iowa
  Archives of the Archdiocese of Dubuque
    Rev. Jean C. Perrodin Papers
  Archives of the Sisters of Charity of the Blessed Virgin Mary
    Acts of Reception, 1833–81
    Annals from the Missions
    Annals of Sister Pulcheria
    Community Register, I
    Council Meetings and Articles of Incorporation, 1864–1900
    Diary of Sister M. Crescentia Markey, 1894–1901, 1904, 1906
    Journal: Statistics I
    Letters and Decrees Register
    Record of Missions
Edmonds, Wash.
  Archives of the Sisters of St. Dominic
    Annals, 1890–1923
    Obituaries to 1948
Fargo, N.Dak.
  Archives of the Sisters of the Presentation of the Blessed Virgin Mary
    Annals, 1880–1938
    Corporation Minutes
    Letters: Early Foundations
    Major Superiors File
    Matters Treated in Chapter
    Mortgage Documents, 1904–21
    Rules and Constitution, 1881

Sacred Heart Academy
St. James Academy
Vow Register, 1859–1935
Farmington, Michigan
Archives of the Sisters of Mercy
Iowa Missions
Sisters of Mercy, Dubuque, Iowa
Through the Years
Fremont, Calif.
Archives of the Sisters of the Holy Family
Annals, 1878–1900
Foundation Day Presentation
Froebel System for Kindergarten
Letters of Sister Dolores
Profession Register, 1872–1910
Published Letters and Notices, 1860–85
Sisters of the Holy Family in the Archdiocese of San Francisco
La Crosse, Wis.
Archives of the Franciscan Sisters of Perpetual Adoration
Account Book, B, 1885–92
Corporation Records, Minutes, 1883–1959
Daily Record, St. Mary's, 1906–10
Diary, Odanah School, 1895–96
Diary, St. Rose Convent, 1883–90, 1893–1900
General Council Minutes, 1898–1926
Inheritances, 1910–34
Mission Accounts, 1886–90
Mission Directories, 1888–1969
Mother Ludovica Letters, 1877–1900
Obituaries, 1858–1921
Our Missions, 1864–1934
Personal Files
Record of Elections, 1883–1907
Register, 1853–1910
Leavenworth, Kans.
Archives of the Sisters of Charity of Leavenworth
Chronicles and Notebooks, 1898–1929
Hospital Registers
Letters, Sister M. Celestia, 1909–15
Mother Superiors' Files
Personal Files
Pioneer Sisters
Profession Register, 1873–1913

Menlo Park, Calif.
  Archives of the Archdiocese of San Francisco
    Religious Orders of Women
Milwaukee, Wis.
  Archives of the School Sisters of Notre Dame
    Candidature Records, 1881–90
    Chronicle of the Congregation, vols. 1 and 2
    Mother Generals: Papers and Circular Letters
  Archives of the School Sisters of St. Francis
    Experiences, Sister M. Emerika, 1904
    Gertrude Bush Papers
    Mother Alexia Hoell Papers
Notre Dame, Ind.
  Archives of the University of Notre Dame
    Clergy and Religious Printed Materials
    Peter A. Baart Papers
    James Gleeson Papers
    Peter Rosen Papers
    John E. Rothensteiner Papers
    Religious Orders, Women; Men
    Scrapbook, Ellen Ewing Sherman, 1879
    Scrapbooks, John J. Hogan, 1870–1913
Omaha, Neb.
  Archives of the Servants of Mary
    Letters: Vicaresses' Administrations
    Missions, 1893–
    Mother Mary Gertrude Papers
    Profession Register, 1897–1915
    Reminiscences, Pioneer Days in America
    St. Matthew's Notebook, 1891–1925
Paola, Kans.
  Archives of the Ursuline Sisters of Paola
    Financial Registers, 1896–1907
    Minutes, Corporation and Chapter Meetings, 1898–1956
    Mother Jerome Schaub Papers
    Mother M. Thomas Reichert Papers
    Record of Receptions and Professions, 1895–1954
Portland, Ore.
  Archives of the Archdiocese of Portland
    Leipzig Research Files, Individual Sisters
  Archives of the Sisters of the Holy Names of Jesus and Mary
    Excerpts from the Oregon Chronicles, 1859–1959
    Foundresses and St. Paul Sisters

Historical Sketches, Christie School
List, Sisters at St. Paul, Oregon, 1861–
Rochester, Minn.
   Archives of the Sisters of St. Francis of Rochester
      Annals, St. Mary's Hospital, 1889–1935
      Chapter Book, 1882–1905
      Chapter Minutes, 1905
      Community Register and Official Reports
      History of the Congregation File
      Mayos: Pioneers in Medicine File
      Mother M. Alfred Moes Papers
      Mother M. Augustine Fricken Files
      Mother M. Matilda Wagner Files
      Novitiate Register, 1903–15
      Obituary Notices, 1895–1938
      Receptions and Professions
      Register, First Vows, 1878–1915
      Register, Members of the Community, 1877–1975
      Register, Novices, 1891–1902
      Reminiscences, Sister Sylvester
St. Joseph, Minn.
   Archives of the Sisters of St. Benedict
      Chronicle, St. Benedict's Convent
      Entrance Records, 1888–1915
      Indian Mission Records
      Memoirs of the Missionaries, 1888–1911
      Mother Aloysia Autobiography
      Records of the Office of the Prioress
St. Louis, Mo.
   Archives of the Daughters of Charity
      Mission Records
      Necrology Records
   Archives of the Franciscan Sisters of Mary (formerly Sisters of St. Mary)
      Annual Reports, St. Mary's 1894–1928
      Chronicles, 1872–1916
      Patient Register, Mt. St. Rose Hospital, 1902–24
      Records, St. Mary's Infirmary, 1877–1912
   Archives of the Sisters of Mercy—Provincial House
      Archbishop Kenrick, Letters, 1860–87
      Chapter Meetings, 1858–1928
      Council Meetings, 1861–1918
      Early History, St. Louis
      Ledger, Finances, Mercy Home, 1912–23

Ledger, Industrial School, 1899–1944
Ledger, St. Catherine's and "The Home," 1904–9
Ledger, Sick Calls, 1904–6
Mercy Home Statistics and History, 1860–93
Mission Records
Mother Katharine Drexel, Letters, 1889–1921
Mother M. De Pazzi Bentley Papers
Sister De Pazzi Specking, Impressions of Life in Novitiate
Statistics, St. Joseph's Convent
Archives of the Sisters of Mercy—St. John's Hospital
Annual Report, 1913–14
Miscellaneous Reports and Statistics
St. John's Hospital, 1871–1936
Archives of the School Sisters of Notre Dame
Chronological Sketches, vol. 1, 1858–1916
Ledger: Applications of Priests for Sisters, 1903–43
Mission Records
Mother Generals Records
Novitiate Register, 1897–1923
Profession Contracts
Profession Register, 1898–1923
Provincials' Papers
Sisters of St. Louis, pre-1900
Sisters of Southern Province, Alphabetical Record
Archives of the Sisters of St. Joseph of Carondelet
Irish Postulants 1898
Members by Place of Birth
Mission Records
St. Paul, Minn.
Archives of the Sisters of St. Joseph of Carondelet
Indian Mission Records
Mother Superiors' Papers
Records of General Chapters, 1869, 1875, 1881, 1908
Register with Necrology, 2 vols., 1852–1949
Registers, St. Joseph's Hospital
Reminiscence, Sister Wilfrida Hogan
San Antonio, Tex.
Archives of the Archdiocese of San Antonio
Religious Orders of Women
Archives of the Sisters of Divine Providence
Canonical Visitation Journal, 1908–15
Circular Letters, Mother Mary Florence, 1890–1925
European Members of the Congregation, 1878–1955

Legal Agreements of Profession, 1901–9
Memoirs of Pioneer Sisters, 1868–1926
Table of Foundations: Opening Dates
Archives of the Sisters of Charity of the Incarnate Word
Letters, Mother Saint Pierre Cinquin, 1869–92
Archives of the Sisters of the Holy Spirit and Mary Immaculate
Bishops' Letters of Introduction, 1909–20
Clippings, Jubilee Celebrations
Contracts, 1914–15
Correspondence, 1910–13
Financial Report and Inventory, 1911–12
General Superiors—Professed Sisters, 1893–1973
Governance Files
Histories
Journals and Reminiscences
Josephite Fathers, Correspondence
Mexico: Short-Term Ministries
Mission Records
Mother Margaret Letters and Estate Papers
Personnel, 1909–11; 1893–1946
Profession Register, 1909–33
Property Records and Tax Receipts, 1884–1958
Seattle, Wash.
Archives of the Archdiocese of Seattle
Religious Women
Archives of the Sisters of Providence
Chronicles, Providence Academy, 1856–1908
Mother Joseph of the Sacred Heart Collection
Records of St. Joseph Hospital
Sacred Heart Province Collection
Sinsinawa, Wis.
Archives of the Sisters of St. Dominic
Annals, 1847–1907
Book of Foundations
Membership to 1899
Mission Records and Annals
Papers of Mother Emily Power
Reception Records, 1900–1910
St. Clara Academy Catalogues, 1867–92
Toledo, Ohio
Archives of the Ursuline Sisters
Letters, Montana Missions
Mother Amadeus Dunne File

Valley City, N.Dak.
  Archives of the Sisters of Mary of the Presentation
    Death Register, 4 vols., 1841–1980
    Historical Sketch of the Sisters of Mary of the Presentation, 3 vols.
    Mission Records
Virginia City, Nev.
  St. Mary of the Mountains Church
    Annals, Daughters of Charity, 1864–97
    Letters, Scattered, 1866–1966
    Newspaper Clippings
Washington, D.C.
  Archives of The Catholic University of America
    E. W. S. Lindesmith Papers
Wichita, Kans.
  Archives of the Adorers of the Blood of Christ
    Annals, Wichita Province, 1901–34
    Council Meetings, 1902–6
    History, St. Francis Convent, 1905–76
    Mission Files

Newspapers

Brooklyn Eagle
New York Times
Salt Lake Herald
San Antonio Daily Express
Southern Messenger
Virginia City Territorial Enterprise

Published Sources

Abbelen, P. M. *Venerable Mother Caroline: A Sketch of Her Life and Character*. St. Louis: Doubleday, 1893.
Barton, George. *Angels of the Battlefield: A History of the Labors of the Catholic Sister-hoods in the Late Civil War*. Philadelphia: Catholic Art Publishing, 1897.
Brouillet, Jean Baptiste. *Bureau of Catholic Indian Missions: Report of the Treasurer, 1876–1884*. Pamphlets in American History: Catholicism and Anti-Catholicism (microfiche, University of Notre Dame Library).
Gleanings of Fifty Years: The Sisters of the Holy Names of Jesus and Mary in the North-west, 1859–1909. Portland, Ore.: Glass and Prudhomme, 1909.
Gouverneur, Marian Campbell. *As I Remember: Recollections of American Society dur-ing the Nineteenth Century*. New York: Appleton, 1911.
Hirst, A. A. "The Memorial Idea." In *The Great American Catholic Missionary Con-*

gresses: Containing Official Procedures, edited by Francis C. Kelley, 435–36. Chicago: J. S. Hyland, 1914.

History of the Franciscan Sisters of the Province of St. Clara in the United States of America, 1873–1915. St. Louis: Herald Press, 1915.

Hoffman's Official Directory, the Catholic Directory, Almanac, and Clergy List. Milwaukee: M. H. Wiltzius, 1900.

Kenedy's Official Catholic Directory. New York: P. J. Kenedy & Sons, 1914.

Lanslots, D. I. *Handbook of Canon Law: For Congregations of Women under Simple Vows*. New York: Frederick Pustet, 1909.

Life of Mother Mary Monholland: A Pioneer Sister of the Order of Mercy. Chicago: J. S. Hyland, 1894.

McGill, Anna Blanche. *The Sisters of Charity of Nazareth, Kentucky*. New York: Encyclopedia Press, 1917.

Memorial of St. Mary's Hospital, Rochester, Minnesota. N.p., 1894.

Minogue, Anna C. *Loretto: Annals of the Century*. New York: America Press, 1912.

Neeb, Mary Joseph. *Memoirs of Fifty Years: Congregation of the Sisters of Divine Providence, San Antonio, Texas, 1846–1916*. San Antonio: Nic Tengg, 1916.

Palladino, L. B. *Indian and White in the Northwest: Or a History of Catholicity in Montana*. Baltimore: John Murphy, 1894.

Reavis, L. U. *St. Louis, the Future Great City of the World*. St. Louis: E. F. Hobart, 1873.

Report of the Commissioner of Indian Affairs. Washington, D.C.: Government Printing Office, 1864, 1867, 1894.

Russell, Matthew. *The Three Sisters of Lord Russell of Killowen and Their Convent Life*. London: Longmans Green, 1912.

Sadlier's Catholic Directory. New York: D. J. Sadlier, 1865, 1889.

Scott, Martin J. *Convent Life: The Meaning of a Religious Vocation*. New York: P. J. Kenedy & Sons, 1919.

Second Annual Report of the Board of Commissioners, 1874. Topeka: Geo. W. Martin, 1875.

Silver Jubilee of the Oblate Sisters of Providence in St. Louis, Missouri, October 1880– October 1905: A Brief History of the Order and Sixteenth Annual Report of St. Frances' Orphan Asylum. N.p., n.d.

Smith, Mary Constance. *A Sheaf of Golden Years, 1856–1906*. New York: Benziger Bros., 1906.

Talbot, Ethelbert. *My People of the Plains*. New York: Harper and Brothers, 1906.

Secondary Sources

Unpublished Sources

Allhoff, Mary Seraphia, SSND. "The School Sisters of Notre Dame in Osage County, Missouri." Master's thesis, St. Louis University, 1943.

Bonner, Dismas W., OFM. "Extern Sisters in Monasteries of Nuns." Ph.D. diss.,
The Catholic University of America, 1963.

Bower, Carita. "'The Women in White' March across the North Dakota Prairies."
Master's thesis, University of North Dakota, 1950.

Ewens, Mary, OP. "The Role of the Nun in Nineteenth-Century America." Ph.D.
diss., University of Minnesota, 1971.

Fecher, Constantine John. "The Longevity of Members of Catholic Religious
Sisterhoods." Ph.D. diss., The Catholic University of America, 1927.

Finck, M. Helena, CCVI. "The Congregation of the Sisters of Charity of the Incarnate Word, San Antonio, Texas, 1625–1924." Master's thesis, The Catholic
University of America, 1925.

Forliti, John E. "The First Thirty Years of the House of the Good Shepherd: St.
Paul, Minnesota." Master's thesis, St. Paul Seminary, 1962.

Hayes, M. Francis Ann, OSF. "Years of Beginning: A History of the Third Order
Regular of St. Francis of the Congregation of Our Lady of Lourdes, Rochester,
Minnesota, 1877–1902." Master's thesis, The Catholic University of America,
1956.

Hollermann, Ephrem, OSB. "The Reshaping of a Tradition: American Benedictine
Women, 1852–1881." Ph.D. diss., Marquette University, 1991.

Homan, M. Caedmon, OSF. "Years of Expansion, 1928–1970: A History of the
Sisters of the Third Order Regular of the Congregation of Our Lady of Lourdes,
Rochester, Minnesota." Unpublished manuscript, 1975.

———. "Years of Vision: A History of the Third Order Regular of St. Francis of
the Congregation of Our Lady of Lourdes, Rochester, Minnesota, 1903–1928."
Master's thesis, The Catholic University of America, 1956.

Mooney, Mary Margaret, PBVM. "Sisters of the Presentation of Fargo: A Centennial History, 1882–1982."

"Mother Mary Caroline Friess: Correspondence and Other Documents." 2 vols.
Edited by Barbara Brumleve SSND and Marjorie Myers SSND. Resource Publication 34, SSND Heritage Research, 1985.

Peters, Rosanna M. "History of the Poor Sisters of St. Francis Seraph of the Perpetual Adoration, 1875–1940." Ph.D. diss., Indiana University, 1944.

Watson, Adolorata, OSM. "No Land Too Far: A Short History of the Servants of
Mary in America." Unpublished manuscript, n.d.

Published Sources

Abbott, Carl. *How Cities Won the West: Four Centuries of Urban Change in Western
North America.* Albuquerque: University of New Mexico Press, 2008.

Abrams, Jeanne E. *Jewish Women Pioneering the Frontier Trail: A History in the
American West.* New York: New York University Press, 2006.

Adams, David Wallace. *Education for Extinction: American Indians and the Boarding
School Experience, 1875–1928.* Lawrence: University Press of Kansas, 1995.

Ahles, Mary Assumpta, OSF. *In the Shadow of His Wings: A History of the Franciscan Sisters*. St. Paul, Minn.: North Central Publishing, 1977.

Anderson, Douglas Firth. "'We Have Here a Different Civilization': Protestant Identity in the San Francisco Bay Area, 1906–1909." *Western Historical Quarterly* 23, no. 1 (February 1992): 199–221.

Apple, Rina D., and Janet Goldman, eds. *Mothers and Motherhood: Readings in American History*. Columbus: Ohio State University Press, 1997.

Archambault, Marie Therese, Mark G. Thiel, and Christopher Vecsey, eds. *The Crossing of Two Roads: Being Catholic and Native in the United States*. Maryknoll, N.Y.: Orbis Books, 2003.

Armitage, Susan, and Elizabeth Jameson, eds. *The Women's West*. Norman: University of Oklahoma Press, 1987.

Baldwin, Lou. *A Call to Sanctity: The Formation and Life of Mother Katharine Drexel*. Philadelphia: Kerryman Press, 1988.

Barkan, Elliott Robert, *From All Points: America's Immigrant West, 1870–1952*. Bloomington: Indiana University Press, 2007.

Barnaba, Mary, OSF. *A Diamond Crown for Christ the King: A Story of the First Franciscan Foundation in Our Country, 1855–1930*. Philadelphia: Walther, 1930.

Beckman, Peter, OSB. *Kansas Monks: A History of St. Benedict's Abbey*. Atchison: Abbey Student Press, 1957.

Berg, Carol J., OSB. "Agents of Cultural Change: The Benedictines in White Earth." *Minnesota History* 48 (Winter 1982): 158–70.

Blatz, Imogene, OSB, and Alard Zimmer OSB. *Threads from Our Tapestry: Benedictine Women in Central Minnesota*. St. Cloud, Minn.: North Star Press, 1994.

Boo, Mary Richard, OSB. *House Made of Stone: The Duluth Benedictines*. Duluth, Minn.: St. Scholastica Priory Books, 1991.

Bradley, Cyprian, OSB, and Edward Kelly DD. *History of the Diocese of Boise, 1863–1953*. Caldwell: Caxton Printers, 1953.

Bridger, Lynn. *Death's Deceiver: The Life of Joseph P. Machebeuf*. Albuquerque: University of New Mexico Press, 1997.

Bruno-Jofré, Rosa. *The Missionary Oblate Sisters: Vision and Mission*. Montreal: McGill-Queen's University Press, 2005.

Buckner, Mary, SCL. *History of the Sisters of Charity of Leavenworth, Kansas*. Kansas City, Mo.: Hudson-Kimberly, 1898; reprint edition, 1985.

Buerge, David, and Cecilia Murray, OP. *Evergreen Land: A History of the Dominican Sisters of Edmonds, Washington*. Seattle: Active Press, 1997.

Butler, Anne M. "Adapting the Vision: Caroline in 19th Century America." In *One Vision: Many Voices*, edited by Virgina Geiger SSND and Patricia McLaughlin SSND, 37–51. Lanham, Md.: University Press of America, 1993.

———. "Building Justice: Mother Margaret Murphy, Race, and Texas." *Catholic Southwest: A Journal of History and Culture* 13 (2002): 13–36.

———. *Daughters of Joy, Sisters of Misery: Prostitutes in the American West, 1865–90*. Urbana: University of Illinois Press, 1985.

———. "The Invisible Flock: Catholicism and the American West." In *Catholicism in the American West: A Rosary of Hidden Voices*, edited by Roberto R. Treviño and Richard V. Francaviglia, 14–41. College Station: Texas A&M University Press, 2007.

———. "Mission in the Mountains: The Daughters of Charity in Virginia City." In *Comstock Women: The Making of a Mining Community*, edited by Ronald M. James and Elizabeth Raymond, 142–64. Reno: University of Nevada, 1998.

———. "Mother Katharine Drexel: Spiritual Visionary for the West." In *By Grit and Grace: Eleven Women Who Shaped the American West*, edited by Glenda Riley and Richard W. Etulain, 198–220. Golden, Colo.: Fulcrum Publishing, 1997.

———. "Pioneer Sisters in a Catholic Melting Pot: Juggling Identity in the Pacific Northwest." *American Catholic Studies* 114, no. 1 (Spring 2003): 21–39.

———. "'There Are Exceptions to Every Rule': Adjusting the Boundaries— Catholic Sisters and the American West." *American Catholic Studies* 116, no. 3 (Fall 2005): 1–22.

———. "'We Had No Assistance from Anyone—Happier to Do It Alone': Montana, the Missions, and Mother Amadeus." In *Portraits of Women in the American West*, edited by Dee Garceau-Hagen, 90–119. New York: Routledge, 2005.

Callahan, Generosa, CDP. *The History of the Sisters of Divine Providence: San Antonio, Texas*. Milwaukee: Bruce Press, 1955.

———. *Mother Angelique Ayres: Dreamer and Builder of Our Lady of the Lake University*. Austin: Jenkins Publishing, Pemberton Press, 1981.

Carriker, Robert C. *Father Peter John De Smet: Jesuit in the West*. Norman: University of Oklahoma Press, 1995.

Carroll, Michael P. *The Penitente Brotherhood: Patriarchy and Hispanic Catholicism*. Baltimore: Johns Hopkins University Press, 2002.

Cetina, Judith G. "In Times of Immigration." In *Pioneer Healers: The History of Women Religious in American Health Care*, edited by Ursula Stepsis CSA and Dolores Liptak RSM, 86–117. New York: Crossroad, 1989.

Chan, Scheng. Douglas Henry Daniels, Mario T. Garcia, and Terry Wilson, eds. *Peoples of Color in the American West*. Lexington, Ky.: D. C. Heath, 1994.

Child, Brenda J. *Boarding School Seasons: American Indian Families, 1900–1940*. Lincoln: University of Nebraska Press, 1998.

Clark, Emily. *Mistresses without Masters: The New Orleans Ursulines and the Development of a New World Society, 1727–1834*. Chapel Hill: University of North Carolina Press, 2007.

———, ed. *Voices from an Early American Convent: Marie Madeleine Hachard and the New Orleans Ursulines, 1727–1760*. Baton Rouge: Louisiana State University Press, 2007.

Coburn, Carol K., and Martha Smith. *Spirited Lives: How Nuns Shaped Catholic Culture and American Life, 1836–1920*. Chapel Hill: University of North Carolina Press, 1999.

Code, Joseph R. *Great American Foundresses*. New York: Macmillan, 1929.

Coogan, Jane M., BVM. *The Price of Our Heritage: The History of the Sisters of Charity of the BVM, 1869–1920*. 2 vols. Dubuque: Mt. Carmel Press, 1978; 1977 Special BVM Edition.

Cordier, Mary Hurlbut. *Schoolwomen of the Prairies and Plains: Personal Narratives from Iowa, Kansas, and Nebraska, 1860s–1920s*. Albuquerque: University of New Mexico Press, 1992.

Cott, Nancy. "Giving Character to Our Whole Civil Polity: Marriage and the Late Nineteenth Century." In *U.S. History as Women's History*, edited by Linda K. Kerber, Alice Kessler Harris, and Kathryn Kish Sklar, 107–21. Chapel Hill: University of North Carolina Press, 1995.

Cummings, Kathleen Sprows. *New Women of the Old Faith: Gender and American Catholicism in the Progressive Era*. Chapel Hill: University of North Carolina Press, 2009.

Davis, Cyprian, OSB, and Jamie Phelps OB, eds. *"Stamped with the Image of God": African Americans as God's Image in Black*. Maryknoll, N.Y.: Orbis Books, 2003.

Dehey, Elinor Tong. *Religious Orders of Women in the United States: Catholic, Accounts of Their Origins, Works, and Most Important Institutions, Interwoven with Histories of Many Famous Foundresses*. Hammond, Ind.: W. B. Conkey, 1930; reprint edition, St. Athanasius Press, n.d.

DeLeon, Arnoldo. *They Called Them Greasers: Anglo Attitudes toward Mexicans in Texas, 1821–1900*. Austin: University of Texas Press, 1983.

Deverell, William, ed. *A Companion to the American West*. Malden, Mass.: Blackwell Publishing, 2004.

Dickson, Lynda F. "African American Women's Clubs in Denver, 1890s–1920s." In *Peoples of Color in the American West*, edited by Scheng Chan, Douglas Henry Daniels, Mario T. Garcia, and Terry Wilson, 224–34. Lexington, Ky.: D. C. Heath, 1994.

Dieker, Alberta, OSB. *A Tree Rooted in Faith: A History of the Queen of Angels Monastery*. Eugene, Ore.: Wipf & Stock, 2007.

Dominicans of San Rafael: First Chapters: The Dominican Congregation of the Holy Name of Jesus in California. San Rafael, Calif.: Dominican Convent of San Rafael, 1941.

Dougherty, Dolorita Marie, CSJ, Helen Angela Hurley CSJ, Emily Joseph Daly CSJ, and others. *Sisters of St. Joseph of Carondelet*. St. Louis: B. Herder, 1966.

Doyle, Mary Ellen, SCN. *Pioneer Spirit: Catherine Spalding, Sister of Charity of Nazareth*. Lexington: University Press of Kentucky, 2006.

DuBois, Ellen Carol, and Vicki L. Ruiz. *Unequal Sisters: A Multi-Cultural Reader in U.S. Women's History*. New York: Routledge, 1990.

Duffy, Consuela Marie, SBS. *Katharine Drexel: A Biography*. Bensalem: Mother Katharine Drexel Guild, 1966.

Duratschek, Claudia, OSB. *Under the Shadow of His Wings: History of the Sacred Heart Convent of Benedictine Sisters, Yankton, South Dakota, 1880–1970*. Aberdeen, S.Dak.: North Plains Press, 1971.

Dwyer, John T. *Condemned to the Mines: The Life of Eugene O'Connell, 1815–1891, Pioneer Bishop of Northern California and Nevada.* New York: Vantage Press, 1976.

Engh, Michael E., SJ. *Frontier Faiths: Church, Temple, and Synagogue in Los Angeles, 1846–1888.* Albuquerque: University of New Mexico Press, 1992.

———. "The Pacific Slope—'When Others Rushed In.'" In *The Frontiers and Catholic Identities*, edited by Anne M. Butler, Michael E. Engh SJ, and Thomas W. Spalding CFX, 143–45. Maryknoll, N.Y.: Orbis Books, 1999.

Faherty, William Barnaby, SJ. *The St. Louis German Catholics.* St. Louis: Reedy Press, 2004.

———. *The St. Louis Irish: An Unmatched Celtic Community.* St. Louis: Missouri Historical Society Press, 2001.

Foley, Thomas W. *Father Francis M. Craft: Missionary to the Sioux.* Lincoln: University of Nebraska Press, 2002.

Fossey, Richard, and Stephanie Morris. "St. Katharine Drexel and St. Patrick's Mission to the Indians of the Southern Plains: A Study in Saintly Administration." *Catholic Southwest: A Journal of History and Culture* 18 (2007): 61–84.

Franks, Karen Marie, OP, ed. *Strength of Our Roots, Faith in Our Vision: Brief History and Biographies, Dominican Sisters of San Rafael, 1850–2000.* San Rafael, Calif.: Dominican Sisters, 2000.

Galvin, M. Camillus, PBVM. *From Acorn to Oak: A Study of Presentation Foundations, 1775–1968.* Fargo, N.Dak.: Sisters of the Presentation, 1969.

Garceau-Hagen, Dee, ed. *Portraits of Women in the American West.* New York: Routledge, 2005.

George, Mary Louis, OSB. *Mother Paula O'Reilly OSB: Foundress of the Benedictine Sisters of Oklahoma.* Tulsa: private printing, 1985.

Geser, Fintan, OSB. *The Canon Law Governing Communities of Sisters.* St. Louis: B. Herder Book, 1939.

Giago, Tim, and Denise Giago. *Children Left Behind: The Dark Legacy of Indian Mission Boarding Schools.* Santa Fe: Clear Light Publishing, 2006.

Gilmore, Julia, SCL, *"Come North!": The Life Story of Mother Xavier Ross, Valiant Pioneer and Foundress of the Sisters of Charity of Leavenworth.* New York: McMullen Books, 1951.

Girgen, M. Incarnata, OSB. *Behind the Beginnings: Benedictine Women in America.* St. Paul, Minn.: North Central Publishing, 1981.

Gloden, M. Cortona. *Sisters of St. Francis of the Holy Family.* St. Louis: B. Herder Book, 1928.

González, Deena J. "The Widowed Women of Santa Fe: Assessments on the Lives of an Unmarried Population, 1850–1880." In *Unequal Sisters: A Multi-Cultural Reader in U.S. Women's History*, edited by Ellen Carol DuBois and Vicki L. Ruiz, 34–50. New York: Routledge, 1990.

Gorman, Thomas K., DD. *Seventy-Five Years of Catholic Life in Nevada.* Reno: Reno Journal Publishing, 1935.

Hackett, Sheila, OP. *Dominican Women in Texas: From Ohio to Galveston and Beyond*. Houston: D. Armstrong, 1986.

Heaton, John W. *The Shoshone-Bannocks: Culture and Commerce at Fort Hall, 1870–1940*. Lawrence: University Press of Kansas, 2005.

Hegarty, Mary Loyola, CCVI. *Serving with Gladness: The Origin and History of the Congregation of the Incarnate Word, Houston, Texas*. Milwaukee: Bruce Publishing, 1967.

Henninger, Mary Gabriel, SSM. *The Sisters of Saint Mary and Their Healing Mission*. St. Louis: Sisters of St. Mary, 1979.

Herron, Mary Eulalia, RSM. *The Sisters of Mercy in the United States, 1843–1928*. New York: Macmillan, 1929.

Hockle, Henrietta, OSB. *On High Ground: A History of the Olivetan Benedictine Sisters, Jonesboro, Arkansas, 1887–2003*. Jonesboro, Ark.: Pinpoint Printing, 2004.

Holland, Mary Ildephonse, RSM. *Lengthened Shadows: An Illustrated History of the Sisters of Mercy of Cedar Rapids, Iowa*. New York: Bookman Associates, 1952.

Howes, Edward H. "Three Weeks That Shook the Nation and California's Capital." *California Historian* (Spring 2002).

Hoy, Suellen. "The Journey Out: The Recruitment and Emigration of Irish Religious Women to the United States, 1812–1914." *Journal of Women's History* 6, no. 4 (Winter/Spring 1995): 65–98.

Hudson, Winthrop S. *Religion in America*. 2nd ed. New York: Charles Scribner's Sons, 1973.

Igler, David. "Engineering the Elephant: Industrialism and the Environment in the Greater West." In *A Companion to the American West*, edited by William Deverell, 93–111. Malden, Mass.: Blackwell Publishing, 2004.

In the Early Days of the Sisters of Charity of the Blessed Virgin Mary. N.p., 1911; 3rd ed., 1943.

In Harvest Fields, by Sunset Shores: The Work of the Sisters of Notre Dame on the Pacific Coast, 1851–1926. San Francisco: Gilmartin, 1926.

James, Ronald M., and Elizabeth Raymond, eds. *Comstock Women: The Making of a Mining Community*. Reno: University of Nevada Press, 1998.

Jolly, Ellen Ryan. *Nuns of the Battlefield*. 4th ed. Providence, R.I.: Providence Visitor Press, 1930.

Kane, Paula, James Kenneally, and Karen Kennelly, eds. *Gender Identities in American Catholicism*. Maryknoll, N.Y.: Orbis Books, 2001.

Kardong, Terrence G. *Beyond Red River: The Diocese of Fargo, One Hundred Years, 1889–1989*. Fargo, N.Dak.: Richtman's Printing, 1989.

———. *Prairie Church: The Diocese of Bismarck, 1910–1985*. Richardton, N.Dak.: Assumption Abbey Press, 1985.

Karolevitz, Robert F. *With Faith, Hope, and Tenacity: The First One Hundred Years of the Catholic Diocese of Sioux Falls, 1889–1989*. Mission Hill, S.Dak.: Dakota Homestead Publishers, 1989.

Kaufman, Polly Welts. *Women Teachers on the Frontier*. New Haven: Yale University Press, 1984.

Kauffmann, Christopher J. *Ministry and Meaning: A Religious History of Catholic Health Care in the United States*. New York: Crossroad, 1995.

———, gen. ed. *American Catholic Identities: A Documentary History*. 12 vols. Maryknoll, N.Y.: Orbis Books, 1999–2003.

Kavanagh, D. J., SJ. *The Sisters of the Holy Family of San Francisco: A Sketch of Their First Fifty Years, 1872–1922*. San Francisco: Gilmartin, 1922.

Kelley, Francis C., ed. *The Great American Catholic Missionary Congresses: Containing Official Procedures*. Chicago: J. S. Hyland, 1914.

Kennelly, Karen. "Faculties and What They Taught." In *Catholic Women's Colleges in America*, edited by Tracy Schier and Cynthia Russett, 98–122. Baltimore: Johns Hopkins University Press, 2002.

Kerber, Linda K., Alice Kessler Harris, and Kathryn Kish Sklar, eds. *U.S. History as Women's History*. Chapel Hill: University of North Carolina Press, 1995.

Kerstetter, Todd. "Spin Doctors at Santee: Missionaries and the Dakota-Language Reporting of the Ghost Dance and Wounded Knee." *Western Historical Quarterly* 28, no. 1 (Spring 1997): 45–67.

Kohler, Hortense Mary, OP. *Rooted in Hope: The Story of the Dominican Sisters of Racine, Wisconsin*. Milwaukee: Bruce Publishing, 1962.

Klingle, Matthew. *Emerald City: An Environmental History of Seattle*. New Haven: Yale University Press, 2007.

Knawa, Anne Marie, OSF. *As God Shall Ordain: A History of the Franciscan Sisters of Chicago, 1894–1987*. Lemont, Ill.: Worzalla Publishing, 1989.

Knecht, Sharon C. *Oblate Sisters of Providence: A Pictorial History*. Virginia Beach, Va.: Donning, 2007.

Kreis, Karl Markus, ed. *Lakotas, Black Robes, and Holy Women: German Reports from the Indian Missions in South Dakota, 1886–1900*. Trans. Corinne Dally-Starna. Lincoln: University of Nebraska Press, 2007.

Kuhns, Elizabeth. *The Habit: A History of the Clothing of Catholic Nuns*. New York: Doubleday, 2003.

Lapomarda, Vincent A., SJ. "St. Mary's in the Mountains: The Cradle of Catholicity in Western Nevada." *Nevada Historical Society Quarterly* 35 (Spring 1992): 58–62.

Lawrence, C. H. *Medieval Monasticism: Forms of Religious Life in Western Europe in the Middle Ages*. London: Longman, 1984; 2nd ed., 1989.

Lennon, Mary Isidore, RSM. *Milestones of Mercy: The Story of the Sisters of Mercy in St. Louis, 1856–1956*. Milwaukee: Bruce Publishing, 1957.

Limerick, Patricia Nelson. *Legacy of Conquest: The Unbroken Past of the American West*. New York: W. W. Norton, 1987.

Ludwig, M. Mileta, FSPA. *A Chapter of Franciscan History: The Sisters of the Third Order of Saint Francis of Perpetual Adoration, 1849–1949*. New York: Bookman Associates, 1950.

Lynch, Claire, OSB. *The Leaven*. St. Paul, Minn.: North Central Publishing, 1980.

Mack, John. "Osage Mission: The Story of Catholic Missionary Work in Southeast Kansas." *Catholic Historical Review* 96, no. 2 (April 2010): 262–81.

Maher, Mary Denis. *To Bind up the Wounds: Catholic Sisters in the U.S. Civil War*. Baton Rouge: Louisiana State University Press, 1989.

Mahoney, Irene, OSU. *Lady Blackrobes: Missionaries in the Heart of Indian Country*. Golden, Colo.: Fulcrum Publishing, 2006.

Mannard, Joseph G. "'What Has Become of Olevia Neal': The Escaped Nun Phenomenon in Antebellum America." *Maryland Historical Magazine* 105 (Winter 2010): 348–67.

Marsh, Margaret. "Motherhood Denied: Women and Infertility in Historical Perspective." In *Mothers and Motherhood: Readings in American History*, edited by Rina D. Apple and Janet Goldman, 216–41. Columbus: Ohio State University Press, 1997.

Matovina, Timothy M. "Lay Initiatives on the Texas *Frontera*, 1830–1860." *U.S. Catholic Historian* 12 (Fall 1994): 107–20.

Matovina, Timothy M., and Gerald E. Poyo, eds. *Presente! U.S. Latino Catholics from Colonial Origins to the Present*. Maryknoll, N.Y.: Orbis Books, 2000.

McBride, Genevieve, OSU. *The Bird Tail*. New York: Vantage Press, 1974.

McCarthy, Thomas P., CSV. *Guide to the Catholic Sisterhoods in the United States*. Washington, D.C.: The Catholic University of America, 1952.

McCrosson, Mary of the Blessed Sacrament, SP. *The Bell and the River*. Seattle: Heath Printers, 1986.

McDonald, M. Grace, OSB. *With Lamps Burning*. St. Joseph, Minn.: St. Benedict's Priory Press, 1957.

McGloin, John B., SJ. *California's First Archbishop: The Life of Joseph Sadoc Alemany OP, 1814–1888*. New York: Herder and Herder, 1966.

McKevitt, Gerald. *Brokers of Culture: Italian Jesuits in the American West*. Stanford: Stanford University Press, 2007.

McNamara, Jo Ann Kay. *Sisters in Arms: Catholic Nuns through Two Millenia*. Cambridge, Mass.: Harvard University Press, 1996.

McNamee, M. Dominica, SNDdeN. *Willamette Interlude*. Palo Alto, Calif.: Pacific Books, 1959.

McNeil, Teresa Baksh. "St. Anthony's Indian School in San Diego, 1886–1907." *Journal of San Diego History* 34, no. 3 (Summer 1988): 187–200.

Metz, Judith, SC. "In Times of War." In *Pioneer Healers: The History of Women Religious in American Health Care*, edited by Ursula Stepsis CSA and Dolores Liptak RSM, 39–68. New York: Crossroad, 1989.

Meyers, Bertrande. *The Education of Sisters: A Plan for Integrating the Religious, Social, Cultural, and Professional Training of Sisters*. New York: Sheed and Ward, 1941.

Mihesuah, Devon A. *Cultivating the Rosebuds: The Education of Women at the Cherokee Female Seminary, 1851–1909*. Urbana: University of Illinois Press, 1993.

Milner, Clyde A., II. "National Initiatives." In *The Oxford History of the American West*, edited by Clyde A. Milner II, Carol A. O'Connor, and Martha A. Sandweiss, 155–93. New York: Oxford University Press, 1994.

Moore, James Talmadge. *Acts of Faith: The Catholic Church in Texas, 1900–1950*. College Station: Texas A&M University Press, 2002.

———. *Through Fire and Flood: The Catholic Church in Frontier Texas, 1836–1900*. College Station: Texas A&M University Press, 1992.

Morris, Charles R. *American Catholic: The Saints and Sinners Who Built America's Most Powerful Church*. New York: Vintage Books, 1997.

Morrow, Diane Batts. *"Persons of Color and Religious at the Same Time": The Oblate Sisters of Providence*. Chapel Hill: University of North Carolina Press, 2002.

Mother Caroline and the School Sisters of Notre Dame in North America. 2 vols. St. Louis: Woodward & Tiernan, 1928.

Mullay, Camilla, OP. *A Place of Springs: A History of the Dominican Sisters of the Springs, 1830–1970*. Columbus, Ohio: Dominican Sisters of St. Mary, 2005.

Murray, Mary Cecilia, OP. *Other Waters: A History of the Dominican Sisters of Newburgh, New York*. Old Brookville, N.Y.: Brookville Books, 1993.

Myres, Sandra. *Westering Women and the Frontier Experience, 1800–1915*. Albuquerque: University of New Mexico Press, 1982.

Naber, Vera M., CSA. *With All Devotedness: Chronicles of the Sisters of St. Agnes, Fond du Lac, Wisconsin*. New York: P. J. Kenedy & Sons, 1959.

Not with Silver or Gold: A History of the Sisters of the Congregation of the Precious Blood, Dayton, Ohio, 1834–1944. Dayton: Sisters of the Precious Blood, 1945.

Nugent, Walter. *Into the West: The Story of Its People*. New York: Alfred A. Knopf, 1999.

Oates, Mary J. "Sisterhoods and Catholic Higher Education." In *Catholic Women's Colleges in America*, edited by Tracy Schier and Cynthia Russett, 161–94. Baltimore: Johns Hopkins University Press, 2002.

O'Brien, Kathleen, RSM. *Journeys: A Pre-Amalgamation History of the Sisters of Mercy, Omaha Province*. Omaha: n.p., 1987.

O'Connell, Marvin R. *John Ireland and the American Catholic Church*. St. Paul: Minnesota Historical Society, 1988.

O'Connor, M. Paschala, OP. *Five Decades: History of the Congregation of the Most Holy Rosary of Sinsinawa, Wisconsin, 1849–1899*. Sinsinawa: Sinsinawa Press, 1954.

Oetgen, Jerome. *An American Abbott: Boniface Wimmer, 1809–1887*. Latrobe, Pa., Archabbey Press, 1976.

O'Grady, John. *Catholic Charities in the United States: History and Problems*. Washington, D.C.: Ransdell, 1930.

Ostler, Jeffrey. "Empire and Liberty: Contradictions and Conflicts in Nineteenth-Century Western Political History." In *A Companion to the American West*, edited by William Deverell, 200–218. Malden, Mass.: Blackwell Publishing, 2004.

Paavola, Richard C., FACHE. *Upon the Rock: A Centennial History of the Sisters of the Presentation of the BVM, Aberdeen, South Dakota, 1886–1986*. N.p., [1987].

Paddison, Joshua. "Anti-Catholicism and Race in Post–Civil War San Francisco." *Pacific Historical Review* 78, no. 4 (November 2009): 505–44.

Passet, Joanne E. *Cultural Crusaders: Women Librarians in the American West, 1900–1917*. Albuquerque: University of New Mexico Press, 1994.

Peterson, Jacqueline. "Sacred Encounters in the Northwest: A Persistent Dialogue." *U.S. Catholic Historian* 12 (Fall 1994): 37–48.

Peterson, Susan C., and Courtney Ann Vaughn-Roberson. *Women with Vision: The Presentation Sisters of South Dakota, 1880–1995*. Urbana: University of Illinois Press, 1988.

"Pioneer Capuchin Letters." *Franciscan Studies* 16 (January 1936).

Polling-Kempes, Lesley. *The Harvey Girls: Women Who Opened the West*. New York: Paragon Books, 1989.

Provenzano, Philippa, trans. *To the Ends of the Earth: Missionary Travels of Frances X. Cabrini*. New York: Center for Migration Studies, 2001.

Renner, Louis L., SJ. *Alaskana Catholica: A History of the Catholic Church in Alaska*. Spokane, Wash.: Arthur H. Clark, 2005.

Riley, Glenda. *Frontierswomen: The Iowa Experience*. Ames, Iowa: Iowa State University Press, 1981.

———. *A Place to Grow: Women in the American West*. Arlington Heights, Ill.: Harlan Davidson, 1992.

———. *Women and Indians on the Frontier, 1825–1915*. Albuquerque: University of New Mexico Press, 1984.

Riley, Glenda, and Richard W. Etulain. *By Grit and Grace: Eleven Women Who Shaped the American West*. Golden, Colo.: Fulcrum Publishing, 1997.

Rocca, Fernando Della. *Manual of Canon Law*. Trans. Anselm Thatcher OSB. Milwaukee: Bruce Publishing, 1959.

Rohrbough, Malcolm J. *Days of Gold: The California Gold Rush and the American Nation*. Berkeley: University of California Press, 1997.

Schier, Tracy, and Cynthia Russett, eds. *Catholic Women's Colleges in America*. Baltimore: Johns Hopkins University Press, 2002.

Schlissel, Lillian. *Women's Diaries of the Westward Journey*. New York: Schocken Books, 2004.

Schoenberg, Wilfred P., SJ. *These Valiant Women: History of the Sisters of St. Mary of Oregon, 1886–1986*. Portland, Ore.: Western Lithograph, 1986.

Schuster, M. Faith, OSB. *The Meaning of the Mountain: A History of the First Century at Mount St. Scholastica*. St. Paul, Minn.: North Central Publishing, 1963.

Segale, Blandina. *At the End of the Santa Fe Trail*. Columbus: Columbus Press, 1932; reprint edition, University of New Mexico Press, 1999.

Simmons, Christina. "Companionate Marriage and the Lesbian Threat." In *Women and Power in American History: A Reader from 1870*, vol. 2, edited by Kathryn Kish Sklar and Thomas Dublin, 183–94. Englewood Cliffs, N.J.: Prentice Hall, 1991.

"Sisters of the Third Order of St. Francis, 1855-1928." *Records of the American Catho-*

lic Historical Society of Philadelphia 40 (1929): 38–64, 123–55, 226–48, 347–81; 41 (1930): 27–68.

Steele, Thomas J., SJ. "*Confradia.*" In *Folk and Church in New Mexico*, 1–20. Colorado Springs, Colo.: Hulbert Center Press, 1993.

Stepsis, Ursula, CSA, and Dolores Liptak RSM. *Pioneer Healers: The History of Women Religious in American Health Care.* New York: Crossroad, 1989.

Stewart, George C. *Marvels of Charity: History of American Sisters and Nuns.* Huntington, Ind.: *Our Sunday Visitor* Publishing Division, 1994.

Stiefermann, Barbandie, OSF. *Stanislaus . . . with Feet in the World: Historical Biography of Mother M. Stanislaus Hegner, Superior General of the School Sisters of St. Francis, 1930–1942.* Baltimore: Gateway Press, 1990.

Supan, Marita-Constance, IHM. "Dangerous Memory: Mother M. Theresa Maxis Duchemin and the Michigan Congregation of the Sisters IHM." In *Building Sisterhood: A Feminist History of the Sisters, Servants of the Immaculate Heart of Mary*, by Sisters, Servants of the Immaculate Heart of Mary, 31–67. Syracuse: Syracuse University Press, 1997.

Synon, Mary, OP. *Mother Emily of Sinsinawa: American Pioneer.* Milwaukee: Bruce, 1951.

Thomas, M. Evangeline. *Footprints on the Frontier: A History of the Sisters of St. Joseph, Concordia, Kansas* Westminster, Md.: Newman Press, 1948.

Thomas, Mary, OP. *The Lord May Be in a Hurry: The Congregation of Dominican Sisters of St. Catherine of Siena of Kenosha, Wisconsin.* Milwaukee: Bruce Publishing, 1967.

Thompson, Margaret Susan. "The Context." In *Building Sisterhood: A Feminist History of the Sisters, Servants of the Immaculate Heart of Mary*, by Sisters, Servants of the Immaculate Heart of Mary, 25–28. Syracuse: Syracuse University Press, 1997.

———. "Discovering Foremothers: Sisters, Society, and the American Catholic Experience." *U.S. Catholic Historian* 5 (Summer/Fall 1986): 273–90.

Thrush, Coll. *Native Seattle: Histories from the Crossing-Over Place.* Seattle: University of Washington Press, 2007.

Thurston, Herbert, and Thomas Meehan. "Catholic Directories." *Catholic Encyclopedia*, 5. New York: Appleton, 1909.

Treviño, Roberto R. *The Church in the Barrio: Mexican American Ethno-Catholicism in Houston.* Chapel Hill: University of North Carolina Press, 2006.

Treviño, Roberto R., and Richard V. Francaviglia, eds. *Catholicism in the American West: A Rosary of Hidden Voices.* College Station: Texas A&M University Press, 2007.

Turbin, Carole. "'And Are We Nothing but Women': Irish Working Women in Troy." In *Women and Power in American History: A Reader from 1870*, vol. 2, edited by Kathryn Kish Sklar and Thomas Dublin, 25–40. Englewood Cliffs, N.J.: Prentice Hall, 1991.

Turley, Mary Immaculata, SHG. *Mother Margaret Mary Healy-Murphy: A Biography.* San Antonio: Naylor, 1969.

Valdez, Mary Paul, MCDP. *History of the Missionary Catechists of Divine Providence*. San Antonio: Archdiocese of San Antonio, 1978.

Vecsey, Christopher. *Traditional Ojibwa Religion and Its Historical Changes*. Philadelphia: American Philosophical Society, 1983; 4th printing, 1993.

Voth, M. Agnes, OSB. *Green Olive Branch*. Chicago: Franciscan Herald Press, 1973.

Weber, David J. *The Spanish Frontier in North America*. New Haven: Yale University Press, 1992.

Weisenburger, Francis P. "God and Man in a Secular City: The Church in Virginia City, Nevada." *Nevada Historical Society Quarterly* 24 (Summer 1971): 3–23.

West, Elliott. "Called Out People: The Cheyennes and the Central Plains." *Montana: The Magazine of Western History* 48, no. 2 (Summer 1998): 2–15.

White, Richard. *"It's Your Misfortune and None of My Own": A New History of the American West*. Norman: University of Oklahoma Press, 1991.

Wilken, Robert L. *Anselm Weber OFM: Missionary to the Navaho, 1898–1921*. Milwaukee: Bruce Publishing, 1955.

Woody, Thomas A. *A History of Women's Education in the United States*. 2 vols. Reprint edition. New York: Octagon Press, 1966.

Index

Page numbers in italics indicate illustrations

Alexia Kerst (OSB). *See* Kerst, Alexia

Alfred Moes (OSF). *See* Moes, Alfred

Allen, Marie Tso, 228

Aloysia Bath (OSB). *See* Bath, Aloysia

Aloysius Lonergan (RSM). *See* Lonergan, Aloysius

Amadeus Dunne (OSU). *See* Dunne, Amadeus

Ambition, in power struggles, 165–67, 183

Americanization: and foreign languages, 294–96; of immigrant nuns, 283–90; of Native Americans, 243, 245

Anderson, Douglas Firth, 366 (n. 7)

Angeliqua, Mary (OSF), 287

Angelique Ayres (CDP). *See* Ayres, Angelique

Annals of Our Lady of the Angels (magazine), 104

Annette Martin (BVM). *See* Martin, Annette

Anselma Felber, Mary (OSB). *See* Felber, Mary Anselma

Anti-Catholicism, 257–58, 269–71

Antone, Juanita, 241–42

Arapahos, 211, 239

Arbor Day, 287

Archbishop, definition of, 315. *See also specific bishops*

Architecture, of monasteries, 3–4

Archivists, record-keeping practices of, xiv–xvii. *See also* Records

Arizona: finances of nuns in, 136, 137; Sisters of St. Joseph of Carondelet in, 44, 51–52, 76–77, 136, 137; travels of nuns to, 44, 51–52, 76–77

Armer, Mary Dolores (Elizabeth) (SHF), 104–6, 335 (n. 92), 336 (n. 101)

Army, U.S., African Americans in, 246–47

Art: cross-cultural, *115*; financial contributions of nuns from, 144–45

ASC. *See* Adorers of the Blood of Christ

Ascetics, desert, 2–3

As God Shall Ordain (Knawa), 5

Assiniboine, 163

Austin (Texas), Sisters of the Holy Cross in, 86–87

Autonomy: financial, 121, 150; in travels, 46–47, 74

Ayres, Angelique (CDP), 34–35

Bagot, Marie Agnes (Victorine) (SMP), 15

Baker City (Oregon), travels of Sisters of St. Francis in, 73

Ballesteros, Michael (SHSp), 257, 258

Baltimore (Maryland), origins of Oblate Sisters of Providence in, 247

Baptism, 297, 372 (n. 127)

Baptista Bowen (PBVM). *See* Bowen, Baptista

Baptist Meyers, Mary (RSM). *See* Meyers, Mary Baptist

Baptist Russell (RSM). *See* Russell, Baptist

Barnabas Siebenhor (CDP). *See* Siebenhor, Barnabas

Bath, Aloysia (OSB), 131

Bavaria, immigration of nuns from, 14, 119–20

BCIM. *See* Bureau of Catholic Indian Missions

Beauty, of West: nuns' appreciation of, 56–59

Begging tours: challenges of, 146–48, 344 (n. 114); definition of, 315; financial contributions through, 146–48; in logging camps, 65–66, 329 (n. 75); nuns influenced by experience of, 71

Beguines, 82

Benedicta Riepp (OSB). *See* Riepp, Benedicta

Benedictine Sisters (OSB): Americanization of, 288; cross-community relationships of, 49; expansion of mission work of, 88–91; finances of vs. Benedictine men, 120; health-care work of, 91–93, 113, 139, 333 (nn. 46, 51), 342 (n. 79); in higher education, 276–77; immigration of, 1, 18; innovations in work of, 104; legal protections for finances of, 130–31; Native American missions of, 109–13, 200, 234, 238; personal wealth in, 121–23, 338 (n. 22); power struggles within, 180–83, 184, 189; shifting traditions in, 291, 292–93; social observations of, 64; spiritual rituals performed by, 297–98; travels of, 59–60; young age of, 24

Benedictine Sisters of Perpetual Adoration (OSB), immigration of, 14–15

Benediction, definition of, 315

Benedict of Nursia, 3

Benicia (California), power struggles of Dominican Sisters in, 155–57

Benitia Vermeersch, Mary (CDP). *See* Vermeersch, Mary Benitia

Bentley, Mary Magdalen de Pazzi (RSM), 168–69, 283, 286, 348 (n. 61)

Berger, Mary Odilia (SSM): immigration of, 14, 15; nursing work under, 96–100; in professionalization of nurses, 281

Biracial children, 222–23

Bishop(s): of archdiocese (archbishops), 315; and begging tours, 146–47; of diocese (ordinaries), 317; gaps in understanding of West, 345 (n. 1); on need for religious women in West, 83, 305; nuns dismissed or disbanded by, 159–61; powers of, 154–61; in power

struggles among nuns, 184; in power struggles with nuns, 161–68, 178–80, 288, 310–11, 370 (n. 87); of provinces (suffragan bishops), 315; on slavery, 36–37; on work of religious women, 87. *See also specific bishops*

Bismarck (Dakota): Benedictine Sisters in, 91–93, 333 (nn. 46, 51); health care in, 91–93, 333 (n. 46), 342 (n. 79)

Blackfeet, 163, 238–39

Blanchet, François Norbert: in power struggles, 156, 158–59, 161; work demands on religious women by, 128, 147

Blandina Segale (SC). *See* Segale, Blandina

Blizzards, 53

Boniface Tummins (OSB). *See* Tummins, Boniface

Boniface Wimmer (OSB). *See* Wimmer, Boniface

Boo, Mary Richard (OSB), *House of Stone*, 5

Boston, Petra (OSP), *231*, 250

Bowen, Baptista (Annie) (PBVM), 79, *79*, 81, 116

Branch houses, definition of, 315

Braun, Lioba (OSB), 109–13

Britt, Mollie, *176*

Brondel, John Baptist, 162–65, 292

Brown, Gabriel (RSM), 51

Bruner, Joanna (SCL), 211

Bruno-Jofré, Rosa, 320 (n. 2)

Bucher, Agnes (OSF), 20, 73, 175, *177*

Buckley, Catherine (FSPA), 237, 359 (n. 28)

Buckner, Mary (SCL), 34

Buffalo Creek Indians, 111–12

Buffalo Soldiers, 247

Building Sisterhood (Immaculate Heart of Mary), 5–6

Bull Bear, Victor, 228

Choir sisters, social class of, 37–38, 292–93

Chollet, Mary Madeline (CCVI), 24

Christmas celebrations, 26, 27

Chronicles, rules for creation and maintenance of, xiv–xvi

Church of Jesus Christ of Latter-day Saints, 138

Cinquin, St. Pierre Jeanne (CCVI): death of, 25; on finances, 149; Mexican immigrant nuns encouraged by, 17; Mexican missions under, 364 (n. 133); in power struggles with bishops, 347 (n. 28); promotion to superior, 24–25; on requirements for admission, 349 (n. 78); on rules of congregation, 172; on spiritual rituals, 297; travels of, 59

Circular letters, on congregational rules, 173–74

Citizenship, U.S., for immigrant nuns, 283, 286

Civil War, American: and Americanization of nuns, 286; nuns' service during, 82–83

Clare, Mary (SCL), 54–55, 327 (n. 39)

Clarita M. Duran (OP). See Duran, Clarita M.

Clarke, Mary Frances (SCL), 126, 149, 172

Class. See Social class

Claus, Caroline, 186

Claver, Petra (SSND), 149

Cloisters: definition of, 315; European vs. American, 3–4, 82

Clothing: death garments, 145; of nurses, 294; shifting traditions in, 293–94; of Sisters of the Holy Family, 105–6, *107. See also* Habits

Code Noir, 36

Coeur d'Alene Indians, 234

Coifs, definition of, 315

College of Saint Teresa, 280

College of the Rosary (Dominican College), 158

Colleges, Catholic: for African Americans, 224; established by nuns, 276–77, 280; nuns prohibited in, 274, 275. *See also* Higher education

Colorado: Dominican Sisters in, 142–43; finances of nuns in, 142–43; immigration of nuns to, 15; Mexican missions in, 259–60; miners' hospitals in, 136–37

Colorado River, 43–44

Colubkille McEnery (CDP). *See* McEnery, Colubkille

Communion. *See* Eucharist

Community, use of term, 9

Concordia, Mary (SSM), 295

Confession, nuns' hearing of, 298, 299

Confessors, definition of, 316

Congregations: abbreviations for, xi–xii; Americanization of, 283–90; cross-community relationships among, 48–49; definition of, 316; disbanding of, 159–61, 178–80; elections in, 288; as families, 74–75; finances of (*See* Finances); incorporation of, 125–27; power struggles within, 178–89, 311–12; professionalization of, 271–83; requirements for admission to, 106, 349 (n. 78); role of vows in, 169–71; rules of (*See* Rules); shifting traditions in, 289–96; support network of, 74–75; transfers of nuns in, 183–84; use of term, 9; withdrawal of nuns from, 184–87, 352 (n. 131); work by (*See* Work). *See also specific congregations*

Conrardy, Lambert L., 88–90, 333 (n. 39)

Conry, James J., 370 (n. 83)

Constitutions, congregational: Americanization in, 288; functions of, 170–71

Contracts: problems with informal, 127–28; rise in use of formal, 131–35

Control. *See* Power struggles; Rules and regulations

Convents: conflicts between old and new ways in, 75–78; control of (*See* Power struggles; Rules); cross-community hospitality in, 48–49, 51, 326 (nn. 18, 24); definition of, 316; elections in, 288; finances of (*See* Finances); nation origins in selection of, 18; nun imposters in, 326 (n. 18); publication of histories of, 4–6; record-keeping practices of, xiv–xvii; role of vows in, 169–71; shifting traditions in, 289–96; social class of sisters in, 37–38, 292–93; support network of, 74–75; travel experiences vs. life in, 44–46; work by (*See* Work)

Conventual priories, 317

Conversions: of Chinese immigrants, 346 (n. 12); of Native Americans, 37, 233

Cordi-Marian Missionary Sisters, 365 (n. 138)

Cornelia, Mary M. Neujean (SNDdeN). *See* Neujean, Cornelia

Correspondence: congregational rules in, 173–74; cultural experiences in, 56–59; humor in, 30

Corrigan, Monica (CSJ), 44, 45, 47, 59, 76–77

Councils, definition of, 316

Crafts, financial contributions from, 144–45

Crespo, Soledad (SHSp), 258

Crow people, 163

CSA. *See* Sisters of St. Agnes

CSC. *See* Sisters of the Holy Cross

CSFN. *See* Sisters of the Holy Family of Nazareth

CSJ. *See* Sisters of St. Joseph of Carondelet

Cultural experiences, of traveling nuns, 56–75

Cultural loneliness, 176

Cultural mixing, of Mexicans and Native Americans, 265–66

Cunigunda Urbany (FSPA). *See* Urbany, Cunigunda

Custer, George A., 353 (n. 16)

Daily life: during travels, 45–46; frugality in, 148–49

Dakota Territory: health-care work of Benedictine Sisters in, 91–93, 333 (nn. 46, 51), 342 (n. 79); immigration of nuns to, 15; Katharine Drexel's travels in, 194–97; shifting traditions in, 291; Sisters of Mary of the Presentation in, 15, 79, 80–81, 291

Damien, Father. *See* Veuster, Damien De

Danger, in travels, 43–44, 52–55, 60–61

Daughters of Charity of St. Vincent de Paul (DC): cross-cultural activities of, 70; in eastern United States, 321 (n. 11); finances of, 145–46, 151; Mexican missions of, 265; migration of, 1, 156; number of, 322 (n. 34); origins of, 82; in power struggles with bishops, 156; professionalization of nurses of, 277–78; spiritual authority of, 298–99, 372 (n. 130); teaching work of, 178; travels of, 54, 77; young sisters of, 22

Daughters of the Purity of Mary, immigration of, 17, 365 (n. 138)

Daughters of the Sacred Hearts of Jesus and Mary, work of, 103

Dawes Severalty Act of 1887, 353 (n. 16)

DC. *See* Daughters of Charity of St. Vincent de Paul

DCJ. *See* Carmelite Sisters of the Divine Heart of Jesus

Death: garments, 145; immigrant, 99; mining disaster and, 102–3; Native Americans and, 220, 231, 246, 295,

297; nuns and, 60, 61, 158, 167, 191, 259, 359 (n. 28)

Debs, Eugene V., 68

De Chantal Enright, Mary (OP). *See* Enright, Mary De Chantal

Deference, in power struggles with bishops, 161, 164, 188

Democracy: in Americanization of nuns, 287–88; in congregational elections, 288

Denver (Colorado): finances of Dominican Sisters in, 142–43; immigration of nuns to, 15

DeSales Kirk, Mary (OP). *See* Kirk, Mary DeSales

Desert ascetics, 2–3

De Smet, Pierre (SJ), 127, 234, 339 (n. 34)

Diaries, cultural experiences in, 56

Diet. *See* Food

Dioceses: bishops of, 317; definition of, 316

Discipline, inside convents, 168–70. *See also* Rules

"Discovering Foremothers" (Thompson), 6–7

Divine Office, definition of, 9, 316

Dolores Armer, Mary (SHF). *See* Armer, Mary Dolores

Domatilla DuRocher, Mary (OSF). *See* DuRocher, Mary Domatilla

Domestic labor: by African American orphans, 251; by nuns for religious men, 87, 128, 159, 339 (n. 41); by nuns in private sphere, 136; opportunities for, 80

Dominican Sisters (OP): Americanization of, 290; anti-Catholicism and, 269; begging tours of, 147–48; education of, 34; frugality of, 148–49, 150; health-care work of, *278*, 342 (n. 72); higher education for, 275; in natural disasters, 61; number of, 20; as per-

manent residents of West, 300–301; personal wealth in, 124, 338 (n. 19); in power struggles with bishops, 154–58; power struggles within, 184; professionalization of, 272–74, *278*, 367 (n. 24); rules of, 173, 174; shifting traditions in, 293–94, 371 (nn. 103, 107); social observations and interactions of, 64–66, 329 (n. 75); teaching work of, 140, 142–43, *143*, 155, 272–74, 343 (n. 94), 367 (n. 24); travels of, 59; work demands on, 131; young nuns of, 22

Dominic of Osma, 3

Donaghoe, Terence J., 126

Donations, requests for, 145–46. *See also* Begging tours

Dougherty, Cecilia (BVM), 174, 272–73, 288

Dowries, 123–24

Doyle, Mary, 86–87

Drexel, Anthony, 354 (n. 43)

Drexel, Elizabeth: death of, 208–9; early life of, 192–93; family of, 192–93; and Katharine's entry into sisterhood, 207; personal wealth of, 192–93, 198, 204–5; on Philomene Ketten, 111, 200; travels of, 194–97, 199–200

Drexel, Emma Bouvier, 192–93, 203

Drexel, Francis, 192–93, 204–5

Drexel, Josephine, 222

Drexel, Katharine (SBS), 191–229; in African American education, 192, 221, 252; and Americanization in education, 284; beatification ceremony for, 228–29; code of conduct of, 226–27; congregation established by, 192, 208–10 (*See also* Sisters of the Blessed Sacrament); construction of schools and other buildings by, 197–202; death of, 191, 226; early life of, 192–97; entry into sisterhood, 203–7, 354 (n. 43); expansion of mission activities under, 213-14; on families of Native Americans, 238; family of, 192-93, 204-5, 208-9, 226; financial records of, 203, 215; first initiatives for Native Americans, 197-203; first interactions with Native Americans, 194-97; frugality of, 149; gaps in understanding of Native Americans, 198, 199, 202, 219-23; guidelines for contributions of, 215-16, 222-23; health problems of, 223-25; in higher education, 224, 239; influence and legacy of, 191-92, 225-29; leadership skills of, 210, 226; loans made by, 215; missions of congregation under, 192, 211-13, 216-21; misuse of donations of, 203, 211, 222-23; motivations for philanthropy of, 198, 226-27; on Native American nuns, 224-25; personal wealth of, 123, 149, 192-93, 198, 204-5; photographs of, *191, 240*; in power struggles, 211-13; racial views of, 222-23, 226-28; on reservation system, 197; sense of humor of, 28; in Sisters of Mercy, 206-8; and Sisters of St. Francis, 198, 204, 212, 213-15; travels in Dakotas, 194-97; travels in Indian Territory, 221-23; travels in Minnesota, 199-200; travels in Wyoming, 211-12. *See also* Native American education

Drexel, Louise: death of, 226; family of, 192; and Katharine's entry into sisterhood, 207; personal wealth of, 192-93, 198, 204-5; travels of, 194-97, 199-200

Dubuis, C. M., 24-25

Dubuque (Iowa), Sisters of Charity of the BVM in: finances of, 126; rules of, 171-73; teaching work of, 94-96

Duchemin, Marie Therese Maxisa (IHM), 36

Duluth (Minnesota), power struggles of Benedictine Sisters in, 181-82

Dunne, Amadeus (OSU): on Cheyenne mission, 56, 72; photograph of, *196*; in power struggles with bishops, 161-68; on rules of congregation, 174, 188; on shifting traditions, 291-92; travels of, 56-57; on western life, 72, 75-76; and withdrawal of nuns, 185

Duquenne, Loyola (SNDdeN), 156

Duran, Clarita M. (OP), 338 (n. 19)

Durango (Colorado), Mexican missions in, 259-60

DuRocher, Mary Domatilla (OSF), 280-81

Earthquakes, 61-62

Economy: nuns' observations on, 63-69; women's labor in, 79-80

Education: of African Americans, 123, 221, 224, 247-55; Americanization in, 284, 287; of health-care workers, 278, 280-83; higher (*See* Higher education); of immigrants, 69-70; kindergarten, 108, 336 (nn. 100, 101); languages used in, 294-95; of Mexicans and Mexican Americans, *256*, 257-58, 261-64; of Native Americans (*See* Native American education); of nuns, 32-36; poverty as barrier to, 63-64; in public schools, 140-41, 272, 287; sense of humor in, 28-29; in shifting traditions of religious life, 291-92; taxes on students in, 64; of teaching nuns, 32-36, 272-77, 282-83; of young miners, 102-3

Eichman, Liguori (SBS), 221, 240-41

Elections: congregational, 288; U.S., 287

Elizabeth Ann Seton (SC). *See* Seton, Elizabeth Ann

Elizabeth Vermeersch (CDP). *See* Vermeersch, Mary Benitia

El Paso (Texas): Daughters of Charity in, 265, 277–78; Mexican missions in, 265; professionalization of nurses in, 277–78; sisters' interactions with immigrants in, 70

Emerentiana (CSC), xv–xvi

Emily Power (OP). *See* Power, Emily

Emmanuel, Claus (FSPA). *See* Claus, Caroline

Emmanuel, Phelan (OP). *See* Phelan, Emmanuel

Emma Short (SHSp). *See* Short, Emma

Emotional toll, of western missions, *176*, 177

Employment opportunities, for men vs. women, 74, 79–80. *See also* Work

Enclosure: in conflict with work of western missions, 97–99, 105, 113–14; for nuns vs. sisters, 9; shift away from tradition of, 290–92

English immigrants, nuns as, 15, *16*

English language: in Americanization of nuns, 283–84; in shifting traditions, 294–96

Enright, Mary De Chantal (OP), 338 (n. 19)

Entrance: definition of, 316; photographs taken to celebrate, *21*

Epidemics, health care by nuns during, 220, 246, 368 (n. 41)

Ernesta Funke, Mary (SSND). *See* Funke, Mary Ernesta

Ethnic groups, 231–66; decline in spiritual identity of, 70; legacy of nuns' work with, 308–9; nuns' relationships with, 231–33. *See also specific groups*

Eucharist: definition of, 316; rules for handling of, 298–99

Eureka (Missouri), farm work of Sisters of Mercy in, 84–85

Europe: financial support from, 119–21; history of monasticism in, 2–4, 81–82; immigration of nuns from, 14–18; remote administration from, 153–54; shifts in United States away from traditions of, 289–96; work for religious women in, 81–82

Euste, Magdalen (OSB), 184

Evangelist (SBS), 30–31

Evangelist, Mary Jennings (SHSp). See Jennings, Mary Evangelist

Excommunication, definition of, 316

Extern sisters: definition of, 318; social class of, 37–38

Facemaz, St. John (CSJ), 47–48

Faith, personal, of nuns, 39–41

Families: congregations as, 74–75; immigrant, 69–70; nuns' observations on, 63–64; nuns' separation from, 47, 50; separation of Native American, 201–2, 221, 234, 238; social work with poor, 105–8

Fancywork, financial contributions from, 144–45

Fargo (North Dakota), Sisters of Mary of the Presentation in: arrival of, 15; shifting traditions of, 291; work of, 79, 80–81

Faribault (Minnesota), teaching work of Dominican Sisters in, 140

Farm labor: by Native Americans, 234; by women, 80, 84–85

Fear, hiding signs of, 54–55

Febronie Fontbonne (CSJ). *See* Fontbonne, Febronie

Federal government, in Native American education, 234, 244, 358 (n. 15)

Felber, Mary Anselma (OSB), 14–15

Feltin, St. Andrew (CDP), 160–61, 178, 188, 370 (n. 87)

Feminist scholarship, 5–7

Fibronia Vandanaigue (SNJM). See Vandanaigue, Fibronia

Finances, 117–52, 305–7; articles of incorporation and, 125–27, 130, 158; begging tours in, 146–48; contracts and, 127–28, 131–35; eastern laity's contributions to, lack of, 195, 353 (n. 13); European contributions to, 119–21; frugality in, 148–50, 152; of hospitals, 91–93, 134–37, 334 (n. 55), 342 (n. 72); lack of church contributions to, 117–18, 305; legal protections for, 125–35; personal talents of nuns in, 141–50; personal wealth of nuns in, 121–25; in power struggles with bishops, 120, 157–58; private industry in, 135–39; of religious men vs. women, 120; results of efforts to stabilize, 150–52, 305–6; teachers' contributions to, 139–44; work conflicts and, 128–32, 306

Florence Walter (CDP). *See* Walter, Florence

Fontbonne, Febronie (CSJ), 1

Food: distribution in Mexican missions, 260, 261–62; distribution in Native American missions, 213; and physical labor, 84; sameness in American style of, 63

Footprints on the Frontier (Thomas), 5

Foreign languages. *See* Languages

Forrest, Leonie (CSJ), 293

Fort Dodge (Iowa), finances of Sisters of Charity of the BVM in, 144

Fort Sumner Treaty (1868), 358 (n. 21)

France: Daughters of Charity in, 82; immigration of nuns from, 14, 15, 17–18; Sisters of Divine Providence in, 320 (chap. 1, n. 1)

Frances Xavier Cabrini (MSC). *See* Cabrini, Frances Xavier

Francis (DC), 1

Franciscan Sister of Christian Charity (OSF), *1*

Franciscan Sisters (OSF): Americaniza-

tion of, 288; frugality of, 148; health-care work of, 93–94, 334 (nn. 55, 58); innovations in work of, 103, 104, 335 (n. 88); professionalization of nurses of, 278–81; rules of, 175, 177; shifting traditions in, 295; social observations of, 63–64; teaching work of, 239, 284, 343 (n. 102); work contracts of, 132–34; young nuns of, 22

Franciscan Sisters of Perpetual Adoration (FSPA): finances of, 148, 338 (n. 25); frugality of, 148; holiday celebrations of, 26; Native American missions of, 199, 235–37; personal talents of, 144–45; personal wealth of nuns in, 338 (n. 25); shifting traditions in, 294, 295; spiritual authority of, 297; teaching work of, 344 (n. 103); withdrawal of nuns from, 186

Franciscan Sisters of the Immaculate Conception (OSF): finances of, 130–31; origins of, 340 (n. 55)

Francis of Assisi, 3

Francis Seibert (OSU). See Seibert, Francis

Franco, Mary Joseph (CSJ), 231–32, 246

Frederica Law (OSF). *See* Law, Frederica

Frederica McGrath (DC). *See* McGrath, Frederica

Freemasons, hospitals supported by, 93

Friars, definition of, 316

Friess, Caroline (SSND): and Americanization, 283, 285, 286; on anti-Catholicism, 269; on class divisions, 38; on diverse backgrounds of nuns, 39; on education of nuns, 34; finances of congregation under, 119–20, 129, 130, 149; on frugality, 149; on German immigrants, 63, 69–70; on immigrant nuns, 22; observations of society by, 63; on professionalization of teachers, 272–73; on rules of congregation, 172, 175; sense of humor of, 26; on shifting traditions, 291, 294–95; on transfer requests, 184; travels of, 54, 63; on withdrawal of nuns, 184–85

Froebel method, 108

Frugality, 148–50, 152

FSPA. *See* Franciscan Sisters of Perpetual Adoration

Funke, Mary Ernesta (SSND), 173

Gabriel Brown (RSM). *See* Brown, Gabriel

Gainesville (Texas), teaching work of School Sisters of Notre Dame in, 141

Gallagher, Nicholas, 178–80

Galveston (Texas): Dominican sisters in, 61; hurricane of 1900 and, 60–61; Ursuline nuns in, 61

Gannon, Pauline (OP), 275

Garrick, de Sales (PBVM), 290–91

Gender discrimination, prevalence of, 10, 310

Gender roles: history of in Catholic Church, 2–3, 10, 81–82, 309–10; nuns' views on, 38–39, 309–10; scholarship on, 5–7

Generalate, definition of, 316

Generosa Callahan (CDP). *See* Callahan, Generosa

German immigrants: financial support for missions for, 119–20; health care for, 96–100; number of, 16; nuns as, 14, 18, 96; nuns' interactions with, 63, 69–70

Gibbons, James, 30–31

Gilded Age, 192

Gilmour, Richard, 162–63, 164, 165

Goemaere, Mary of the Cross (OP), 154–55, 158, 188

Gold, in California, 154

Grand Ronde Mission (Oregon), 89–91, 333 (n. 37)

Grand Ronde valley (Oregon), 333 (n. 37)

Great Northern and Pacific Railroad, 136

Gregory XVI, Pope, 36

Griffin, Mary Regina (OP), 124

Grilles, definition of, 316

Gross, William H., 357 (n. 108)

Gros Ventres, 163

Guilelma (OP), 301

Guimpes, 294, 371 (n. 107)

Guinaw, Mary Gertrude (OSM), 15, 283, 341 (n. 62)

Haas, Marianne (SSND), 273

Habits (dress): anti-Catholicism and, 269; definition of, 316; frugality in maintenance of, 149; Mexican government's ban on, 257; of Oblate Sisters of Providence, 251–52; in public schools, 141, 287, 343 (n. 90); shifting traditions in, 293–94, 371 (n. 107); Sisters of the Holy Family's modification of, 105–6, *107*

Hanna, Edward J., 184

Hawaii, 320 (intro., n. 5), 333 (n. 39)

Hayes, Ignatius (OSF), 340 (n. 55), 357 (n. 108)

Hayes, Juliana (SBS), 228

Hazotte, Agnes (CSA), 179–80

Health, of nuns, 85–86

Health-care work, by nuns: in Civil War, 82–83; contracts on, 134–35; education for, 278, 280–83; in homes, 96–100, 281; for industry workers, 135–39, 271; for Mexicans and Mexican Americans, 259; for Native Americans, 213–14, 220; professionalization of, 277–83; in relief operations, 102–3; subscriptions and insurance in, 136–37, 139, 271. *See also* Hospital(s)

Healy-Murphy, Margaret Mary (SHSp):

in African American education, 252–55, 362 (n. 112); in Mexican American education, 256–57; personal wealth of, 123; on racial diversity of congregation, 256–57, 260, 364 (n. 130)

Helena (Montana), work contracts of Sisters of Charity in, 134–35

Helen Kyle (SSM). *See* Kyle, Helen

Henry, William, 247

Herker, Marianna (SSM), 334 (n. 74)

Hierarchy, of nuns, 168–70

Higher education: for African Americans, 224; for nursing nuns, 278, 280–83; for teaching nuns, 272–77, 282–83

Hildegund (OSB), 28

Hill, James J., 136

Hoffman's Catholic Directory, 19

Hogan, Wilfrida (CSJ), 33–34

Holiday celebrations: in Americanization of nuns, 285–86, 287; humor in, 26, 27–28

Holly, Mary Joseph (DC), 148

Holy See, definition of, 316

Home health care, by nuns, 96–100, 281

Hospital(s): contracts on work of, 134–35; financing of, 91–93, 134–37, 334 (n. 55), 342 (n. 72); industry, 135–39, 271, 341 (n. 67); nuns' management of, 91–94, 96; patient payments to, 136–37, 342 (n. 72); professionalization of, 277–83. *See also* Health-care work, by nuns

Hospitality: cross-community, 48–49, 51, 326 (nn. 18, 24); and nun imposters, 326 (n. 18); Sisters of St. Francis's tradition of, 213

Household work. *See* Domestic labor

House of Stone (Boo), 5

Housing: contracts on, 132; problems with, 127, 132, 156, 307, 339 (nn. 37, 39)

Houston (Texas), Mexican missions of Sisters of Divine Providence in, 261–64

Hughes, John (SMP), 159

Humor, nuns' sense of, 25–32

Hurricanes, 60–61

Identity, of nuns: Americanization of, 283–90; reconciliation of religious and regional, 303–13

Ignatius Hayes (OSF). *See* Hayes, Ignatius

Ignatius Mary Lynch (RSM). *See* Lynch, Mary Ignatius

Ignatius McFarland (OSU). *See* McFarland, Ignatius

Ignatius Walker (RSM). *See* Walker, Ignatius

IHM. *See* Sisters of the Immaculate Heart of Mary

Immaculate Conception School (Houston), 261

Immaculate Heart of Mary, *Building Sisterhood*, 5–6

Immigrant(s): languages spoken by, 45; number of, 15, 16; nuns' interactions with, 63, 69–70; poverty among, 63; schools for, 69–70

Immigrant nuns, 14–22, 304; Americanization of, 283–90; citizenship for, 283, 286; journeys of, 14–18, 304; languages spoken by, 15, 18, 45, 283–84; motivations of, 14, 23–24; national origins of, 14–18; number of, 17, 18–22; as permanent residents of West, 299–301; young age of, 22–25

Imposters, nun, 326 (n. 18)

Income. *See* Finances; Salaries

Incorporation, articles of, 125–27, 130, 158

Independence Day celebrations, 285–86

Indians. *See* Native American(s)

Indian Territory: Katharine Drexel's travels in, 221–23; land distribution in, 222; Sisters of Mercy in, 101–3, 335 (n. 82)

Industrial School (St. Louis), 100–101

Industry hospitals: anti-Catholicism and, 271; in finances of nuns, 135–39, 341 (n. 67)

Inez (RSM), 209, 211

Inheritance, 124–25, 338 (n. 25)

Innocentia (SSND), 174

Institutes: definition of, 316; use of term, 9

Insurance, health, 137, 139, 271

International travel, by nuns, 23–24

Inventing Catholic Tradition (Tilley), 7

Iowa, Sisters of Charity of the BVM in: finances of, 126, 144; rules of, 171–73; teaching work of, 94–96

Ireland, John, 285

Irish immigrants: number of, 16; nuns as, 13–14, 23–24, 254, 321 (n. 20)

Italian immigrants: missions focused on, 15; number of, 16; nuns as, 15; nuns' interactions with, 68–69, 70

James, Mary (OP), 142

Javete, Mary Magdalen (SHF), 106

Jeager, Agnes, 231–32, 246

Jefferson (Texas), power struggles of Sisters of St. Agnes in, 178–80

Jennings, Mary Evangelist (SHSp), 24, 254

Jesuits, Native American languages studied by, 243–44, 360 (n. 67)

Joanna Bruner (SCL). *See* Bruner, Joanna

Johanna Holly (DC). *See* Holly, Mary Joseph

John Hughes (SMP). *See* Hughes, John

Joseph, Mary (RSM), 101–2

Josephine Cantwell (SCL). *See* Cantwell, Josephine

Joseph Pariseau (SP). *See* Pariseau, Joseph

Judge, Mary, 137, 138

Juliana Hayes (SBS). *See* Hayes, Juliana

Kansas: Sisters of Charity of the BVM in, 94–96, 334 (n. 65); teaching work in, 64, 94–96, 328 (n. 70), 334 (n. 65). *See also* Sisters of Charity of Leavenworth

Kansas City (Missouri), teaching work in, 47

Katharine Drexel (SBS). *See* Drexel, Katharine

Kenrick, Peter Richard, 97, 168, 247–48

Kentucky. *See* Sisters of Charity of Nazareth

Kerst, Alexia (OSB): hospital management by, 92; personal wealth of, 121–23; in power struggles, 181–83

Kerst, Anna M., 121

Kerst, Peter, 121–22

Kerst, Scholastica (OSB): election of, 370 (n. 87); hospital management by, 91–92, 96, 333 (nn. 46, 51); personal wealth of, 121–23; photograph of, *181*; in power struggles, 180–82, 188

Ketten, Philomene (OSB): Drexels and, 111, 200; work with Native Americans, 109–13, 200

Kilian Schoeller (OSF). *See* Schoeller, Kilian

Kindergarten, 108, 336 (nn. 100, 101)

Kingsville (Texas), immigration of nuns to, 17

Kinsella, Thomas F., 267

Kirk, Mary DeSales (OP), 338 (n. 19)

Knawa, Anne Marie (OSF), *As God Shall Ordain*, 5

Kopp, Marianne (OSF), 320 (n. 5)

Krebs (Indian Territory), Sisters of Mercy in, 101–3

Kyle, Helen (SSM), *303*

Labor. *See* Work

Laborers: health care for, 135–39; nuns' interactions with, 64–69

Labor strikes, 66–68

Mother generals: enforcement of rules by, 175–77; frugality of, 149; records of, xv

Motherhood, nineteenth-century mores on, 22–23

Motherhouses: bonds with permanent residents of West, 299–301; definition of, 316; oversight of congregations by, 172–77, 187–88; record-keeping practices of, xv

Mother superiors, election of, 288

Mount Saint Mary's Academy (Omaha), 48

Moye, John Martin, 320 (n. 1)

MSC. *See* Missionary Sisters of the Sacred Heart of Jesus

Munoz, Father, 259

Music: humor in, 25–27; in Native American missions, 239–42; value of teachers of, 142–44, *143*, 343 (n. 94)

Musical instruments, 143–44

Names, of nuns, 10

Native American(s), 232–46; adaptations to Catholicism by, 241; Americanization of, 243, 245; baptism of, 297, 372 (n. 127); in beatification ceremony for Katharine Drexel, 228–29; ceremonial practices of, 219–20; deconstruction of societies of, 195–96, 353 (n. 16); education of (*See* Native American education); farms of, 234; forced conversions of, 37, 233; gaps in missionaries' understanding of, 198, 199, 201, 202, 219–23; impact of reservation life on, 197; interracial marriage and children of, 222–23; Katharine Drexel's first interactions with, 194–97; languages of, 242–44, 360 (n. 67); legacy of nuns' work with, 308–9; Mexican Americans worshipping with, 265–66; migration to West by, 16–17; missions to (*See* Native American missions); as nuns, 224–25, 228, *240*; poverty of, 195, *196*, 200, 244; and racism, 37, 226–27, 245, 247; relocation to reservations, 234, 353 (n. 16); responses to white expansionism, 233–34; whites' treatment of, 112–13, 233–34, 244–45, 337 (n. 111); in Wounded Knee Massacre, 246–47

Native American education: acceptance by tribes, 219, 234–39; by Benedictine Sisters, 110–11, 200; for biracial children, 222–23; content and philosophy of, 236; criteria for Katharine Drexel's contributions to, 215–16, 222–23; federal support for, 234, 244, 358 (n. 15); by Franciscan Sisters, 239; music in, 239–42; nuns' relationships with students in, 232–46; progress of students in, 238–39; in public schools, 140; schools built by Katharine Drexel for, 197–202; separation of families for, 201–2, 221, 234, 238; by Sisters of St. Francis, 212, 213–15; by Sisters of St. Joseph, 239; by Sisters of the Blessed Sacrament, 216–17, 219–25; by Ursuline nuns, 238–39

Native American missions, 191–229; acceptance by tribes, 196–97, 199, 219, 234–39; of Benedictine Sisters, 109–13, 200, 234, 238; challenges of, 89, 110, 195–96; food distribution in, 213; of Franciscan Sisters, 199, 235–37; health care in, 213–14, 220; Katharine Drexel's early initiatives for, 197–203; Katharine Drexel's first visits to, 194–97; legacy of nuns' work in, 308–9; motivations for, 233; music in, 239–42; nuns influenced by experience of, 246; power struggles over, 211–13; schools in (*See* Native American education); of Sisters of

Charity of Leavenworth, 211; of Sisters of Mercy, 353 (n. 17); of Sisters of Providence, *202*, 234; of Sisters of St. Francis, 198, 212, 213–15; of Sisters of the Blessed Sacrament, 192, 211–13, 216–25; of Sisters of the Holy Names, 235, 242; spiritual rituals performed by nuns in, 297–98; of Ursuline nuns, 56, 71–72, 163, *196*, 238–39, 244–45

Nativism, 269

Natural disasters: on Native American farms, 234; nuns' experience with, 60–62, 329 (n. 87). *See also* Storms

Nature: Native American students' need for, 242; nuns' experience of, 56–62, 304–5

Navajos, 220–21, 358 (n. 21)

Nazareth (Kentucky). *See* Sisters of Charity of Nazareth

Nebraska: hospitality of Sisters of Mercy in, 48; immigration of nuns to, 15

Needlework, financial contributions from, 144–45

Néraz, John C., 25, 160–61, 178, 347 (n. 28), 370 (n. 87)

Neujean, Cornelia (SNDdeN), *267*

Nevada, Daughters of Charity in: finances of, 145–46, *151*; spiritual authority of, 298–99, 372 (n. 130)

New Mexico: cultural mixing of Mexicans and Native Americans in, 265–66; humor of nuns in, 29; Native American missions in, 216–20; Sisters of Loretto in, 53–54; Sisters of the Blessed Sacrament in, 216–20

New Orleans (Louisiana): African American education in, 224; racial views of Ursuline nuns in, 36

Newspapers, requests for donations in, 145–46

North Dakota. *See* Dakota Territory

Novena, definition of, 316

Novices: definition of, 316–17; education of, 32–36; number of, 19; physical labor by, 84–85; sense of humor of, 25–27; as teachers, 272, 366 (nn. 13, 17)

Novitiate, definition of, 317

Nuns: African American, 228, 247–52, 357 (n. 108), 364 (n. 130), 368 (n. 57); definition of, 9, 317; dismissal of, 159–61, 178–80; education of, 32–36; finances of (*See* Finances); gaps in scholarship on, xiii–xiv; hierarchy of, 168–70; history of scholarship by and on, 4–7; identity of (*See* Identity, of nuns); immigration of (*See* Immigrant nuns); imposters of, 326 (n. 18); Mexican, 17, 256–58, 263–64; motivations for becoming, 23–24; motivations for moving to West, 2; names of, 10; Native American, 224–25, 228, *240*; number of, in United States, 18–22; origins of, 2; sense of humor of, 25–32; vs. sisters, 9, 317; stereotypes of, xiv, 55, 308; transfers of, 183–84; travels of (*See* Travel); use of term, 9; views on gender, 38–39, 309–10; views on race and class, 36–38, 292–93; withdrawal from sisterhoods, 184–87, 352 (n. 131); work of (*See* Work); young, 22–25

Nurses, nuns as: African American, 368 (n. 57); in Civil War, 82–83; clothing of, 294; education of, 278, 280–83; in homes, 96–100, 281; in hospitals, 92–94; professionalization of, 277–83, *278*; work contracts for, 134–35. *See also* Health-care work, by nuns

Oaxaca (Mexico), Sisters of the Holy Ghost in, 257

Obedience, vow of, 169–71. *See also* Rules and regulations

Obedientiary priories, 317

Phelan, Emmanuel (OP), 300–301

Philomene Ketten (OSB). *See* Ketten, Philomene

Politics, U.S., nuns' responses to, 286–87

Poor, the. *See* Poverty

Pope, definition of, 317

Portland (Oregon), Sisters of the Holy Names in: anti-Catholicism and, 270; as permanent residents, 299–300; teaching work of, 89–91

Postulants (candidates): definition of, 317; education of, 32–36; foreign motherhouses as barrier to, 300; number of, in United States, 19, *21*; physical labor by, 84–86; requirements for admission of, 106, 349 (n. 78); sense of humor of, 25–27; as teachers, 272, 366 (n. 13), 366 (n. 17)

Poverty: as barrier to education, 63–64; legacy of nuns' work with, 307–8; of Native Americans, 195, *196*, 200, 244; nuns' observations on, 63–69; nuns' vow of, 121, 148, 169–71, 307; nuns' work on in urban areas, 104–9; origins of nuns' work with, 81–82

Power(s), 153–89; of bishops, 154–61; of congregational rules, 169–77; to dismiss or disband nuns, 159–61, 178–80; and hierarchy of nuns, 168–70

Power, Emily (OP): on education of nuns, 34; on finances, 149, 150; on lay sisters, 293; on professionalization of teachers, 272–74; on rules of congregation, 173, 174

Power struggles, 153–89, 309–12; between bishops and nuns, 161–68, 178–80, 288, 310–11, 370 (n. 87); within convents, 178–89, 311–12; finances in, 120, 157–58; over Native American missions, 211–13; remote administration of church in, 153–54, 177; women's work in, 159

Prayer, shifting traditions in, 292–93

Prendergast, John J., 104–5

Prescott (Arizona), finances of Sisters of St. Joseph of Carondelet in, 136, 137

Presidents, U.S., nuns' respect for, 286–87

Priests: in finances of religious women, 120, 126, 128–30, 146; nuns' access to, 187; on rule violations, 175; shortage of, 83, 259, 332 (n. 15), 365 (n. 141); solitary experience of vs. nuns, 83–84; and spiritual authority of nuns, 296–99; on work by religious women, 87, 88–89, 94–96. *See also specific priests*

Priories, definition of, 317. *See also* Monasteries

Privacy, in travels, 45, 46–47

Private sphere: health care in, 135–36; work contracts in, 134–35

Professed, definition of, 317

Professionalization, of nuns, 271–83, 311; as nurses, 277–83, *278*; as teachers, 272–77, 282–83

Property, personal, of nuns, 121, 123–25

Protestant(s): education of, 141; Native American missions of, 110; nuns' prejudices against, 270–71; women, as missionaries, 330 (n. 111); working with Catholic nuns in health care, 94, 279

Provinces, definition of, 317

Publications, church: by nun historians, 4–6; review process for, 4–5

Public schools, nuns as teachers in, 140–41, 272, 287

Public transportation, nuns' experiences with, 45–46

Pullman, George W., 66

Pullman Strike of 1894, 66–68, 75

Race: Catholic views on, 36–37, 227–28; Katharine Drexel's views on, 222–23, 226–28

tion of, 9, 317; extern, 37–38, 318; lay, 37–38, 292–93; number of in United States, 18–22; vs. nuns, 9, 317; use of term, 9. *See also* Nuns; Women, religious

Sisters, Servants of the Immaculate Heart of Mary (IHM), 364 (n. 138)

Sisters' College, of The Catholic University of America, 275–76

Sisters in Arms (McNamara), 6

Sisters of Charity of Cincinnati (SC): anti-Catholicism and, 271; expansion of mission of, 103–4; innovations in work of, 103–4

Sisters of Charity of Leavenworth, Kansas (SCL): Americanization of, *289*; cross-community relationships of, 49; financial protections for finances of, 125–26, 127, 134–35; Native American missions of, 211; travels of, 54–55, 57, 70–71, 326 (n. 25), 327 (n. 39); work contracts of, 134–35; work demands on, 127, 339 (n. 41)

Sisters of Charity of Nazareth (SCN): expansion of mission of, 170; racial views of, 36

Sisters of Charity of the Blessed Virgin Mary (BVM): Americanization of, 288; finances of, 124, 144, 149; frugality of, 149; higher education hosted by, 276; humor in, 25–26; personal wealth in, 124; photograph of, *117*; professionalization of, 272–73; rules of, 171–73; teaching work of, 94–96, 144, 272–73, 334 (n. 65); terminology for, 9–10; withdrawal of nuns from, 352 (n. 131); work demands on, 132

Sisters of Charity of the Incarnate Word (CCVI): finances of, 149; Mexican missions of, 260, 364 (n. 133); rules of, 172; shifting tra-

ditions in, 292, 371 (n. 98); spiritual rituals performed by, 297; teaching work of, 362 (n. 112); weather disasters and, 61; work demands on, 132; young nuns of, 24–25

Sisters of Divine Providence (CDP): Catechists program of, 262–64, *263*; education of, 34–35; expansion of mission work of, 88; finances of, 140, 148; frugality of, 148; ideals of, 14; immigration of, 13–14; Mexican missions of, 260–64; number of, 20; origins of, 320 (chap. 1, n. 1); in power struggles, 160–61, 263–64; rules of, 173; teaching work of, 140, 362 (n. 112); work demands on, 131–32; young nuns of, 25

Sisters of Loretto (SL): expansion of mission work of, 88; finances of, 131, 140; teaching work of, 140; travels of, 53–54, *58*, 327 (n. 31); work demands on, 131

Sisters of Mary of the Presentation (SMP): immigration of, 15; travels of, 59

Sisters of Mercy (RSM): Americanization of, 286; cross-community relationships of, 48, 49, 51; expansion of mission work of, 88; farm work by, 84–85; finances of, 137, 148, 149, 342 (n. 72); frugality of, 148, 149; health-care work of, 137–38, 342 (n. 72); hierarchy of nuns of, 168–69; Irish nuns in, 321 (n. 20); Katharine Drexel in, 206–8; Mexican missions of, 259; migration of, 156, 346 (n. 10); Native American missions of, 353 (n. 17); number of, 18, 20; origins of, 100; orphanages of, 362 (n. 106); in power struggles with bishops, 156, 346 (n. 10); power struggles within, 183; teaching work of, 100–103, 168–69, 248; travels of, 48; withdrawal of nuns from, 352 (n. 131); work demands on, 132

Sisters of Notre Dame de Namur (SNDdeN): earthquakes and, 61; migration of, 155–56, 158; number of, 19; as permanent residents of West, 300; in power struggles with bishops, 155–56, 158

Sisters of Providence (SP): Americanization of, 283–84; begging tours of, 147, *147*; cross-community relationships of, 49; immigration of, 1; Native American missions of, *202*, 234; as permanent residents of West, 299–300; shifting traditions in, 294, 295–96, 371 (n. 110); teaching work of, 234

Sisters of St. Agnes (CSA): power struggles in, 178–80; teaching work of, 178–79

Sisters of St. Francis of Philadelphia (OSF): influence of western life on, 73–74; Katharine Drexel's donations to, 198; Native American missions of, 198, 212, 213–15; travels of, 73–74; work contracts of, 132, 134

Sisters of St. Francis of Rochester (OSF): Mayo Clinic and, 93–94; professionalization of, 278–81, 367 (n. 23); teaching work of, 343 (n. 102), 367 (n. 23)

Sisters of St. Francis of the Holy Family (OSF), higher education for, 276

Sisters of St. Joseph (SSJ): in higher education, 277; teaching work of, 284

Sisters of St. Joseph of Carondelet (CSJ): cross-community relationships of, 49, 51; cross-cultural art and, *115*; frugality of, 149; health-care work of, 136–37, 342 (n. 72); higher education for, 275; immigration of, 1, 17–18; legal protections for finances

of, 126–27; number of, 20; photograph of, *xiii*; shifting traditions in, 293; teaching work of, 33–34, 144, 239, 248, 284; travels of, 1, 43, 43–44, 45, 47, 49–52, 56, 59, 76–77

Sisters of St. Mary (SSM): African American missions of, 368 (n. 57); Americanization of, 286; finances of, 148; health-care work of, 96–100, 281–82, *282*, 342 (n. 79); holiday celebrations of, 26; origins of name, 98; professionalization of, 281–82, *282*; spiritual rituals and, 297

Sisters of St. Mary of Oregon (SSMO), travels of, 59

Sisters of the Blessed Sacrament (SBS): African American missions of, 192, 221; change to name of, 228; on cultural mixing of Mexicans and Native Americans, 265–66; expansion of mission of, 216–19; fiftieth anniversary of, 225; finances of, 225, 226; Native American missions of, 192, 211–13, 216–25, *218*; origins of, 192, 209–10; in power struggles, 211–12; public opinion of work of, 224; sense of humor of, 29–31; travels of, 46–47, 66–68, 75, 329 (n. 87)

Sisters of the Blessed Sacrament for Indians and Colored People. *See* Sisters of the Blessed Sacrament

Sisters of the Good Shepherd (RGS-CGS), 40; finances of, 136; number of, 19

Sisters of the Holy Cross (CSC): records of, xiv–xvi; work of, 86–87, 138

Sisters of the Holy Family of Nazareth (CSFN): European roots of, *171*; New Mexico mission of, *171*

Sisters of the Holy Family of San Francisco (SHF): clothing worn by, 105–6, *107*; in earthquake of 1906,

Standards of living, 307

Standing Rock Reservation (Dakota), 234

Stanislaus (OSU), 163–64, 347 (n. 42)

Stanislaus, Mary (OSF), 73, 330 (n. 108)

State certification: of nurses, 280, 281–82; of teachers, 140, 272–73, 275

Steamboats, nuns' travels by, 54

Stephan, Joseph, 194, 195, 224, 227

Stereotypes, of nuns, xiv, 55, 308

Storms: hurricanes, 60–61; tornadoes, 93; during travels, 53, 329 (n. 87); winter, 53, 60

Strikes. *See* Labor strikes

Studer, Pancratia (ASC), 31–32

Stueber, Marylu (FSM), xvi

Subscription services, for health care, 136–37, 271

Suffragan bishops, definition of, 315

Swiss immigrants: death of Sister Wilhelmina, 60; nuns as, 14–15

Sylvester (OSF), 93–94

Tabasco (Mexico), Sisters of the Holy Ghost in, 257–58

Tacoma (Washington), work contracts of Franciscan Sisters in, 132–34

Taft, William Howard, 286–87

Talbot, Ethelbert, 353 (n. 17)

Tash-quin, Teresa, 241–42

Taxes, on students, 64

Teachers, nuns as: certification of, 140, 141, 272–73, 275; challenges of work of, 94–96, 100–103; in conflict with other duties, 94–96; education of, 32–36, 272–77, 282–83; financial contributions of, 139–44; intercongregational cooperation of, 274–75, 336 (n. 101); music, 142–44, *143*; professionalization of, 272–77, 282–83; in public schools, 140–41, 272, 287. *See also specific congregations*

Terminology, Catholic, 9–10, 315–18

Texarkana (Texas), power struggles of Sisters of St. Agnes in, 178–80

Texas: Daughters of Charity in, 178, 265, 277–78; Dominican Sisters in, 61; hurricane of 1900 in, 60–61; immigration of nuns to, 17; Mexican missions in, *256*, 257, 261–64, 265; Missionary Catechists of Divine Providence in, 262–64, *263*; nuns' interactions with immigrants in, 70; power struggles in, 160–61, 178–80; professionalization of nurses in, 277–78; School Sisters of Notre Dame in, 141; Sisters of Divine Providence in, 13–14, 140, 160–61, 261–64; Sisters of St. Agnes in, 178–80; Sisters of the Holy Cross in, 86–87; Sisters of the Holy Ghost in, *256*, 257; teaching work in, 86–87, 140, 141, 178; Ursuline nuns in, 61

Theatine Fathers, 259

Thomas, Mary Evangeline (SSJ), 355 (n. 69); *Footprints on the Frontier*, 5

Thomasine (CSA), 178, 179, 180

Thompson, Margaret Susan, "Discovering Foremothers," 6–7

Tief, Francis, 277

Tierney, Adeline (OP), 23

Tilley, Terrence W., *Inventing Catholic Tradition*, 7

Tomazin, Ignatius, 109, 110, 336 (n. 102)

Toner, David, 185–86

Tornadoes, 93

Tradition, Catholic: changes to in United States, 289–96; as made vs. given, 7

Trains. *See* Railroad(s)

Travel, by nuns, 43–78, 304–5; appreciation for western landscape in, 56–59; conflicts between old and new demands in, 75–78; cross-community hospitality in, 48–49, 51; cultural experiences of, 56–75; danger in, 43–44, 52–55, 60–61; foreign languages in, 45; humor in, 28, 29–30; immigrants in, 69–70; influence on nuns, 69–78; interactions with society in, 45, 47–49, 64–69; international, 23–24; nature in, 56–62, 304–5; observations of society during, 62–69; physical experiences of, 44–56; resistance to, 72–74; rules and regulations during, 46–47, 75–77; self-reliance in, 46–47, 74; vs. single laywomen, 74

Troy, Catherine (RSM), 335 (n. 82)

Tucson (Arizona), travels of Sisters of St. Joseph of Carondelet in, 44, 51–52, 76–77

Tummins, Boniface (OSB), 92–93, 113

Turner, Frederick Jackson, 5

Uniformity, American tendency toward, 63

Union Pacific Railroad, 138

University of Minnesota, 276

University of Notre Dame, 86, 87

Urban areas, challenges of work in, 104–9

Urbany, Cunigunda (FSPA), 237

Ursuline nuns (OSU): cross-community relationships of, 49; finances of, 143, 144, 162–63; holiday celebrations of, 26; influence of western life on, 71–72, 75–76; innovations in work of, 103; international union of, 165–66, 348 (n. 53); Native American missions of, 56, 71–72, 163, 196, 238–39, 244–45; in natural disasters, 61; in power struggles with bishops, 161–68; priests' experience vs., 332 (n. 18); racial views of, 36; rules of, 174; shifting traditions in, 291–92; teaching work of, 143, 144, 238–39; travels of, 54, 56–57, 71–72; withdrawal of

sisters from, 185–86; work demands on, 132

Utah: health care in, 137–38; Sisters of Mercy in, 137–38; Sisters of the Holy Cross in, 138

Vandanaigue, Fibronia (SNJM), 176

Vatican: and Americanization of nuns, 285; congregational rules approved by, 171; definition of, 318

Vatican II, 228

Vermeersch, Mary Benitia (Elizabeth) (CDP), 260–64

Veronica (SBS), 29

Veronica Zygmanski (OSB). See Zygmanski, Veronica

Veuster, Damien De, 320 (n. 5), 333 (n. 39)

Vicariate, definition of, 318

Vilarrasa, Francis Sadoc: positions of authority held by, 154, 345 (n. 6); in power struggles, 154–55, 156, 157, 158

Virginia City (Nevada), Daughters of Charity in: finances of, 145–46, 151; spiritual authority of, 298–99, 372 (n. 130)

Visitations, in enforcement of rules, 175–77

Vocabulary, Catholic, 9–10, 315–18

Voting rights, for women, 288

Vows: and controls inside convents, 169–71; definition of, 318; functions of, 170; origins of, 170; release from, 184–86

Wagner, Matilda (OSF), 295

Wagons, nuns' travels by, 43–44, 51–55

Walker, Ignatius (RSM), 348 (n. 61)

Walter, Florence (CDP), 25, 153, 173

War: and Americanization of nuns, 286, 287; nuns' service in, 82–83

Washington: Dominican Sisters in, 64–66, 300–301, 329 (n. 75); Franciscan Sisters in, 132–34; Italian immigrants in, 70; nuns as permanent residents of, 300–301; social observations and interactions of nuns in, 64–66, 329 (n. 75); work contracts of nuns in, 132–34

Weather: dangers of, 53, 60, 329 (n. 87); misleading reports of, 89, 90

Wegman, Gustave, 14

West, American: appreciation for aesthetic of, 56–59; boundaries of, 8; diversity of region, 7–8; gaps in knowledge about nuns in, 19; history of scholarship on, 4–8; immigration to (*See* Immigrant[s]); lack of attention paid to nuns in, 35–36; local communities of, 69–75; migration to, 16–17, 22–25, 44 (*See also* Travel); motivations for moving to, 2; number of religious women in, 19–20; nuns as permanent residents of, 299–301; shifting traditions in, 289–96

White Earth Reservation (Minnesota): Benedictine Sisters in, 109–13, 200, 238, 297–98; Drexels' visit to, 199–200; spiritual rituals at, 297–98

Whitman, Marcus, 330 (n. 111)

Whitman, Narcissa, 330 (n. 111)

Widows, admitted to Sisters of the Holy Family, 106, 336 (n. 96)

Wild Rice (North Dakota), immigration of nuns to, 15

Wilfrida Hogan (CSJ). *See* Hogan, Wilfrida

Wilhelmina (OSB), 60

Willibalda Scherbauer (OSB). *See* Scherbauer, Willibalda

Wimmer, Boniface, 24, 120

Wimples (coifs), definition of, 315

Wind River Reservation (Wyoming), 211–12

Windthorst (Kansas), teaching work in, 64, 328 (n. 70)

Winter storms, 53, 60

Wisconsin: Dominican Sisters in, 20, 22, 142, 149, 272–73, 343 (n. 94); finances of nuns in, 149; Franciscan Sisters of Perpetual Adoration in, 199; Native American missions in, 199; number of nuns in, 20; professionalization of nuns in, 272–73; teaching work in, 142, 272–73, 343 (n. 94); young nuns in, 22

Women, religious: definition of, 317; gendered set of regulations for, 3, 81–82; history of scholarship by and on, 4–7; motivations for becoming, 23–24; number of in United States, 18–22; priest shortage in need for, 83, 305; Protestant, 330 (n. 111); religious men's attitudes toward, 2–3; opportunities for vs. single women, 74–75, 80. *See also* Nuns; Sisters

Women, single, opportunities for: vs. religious women, 74–75, 80; vs. single men, 74, 79–80

Work, by women, 79–116, 305–6; achievements of, 113–16, 268; in Civil War, 82–83; contracts on, 127–28, 131–35; demands regarding, 87, 128–32, 134, 159, 306; domestic (*See* Domestic labor); enclosure in conflict with, 97–99, 105, 113–14; in Europe, 81–82; expansion of, 88–91; farm labor, 80, 84–85; goals of, 80; in health care (*See* Health-care work, by nuns); history of, 81–87; legal protections for, 125–35; vs. men, 74, 79–80; with Native Americans in rural areas, 109–13; physical labor, 80, 84–87; priest shortage and, 83; professionalization of, 271–83; redefining of, 80, 83, 103–4, 108–9; religious men in conflict with women over, 87, 88–89, 94–96; by single vs. religious women, 74–75, 80; social work with urban